ADAPTIVE

ECONOMIC

MODELS

Publication No. 34
of the Mathematics Research Center
The University of Wisconsin — Madison

ACADEMIC PRESS RAPID MANUSCRIPT REPRODUCTION

Adaptive Economic Models

Edited by Richard H. Day / Theodore Groves

Proceedings of a Symposium
Conducted by the Mathematics Research Center
The University of Wisconsin—Madison
October 21–23, 1974

Academic Press
New York • San Francisco • London   1975

A Subsidiary of Harcourt Brace Jovanovich, Publishers

ACADEMIC PRESS, INC.
111 Fifth Avenue, New York, New York 10003

United Kingdom Edition published by
ACADEMIC PRESS, INC. (LONDON) LTD.
24/28 Oval Road, London NW1

Library of Congress Cataloging in Publication Data

Main entry under title:

Adaptive economic models.

    (Publication – Mathematics Research Center,
University of Wisconsin—Madison; no. 34)
    Includes bibliographies and index.
    1.   Economics —Mathematical models—Congresses.
I. Day, Richard H.   II.   Groves, Theodore.
III.   Wisconsin. University—Madison. Mathematics
Research Center.   IV.   Series: Wisconsin. University—
Madison. Mathematics Research Center. Publication; no. 34.
QA3.U45   no.34   [HB135]   510'.8s   [330'.01'51]
ISBN 0–12–207350–9   75-28274

Contents

CONTENTS

CONTENTS

Preface

The purpose of this book is to consider adaptive processes in economics, that is, the field of adaptive economics. It is too early to identify the precise boundaries of adaptive economics and perhaps there would be no point in doing so, even were it feasible. Nonetheless, it is possible to discern the character of part of this new domain, to outline some of its essential features, and to report on its general appearance from several quite different points of view. Just as the travelogs of early explorers induced poineers to venture into relatively uncharted, yet fertile, country, so we hope the exercises assembled here will encourage further research by adventurous colleagues in this very rich field.

All of the papers and abstracts included here were presented at the Symposium on Adaptive Economics sponsored by the Mathematics Research Center at the University of Wisconsin, Madison, October 21-23, 1974, with the financial support of the United States Army under Contract No. DA-31-124-ARO-D-462. Although it was possible to include only a tiny fraction of the papers suggested for the program and though significant gaps in subject matter are evident, an effort was made to place on the symposium program contributions from as wide a range of research in the field of adaptive economics as possible. All papers on the program are included herein, either in full or in abstract.

The program committee of the symposium was:

Richard H. Day, Chairman, *University of Wisconsin, Madison*
Theodore Groves, *Northwestern University*
Jacob Marschak, *University of California at Los Angeles*
Dale Rudd, *University of Wisconsin, Madison*

Gladys Moran served as administrator and was aided by Judy Siesen. The manuscripts were typed by Carol Chase. The timely completion of this volume was made possible by the splendid cooperation of the various authors.

R.H.D.
T.G.

Adaptive Processes and Economic Theory
Richard H. Day

CONTENTS

1. INTRODUCTION

The world economy is an intricate, evolving game with nearly four billion players. The players, whose number is growing at a rapid rate, each possess some freedom of choice and each draws on a specific, perhaps unique, configuration of numerous personal attributes. They are organized into literally millions of overlapping organizations: families, enterprises, political and social groups, all having something, more or less, to do with the allocation and utilization of resources, the accumulation of wealth and the exploitation of the natural environment.

Economic theorists have very often chosen to view this complex world as populated by a non-adaptive being, homoeconomicus, a being who is omniscient, perfectly rational and whose behavior is assumed to

1

be in equilibrium. The theory that flows from this view is designed to answer questions about the existence and character of equilibria and how equilibria vary with changes in the data. It is, in short, the theory of adapted systems. But the economic game is in reality played in an environment of tortuous complexity, not by homoeconomicus, but by an adaptive person, who is only partially informed and whose foresight is imperfect. His behavior is evidently conducted out of equilibirum.

Nonetheless, our traditional paradigm is useful, partly because it helps characterize goals toward which an adaptive process might tend, partly because the concept radically simplifies the logical structure of economic theory and thus renders manageable the manifold complexity of the real world. It is probably correct to infer that economics could not have reached its present position of scientific rigor and practical importance in affairs if equilibrium economics had not been developed. Yet, it must be acknowledged that, from a scientific point of view, our job is not complete until we understand the dynamic, adaptive processes that bring about -- or fail to bring about -- equilibria. Because existing economies often appear to be maladaptive -- sometimes acutely so -- we are aware of the need to understand how they really work. It is thus for both purely scientific and imminently practical purposes that we seek progress in adaptive economics.

Adaptive economics is here defined to be the study of economic processes using concepts of adaptation. Many such concepts have arisen in various scientific fields, but as the literature dealing with them is often vague or tailored to the needs of a narrow specialty I have taken it as one purpose of this paper to provide a formally precise framework of definitions. Hopefully, this framework will bring out the general concepts in a way that is consistent with usage in many fields and at the same time provide a starting point for economic analysis. A second purpose is to indicate how -- in my opinion -- "economizing" or "optimizing" must be construed if it is to have adaptive content. A general model of adaptive economizing is posed, a model that incorporates strategic considerations

2

of the dynamic programming genre, but which is based on the behavioral principle of bounded rationality. As a third purpose I have attempted, though with extreme brevity, to indicate how economic theory has incorporated one or another of the several concepts of adaptation. In concluding sections suggestions for emphasis in future research are presented together with a final reminder of the limitations subject to which those efforts must be pursued.

2. ADAPTIVE SYSTEMS

2.1. The Adaptive System

The theory of adaptation must begin with a breakdown of reality into two parts, one representing the behavior of a part of the process of special interest which we may -- quite arbitrarily -- call the agent, one representing other parts of reality, which -- equally arbitrarily -- we call the environment.[1] Adaptation may then be defined quite generally as the adjustment of the agent to his environment. The "agent" may be a person, a household, a firm, a group of firms, or even an entire economy, depending on the purpose at hand. The "agent" therefore must be understood here to be a purely formal entity.

An organism is sometimes called "adaptive" if it behaves in a way that favors its own survival. It is also then said to exhibit "fitness" to its environment. To formalize survival and demise the concept of an admissible act must be introduced. Such an act is one that is consistent with the existence of the agent. Also, the environment should be allowed to continue to exist even though the agent under consideration performs an inadmissible act or goes out of existence. The concept of survival is further complicated by the fact that the set of admissible acts is, in general, a variable of the system. Survival is possible as long as this set is nonempty. Moreover, the agent survives indeed only if he generates an admissible act.[2]

3

The output of the agent is an act, a, belonging to an action set $\mathbb{A}$. The output of the environment is an environmental state, s, belonging to a state set $\mathbb{S}$. Again, those terms have no intrinsic meaning and are relative to the purpose at hand. The set of admissible acts is denoted A_t and it belongs to the set $\mathcal{P}(\mathbb{A})$ of the action space $\mathbb{A}$. The dependence of this set on the previous situation is represented by an admissibility correspondence: $\mathfrak{A} : \mathbb{A} \times \mathbb{S} \to \mathcal{P}(\mathbb{A})$. The mechanism connecting act to previous acts and the existing state may be called an adaptor and we shall denote it by the symbol $\alpha : \mathbb{A} \times \mathbb{S} \to \mathbb{A}$. The mechanism connecting succeeding states with the previous state and the agent's act may be called a transitor. Two such transitors must be distinguished, one which is denoted $\omega_p : \mathbb{A} \times \mathbb{S} \to \mathbb{S}$ and which represents the situation when the agent survives, and one denoted $\omega_\emptyset : \mathbb{S} \to \mathbb{S}$ which governs the environmental transition when the agent can find no admissible act or "dies".[3] In the present paper it shall be supposed that the adjustment of agent and environment to one another takes place at discrete intervals.[4]

The condition for survival at period t is:

(S)
$$A_t \neq \emptyset \text{ and } a_t \epsilon A_t .$$

When demise occurs the system collapses to the environment. Hence, the adaptive process consists of two distinct regimes: the first which governs behavior when the agent is active:

(1)
$$A_{t+1} = \mathfrak{A}(a_t, s_t)$$

(2)
$$a_{t+1} = \alpha(a_t, s_t) \left.\right\} , \quad A_t \neq \emptyset \text{ and } a_t \epsilon A_t ,$$

(3)
$$s_{t+1} = \omega_p(a_t, s_t)$$

the second when the system collapses to the environment,

(4)
$$s_{t+1} = \omega_\emptyset(s_t), \quad A_t = \emptyset \quad \text{or} \quad a_t \notin A_t.$$

Because of the possibility of demise the usual solution concepts for discrete dynamic systems must be extended. Given an initial situation (a_0, s_0) a process is called viable as long as the survival condition (S) holds. If condition (S) holds for τ periods but fails for period $(\tau+1)$ then the system is τ-viable for (a_0, s_0). If condition (S) holds for all $t > 0$ then the system is ∞-viable (or viable for short) for (a_0, s_0).[5]

2.2. Homeostasis

The concept of homeostasis is a particular formalization of the idea that agents behave -- or seek to behave -- in ways that favor their own survival. The agent is described by a vector of characteristic variables whose values must lie in a critical set to insure his survival. The value of the characteristic variable vector is determined by an outcome function whose arguments are the agent's act and the environmental state. When the agent acts so that its outcome function maps into its critical set it is said to exhibit homeostasis.[6] Apparently, much economic behavior must be understood in such terms. It would appear that the search for rules of economic adaptation that exhibit homeostasis must be a major preoccupation of a society faced with rapidly changing environmental states, scarce resources and fierce competition.

Homeostatic rules are found somehow or other by meta-adaptive processes, either by trial and error as in evolution, or by design synthesis as in cultural adaptation. (See below §2.4). We do not derive such rules here but rather present an abstract model of the concept in terms of the adaptive system (1)-(4). Let the vector of critical variables be denoted by c belonging to a critical characteristic set $\mathbb{C}$. The outcome function which shows how the current situation affects the critical variable vector may be denoted by $\gamma: \mathbb{A} \times \mathbb{S} \to \mathbb{C}$. The critical region or set of values of the critical variable vector compatible with the agent's existence is denoted C_{t+1} and belongs to the set $\mathbb{P}(\mathbb{C})$ of subsets of the set $\mathbb{C}$. The operator that expresses the dependence of C_{t+1} on the current situation is denoted by $\mathfrak{Q}: \mathbb{A} \times \mathbb{S} \to \mathbb{P}(\mathbb{C})$. It determines the critical region according to

$$(5) \qquad\qquad C_{t+1} = \mathfrak{Q}(a_t, s_t) .$$

Given the previous situation the critical variable vector is $c_{t+1} = \gamma(a_{t+1}, s_{t+1})$. The agent exhibits homeostasis if, in choosing a_{t+1},

$$(6) \qquad\qquad c_{t+1} = \gamma(a_{t+1}, s_{t+1}) \in C_{t+1} .$$

By defining

$$(7) \qquad\qquad \mathfrak{A}(a_t, s_t) := \{a \mid \gamma(a, \omega(a_t, s_t)) \in \mathfrak{Q}(a_t, s_t)\}$$

we have the admissibility operator, equation (1).

  It is important to note that a homeostatic process as defined here need not always exhibit homeostasis. Let a "compatibility" correspondence $\mathfrak{S}: \mathbb{A} \to \mathbb{P}(\mathbb{S})$ be defined as

$$\mathfrak{S}(a_t) := \{s \mid A(a_t, s) \neq \emptyset\} = \{s \mid \exists a \ni \gamma(a, s) \in \mathfrak{Q}(a_t, s)\} .$$

A viable adaptor is now one for which there exists $U^0 \subset \mathbb{A} \times \mathbb{S}$ such that for all $(a, s) \in U^0$, (i) $\omega(a, s) \in \mathfrak{S}(a)$, (ii) $\alpha(a, s) \in \mathfrak{A}(a, s)$, and (iii) $[\alpha(a, s), \omega(a, s)] \in U^0$. These conditions are respectively compatibility, homeostasis and closure. Such a process exhibits homeostasis forever for any initial conditions in U^0. Such ∞-viable processes must, at best, be regarded as approximations of real world systems.

2.3. Systems of Adaptors

  The environment of a given economic agent includes other agents and the agent himself may be thought of -- in so far as his actual mode of behavior is concerned -- as a collection of coordinated adaptive functions. In this way one arrives at the concept of a system of adaptors. There are three distinct but closely related types of such systems. These are (1) the adaptive economy, (2) the adaptive organization, and (3) the adaptive algorithm.

The adaptive economy is a collection of agents who adapt to each other and to the "outside" environment. It includes cases in which the number of agents is so large that direct adaptation to other agents, even through feedback, would require so many linkages that effective action would be unthinkable. In such systems adaptation to other agents occurs, in part, indirectly through the environment. For example, the "market", by means of prices, communicates information about the entire system to each agent without his having to monitor any but his own economic activity. In this way markets economize interagent linkages.[7] Of course, direct (lagged) linkages in the form of "conjectural variations" are also included in the notion of an adaptive economy and have been studied in well known theories of oligopoly that go back to Cournot.[8]

The adaptive organization is a collection of agents who adaptively coordinate their activity, achieve some common purpose and share some benefits. A hierarchy or multi-level structure may exist among these linkages in which agents play differentiated roles, in this way coordinating activity to take advantage of specialization. The adaptive economy includes, of course, the notion of a collection of adaptive agents some of whom are adaptive organizations.[9]

For many purposes the theorist may wish to suppress the internal structures of adaptation within organizations and focus on adaptation among them. For others, the internal adaptive process may be the focal point of interest. When it is, the concern is with the adaptive algorithm, a collection of adaptors which is coordinated for the purpose of solving specific problems. The notion of an adaptive algorithm is quite general, for individual agents, organization and economies solve problems: they consume, produce and coordinate supply and demand. However, its explicit use may embroil the conomist in too much detail for the purpose at hand and he may prefer to treat the agent or organization as a kind of black box.

To formalize the general, multiadaptor process which includes the three types just described a population or set P of adaptors or agents is considered with individual members identified by the index i. The act of each agent is denoted by a_{it} which belongs to the actions set $\mathbb{A}_i$. A multiact consisting of the vector $a_t := (a_{it})_{i \in P}$ is the vector of all the agents' acts and belongs to the multiaction set $\mathbb{A} := X_{i \in P} \mathbb{A}_i$. Each agent possesses an admissibility correspondence $\mathfrak{A}_i$ and an adaptor α_i. The equations describing the behavior of the multiadaptor process when all the agents survive (that is when condition (S) holds for each agent) are:

$$
\left. \begin{array}{ll}
(8) & A_{i,t+1} = \mathfrak{A}_i(a_t, s_t), \\[2ex]
(9) & a_{i,t+1} = \alpha_i(a_y, s_t), \\[2ex]
(10) & s_{t+1} = \omega_P(a_t, s_t) .
\end{array} \right\} \quad A_{it} \neq \emptyset \text{ and } a_{it} \in A_{it}, \text{ all } i \in P .
$$

The system collapses to

$$
(11) \qquad s_{t+1} = \omega_\emptyset(s_t), \quad A_{it} = \emptyset \text{ or } a_{it} \notin A_{it}, \text{ some } i \in P,
$$

that is, when any one adaptor does not survive.

By defining $\alpha(.\,,\,.) := [\alpha_j(.\,,\,.)]_{i \in P}$, $\mathfrak{A}(.\,,\,.) := [\mathfrak{A}_i(.\,,\,.)]_{i \in P}$ and $A_t := [A_{it}]_{i \in P}$ the multiadaptor process is seen to be merely an elaboration of (1)-(4). However, the modeller may want to recognize delays of various lengths within the multiadaptor system. The whole system may involve partial processes that proceed according to short time periods and other partial processes that adapt at longer intervals. Examples in economics organizations occur in abundance. Buyers for a store may modify their activity on a daily basis, while top management may modify its long run investment plan in new stores and renovations anually. Another example is the concept of sequences of temporary equilibria for an economy in which during each period the economy satisfies temporary equilibrium conditions. The economy is implicitly assumed to possess a convergent tatonnement process which brings about each temporary equilibrium. But if represented explicitly instead of assumed implicitly this tatonnement process would be adaptive and time consuming.[10]

2.4. Meta-Adaptation

Changing Structure. The formal structure of an adaptive process consists of the operator triple $(\mathfrak{A}, \alpha, \omega)$, which, as we have seen, includes the multiadaptor systems in which the operators $\mathfrak{A}$ and α are composed of the corresponding operators for each agent in the population of agents. If we are to consider how a given process comes into being or if we are to inquire how a system changes (or may be changed) from one structure to another then we come to a more complex type of adaptation which may be called meta-adaptation.

Two forms of meta-adaptation may be distinguished. These are evolution and cultural adaptation. Evolution involves a variable population of agents which is determined at any time by the previously existing population interacting with its environment through forces of competition and selection. Each population behaves according to some adaptive process, described by its members' α operators. Presumably all living things are subject to this evolutionary process. For human populations it includes an additional feature which involves the creation of new rules of adaptation which may or may not be passed on to future generations. In the terms defined so far the effect of this process is to select α operators for a given population. This is so important that society as a whole and many of its institutions set aside resources for the use of specialists in this function. In present day economies these specialists

9

include economists, management scientists and engineers. Individuals, too, set aside resources, time and money for learning through education and training new modes of behavior. For want of a better term we call this second form of meta-adaptation <u>cultural adaptation</u>.

    <u>Evolution</u>. A part of the flavor of evolution has been recognized in the adaptive process, that part involving survival or demise of an agent. But the general concept goes much beyond this notion to include progression in the <u>population</u> of agents. The evolutionary process "produces" a new population through forces acting on the preceding population in a manner influenced by the activities of the preceding population of agents and the state of the environment. The concept of evolution was of course developed to explain the progress of biological populations, but its application to populations of socio-economic organizations is an obvious analogy not without relevance.[11] Bankruptcy and the reorganization of resources into new or surviving firms is an example to which we have already attended. This suggests of course that in the application of evolutionary concepts to economics one should distinguish between "agents" identified for analysis and the human participants in the process. Indeed the natural agent for analysis in economics is often the institution: an organization of rules and procedures for regulating purposeful activity by its members.

    To define evolution in a very general form shall be our objective here. To do so we must make all of the mappings or operators introduced so far contingent on the existing population of agents. The population of agents P is now a variable P_t belonging to a set of "potential" agents $\mathbb{P}$. The multiact of the population is now denoted by $a_{pt} :=$ $(a_{it})_{i \in P_t}$. It belongs to the multiact set $\mathbb{A}_{pt} := X_{i \in P_t} \mathbb{A}_i$. With each population $P_t \subset \mathbb{P}$ is associated a transitor $\omega_{pt} : \mathbb{A}_{pt} \times \mathbb{S} \to \mathbb{S}$. With each "potential" agent $i \in \mathbb{P}$ is associated an admissibility correspondence $\mathfrak{A}_{ipt} := \mathbb{A}_{pt} \times \mathbb{S} \to \mathcal{P}(\mathbb{A}_i)$ which defines the agent's possible acts given the preexisting population and the current situation (a_{pt}, s_t). Also, the

10

agent possesses an adaptor $\alpha_{ipt} : A_{pt} \times \mathcal{S} \to A_i$ which describes his act as it depends on the preexisting population and situation. An existence condition now defines the emerging population:

(12) $\qquad P_{t+1} = \mathfrak{C}_{pt}(P_t,\ a_{pt},\ s_t) := \{i \in \mathbb{P} \,|\, \alpha_{ipt}(a_{pt},\ s_t) \in \mathfrak{U}_{ipt}(a_{pt},\ s_t) \neq \emptyset\}$

which states that the new population consists of those agents who have something they can do and manage to do it. With this we have the modification of (9) - (11) given by

(13) $\qquad\qquad A_{i,t+1} = \mathfrak{U}_{ipt}(a_{pt},\ s_t)$

(14) $\qquad\qquad a_{i,t+1} = \alpha_{ipt}(a_{pt},\ s_t)\ \Big\}\ \ P_t \neq \emptyset$

(15) $\qquad\qquad s_{t+1} = \omega_{pt}(a_{pt},\ s_t),$

and

(16) $\qquad\qquad s_{t+1} = \omega_{\emptyset}(s_t),\ \ P_t = \emptyset\ .$

Because for some purposes of analysis the population in question may be a body of institutions instead of persons, that is, it may be thought of as a body of corporate persons with potentially infinite life spans, it is not unreasonable to consider examples of (12)-(16) for which there exists a fixed population, say $\overline{P} \subset \mathbb{P}$ such that for some initial situation $P_0 = \overline{P}$, a_{p0}, s_0,

(17) $\qquad\qquad\qquad \overline{P} = (\overline{P},\ a_{pt},\ s_t)$

for all t. This would imply the existence of a stationary institutional structure given which the system reduces to the multiadaptor process (8)-(11).

11

Cultural Adaptation. The existence condition (12) implies, in the absence of a stationary population (17), a certain profligacy of evolution for it means that agents have no second chance with respect to non-adaptive behavior. Human agents, on the contrary, do get second chances by modifying their strategies or modes of behavior when threatened with demise. This leads to the second form of meta-adaptation, which goes on simultaneously with the ordinary process of adaptation, and enables given agents to survive in the face of evolutionary forces that would spell their demise if they did not acquire new modes of behavior. It also enables them to "improve" their performance in the sense of some performance criterion such as the outcome function (6). Leaving evolution aside for the moment, the process is formalized within the framework of the adaptive process (8)-(11) by defining a cultural adaptation operator $\mathfrak{C}$ that acts on a set of potential adaptors $\mathcal{A}$ to generate an adaptor, possibly the same as before, possibly distinct and involving a new mode of behavior. Instead of (8)-(11) we now have

$$(18) \qquad A_{t+1} = \mathfrak{A}(a_t, s_t)$$

$$(19) \qquad \alpha_{t+1} = \mathfrak{C}(\alpha_t, a_t, s_t) \in \mathcal{A}$$

$$(20) \qquad a_{t+1} = \alpha_t(a_t, s_t)$$

$$(21) \qquad s_{t+1} = \omega_p(a_t, s_t)$$

The survival condition (S) is now modified to become

$$(S') \qquad \alpha_t(a_t, s_t) = \mathfrak{C}(\alpha_{t-1}, a_{t-1}, s_{t-1})(a_t, s_t) \in \mathfrak{A}(a_t, s_t) \neq \emptyset$$

which states that cultural adaptation modifies behavior (at least when necessary) in such a way that behavior is admissible. When the system fails it collapses to (11) as before. However, just as in the case of the

12

stationary population $\overline{P}$ (which is here assumed) one can think of a stationary $\overline{\alpha}$ of (19) given which the system reduces to the ordinary adaptive process (8)-(11). By defining a suitable metric on the space of adaptors the stability of cultural adaptation can also be discussed.

The process represented by equation (19) is complex, involving investigation, synthesizing and education or learning. Hence, it must be thought of as being itself a system of adaptors representing these various functions. Rather than go into such details here, however, let us instead consider the broad process of cultural evolution that emerges when the processes of evolution and cultural adaptation are combined.

Cultural Evolution. [12] Putting together evolution and cultural adaptation yields an abstract model which allows for the response of agents to their environment, the modification of strategies or modes of behavior by given agents, and the modification of the population of agents. With obvious changes in notation we have

$$(22) \qquad\qquad A_{i,t+1} = \mathfrak{A}_{ipt}(a_{pt},\ s_t)$$

$$(23) \qquad\qquad \alpha_{ip,t+1} = \mathfrak{C}_{ipt}(\alpha_{pt},\ a_{pt},\ s_t)$$

$$(24) \qquad\qquad a_{i,t+1} = \alpha_{ipt}(a_{pt},\ s_t)$$

which describe the (potential) behavior of each agent $i \in \mathbb{P}$. The surivial condition is now, instead of (12),

$$P_{t+1} = \mathfrak{E}_{pt}(P_t,\ \alpha_{pt},\ s_t) :=$$

$$(25) \qquad \{i \in \mathbb{P}\,|\,\alpha_{ipt}(a_{pt},\ s_t) = \mathfrak{C}_{ipt}(\alpha_{p,t-1},\ a_{p,t-1},\ s_{t-1})\ \cdot$$

$$(a_{pt},\ s_t) \in A_{i,t+1} = \mathfrak{A}_{ipt}(a_{pt},\ s_t) \neq \emptyset\}$$

in which $\alpha_{pt} := (\alpha_{ipt})_{i \epsilon P_t}$. Equation (25) states that the emerging population consists of those agents who have something to do and, perhaps with the help of changes in their mode of behavior, do it. Evolution selects out maladaptive behavior, a threat against which cultural adaptation is a defense, which may or may not be effective. The transitors for the process are the same as in the evolutionary process, namely (15) and (16).

Possible Simplifications for Modelling. The abstract models of evolution and of cultural evolution share the property that the individual agent matters. However, as the "agent" is itself an abstraction and may stand for an organization of people or activities, the model need not be as detailed as it may first seem to be the case. Indeed, given appropriate definitions of the "agent", highly aggregated units of economic activity may be represented in such a model.

The operational consideration of building workable models within available model building resources may force attention, however, to an alternative formalization of evolutionary processes in which the population of agents is replaced by a vector of characteristics of a population such as the number of agents, their age and sex distribution, etc. Evolution consists then not of a transition from one population to another, but from one population characteristic vector to another. From a purely formal point of view, the vector of characteristics would be a component of the environmental state, and the evolutionary operator would be a part of the transitor ω. In this way an evolutionary process might be formally reduced to the simpler structure of the multi-adaptor process (8)-(11) or more generally to the cultural adaptation process (18)-(21).

3. MODELLING ADAPTATION

3.1. Adaptive Mechanisms

So far the interaction of agents and environment has been considered. Now the question is taken up, "How do agents adapt?" From the point of view of analytical theory this question is answered by constructing

mechanisms that adjust behavior to environmental states. But when the
black box "agent" is opened up hierarchies of adaptive systems are found
and involve mechanisms of considerable complexity even in the simplest
organisms.

The elemental decomposition of an adaptive agent is into two
constituent parts, that of _sensor_ which filers and processes information
about the environment and that of _effector_ which responds in terms of behavior to the informational cues. Very simple combinations of these two
elements can have great survival power as is effectively illustrated by
Lotka's example of the mechanical mouse.[13] Thermostats and other useful servomechanisms have a similar structure.[14] To model effectively
economizing behavior, however, a decomposition of these two constit-
uents must be recognized. The sensor function may be broken down into
observation, information storage and information processing which results
in planning data. The effector function may be broken down into planning
and implementing activities. The latter distinction recognizes that plans
are not always realized and that the administrator in an organization must
react to the unfolding situation according to an adaptive procedure quite
different from the "decision-maker" or planner. Many organizations in-
stitutionalize this distinction in separate staff and command systems.
Individuals embody it in separate reflective and decisive activies. Cultural change may be thought of in similar terms, in which the subsystems
governing the selection of adaptors or behavioral rules is based on an
orchestration of activities in which the observation and data generating
functions are called investigation, the planning function in which new
rules are synthesized is called theorizing or model building, and the implementation function involves education, training, or indoctrination. In
the context of economic behavior modification, management science and
operations research are disciplines involved in this process of cultural
change.

The several functions just outlined can be summarized by separate
operators, one for _observing_ $\sigma : \mathbb{A} \times \mathbb{S} \to \mathbb{O}$ in which $\mathbb{O}$ is the

15

observation set, one for <u>information storing</u> or remembering $\mu : \mathbb{O} \times \mathbb{A} \times \mathbb{S} \to \mathbb{M}$ in which $\mathbb{M}$ is an information set, one for <u>data processing</u> $\pi : \mathbb{M} \times \mathbb{A} \times \mathbb{S} \to \mathbb{D}$ in which $\mathbb{D}$ is a data set, one for <u>planning or programming</u> $\delta : \mathbb{D} \times \mathbb{A} \times \mathbb{S} \to \mathbb{X}$ in which $\mathbb{X}$ is a program set, and one for <u>implementing or administering</u> $\iota : \mathbb{X} \times \mathbb{A} \times \mathbb{S} \to \mathbb{U}$ in which $\mathbb{U}$ is an action proper set.[15] The activity of the agent is then represented by the action $a_t := (o_t, m_t, d_t, x_t, u_t)$ and (for example) by the equations,

$$(26) \qquad o_{t+1} = \sigma(a_t, s_t) \qquad \text{observing}$$

$$(27) \qquad m_{t+1} = \mu(o_{t+1}, a_t, s_t) \qquad \text{remembering or storing}$$

$$(28) \qquad d_{t+1} = \pi(m_{t+1}, a_t, s_t) \qquad \text{processing}$$

$$(29) \qquad x_{t+1} = \delta(d_{t+1}, a_t, a_t) \qquad \text{planning}$$

$$(30) \qquad u_{t+1} = \iota(x_t, a_t, s_t) \qquad \text{implementing}$$

Combined with (1)-(4) a particular kind of multiadaptor process emerges in which

$$(31) \qquad \alpha(a_t, s_t) := [\sigma(a_t, s_t), \ldots, \iota(\delta(\pi(\mu(\sigma(a_t, s_t), \ldots, a_t, s_t)].$$

It would be far too ambitious here to attempt a survey of all the mechanisms that have been or might be used to represent the working of these several functions. Instead three "canonical" categories will be summarized (i) the system of switches and rules, (ii) learning algorithms and (iii) economizing or explicit optimizing. It is the latter category that brings us (as economists) home, but to a home extensively remodelled, so to speak, from the adaptive point of view.

3.2. Switches and Rules

Unavoidably, one must begin with the notion of a function or set of ordered pairs, the first member of which is the input (argument), the second which is the output (image), of the adaptor. When the function can be represented by a closed form expression or formula that describes how the image of each possible argument can be obtained it is called an operator or a rule. A rule for an adaptor, then, generates an act for each possible state.

Rules may be derived from economizing arguments. They may be identified by a statistical analysis of inputs and outputs when the agent is regarded as a "black box". In the case of persons and organizations rules may be identified by direct observation. In the latter case one speaks of behavioral rules. The identification and study of behavioral rules in representing adaptive behavior in economic organizations is the province of behavioral economics.[16]

Not all functions used in mathematics can be computed. When they can they are called computable or recursive. A procedure for computing an image for a given argument is called an algorithm. A functional rule or operator may, from this point of view, be regarded as the "equilibrium" of some algorithm for computing the function it represents. It is for this reason that many of the simplest and most mechanical models of economic behavior possess hidden or implicit conditions for temporary equilibrium, a technique for simplifying the full dynamic structure of economic behavior. If one is to make explicit the full structure of adaptation one must appeal to the class of simplest functions or rules from which algorithms for all other rules may be constructed. Adaptive behavior is founded on the existence of such rules.

Among the simplest rules is the switch, which has the function of changing action from one mode to another depending on the environmental state. Such mechanisms are not unknown in socioeconomic modelling, a famous example of which is Hick's trade cycle model. Just as elemental numerical algorithms for computing functions consist of

systems of switches and simple arithmetical rules, so dynamic models
of directly observable behavior in economic organizations have employed
analogous systems. Not only behavioral economic models but also "system dynamics" models[17] can be reduced to systems of switches and rules
in the sense defined here.

A general form of an adaptor that behaves according to different
rules depending on which environmental state attains is

$$(32) \qquad \alpha(a_t, \ s_t) := \Sigma_{k \in K} \ \Delta(s_t, \ S^k) f^k(a_t, \ s_t)$$

in which the switching sets $\{S^k, \ k \in K\}$ form a partition of the state
space $\mathbb{S}$ and in which the family of rules $\{f^k : \mathbb{A} \times \mathbb{S} \to \mathbb{A}, \ k \in K\}$ gives
a complete description of behavior given any environmental state. Such
systems exhibit threshold behavior, for, as the environmental state
crosses the threshold of one switching set to another the system behavior
changes, perhaps in a qualitatively striking manner.

An important special case is the logical net in which each output
function assumes only one of two discrete states, zero or one. In this
form adaptation is severely "mechanical", yet exhibits an astonishingly
wide range of behavior. Even very simple examples of such systems,
simple enough that their structures can be graphed on a page, can exhibit selective response to environmental change, memory, conditioned
response and so on.[18] Designed to model neural activity, the logical
net per se is not presented here as a candidate for an adaptive economic
model, but as a potential component for such models which might be used
to represent one or more agents who exercise policies which, in effect,
operate as simple, on-off switches. Moreover, if one were to attempt a
complete explication of adaptation, the logical net would appear to be
close to the simplest adaptive structure out of which all "higher level"
adaptive processes such as those to be considered below, would have to
be constructed.

18

3.3. Learning

Economizing behavior as described, for example, by the marginalist Marshall involved incremental changes toward an economically improved state. Optimality or full equilibrium only occurred with the pas-
sage of time through a converging sequence of adjustments. His focus,
however, like that of many of his contemporaries, was on the characteristics of the state of equilibrium, assuming it was brought about. But if
one is to understand fully the adaptive mechanism that underlies economizing then one must study the process of marginal adjustment itself
and ask under what conditions it will bring about optimality and with
what speed. And, as explicit optimizing takes time, involves the consumption of other resources and is far from easy, the process of optimizing itself is a part of the economizing problem. To investigate such
issues learning algorithms must be constructed that describe economizing
as an adaptive process.[19]

The canonical form for learning algorithms is the system of
switches and rules (32) in which the switching sets are determined by
performance measures. Learning takes place whenever behavior is modified in response to changes in these measures of performance. Successful learning is implied by an improvement in performance. This may
occur as the result of a fixed adaptor or as the result of cultural adaptation in which the adaptor or mode of behavior is modified. Simple examples can readily be constructed using three elemental principles of
learning: (A) successful behavior is repeated; (B) unsuccessful behavior is avoided; (C) unsuccessful behavior is followed by a search
for alternative modes of behavior; (D) behavior becomes more cautious
in response to failure. Models incorporating (A)-(C) have been the basis
of behavioral economic theory as developed by Cyert and March. I have
shown elsewhere that such models, augmented by (D), can converge to
the economists' traditional optimal economic equilibrium.[20] The latter
result was obtained only in an extremely simple case and the former
work, while immensely important, has led a life outside the mainstream

of the profession. Clearly, a great deal more attention needs to be focussed here if an adaptive economic theory is to be fully developed.

Nonetheless, it must be admitted that for many modelling purposes the use of systems of switches and rules is too detailed. "Higher level" adaptive mechanisms are desired that subsume the computational or behavioral details by which behavior is generated within a given period, and yet which retain the essential features of adaptation between periods. The basic mechanisms for this are the explicit optimizing model and the concept of temporary equilibrium. They are devices for subsuming the learning process of agents and for subsuming the process of interaction among agents by which their behavior becomes consistent one with another, that is, viable. [21]

3.4. Optimizing

Global optimizing. The economist's notion of optimality provides the formal basis for evaluating alternative adaptors, sets the stage for a consideration of adaptive optimizing strategies and illuminates the difference between adaptive and nonadaptive or optimally adapted systems. For this reason a general canonical structure of global optimizing behavior is presented first. "Once and for all optimizing" is defined. Then "rolling global optimizing" and the concept of "consistency" is discussed as a principle of global optimality. These problems are then related to the adaptive system by transforming them into the "design systhesis problem", the problem of deriving globally optimal adaptors. After this discussion optimizing is looked at from the explicitly adaptive point of view.

Once-and-for-all optimizing. In global optimizing theory the past is ignored; and it can be, for the set of all future possibilities is known through a perfect knowledge of environmental structure, which, in the present context, means an exact knowledge of the operators $\mathfrak{U}$, ω, and the initial conditions (a_t, s_t). The problem of the agent is to obtain a best trajectory $_{t+1}(a, s) := (a_{t+1}, s_{t+1}, a_{t+2}, s_{t+2}, \ldots)$ for the system

20

given that he knows $(a_t, s_t, \mathfrak{A}, \omega)$. The set of feasible trajectories (viable solutions) is determined by the correspondence

$$(33) \quad \mathfrak{A}^\infty(a_t, s_t, \omega, \mathfrak{A}) := \{_{t+1}(a, s) \mid a_{i+1} \in \mathfrak{A}(a_i, s_i), \; s_{i+1} = \omega(a_i, s_i),$$
$$i = t, \ldots, \infty\} \, .$$

A comparison among trajectories is made possible by a utility function $\Phi^\infty : (\mathbb{A} \times \mathbb{S})^\infty \to \mathbb{R}$ which assigns a value $\Phi^\infty[_{t+1}(a, s)]$ to each trajectory. The best value (if it exists) is

$$(34) \quad \Phi^{\infty\#}(a_t, s_t, \omega, \mathfrak{A}) := \sup_{_{t+1}(a, s) \in \mathfrak{A}^\infty(a_t, s_t, \omega, \mathfrak{A})} \Phi^\infty(_{t+1}(a, s))$$

and the set of best trajectories satisfying (33) is

$$(35) \quad A^{\infty\#}(a_t, s_t; \omega, \mathfrak{A}) := \{_{t+1}(a, s) \mid \Phi^\infty(_{t+1}(a, s)) \geq \Phi^{\infty\#}(a_t, s_t; \omega, \mathfrak{A})\}$$
$$\cap \, \mathfrak{A}^\infty(a_t, s_t; \omega, \mathfrak{A}) \, .$$

One may note that most economic control theory models that fall into this general class assume the existence of a utility function $\Phi_i = \beta^i \Phi$ in which $\beta \in \mathbb{R}$, $0 < \beta < 1$ with

$$(*) \quad \Phi^\infty[_{t+1}(a, s)] := \Sigma_{i=t+1}^\infty \Phi_i(a_i, s_i) = \Sigma_{i=t+1}^\infty \beta^i \Phi(a_i, s_i)$$

and

$$(**) \quad (a_t, s_t) := A^0 \subset \mathbb{A} \, .$$

Preferences may in fact be poorly represented by (*) and in reality admissibility is an evolving set unlike (**).

21

Rolling global optimizing and consistency. Now plans are not made once and for all. They are reevaluated and reconstituted as time passes. Therefore, a sensible restriction on any criterion of global optimality is a principle of optimality which asserts that no matter at what time after t a new plan is drawn up and regardless of what state prevails at that time, the optimal sequence planned for the future is optimal with respect to the state resulting (or that would result) from the initial plan.[22] Another, simpler way of putting this is that a globally optimal plan must be consistent with respect to subsequent plans.[23] To formalize this idea an additional time index must be used that distinguishes a trajectory of events $_t(a, s)$ from the time at which those events are planned. Let (a_t^i, s_t^i) be the event planned or programmed at time t to take place at time t+i, and let $(a_t^0, s_t^0) = (a_t, s_t) = (a, s)_t$ be the initial condition. Also let $^1(a, s)_t := (a_t^1, s_t^1, a_t^2, s_t^2, \ldots)$ be the trajectory of events planned or programmed at time t. Given perfect knowledge as before we have the feasibility correspondence

$$(36) \quad \mathfrak{A}^\infty(a_t, s_t, \omega, \mathfrak{A}) := \{^1(a,s)_t \,|\, a_t^{i+1} \in \mathfrak{A}(a_1^i, s_1^i), \; s_t^{i+1} = \omega(a_t^i, s_t^i), \; i=t, \ldots \} \; .$$

The best value function

$$(37) \qquad \Phi^{\infty\#}(a_t, s_t, \omega, \mathfrak{A}) := \sup_{^1(a, s_t) \in \mathfrak{A}^\infty(a_t, s_t, \omega, \mathfrak{A})} \Phi^{\infty}(^1(a, s)_t)$$

and the rolling optimizing correspondence,

$$(38) \quad \mathfrak{A}^{\infty\#}(a_t, s_t, \omega, \mathfrak{A}) := \{^1(a, s)_t \,|\, \Phi^\infty(^1(a, s)_t \geq$$
$$\geq \Phi^{\infty\#}(a_t, s_t, \omega, \mathfrak{A})\} \cap \mathfrak{A}^\infty(a_t, s_t, \omega, \mathfrak{A}),$$

assuming that all of these exist. The requirement of consistency is now that imminent plans are realized and that one does not change ones mind as time passes, i.e.,

<u>Condition C</u> $(a_t^1, s_t^1) = (a_{t+1}, s_{t+1})$ and $(a_t^i, s_t^i) = (a_{t+i-1}^1, s_{t+i-1}^1)$,

holds. Whenever condition C holds the possible behavior generated by
(38) is the same as that generated by (35) and that justifies the term
global optimality used in connection with the earlier model.

Not all models of the form (36)-(38) will meet condition C. In
fact consistency (principle of optimality) apparently requires assumption
(*) above. Much more importantly, one must notice that (36)-(38) require
<u>perfect knowledge</u> of ω and $\mathfrak{A}$ as well of the initial conditions (a_t, s_t).
All of this is in strong contrast to the models described in §3.1-3.2.
However, before returning to adaptive considerations let us recast global
optimizing into the design synthesis problem: that of determining not a
trajectory <u>per se</u> but an adaptor that will, together with the environment,
generate one.

Assuming that (*) holds and using the dynamic programming point
of view we derive from (33)-(35) the problem of reduced dimension

$$(39) \quad \Phi^{\infty\#}(a_t, s_t, \omega, \mathfrak{A}) = \sup_{\substack{a_{t+1} \epsilon \, \mathfrak{A}(a_t, s_t) \\ s_{t+1} = \omega(a_t, s_t)}} [\,\Phi(a_{t+1}, s_{t+1}) + \beta\Phi^{\infty\#}(a_{t+1}, s_{t+1}, \omega, \mathfrak{A})]$$

The problem of globally optimal design synthesis is the discovery of a
transformation $\tau(a, s) = [\alpha(a, s), \omega(a, s)]$ which solves (39). If $\mathcal{A}$
is the set of possible adaptors let

$$(40) \quad \mathfrak{J}(\mathfrak{A}, \omega) := \{(\alpha, \omega) \,|\, \alpha \epsilon \, \mathcal{A}, \ \alpha(a, s) \epsilon \, \mathfrak{A}(a, s), \ (a, s) \epsilon \, \mathbb{A} \times \mathbb{S}\}$$

Then (37) can be rewritten as

$$(41) \quad \Phi^{\infty\#}(a_t, s_t, \omega, \mathfrak{A}) := \sup_{\tau \epsilon \, \mathfrak{J}(\mathfrak{A}, \omega)} \{\Phi[\tau(a_t, s_t)] + \beta\Phi^{\infty\#}[\tau(a_t, s_t, \omega, \mathfrak{A})]\}$$

A strategy $\tau^\# = (\alpha_\omega^\#, \omega)$ satisfying (41) is the globally optimal strategy
for the environmental structure ω and defines an optimally adapted discrete adaptive process by using $\alpha_\omega^\#$ in (1)-(4).

Comment. In addition to requiring perfect knowledge of the environment, existence of rolling solutions has been presumed (no small presumption). Consistency imposes a stronger restriction yet. Moreover, the existence of a complete and unchanging preordering over all trajectories as represented in Φ^∞ may be questioned as a realistic component of decision making. Consequently, such models might be used to characterize what is meant by perfectly adapted behavior. Such a characterization, however, is still further complicated when these concepts are applied to multi-adaptor systems. One must then introduce the notion of Pareto maximal trajectories and multiadaptors. That will not be done here, however. Instead, we turn to a reconsideration of explicit optimizing from an adaptive point of view.

Adaptive optimizing strategies. In spite of what has just been observed about global optimizing, human behavior is at least in part, if not in general, predicated on strategic considerations, that is upon an understanding -- imperfect and evolving -- of the system structure within which action is determined. Any choice simultaneously controls the system and generates new information about its structure. As a result the agent is simultaneously "investigator and director" and is faced with the problem of dual control, that is, of figuring out both how to learn and what to do.[24] To apply the global optimizing model the agent must learn about the situation (a_t, s_t), the structure of the environment $(\mathfrak{A}, \omega)$ and his preferences as represented by Φ^∞.

Let actions planned or programmed at time t for the period $t+i$ be a vector $\hat{a}_t^i := (\hat{o}_t^i, \hat{m}_t^i, \hat{d}_t^i, \hat{u}_t^i) \in \hat{\mathbb{A}}$ the perceived action space, so that the strategic aspect of planning explicitly includes the dual nature of behavior. Let $\hat{s}_t$ be the perceived state in $\hat{\mathbb{S}}$, the set of perceived states. Let $w_t \in \mathbb{W}$ be a vector of variables that determine the current structure of the environment and of preferences. Now, for the purposes of planning all of the operators involved in global optimizing must be based on what the agent knows. Hence, we let $\hat{\mathfrak{A}}(\hat{a}_t^i, \hat{s}_t^i, w_t)$ be the perceived admissibility correspondence, $\hat{\omega}(\hat{a}_t^i, \hat{s}_t^i, w_t)$ the perceived transitor and

24

$\Phi^\infty[{}^1(\hat{a},\ \hat{s})_t,\ w_t]$ be the perceived utility function representing current preferences. Now the space of perceived trajectories based on current knowledge is

(42) $\qquad \hat{\mathfrak{A}}^\infty(\hat{a}_t,\ \hat{s}_t,\ w_t) := \{{}^1(\hat{a},\hat{s})_t\,|\,\hat{a}_t^{i+1}\,\epsilon\,\hat{A}(\hat{a}_t^i,\hat{s}_t^i,w_t),\ \hat{s}_t^{i+1}=\hat{\omega}(\hat{a}_t^i,\hat{s}_t^i)\}$.

The "best value function" is

(43) $\qquad \Phi^{\infty\#}(\hat{a}_t,\hat{s}_t,w_t) := \underset{{}^1(\hat{a},\hat{s})_t\,\epsilon\,A(\hat{a}_t,\,\hat{s}_t,w_t)}{\sup}\ \Phi^\infty[{}^1(\hat{a},\hat{s})_t,w_t]$

and the rolling, global optimizing correspondence is

(44)
$$\hat{\mathfrak{A}}^{\infty\#}(\hat{a}_t,\hat{s}_t,w_t) := \{{}^1(\hat{a},\hat{s})_t\,|\,\Phi^\infty[{}^1(\hat{a},\hat{s})_t\geq\Phi^{\infty\#}[\hat{a}_t,\hat{s}_t,\hat{w}_t]\}$$
$$\cap\ \mathfrak{A}^\infty(\hat{a}_t,\hat{s}_t,w_t)\ .$$

The data upon which a plan is predicated is $d_t = (\hat{a}_t,\ \hat{s}_t,\ w_t)\,\epsilon\,\mathbb{D}$ the data space. The plan is now the trajectory or scenario $x_t := {}^1(\hat{a},\hat{s})_t\,\epsilon\,\mathbb{X}$. An adaptive, dual controller or strategic optimizing operator is a mapping $\delta : \mathbb{D} \to \mathbb{X}$,

(45) $\qquad\qquad\qquad x_t = \delta(d_t)\,\epsilon\,\hat{\mathfrak{A}}^{\infty\#}(d_t)\ .$

This planning operator is based on the perception of possibilities and preferences and must be imbedded in the structure of actual events as determined by equations (26)-(30) which determines what is <u>actually</u> observed, remembered, processed and implemented as time goes on. Thus, the complete model of the adaptive agent who behaves according to strategic considerations is (1)-(4) with the adaptor α determined by (31) and (45).

Now it must be noted that, while a dynamic programming model could be derived from the strategic plan (42)-(44) using the planning index i, just as (39)-(41) was derived from (33)-(35), the resulting "optimal strategy" would be optimal only for the currently perceived environmental situation and would be optimal for the true situation only with luck, or in the limit if d_t leads to better and better approximations of $(a_t, s_t, \mathfrak{A}, \omega)$ and if the adaptive utility function $\Phi(.,.,w_t)$ approaches stationarity as t grows large. Consequently adaptive optimizing strategies, though perhaps based on "globally optimal" and "consistent" plans (which satisfy a principle of optimality in the planning index i), will not necessarily lead to globally optimal or consistent behavior. In effect they involve approximate optimization with feedback, the effects of which are accounted for only approximately by the agent. They are, indeed, simply one way of figuring out how to behave when one is partially informed. [25]

Adaptive optimizing tactics and bounded rationality. If, from the adaptive point of view, global optimizing and optimal strategies must be interpreted in this way, then we must ask how good they really are, how they compare with alternative, less "sophisticated" modes of behavior and whether or not they are worth the trouble? It is not possible to go into these questions here. It is sufficient to be reminded that the derivation of optimizing solutions is costly and is based on very restrictive assumptions. Moreover, even under assumptions for which solutions are known to exist, computational algorithms are available for only a limited subset of cases and in those the amount of detail is limited by computational capability. Thus rationality is bounded by perception, logical power and economic capacity. Adaptive man is, to use Simon's term, boundedly rational.

Moreover, adaptive man tends to ask, "If I am to learn a great deal in the future about what is, what might be and what I want, why should I make long horizon plans in the first place, or place too much faith in strategic considerations, however sophisticated? Should I rather incorporate strategic considerations only when I have evidence that far-sighted behavior pays off, and limit the scope of possible plans to some perceptively safe-enough set as dictated by my sense of caution?" If the answer to the latter is affirmative then adaptive man is described by cautious, local, approximate optimization, that is, by adaptive optimizing tactics which account for only a part of the total situation.[26] In formal terms the behavior of such a man is described not by an optimal control or dynamic programming model, but by a sequence of optimizations with feedback, that is, by a recursive programming model which represents the essentially tactical nature of adaptive man's struggle with reality.[27]

Adaptive algorithms. To the extent that tactics involve explicit optimization they constitute a problem the solution to which must be intuited directly or computed by means of an algorithm. Such an algorithm must ultimately reduce to a set of switches and rules which "learns" the optimal solution through a sequence of local explorations of the "true" decision problem. Therefore, when human behavior is represented by means of an explicit optimization model, even of the adaptive genre, either a part of the adaptive mechanism has been subsumed (implicitly assumed to function effectively) or the modeller has invoked the "positivist" proposition that (without explaining how) agents behave "as if" they optimize.

Because of the extreme complexity of human economic activity it is a matter of convenience, if not necessity, to use explicit optimizing models of behavior, precisely because they "short circuit" the complete network of adaptive behavior. However, the adaptive tactical point of view described above should be useful in guiding the modeller when he wishes to understand the actual working of the economy. Moreover, the investigation of adaptive algorithms with the structure described in §3.1-3.2 needs vastly more attention than it has received so far.

27

4. EPILOG: TOWARD AN ADAPTIVE ECONOMICS

4.1. The Questions of Adaptive Economics

If a major new emphasis on adaptive economics is to be launched it may be well to ask how such an enterprise should be guided.

Let us begin with the proposition that the first task of adaptive economics should be to characterize in formal theoretical terms how economies really work: how and under what conditions imperfectly informed agents adjust out of equilibrium to one another and to the system as a whole. Given that survival cannot be realistically assumed in such a world, explicit mechanisms based on learning and adaptive optimizing tactics that maintain viability for individual agents and the economy as a whole must be investigated. Moreover, in that pursuit it would appear to be useful to attempt a characterization of economic survival and viability for the population of agents as a whole while allowing for demise of individual members. Thus economy wide viability may allow for entry and exit of organizations and individual agents.

The second task is a study of the dynamic properties, including the long run properties, of such adaptive systems. Within this context, the existence of stationary or steady states and their socioeconomic efficiency can be investigated. But the latter must not become the focus. Instead, the focus must be on homeostasis, viability and stability of the process. Policy-oriented research in this field should aim at identifying control mechanisms of an adaptive nature that can improve economic performance, primarily from the point of view of viability (homeostasis) and secondarily from the point of view of efficiency. In this way the economic theorist can become more than an apologist for the prevailing system. Instead, he can help improve the mechanism by which a socioeconomic system changes mode of behavior in the interest of its survival and the betterment of its members.

In all of this endeavor a radical reorientation of the axiom structure of economics needs to be considered. Though the original utilitarian

28

and technological assumptions of economic theory were based on intro-
spection and observation, modern theory, with its enthusiastic use of
Occam's razor, has -- along with redundant postulates -- shaved off
much of the reality of economic life, eliminating essential aspects that
cause real economies to work much differently than their theoretical
counterparts. When the economy is working well there seems to be little
reason, and less need, for realistic theories. Moreover, there is a tendency to eliminate those mechanisms instituted when viability and stability were threatened. Then, when the economy misbehaves, the economist has relatively little to offer, both because his theories cannot explain maladaptive behavior and because he has been a party to the de-
struction of those seemingly redundant mechanisms that suddenly become
useful. He finds himself discredited by events.

What is needed is, firstly, the systematic identification and
classification through direct observation and interviews of common modes
of behavior and, secondly, their formalization into coherent axiom structures. The idea here is not to reduce economics to a merely descriptive
exercise with the sole purpose of cataloguing countless special cases.
Rather the idea is to provide believable axiom structures with a view to
establishing more credible deductions about economic behavior and performance.[28]

4.2. Problems of Method: Modelling, Analysis and Simulation

Theoretical exercises that accomodate adaptive components within the context of extremely simple models can yield general analytical
results of great interest and usefulness. Obviously, however, the adaptive approach will, when pursued very far, lead to models of great complexity and variety. For this reason some theorists will advocate aban-
doning them in favor of the simpler, more uniform orthodox theories of
equilibrium and global optimization. In my view it would be a mistake
to follow their advice.

Instead, the activity of investigating models of increasing behavioral complexity should be expanded and, where necessary, computer
simulation should be exploited. Model simulation can never yield general inferences from a given system of assumptions but it can yield specific inferences of great variety and interest. The reluctance of economists to embrace this approach creates a vacuum into which scientists
from other disciplines will eventually flow. The result may well be that
economists, who now hold sway over the interpretation and control of
the economic world, much as the Shamans held sway over the unseen
world long ago, will, like the latter, eventually lose out to those who
interpret the world in more useful and evidently more realistic terms. [29]

4.3. Dialectic

While calling for a vast extension of economic theory we must at
the same time recognize the limits of theory in general and of adaptive
theory in particular. The basis of adaptation is the incompleteness of
knowledge, the inability to comprehend all the properties of complex
systems, the limits on inferring structure from behavior and the limits of
economic constraints placed on theoretical analysis and simulation. It
is likely that man will always face surprise, unanticipated events and
unanswered questions.

In consequence, our understanding of the world system changes,
and our values and preferences are modified with experience. Because
of limited perception, analytical skill and communication arts, both understanding and values are subject to argument, persuasion, and debate.
Hence, from the most general point of view the values and understandings
upon which planning and cultural evolution are based emerge from a dialectical process whose outcomes are not "state determined" in any manner
that can be wholly grasped by mathematical models. Thus, if I have described a starting point for adaptive economics, that point is merely the
beginning of an essentially endless task.

That the content and usefulness of economic theory can be greatly extended by an appeal to concepts of adaptation as summarized here seems evident. Such an effort comprises a project of the greatest scientific and practical importance. But, to paraphrase Georgescu-Roegen, no analytical model, however sophisticated and complete, can exhaust the content of reality, nor can it provide a blueprint for policy.[30] Even the best and most complete will be no more than an analytical simile. Still, analytical similes may be the closest one can ever come to definitive understanding and description of the evolving world of human affairs. If that is so, the imperfection of our theories should not stand as a deterrent to their further elaboration and use.

NOTES

[*]The writer is grateful to A. Cigno and B. Hool who provided numerous useful suggestions for the preparation of this manuscript. He was also aided by numerous stimulating conversations with T. Groves, T. Heidhues, M. Petit, G. Johnson and especially U. Renborg.

[1]"The first heroic step is to divide actuality into two parts - one representing the partial process in point; the other, its environment (so to speak) separated by a boundary consisting of an arithmomorphic void," Georgescu-Roegen [1970, p. 2].

[2]Technical and financial feasibility have always been central in neoclassical microeconomic theory, but in a static context.

[3]The adaptor and transitors, α, $\omega_{\emptyset}$, ω_p may be stochastic, i.e., generate random outputs. The stochastic case is not developed in this paper though the models presented can be elaborated from this point of view, when they are, none of the conclusions are modified in substance.

[4]A continuous time adaptive system can be formulated. The present approach may be considered as an approximation to such a system.

31

[5]Economic theorists have, in order to simplify, taken care to insure viability so that (4) is not involved. In a static setting this is carefully brought out in Debreu [1958].

[6]The term homeostasis was coined by Cannon [1939] who (writing in the great depression) elaborated on the concept's relevance for understanding economic viability. The only economist to have made any significant use of either the term or the idea is Boulding [1950]. The present formalization is based on Ashby [1967].

[7]Adam Smith's concept of a market within which agents pursue their self-interest to their mutual benefit is perhaps the central theme of economics. In its classical form this is a dynamic concept involving some of the essential features of adaptive processes. Even Walras' formalization of the theory, which focusses on competitive equilibrium (in our terms, on a state of adaptedness), retains, in the concept of tatonnement, an explicitly adaptive character. The latter unfortunately involves a stylization of the market which has few real counterparts. Marshall's treatment of the market economy also incorporates a number of adaptive features. Replete with biological analogies, it describes the process by which low cost firms drive out high cost competitors, how firms adapt to the market environment by adjusting investment to prevailing quasi-rents and how marginal changes carried out in disequilibrium converge to long-run equilibrium through a series of temporary, or short-run, equilibria. Marshall's conception of market dynamics is a direct descendent of Malthus' "struggle for existence" that inspired Darwin at precisely the time the neoclassical founding fathers were formalizing the classical concept of the market economy. But the adaptive and evolutionary character of economic dynamics has in this century received much less attention than statics. Marshall, indeed, is remembered primarily for his contribution to static equilibrium theory.

[8]Other contributions to an explicitly adaptive conception of economic behavior are Cournot's and Stackelberg's duopoly models, and Chamberlin's monopolistic competition. Because the competitors in these models do not arrive at efficient long run equilibria, incentives to modify strategies (not perceived by Cournot's firms) exist. For this reason, modern economists have looked for other stylizations, based on game theory, to formulate competition theory. In doing so the theory has lost its adaptive character. But even the static point of view has failed to escape the unhappy result that flows from the study of forms of competition: namely, that the final resting place depends on the information in the hands of the participants and on the particular tactics or strategies they use in adapting to their competitors' activities. The adaptive theory of market competition must inevitably involve special case after special case.

[9]Recent developments in decentralized decision theory have an essentially adaptive character. A classic example is Malinvaud [1967]. See See also Mesarovic et al. [1970].

[10]The temporary equilibrium method was originated by Cournot, elabororated by Marshall and Hicks, and is being used in the contemporary monetary, general equilibrium literature reviewed by Hool elsewhere in this volume. From the present point of view it is a device for expressing the "short-run" adaptive mechanisms that underlie the exchange of money and commodities. Once the existence of temporary equilibria is established, it enables one (with heroic implicit assumptions) to pass on to a consideration of longer-run adaptations involving the sequence of temporary equilibria.

[11]A small but suggestive literature on economic evolution in the sense used here exists. See Winter [1964]. A recent attempt to describe economic development using a version of the theory described by Wynne-

Edwards [1972] is Culbertson [1973]. A careful reading of Marshall suggests that he was much more influenced by the concept than is often remembered.

[12] I believe the following formalization is consistent with anthropological usage. See for example, Childe [1951].

[13] Lotka's brilliant Elements of Mathematical Biology [1924] contains this and numerous other cogent insights into the nature of biological and economic adaptation and evolution.

[14] See Simon [1956] and [1957].

[15] Marschak [1968] was an early advocate for explicitly accounting for these separate functions.

[16] See Simon [1956], [1957], March and Simon [1958], and Cyert and March [1963]. For a concise review see Day [forthcoming].

[17] See Forrester [1961].

[18] See Stewart, D. J. [1967].

[19] See Winter's chapter in this volume.

[20] See Day and Tinney [1968]. A far more powerful analysis is found in the joint work of Radner and Rothschild. See the latter's chapter in this volume.

[21] On temporary equilibrium see note 10 above.

[22] See Bellman [1957] or Karlin [1955].

[23] On consistency see Strotz [1966]. On the axiomatic foundations for (*) to which both consistency and the principle of optimality are related see Koopmans [1972].

[24]See Marschak [1963], [1972], and Fel'dbaum [1965].

[25]I believe this argument to be true even for the Bayesian formulation of (42)-(44). Any notion of optimality must be contingent on an environmental structure -- even if the latter is stochastic.

[26]Let it be emphasized again we are talking about the way people are, not how they should or wish to be. See Day [1971].

[27]For a review of recursive programming theory and empirical applications see Day and Cigno [forthcoming].

[28]In doing so a large and useful literature of institutional case studies and surveys can be drawn upon.

[29]A prominent example of a massive invasion using adaptive modelling is J. W. Forrester, who was originally an electrical engineer. See Forrester [1974]. See also the IEEE Journal Systems, Man and Cybernetics.

[30]Georgescu-Roegen, N. [1966, p. 116].

REFERENCES

Ashby, W. R. [1967], "The Set Theory of Mechanism and Homeostasis," in D. J. Stewart (ed.), Automation Theory and Learning Systems, Washington, D. C.: Thompson Book Co.

Bellman, R. [1957], Dynamic Programming, Princeton: Princeton University Press.

Boulding, K. E. [1962], A Reconstruction of Economics, New York: Science Editions, Inc.

Cannon, W. B. [1939], The Wisdom of the Body (revised edition), New York: W. W. Norton and Co., Inc.

Childe, V. G. [1951], Social Evolution, London: Watts and Co.

Culbertson, John [1973], Economic Development: An Ecological Approach, New York: Alfred A. Knopf.

Cyert, R. M. and J. G. March [1963], A Behavioral Theory of the Firm, Englewood Cliffs, New Jersey: Prentice-Hall.

Day, R. H. [forthcoming], "Behavioral Economics" in Beckmann, Menges and Selten (eds.), Handwörterbuch der Mathematischen Wirt- schaftswissenschaften, Opladen: Westdeutscher Verlag.

_____ [1971], "Rational Choice and Economic Behavior," Theory and Decision, 1:229-251.

Day, R. H. and A. Cigno (eds.) [forthcoming], Recursive Programming Models of Economic Change, Amsterdam: North-Holland Pub- lishing Co.

Day, R. H. and E. H. Tinney [July-August 1968], "How to Cooperate in Business Without Really Trying: A Learning Model of Decentral- ized Decision Making," Journal of Political Economy, 76:583-600.

Debreu, G. [1959], Theory of Value, New York: John Wiley and Sons, Inc.

Dobzhansky, T. [1972], "Natural Selection in Mankind," in Harrison and Boyce (eds.), Oxford: Clarendon Press.

Fel'dbaum, A. A. [1965], Optimal Control Systems, New York: Academic Press.

Forrester, J. W. [1961], Industrial Dynamics, Cambridge: MIT Press.

_____ [1974], "Understanding Social and Economic Change in the United States," Address delivered at the Summer Computer Simulation Conference, Houston, Texas, July 10.

Georgescu-Roegen, N. [1970], "The Economics of Production" (Richard T. Ely Lecture), American Economic Review, 60:1-9.

_____ [1966], Analytical Economics, Cambridge: Harvard University Press.

Karlin, S. [1955], "The Structure of Dynamic Programming Models," Naval Logistics Research Quarterly, 2:285-294.

Koopmans, T. C. [1972], "Representation of Preference Orderings Over Time," in C. B. McGuire and R. Radner (eds.), Decision and Organization, Amsterdam: North-Holland Publishing Co.

Lotka, A. J. [1924], Elements of Mathematical Biology, New York: Dover Publications, Inc., Dover Edition, 1956.

Malinvaud, E. [1967], "Decentralized Procedures for Planning," in E. Malinvaud and M. O. L. Bacharach (eds.), Activity Analysis in the Theory of Growth and Planning, London: Macmillan, St. Martin's Press.

March, J. G. and H. A. Simon [1968], Organizations, New York: John Wiley and Sons.

Marschak, J. [1963], "On Adaptive Programming," Management Science, 9:517-526.

_____ [1968], "Economics of Inquiring, Communicating, Deciding," American Economic Review, 58:1-18.

_____ [1972], "Optimal Systems for Information and Decision," in Techniques of Optimization, New York: Academic Press, Inc.

Mesarović, M. D., D. Macko, and Y. Takahara [1970], Theory of Hierarchical Multilevel Systems. New York: Academic Press.

Radner, R. and M. Rothschild [1975], "On the Allocation of Effort," Journal of Economic Theory, Vol. 10, No. 3.

Simon, H. A. [1956], Administrative Behavior, New York: MacMillan.

_____ [1957], Models of Man, New York: Wiley.

Stewart, D. J. [1967], "Logical Nets and Organisms that Learn," in Stewart (ed.), Automation Theory and Learning Systems, Washington, D. C.: Thompson Book Co.

_____ (ed.) [1967], Automation Theory and Learning Systems, Washington, D. C.: Thompson Book Co. Papers by Andrew, Ashby, Genge, Pash, Shephardson, Stewart.

Strotz, R. [1966], "Myopia and Inconsistency in Dynamic Utility Maximization," Revised Economic Studies, 165-180.

Winter, S. G. [1964], "Economic Natural Selection and the Theory of the Firm," Yale Economic Essays, 4:225-272.

_____ [1971], "Satisficing, Selection, and the Innovating Remnant," Quarterly Journal of Economics, 85:237-261.

Wynne-Edwards, V. C. [1972], Animal Dispersion in Relation to Social Behavior, New York: Hafner Publishing Co., Inc.

Biological Systems as Paradigms for Adaptation
Robert Rosen

CONTENTS

1. INTRODUCTION

One of the most troublesome, as well as one of the most stimulating characteristics of the growth of knowledge during the past decades is the appearance of homologous modes of behavior at many different and apparently unrelated levels of organization. Such developments are troublesome because a concept or method required by a researcher in a particular field may have been formulated, not in his own field, but in a completely different one, to which, according to our traditions of intense specialization, he may never normally have access. Thus, at best, there follows an inefficient duplication of results in many different specialties, and at worst a paralysis of important fields until such time as appropriate insights can be developed from within these fields themselves.

Nevertheless, this insistent reappearance of homologous behaviors in many apparently independent areas could not occur unless there exist deep formal relationships between these areas. One of the most exciting tasks of contemporary theoretical science is to discern and articulate these relationships, and examine their implications and consequences. The benefits accruing from these theoretical activities are many. For one thing, they allow the development of new kinds of unifying principles, with their attendant economies of thought which we must have if we are not to be overwhelmed by torrents of specialized new knowledge. Perhaps even more important, such unifying principles will allow us to effectively transfer knowledge and insights obtained in a particular special context to entirely new contexts, in which they may be all-important but not readily visible.

Just at present, many different kinds of specialists are concerned with understanding those modes of behavior of systems which are commonly called <u>adaptive</u>. Adaptive behavior is, of course, most prominent in biological organisms, and in populations of these organisms. But it is equally of the essence in engineering technology, where the fabrication of "adaptive control" systems dominates whole fields; and, perhaps most importantly for us in the long run, it is at the center of the technologies we require to control our own human institutions, especially in the economic and political realm.

Let us concentrate on economics, the theme of the present conference. Just at present, our own economy seems to be escaping from our control, as it did in the 1930's and many times before that. Since, as Alan Bullock remarked, the unique quality of economic upheaval is that "of reaching down and touching every single member of the community in a way which no political event can", such a loss of control can have the most tragic and far-reaching consequences. Despite the best efforts of

40

our professional specialists in economics, control is not visibly being regained. Moreover, the obvious measures which have been taken to regain control have actually seemed to exacerbate the situation.

The fact that our economic system has responded to attempts to control it in surprising and unexpected ways has often been offered as an illustration that complex systems are "counter-intuitive". What does such a statement mean? It means simply that those intuitions regarding system behavior which we presently possess were formed on systems which are in some sense simple, and that the properties of these simple systems do not generalize in any obvious way. In fact, at present we simply do not have any real intuition regarding the way in which complex systems behave, and this fact, more than anything else, is responsible for the interconnected body of problems which the Club of Rome has called la problématique. In the economic realm, it is clear that we cannot wait for such insights to develop from within economics itself; we must, if possible, be able to import such insights as are available from other disciplines and reformulate them in an economic context.

The aim of the present paper is to indicate how concepts arising from biology, which is the study of the class of complex systems with which we have had the most experience, can be formulated in such a way that they can be a source of insight into man's social systems. Such an approach has been suggested, from a variety of points of view, by many biologists of past and present generations (cf. e.g. Cannon 1933, 1942; Bonner 1955; Hardin 1963; Hollings 1969; Salk 1972, 1973). In this work we shall consider the special context of adaptive behavior. This is only a fragment of the many ways in which systems concepts can be transferred from one field to another, but it is an important one, and is itself rich enough so that we will be able only to provide an outline in this brief space.

In Section 2 below, we shall set forth some general strategic principles for dealing with broad, ambiguous systemic concepts like adaptation. In Section 3, we shall set forth some generalities regarding

41

adaptive mechanisms in biology. In Section 4, these adaptive mechanisms will be classified according to their flexibility and generality; and finally in Section 5 we shall consider some of the implications of the preceding sections bearing on the problems we face in dealing with human systems.

2. SOME GENERALITIES ON "ADAPTATION"

The term "adaptive", like so many other functional or behavioral terms which dominate the study of complex systems, is employed in a bewildering number of different ways. Moreover, such concepts as "adaptation", as well as cognate concepts like "memory", "learning", "fitness", "development", "intelligence", and many others, seem to be embarassingly qualitative material on which to try to base a hard predictive science. Yet it is precisely these qualitative, functional concepts which embody what we really want to know about complex systems, and we cannot sidestep the problem of how to deal with them.

The root of the difficulty in dealing with functional concepts is that they cannot readily be defined formally, but only ostensively. This involves identifying a spectrum of examples or instances of the behavior we wish to study, manifested by systems of widely differing structural properties. A term like "memory", for example, can legitimately be applied to inorganic systems exhibiting hysteresis, to technological artifacts, and to many different aspects of biological behavior. There is no obvious structural similarity between these diverse systems, and hence the mechanisms by which memory is manifested in these different systems are likewise different. Since we are accustomed to defining qualitative behavioral properties in terms of quantitative structural ones, we reach an impasse when the same kind of behavior arises out of unrelated structures. This indeed is one of the crucial problems with reductionism in biology and the behavioral sciences.

42

One kind of strategy for dealing directly with functional concepts like "adaptation" which is proving effective is the following: Since adaptive properties are defined ostensively, in terms of a spectrum of examples, let us see if we can assign these various examples to a number of classes, such that within each class, the behavior we regard as adaptive can be identified with a specific kind of structural property. Thus, within each class, the qualitative term "adaptation" becomes identified with specific, quantitative aspects of system structure, and hence amenable to conventional modes of system investigation. These identifications, and hence the very meaning of "adaptation", will of course differ from class to class. But each sense in which the term "adaptation" can be meaningfully used will correspond to a class of systems in which the term is connected to an explicit kind of structure and organization. Thus, when a new system is encountered which exhibits adaptive behavior in some sense, the main problem will be to determine into which such class the new system most appropriately falls.

Stated another way: within each class, the broadly qualitative concept of "adaptation" receives a much narrower quantitative definition, which only captures a fragment of its general meaning. Within each class, we thereby lose generality, but gain the capacity to deeply investigate the implications of "adaptation" within the class. Generality is recaptured by considering many such classes.

This procedure, like so much else in system theory, had its conceptual origins in the study of mechanical systems, especially in the work of Galileo, Newton, Lagrange and others. The basis of mechanics as a science was laid by taking <u>qualitative</u> terms like "force", "momentum", "energy", "power", etc., and constraining them in a narrow quantitative fashion appropriate for the study of systems of material particles. Thus, within the framework of mechanics, enormous advances were possible, while outside of physics these same functional terms retain their broad and contradictory connotations, and hence have remained largely useless for scientific purposes.

Further, we should note that many different kinds of questions can be asked about classes of behaviors like those which we call "adaptive". Given a spectrum of examples of adaptation in different kinds of systems, we can ask such questions as:

1. How shall we most effectively describe and understand specific instances of adaptation?

2. Given a specimen of adaptive behavior, how did the adaptive mode arise from a previous non-adapted state?

3. Given a system which is in some sense non-adapted, how can we make it adaptive?

It is this third question which is of primary interest for technological and economic applications. The first two questions have been broadly studied in a wide variety of biological contexts. Clearly, if we can answer question (2) in a variety of different classes defining different interpretations of adaptation, we will be well along towards answering (3) in any given situation. But we cannot define these classes effectively without solving question (1). In what follows, therefore, we shall attempt to sketch how the general strategy we have outlined can be implemented, utilizing a spectrum of biological examples of adaptive behavior. These will fall into definite classes, in each of which the questions (1), (2), (3) above can be meaningfully posed, and whose solutions in each class become a technical matter. We shall then see to what extent we can "export" the insights so obtained to the generation of specific algorithms required for solving problem (3) in applied fields.

3. SOME BIOLOGICAL ASPECTS OF ADAPTATION

In this section, we shall briefly outline some of the main ideas derived from the study of adaptive processes in biological systems, and which will be important to us later. Our treatment is necessarily a sketchy one, and the interested reader is referred to the references for fuller discussions. We have separated the material in this section into eight parts, each dealing with a relatively self-contained idea.

3.1. Evolution: An Adaptive Mechanism for Generating Adaptations

To a biologist, the sum total of the behaviors and structures through which an organism copes with its surroundings is summed up in a single word: fitness. The concept of fitness plays an analogous role in biology to that played by money in economics; it provides a common currency in terms of which diverse biological processes may be compared (cf. e.g. Fisher 1930; Thoday 1953). Roughly speaking, fitness is determined by the relative capacity of an individual organism to leave offspring; the more fit an organism for a particular environmental niche, the more offspring it will tend to leave. Therefore, to the extent that an organism's fitness is passed on to its progeny, the population to which it belongs will tend to become enriched in fit organisms.

Given a biological individual, its structures and behaviors arise from an interplay between its genome and the environmental circumstances of its development. The correlation of fitness with production of offspring means that, at the genetic level, a fit organism contributes more of its genes to the "gene pool" of the population to which it belongs than one which is less fit. In this way, the composition of this gene pool changes with time, in a way corresponding to increasing fitness.

From the standpoint of an individual organism, fitness and adapted- are closely related concepts. The relation between them is analogous to the economic relation between money and wealth; the first provides a common numerical measure in terms of which the diverse forms of the second may be compared to each other. But the two concepts are not identical, and the various distinctions between them should always be kept in mind (cf. for another kind of discussion Dobzhansky 1968).

What we have described above is a thumbnail sketch of the modern theory of natural selection and its genetic underpinning. Selection occurs through differential reproductive rates as a function of fitness for a particular environmental niche. Insofar as selection tends to increase fitness, it tends to generate adaptations. In this sense, evolution itself is the adaptive process par excellence. Indeed, the most general and

45

interesting formal treatment of adaptive systems (Holland 1970) is basically a paraphrase of the evolutionary process. Moreover, the evolutionary process has provided mathematicians with practical tools for solving extremization problems (e. g. Bremmermann 1966). Indeed, in biological terms, if we suppose that a sequence of increasingly fit organisms in an evolutionary process approaches a limit, in which fitness is maximal, then such a limiting organism can be regarded as optimal for its environmental niche; this is the intuitive relation between evolution and considerations of optimal design of organisms (cf. Rosen 1967).

It should be noted that the strategy of evolution is, in human terms, an extravagant one. It is not incorrect to say that evolution proceeds by making all possible experiments (and hence all possible mistakes), continually eliminating those which are less fit. The redundancy and prodigality of this kind of strategy for producing adaptations makes it unlikely that we would want to copy this particular strategy in generating adaptations. But evolution provides a kind of existence proof, showing that there exists at least one mechanism, or algorithm, for generating adaptation. If one such algorithm exists, however, other equivalent ones must also exist; understanding any one of them will provide clues to the formulation of others (cf. Salk loc. cit.).

3.2. The Concept of the Individual

Broadly speaking, adaptation refers to those processes of structural or behavioral modifications which permit organisms to function more effectively in a particular kind of environment. Adaptation is a process, which results in a state of adaptedness; as we have seen, the most stringent test of adaptedness is survival, either of an individual organism, or of its progeny.

The individual organism is the basic unit on which selection acts. The concept of adaptedness becomes quite meaningless apart from the standpoint of the individual whose survival is favored by the adaptation. As many authors have pointed out (Weiss 1949, Pittendrigh 1958),

adaptation must be _for_ something, and that something must be a property
embodied by individual organisms. A particular physiological mechanism,
by itself, it not an adaptation of anything or for anything; it becomes so
only when integrated into an organism whose survival it favors.

This much may seem trivial, but it will become quite important to
us in the next section. For in speaking of any adaptation, we must first
be able to identify the individual to which the adaptation refers, and on
whose survival it bears. We feel we have no difficulty doing this at the
biological level; we do not hesitate to identify a bacterial cell as a
meaningful individual, or a tree, or a dog. But what of a cell culture?
An ecosystem? A termite nest? A pair of termite nests? Our instinct in
these situations becomes less categorical. Indeed, both the concepts of
"individual" and of "survival" are exceedingly subtle and difficult ones,
for which an analysis like that we suggested for the concept of "adaptation" might likewise be appropriate. And we must meet these notions
squarely at the very outset of any discussion of adaptation, as well as
in many other discussions of the human implications of the biological
sciences (Salk, _loc. cit._).

The examples we have just cited leads us into the next general
concept which must be mentioned.

3.3. The Hierarchical Structure of Biological Organizations

The process of biological evolution began long ago with the proliferation of individual cellular units. Since such cells are individuals
with a well-defined notion of survival, we can speak of their adaptations
to a host of environmental circumstances. But at some point, we find an
emergence of associations between these units, to form entirely new
kinds of individuals (colonies, multicellular organisms) at a higher level
of organization. These must then, as individuals, adapt in their turn.
The most conspicuous way in which they can adapt is to _differentiate_; to
elaborate an unending complexity of organs and organ systems, which
may be regarded, at the cellular level, as a manifestation of a cellular

47

capacity to adapt, not directly to the external environment, but rather to the organism of which the cell is a part.

The organs which have arisen in the course of evolution of multicellular organisms are the instruments through which these organisms manifest adaptation. But it must be stressed that the association of differentiated cells into organs do not comprise an intermediate evolutionary stage in the generation of multicellular individuals; they only represent a convenient way of analyzing the adaptations of those individuals. For this reason, it is misleading to introduce an "organ" level into the biological hierarchy; in a certain sense, the physiological organs of a multicellular individiaul are epiphenomena, visible and meaningful only from the standpoint of the whole organism of which they are a part. These organs themselves, then, cannot be considered as biological individuals in their own right, and it is therefore not correct to speak of their "survival" and "adaptation" in the same sense as we do of individual cells or multicellular organisms. As we shall see, this is a crucial aspect of our subsequence discussion; see also §3.5 below.

Now just as we envision multicellular individuals arising from associations of individual cells, so we can imagine emerging associations of multicellular organisms. Some of these supra-organismic associations we may wish to call societies, and to consider as individuals in their own right. If so, we can meaningfully ask such questions as: what is meant by the survival of such individuals? How do they manifest adaptation? such questions arise naturally out of the biological context we have developed, and will be considered in more detail in the next section; for the moment we only note that, in addressing such questions, we can use multicellularity as a paradigm.

The idea that we can treat societies as a new emergent level of adaptive individuals, i.e. as "super-organisms", is of course not new, and has had a long and controversial history. We refer the reader to the discussions of Emerson (cf. Emerson 1952) for the most convincing theoretical support for this idea. However, if it is true that we can regard

48

"societies" as adaptive individuals in their own right, then our remark
that "multicellularity is a paradigm" can be regarded as a consequence,
or corollary, of the evolutionary process itself. For adapting individual
organisms, at any level, in the face of analogous selection pressures,
tend to elaborate analogous adaptations; this is the phenomenon of <u>con-
vergent</u> <u>evolution</u>. The mechanisms by which diverse organisms undergo
adaptation in analogous environmental situations are, of course, likewise
diverse, but the adaptations themselves tend to be similar. Thus, if it
is true that "societies" can be regarded as adaptive individuals, and if
it is true that the selection pressures on them can be analogized to those
impinging on multicellular organisms, then the principle of convergence
implies precisely that multicellularity will be a paradigm for understanding adaptation at the societal level. This is the sense in which our assertion should be understood.

3.4. Biological Hierarchies: Evolutionary Aspects

We noted above that, in effect, one kind of adaptation which could
be manifested by individual cells was to associate into supra-cellular
organizations, which could then themselves evolve and adapt as individuals. Now individual free-living cells can exhibit remarkable adaptive
powers. By contrast, the most primitive multicellular organisms, <u>as</u>
<u>individuals</u>, exhibit a correspondingly far more primitive degree of adap-
tation. Doubtless, the assumption of multicellular modes of organization
ultimately makes possible an evolutionary <u>capability</u> to manifest much
higher and more elaborate modes of adaptation than is possible at the
cellular level; but the point is that, <u>at the outset</u>, multicellular modes
of organization were more primitively adaptable than unicellular ones,
and it took eons before the superior latent possibilities for adaptation in
multicellulars could be manifested. And in order to make such real evolutionary progress possible, it was necessary to appear to take a step
backward.

The same thing is true at the next higher level. Insofar as a social
aggregation can be regarded as an individual, its adaptive capabilities

49

are far more primitive than those manifested by the organisms which compose it. We can ask whether multicellularity is paradigmatic for this aspect also; i.e. can social organizations become more complexly adaptive than the organisms of which they are composed? If so, what are the requirements? We shall consider such questions further in Part 5 below.

3.5. On the Health of a Complex Organism

It is a truism to point out that the organs of a complex organism do not act independently. If they could act independently, then we would be justified in regarding any one of them as itself an "individual", and we could speak of its adaptibility. We would then find the paradoxical situation that, by optimizing the adaptability of each organ independently, we will in general kill the organism. For instance, we might be tempted to argue as follows: an efficient circulatory system, say, is essential to the health of a human being. Therefore whatever facilitates the circulation is good; whatever hinders the circulation is bad. Now it is a fact that the main stress on the heart arises from the necessity to force blood through the capillaries of peripheral organs; therefore to minimize the stress on the heart means to minimize the peripheral organs (e.g. kidneys, liver, lungs, brain). In a certain sesne, health is maintained precisely because individual organs cannot be treated as adaptive individuals in their own right; as soon as they become so, health is disturbed (cf. Salk. loc. cit.). In biology, such Pyrrhic "adaptations" as the one just discussed cannot arise, for selection acts on the level of the whole individual organism, and not directly on its parts.

On the other hand, the fact that it is the survival of the whole organism, and not of any particular organ acting independently, on which selection acts, does not in theory preclude the manifestation of adaptive powers by organs in their own right. After all, a multicellular organism is a collection of individual cells, each of which is separately adaptive; therefore there is no reason a priori why an organism cannot likewise be built out of a family of interacting organs which are likewise separately

50

adaptive. As we shall see later, however, it is a fact that biological modes of organization do not tend to employ organs of adaptation which are themselves directly adaptive; apparently the constraints which have to be imposed on a population of adapting individuals in order for that population to comprise a higher-level adaptive individual are too severe to be easily manifested at the "organ level".

3.6. On Emergence and Emergent Novelty

In the first paragraph of this section, we dealt briefly with the evolutionary view of the origin of adaptations. The picture we drew there was in the main one of refining and elaborating structures and processes already present. Yet the most striking characteristic of evolution is its discontinuities; transitions from marine to terrestrial; from invertebrate to vertebrate; from unicellular to multicellular; transitions which are not a matter of degree but of kind. Such appearances of entirely new structures, playing entirely new functional roles, is generally what is referred to as emergence, and it seems incompatible with the picture we gave.

New structures must come from somewhere. At the very lowest level, they must imply the presence of new genes. Where can new genes come from? From mutation, clearly. But mutation is only a partial answer. Equally important are the numerous mechanisms which generate redundancy at the genetic level; to give many copies of a gene where only one was available before. With such redundancy comes the capability for independent variation where none was previously present; and as we saw earlier, the formula redundancy + selection = adaptation is the evolutionary formula.

The generation of redundancy is a first step for the elaboration of new structures, and it is easy to imagine how entirely new activities could arise in this way, by accretion. But there is another, more subtle, and perhaps more interesting mechanism whereby new functions can originate; this is most frequently called the Principle of Function Change. Speaking broadly, any organ, and in general any physical system which

exhibits a particular functional activity, has implicit in it the capacity
to manifest many other kinds of activities. A small change in selection
in the environment can cause an organ, originally adapted for one kind
of purpose, to switch over into an entirely different one. Function change
thus displays a kind of opportunism characteristic of evolutionary adaptation. It also helps to explain how complex organs, like the eye, could
have evolved at all, since an eye conveys no advantage until it sees,
and it cannot see until it has evolved.

The system-theoretic realities underlying the possibility of function
change, which we have discussed elsewhere (Rosen 1974) have a number
of other profound consequences of importance for a study of adaptation.
For they imply that, as a general rule, attempts to control a subsystem
of a complex system will induce unpredictable changes in other subsystems ("side effects") one of the consequences of which is often a modification or loss of the very control it was intended to exert. These properties are at the root of the dialectical qualities of complex systems; in
the long term they can cause the most drastic and calamitous effects,
but in the short term, they play a most important role in adaptation; all
the more important because it has been so conspicuously neglected in
technical treatments of adaptive systems.

Function change, then, is not an accretion but a re-organization.
At the physiological levels, we can also find spectacular cases of such
re-organization, apparently as discontinuous as the transition from invertebrate to vertebrate, in the phenomena of insect and amphibian
metamorphosis.

3.7. Evolution and Progress

In biology, it is clear that evolutionary mechanisms have elaborated successively more elaborate and complex organisms, in some
commonly accepted intuitive sense. Therefore it is easy to believe that
evolution is synonymous with "progress". This kind of view is difficult
to defend on any grounds (cf. Williams 1966 for a good discussion).

Insofar as we can attach any meaning to a progressive trend in evolution, it must involve transitions from "special-purpose" organisms to "general-purpose" ones; or to use another kind of computer-originated jargon, from adaptations of hardware to adaptations of software. Under a given set of environmental circumstances, there is no reason to prefer a general-purpose design over a special-purpose one; perhaps quite the contrary. This is one way to understand the persistence of "primitive" forms which have always provided a counter-argument to notions of evolutionary progress. Indeed, there is a certain sense in which it is true that the evolution of "higher" forms favors the persistence of lower ones, since the activities of the "higher" forms tend to create many new environmental niches into which more primitive ones can move.

4. A CLASSIFICATION OF ADAPTIVE MECHANISMS

In accord with the general strategy laid down in Part 2 for dealing with the complex and ambiguous concept of "adaptation", we will now attempt to construct a classification of adaptive mechanisms, such that all the mechanisms falling into the same class will exhibit some kind of commonality, while those falling into different classes will exhibit a corresponding diversity. Like any taxonomy, the classification to be developed is intended as a tool to facilitate analysis, by narrowing and localizing the domain of the analysis. As in any complex situation, the basis we use for the classification is not the only one possible, and other useful ones can be imagined. Nevertheless, it is hoped that the one adopted will possess some utility for our purposes.

The adaptive mechanisms which provide our main point of departure are mainly those exhibited in the physiology of organisms however, wherever possible, examples are drawn from technology or from social and behavioral levels of organization.

4.1. Class I: Feedback Homeostats

We call a homeostat any process or mechanism whereby some

53

system quantity can be maintained at a constant level, within a class of randomly fluctuating environments. Homeostats are the most familiar adaptive mechanisms, partly because so many biological adaptations are of this type, and partly because we can build certain kinds of homeostats for ourselves.

In formal terms, any homeostat can be decomposed into two sub-systems: a controlled system and a controller. (It is to be emphasized that, in many cases, this decomposition is a purely formal one, and need not correspond to any simple decomposition of a real system into separate "organs".) We desire to maintain some function of the state of the controlled system at a constant level, in the face of randomly fluctuating environments environments producing deviations from constancy.

The characteristic property of the feedback homeostat is that the controller looks only at the controlled system, and not at the environment. From the deviation of the state of the controlled system away from the desired one, the controller evaluates an error function; from the value of the error function, the controller then modifies the dynamics of the controlled system in such a way as to diminish the error.

Biological examples of such feedback homeostats are: (1) the pupillary servomechanism (Stark 1959), ensuring a constant flux of light on the retina; (2) the retinal mechanism for light and dark adaptation, ensuring a constant rate of retinal excitation at different light intensities (Bartlett 1965); (3) thermoregulation in warm-blooded animals (Milsum 1965); (4) adaptive enzyme formation in bacteria, ensuring a constant flow of metabolites through the cell in the face of ambient variations of carbon source (Hinshelwood 1953); (5) regeneration phenomena and the healing of wounds. Engineering examples of feedback homeostats, of course, also abound.

Formally, we are well equipped for understanding and describing any given feedback homeostat. There is a sense in which any dynamical system, in the neighborhood of an asymptotically stable steady state, can be regarded as a feedback homeostat (cf. Rosen 1971). Moreover,

there is a close relation between such homeostats and optimality problems; for when some system quantity is conserved (i.e. held constant)
some related quantity is typically extremized. In engineering applications, emphasis is usually given to the conserved quantity; in biology
one tends to stress the extremized one (because it is easier to detect
selection through such quantities).

Let us list some of the general properties of feedback homeostats,
which hold true independent of the specific structural details involved in
their operation:

1. Feedback homeostats are special-purpose systems. Once
fabricated and operating, their behavior is obligate.

2. Feedback homeostats operate as a result of randomness in
their environment. Typically, however, only one aspect of the environment is important. For instance, a thermostat designed to keep water
from boiling will fail if the pressure is lowered. Thus, these homeostats
can be "fooled".

3. There is no memory trace; the present activity of a feedback
homeostat is independent of its past behavior.

4. In biological feedback homeostats, the special-purpose
"hardware" required for their activity is difficult to modify for other
purposes; in some sense their generation is irreversible.

4.2. Class II: Feed-Forward Homeostats

The feedback homeostats were characterized by the fact that the
controller senses only the state of the controlled system, and not the
environment directly. We now envisage a new type of controller, with
the following additional properties:

1. The controller can sense an environmental quantity q, whose
present value is correlated to some future value of the state p of the
controlled system.

2. The correlation between $q(t)$ and $p(t + \tau)$ is "wired in" to the
controller.

3. The controller can modify the dynamics of the controller system in accord with the present values of q and p, so as to maintain constant some function of p.

Adaptive mechanisms of this type are radically different from those of the feedback homeostats. They introduce a notion of prediction which was previously absent. Further, we can say that the controller embodies a model of the external world, in the correlation between q and p, in terms of which it can select, or choose, an appropriate behavior for the controlled system.

Feed-forward homeostats have certain advantages over feedback homeostats. For one thing, controller operation is no longer primarily off an error signal. In an error-driven system, the behavior of the system has necessarily deteriorated before the controller can begin to act. Since any feedback loop has an intrinsic time constant, it can happen that performance has irreversibly deteriorated before control is instituted. Further, in environments which fluctuate too rapidly, the entire control system will track the fluctuations rather than exhibit homeostasis. The feedforward homeostat avoids these difficulties completely.

Examples of such anticipatory control abound in biology. Plants prepare for winter on the basis of day length rather than ambient temperature. Animals which require high humidity tend to be photophobic, moving to regions of low light intensity. Behavioral phenomena such as "imprinting" (in which a newly hatched bird will follow the first large moving object it sees) and many unconditioned reflexes are of this type. In our technology, we can also find examples: the automatic setting of aperture and shutter speeds in cameras, or in the control of chemical plants through analog simulations (Greene 1973) (This paper also contains a most imaginative discussion of the synthesis of such homeostats).

Our capacity to recognize and describe homeostats operating through feed-forward or anticipation is much more sharply circumscribed than is the case with feedback systems. The very word "anticipatory" is excluded by physicists and system modellers, because of a host of unpleasant mystical associations (Zadeh and Desoer 1963). As a result, when we encounter a homeostatic process, we almost invariably attempt to understand it in terms of feedbacks; we can always _simulate_ an anticipatory system by a generally far more complex feedback system, but we cannot thereby understand it. Indeed, we have almost no understanding of the dynamical correlates of these systems. Yet they are of the essence in many important biological and behavioral mechanisms.

Some of the essential properties of feedforward homeostats are the following:

1. The "model" of the external world embodied in the controller introduces the incipient concept of "software" into the adaptive process; by changing the "model" we can modify the entire system without completely redesigning it.

2. A feedforward homeostat requires a sensory mechanism for direct access to the environment.

3. Feedforward homeostats operate off _regularities_ in the environment (embodied in the correlation between q and p) rather than off randomness (which as we have seen generates the error signal to which a feedback homeostat responds).

4. The feedforward homeostats have no memory trace; i.e. their present activity is independent of their past, and their behavior is still hardware-dependent.

4.3. Class III: Feedback Homeostats with Memory

In this class, we consider feedback homeostats which can make a "memory trace" of previous experience, and employ such memory traces to modify or modulate their present behavior.

In their simplest form, homeostats in this class can be regarded as able to modify their set-points and/or time constants, as a function of their own past behavior and that of the controlled system. In order for such a modification to be adaptive, some kind of improvement in the performance of the homeostat must result from it. Such an improvement generally takes the form of enlarging or otherwise modifying the class of environments in which homeostasis can be maintained.

Any system which can lay down a memory trace, which has a means of access to its memory traces, and can utilize this access to improve its overall activity, can be said to be a learning system. Perhaps the best biological example of this class of adaptations is found in the immune system. This system, universally present in higher organisms, can "remember" exposure to foreign antigens, so that on re-exposure an appropriate defensive response is made. In crude terms, the laying down of a memory trace in the immune system may be regarded as a set-point modification, since states of the controlled system (i.e. the circulating proteins) which previously provoked no error signal to the controller will subsequently do so. On the other hand, a variety of facilitation phenomena (e.g. in the central nervous system) in which an appropriate response to a new environmental situation becomes easier to perform on repetition, can best be regarded as a change in the time constant. Many other examples of this kind of "memory" can exist; populations of micro-organisms originally sensitive to antibiotic, or of insects sensitive to insecticide, recover more quickly after previous exposure to the toxic material (due, of course, to selection for resistance during past exposures).

The existence of a memory trace introduces a new kind of irreversibility into the functioning of a feedback homeostat. We remarked previously that a feedback homeostat without memory is a special-purpose device. The introduction of memory typically does not alter this characteristic; a change in set-point and/or time constant still leaves us with a special-purpose device. Thus, in the most general terms, a feedback homeostat with memory exhibits a kind of hysteresis.

4.4. Class IV. Feedforward Homeostats with Memory

We place in this class those systems which have the properties of feedforward homeostats, which can make memory traces of past behavior, and employ these traces to modify their subsequent activity.

Just as the feedback homeostats with memory could utilize past behavior to modify their set point and/or time constant, the feedforward homeostats with memory can employ their past behavior to modify their internal models; i.e. their correlations between present values of environmental quantities and subsequent values of the states of the controlled system. Thus, in a certain sense, these systems are capable of reprogramming themselves, or of modifying their own software. It is in this class that we find the bulk of the "adaptive control systems" of the mathematical and engineering literature (cf. for example Yakowitz 1969) as well as those systems considered in the literatures devoted to artificial intelligence and self-organization.

Ironically, the feedforward homeostats with memory must employ features of the Class I feedback homeostats in their operation. For they must employ an error signal (i.e. a deviation from a predicted or desired state) in order to modify their internal model. They thus suffer from the limitations of all feedback systems. Nevertheless, there is an enormous gain in adaptive power in systems which can modify their models of the world on the basis of part experience. For in this class fall all the learning and conditioning behaviors which are exhibited by the higher organisms.

As a very special, but most important, case, we can consider the situation in which the initial "wired-in" correlation between the environmental quantity q sensed by the controller and the state p of the controlled system is random. In this case, we can regard the initial behavior of the system as completely unadapted. Since the system is by hypothesis capable of modifying this correlation as a function of past experience, the behavior of such a system will continually improve until its internal model forms a best-possible approximation to the actual correlation between q and p which is manifested in the world.

4.5. Class V: Universal Adaptive Systems

The Class IV systems are limited by the fact that they have, by hypothesis, only one sensory modality; i.e. only one environmental quantity which they can perceive. If we give to such systems an un-limited access to their environment, then in principle they can establish correlations between any environmental quantity and the states of the controlled system, and function effectively in any environment. Another way of doing this is to give a Class IV system a set of effectors with which it can manipulate the environment. With this capability the system can create new sensory modalities for itself, by fabricating instruments capable of directly measuring environmental quantities to which it does not have direct sensory access. The total activities of individual human beings may be said to approach this class of universal adaptability. Such systems are constrained only by the limitations imposed by the utilization of feedbacks in the modification of their internal models (but this is a serious constraint); otherwise they are entirely general-purpose systems.

The classification we have presented above seems to encompass those modes of adaptation which are of biological and technological importance. We have restricted attention to homeostats, but it is a simple matter to enlarge the discussion of each class so as to encompass any type of regulatory behavior. More specifically, any regulatory process involves keeping the state of some controlled system from leaving a particular set of states. The characteristic function of this set associates with each state the number zero or one; we desire to maintain this function at the value one, and this places us once again in the situation of homeostasis.

Notice too that our classification is in order of increasing flexibility of performance. The feedforward homeostats are in many ways improvements over the feedback homeostats; the homeostats with memory are in many ways improvements over the homeostats without memory; the homeostats with multiple sensory modalities are improvements over those with few modalities, etc. Thus, if we wish to build an adaptive system, or convert an unadapted system into an adapted one, we should get as close to Class V as possible. We shall now turn to the question of how, and when, to attempt such a conversion in the context of human systems.

5. IMPLICATIONS FOR SOCIETIES AND THEIR INSTITUTIONS

The main thrust of the present work is that deep system-theoretic homologies make it possible to obtain insights into adaptive processes in the human realm by means of appropriately utilizing our understanding of biological adaptations. In the present section, we shall attempt to explore some of the possibilities in this direction. Because of my own professional limitations, I shall have to content myself with generalities which, I hope, will suggest to those with greater competence in the human sciences what may be some fruitful lines of approach to take (and, perhaps more significantly, what lines to avoid).

One of the main reasons for asking questions about the adaptations of social systems and their institutions is a dissatisfaction with their current performance, and a sense that such poor performance (as measured by some standard) arises from a state of non-adaptation or maladaptation. As noted above; biology deals with just such questions, and in particular with the evolutionary, physiological and behavioral transitions from un-adapted or maladapted states to adapted ones. Therefore, the question becomes one of translating the basic aspects of biological adaptations into the social and institutional realms, and seeing what we can learn thereby.

The first question which biology teaches us to ask (cf. Section 3.2 above) is this: what is the individual whose survival is to be favored by adaptation? As we have seen, this is not a trivial question, even in biology. In the social realm, our intuitions are even weaker, for there are many candidates for such a role. At the lowest level, a society is composed or organisms who are, themselves, already adaptive individuals in the biological sense. In our own society, such entities as a corpora-tion, a city, a political party, a trade union, a university, a fraternal organization, a boy scout troop, and hundreds of others, have many of

61

the properties of coherence which we would associate with "individuals". Some of these in turn comprise systems, or institutions, which also possess such properties: a judicial system, an economic system, a political system, an educational system, and so on. And cutting across these structures in complex ways, we find still other presumptive "individuals"; nations, classes, cultures, etc. It is important to bear in mind that these entities are not disjoint; the same individual citizen can, and generally does, simultaneously or sequentially play a role in many of them.

Suppose that we have chosen some one of the above presumptive "individuals", and decided that it must in fact be treated as a real organism, whose survival is to be furthered by adaptation. According to the classification presented in the preceding section, we can render such a system adaptive in a variety of ways, by attaching to it a controller belonging to one or another of the five classes we discussed. Let us see what is involved in this process, considering only the simplest case in which a quantity is to be maintained constant (or equivalently, a quantity is to be extremized).

At the outset, it is necessary to know the following: (a) how the quantity to be controlled depends on the state of the controlled system; (b) how the state of the controlled system itself depends on modifications of its state variables and/or parameters, so that a choice of control variables (i.e. variables to which a controller may be coupled) can be made. That is, we have to solve a problem of system identification for the controlled system.

Once this problem of system identification is solved (and it should be emphasized that the solution of such a problem does not, in general, require a complete characterization of the controlled system), it is in principle possible on this basis alone to construct a controller belonging to Class I or Class III (i.e. a feedback homeostat). The operation of the feedback controller embodies, through its activities, the model of the controlled system which led to its construction, so that if the model is incorrect, so too will be the control which is exerted. The Class III

62

controllers can obviate this defect to a certain extent, since they have
the capability of, in effect, revising their model of the controlled system on the basis of the response of that system. However, the intrinsic
long time constant of such a hierarchy of feedback loops, and the ease
with which such systems can be fooled (primarily because they take no
direct account of the environment, but only of the controlled system's
response to the environment) make them unsatisfactory as the sole adaptive mechanisms available to further an individual's survival. Indeed,
no biological organism manifests only Class I and Class III adaptations;
we might say in general that particular organs of biological individuals
tend to be of this type, but the presence of only such adaptations in a
biological structure means that it is not itself a biological individual on
which selection acts to further survival.

Returning then to our social "individual", it follows that we must
also provide it with a capability belonging to at least Class II. That is,
we must give the controller a direct capacity to sense the environment,
and the ability to predict the behavior of the controlled system from the
present state of the environment. Before we can do this, we must solve
two more system identification problems; (a) we must solve such a problem for the ambient environment of the controlled system, and (b) we
must solve such a problem for the composite of the controlled system
and the environment. Only in this manner can we decide what environmental quantity can best serve as a predictor, and on the correlation
between this predictor and the state of the controlled system which is to
be embodied in a Class II controller.

As we have noted, it is the presence of Class II controllers which
underlies much of our intuitions about the identification of biological
individuals. And the essence of Class II controllers involves two main
features: direct access to the environment, and a predictive model of
the effect of the environment on the controlled system. Without these,
we are not yet dealing with a real individual (in the adaptive sense), but
with a possible part of such an individual.

63

For many purposes, Class II controllers are better than Class I or Class III, because (a) they do not work off an error signal, and (b) although they are still special-purpose devices, there is a shift of emphasis from hardware to sfotware. This means that there is less of a danger of obsolescence of the control mechanism as circumstances change, and a greater capacity for the introduction of new control mechanisms through function-change (cf. Section III.7 above) in the course of time. This is even more true with Class IV controllers (although, as noted, the Class IV controllers tend to require feedback loops with rather long time constants in generating their adaptive behavior). Nevertheless, it seems to be true that many social problems have their origin in the accumulation of obsolete and obsolescent special-purpose hardware. In biology, of course, such a problem is solved by a simple mechanism; extinction.

In general, we see that once we have decided upon the social entity which we wish to behave as an adaptive individual, it is appropriate to equip it with the most powerful and flexible adaptive mechanisms possible. If we know that we will always want to keep a particular kind of quantity constant (or equivalently, extermize some related quantity) in a narrow range of environments, then it is reasonable to utilize Class I or Class III homeostats for this purpose; this is what organisms do with respect to their internal physiological processes. In all other cases, it is necessary to equip the controllers with direct sensory access to the environment, and with models of the effect of the environment on the controlled system; i.e. with controllers of Class II, IV and V is possible. This is what organisms do for their "behaviors".

Now all of these adaptive mechanisms will only bear upon the survival of the chosen "individual" to which they pertain. If that "individual" is but one of a population of such "individuals" (e.g. if it is a corporation, or a political party) then the possession of such adaptive mechanisms by a small number of the members of the population confers upon them a powerful selective advantage. The other members of the population will then have to acquire

64

similar or compensating adaptations, or else they will be eliminated in one way or another. Such a population of competing adaptive individuals will not, in general, comprise a higher-level adaptive individual, and the adaptations developed in the population will in general tend to work against such higher-level properties emerging (cf. Section 3.5 above). That is, Class II or IV adaptive mechanisms, bearing on the survival of an individual corporation, say, will not (unless very stringent constraints) are satisfied) bear on anything but the survival of that corporation; they will, in particular, not bear upon the survival of an economic system of which the corporation is a part, or upon the survival of the society of which that economic system is a part. Stated in yet another way, a corporation with Class II or IV controllers will not in general be an adaptive organ for any higher-level individual; in general, its own adaptive capacities will actually preclude such a role from being played. It is for this reason that we always find, in biology, a modification or loss of the adaptive capabilities of individual units when they become integrated into a higher-level adaptive individual.

For these reasons, a motto like "What's best for GM is best for America" cannot but be an absurdity. To treat "GM" as a free adaptive individual furthering its own survival will, in general, preclude "America", as a similar individual at another hierarchical level, from similar capabilities. If such a motto is to make any sense at all, it is necessary to recognize the subtleties and complexities embodied in the simple word "best". And the discussion thus devolves once again on the specification of the individual whose survival an adaptive mechanism is to foster and promote. Now that we have seen the significance of this question in the human realm, let us return to a consideration of biological mechanisms to see how we might go about answering it.

We noted above (Section 3.3) that multicellularity is a paradigm for the generation of higher-level adaptive individuals by associations of lower-level ones. We also noted there that, at least at the outset, the adaptive capacity of an association of such individuals is smaller

65

than that of the individuals of which it is comprised. Now we ask: how can such associations be established in the first place, and how can they be maintained in the face of the centrifugal adaptive capacities of the constituent units ?

The simplest biological mechanism for fostering and maintaining such associations is complementation. In crudest terms, consider a population of two types of cells, denoted by A and B. Suppose that A requires for its growth some metabolite x, which it is unable to produce for itself, while B requires a similar metabolite y. If A produces y, and B produces x, it is clear that an association of A and B cells will be viable where neither would be viable separately. Such a symbiosis could provide the basis for the further evolution of the symbiotic population, and this mechanism has been proposed for a wide variety of basic biological phenomena, from the origin of cellular organelles like mitochondria and chloroplasts (Sagan 1967) to the origin of sex (Beadle and Coonradt 1944) to the origin of societies. In a limiting case, of course, it degenerates into parasitism.

It is clear that such a symbiotic association would disintegrate if either of the co-operating units became entirely self-sufficient; i.e. perfectly adaptive in its own right. Therefore, if a symbiotic association based on co-operation is to survive and evolve, the mutual inter-dependence between the complementary individuals must strengthen and not weaken; the advantages to the co-operative mode must be intensified, not by the unrestricted increase of adaptive power on the part of the constitutent units, but on the part of the association. So we are led once again to the curious conclusion that it is through the defects in the adaptive capabilities of biological units that higher-level associations with new properties can be generated and maintained; too great an adaptive capacity in the units precludes or destroys such associations.

Now we have observed several times that the motivation for considering questions of adaptation in a social context is a feeling that our social organizations are malfunctioning, and that we must make them, in some sense, adaptive. On the basis of the above discussion, we must suggest that at least some of the perceived maladaptation arises from the fact that our social organizations are, in fact, too adaptive. They have, in effect, too comprehensive a view of what constitutes their own survival; too much access to their environmental variables; too many models correlating behavior and environment, for them to admit integrating mechanisms which would ensure a mutually beneficial symbiosis which could then be refined and improved. Too much adaptive capacity, at too low a level, generated by too much special-purpose hardware, is indeed a serious problem, but one which our biological experience will help us to recognize and approach seriously (if that is what is desired).

At a more technical level, if we decide that we do indeed wish particular kinds of social units to behave as adaptive individuals, then it may indeed be the case that their malfunctioning arises from imperfect adaptive mechanisms. In the classification we have given above, we can ask how the adaptations belonging to the various classes can malfunction. Let us then briefly consider this question.

Class I homeostats can malfunction because they have an incorrect set-point, ensuring homeostasis at an incorrect level of the controlled variable. Or they may malfunction because of a poor choice of control variables, which does not allow a necessary control to be effected, or by a poor choice of coupling of the controller to the controlled system. They may malfunction because of a poor sensing of the state of the controlled system by the controller. Finally, they may malfunction because the time constant of the control loop is too great for the environment in which the system is called upon to operate.

Class II homeostats can malfunction because they have an incorrect wired-in model of the correlation between the controlled system and the environment. Like the Class I homeostats, they may also malfunction because of an incorrect choice of control variables, poor sensory mechanisms, and/or poor effectors.

Class III homeostats obviate many of the defects of the Class I homeostats. However, they cannot compensate directly for poor sensors or effectors. And they introduce a further possibility of intolerable delay in adaptive behavior because of the cascading of feedback loops.

Class IV controllers likewise obviate the defects of Class II, but introduce a possibly intolerable lag in adaptive behavior because of the introduction of error-actuated feedback.

The Class V controllers can obviate all of the problems of the previous classes, because they can modify and extend their own modes of coupling with both the environment and with the controlled system. But they, too, may suffer from intolerable lag effects.

Finally, all controllers will encounter the difficulties involved in Function Change and the generation of unforeseeable side-effects introduced into the controled system as a consequence of the implementation of the control itself (Rosen 1974).

Now each of these malfunctionings gives rise to a specific syndrome, much like a medical syndrome in a human patient, which allows these various modes of malfunction to be distinguished from one another, and suggests the appropriate therapeutic measures to be undertaken. These will be dictated by the specific structure of the homeostat in question. Thus, an incorrect set-point in a thermostat may be most easily corrected by changing the set-point, or may best be compensated for by altering the coupling between the thermostat and the heat source (in mechanical thermostats, the former is usually more appropriate; in organisms it is often the latter). In any case, a study of such "syndromes" and their corresponding "therapies", in broad system-theoretic terms, should do much to facilitate the correction of true malfunctions in societal adaptive mechanisms.

6. CONCLUSION

The thrust of the above discussion is that we have much to learn about the nature of our own social technology from a study of comparable processes occurring in biological systems. Particularly in the study of adaptive mechanisms, it is important to avail ourselves of the experiences preserved for us in the biological record, when translated into an appropriate societal context. The most important lesson, as well as the most elementary, which a consideration of biological adaptation leads to, is to ask what a particular mode of adaptation is to be for; unless we are able to answer such a question correctly from the outset, we may face an endless cascade of further problems.

Once having decided upon generating a particular mode of adaptation, biology provides us with algorithms for generating that adaptation. These algorithms may be applied directly, or converted into more effective ones. Particularly in the area of predictive control, in which our social adaptations are singularly defective, we have a great deal to learn from a study of sensory mechanisms in organisms and the manner in which they guide adaptive responses. A study of anticipatory control is not yet even in its infancy, despite the universality of this mode in the biological realm.

In sum, for a long time to come, our social adaptations will have to depend primarily upon our own individual biological adaptative capabilities. This is a heavy responsibility, which we are slowly coming to recognize; we will need all of our experience and all of our ingenuity if we are to be able to bear it well.

ACKNOWLEDGEMENT. This paper was prepared in part while the author was in residence at the Salk Institute for Biological Studies. The hospitality of Dr. Salk, as well as many basic discussions on the role of biology in understanding the nature of man and his institutions, are gratefully acknowledged.

REFERENCES

Bartlett, N. R. [1965], "Dark Adaptation and Light Adaptation" in Vision and Visual Perception (C. H. Graham, ed.) 185-207. John Wiley and Sons, New York.

Beadle, G. W. and Coonradt, V. L. [1944], Genetics 24, 291-308.

Bonner, J. T. [1933], Cells and Societies. Princeton University Press, Princeton, New Jersey.

Bremmermann, H. J., Rogson, M., and Salaf, F. "Global Properties of Evolutionary Processes", in Natural Automate and Useful Simulations. (Pattee, Edelsack, Fein and Callahan, eds.), 3-41. Spartan Books, Washington, D. C.

Cannon, W. B. [1933], "Biocracy". Tech. Rev. 35, 203-206.

———, [1942], The Body as a Guide to Politics. Watts, London.

Dobzhansky, T. [1963], "Adaptedness and Fitness", in Population Biology and Evolution (R. C. Lewontin, ed.) 109-121. Syracuse University Press, Syracuse, N.Y.

Emerson, A. E. [1952], "The Supra-organismic Aspects of Society" Coloques Int. Centre Nat. Recherche Sci., Vol. 34, pp. 333-353.

Fisher, R. A. [1930], The Genetical Theory of Natural Selection. Clarendon Press, Oxford.

Greene, P. H. [1972], "Problems of Organization of Motor Systems" in Progress in Theoretical Biology 2 (R. Rosen and F. M. Snell, eds.), 303-338.

Hardin, G. [1963], "The Cybernetics of Competition: A Biologist's View of Society". Perspect. Biol. and Med. 8, 61-84.

Hinshelwood, C. N. [1953], "Adaptation in Microorganisms and its Relation to Evolution". Symp. Soc. Exp. Biol. 7, 31-42.

Holland, J. [1970], "Outline for a Logical Theory of Adaptive Systems", and "Hierarchical Descriptions, Universal Spaces and Adaptive Systems", in Essays on Cellular Automata (A. W. Burks, ed.) 297-369. University of Illinois Press, Urbana, Ill.

Hollings, C. S. [1967], "Stability in Ecological and Social Systems" in Diversity and Stability in Ecological Systems. Brookhaven Symp. 1967.

Milsum, J. [1965], Biological Control Systems Analysis. McGraw-Hill, N. Y.

Pittendrigh, C. S. [1958], "Adaptation, Natural Selection and Behavior", in Behavior and Evolution (A. Roe and G. G. Simpson, eds.) 390-416. Yale University Press, New Haven, Ct.

Rosen, R. [1967], Optimality Principles in Biology. Butterworth's, London.

_____, [1971], Dynamical System Theory in Biology. John Wiley and Sons, New York.

_____, [1974], "Some Temporal Aspects of Political Change", Int. J. Gen. Syst. $\underline{1}$, 93-103.

Sagan, L. [1967], "On the Origin of Mitosing Cells". J. Theoret. Biol. $\underline{14}$, 225-274.

Salk, J. [1972], Man Unfolding. Harper and Row, New York.

_____, [1973], The Survival of the Wisest. Harper and Row, New York.

Stark, L. [1959], "Oscillations of a Neurophysiological Servomechanism", in Selected Papers in Biophysics. Yale University Press, New Haven.

Thoday, J. M. [1953], "The Components of Fitness". Soc. Symp. Exp. Biol. VII, 96-113.

Weiss, P. [1949], "The Biological Basis of Adaptation", in Adaptation (J. Romano, Ed.), 1-22. Cornell University Press, Ithaca, N.Y.

Williams, G. C. [1966], Adaptation and Natural Selection. Princeton University Press, Princeton, New Jersey.

Yakowitz, S. J. [1969], Mathematics of Adaptive Control Processes. American-Elsevier Publishing Co., New York.

Zadeh, L. A. and Desoer, C. A. [1963], Linear System Theory. McGraw-Hill, New York.

EPILOG

As a result of participating in the Conference on Adaptive Economics, it appears that there are many specific examples of parallel developments between the biological and economic sciences. For instance, the kinds of analysis employed by Drs. Cyert and DeGroot in their discussion of adaptive utility is closely related to that employed in "mathematical learning theory", which considers how organisms modify their behavior (i.e. "learn") as a function of reinforcement schedules. Dr. Shubik's paper concerned the inter-relationships between dynamical structures (e.g. goods and services) and certain symbolic descriptions of them (contracts), which is highly reminiscent of the phenotype-genotype dualism which dominates biology; his concern with behavior far from equilibrium is strongly reminiscent of the concern with "symmetry-breaking" as a means for understanding developmental processes in organisms. Dr. Lloyd spoke explicitly about niche selection models in ecology as a paradigm for understanding how a firm might evaluate its chances of moving successfully into a new industry. Dr. Powers' discussion of design in the chemical industry are closely related to algorithmic and heuristic methods in artificial intelligence, a cognate field to the study of intelligent behavior in organisms. Many more examples might be drawn from the papers presented at the Conference. Conversely, numerous papers are appearing which seek to analyze problems of energy flows in ecosystems, or in metabolizing organisms, in frank economic terms. These developments point to a fruitful confluence of hitherto separate biological and economic disciplines, which conferences like the present one may catalyze most effectively.

Optimization and Evolution in the Theory of the Firm
Sidney G. Winter

CONTENTS

1. INTRODUCTION

The controversy that I review in this paper was already an old one when I began my own first attempt to get the matter clear. That was more than fifteen years ago. In the meantime, an enormous volume of economic theory has flowed over the editorial dams and into the sea of print. Most of this stream has avoided the controversy, and, in fact, has managed to progress as if the snag did not exist at all. I suspect that, on the maps

73

of most theorists, it appears lodged in about the same place that it was
a quarter century or more ago, and perhaps those of us who think it important are perceived as being lodged there with it. Such maps, I shall
argue, are out of date. New channels are being cut. And the debris of
that old controversy may be shifting in such a way as to constitute a
hazard to navigation in the mainstream.

In support of this view, I offer an argument with three main parts.
First, I state the principal objections to the use of optimization assumptions as a foundation for the theory of the firm. I then review the case
against using loosely formulated "natural selection" arguments as a sort
of auxiliary defense for the traditional optimization assumptions. In
Section IV, I sketch the elements of an evolutionary theory that is not a
prop for, but an alternative to, the optimization approach. A concluding
comment evaluates the prospects for major change at the foundations of
the theory of the firm.

As this plan indicates, very high level theoretical commitments
are at issue here. It would therefore be appropriate to preface the discussion of the theory of the firm with some consideration of the philosophical problems involved in "choosing" between alternative sets of high
level theoretical commitments. Serious consideration of those problems
would, however, occupy a lot of space, and one can entertain a reasonable doubt as to whether the arguments would substantially alter any
reader's reaction to the subsequent discussion of the theory of the firm.
I therefore propose to forego that lengthy methodological preamble. Instead, I will state the indispensable "non-controversial" conclusions of
the omitted discussion in the form of assumptions about what "everybody
knows."[1]

Everybody knows, I assume, that the problem of comparing sets
of high level theoretical commitments is not the same as the problem of
comparing particular, fully specified predictive models aimed at a particular class of quantitative phenomena. To put the matter in our own
jargon, the more diversity there is in the bundle of situations in which

a theoretical idea is applied, the greater are the conceptual difficulties in defining a good index number to represent the idea's performance. Secondly, everybody knows that the rules that characterize the acceptable modes of empirical application of a theory are, on the one hand, properly considered as part of the theory itself -- but, on the other hand, they are rarely very explicit, and they are subject to change in the light of experience.

We know, therefore, that is is not a simple matter to describe how empirical observations bear (or ought to bear) on the acceptability of high level theories. The empirical situation surveyed from a particular theoretical viewpoint, always contains some facts that are more or less anomalous, troublesome or recalcitrant, along with some that are more of less supportive and encouraging. The question of how theory should adapt to the troublesome ones -- whether with radical change, incremental adjustment, or "benign neglect" -- is not decidable by reference to the facts themselves. Ex post, one can give the answer: How the theory adapted reveals what the facts meant. But this is just to say that, ex ante, the question of what the facts mean is really inseparable from the question of what ought to be done about them, in terms of revising theory.

Although I now begin my main argument with an examination of some empirical issues, the interpretation of these issues is clearly influenced by, and bound up with, their relationship to the choice between theoretical systems.

2. THE THEORY OF THE OPTIMIZING FIRM: A THREEFOLD CRITIQUE

2.1. Empirical Truth

The first count of the indictment is simply put: It is not true, as an empirical matter, that firms optimize. But while the statement is simple, an attempt to document it must rest on an operational interpretation. Very likely, the interpretation put forward here is not one that most economists would find entirely natural. For the moment, at least,

this disagreement at the semantic level is irrelevant: Given the interpretation set forth below, there remains a question of empirical fact on
which some available empirical evidence bears. One can ask where the
weight of that evidence lies, and hence whether the indictment, as interpreted, stands.

A first, and crucial, interpretive comment is that the statement
is to be understood as relating to events occurring "inside" firms, i.e.,
to the decision processes of organizations called firms. Secondly, it
is not a statement that relates merely to the results of these processes
-- i.e., to overt actions taken. Although evidence relating to actions
is relevant, it is obvious that any given action, including an optimal
one, might be taken for reasons having nothing to do with optimization,
and hence that the optimality of actions taken cannot be decisive evidence that optimization occurs. Similarly, evidence bearing on the motivation of action cannot be decisive for optimization, because there
are many ways of "striving" for a goal (e.g., more profit) that do not
constitute optimization. Indeed, the literature of economics is riddled
with "striving" models that turn out, on close examination, to have only
a superficial claim to being optimization models. There is, for example,
the large class of models in which the optimization problem is posed in
essentially static terms, while the firm acts by ad hoc rules in an essentially dynamic environment. Finally, the statement should be understood as referring to all, or substantially all, firm decisions. That a
handful of firms optimize all the time, or that a few types of decisions
are typically optimized, is not enough to make it true (in the intended
sense) that "firms optimize."

What would support the claim that firms optimize would be evidence that firm decision processes characteristically proceed by developing a number of fairly comprehensive alternative strategies for the firm
as a whole, and then comparing them systematically according to some
criterion, and acting according to the one that seemed best. In short,
supportive evidence would be evidence indicating that they behave in

76

the way that a naive reading of the optimization models of economics would lead one to expect. Of course, one would not necessarily expect the participants to use the language of economic theory in describing the process. One would not expect to find comparison algorithms that proceeded to the point of picking a true optimum out of a continuum of possibilities; reasonable finite approximations to the choice set would do. One would not expect to find supernatural feats of foresight implicit in the process; rather one would expect to see signs of explicit recognition of the major uncertainties, and a systematic, non-superstitious attempt to deal with those uncertainties. And one would expect to hear, and discount, a certain amount of self-serving misrepresentation of the process and its goals.

After these, and other, commonsensical qualifications have been allowed for, the resulting image of optimization is an image of decision behavior involving systematic, global comparison of coherent alternatives before action is taken. Comparisons must be global in the sense that radical changes of strategy must not be ruled out of consideration merely because they are radical -- the case against such change must be subject to review. The alternatives must be coherent in the sense that the interactions among the decision variables controlled by the firm must be recognized and allowed for. And it is implicit, of course, that systematic comparison involves stable decision criteria. Altogether, this is an image of something that firm decision processes really could be like; it is not an exercise in logic to show that this is a false picture of decision process realities. It might be regarded as a reasonable -- or "not unreasonable" -- guess.

Does anyone think that this logically possible picture is also empirically accurate? In particular, do most economists think so? Most economic theorists? As far as I can tell, an opinion poll would show an overwhelming "no opinion" response. This is because orthodox doctrine maintains that our theoretical business can be conducted without an answer to this question. The validity of this doctrine will be considered

77

in Section III. For the moment, it suffices to note that there is still an empirical issue here, regardless of whether economists care, or ought to care, about it.

The empirical evidence is not, of course, as abundant or systematic as one would like. (Undoubtedly, this is attributable in part to the fact that economists don't think they need an answer.) However, the tendency of this evidence is quite clear, given the specific interpretation of the question set forth above. That is, once one stipulates that evidence on motivation and "striving" behavior is not of direct relevance, and that evidence on the globalness of search and consideration of coherent alternatives is of direct relevance, the pieces fall into place. Most of what economists cite, when they do feel compelled to offer evidence supportive of optimization assumptions (and relating to internal events of firms), is evidence on motivation and striving behavior. It supports the conclusion: There is a lot of striving, and specifically a lot of profit-motivated striving in firm behavior. Critics of the optimization approach sometimes question the relative importance of this type of behavior; they rarely challenge its existence. However, such critics also cite evidence that calls into serious and direct question the prevalence of optimization as defined here -- and to that evidence there is not, as far as I know, a serious reply.

To illustrate the point about "striving" evidence, I refer to the protracted discussion of pricing behavior. As Scherer has concisely said, "Case studies reveal that the use of full cost pricing procedures is widespread."[2] In discussion of this evidence, a good deal of emphasis is often placed on the fact that these procedures are not always adhered to rigidly, and that some of the exceptions are rationalizable on marginalist grounds.[3] It seems reasonable to interpret some of these exceptions, at least, as evidence of a striving for greater profit than adherence to the rule would allow. Is it evidence for optimization, as understood here? Not, I think, unless supplemented by a showing that the pricing rule was well calculated for the cases in which it was

78

followed, and that the prices in the exceptional cases were determined by something more systematic than a rough incremental adjustment in a plausible direction. Certainly the case study evidence calls the first of these requirements into question (especially because of the high historical presistence of markup factors). As for the second, there is little evidence, but surely the "marginalists" are not entitled to a presumption that firm response to exceptional cases is better calculated than the routine responses -- one might well presume the reverse.[4]

Aharoni's study [1966] of the foreign investment decision process is one illustration of the kind of evidence that hits directly at optimization assumptions. He interviewed managers in U.S. firms in search of an answer to the question: Why it is that there is so little response to the tax incentives for direct foreign investment offered by less developed countries? His findings indicated that a sharp distinction had to be made between firms that had undertaken one or more foreign investment projects in the past, and those that had not. For the latter firms, changes in tax conditions abroad were essentially invisible and irrelevant. Foreign investment was "too risky" -- a perception that was not founded on actual calculations of risks and returns, but rather was the rationale for not undertaking such calculations. In short, what was perceived as a radical change of firm policy was excluded from consideration prior to, not as a consequence of, the comparison of alternatives.

More recently, Eliasson has studied corporate planning procedures in a group of U.S. and foreign firms -- typically, large and successful ones [1974]. If "global" comparison of alternatives is characteristic of most firm decision making, the planning activities of these firms should reflect this fact. Eliasson comments as follows on his findings:

> "The impact of tradition seems to me paramount in planning. The basic effort at the early stages of planning was directed towards the problem of staying on and performing well in established markets and maintaining established positions

79

(market shares). Suggestions in preliminary planning documents by planners to do something entirely new in some areas, even on a 10 year horizon, would probably be weeded out in the reviewing process. This was not considered a matter for planners. With a few exceptions (firms with conglomerate features), I found very little effort (even in very long range plans) spent on planning to enter entirely new markets, and still less (i.e., practically nothing) on direct efforts to contract in and leave (gradually) long established markets."

-- Eliasson [1974, pp. 211-12]

He goes on to paraphrase as follows the "policy" that underlay such planning in one firm: "We have been producing on the basis of these raw materials for more than 50 years with success and we have made it a policy to continue to do so."[5]

There is other case study evidence of a formal and scholarly sort.[6] There is a much richer vein of more journalistic material; for example, the "How X Corp. Got in Trouble" genre is standard fare in Fortune. The admissibility of such evidence may be questioned: The journalists presumably do not have the advantage of advanced training in economic theory and hence may not distinguish carefully enough between failures to optimize and mere bad luck suffered by an optimizing firm in an uncertain world. However, these problems of interpretation are sufficiently resistant even to our own trained minds that we should probably not scorn the journalists' testimony. Here, then, is a capsule account of a classic fiasco:

"Seldom has a corporate crisis been compounded of so many errors of commission and omission as General Dynamics' $425-million troubles with its 880 and 990 jet transport planes. G. D.'s management failed to recognize that this age requires not only technological superiority but management superiority as well. It failed to establish a detection apparatus that would have signalled trouble in time. It failed to permit only programs which would not threaten the whole company, and failed to stop one enterprise when its failings became apparent. Instead it kept sending good money after bad in the hope that one lucky coup would square all accounts."   -- Smith [1966, p. 67]

To translate the details of this episode from the "errors" language into the "bad luck" language may be possible in principle, but few would take it seriously. The task is particularly difficult because the size of the loss involved tends to foreclose the "it doesn't pay to be perfect" rationale for mistakes.

Before leaving the question of the empirical truth of optimization assumptions, some mention should be made of the influence of normative decision theory on actual decision practice. It is undoubtedly a fact that some decisions are routinely produced as the outcomes of systematic optimizing computations, while in other cases managers are routinely informed of the results of such computations before taking action. Is this fact evidence that firms optimize in the sense defined above? There are several grounds for a negative answer, but the most important point is that the <u>scope</u> of the optimization procedures employed is narrow. That is, the "substantially all decisions" requirement is not met. Like the routine acceptance of the lowest bid by a purchasing department, like the "marginalist" cost accounting of Earley's "excellently managed companies," the more sophisticated techniques of management science yield imperfect suboptimizations of limited scope. They may be indicative of a higher level "striving," but, empirically, they are not embedded in a higher level optimization. As the discussion below points out, this should not be surprising.

2.2. The Logic of Calculation Cost[7]

Given evidence that some particular observed behavior is not optimal in some specific sense, the traditional response in economic theory is to reconsider the "sense." One asks what costs or objectives may be present in the real situation that have not been properly accounted for in the optimization calculus. This heuristic principle is admirably effective at bringing all possible empirical issues within the scope of the theory, so that question posed is not <u>whether</u> the theory is consistent with the facts, but <u>how</u> it is consistent with them. Given this principle, the sort of empirical challenge sketched above is doomed to failure from the start: The findings of Aharoni or Elliason, even the apparently gross blundering of General Dynamics, can only serve to suggest an intriguing range of puzzles concerning optimization in the face of information costs, uncertainty, and perhaps managerial objectives that diverge from stockholder interests.

On one set of methodological criteria, the objection to this "superoptimization" principle is that it eliminates the empirical content of the theory that firms optimize. However, as has been briefly suggested in the introduction, this sort of criticism cannot strike against high level theoretical commitments with anything like the force that it has against fully specified, and purportedly predictive, models. Whatever the _empirical_ content of such commitments may be, they ordinarily have a lot of content in the form of guidance for research; they suggest ways of approaching the problems of constructing predictive models. Whether that guidance is adequate, or the best available, is the central issue, and it will not be resolved by any amount of carping about the low empirical content of high level assumptions.

There is, however, an alternative way to illuminate the central issue. One can set down some assumptions characterizing a hypothetical world in which the research effort is taking place. One can then ask how the effort will fare in this hypothetical world, given that it is guided by a particular set of high level commitments. The likely varieties of "success" that the effort will enjoy may be characterized -- and the likely forms of "failure." One can then assess the significance of the conclusions reached about the performance of the research effort in the hypothetical world -- which involves reflecting on the plausibility of the assumptions characterizing that world. If their plausibility is high, the exercise may be considered to have yielded useful insight to the actual merits and limitations of the sort of research program considered.

82

Following this plan, let us consider the fate of research guided by the high level (non-refutable) commitment "firms optimize" in the hypothetical world characterized by the following assumptions: (1) Every act of communication and calculation is costly, in terms of valued alternatives foregone. (2) Optimization requires a positive amount of calculation.

Combining (1) and (2), we conclude that, in the hypothetical world, optimization is costly. Now consider the costs of a particular optimization in relation to the scope of that optimization itself. Either they are neglected -- in which case we label this particular example a "suboptimization" -- or they are not -- in which case we may label this a "true" optimization or "superoptimization," provided that no other costs or considerations have been neglected. The latter alternative -- the optimization whose scope covers all consideration including its own costs -- sounds like it may involve the logical difficulties of self- reference. To demonstrate this -- to prove logically that there is no super- optimization -- would require the development of a formal framework within which the statement could be interpreted. That would be an interesting project. But whatever the outcome of that project, it is clear that "optimization" as ostensively defined by pointing at appropriate portions of decision theory literature does not involve self-reference. Carrying this definition of optimization into our hypothetical world, we conclude that in it there are no superoptimizations. There may, at best, be suboptimizations.

What will become of the research effort founded on "firms optimize?" A lot obviously depends on characteristics of the hypothetical world not specified in the above assumptions. Given the presence of a substantial amount of suboptimizing, and assuming that the correct motivational assumptions are guiding the research, much of the structure of reality may be uncovered and explained. The principle that the considerations apparently neglected at one level are correctly balanced at some higher level may be applied with considerable success. If calculation costs are actually quite small in relation to other sorts of costs, it could be that much of the "interesting" economics of the hypothetical world is understandable as the results of suboptimizations relatively low in the hierarchical structures of calculated decisions. The fact that the pyramids have tops -- decisions not patterned by the results of higher level calculations -- might not matter very much.

Alternatively, it might be that the calculation costs are high in this hypothetical world and the "pyramids" are low. While a good deal of calculation and suboptimization goes on, it occurs in fairly shallow structures, topped by -- or perhaps buried under -- a range of decisions, "policies" and prejudices that are not patterned as the consequence of comparisons of alternatives. (They may, of course, be patterned in other ways.) In this world, the practitioners of the "firms optimize" paradigm will draw encouragement from their success in explaining those aspects of their reality that reflect the presence of the suboptimizations that do occur. They will be even more encouraged on the occasions when phenomena inexplicable at one level of analysis fall neatly into place when considered as the result of more subtle calculation at a higher level. Such instances will show that faith in their high level commitment is not misplaced, that, in fact, greater success rewards greater devotion. Furthermore, at any given time they will perceive their research task as unfinished: Noting that predictive models of optimizing behavior are always narrower in scope than the "true" optimization problems confronting the actors, and also that prediction errors occur, they will interpret the former as the cause of the latter and thus define their research problems. The fact that the amount of actual (sub) optimization going on is limited, and that the "elite" decisions of the shallow hierarchies are necessarily uncalculated, will pose no serious obstacles to the _pursuit_ of the research program -- only to its success. The pursuit will be encouraged, not only by sorts of achievements mentioned above, but also by spurious correlations between the predictions of optimization theory and the consequences of mechanisms actually at work in the

84

system. Such correlations may, in particular, provide sufficient fuel to keep the research effort moving even when it is far outside of the realm in which systematic comparisons of alternatives are a major influence structuring behavior. Some prediction errors may result from the misinterpretation of these correlations. But the success of the research effort will be much more significantly limited as a result of its neglect of the study of the mechanisms actually governing outcomes over the wide range of behavior that is not calculated. The principal handicap will not be the tendency to "see" optimizations that aren't there, since this tendency will be at least partially checked by closer observation of reality. The troublesome thing will be the failure to study what is there.

Enough of this parable. Few will want to quarrel, presumably, with the assumption that calculation is costly. Given the interpretation offered above of what optimization means -- and specifically, that the term relates to how decisions are arrived at rather than to what they are -- few will dispute the assumption that optimization involves some calculation. Given these premises, the conclusion that there is no super-optimization follows, as a matter of logic, for the real world just as for the hypothetical one. In this sense, the image of firm optimizing behavior that, in the discussion above, was granted the status of a "reasonable guess" appears not so reasonable, so far as the demand for "globalness" is concerned.

There remains the crucial question as to which of the two variants of the hypothetical world the real world more closely resembles. Perhaps the ultimate dead end of the optimization approach is so far down the road as to be of no immediate practical significance. The alternative view (i.e., the other extreme) is that we have already devoted a lot of theoretical effort to exploring that dead end, but have failed to diagnose the difficulty.

2.3. Fruitfulness

Even in the context of this rather belligerent essay, a sweeping charge that the optimization approach is "unfruitful" seems excessive

-- and difficult to sustain. There is no question, at least in my mind, that the approach has yielded an enormous wealth of insight into the workings of economic reality, and has provided an exceedingly valuable organizing framework for research on a wide range of superficially disparate aspects of that reality. Equally clearly, however, there are characteristic biases and "blind spots" associated with the approach. Some of these involve issues that are of central importance in the comparison of the conventional and evolutionary perspectives.

Thoroughgoing commitment to optimization seems to be associated, in the actual practice of theorists, with a strong propensity to focus on equilibrium positions and to suppress the problem of how equilibrium is achieved. Of course, "equilibrium" is here to be understood, not in the narrow sense of a static condition which would tend to persist in the absence of exogenous change, but rather in the sense of a condition in which the expectations of all economic actors are realized. Also, the problem of how equilibrium is achieved is often not suppressed entirely, but is attacked with methods and assumptions that are essentially foreign to the spirit of the underlying characterization of actors as optimizers.

Though it is not logically inevitable that an analysis of optimal behavior must be an analysis of situations in which expectations are realized, there are definite reasons why it tends to be inevitable as a matter of theoretical practice: If actual outcomes of an economic process violate the expectations of the actors involved, then presumably these actors will learn from the discrepancies and modify their behavior. Different outcomes will then appear, followed by further modifications of behavior. However, in attempting to develop theoretical models that explicitly incorporate the idea that individual actors respond differently through time as they gradually learn about their own decision problems, one is increasingly forced to the view that a theory about the economic events should subsume a cognitive theory for the individual actors -- i.e., a characterization of the actors in their naive state and of the processes by which they learn. The need for such a cognitive theory -- and the correlative requirement for testing the theory by observation of the decision processes of individual actors -- is precisely what has characteristically been denied or elided by adopting the optimization approach. It is not surprising, therefore, that the optimization approach is, predominantly, an approach to equilibrium analysis. The signal virtue of the approach is precisely the enormous simplification that is achieved by assuming that the necessary learning has somehow got done.

There are major drawbacks to a theory that works to greatest advantage in the analysis of equilibrium positions. The first, concisely put, is that the world contains a lot of interesting disequilibrium phenomena, and research on these tends to be neglected or distorted because of the characteristics of the accepted theoretical framework. As seems to be inevitable in this sort of discussion, a concise statement of the problem is oversimplified: What sorts of things count as "disequilibrium phenomena" depends on precisely what one means by "equilibrium" in a specific theoretical context. However, as long as that meaning includes the "expectations realized" connotation, the complaint holds. It strains credulity to suppose that the great economic transformations of the modern world constitute an unfolding of events such that expectations are realized, however loose the meaning that one might attach to the latter notion.

Even if economic life were considerably tamer than it is, and more plausibly viewed as a sequence of proximate equilibria, the over-attention to equilibrium analysis still could not be justified. For, as Hahn said not long ago, "The most intellectually exciting question of our subject remains: Is it true that the pursuit of private interest produces not chaos but coherence, and if so, how is it done?" [1970, pp. 11-12]. Studies of the existence and properties of equilibrium positions can make only a limited contribution to our understanding of how it is done. To understand whether coherence could (logically) arise under specified circumstances, and what it would be like if it did, is

87

not to understand _how_ the coherence arises. Furthermore, an account of how it is done can hardly be considered satisfactory if it is based on characterizations of the behavior of individual economic actors that are mere abstract building blocks for the larger scheme, having, avowedly, no definite empirical link to the behavior of the real actors. Such an account does not even _aspire_ to being a fully credible answer to our "most intellectually exciting question"; no wonder it fails to achieve that goal.

A second major bias associated with the optimization approach is a drastic overemphasis on prices and market processes as social mechanisms of information transmission. This bias is not, of course, independent of the one toward equilibrium analysis. They both reflect, and are partly derived from, the theoretical preoccupation with issuing resounding normative statements about the efficacy of the invisible hand. We know how to go about proving the Pareto optimality of equilibria in theoretical systems in which prices provide the necessary coordinating information, while actors have essentially unlimited memories and computation power, and contracts are costlessly enforced. We do not know how to -- and very likely it is not true -- for a system in which relevant economic information is routinely transmitted by the daily newspaper, or, indeed by any one of a large number of obviously significant social institutions. The list comprises, for example, the mass media, the schools and other educational institutions, the family, business firms (in advertising, training programs, etc.), trade journals and academic journals, courts, government regulatory agencies, etc., etc. And not only are we unable to prove our conventional sorts of efficiency results for systems in which these "complications" are represented, but we are largely lacking in accepted ways of expressing other sorts of normative conclusions, of a kind that might be helpful in policy design. If anything, applied policy evaluation is more significantly afflected by these biases than is theoretical research. Perhaps this is because the compulsion to reach normative conclusions operates even more strongly in this area, and the

only familiar path to such conclusions involves overstatement of the normative significance of market prices.

It is true that, in the last decade or so, there have been great advances in theoretical understanding of the economics of information and
the functioning of informationally imperfect markets.[8] At the same time,
the human capital approach has supplied the theoretical underpinnings for
a major wave of empirical research on the economics of education and
training. The problem of incentives for the production of new technological information has received some further attention. Virtually all of these
advances have, concededly, been made within the framework of the optimization approach. Thus, it is far from true that the "bias" here attributed to that approach has resulted in a total neglect of theoretical study
of situations in which economic information other than price information
plays a significant role. But the overall theoretical structure remains
very unbalanced. Competitive general equilibrium theory is still the dominant interpretation of the "coherence" of the system as a whole; as a
consequence, the various advances made in understanding of the problems
of information economics appear as commentary on that interpretation, or
as further additions to an already long list of important qualifications to
the competitive equilibrium/Pareto optimality story. There is little sign
of a serious quest for an alternative appraisal of the system as a whole,
an appraisal that would give full weight both to the information-theoretic
limitations of market systems and to the role of non-price, non-market
information flows in economic organization and change. Rather, there is
a sort of nostalgia for the good old efficiency theorems, and an apparent
reluctance to take more than incremental steps away from theoretical ter-
rain where those theorems hold.

3. "AS IF" OPTIMIZATION AND THE NATURAL SELECTION ARGUMENT

3.1. "As If" Optimization

It is time now to return to the question of the empirical truth of
optimization assumptions and to scrutinize those familiar arguments that

declare this question to be largely irrelevant to the validity and utility of the theories founded on those assumptions. The position set forth in Friedman's classic essay has been discussed and disputed at length in the substantial literature of economic methodology. For the most part, that literature addresses the issues at the level of general scientific principles; it is, notably, long on references to the accomplishments of physics and the works of philosophers of science, and short on detailed examination of the methodological status of particular economic models.[9] The present discussion is focused on the intermediate-level problem of the status of optimization assumptions in the theory of the firm. It presumes that this problem cannot be fully resolved by reference to methodological principles, whatever the correct ones might be, but rather must be considered in relation to the available theoretical alternatives and the empirical facts.

On the problem of the status of optimization assumptions, (although perhaps not on the broader questions of methodology) the Friedman position is, I think, the dominant view in the discipline. When questions are raised about the descriptive accuracy of the optimization assumptions in a particular model, or when an attempt is made to claim behavioral realism as a significant virtue of a non-optimizing approach, the response is almost invariably a paraphrase of Friedman. There is, accordingly, no better way to begin a statement and critique of this orthodox position than by quoting a fragment from the locus classicus

> "... -- unless the behavior of businessmen in some way or other approximated behavior consistent with the maximization of returns, it seems unlikely that they would remain in business for long. Let the apparent immediate determinant of business behavior be anything at all -- habitual reaction, random chance, or whatnot. Whenever this determinant happens to lead to behavior consistent with the rational and informed maximization of returns, the business will prosper and acquire resources with which to expand; whenever it does not, the business will tend to lose resources and can be kept in existence only by the addition of resources from outside. The process of "natural selection" thus helps to validate the (maximization of returns) hypothesis -- or rather, given natural selection, acceptance of the

90

hypothesis can be based largely on the judgment that it summarizes appropriately the conditions for survival."

-- Friedman [1953, p. 35]

The contributions of Machlup to the marginalist controversy of
the forties, and his more recent review of the issues of that debate, form
another important segment of orthodox scripture on these matters. Particularly useful for present purposes are the following:

> "Business men do not always "calculate" before they make
> decisions, and they do not always "decide" before they act.
> For they think that they know their business well enough
> without making repeated calculations; and their actions are
> frequently routine. But routine is based on principles which
> were once considered and decided upon and have then been
> frequently applied with decreasing need for conscious choices.
> The feeling that calculations are not always necessary is
> usually based upon an ability to size up a situation without
> reducing its dimensions to definite numerical values.
>
> -- Machlup [1946, p. 525]

> "The question is not whether the firms of the real world
> really maximize money profits, or whether they even strive
> to maximize their money profits, but rather whether the
> assumption that this is the objective in the theoretical firms
> in the artificial world of our construction will lead to con-
> clusions -- "inferred outcomes" very different from those
> derived from admittedly more realistic assumptions."
>
> -- Machlup [1967, pp. 14-15]

It is striking that these statements come so close to being consistent with the empirical points made in the preceding section. The image of what firms are really like that is evoked by phrases like "habitual
reaction, random chance, or whatnot" and "they do not always 'decide' "
and "their actions are frequently routine" is not obviously in conflict with
the image presented by Aharoni and Eliasson, or by Cyert and March.
Perhaps we all know, and agree, at least in a general way, what firms
are "really" like. Perhaps we could even agree that, in a general characterization of the immediate determinants of firm behavior, abstract concepts like "profit maximization" are much less useful than concepts like

91

"routine" and "habitual reaction" -- and not because the latter are less abstract, but because they are more true, i.e., descriptively accurate.

According to the Friedman-Machlup position, the empirical questions posed and examined in the preceding section are not significantly in dispute, but they are irrelevant. What is central to that position is the "as if" principle, i.e., the claim that actual behavior "some way or other" approximates behavior "consistent with the maximization of returns." The methodological literature has, for the most part, treated this claim as raising a general issue of scientific principle, namely, the legitimacy of theory founded on admittedly unrealistic assumptions. It will be argued here that the particular case of the theory of the firm involves not merely this general issue, but also questions of a more specific and substantive nature. These arise because the "as if" principle is not advanced baldly, but with supporting arguments directed to the particular case of firm behavior. The "natural selection" argument, as set forth by Friedman above, is one such. Machlup, in his use of the analogy of a driver calculating how to overtake a truck, made a different point but to similar effect. Essentially, the point of the analogy is that adaptive behavior, based on rough calculations and feedback, will respond to changes in the decision situation in much the same way that optimizing behavior would. These two arguments by Friedman and Machlup will be treated here as representatives of the class of auxiliary defenses for optimization assumptions. Such defenses provide specific grounds for believing that firms behave, in significant respects, "as if" they were optimizing, even though direct evidence on decision processes may fail to corroborate the existence of optimization itself.

Let us defer for the moment the question of the validity of these auxiliary defenses. Suppose they are substantially valid, in the sense that the mechanisms cited do operate in reality and do confer a degree of predictive success upon some implications of optimization theories. Does it then follow that the auxiliary defenses are also an adequate response to the charges of unrealism, and legitimate reasons for proceeding with "as if" theorizing? In spite of the weight of disciplinary opinion and practice favoring an affirmative answer to this question, it seems to me that the correct answer is no. It is really a simple matter of the unacceptability of procedures that yield the right answers for the wrong reasons -- when it is known that the reasons are wrong, and even the general character of the right reasons is also known. While there may be practical men who will stoutly contend that it is only the answers that matter, and certainly there are propagandists who consider the political moral of a story more important than the accuracy of its facts, it is hard to think of another area of scientific or scholarly activity where this sort of bottom-line pragmatism holds sway. Indeed, a serious concern with the validity of the premises, reasoning and facts supporting a conclusion is a hallmark that distinguishes a scientific or scholarly approach from a practical or propagandistic one.

There is no denying that, in scientific inquiry, it can be a subtle task to determine the "right reasons" underlying the observed phenomena. Deep problems involving the very meanings of "explanation" and "truth" can certainly arise. In the instant case, however, the subtleties and deep problems are not the major issue. The auxiliary defenses themselves are plausible sketches of what a real explanation might be like, and are advanced as such by the proponents of "as if" theorizing. We are not required to judge the implications of hypothetical facts in a hypothetical clash among equally hypothetical explanations; rather, the facts and the alternatives can be taken as stipulated. The major remaining issue concerns the propriety of subordinating the real explanation to an unreal and contrived one, investing great effort in refining the latter while casting the former in the role of a vague excuse for doing so. On this issue, the general principle that scientific inquiry ought to pursue the "right reasons" speaks clearly and decisively.

To underscore the applicability of this rather conventional but important principle, it is helpful to consider "as if" theorizing in relation to the identification problem of econometrics. In that context, the "as if" principle can be regarded as saying that optimization assumptions are an acceptable foundation for the theory of the firm because the theory leads to useful reduced form equations, and because the "true" explanation leads (or may well lead) to those same reduced form equations. Thus, the principle discounts entirely the advantages of structural estimation, and hence also the contributions of correct theory to structural estimation. As is well known, the central advantage is the ability to generate accurate predictions when the structure changes in specified ways.[10] There is no peculiar feature of the problem of firm behavior, or of the auxiliary defenses, that makes this consideration less important in this context than it is in general.

In fairness, it should be noted that some of the arguments offered for the "as if" principle suggest a considerably more innocuous interpretation of it than the one attacked above. On this alternative reading, the principle is primarily a response to the practical exigencies of economic research. Optimization theories are defended, not out of fundamental indifference to the "right reasons," but in the belief that, over a wide range of problems and research budgets, a deeper analysis of firm behavior is not worth the time and effort. Thus, Friedman said in his classic essay: "Complete 'realism' is clearly unattainable, and the question whether a theory is realistic 'enough' can be settled only by seeing whether it yields predictions that are good enough for the purpose in hand, or that are better than predictions from alternative theories."[11]

This emphasis on predictions "good enough for the purpose in hand" suggests that the problem under discussion is not the criteria for judging scientific theories, but the utility of approximation schemes. The point made is that a deliberate neglect of known complications may be perfectly sensible, given the "purpose in hand" (and also given, presumably, the size of the research budget or an impression of the marginal utility of accuracy). Friedman's discussion of the law of falling bodies, and other passages as well, make it clear that the "as if" principle is intended, at least in part, as a characterization of the deliberate use of approximations. Machlup's review of the issues in his presidential address strikes the same note very strongly: "I conclude that the choice of the theory has to depend on the problem we have to solve. "[12]

There can be no real quarrel with this pragmatic approach insofar as it relates to choices of approximate prediction methods for particular problems. There is a very serious quarrel, however, with the suggestion that such choices are prototypical examples of choice between competing theories -- and in Friedman and Machlup, there is more than a suggestion to this effect. Questions of scientific truth and explanation are at quite a different level than questions of the utility of approximation schemes. It may be reasonable to disregard known causal factors for the purposes of simplifying a particular calculation. But there is no warrant for ignoring such factors in a statement of the theory of the situation; the theory is after all, an attempt to state what the causal factors are. Ignoring air resistance may be acceptable in a calculation concerning a particular falling body; it certainly is not acceptable at the foundations of a theoretical account of how bodies fall in the earth's atmosphere.

What this all comes down to is a series of questions that I hope I have made troublesome: If the auxiliary defenses are valid and the true explanation for the successes of optimization theories, why should they not be considered as the appropriate foundation for the theory of the firm, while the optimization theories are treated as approximation schemes? What is wrong with the naive view that something called the "theory of the firm" ought to be a defensible attempt at truth about firm behavior, whereas an approximation scheme needs only to be defended as an approximation scheme? If optimization theories are essentially approximation schemes, how can useful progress in their development be expected if the fact that they are approximations is forgotten and the study of the real mechanisms underlying their predictive success is ignored? And of what value, to positive theory, are highly refined optimization models, given that the refinements typically leave unmodified the crudest feature of the approximation to real behavior, the optimization assumption itself?

95

3. 2. Critique of the Natural Selection Defense

The foregoing discussion proceeds on the assumption that the aux-iliary defenses are substantially valid, and specifically that they offer support for the use of optimization theories as approximations. I now propose to reexamine this assumption as it relates to the natural selection argument. It will be argued that this defense, in the form offered by Friedman and casually endorsed by many other writers, provides an extremely vague and incomplete account of the presumptive "true explanation" for the success of optimization theories. (This, of course, is not surprising, given that the purpose of this account is not to further understanding of the true explanation, but to foreclose the study of it.) It will be further argued that, when the vagueness of the account is reduced by completing the implicit model in plausible ways, the result is that the scope of the support for optimization theories is very narrow. This underscores the importance of the considerations put forward above: If there is a substantial class of interesting phenomena where there is no reason to expect the available approximation schemes to be effective, it becomes all the more important to develop a more fundamental theory that explains both the range of validity of the approximations and the phenomena that lie outside that range.

Since most of the points made here are discussed in detail in my earlier papers [1964, 1971],[13] I will present only a brief summary.

1) What are the genes? A theory of natural selection must characterize the basic sources of continuity in the evolutionary process. In the biological case, this basic source is the genetic transmission of characteristics. If there were no causal link between the characteristics of the nth generation and the characteristics of the $n+1^{st}$, there could be no natural selection and no evolution. The Friedman proposal, as quoted above, apparently claims that natural selection can operate regardless of the nature of the firms, and it is only on the basis of this incorrect claim that one can reach the conclusion that the study of actual firm behavior is not of central importance. A correct use of the biological

analogy makes the behavioral study of the firm correspond, at least in part, to genetics.

2) Actions v. rules of action. The environment does not act directly on genes or genotypes. It acts upon the actual historical individuals, whose characteristics and behaviors are determined in part by the environment itself. In particular, a genetically determined trait that confers superiority only in environments that never occur is not favored by selection pressures. Let us suppose, tentatively, that what corresponds to a geneotype in the theory of the firm is a rule of action or strategy. What the environment operates on, and rewards and punishes, is not the rule but the actions evoked from the rule by variables in the environment itself. This is a major objection to any claim that economic natural selection tends to produce situations in which the surviving rules are optimizing ones.

3) Entry, exit and dynamics. It is quite clear that, in reality or in any reasonable model, a temporary departure from optimization does not necessarily threaten the survival of a firm. Furthermore, a particular behavioral pattern could persist indefinitely in the economy in spite of the relatively speedy demise of each and every firm displaying it. All that is required is a continuing flow of entry of firms of this unfortunate type. Hence, a natural selection argument that validly reaches conclusions about the characteristics of surviving firms is necessarily an argument about a dynamic process, in which the specifications of entry and exit conditions are critical. No concern with these matters is evinced when the natural selection argument is casually invoked in support of optimization assumptions.

4) Investment policies. Fundamental to the natural selection argument is the assumption that a firm that behaves optimally will, in Friedman's words, "prosper and acquire resources with which to expand." In fact, such firms must actually expand, if the survival of non-optimizers is to be threatened. A definite assumption concerning investment policies is involved. At the behavioral level, it may certainly be doubted that a

desire for an expanded scale of operation is a universal concommitant of business success. And it may be noted that, for firms that are large enough relative to the market, this assumption is in _conflict_ with present value maximization. Hence, as many authors have pointed out, the force of the selection argument is greatly reduced in any context where firms are sheltered from competitive pressures.

5) _Scale dependence._ The question arises as to whether an optimizing firm that expands its operations is still an optimizing firm. In general, the scale of the firm must be admitted as a parameter of the firm's rules of action. When the firm expands, it necessarily behaves differently. If scale enters the rules as other than a multiplicative factor, expansion cannot be interpreted as merely "more of the same" behavior.

6) _Time dependence._ Models of _intertemporal_ optimization by firms have received much attention in recent years. It is therefore worth noting that time-dependence of firms' rules of action creates difficulties for the natural selection argument that are similar to, but perhaps more severe, than those created by scale dependence. An evolutionary contest among time-dependent rules is a peculiar thing. Unless the contest is restricted to rules that are in some sense cyclic or repetitive, there is, in effect, only a single generation in all of history. History's verdict on the behavior of that one generation will be rendered at the end, but that is too late to be of much help in understanding history itself.

Insofar as the above points complain of the vagueness of the natural selection defense, my own papers provide the basis for a reply. They set forth examples of economic selection processes that can be modeled as complete dynamic systems. Conditions are given under which the asymptotic behavior of these dynamic systems is indeed in conformity with the "as if" maximization principle. In this sense, Friedman's auxiliary defense can be made to work. But it must be emphasized that the scope of this defense -- as indicated by the assumptions of the theorems -- is narrow. To begin with, the results relate

98

only to long run tendencies under static conditions. The rates of approach to the long run conditions, as well as the shape of events along
the way, obviously depend on the specifics of firm behavior and on the
initial conditions. Secondly, the existing results are restricted to the
optimality of equilibrium actions -- they say nothing about the optimality
of the rules. Finally, the long run results rest on the denial by assumption of some of the difficulties raised above, especially points 4 - 6.

It is possible -- even likely -- that somewhat weaker sufficient
condition for "as if" maximization can be found. But it is very unlikely
that a theorem will be proved showing the evolution does not take time,
or that selection operates on totally unmanifested characteristics. In
fact, it is unlikely that more refined logic will demonstrate the substantive unimportance of any of the criticisms made above.

The natural selection argument does provide some support for the
"as if" optimization approach -- but not enough to justify all the varied
uses of that approach in the theory of the firm. And, emphatically, it
does not provide justification for the neglect of theoretical and empirical
study of actual firm decision processes. This same conclusion can, I
think, be convincingly established for the other auxiliary defenses; in
particular, it can be established for the claim that reasonable adaptive
behavior is "as if" optimizing. As in the case of natural selection, careful consideration will show that this defense is valid, but only in a suitably restricted sense, and in a narrow range of situations. It will be
found that large portions of orthodox theoretical practice remain unsupported and probably unsupportable by the adaptive behavior argument,
just as they are unsupported by the natural selection argument. And thus,
the verdict will again be that optimization models are useful for approximation purposes, under some conditions, but their place at the foundations of the theory of the firm is undeserved.

4. AN EVOLUTIONARY FRAMEWORK

4.1. Broadening the Postulational Basis of Theory

Much of the argument of the preceding section is essentially a reiteration and elaboration of points well made by Koopmans in 1957:

> "But if this (natural selection argument) is the basis for our belief in profit maximization, then we should postulate that basis itself, and not the profit maximization which it implies in certain circumstances. We should then postulate that entrepreneurial policies unsuitable for economic survival are applied by only a minority of enterprises which exhibit a high rate of economic mortality.
>
> "Such a change in the basis of economic analysis would seem to represent a gain in realism attributable to a concern with the directly perceived descriptive accuracy of the postulates. It would lead us to expect profit maximization to be most clearly exhibited in industries where entry is easiest and where the struggle for survival is keenest, and would present us with the further challenge to analyze what circumstances give to an industry that character. It would also prevent us, for purposes of explanatory theory, from getting bogged down in those refinements of profit maximization theory which endow the decision makers with analytical and computational abilities and assume them to have information-gathering opportunities such as are unlikely to exist or be applied in current practice. It seems that nothing is lost, and much may be gained, in thus broadening the postulational basis of economic theory."
>
> -- Koopmans [1957, pp. 140-41]

The present section sets forth the elements of a theoretical scheme that is an attempt to carry out the Koopmans program of "broadening the postulational basis of economic theory." The purpose of the discussion is to explicate concepts and mechanisms, and to characterize the underlying commitments that distinguish this approach from the orthodox one. No formalisms, specific models, theorems, equations or numbers are presented. It would be an error to suppose, however, that there is a major unbridged gap between this verbal proposal and the tasks of formal theory construction, model building, and quantification. The existence of the gap is readily conceded; it is a virtue of the proposal that it suggests a great deal of theoretical work that needs doing. However, Richard Nelson and I have already strung a few suspension bridges across that gap.[14] We claim that it is possible both to get across and to make progress on the other side. That work can speak for itself, however, and we would emphasize in any case the possibility that others may find much better crossings and more interesting territory on the other side than we have discovered.

We refer to the general proposal here described as <u>evolutionary</u> theory. As in evolutionary biology, the natural selection idea is central to the scheme. We do not, however, assign to the natural selection argument the role that Koopmans apparently had in mind; we do not argue that selection is the chief reason why approaches to profit maximization may, in some cases, occur. <u>We certainly do not underestimate the significance of various forms of learning and adaptive behavior in this connection.</u> Rather, we propose the evolutionary theory as an organizing framework within which to examine, and perhaps synthesize, alternative theoretical accounts of individual firm behavior. The value of this organizing function can be better assessed after the evolutionary framework has been sketched out.

4.2. Routines as Genes

The first element of the structure is an answer to the first critical question of the preceding section, "What are the genes?" The answer has already been suggested: The essential contunuity underlying the process of evolutionary change is the continuity of routinized behavior. That a great deal of firm decision behavior is in fact routinized can hardly be disputed; this is a central "stylized fact" about the realities of firm decision processes. Accounts of routinized or "rule of thumb" decision procedures can be cited that cover decision situations from pricing practices in retail stores to such "strategic" decisions as advertising or R and D effort, or the question of whether to invest abroad. Hardly any extended report of actual decision behavior fails to note the presence of a good deal of "inertia" -- frequently, it appears, more inertia than can readily be explained on the assumption that the firm is optimizing something. Judging by the anecdotes I have heard, I suspect that a great many economists have had frustrating confirmation of this point in their everyday experience as consumers: It is not uncommon to find firms adamantly refusing to budge from established routine -- refusing for example, to even quote a price at which better, quicker or otherwise different service would be available.

It is, of course, possible to dismiss all this as accounts of epiphenomena, compounded partly of the results of unobservable superoptimizing, and partly of atypical and aberrant behavior. The position here is to the contrary: The evidence is a reflection of the role of business firms in the economic system. That role is, first of all, to serve as a repository of economic capabilities, to simply maintain and transmit through time the ability to do something that is more or less useful. To modify a familiar phrase, the institutional role is essentially that of "remembering by doing." Unrealistic expectations concerning the amount of flexibility and responsiveness displayed by firms arise from an underestimate of the importance and difficulty of the task of merely continuing the routine performance, i.e., of preventing undesired deviations. Successful performance of that task is, at least in ordinary circumstances, a prerequisite for the ability to pursue profits by more sophisticated means such as responding to new opportunities. Some firms fail to satisfy that first prerequisite at all, while many others achieve it but never reach the more sophisticated level of operation.

4.3. Innovations as Mutations

Behavioral routines do change over time, in both desired and undesired ways. Such changes correspond to mutations in the biological theory, and without them there could be no long-term evolutionary change. Insofar as these changes are unintended and undirected, as many of them certainly are, the biological analogy is very close, and

102

perhaps it can be extended to the realm of theoretical results. But a slavish pursuit of the biological analogy would be counterproductive, for it is quite clear that the bulk of what we count as interesting long-term change in business behavior is not the product of blind chance. Rather, it is deliberate innovation, the product of directed effort, typically undertaken in response to identifiable economic stimuli, and motivated by profit consideration. Thus, with a considered step away from the biological theory, it is proposed that deliberate innovations, large and small, be counted as the most significant subset of the changes in routine behavior.

To concede that innovation is deliberate and profit-motivated is not to retreat back into the optimization framework. It is precisely in this area that the distinction between profit-motivated action and profit-maximizing action is most significant. What the evolutionary theory ultimately needs here is a theoretical account of the cognitive processes involved in innovative behavior. Such an account should, first of all, relate comfortably to available facts about such behavior, rather than requiring an artificial isolation from them. Ideally, the theory should be effectively linked to more general theories of individual and organizational problem-solving behavior, and also generate refutable hypotheses concerning market events of that sort that economists are typically interested in. This is clearly a tall order, and a long term goal. But some progress in the appropriate direction can be made even in the context of highly simplified models. The continual and global scan of alternatives assumed in optimization theory can be replaced by models that recognize search for new methods to be sporadic, problem-oriented, and local. The fact that the outcomes of the search processes are not predictable in detail, either by participants or outside observers, can be accorded explicit recognition by making these outcomes probabilistic. That such search draws upon information sources external to the firm, and thus is a type of non-market interaction in the system, can also be treated explicitly, though necessarily in a highly stylized way. Finally, to the extent that simple suboptimization procedures play a role in the evaluation of new methods, these too can be incorporated as features of the search model -- with due recognition for the fact that the prices and parameters employed in such calculations may have other behavioral rules of the firm as their direct source, and relate only indirectly to external conditions.[15]

In sharp contrast to the optimization approach, the routine/innovation dichotomy of evolutionary theory suggests that accurate prediction of firm behavior is likely to be most feasible precisely when the behavior is not strongly profit-motivated -- i.e., when there are not strong pressures leading firms to modify routines, and directly observable decision rules may be expected to continue to prevail in the future. When the opposite condition obtains, it may be easy (for anybody's theory) to predict the general direction of the response that will be made to particular pronounced changes in the profit incentive situation. Accurate quantitative prediction is another matter. Orthodoxy contends that the problem is simple, at least in principle; it is just a matter of movements in a pre-existing and sharply defined opportunity set. The present proposal suggests that anticipating the quantitative details of strongly motivated human problem-solving behavior is not, in principle, simple -- especially for outside observers who may lack both the motivation and the detailed data on the "givens" of the problem.

4.4. The Set of Possible Routines

Although the present discussion is not directed toward formalization of the theory, there is one indispensable first step toward formal modeling that must be mentioned here, to corroborate the claim that formalization is possible. A formal discussion of "routines" and "changes in routine" requires a formal characterization of what a routine is, and what it might change to. At the most abstract level, a routine is simply characterized as an element of some set of possible routines, and a "change in routine" for a given firm involves a replacement of one element of that set by another. This is adequate for highly abstract discussion, but, obviously, a specific analytical purpose will ordinarily suggest a set of possible routines that has much more specific structure. (In a study of markup pricing rules, the set of possible routines may be identical with a set of alternative markup percentages, while other aspects of behavior are assumed to be identical among firms and immutable across time.) The same theoretical language and formalisms can be employed in discussing an extremely wide range of situations, differing greatly in levels of complexity and detail, as well as in issues considered. This presents considerable advantages, along with some dangers of self-deception. Shubik has criticized orthodoxy, as taught at "advanced" levels, because it does not "bother to differentiate between General Motors and the local candy store."[16] There are dangers of replicating that defect, but they are presumably held in check by evolutionary theory's receptivity to direct information on firm decision processes.

4.5. Search Triggers

Since evolutionary theory differentiates sharply between the persistence of current routines and the more subtle processes of innovation, it is of obvious importance to identify the conditions that evoke the latter behavior rather than the former. In this connection, there are two broad hypotheses, that may conveniently be labeled "carrot" and "stick." The "stick" hypothesis says that the thing that most typically and effectively rouses individuals and organizations out of their routinized lethargy is trouble. The appropriate notion of "trouble" is "performance at less than aspiration level" -- a formulation that recognizes that the sorts of objective events that constitute trouble may differ from individual to individual or organization to organization. The essential doctrine of the "stick" position is that performance is frequently above aspiration level, and that extended periods of zero or low search activity therefore occur. The "carrot" view denies the existence of a motivational asymmetry or discontinuity between high performance and low, arguing that the only acceptable interpretation of "aspiration level" is the preferred outer limit of the objectively available opportunities. Furthermore, the argument runs, the ability to finance investment in change will, if anything, be higher when the proposed change is a response to an improvement in the objective opportunities than it is when the response is to deterioration.

Although both carrots and sticks are mentioned in elementary textbooks, and occasionally in informal discussion at advanced levels, the formal versions of orthodox theory are fully committed to the "carrot" position. The profit-maximizing zeal never flags; routine or satisficing behavior can be interpreted only as instrumental to the vigorous pursuit of higher level objectives. The commitment of evolutionary theory to the "stick" hypothesis is equally strong. And just as orthodoxy prefers to think of routines as instrumental in higher level optimizations, it is natural in the evolutionary approach to think of observed suboptimizing behavior as a facet of some higher level routine or policy that is reviewed only infrequently, and in response to trouble. There is a sort of symmetry here -- but the logic of calculation cost cuts sharply in favor of the view that calculated decisions are made within a context formed by relatively uncalculated assumptions and policy commitments.

Although a large difference in point of view separates the "carrot" and "stick" approaches, the general ideas have little empirical content. To add content to the notion that search for alternatives is triggered by trouble, it is first of all necessary to characterize the sorts of adjustments that are made routinely. For example, markup pricing rules provide a routinized response to cost increases, so cost increases, as such, do not directly imply "trouble" or trigger search. It is then necessary to define the events that do mean trouble, equivalently, to model the determination of the aspiration level. Plausible candidate models are easy to propose -- and easily shown to differ sharply in their implications. A model that identifies profit aspirations with some fixed rate of return behaves quite differently from one that relates aspiration to past

performance of the same firm, which in turn differs from one that relates
it to contemporaneous performance of other firms in the industry. Theoretical and empirical exploration of these sorts of differences constitutes
a major research task within the evolutionary approach.

4.6. Investment, Finance and Capital Markets

As was noted in the critique of the natural selection argument,
the character of firm investment policies is a crucial determinant of the
extent to which the successful firms in a given environment exert pressures for adaptation or contraction on the less successful firms. The
questions that arise in this connection include the motivations of the
decision makers, the role of perceptions of market power, and the nature
of the routinized procedures that support the investment decision process. However, the sharpest contrasts with the orthodox approach arise
in the treatment of the financing of investment. It is natural in orthodoxy to adopt an assumption of perfect capital markets as at least a first
approximation. This avoids the complexities of modeling an imperfect
capital market, and has the considerable advantage of making present
value maximization an unambiguous decision criterion. The corresponding first approximation in the evolutionary approach is that there is no
capital market at all, i.e., that investment is financed entirely out of
retained earnings. This also avoids the problem of modeling an imperfect capital market, and it defers a confrontation with the question of
whether some types of poor business performance might be indefinitely
sustained (in the aggregate, if not in individual firms) by a continuing
infusion of new capital.

When the first approximations are left behind, the important
problems that arise concern the information processing functions of the
capital market. If future business success were readily predictable,
but not highly correlated with current and past success, one would expect to find heavy reliance on external finance and weak correlations
between investment levels and realized success. However, to the

107

extent that prediction is difficult and perhaps complicated by moral hazard problems, one would expect to find lending decisions governed by relatively crude extrapolations of past performance, and by the application of routinized tests for current financial soundness to potential borrowers. Procedures of this type can be interpreted as being a response more to the problem of effectively processing the currently available data than to the implicit prediction task. Needless to say, one would not expect to find lenders willing, on the basis of these sorts of calculations, to fix an interest rate and let the borrower decide the amount of the loan.

Viewed from this perspective, the functioning of "imperfect" capital markets is not seen in terms of degrees of departure from a baseline of perfection, but in terms of degrees of enhancement of the differential firm growth phenomena that would arise if there were no institutionalized lending at all. Direct study of the information processing routines employed becomes fundamental to the understanding of roles of such lenders in different economic contexts.

4.7. Theoretical Tasks

There are other elements of the evolutionary approach that have barely been suggested above. It offers, for example, a convenient framework for the discussion of non-market information flows, including the flows of information associated with technical advance. The concept of enterpreneurship, which fits very uncomfortably in the orthodox scheme, is admissible, and clarified, in the evolutionary one. These and related matters are discussed in more detail in recent work by Nelson and myself. Enough of the framework has been developed here to make it possible to discuss what the framework might be good for; specifically, to consider the objectives of theoretical inquiry within it.

The canonical question of evolutionary theory is this: Consider a group of firms, operating according to specified routines -- subject to modification by specified search rules -- in a specified market environment. Let the specification of the environment include, for example, the conditions of determination of the market prices confronting the firms, the behavior of financial institutions, and the rules governing entry and exit from the group, and the functioning of exogenous sources of information about new routines. Given a complete dynamic system of this type, and given the initial conditions, the question is, what next? What behavior will the system exhibit in the short run, the intermediate, the long? In particular, how do the consequences of differential profit performance by different firms shape the course of events in the system? Which classes of routine behaviors are capable of protracted coexistence with each other, without producing, out of their own dynamic logic, pressures for change? What classes are mutually incompatible or antagonistic, and in what time frame is the clash likely to become acute?

There are many possible objections to this proposed canonical form; I consider three of them. The first is that it is too roomy; the class of questions characterized is very large. This objection would certainly have great force if the routine behaviors to be imputed to firms were to be chosen on the basis of nothing more than undisciplined speculation. But the proposal is not for such speculation, it is for drawing to the maximum possible extent on the guidance available in the empirical literature on firm decision making. Further guidance may be found in the textbooks of business school courses. And when an empirical basis is lacking entirely, plausible adaptive or suboptimizing rules can be postulated.

A second possible objection is that the problem is too complicated, and perhaps intractable. The answer is orthodox: Theorists are perfectly entitled to divide the difficulties and to study simplified models for the sake of building understanding. Also, the degree of intractability that one imputes to a model depends rather strongly on the sorts of conclusions one expects to get out of it. Qualitative results concerning asymptotic behavior, for example, may be obtainable for dynamic systems of quite a high degree of complexity. Studies of this kind ought to be regarded as exercises in the logic of the canonical problem rather than as predictions, but that is no reason not to undertake them.

A third complaint might be that, with the possible exception of theorems concerning asymptotic behavior, interpretable qualitative predictions may be impossible to obtain for dynamic systems of the sort described. There is probably a large measure of validity in this complaint. But it might not be a bad thing if theorists were more concerned with providing guidance for attempts at accurate quantitative prediction and less concerned with generating qualitative hypotheses and interpretive fables.

To pursue this last point a bit further, it is clear that the canonical problem implicitly suggests quite a different relationship between theoretical and empirical research than the one that currently prevails. The practice of taking empirical facts about business behavior as **premises** of theoretical argument -- on the mere ground that they are facts -- is virtually unknown. In line with the "as if" doctrine, it is the conclusion of the argument that might possibly have empirical relevance, not the premises. Relatedly, the addiction of empirical research to the lagged dependent variable is widely regarded as an embarrassment; the derived theoretical puzzle is to work out an appropriately subtle super-optimization rationale for this practice. By contrast, from the evolutionary point of view, the first task is simply accurate description of the patterns of behavior that display inertia. That the inertia itself exists, and can be utilized as the basis for successful prediction, is not a puzzle but a premise. The real puzzles begin with the attempt to explain the statistical effects of the exogenous variables without resorting to fictions about decision behavior, and then to indicate how to further reduce the prediction errors. The hope is that, under combined empirical and theoretical attack, the dynamics of an economic situation involving interacting firms might be understood well enough to generate intermediate-term predictions of high precision and substantive significance -- a level of success well beyond that of naive extrapolation, or of methods

that are constrained by methodological principle to forego the attempt
to estimate the true structure.

5. CONCLUSION

It is sobering to consider the possibility that behavior of economic theorists might be governed by the same evolutionary logic that
has been proposed here as an interpretation of the behavior of business-
men. I fear that it is. The theoretical use of the optimization approach
has become highly routinized. The capacity for significant incremental
adjustments to environmental change is also routinized. One might
imagine that the continued pursuit of the optimization approach is merely
the continuing verdict of a superoptimization process, one that carefully
compares the marginal returns to different lines of theoretical endeavour.
But one would be imagining. There is no such superoptimization going
on; the amount of effort devoted to reviewing the high level commitments
is negligible compared to the effort devoted to the more routinized activities that the commitments support. And this is no reflection on the
rationality or motivation of theorists; it is merely a reflection of the
ambiguities of rationality in a world of positive calculation costs. The
picture seems complete, and the prediction distressingly clear. Routines will persist -- unless, of course, there is trouble.

Is there trouble? Whether there is trouble does not depend directly on objective performance. As was explained above, the sort of
trouble that matters is perfornamce below aspiration levels. The aspirations relevant to theorizing about firm behavior are obviously diverse.
Leaving the areas of mundane incentives and intellectual fads aside,
there remain such large differences as those between, for example, the
theoretical aspirations relevant in general equilibrium analysis and the
aspirations relating to the theory of the regulated firm. Thus, it is difficult to generalize about the operative aspirations.

It is less difficult to cite some possible aspirations that do not
seem to figure strongly in the theory-building process. Highly precise

111

quantitative prediction is one such; if such prediction were highly valued in itself, much greater interest would necessarily attach to the specific quantitative rules actually employed in many decision situations.[17] Another non-aspiration is comprehensiveness -- it is entirely accepted that a different model of firm behavior is appropriate according to whether the question at hand involves investment, price determination, cash holdings, etc., etc. Models intended for empirical implementation are especially likely to be carefully aimed at specific data targets; they are subject to scrutiny for conformity to optimization principles, but rarely pretend to offer empirical predictions on other aspects or consequences of the behavior of the same firms.

Finally, there is the related non-aspiration of dynamic completeness, i.e., of providing enough dynamic equations to determine all the firm decision variables that appear in the model, for arbitrary initial conditions and time paths of environmental data. All of these lacunae in the scheme of theoretical aspirations are quite understandable consequences of the general acceptance of the "as if" principle and of the intrinsic information-theoretic ambiguities of the optimization approach itself. As long as they remain, there is little chance that the results obtained from the optimization approach will fall short of the prevailing aspirations. In a manner quite consistent with familiar notions of aspiration adjustment, a protracted failure to achieve certain kinds of results has produced a situation where those results are no longer aspired to, and are even of doubtful legitimacy as objectives. Thus, the initial presumption that established routines will persist apparently stands.

There is one important qualification to this prognosis. It is possible that the calculation cost problem constitutes a source of long run instability in the routines of optimization theory. Economists are presumably concerned with the implications of scarcity, and it is hard to believe that an economic theory founded on the denial of a fundamental scarcity can be viable indefinitely. Perhaps what we are witnessing is a painfully protracted reductio ad absurdum from flawed basic premises.

112

The conclusion of the reductio may one day be drawn. If it is, the discipline may or may not turn to the evolutionary approach advocated here. But it will have to turn to something.

NOTES

[1] The conclusions that I here treat as non-controversial can, I believe, be supported very effectively by arguments drawn from Kuhn [1970], Polanyi [1962], and Quine [1961]. I fear that the present paper may have very little to say to any reader who, though familiar with the works cited, finds them totally unconvincing.

[2] Scherer [1970], p. 175. In the same connection, see Silberston [1970] p. 545.

[3] Comments along this line may be found in, for example, Friedman [1953], Machlup [1946, 1967] and Silberston [1970]. See also the analysis by Gordon [1948, pp. 284-85].

[4] The point here is that what the "exceptional" cases present may merely be strong temptations to deviate from the established rule, rather than solid grounds for doing so. To distinguish the valid exceptions to a rule from the temptations is not always easy.

[5] Eliasson [1974, p. 212].

[6] Reference should be made, in particular, to the four case studies summarized in the well known volume by Cyert and March [1963].

[7] The difficulty examined in this section has been noted, in one formulation or another, by a number of authors. See, for example, Day [1971], Marschak and Radner [1972, Chapter 9], Radner [1968]. I discussed it myself in [1964, p. 262-64]. The term "superoptimization" is employed in this connection by Mirrlees and Stern [1972].

[8] See Hirshleifer [1973], and Rothschild [1973], for surveys of recent work in these areas.

[9] Perhaps it is this orientation that accounts for the fact that the contributions of the philosophers to the discussion are unusually clear and helpful relative to the discussion as a whole. Personally, I recommend Nagel [1963] and Massey [1965].

[10] A classic exposition of this point is that of Marschak [1953].

[11] Friedman [1953, p. 41].

[12] Machlup [1967, pp. 30-31].

[13] For background on the biological theory referred to here, an excellent elementary source is Wilson and Bossert [1971].

[14] See references [Nelson and Winter, 1973; Nelson and Winter, 1974; Nelson, Winter and Schuette, forthcoming; and Nelson and Winter, forthcoming].

[15] See the previously cited Nelson and Winter papers for illustrative efforts along the lines just described.

[16] Shubik [1970, p. 413].

[17] Under perfectly reasonable assumptions about the goals of economic inquiry, the department store pricing model in the Cyert and March volume could be regarded as a signal achievement in the theory of the firm. (see also Baumol and Stewart [1971]). But such a degree of emphasis on precise prediction is obviously not characteristic of the discipline.

REFERENCES

Aharoni, Y. [1966], The Foreign Investment Decision Process, (Cambridge: Harvard University Press).

Alchian, A. A. [1950], "Uncertainty, Evolution and Economic Theory," Journal of Political Economy, v. 58, pp. 211-22.

Baumol, W. J. and M. Stewart [1971], "On the Behavioral Theory of the Firm," in R. Marris and A. Wood, (eds.), The Corporate Economy: Growth, Competition and Innovative Potential, (Cambridge: Harvard University Press), pp. 118-43.

Cyert, R. and J. G. March [1963], A Behavioral Theory of the Firm, (Englewood Cliffs, N. J.: Prentice Hall, Inc.).

Day, R. H. [1971], "Rational Choice and Economic Behavior," Theory and Decision, v. 1, pp. 229-51.

Day, R. H., S. Morley and K. R. Smith [1974], "Myopic Optimizing and Rules of Thumb in a Micro-Model of Industrial Growth," American Economic Review, v. 64, pp. 11-23.

Earley, J. S. [1956], "Marginal Policies of 'Excellently Managed' Companies," American Economic Review, v. 46, no. 1, pp. 44-70.

Eliasson, G. [1974], Corporate Planning -- Theory, Practice, Comparison, (Stockholm: Federation of Swedish Industries).

Farrell, M. J. [1970], "Some Elementary Selection Processes in Economics," Review of Economic Studies, v. 37, pp. 305-319.

Friedman, M. [1953], "The Methodology of Positive Economics," Chapter 1 in Essays in Positive Economics, (Chicago: The University of Chicago Press).

Gordon, R. A. [1948], "Short Period Price Determination in Theory and Practice," American Economic Review, v. 38, pp. 265-88.

Hahn, F. H. [1970], "Some Adjustment Problems," Econometrica, v. 38, pp. 1-17.

Hirshleifer, J. [1973], "Where Are We in the Theory of Information," American Economic Review, v. 63(May 1973), pp. 31-39.

Koopmans, T. C. [1957], Three Essays on the State of Economic Science, (New York: McGraw Hill Book Co.).

Kuhn, T. S. [1970], The Structure of Scientific Revolutions, 2nd ed., (Chicago: University of Chicago Press).

Machlup, F. [1946], "Marginal Analysis and Empirical Research," American Economic Review, v. 36, pp. 519-54.

_____ [1967], "Theories of the Firm: Marginalist, Behavioral, Managerial," American Economic Review, v. 57, pp. 1-33.

Marschak, J. [1953], "Economic Measurements for Policy and Prediction," Chapter 1 in W. C. Hood and T. C. Koopmans, (eds.), Studies in Econometric Method, (New York: John Wiley and Sons).

Marschak, J. and R. Radner [1972], Economic Theory of Teams, (New Haven: Yale University Press).

Massey, G. J. [1965], "Professor Samuelson on Theory and Realism: Comment," American Economic Review, v. 55, pp. 1155-63.

Mirrlees, J. A. And N. H. Stern [1972], "Fairly Good Plans," Journal of Economic Theory, v. 4, pp. 268-88.

Nagel, E. [1963], "Assumptions in Economic Theory," American Economic Review, v. 53, pp. 211-19.

Nelson, R. R. and S. G. Winter [1973], "Toward an Evolutionary Theory of Economic Capabilities," American Economic Review, v. 63, pp. 440-49.

_____ [1974], "Neoclassical vs. Evolutionary Theories of Economic Growth: Critique and Prospectus," The Economic Journal, v. 84, pp. 886-905.

_____ and H. L. Schuette [forthcoming], "Technical Change in an Evolutionary Model," Quarterly Journal of Economics.

_____ [forthcoming], "Factor Price Changes
and Factor Substitution in an Evolutionary Model," The Bell
Journal of Economics and Management Science.

Nerlove, M. [1972], "Lags in Economic Behavior," Econometrica,
v. 40, pp. 221-51.

Polanyi, M. [1962], Personal Knowledge: Towards a Post-Critical
Philosophy, (New York: Harper Torchbooks).

Quine, W. V. [1961], "Two Dogmas of Empiricism," in From a Logical
Point of View, 2nd ed., (New York: Harper Torchbooks).

Radner, R. [1968], "Competitive Equilibrium Under Uncertainty,"
Econometrica, v. 36, pp. 31-58.

Rothschild, M. [1973], "Models of Markets with Imperfect Information:
A Survey," Journal of Political Economy, v. 81, pp. 1283-1308.

Scherer, F. M. [1970], Industrial Market Structure and Economic Performance, (Chicago: Rand McNally and Co.).

Schumpeter, J. A. [1955], The Theory of Economic Development,
(Cambridge: Harvard University Press), first published in
German, 1911.

_____ [1950], Capitalism, Socialism and Democracy,
3rd ed., (New York: Harper and Brothers).

Shubik, M. [1970], "A Curmudgeon's Guide to Microeconomics,"
Journal of Economic Literature, v. 8, pp. 405-34.

Silberston, A. [1970], "Price Behaviour of Firms," The Economic Journal,
v. 80, pp. 511-82.

Simon, H. A. [1965], Administrative Behavior, 2nd ed. (New York: The
Free Press [paperback]).

_____ [1955], "A Behavioral Model of Rational Choice,"
Quarterly Journal of Economics, v. 69, pp. 99-118.

Smith, R. A. [1966], Corporations in Crisis, (New York: Anchor Books).

Wilson, E. O. and W. H. Bossert [1971], A Primer of Population Biology,
(Stanford, Connecticut: Sinauer Associates, Inc.).

Winter, S. G. [1964], "Economic 'Natural Selection' and the Theory of the Firm," Yale Economic Essays, v. 4, pp. 225-272.

_____ [1971], "Satisficing, Selection and the Innovating Remnant," Quarterly Journal of Economics, v. 85, pp. 237-61.

The author is professor of economics at the University of Michigan. I am indebted to Richard Nelson for many helpful discussions of the matters treated here. The influence of J. A. Schumpeter [1955, 1950], and H. A. Simon [1965, 1955] (and other work) is so pervasive in the paper that it seems appropriate to mention it here rather than at some arbitrary point in the text. Also, the well known article by A. Alchian [1950] was a major stimulus to the development of the evolutionary approach described in section four. The support of this research by the National Science Foundation under grant GS-35659 is gratefully acknowledged.

118

The Market Adaptation of the Firm
Cliff Lloyd, David Rapport, and James E. Turner

CONTENTS

1. INTRODUCTION

Traditional theories of the firm have relatively little to say about the actual growth path of output (see however Day, Morley and Smith [1974] and Day and Tinney [1969]). To say simply that the firm maximizes profit (assuming adequate knowledge) tells nothing at all about the adjustment process by which the firm would move from one production level to another when circumstances change. It also tells us nothing about the way in which the firm would behave to seek profit in the absence of complete knowledge. A similar lack of explanation exists regarding the entry of firms into the production of new commodities. If firms enter those industries in which excess profits are being earned and leave those where losses are made, what happens in industries where some firms are experiencing losses while others are enjoying excess profits.

Suppose, for example, that it is known that Chevrolet is making excess profits. What is the entering firm to do? Take up the production of Chevrolets? It would presumably face a considerable law suit if it did so. Perhaps it could produce the Edsel?

In this paper, we develop a general view of the adaptation of the firm to its environment. In Section 2, we present a model of the growth of the output of a monopolistic firm in the absence of extensive information. In Section 3, we discuss how a firm with a definite commodity in mind can decide whether to enter a given established market. In Section 4, we consider how the firm could determine what sort of product it could create in order to take advantage of perceived profit opportunities. This problem of niche selection by the firm has, to our knowledge, rarely been formally discussed (Chamberlin [1953]). In our discussion we will consider firms which are multi-product in principle. However, we will be concerned with the growth path of output and marketing of a single product.

2. THE GROWTH OF OUTPUT

The multi-product firm must decide which of the outputs of its products (or divisions) to expand and which to contract. What governs such decisions in the absence of the perfect knowledge commonly assumed in economic models ? We will suppose that, under normal circumstances (i.e., except when the firm is actually entering a new market), the firm will expand output of those products that are making greater than normal profits and contract those that are making losses (Winter [1971]). There is some evidence for this view of output decision making. Firms do seem to have a clear concept of a satisfactory rate of return on invested capital (Simon [1965]) and there is some indication that firms do attempt to grow as large as possible subject to the satisfactory return condition (Baumol [1959]).

For simplicity, let us consider a monopolistic firm with output rate $X(t)$ at time t. Suppose that an output of X^o is required before sales are sufficient to return normal profits. Suppose further that profits remain above normal for outputs up to a level K. Thus X^o is the minimum output level and K is the maximum output level to achieve normal profits. We suppose that the firm (or division) will exhibit positive

120

growth $(dx/dt > 0)$ if $X^O < X < K$ and negative growth $(dx/dt < 0)$ if $X < X^O$ or $X > K$. An approximation (around X^O and K) to any equation having these properties is given by

(1)
$$\frac{dX}{dt} = r(X - X^O)(1 - X/K) \; .$$

This is the equation of logistic growth familiar in the study of the dynamics of population growth in ecology (MacArthur [1972]). The constant r sets the time scale of the growth process.

According to the model, the growth of output is a monotonic increasing function of excess profits. The simplest possible model identifies the growth rate and the excess profit rate,

(2)
$$\frac{dX}{dt} = r(X-X^O)(1 - X/K) = \gamma \Pi(X)$$

where γ is a positive constant. Equation (2) expresses the basic assumption of the model that the firm increases the output of those products that earn profit (above the normal level) and decrease those that make losses.

The traditional theory of the firm has been concerned almost exclusively with profit maximizing behavior under conditions of very complete knowledge. Little has been incorporated about how an imperfectly informed firm might decide to expand its output (see however Day, Morley and Smith [1974]; Simon [1965]; Cyert and March [1963] and Winter [1971]). Without additional information, it seems quite unreasonable to suppose that the firm would expand its output in the face of losses. On the other hand, the idea that output of those commodities earning excess profits will increase is as old as the "invisible hand". If the firm is seeking opportunities of excess profits, what is more reasonable than that it take advantage of such opportunities in its own product line? Perhaps a major reason to increase production is to prevent other firms from entering the market to take advantage of opportunities for excess profits (Bain [1968, Chapter 8]). On these grounds, we argue that any reasonable equation describing growth under information insufficient for maximization should associate positive growth with excess profits and zero growth with zero excess profits. Equations (1) and (2) provide an approximation to any such reasonable equation.

The time path of output given by equation (1) has one other very reasonable property. Students of marketing have observed that new products exhibit a typical life cycle of sales (Kotler [1972, Chapter 12]. The characteristic form that they attribute to the life cycle is shown in Figure 1. The logistic equation gives rise to the growth pattern shown

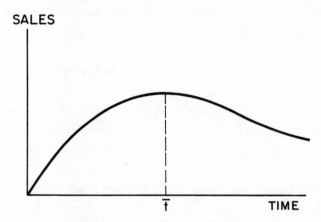

Figure 1. Typical Life Cycle Pattern of Sales

in Figure 2. Note that, from the inflection point at $X = 1/2(X^o + K)$, the logistic curve is similar to the life cycle curve to the left of its maximum at $\bar{t}$.

The downturn of the life cycle curve to the right of $\bar{t}$ is explained in terms of the introduction of competing commodities and product obsolescence. Product obsolescence would be represented in the logistic growth model by shrinkage of K at times greater than $\bar{t}$ which clearly would lead to a downturn in the logistic curve. A time lag in the response of the growth rate to profit levels would give rise to an overshoot of the equilibrium size K

122

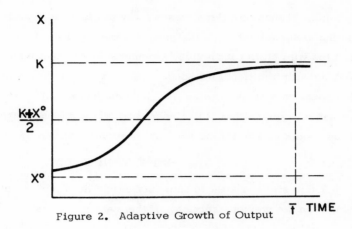

Figure 2. Adaptive Growth of Output

followed by a downturn in the growth curve. Moreover, after this model is generalized in the next section to describe competition, it will be seen that competition also helps to account for the characteristic shape of the life-cycle curve. Finally, note that the portion of the logistic growth curve which is not in conformity with the observed life cycle pattern (i.e. where $X < 1/2(K+X^o)$) would never be observed for firms that begin production at levels much above the minimum X^o.

It would be premature to claim complete generality for the life cycle curve. Its shape at very low levels of output in particular is nec- essarily somewhat conjectural. Firms normally begin production at some finite rate of output, not be easing up from zero. Accordingly, the life cycle curve near the origin may never be observed. Indeed, if a firm behaving according to the logistic growth model began production at a rate of output reasonably near to $X = 1/2(K+X^o)$ and if it were later con- fronted (as the life cycle curve requires) with competition and obsoles- cence, and if we were to sketch the product's growth path, we would pre- sumably draw exactly the life cycle curve. Accordingly, not only is the growth path given by the logistic growth model consistent with the life cycle curve, under appropriate conditions it predicts it.

123

In brief there are three reasons why the logistic growth model is appealing as a description of the growth of output of the firm. (1) When associated with profits it provides a reasonable explanation very much in keeping with traditional economics of how the firm with limited information could control its growth. (2) It is an approximation to any such "reasonable" explanation. (3) Under appropriate circumstances it predicts behaviour of exactly the sort that observers take to be typical.

3. COMPETITION AND ENTRY

It is a simple matter to introduce competition into the structure developed in the previous section. If there are two firms in the industry, presumably the outputs of each firm, $X_1(t)$ and $X_2(t)$, will negatively affect the profits of the other firm. In particular, if the sale of one unit of the second commodity decreases the maximum profitable sales of the first commodity by α_1 units, then the growth of the output of the first firm should cease at the level $K_1 - \alpha_1 X_2$. This leads to the following explicit model for the growth rate

(3)
$$\frac{dX_1}{dt} = r_1(X_1 - X_1^O)(1 - X_1/K_1 - \alpha_1 X_2/K_1) = \gamma_1 \Pi_1(X_1, X_2) .$$

This equation is familiar to population ecologists and is used to model two competing populations. Together with the corresponding equation for X_2,

(4)
$$\frac{dX_2}{dt} = r_2(X_2 - X_2^O)(1 - X_2/K_2 - \alpha_2 X_1/K_2) = \gamma_2 \Pi_2(X_1, X_2) .$$

The two equations are known as the Lotka-Volterra system (MacArthur [1972], Boulding [1962, p. 483], and Lotka [1956]).

Equations (3) and (4) allow us to say a great deal about entry. In particular, the model describes the consequences to a firm of introducing a given product into an established market where competing commodities are already being sold. For example, suppose that firm 1 is established alone in the market and that its growth path is given by equation (1). A second firm considering entry will have a growth path given by equation (4). The larger the sales of the first firm the more damaging it will be to the entry prospects of the new firm. The first firm will not expand output beyond K_1. Accordingly, if (4) yields positive profit and growth at $X_1 = K_1$, then the second firm can enter. The feasible entry sizes are X_2 in the range

$$(5) \qquad X_2^o < X_2 < K_2 - \alpha_2 K_1 \ .$$

For output levels in this range, the second firm can profitably enter and survive.

Firm 2 will not, in general, know if inequality (5) is satisfied because it will not, in general, know the value of K_1. Indeed it need not know K_2 either, although it would presumably have some estimates of both K's and of α_2. So long as firm 1's output level is not too large it will be possible, and initially profitable, for firm 2 to enter. Thereafter, a variety of possibilities arise as the firms compete for the market.

Both firms can coexist, at least temporarily, at output levels X_1 and X_2 in the ranges

$$X_1^o < X_1 < K_1 - \alpha_1 X_2$$

$$(6)$$

$$X_2^o < X_2 < K_2 - \alpha_2 X_1$$

In this event, the outputs of both firms increase and, as they grow, they exploit more and more of the market. The four possible outcomes of the competition depend on the degree of competition (measured by α_1 and α_2) and are summarized in the following table. The fourth outcome is indeterminate in the sense that the outcome depends on the initial production levels of the two firms.

Table I: Four Possible Outcomes of Competition

(i)   Coexistence

$$\alpha_1 < (K_1 - X_1^0)/K_2, \quad \alpha_2 < (K_2 - X_2^0)/K_1$$

(ii)   First firm eliminates second

$$\alpha_1 < (K_1 - X_1^0)/K_2, \quad \alpha_2 > (K_2 - X_2^0)/K_1$$

(iii) Second firm eliminates first

$$\alpha_1 > (K_1 - X_1^0)/K_2, \quad \alpha_2 < (K_2 - X_2^0)/K_1$$

(iv)   Indeterminate outcome

$$\alpha_1 > (K_1 - X_1^0)/K_2, \quad \alpha_2 > (K_2 - X_2^0)/K_1$$

The outcome of competition is seen to depend critically on the strength of the competitive interaction between the two firms. The effects of the competition are illustrated graphically in Figure 3.

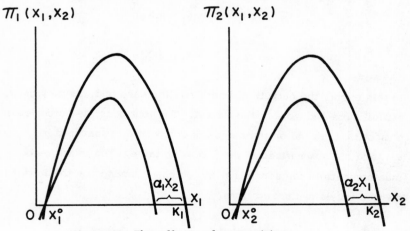

Figure 3. The effects of competition

The effect of a competing firm is to decrease the maximum profitable output level. Competitive displacement occurs when either $\alpha_1 X_2 > K_1 - X_1^o$ or $\alpha_2 X_1 > K_2 - X_2^o$ when, in terms of Figure 3, one firm or the other would be literally squeezed out of the market.

4. FINDING A NICHE

An important activity of the top management of firms is the consideration of possible new products. According to traditional economic theory, the firm will enter markets where excess profits are being earned. This is not a sufficient explanation in a market with differentiated products. It is not at all unusual, for example, to see one automobile (e.g. Dodge or Mercury) making large profits while another ostensibly similar automobile (e.g. Hudson) is making losses. Clearly the entering firm will want to produce a car similar to the Dodge and unlike the Hudson. But what does that mean? In this section we will attempt to clarify this question. We will also show how, once it is answered, the Lotka-Volterra structure can be used to determine the advisability of entry.

Suppose, following Lancaster [1966], that each commodity may be described in terms of a set of relevant linear characteristics. Thus we might describe a car in terms of its horsepower, top speed, miles per gallon, the time that it takes to accelerate from 0 to 60 miles per hour, etc.

An illustration may be in order. Consider the characterisation of a candy in terms of its chocolateness and its sweetness. The former may be measured in terms of the amount of cocoa per pound of candy, the latter in terms of the amount of sugar. We could then define the relevant characteristics space as the positive quadrant of a two dimensional Euclidean space with sugar content on one axis and cocoa content on the other. Each point in this space will define a different candy varying all the way from bitter chocolate to pure cane sugar.[1] Each possible candy combining sugar and chocolate can be defined as a point in this characteristics space.

127

Relevant to any industry there will be a characteristics space, C, each point in which defines a possible product (analogous to a biological niche). Associated with each such point it would be possible for the firm to estimate a total demand for that commodity at a price sufficient to cover cost plus the usual mark-up. Thus, if Z_i is the amount of characteristic i we may define a quantity mapping

$$(7) \qquad Q = h(Z_1, Z_2, \ldots, Z_n).$$

From the n-dimensional characteristic space $C_n = \mathbb{R}^n$ to the real line where Q is the quantity demanded of the commodity defined by the point $(Z_1, Z_2, \ldots, Z_n)$. We call this a quantity mapping to avoid confusion between it and the classical demand function.

Suppose now that the firm chooses to produce some specific commodity represented by a particular point Z^o in C_n. The firm will choose a price, P^o adequate to cover costs plus the standard markup.[2] Associated with Z^o and P^o will be a probability density function over the characteristics space C_n, representing for each element of volume in C_n the relative proportion of the demand for products in that volume that is satisfied by Z^o at P^o (i.e. the proportion that will buy Z^o) in the absence of alternative products. This function $f^o(Z_1, Z_2, \ldots, Z_n)$ will be called the demand density function. The superscript on f indicates that $f^o(Z_1, Z_2, \ldots, Z_n)$ is defined as a function of the particular initial point Z^o and P^o.

The firm's choice of product to introduce will be based upon three distributions. The most basic defines the potential sales of a monopolistic firm producing the commodity Z^o. It is given by

$$(8) \qquad Q^o = \int_{C_n} h^o(Z)dZ = \int_{C_n} h(Z)f^o(Z)dZ,$$

where $Z = (Z_1, \ldots, Z_n)$ varies in C_n. Recall however that maximum profitable sales are given by K. If customers are dealt with on a first come first serve basis the distribution of sales over C_n would spread out below $h^o(Z)$ in a distribution function $\beta h^o(Z)$ such that

$$(9) \qquad K = \int_{C_n} \beta h^o(Z)dZ = \beta Q^o .$$

Of course $\beta \leq 1$, since the firm cannot sell more than the market will absorb. Note that $\beta = K/Q^o$ is the portion of the market for Z^o that the firm can profitably supply. The smaller is β the more such firms the market can absorb. Pure competition is simply the case in which β approaches zero. And when $\beta = 1$ the firm would be able profitably to satisfy the entire market on its own. A final relevant distribution is given by the minimum sales requirement

$$(10) \qquad X^o = \int_{C_n} \delta h^o(Z)dZ = \delta Q^o .$$

If a range of profitable output is to exist, $\delta < \beta$.

To illustrate in detail the use of these concepts in the analysis of new product introduction where β is near 1 we consider the special case of two competing firms producing commodities in a two dimensional characteristics space. We will assume that the two characteristics are uncorrelated. Suppose that the first firm is producing a commodity de-fined by the coordinates (Z_{11}, Z_{12}). The second firm is considering mar-keting a commodity defined by the coordinates (Z_{21}, Z_{22}). Suppose that the distribution of potential sales for each firm is normal in the absence of competition (this is for explicit computation only),

$$h_1^o(Z_1, Z_2) = \frac{Q_1^o}{2\Pi\sigma_{11}\sigma_{12}} \quad \exp\left[\frac{-(Z_1 - Z_{11})^2}{2\sigma_{11}^2} - \frac{(Z_2 - Z_{12})^2}{2\sigma_{12}^2}\right]$$

(11)

$$h_2^o(Z_1, Z_2) = \frac{Q_2^o}{2\Pi\sigma_{21}\sigma_{22}} \quad \exp\left[\frac{-(Z_1 - Z_{21})^2}{2\sigma_{21}^2} - \frac{(Z_2 - Z_{22})^2}{2\sigma_{22}^2}\right]$$

The total profitable output for firm one in the absence of competition is K_1 and for firm two is K_2. The distribution of sales of firm one is then given by

$$D_1(Z_1, Z_2) = \beta_1 h_1^o(Z_1, Z_2)$$

in the monopoly case, and for firm two by

$$D_2(Z_1, Z_2) = \beta_2 h_2^o(Z_1, Z_2) .$$

The overlap of the functions $D_1(Z_1, Z_2)$ and $D_2(Z_1, Z_2)$ can be taken as an index of the degree of competition between the two firms. To study the dynamics of the competition using the methods of the previous section, we must determine α_1 and α_2. A reasonable model for these coefficients in this framework is given by[3]

$$\alpha_1 = \frac{\int_{-\infty}^{\infty}\int_{-\infty}^{\infty} D_1(Z_1, Z_2)D_2(Z_1, Z_2)dZ_1dZ_2}{\int_{-\infty}^{\infty}\int_{-\infty}^{\infty} D_1(Z_1, Z_2)^2dZ_1dZ_2}$$

(12)

$$\alpha_2 = \frac{\int_{-\infty}^{\infty}\int_{-\infty}^{\infty} D_2(Z_1, Z_2)D_1(Z_1, Z_2)dZ_1dZ_2}{\int_{-\infty}^{\infty}\int_{-\infty}^{\infty} D_2(Z_1, Z_2)^2dZ_1dZ_2}$$

Note that α_1 and α_2 have symmetric formulas and both reduce to 1 when the two firms are identical. Also, α_1 and α_2 are small when there is relatively little overlap in the distributions of demand of the two firms. Performing the integrations, we find

(13)

$$\alpha_1 = \frac{\beta_2 Q_2^o 2\sigma_{11}\sigma_{12}}{\beta_1 Q_1^o \sqrt{(\sigma_{11}^2 + \sigma_{21}^2)(\sigma_{12}^2 + \sigma_{22}^2)}} \exp\left[-\frac{d_1^2}{2(\sigma_{11}^2 + \sigma_{21}^2)} - \frac{d_2^2}{2(\sigma_{12}^2 + \sigma_{22}^2)}\right]$$

$$\alpha_2 = \frac{\beta_1 Q_1^o 2\sigma_{21}\sigma_{22}}{\beta_2 Q_2^o \sqrt{(\sigma_{11}^2 + \sigma_{21}^2)(\sigma_{12}^2 + \sigma_{22}^2)}} \exp\left[-\frac{d_1^2}{2(\sigma_{12}^2 + \sigma_{22}^2)} - \frac{d_2^2}{2(\sigma_{11}^2 + \sigma_{21}^2)}\right]$$

where $d_1 = |Z_{11} - Z_{21}|$ and $d_2 = |Z_{12} - Z_{22}|$. These coefficients in the Lotka-Volterra model determine the dynamics of the competition and the effect of the distributions of demand on the outcome of competition.

To study formulas (13) in detail, consider the special case $\sigma_{11} = \sigma_{21} = \sigma_1$ and $\sigma_{12} = \sigma_{22} = \sigma_2$. (The demand distribution of each firm is equally spread in each of the two characteristics.) In this special case,

(14)

$$\alpha_1 = \frac{\beta_2 Q^o}{\beta_1 Q_1^o} \exp\left[\frac{-d_1^2}{4\sigma_1^2} \frac{-d_2^2}{4\sigma_2^2}\right]$$

$$\alpha_2 = \frac{\beta_1 Q_1^o}{\beta_2 Q_2^o} \exp\left[\frac{-d_1^2}{4\sigma_2^2} \frac{-d_2^2}{4\sigma_1^2}\right]$$

The qualitative features of these formula should be apparent. If d_1 and d_2 are large, the commodities of the two firms are very different and the competition coefficients are small. If β_2 is small relative to β_1 so that firm two is capable of satisfying a relatively small portion of its niche when compared to what firm 1 can do in its niche, then α_1 will be small and α_2 large. The reason, of course, is that dealing on a first come first serve basis, firm two will satisfy little of its own market and

131

hence little of the overlap between markets.

Referring to Table I, the four outcomes of competition can now be related to the parameters describing the demand distributions for the competing products. For example, coexistence occurs when

$$\alpha_1 < \frac{(\beta_1 - \delta_1)Q_1^o}{\beta_2 Q_2^o} \quad \text{and} \quad \alpha_2 < \frac{(\beta_2 - \delta_2)Q_2^o}{\beta_1 Q_1^o}$$

or when

$$\frac{\beta_2 Q_2^o}{\beta_1 Q_1^o} \exp\left[\frac{-d_1^2}{4\sigma_1^2} \quad \frac{-d_2^2}{4\sigma_2^2}\right] < \frac{(\beta_1 - \delta_1)Q_1^o}{\beta_2 Q_2^o}$$

(15)

$$\frac{\beta_1 Q_1^o}{\beta_2 Q_2^o} \exp\left[\frac{-d_1^2}{4\sigma_2^2} \quad \frac{-d_2^2}{4\sigma_1^2}\right] < \frac{(\beta_2 - \delta_2)Q_2^o}{\beta_1 Q_1^o}$$

These conditions reduce to

$$\frac{d_1^2}{4\sigma_1^2} + \frac{d_2^2}{4\sigma_2^2} > \text{Log}_e\left[\frac{\beta_1^2 Q_1^{o^2}}{\beta_2(\beta_2 - \delta_2)Q_2^{o^2}}\right]$$

(16)

$$\frac{d_1^2}{4\sigma_2^2} + \frac{d_2^2}{4\sigma_1^2} > \text{Log}_e\left[\frac{\beta_2^2 Q_2^{o^2}}{\beta_1(\beta_1 - \delta_1)Q_1^{o^2}}\right]$$

In words, firm 2 to guarantee coexistence with firm 1 must establish itself at a point in the characteristics space that satisfies these two inequalities. The niche of the first firm relative to the second firm can be considered to be that area of characteristics space about (Z_{11}, Z_{12}) inside the two ellipses defined by (16).

This calculation of the dynamics of competition in a special case provides some general insight into the problem of market entry. The parameters β_1 and β_2 measure each firm's ability to satisfy its market niche. The parameters Q_1^o and Q_2^o measure the sizes of the niches.

If β_1 is large relative to β_2, the likelihood that the second firm will coexist with the first firm is decreased. Similarly, if Q_1^o is large relative to Q_2^o. Put another way, the larger is the equilibrium size of firm 1 relative to that of firm 2 the less likely it is that firm 2 will survive competition with firm 1. By adjusting the several parameters of the model we will be able to study the qualitative features of competition between firms.

5. CONCLUDING REMARKS

In this paper we have attempted to contribute to the development of a more descriptive view of the firm without the sacrifice of mathematical precision. The firm emerges as a profit seeker rather than a profit maximizer. It is governed by rules of thumb in its day to day operations (see section 2) but capable of quite sophisticated considerations in connection with the introduction of new products. This reflects the fact that top level management is very concerned with the new product decision. Indeed discussion of the model developed in this paper with marketing researchers disclosed striking similarities between the concepts presented here (e. g. the demand density function) and notions with which they were working.

The model that we have presented is quite consistent with the idea of satisficing. Thus the output levels X^o and K may be, respectively the least output and the greatest output consistent with satisfactory profits. Similarly, a firm which maximized output subject to a profit constraint could reasonably attain its maximum output point as described in our model. On the other hand if K is taken as the maximum profitable level of output then the model has the interesting implication that, in final equilibrium, all firms will produce at a level of output that allows exactly normal profits.

We have been concerned with the growth of output and with niche selection because we feel that these decisions are considered most important by the firm. The notion being that the firm "maximizes" profit by trying to be in the right business at the right time rather than by concentration on producing an output that yields the traditional marginal equalities. We plan to develop these views further in later papers.

NOTES

[1]The reader familiar with Lancaster's work will notice that we have a rather less restrictive notion in mind than he used. We do not require that each commodity define a one dimensional subspace.

[2]Assume the firm finds a price, P^O, such that, where $X^O = g(P^O)$, $k = q(P^O)$, ε is the standard mark-up and C is the cost, for outputs X such that $X^O \leq X \leq K$, $P^O \geq (1+\varepsilon)C$.

[3]For a brief development of this framework see MacArthur [1972, p. 40-42].

REFERENCES

Bain, J. S. [1968], Industrial Organization, 2nd Edition, John Wiley, New York, Chapter 8.

Baumol, W. J. [1959], Business Behavior, Value and Growth, MacMillan, New York.

Boulding, K. [1962], A Reconstruction of Economics, Science Editions Inc., N. Y., p. 483.

Chamberlin, E. H. [1953], The Product as an Economic Variable, Quarterly Journal of Economics, pp. 1-29.

Cyert, R. M. and J. G. March [1963], A Behavioral Theory of the Firm, Prentice-Hall, Englewood Cliffs.

Day, R. H. and E. H. Tinney [1969], "Cycles, Phases and Growth in a Generalized Cobweb Theory", The Economic Journal, pp. 91-108.

134

Day, R. H., S. Morley and K. R. Smith [1974], "Myopic Optimizing and Rules of Thumb in a Micro-Model of Industrial Growth", American Economic Review, pp. 11-23.

Kotler, P. [1972], Marketing Management: Analysis, Planning and Control, 2nd Edition, Prentice-Hall, Chapter 12.

Lancaster, K. J. [1966], "A New Approach to Consumer Theory", Journal of Political Economy, Vol. 74.

Lotka, A. J. [1956], Element of Mathematical Biology, Dover.

MacArthur, R. H. [1972], Geographical Ecology, Harper and Row, Publishers, Inc.

Simon, H. [1965], Administrative Behavior, Free Press, New York.

Winter, S. [1971], "Satisficing, Selection and the Innovating Remnant", Quarterly Journal of Economics, pp. 237-261.

Learning by Firms about Demand Conditions
Alan P. Kirman

CONTENTS

1. INTRODUCTION

It is clear that firms are, in general, imperfectly aware of their environment. In other words, if asked, they could, at best, give an incomplete description of the economic system of which they are a part. Furthermore, even if one sets aside the complete general system and focuses on that subsection which directly involved the firm, then the firm is still unlikely to be able to give a precise description. The firm will realise that its view of the world is imperfect since the outcome of its actions will not always coincide with its predictions. A reasonable response would then be for the firm to change its model or the parameters of its models in the light of the observations that it makes. In other words the firm adapts its behaviour to its changing picture of the world in which it operates. The literature contains descriptions of models of firms which behave in this way.

The firm's picture of the world may be erroneous in two ways. In the first place its description of the structure of the system may be correct but it may have a false estimate of the parameters. Secondly, it could have an incorrect model of the true structure, and might persist in this view, attributing its prediction errors to its incorrect estimation of the parameters. Indeed, as will become evident, it may develop an inaccurate picture of the world which nevertheless generates exactly the information it does in fact observe. The firm may well be satisfied with this situation and there is little evidence to suggest that such unjustified complacency is uncommon.

A natural reaction to a situation in which the economic mechanism is complex, is to replace those parts of the mechanism which are too difficult or too costly to evaluate, by a stochastic term. This is, of course, the explanation of the "error term" in economic models, offered by econometric texts. The firm must make some estimate of the nature of the distribution of such a term and then will set about trying to establish values of the parameters of its model. Again, if the firm has the wrong model, in the sense that the observed "errors" are very different from those that one might expect from its specification of the distribution, then there is a basic problem. Suppose that the firm was acting as a Bayesian and revising its prior distribution of the parameters of the error population. Then, if it has a view inconsistent with the true nature of that population, there is no reason, in general, to expect the learning process to converge.

In this paper we shall consider a very simple duopoly problem in which firms are in error in the sense that they specify an incomplete model and add a random error term. We shall see from examples that in very special cases the firms, by learning, will arrive at the equilibrium position they would have reached had they been fully informed. In other cases however their learning process leads to "equilibria" which are different from the "true" equilibrium. Indeed their behaviour is rather perverse in that, far from informing themselves about the true mechanism at work, they construct an incorrect picture of the world but one in which their behaviour would be optimal. Thus rather than gather information they construct a model to justify what they are doing!

2. A REVIEW OF THE LITERATURE

Before proceeding to analyse the simple duopoly model it is worth having a brief look at some related models in the literature. Cyert and

DeGroot [1971], [1973], [1974] have analysed three models which have a family relationship to those in this paper. In their first paper [1971] they consider a duopoly model in which both firms are price setters. One firm would like to raise its price if it could be sure that the other would match the increase. Thus both firms are below the market monopoly price and joint increase would be profitable. However the first firm is not sure what is the extent of its competitor's willingness to match its increase. If the other firm does not match then the first firm makes a loss. To handle this situation it establishes a prior probability distribution on θ the maximal price which will be matched, then experiments and revises its distribution in the light of its observations. The basic result is that if the learning firm is using a uniform prior distribution then when the interval for θ becomes small the firm will cease to experiment and the kinked demand curve is an adequate description of the situation.

It is interesting to note that in their paper Cyert and DeGroot have separated out two ways of learning. The firm's original prior is presumably formed as a result of external information. Subsequent revision of that distribution occurs entirely as a result of experimentation. Somehow the flow of external information stops. This problem is important and is relevant in the analysis presented below. It would be more reasonable in a general model to incorporate both sorts of learning simultaneously, and to allow the firm to continue to learn from its external sources of information as well as from the consequences of its actions.

In Cyert and DeGroot's 1973 contribution a duopoly situation is considered in which the two firms each have a "coefficient of cooperation". In other words they maximise their own profit plus a fraction of their opponent's profit. Thus firm one, whose output is q seeks to maximise

$$\pi_1(q,\ r) + \gamma\pi_2(q,\ r)$$

where π is profit and, r is the output of the second firm and γ the coefficient of cooperation. A symmetric situation holds for the second firm. The authors consider multi period models in which the sum of profits is maximised. By backward induction they construct a sequence of reaction functions, one for each period. The limit functions of that sequence are mutually optimal, i.e. given each other's current behaviour neither has an incentive to move.

The authors then go on to consider adaptive or learning behaviour in which each firm now forms a prior distribution on the values of its opponent's maximum level of cooperation. By raising its own level of cooperation a firm hopes to stimulate a similar reaction from its adversary. Recognising the value of this move, the firms will repeat the process. What the optimal coefficient of cooperation is, depends on the prior judgement as to the opponent's reaction. This judgement is modified over time and the process moves from a non cooperative equilibrium to a joint maximisation position.

The third paper by Cyert and DeGroot considers a learning process by which firms might move to a situation in which Muth's [1961] "rational expectations" hypothesis holds. The latter hypothesis might best be described as specifying that the equilibrium value of the economic model should coincide with the weighted average of firms' expectations about that value. The part of that paper most related to the analysis here is that in which firms have the "wrong" model of price formation. The firm believes that the price in the next period p_{t+1} is related to that in the current period by the relation

$$p_{t+1} = ap_t + v_{t+1}$$

where v_{t+1} is a random error term. The error terms in each period are identically distributed with mean 0 and known variance σ^2. The firm at time t forms a prior distribution about the value of "a" given its observations up to that point. This distribution is taken to be Normal with mean m_t and variance v^2. In reality the price is determined as follows:

140

$$p_{t+1} = \frac{\gamma}{\beta} m_t p_t + v_{t+1}$$

where an γ and β are fixed parameters of the mechanism. The question is, does the learning process based on the wrong model converge? If $(\gamma/\beta) |m_\tau|$ becomes less than one then, in fact, it does. Monte Carlo simulation showed that when the process converged it did so to a value of m_t close to zero. In other words p_t was esssentially the error term and the two models, the "true" and the "perceived" model did, in fact, coincide. Thus learning led to a "correct" view of the world. It will be seen in our analysis that the equilibrium will not, in general, correspond to a correct view of the world as soon as more than one parameter has to be estimated.

In a recent paper Arrow and Green [1973][1] have discussed the problem of the existence of equilibrium in simple oligopoly models where firms make inferences about the model facing them. They give examples where equilibrium may or may not exist and also emphasise the somewhat unexpected nature of these equilibria when they do exist. Further, they discuss the attainment of the equilibrium as a result of a learning process for a model which is akin to that treated below. Their model has a "true" joint profit function for all firms and has each firm with a "personal" model different from the true one. The personal model varies, just as ours, from the true one in that the only variable perceived to affect own profit is the action of that firm itself. There are two features which are different from our first model. In the Arrow-Green model there is uncertainty, i.e. randomness in both the "true" and the "personal" models. In ours randomness in the personal models replaces that part of the purely deterministic model which firms cannot or do not explain. Secondly by learning the firms move from ignorance to the "true" equilibrium, whereas those in Arrow and Green's model move to any one of a number of equilibria which are determined by their priors. This result is very similar to what happens in our second model.

3. A SIMPLE MODEL

Ignorance, as we have observed, like error may take several forms. Here we will consider the case of duopolists who have a restricted view of the world and who escape from the incompleteness of their description by introducing stochastic disturbance. Let us suppose that the demand facing the duopolists is given by <u>The True Model</u>

(1)
$$d_1(p_1, p_2) = \alpha_1 - \beta_1 p_1 + \gamma_1 p_2$$

$$d_2(p_1, p_2) = \alpha_2 - \beta_2 p_2 + \gamma_2 p_1$$

For convenience we shall impose symmetry on this system and let $\alpha_1 = \alpha_2 = \alpha$, $\beta_1 = \beta_2 = \beta$ and $\gamma_1 = \gamma_2 = \gamma$. Now however consider the situation the two firms believe themselves to be facing. They each consider the demand facing them to be a function of their own price. They explain the deviations that they observe from this model by introducing a stochastic error term. Thus the firms believe themselves to face the following situation <u>The Perceived Model</u>

(2)
$$d_1(p_1, t) = a_1 - b_1 p_1 + \varepsilon_1(t)$$

$$d_2(p_2, t) = a_2 - b_2 p_2 + \varepsilon_2(t)$$

where for example the $\varepsilon_i(t)$ are believed by firm i to be independently identically Normally distributed with mean 0 and unknown precision ν_i i.e. variance $\frac{1}{\nu_i}$. Each firm will set about trying to learn the values of the parameters of its model. It is clearly unrealistic that in a duopolistic situation a firm should be unaware of the effect of the price of its rival. However this should be regarded as an approximation of an oligopolistic market with many firms, where the individual firms simply put the behaviour of their competitors into a stochastic hat. Such unwillingness to make specific allowance for competitive behaviour is by no means uncommon among firms when estimating demand. Thus even though such behaviour may not be appropriate or optimal, the model here is a rudimentary description of the behaviour of some producers.

The aim of each firm is to maximise its expected profit in each period; expected, since it is uncertain about the parameters of the model. Now we must draw attention to an important feature of the model. The firm in setting its price, in fact, together with the action of its rival, generates a new observation which in turn provides information about the true model. However the assumptions that we have made imply that the firm will not believe that its own action will in any way influence the value of the error term actually observed. Hence it simply maximises expected profit using the best estimates of the parameters of the model given the data observed to date. Now in more complicated models the firm would have to weigh two things: first, the profit to be obtained from charging a certain price and second, the information to be gained from the results of its own action. There will frequently be a conflict between the aims of gaining maximum information and maximising short run profit. In our model the firms do not have to worry about the optimum degree of experimentation.

To further simplify matters we shall incorporate an old assumption that the two firms have constant costs and indeed that these costs are zero. Thus one might picture Cournot's two purveyors of spring water situated on each side of a hill each blissfully unaware of each other's existence, viewing the fluctuations in their demand as being due to changes in the weather or inexplicable traits in the character of tourists.

Each firm then chooses $p_i(t)$ to maximise

$$p_i(t)E(d_i(p_i(t), t)),$$

At time t the firm will have estimates of its parameters $\hat{a}_i$ and $\hat{b}_i$ say $\hat{a}_i(t)$ and $\hat{b}_i(t)$. Then if $E(\varepsilon_i(t)) = 0$ it is clear that the optimal price is

$$(3) \qquad p_i(t) = \frac{\hat{a}_i(t)}{2\hat{b}_i(t)}$$

Now returning to the true model we see that the process of estimation and reestimation by the two firms generates a sequence of prices. Before examining the problem of convergence let us first consider what the outcome would be were the two firms aware of the true model. In this case we would look for the Nash equilibrium of the two person non-cooperative game defined by the true model.

If firm 2 in this situation were to charge some price p_2 firm 1's best reaction would be to choose p_1 to

$$\underset{p_1}{\text{Max}} \quad \pi_1(p_1, p_2) = p_1[\alpha - \beta p_1 + \gamma p_2]$$

Then,

$$\frac{\partial \pi_1}{\partial p_1} = \alpha - 2\beta p_1 + \gamma p_2 = 0 \ .$$

Thus we have firm 1's "reaction function",

$$(4) \qquad p_1 = \frac{\alpha + \gamma p_2}{2\beta}$$

and similarly for firm 2,

$$(5) \qquad p_2 = \frac{\alpha + \gamma p_1}{2\beta}$$

But using the symmetry of the model the equilibrium p_1^* and p_2^* are clearly given by

$$(6) \qquad p_1^* = p_2^* = \frac{\alpha}{2\beta - \gamma} \ .$$

Thus the non-cooperative solution coincides with the standard monopoly

144

solution where γ is zero. The questions are, first, what values of the parameters a_1 and b_i would produce the solution given by (6), and second, of these values, which would persist if achieved? Clearly if each firm were to estimate its parameters as follows at some time t,

(7)
$$\hat{a}_1(t) = \alpha + \gamma p_2^* \quad \text{and} \quad \hat{b}_1(t) = \beta$$

$$\hat{a}_2(t) = \alpha + \gamma p_1^* \quad \text{and} \quad \hat{b}_2(t) = \beta$$

then they would, in fact, have arrived at the true model. Note that we can rewrite part of (7) as

(8)
$$\hat{a}_1(t) = \hat{a}_2(t) = \frac{2\alpha\beta}{2\beta - \gamma} .$$

With these estimates each firm will expect a demand of $\dfrac{\hat{a}_i}{2}$. But from (1) it is clear that the demand will be

(9)
$$d_1(p_1^*, p_2^*) = \frac{\alpha\beta}{2\beta - \gamma} = \frac{\hat{a}_1}{2}$$

and similarly for firm 2. Thus if the firms arrived at these estimates the equilibrium would persist. Is it possible that by a process of systematic revision of their estimates of the parameter values that the firms will arrive at this position?

4. PARTIAL IGNORANCE

Let us consider the case of firms in partial ignorance. Suppose that they, in fact, know or believe with certainty that $\hat{b}_i = \beta$. Thus the area of uncertainty for them is confined to the values of their respective parameters a_i. Now we can view each firm as observing at time t a value of the random variable s_i. Thus,

(10)
$$d_i(p_i, t) = s_i(t) - \beta p_i$$

145

where

(11) $$s_i(t) = a_i + \varepsilon(t) \ .$$

Now it believes that s_i is distributed as $N(a_i, \nu_i)$ and its problem is to estimate the parameters and, in particular, the mean of that distribution. If the firm has as its prior distribution of a_i a Normal distribution with mean μ_i and precision τ_i, then after a sample of n values of s_i the posterior distribution will be Normal with mean

(12) $$\mu_i' = \frac{\tau_i \mu_i + n\nu_i \bar{s}_i}{\tau_i + n\nu_i} = \frac{n\nu_i}{\tau_i + n\nu_i} \bar{s}_i + \frac{\tau_i}{\tau_i n\nu_i} \mu_i$$

and

$$\tau_i = \tau + n\nu_i \ .$$

Thus, as is well known, the mean of the posterior distribution is a convex combination of the sample mean $\bar{s}_i$ and the mean μ_i of the prior distribution. (See DeGroot [1970], pp. 167-168). Now let us go one step further and stipulate that the firm has no knowledge a priori about the value of a_i. By making this assumption we overcome a conflict mentioned earlier. We now no longer have external information obtained before experimentation. All the information is obtained as a result of the observations made after each action is taken. How might we best describe this situation of complete uncertainty about a_i? A standard procedure is to assume that the distribution of a_i is uniform over the real line. This is clearly an improper distribution since its integral over the real line is infinite. However after a random sample $s_i(1)$, $s_i(2)$, ..., $s_i(n)$ for a distribution assumed to be Normal with unknown mean μ_i and known precision ν_i the posterior distribution will be Normal with mean $\bar{s}_i$ and precision $n\nu_i$, (see DeGroot [1970], pp. 190-191). Starting from a position where nothing is known about a_i and revising in the way

suggested we can show that the two firms will converge to the non-cooperative equilibrium.

Before proving the theorem it is interesting to note that the procedure just described is formally equivalent to "fictitious play" for the
game described by the true model. In fictitious play the true model is
known but neither player is sure of what the other is going to do. Each
considers that the other has a distribution over prices and tries to anticipate the next more of its opponent by looking at the frequency distribution of the latter's actions in the past. Thus at each period the firm
chooses that price which would, if played consistently, have done best
in total against the moves that the opponent played. Thus in our model
firm 1 would seek to find $p_1(t)$ such that

$$(13) \quad p_1(t)[\alpha - \beta p_1(t) + \gamma \overline{p}_2(t)] \geq p_1[\alpha - \beta p_1 + \gamma \overline{p}_2(t)], \quad \forall \, p_1 > 0$$

where

$$\overline{p}_2(t) = \frac{1}{t} \sum_{k=0}^{t-1} p_2(t)$$

i.e. to solve

$$(14) \qquad \qquad \underset{p_1}{\text{Max}} \quad p_1[\alpha - \beta p_1 + \gamma \overline{p}_2(t)]$$

But note that in our case, where the firm is learning about a_1, it will
try at period t to act so as to solve

$$(15) \qquad \qquad \underset{p_1}{\text{Max}} \quad p_1 E(d_1(p_1, t))$$

that is to solve

$$(16) \qquad \qquad \underset{p_1}{\text{Max}} \quad p_1[E(s_1(t)) \mid s(0), \ldots, s(t-1)) - \beta p_1]$$

or,

(17)
$$\underset{p_1}{\text{Max}} \quad p_1[\bar{s}_1(t) - p_1] \; .$$

But of course, in fact

(18)
$$\bar{s}_1(t) = \alpha + \gamma \bar{p}_2(t)$$

so the problem of the Bayesian with no information about a_i reduces to that in (14). We can now adapt a proof of Deschamps [1973] for the fictitious play problem to prove the following.

THEOREM. If both firms i have as their model $d_i(p_i, t) = a_i - b_i p_i + \varepsilon_i(t) = s_i - b_i p_i$ and believe s_i to be normally distributed with unknown mean μ_i and known precision ν_i, and they have improper uniform prior distributions for μ_i then choosing $p_i(t)$ to maximise expected profit at t gives

$$\underset{t \to \infty}{\text{Lim}} \quad p_1(t) = \underset{t \to \infty}{\text{Lim}} \quad p_2(t) = \frac{\alpha}{2\beta - \gamma}$$

if $\gamma < 2\beta$.

PROOF. Recall that $p_i(t) = \dfrac{\hat{a}_i(t)}{2\beta}$ so that $\dfrac{\bar{s}_i(t)}{2\beta}$ is the expected profit maximising price for firm i. Hence

(19) and
$$p_1(t) = \frac{\alpha + \gamma \bar{p}_2(t)}{2\beta}$$

$$p_2(t) = \frac{\alpha + \gamma \bar{p}_1(t)}{2\beta} \; .$$

We will first show that $\bar{p}_i(t) \to \dfrac{\alpha}{2\beta - \gamma}$. Note that

(20)
$$\bar{p}_1(t) = \frac{1}{t} (p_1(t - 1)) + \frac{t-1}{t} \bar{p}_1(t - 1) \; ,$$

that is,

(21) $\qquad \bar{p}_1(t) = \dfrac{\alpha + \gamma \bar{p}_2(t-1)}{2\beta t} + \dfrac{2\beta(t-1)}{2\beta t}\, \bar{p}_1(t-1)$.

Define

(22) $\qquad u_t = \bar{p}_1(t) - \dfrac{\alpha}{2\beta - \gamma}$

and

$\qquad v_t = \bar{p}_2(t) - \dfrac{\alpha}{2\beta - \gamma}$.

Our object is then to show that $u(t)$ and $v(t) \to 0$. Now

(23) $\qquad \bar{p}_1(t) = \dfrac{1}{2\beta t}\left[\alpha + \gamma\left(v_t + \dfrac{\alpha}{2\beta - \gamma}\right) + 2\beta(t-1)\left(u_{t-1} + \dfrac{\alpha}{2\beta - \gamma}\right)\right]$.

Substituting from (22) and rearranging, we get

(24) $\qquad u_t = \dfrac{t-1}{t}\, u_{t-1} + \dfrac{\gamma}{2\beta t}\, v_{t-1}$

and symmetrically for v_t. Our system can now be written

(25) $\qquad \begin{bmatrix} u_t \\[2mm] v_t \end{bmatrix} = \begin{bmatrix} \dfrac{t-1}{t} & \dfrac{\gamma}{2\beta t} \\[3mm] \dfrac{\gamma}{2\beta t} & \dfrac{t-1}{t} \end{bmatrix} \begin{bmatrix} u_{t-1} \\[2mm] v_{t-1} \end{bmatrix} = \prod_{k=1}^{t} \begin{bmatrix} \dfrac{k-1}{k} & \dfrac{\gamma}{2\beta k} \\[3mm] \dfrac{\gamma}{2\beta k} & \dfrac{k-1}{k} \end{bmatrix} \begin{bmatrix} u_0 \\[2mm] v_0 \end{bmatrix}$

Let $\rho = \dfrac{\gamma}{2\beta}$. Then rewrite (25) as

(26) $\qquad \begin{bmatrix} 1 & 1 \\[4mm] 1 & -1 \end{bmatrix} \begin{bmatrix} \displaystyle\prod_{k=1}^{t} \dfrac{k-1+\rho}{k} & 0 \\[6mm] 0 & \displaystyle\prod_{k=1}^{t} \dfrac{k-1-\rho}{k} \end{bmatrix} \begin{bmatrix} \dfrac{1}{2} & \dfrac{1}{2} \\[4mm] \dfrac{1}{2} & -\dfrac{1}{2} \end{bmatrix}$

But $\lim\limits_{t \to \infty} \prod\limits_{k=1}^{t} (1 - \frac{\varepsilon}{k}) = 0$. Hence if $\rho < 1$ i.e. if $\gamma < 2\beta$ then

$$\lim_{t \to \infty} u_t = \lim_{t \to \infty} v_t = 0 .$$

Hence

$$\lim \overline{p}_1(t) = \lim \overline{p}_2(t) = \frac{\alpha}{2\beta - \gamma} .$$

But recall that

$$p_1(t) = \frac{\alpha + \gamma \overline{p}_2(t)}{2\beta} .$$

Hence

$$\lim_{t \to \infty} p_1(t) = \frac{\alpha + \gamma(\frac{\alpha}{2\beta - \gamma})}{2\beta} = \frac{\alpha}{2\beta - \gamma} . \qquad \text{Q.E.D.}$$

Provided the effect of the opponent's price is not too important in determining demand in the true model, the firms proceed by learning about an "incorrect" model but arrive at a "correct" solution.

5. NAIVE ECONOMETRICS

In the previous section we assumed that, in some mysterious way the firms knew the true value of the parameter β and took this as their fixed value of b_i. Since there is no reason to believe that the ignorance of the firms will be confined to the parameters a_i we now consider a situation in which the firms try to establish the values of both their parameters a_i and b_i. Suppose that those controlling the firms have had at some stage a brief encounter with econometrics and decide to estimate their parameters by ordinary least squares. Thus at each point t the firms will be making estimates $\hat{a}_i(t)$ and $\hat{b}_i(t)$ as follows:

$$(27) \qquad \hat{b}_i(t) = \frac{\sum\limits_{k=1}^{t-1} (d_i(k) - \bar{d}_i(t))(p_i(k) - \bar{p}_i(t))}{\sum\limits_{k=1}^{\tau-1} (p_i(k) - \bar{p}_i(t))^2}$$

and

$$\hat{a}_i(t) = \bar{d}_i(t) + \hat{b}_i(t)\bar{p}_i(t) \ .$$

Note however that the system is recursive since at each point the firms will set $p_i(t) = \dfrac{\hat{a}_i(t)}{2\hat{b}_i(t)}$. From the equation of the true model

$$d_1(t) = \alpha - \beta \ \frac{\hat{a}_1(t)}{2\hat{b}_1(t)} + \gamma \ \frac{\hat{a}_2(t)}{2\hat{b}_2(t)} \ .$$

The use of ordinary least squares estimates can, of course, be justified from a Bayesian viewpoint (see Zellner [1971]). In fact, our model is a special case of the Dynamic Linear Model in statistics and ordinary least squares estimation is a special version of the updating procedure provided by the Kalman Filter (see Stevens and Harrison [1974]).

The problem of updating a misspecified model in this general framework will be the subject of a later paper. Here we will content ourselves with examining the effects of the elementary econometric procedure in the simple linear duopoly model. When considering the problem of convergence it is important to specify the nature of possible equilibria. Note that to each observed pair of prices (p_1, p_2) corresponds a quadruple of parameters (a_1, a_2, b_1, b_2) for which these prices are optimal and which realise, via the true model, the expected demand. Thus if the firms have estimates of their parameters:

$$(28) \qquad \begin{aligned} \hat{a}_1 &= 2\alpha - 2\beta p_1 + 2\gamma p_2 \ , \qquad & \hat{a}_2 &= 2\alpha - 2\beta p_2 + 2\gamma p_1 \ , \\[2mm] \hat{b}_1 &= \frac{\alpha}{p_1} - \beta + \gamma \ \frac{p_2}{p_1} \ , \qquad & \hat{b}_2 &= \frac{\alpha}{p_2} - \beta + \gamma \ \frac{p_1}{p_2} \ ; \end{aligned}$$

151

since $d_1 = \dfrac{\hat{a}_1}{2}$ and $d_2 = \dfrac{\hat{a}_2}{2}$, p_1 and p_2 are optimal for these values of $\hat{a}$ and $\hat{b}$ and the firm's expectations will be fulfilled.

Since neither the parameters nor the prices they generate bear any resemblance to the "true model" we shall refer to these situations as "pseudo equilibria" even though this term has been used elsewhere in a rather different context. It would seem that an initial coincidence of estimates to such a pseudo equilibrium would be highly unlikely. Hence one might hope that starting from some other position, the information generated by setting prices and observing the resultant quantities demanded would be sufficient to lead the firms to the true equilibrium. To see whether this was the case the behaviour of firms was simulated from arbitrary initial positions. The results were, in a sense, unexpected. The process converged rapidly but not to the true equilibrium. In other words the pseudo equilibria were not only stable but attracting states. The description of what happens to the firms is intriguing. They are not aware of the true values of the parameters; they persist in trying to estimate the parameters of the wrong model; yet, they end up in a position where their behaviour is justified. Thus they are ignorant, incompetent but happy.

An examination of tables 1 and 2 show the prices to which the process converge for the given values of the initiating prices. As the equilibrium is heavily dependent on the initial position, it is worth noting that the process was initiated by choosing prices for the firms in the first two periods at random. This was a matter of convenience but it can be shown that starting with a prior distribution leads to the same results. It is worth observing that in the simulations the prices set by the firms were established to the second decimal place after 20 iterations. After a few initial convulsions the firms rapidly took a hold on themselves and settled down to a pseudo-equilibrium.

In the tables the value of γ is reduced while the other parameter values are held constant. It can be seen that the limit process approached

Table 1.

$$\alpha = 10 \qquad \beta = .55$$

γ	$p_1(1)$	$p_2(1)$	$p_1(2)$	$p_2(2)$	$p_1(300)$	$p_2(300)$	$b_1(300)$	$b_2(300)$	p_1^*	p_2^*
.005	1	5	2	6	9.15	9.28	0.55	0.54	9.2	9.2
.05	1	5	2	6	9.86	10.75	0.52	0.47	9.5	9.5
.1	1	5	2	6	10.89	12.16	0.48	0.42	10.0	10.0
.2	1	5	2	6	12.44	11.98	0.45	0.47	11.1	11.1
.3	1	5	2	6	13.62	12.50	0.46	0.52	12.5	12.5
.4	1	5	2	6	15.12	13.87	0.47	0.53	14.3	14.3
.005	1	10	5	9	9.12	8.65	0.55	0.58	9.2	9.2
.05	1	10	5	9	9.30	7.52	0.57	0.70	9.5	9.5
.1	1	10	5	9	9.44	7.20	0.59	0.78	10.0	10.0
.2	1	10	5	9	9.71	7.01	0.63	0.89	11.1	11.1
.3	1	10	5	9	9.93	6.88	0.67	0.99	12.5	12.5
.4	1	10	5	9	10.04	6.68	0.71	1.13	14.3	14.3
.005	5	20	3	15	9.07	9.15	0.56	0.55	9.2	9.2
.05	5	20	3	15	9.0	9.57	0.62	0.58	9.5	9.5
.1	5	20	3	15	9.25	9.43	0.63	0.62	10.0	10.0
.2	5	20	3	15	10.16	6.33	0.56	0.96	11.1	11.1
.3	5	20	3	15	13.22	13.17	0.51	0.51	12.5	12.5
.4	5	20	3	15	12.53	8.93	0.55	1.07	14.3	14.3

153

Table 2.

$\alpha = 10 \quad \beta = .55$

Y	$p_1(1)$	$p_2(1)$	$p_1(2)$	$p_2(2)$	$p_1(300)$	$p_2(300)$	$\hat{b}_1(300)$	$\hat{b}_2(300)$	p_1^*	p_2^*
.4	2	4	4	2	33.27	33.27	.15	.15	14.3	14.3
.1	2	4	4	2	11.08	11.08	.45	.45	10.0	10.0
.05	2	4	4	2	9.98	9.98	.50	.50	9.5	9.5
.4	1	2	3	4	15.56	16.82	.53	.48	14.3	14.3
.1	1	2	3	4	11.05	11.37	.46	.44	10.0	10.0
.05	1	2	3	4	9.96	10.15	.51	.49	9.5	9.5
.4	10	12	12	10	33.28	33.28	.15	.15	14.3	14.3
.1	10	12	12	10	10.06	10.06	.54	.54	10.0	10.0
.05	10	12	12	10	9.66	9.66	.53	.53	9.5	9.5

the true equilibrium prices p^* as γ declined. Note that in the symmetric runs in table 2, the higher the value of γ the higher the prices set by the firms and the higher their profits. This was not however uniformly true for the asymmetric starting prices in table 1.

The intractable nature of the analytic treatment of the convergence problem sheds some light on the results obtained by simulation. The limit values of the parameters are undefined, i.e. of the form $\frac{0}{0}$, but this is not unexpected as the spread of the observations diminishes if the process is convergent. Thus it seems that the effectiveness of the ordinary least squares procedure is too quickly reduced if the observations tend to a limit. It may be that adding an error term to the true equations would maintain the spread and lead to learning more about the true system, or rather establishing values of the parameters of their individual models compatible with those of the true model.

One way of characterising the behaviour of the firms is to say that they are not learning about the true nature of the world but rather adapting their view of the world to justify their current behaviour. Note that in the individual models the effect of the opponent's price is put into the error term. But the estimating procedure is precisely aimed at minimising these errors. Thus the firms are inevitably moved to a "wrong" position. Of course it is true that this will occur whenever one is estimating a misspecified model by standard procedures.

In conclusion then, the simple example discussed here does suggest that learning by firms with wrong models may, if they are sufficiently well informed initially, lead to the equilibrium of the "full information game". However when the firms have individual models and little information about any of the parameters they may well settle to a position where their beliefs have no relation to the true situation but where their observations continually confirm them in these beliefs.

ACKNOWLEDGEMENTS

I am grateful to A. Dixit, G. Fisher, P. J. Harrison and D. Leech for their helpful comments.

NOTE

[1] I am grateful to S. Grossman who drew my attention to Arrow and Green's paper when I presented the first version of this paper at Wisconsin.

REFERENCES

Arrow, K. and J. Green [1973], "Notes on Expectations Equilibria in Bayesian Settings", Working Paper No. 33, The Economics Series, Institute for Mathematical Studies in the Social Sciences, Stanford.

Cyert, R. M. and M. H. DeGroot [1971], "Interfirm Learning and the Kinked Demand Curve", Journal of Economic Theory, Vol. 3, No. 3.

——————————————— [1973], "An Analysis of Cooperation and Learning in a Duopoly Context", American Economic Review, Vol. 63, No. 1.

——————————————— [1974], "Rational Expectations and Bayesian Analysis", Journal of Political Economy, Vol. 82, No. 3.

DeGroot, M. H. [1970], Optimal Statistical Decisions, McGraw-Hill, New York.

Deschamps, R. [1973], "An Algorithm of Game Theory Applied to the Duopoly Problem", C.O.R.E. Discussion Paper No. 7323, C.O.R.E., Louvain.

Muth, J. [1961], "Rational Expectations and the Theory of Price Movements", Econometrica, Vol. 29, No. 3.

Stevens, C. F. and P. J. Harrison [1974], "Bayesian Forecasting: Paper II. The Dynamic Linear Model", University of Warwick Statistics Department mimeo.

Zellner, A. [1971], "An Introduction to Bayesian Inference in Econometrics", John Wiley, New York.

Output Decisions by a Firm: An Example
of a Dual Control Problem with Information Externalities
Masanao Aoki

CONTENTS

1. INTRODUCTION

There seems to be an increasing number of economists who attempt to explore consequences of replacing the assumption of perfect and
complete information by that of imperfect and/or incomplete information
in modeling macro--as well as micro-economic phenomena.[1] Several approaches are possible in examining the implications of dropping this
standard assumption and adopting that of imperfect and/or incomplete
information. Models with inperfect or incomplete information contain
several features that are not found in models with complete and perfect
information. First of all, in such models economic agents do not have
perfect information and foresight; hence they must learn. The issue of
information externalities therefore arises naturally, although the learning
process of an economic agent is made independent of his actions in some

models, in order to allow the investigators to concentrate their efforts
on examining other aspects of the imperfect information assumption.

We focus our attention on information externalities and examine
a model in which economic agents possess non-identical information[2]
and in which an interaction exists between the actions of economic agents
and their experiences, and hence the information learned by them or by
other economic agents. Economic agents recognize the influences of
their own actions as well as the actions by other agents on their experiences and consequently on their learning.

Economists are familiar with the problem of information externalities in an essentially static setting in which "informational" variables
are updated over time, such as, for example, in the two-armed bandit
problem. "Physical" states, however, do not evolve with time but remain
the same. Interactions between actions and information have been recognized to exist and dealt with explicitly in a dynamic context in the case
of centralized information (i.e., when all decision makers have the same
information or a representative agent assumption is adopted) as a problem
of dual control in control literature. For example, when the precision of
the estimation of some imperfectly known parameter of a dynamic system
depends on his own past actions, dual control effects are said to exist.[3]

Although the sets of circumstances are different, economists and
control engineers face the same problem of designing actions to minimize
some meausre of the combined effects of estimation and consequences of
actions involving a tradeoff between learning more quickly and more advantageous actions while learning. Economists are more familiar with
this tradeoff in static problems with a decentralized information pattern
(i.e., economic agents do not necessarily have identical pieces of information) while control engineers usually encounter it in a context of dynamic systems with centralized information patterns.

What is needed, it seems, is to examine information externalities
in a combination of the hypotheses of decentralized information patterns
and a dual control formulation (which has been developed for centralized

information pattern) which incorporates dual control effects, i.e., information externalities in microeconomic optimization problems by economic agents. From now on, we refer to dual control effects in this broader sense of information externalities, i.e., an economic agent's information or learning is influenced by his own actions as well as the actions of other agents of which he is ignorant. We show for the model of this paper that this approach leads to a very complicated optimal decision problem. It therefore would seem unreasonable to insist on optimizing procedures in the face of such enormous information processing demands. What Simon termed behavior of bounded rationality might then seem to be more realistic [Simon 1972]. We then suggest, as an alternative to the optimal decision policy, an iterative performance improvement scheme, which is based on stochastic approximation and is a plausible behavioral (suboptimal) decision rule in imperfect information world. We leave the detailed analysis of this approach to another paper, however. See Aoki [1974].

Recent concerns expressed by some economists on existence and nature of equilibrium in imperfect information economic models can also be formulated properly in this broader version of the dual control framework, i.e., in the decentralized dual control theoretic formulation. This formulation also permits investigation of economic models in which information becomes obsolete, for example, because some exogneous parameter (state of the world parameter) undergoes random changes while economic agents are learning and acting. See Britto [1972]. We will not discuss this last possibility to any extend in this paper, however. [4]

In this paper, we construct a model which is dynamic not only in terms of information variables, for example, estimates of the state of the world parameters that are changing with time, but also in terms of other endogenous variables (state variables) that are changing with time as well. We shall then examine, in the context of a particular market situation, the nature and amount of information processing that is demanded of economic agents to reach optimal output decisions. We do this

without assuming that an equilibrium has been reached in learning, as
for example Lucas and Prescott do in their paper [1971]. This microeconomic model is then used, as a vehicle of discussion, to illustrate
a kind of information externalities that could be present in some market
situations. These externalities present economic agents with an inordi-
nate information processing task. We argue at the end of the paper that
it is much more realistic for economic agents to purse some decision
policies which are suboptimal, yet which do not demand as much in terms
of effort in reaching the decision (solution efforts).[5]

The model of this paper may be too specific to suit the taste of
some economists. The use of this model permits us, however, to spell
out explicitly and to bring into focus sharply certain technical and conceptual difficulties economic agents face and the nature and amount of
information processing the agents must perform in reaching optimal or
suboptimal decisions under an imperfect information assumption.

Our model in this paper is a dynamic extension of the Marshallian
quantity adjustment model recently used by Leijonhufvud [1974]. It is a
model of an industry composed of n firms producing a homogeneous
perishable good. The number of firms is assumed to remain constant for
expositional convenience. Each firm must decide on the output for the
next market day as the production delay is taken to coincide with one
market day. Firms realize that their output decisions jointly affect the
market clearing price on the next day, but do not know the output decisions of the other firms. We assume that firms do not form coalitions
because coalition formation is a resource consuming activity even when
n is only moderately large. Firms observe market clearing prices each
day.

The paper is organized as follows: We describe the model formally in Sec. 2. We then derive, in Sec. 3, the difference equation which
governs the behavior of the outputs over successive market days, given
adjustment step size decisions by the firms. In Secs. 4.1 - 4.3, we
consider how firms may attempt to predict future market clearing prices

160

and maximize expected future profits by postulating certain reaction patterns by the other firms, and show that they are governed by the n-th order stochastic difference equation, the coefficients of which are functions of all the firms' current and past decisions. In Sec. 4.4 we sketch an iterative performance improvement scheme which demands less in terms of information processing than the optimal procedure. We conclude the paper in Sec. 5.

2. THE MODEL

We first describe Leijonhufvud's deterministic model and then describe the model to be used in the rest of the paper.

Leijonhufvud based his model of output adjustments of a representative firm on a Marshallian model given by

(M.1) $$p^d = d(q)$$

(M.2) $$p^s = s(q)$$

(M.3) $$\Delta q = h\{s(q) - d(q)\}$$

where $h < 0$ is a constant determining the adjustment step-size, q is the actual output rate, p^d is the maximum price at which consumers are willing to absorb a given rate of output and p^s is the minimum price required to induce producers to continue a given rate of output. $d(\cdot)$ is the demand price schedule, and $s(\cdot)$ is the supply price schedule.

In the above Marshallian quantity adjustment scheme, the demand price p^d must be known for the representative firm to adjust the output rate according to (M.3). Since p^d is not actually known, Leijonhufvud replaces (M.3) with (M.3') which is taken to be the adjustment scheme[6] for the representative firm

(M.3') $$\Delta q_t = h \cdot [p^s(q_t) - p_t^*] ,$$

where

$$\Delta q_t = q_{t+1} - q_t ,$$

and where

$$p_t^* = d(q_t)$$

is the market clearing price for the actual output rate, q_t.[7] The quantity adjustment equation (M. 3') takes the place of the more familiar cobweb type quantity adjustment equation.

Leijonhufvud next considered a disaggregated version of (M. 3') in an industry composed of n firms producing a single homogeneous non-storable good. In this paper we assume adjustments are not carried out exactly. Instead, we assume that the j-th firm's output adjustment is determined by

(1)[8]
$$\Delta q_{jt} = h_{jt}\{s_j(q_{jt}) - p_t^*\} + \zeta_{j,t} \qquad j = 1,\ldots,n$$

where $\{\zeta_{j,t}\}$ is a sequence of exogenous disturbances and the market clearing price is given by the joint output rates of n producers,

$$p_t^* = d(Q_t) + n_t ,$$

where

(2)
$$Q_t = \sum_{j=1}^{n} q_{jt} ,$$

and where n_t is some exogenous disturbance, assumed to be independent of the ζ's. Each firm observes p_t^* and knows his own output and supply price schedule but not the other firms' outputs or supply price schedules.

162

Equations (1) and (2) explicitly introduce the individual firms' behavior and their interactions at the market level. With these interactions explicitly spelled out, we can ask and answer some interesting questions. For example, can the market be in equilibrium in the sense that the market clearing price remains the same on several consecutive market days (assuming a deterministic model with no random disturbances) while individual firms are not necessarily in equilibrium? This is a question on the nonuniqueness of equilibrium states on the microeconomic level. See Appendix 1. Although we could treat $p^s(\cdot)$ and $d(\cdot)$ as general nonlinear functions parameterized by unknown parameter θ in some compact set Θ, we analyze the adjustment mechanisms (1) and (2), in the most part of the paper, assuming that the firms' supply price schedules are affine in q,

$$(3) \qquad s_j(q) = \alpha_j + \beta_j q, \quad j = 1, \ldots, n$$

where α's and β's are deterministic scalars. We assume also that the market clearing price is linearly related to the total amount of the good put on the market by

$$(4) \qquad p_t^* = \gamma - \delta Q_t + n_t .$$

We assume γ, δ, α_j, β_j, $j = 1, \ldots, n$ all come from a compact set in R_+^{n+2} .

3. DIFFERENCE EQUATIONS FOR OUTPUT RATES

From (1) and (3), we see that

$$(5)^9 \qquad q_{t+1} = H_t \alpha + (I + H_t B) q_t - H_t e p_t^* + \zeta_t$$

where

163

$$\alpha = (\alpha_1, \ldots, \alpha_n)'$$

$$H_t = \operatorname{diag}(h_{1t}, \ldots, h_{nt})$$

(6)
$$B = \operatorname{diag}(\beta_1, \ldots, \beta_n)$$

$$e = (1 \ldots 1)'$$

$$\zeta_t = (\zeta_{1t}, \ldots, \zeta_{nt}) \ .$$

We assume that h_{jt} is chosen from a closed interval I on the positive real axis, $j = 1, \ldots, n$ for all $t = 0, 1, \ldots$. Hence the vector $h_t = (h_{1t}, \ldots, h_{nt})'$ is in the compact set $I \times I \times \ldots \times I$.

From (4) and (5), we obtain the stochastic difference equation governing q_t,

$$q_{t+1} = \Phi_t q_t + C_t + \xi_t$$

where
(7)
$$C_t \equiv H_t(\alpha - \gamma e)$$

$$\Phi_t \equiv I + H_t B + \delta h_t e'$$

and where

$$\xi_t \equiv \zeta_t - H_t n_t \ .$$

When h_{jt} is constant for all t, then Φ_t, H_t and h_t all become constant. In that case, it is more convenient to rewrite (7) as

(7A)
$$\Delta q_{t+1} = \Phi \Delta q_t + \Delta \xi_t$$

where

$$\Delta \xi_t = \Delta \zeta_t - H \Delta n_t \ .$$

The third term in Φ_t represents interaction or cross-coupling of different firms' output rates caused by the fact that all firms react to a common signal, the market clearing price. Firm j knows the value of his own current and past decision variable, the parameters of his own supply price schedule and the current and past market clearing prices. Equation (7) is a state space representation of the dynamics of the output rate of the industry, describing time paths of the firms' output rates. Each firm is assumed to know that the price moves according to (6) and (7). Firms, however, do not know Φ_t nor γ exactly. Thus, all firms have the same structural model of the industry. However they do not all have the same information about the model's parameters (which uniquely specify the model in the class of similar models). In other words, firms' information patterns are decentralized. See Appendix 1 for further discussion of (7).

4. FORMATION OF FUTURE PRICE EXPECTATIONS AND OUTPUT DECISIONS

Having formally described the model, the next stage of investigation normally would be to examine an individual firm's intertemporal (expected) profit maximization problem if information processing cost is ignored completely. But as stated in Part 1, we do not adopt the rational expectation assumption since our interest is in the disequilibrium dynamic behavior of the firms. We derive the (stochastic difference) equation used by the firms to predict the market clearing prices, or examine how future price expectations are formed and updated by firms. Because of the assumed imprecise knowledge of other firms' supply price schedules, and the ignorance of the output rate decisions made by the other firms, the coefficients of the stochastic difference equations governing the future prices are unknown. Furthermore (as we show later) they are complicated algebraic functions of α's and β's as well as decisions taken by all the firms in the past. See (10) - (12) below. Thus, even if we were to make an initial assumption about the joint probability distribution of α's and β's on some economic grounds, the posterior probability distribution of these coefficients would usually be analytically intractable to determine.

To proceed with analysis, we assume that the firms change their adjustment step sizes only occasionally so that there are market days with no step size changes by any firm.[10] On these days, Φ_t in (7) becomes a constant matrix and the difference equation for the future market clearing prices becomes a little simpler. Under this assumption we now derive a personal (subjective) model used by firm 1 in predicting the market clearing price on the next day. This will be used later to discuss firm 1's choices of step sizes to maximize its subjectively estimated profits.

The ensuing analysis clearly indicates that the required information processing or learning by firms may be too much to be carried out so that firms would not be likely to engage in this sort of optimal or sophisticated price prediction activities in making their output decisions.

We now derive the equation governing the future prices explicitly and examine what is implied if parameters are to be learned adaptively or if some intertemporal optimization problems are to be solved.

4.1. The Firm's Personal Model of Future Prices

We now derive a set of differential equations for Δp_t^* and Δq_{1t}, assuming no step size changes by any firm. See footnote 10 and Appendix 2 for alternate assumptions. With constant step sizes, Φ_t and h_t become constant and thus the time subscript will be dropped.

Partition Δq_t, Φ and h conformably as

$$\Delta q_t = \begin{pmatrix} w_t \\ v_t \end{pmatrix}$$

where we write w_t for Δq_{1t} for a shorter notation and v_t is the $(n-1)$-dimensional vector composed of $\Delta q_{2t}, \ldots, \Delta q_{nt}$;

166

(8)
$$\Phi = \begin{pmatrix} a & h_1 \delta f' \\ \delta \bar{h} & E \end{pmatrix}$$

where E is the $(n-1)$ by $(n-1)$ matrix, and from (7),

$$a = 1 + h_1(\beta_1 + \delta),$$

$$f' = (1, \ldots, 1) : \text{ an } (n-1)\text{-vector},$$

$$\bar{h} = \begin{pmatrix} h_2 \\ \vdots \\ h_n \end{pmatrix} : \text{ other firm's decision vector},$$

and

$$E = \delta \bar{h} f' + \text{diag}(1 + h_2 \beta_2, \ldots, 1 + h_n \beta_n) .$$

From (7), we analogously obtain

(9)
$$w_{t+1} = a w_t + h_1 \delta f' v_t + \eta_t + \delta h_1 n_t ,$$

$$v_{t+1} = \delta \bar{h} w_t + e v_t + \epsilon_t + \delta \bar{h} n_t$$

where we write η_t for $\Delta \zeta_{1t}$ and $\epsilon_t = (\Delta \zeta_{2t}, \ldots, \Delta \zeta_{nt})$.

Note that $f' v_t$ is the change in the industry's output rate, excluding that due to firm one. If the parameters in (9) are all known and if noise characteristics are all known (such as, for example, Gaussian and with known means and covariance matrices), then a recursive scheme for predicting $f' v_t$ (the output rate change by the rest of the industry) or equivalently for predicting p_{t-1}^* may be obtained. To simplify our development somewhat, suppose δ is known to firm one. Then a in (9) is known to firm one. None of the system parameters governing the dynamics of $\{v_\tau\}$ is known to firm one, however. Eqution (9), with firm one's subjective estimate of h and E or a joint probability distribution of $h_2, \ldots, h_n$, would constitute firm one's personal model of this market situation. Firm one uses this subjective model to compute the conditional expectation of v_t, given what it knows at time t. We denote the information of firm one by ϑ_t.

The market clearing price p_t^* becomes known to all firms at the end of the t-th market day. Firm one also knows q_{1t} at the end of the t-th day. Knowing p_t^* and choosing an adjustment step size h_1, the output available at the beginning of the (t+1)-st market day is

$$q_{1t+1} = q_{1t} + h_1 \{s_1(q_{1t}) - p_t^*\} + \zeta_{1t} .$$

The effect of v_t on Δp_{t-1}^* may be written as

(10) $$\Delta p_{t-1}^* + \delta w_{t-1} = -\delta f' v_{t-1} + n_{t-1} .$$

Since Δp_{t-1}^* and w_{t-1} are known to firm one, this equation may be regarded as a noisy observation made on $f' v_{t-1}$. Firm one has another observation on $f' v_{t-1}$ at the end of the t-th day by

(11) $$w_t - a w_{t-1} = \delta h_1 f' v_{t-1} + \quad + \delta h_1 n_t .$$

Thus, we have a dynamic equation for v_τ's,

$$v_{\tau+1} = E v_\tau + \delta \overline{h} w_\tau + \epsilon_\tau + \delta \overline{h} n_\tau$$

(12)[11]
$$y_\tau = \delta \begin{pmatrix} -1 \\ h_1 \end{pmatrix} f' v_{\tau-1} + \begin{pmatrix} n_{\tau-1} \\ \eta_\tau + \delta h_1 n_\tau \end{pmatrix} ,$$

where

$$y_\tau = (y_{1\tau}, y_{2\tau})' \text{ with}$$

$$y_{1\tau} = \Delta p^*_{\tau-1} + \delta w_{\tau-1},$$

$$y_{2\tau} = w_\tau - aw_{\tau-1}.$$

At the end of the t-th market day, $y_{t-1}, y_{t-2}, \ldots$ are available to firm one. Equations (11) and (12) constitute firm one's "personal" model of the industry.

It would be straightforward, if all system parameters are known, to obtain (in principle) $\mathcal{E}(v_t | \mathcal{I}_t) \equiv v_{t|t}$, and hence to obtain $-\delta f' v_{t|t}$, the estimate of price change on the (t+1)-th day due to the output rate change of the rest of the industry, where $\mathcal{I}_t = \{y_t, y_{t-1}, \ldots;$ a priori information$\} = \{q_{1t}, q_{1t-1}, \ldots, p^*_t, p^*_{t-1}, \ldots;$ a priori information$\}$.

Firm one can estimate its own output for the (t+1)-th day by

$$q_{1t+1|t} = q_{1t} + w_{t|t}$$

where

$$w_{t|t} = h_1(\alpha_1 + \beta_1 q_{1t} - p^*_t).$$

When some of the parameters are unknown as in this case (other firms' adjustment step sizes appear in E and h), we must treat the profit maximization problem as a dual control problem in which the step sizes are chosen to compromise between learning unknown parameters quickly and attaining profit maximization. See Appendix 2 for some detail on computing $v_{t|t}$.

The prediction of $p^*_{t+1|t}$ arises when firm one engages in some intertemporal expected profit maximization. This topic is discussed next.

169

4.2. A One-Day Look-Ahead Profit Maximization

To illustrate how firm one's price expectation affects its output decisions, we consider maximizing the expected profit on the next day by firm one. Suppose that firm one finds itself at the end of the t-th market day. Assume that no firms have changed step sizes up to now. Firm one considers changing its step size for the next day. The profit that firm One realizes on the (t+1)st market day is the random variable

$$(27) \qquad J_{t+1} = \{p_{t+1}^* - s_1(q_{1t+1})\}q_{1t+1}$$

where

$$(28) \qquad q_{1t+1} = q_{1t} + w_t .$$

Let

$$(29) \qquad \begin{aligned} \overline{w}_t &= \mathcal{E}(w_t | \mathcal{J}_t) \\ &= h_1\{s_1(q_{1t}) - p_t^*\} \end{aligned}$$

where $\mathcal{J}_t$ is the information set available to firm one at the end of the t-th day. For shorter notation denote Δp_t^* by r_t and $s_1(q_{1\tau}^*)$ by s_τ. Let $J_{t+1|t}$ denote $\mathcal{E}(J_{t+1}|\mathcal{J}_t)$, the expected profit on the next market day. Then from (1), recalling that $w_t = \Delta q_{1t}$ and $r_t = \Delta p_t^*$, and from (3), we may derive

$$J_{t+1|t} = (1 + h_1\beta_1)(p_t^* - s_t)\{q_{1t} + h_1(s_t - p_t^*)\}$$

$$+ \{q_{1t} + h_1(s_t - p_t^*)\}r_{t|t} - \beta_1\sigma_1^2$$

since $\mathcal{E}(y_t\zeta_{1t}|\mathcal{J}_t) = 0$, where $y_{t|t} = \mathcal{E}(y_t|\mathcal{J}_t)$ is firm one's estimate of the price change on the next day. It is more informative to rewrite this as

$$J_{t+1|t} = J_t + \overline{w}_t(p_t^* - s_t) - \beta_1\overline{w}_t(q_{1t} + \overline{w}_t)$$

(30)

$$+ (q_{1t} + \overline{w}_t)r_{t|t} - \beta_1\sigma_1^2$$

where $r_{t|t}$ stands for $\mathcal{E}(r_t|\mathcal{I}_t)$ and where J_t is the profit realized on the t-th market day, $J_t = q_{1t}(p_t^* - s_t)$. J_t is hence known. Since $\overline{w}_t$ is the expected increase in the output to be sold on the (t+1)-th market day and since $p_t^* - s_t$ is the current profit rate (per unit of the output) we can readily interpret (30): The expected increase of the profit on the (t+1)-th day over that of the t-th market day consists of (except for the $-\beta_1\sigma_1^2$ term due to the exogeneous disturbance on the output of the firm) (i) the profit due to the increased output computed at the current rate of profit, (ii) the correction term to (i) to account for the change in the supply price due to increased output and (iii) the expected change in the profit due to the change in the market clearing price. Suppose at time t firm one wishes to choose h_1 which maximized (30). The first order condition is then given by

(31) $$0 = \partial\mathcal{E}(J_{t+1}|\mathcal{I}_t)/\partial h_1,$$

or the optimal step size to determine the output rate for the (t+1)-th market day is given by

$$h_1^o = \{\beta_1 J_t - (p_t^* - s_t)^2 - (p_t^* - s_t)r_{t|t} + q_{1t}\partial r_{t|t}/\partial h_1\}/$$

(32)

$$\{2\beta_1(p_t^* - s_t)^2 + (p_t^* - s_t)\partial r_{t|t}/\partial h_1\},$$

if

$$p_t^* - s_t \neq 0 .$$

From (32), the optimal change in the output rate is given as

$$\overline{w}_t^o = -h_1^o(p_t^* - s_t)$$

(33)
$$= \{-\beta_1 q_{1t} + (p_t^* - s_t) + r_{t|t} - \frac{q_{1t}}{p_t^* - s_t} \frac{\partial r_{t|t}}{\partial h_1} \} \Big/$$

$$\{2\beta_1 + \frac{1}{p_t^* - s_t} \frac{\partial r_{t|t}}{\partial h_1} \} .$$

When $r_{t|t} = 0$ and $\partial r_{t|t}/\partial h = 0$, (32) reduces to

$$\overline{w}_t = (-\beta_1 q_{1t} + p_t^* - s_t)/2\beta_1$$

which is the known result of the profit maximization of a price-taker when p_{t+1}^* is assumed given.

We now turn our attention to the evaluation of expressions $r_{t|t}$ and $\partial r_{t|t}/\partial h_1$. We have already discussed the derivation of $v_{t|t}$ in Sec. 4.1. Since $\overline{w}_t = h_1(s_t - p_t^*)$, firm one has

(34)
$$r_{t|t} = -\delta v_{t|t} - \delta h_1(s_t - p_t^*) .$$

If h_1 is to be changed on the $(t+1)$-th market day, $v_{t|t}$ is not affected. Hence

(35)
$$\frac{\partial r_{t|t}}{\partial h_1} = -\delta(s_t - p_t^*) .$$

Thus from (32) and (33), we obtain

(36)
$$\overline{w}_t = [-(\beta_1 + \delta)q_{1t} + (p_t^* - s_t) - \delta v_{t|t}]/2(\beta_1 + \delta) .$$

It is interesting to note a close resemblance of (36) to (3.6) of Appendix 3 which gives the optimal output change of firm one for a monopolist who owns the n firms (i.e., under centralized information pattern). Except for the presence of $v_{t|t}$ term and the fact that the denominator is $2(\beta_1+\delta)$ rather than $2\beta_1+\delta$, (36) is identical to (3.6) of Appendix 3.

We have shown that in the one-day-look-ahead profit maximization problem, firm one needs to know $r_{t|t}$ or $v_{t|t}$ since

$$r_{t|t} = \mathcal{E}(\Delta p_t^* | \vartheta_t)$$

$$= -\delta(w_t + v_{t|t}) .$$

On the next market day, firm one updates his estimate $v_{t|t}$ to $v_{t+1|t+1}$. (See Appendix 2 for the recursive formula of updating $v_{t|t}$.) Computation of $v_{t|t}$ requires, however, that firm one computes $p(\theta | \vartheta_t)$.

4.3. Parameter-Adaptive Expected Profit Maximization

In case firm one wishes to formulate an intertemporal optimization problem involving profits over the next N market days, the situation becomes very complicated, although straightforward conceptually, since we need $v_{t+\tau|t}$, $\tau = 1, \ldots, N$, and their derivatives with respect to h_1.

In keeping with our basic assumption that firms change the adjustment step size only occasionally, we next discuss firm one's step size decision covering the last k market days in firm one's planning horizon.[12] In other words, we choose h to maximize the conditional expected profit over the next k periods, $\mathcal{E}(J_t | \vartheta_t)$, where we redefine J_τ by

$$J_t = \pi_{t+1} + \ldots + \pi_{t+k}$$

where t+k is the end of the planning horizon, where

$$\pi_{t+\tau} = (p_{t+\tau}^* - s_{t+\tau})q_{1t+\tau}, \quad \tau = 1, \ldots, k$$

and where we let $s_{t+\tau} = s_1(q_{1t+\tau})$. Recall that

$$p_{t+\tau}^* = p_t^* + r_t + \ldots + r_{t+\tau-1}$$

and

$$q_{1t+\tau} = q_{1t} + w_t + \ldots + w_{t+\tau-1}$$

$$= q_{1t} + h\Sigma_{j=0}^{\tau-1}(s_{t+j} - p_{t+j}^*)$$

since

$$w_{t+j} = h(s_{t+j} - p_{t+j}^*) \ .$$

Thus,

$$J_t = \Sigma_{\tau=1}^{k} \pi_{t+\tau}$$

(37)

$$= -\Sigma_{\tau=1}^{k}(s_{t+\tau} - p_{t+\tau}^*)q_{1t} - h\Sigma_{\tau=1}^{k}\Sigma_{j=0}^{\tau-1}(s_{t+\tau} - p_{t+\tau}^*)(s_{t+j} - p_{t+j}^*) \ .$$

By iterating the relation

$$s_{t+1} - p_{t+1}^* = s_t + \beta_1 h(s_t - p_t^*) - p_t^* - r_t$$

$$= (1 + \beta_1 h)(s_t - p_t^*) - r_t \ ,$$

we obtain

(38) $$s_{t+j} - p_{t+j}^* = (1 + \beta_1 h)^j(s_t - p_t^*) - \Sigma_{\ell=0}^{j-1}(1 + \beta_1 h)^{j-1-\ell} r_{t+\ell} \ .$$

Substituting (38) into (37), we can now express $\mathcal{E}(J_t | \mathcal{I}_t)$ as

$$\mathcal{E}(J_t | \vartheta_t) = -\{(1 + \beta_1 h_1)^{k+1} - (1 + \beta_1 h)\}(s_t - p_t^*)q_{1t}/\beta_1 h$$

$$+ \left[\Sigma_{\tau=1}^k \Sigma_{\ell=0}^{\tau-1} (1 + \beta_1 h_1)^{\tau-1-\ell} r_{t+\ell} |_t \right] q_{1t}$$

$$- h\{ \Sigma_{\tau=1}^k \Sigma_{j=0}^{\tau-1} (1 + \beta_1 h_1)^{\tau+j} (s_t - p_t^*)^2$$

$$- \Sigma_{\ell=0}^{\tau-1} (1 + \beta_1 h_1)^{\tau-1-\ell-j} (s_t - p_t^*) r_{t+\ell} |_t$$

$$- \Sigma_{m=0}^{j-1} (1 + \beta_1 h_1)^{\tau+j-1-m} (s_t - p_t^*) r_{t+m} |_t$$

$$+ \Sigma_{\ell=0}^{\tau-1} \Sigma_{m=0}^{j-1} (1 + \beta_1 h_1)^{\tau+j-2-\ell-m} \{ r_{t+\ell} |_t r_{t+m} |_t + R_{\ell,m} \}]$$

where

$$R_{\ell m} = \mathcal{E}\{ (r_{t+\ell} - r_{t+\ell} |_t)(r_{t+m} - t_{t+m} |_t) | \vartheta_t \}.$$

We can see that the first-order condition obtained by $\partial E(J_t | \vartheta_t)/\partial h = 0$ is very complicated and offers little intuitively interpretable basis for choosing h. Besides, we need $r_{t+j} |_t$, $R_{\ell,m}$ and must obtain their derivatives with respect to h. From the market dynamic equation (7) or (9) we have

$$\begin{pmatrix} w_{t+\tau} \\ v_{t+\tau} \end{pmatrix} = \Phi^\tau \begin{pmatrix} w_t \\ v_t \end{pmatrix} \quad \Sigma_{s=0}^{\tau-1} \Phi^{\tau-1-s} \left\{ \begin{pmatrix} \eta_{t+s} \\ \epsilon_{t+s} \end{pmatrix} + \delta \begin{pmatrix} h_1 \\ h \end{pmatrix} n_{t+s} \right\}.$$

Thus, from $r_{t+\tau} = -\delta(w_{t+\tau} + f' v_{t+\tau})$,

$$r_{t+\tau} |_{t,\theta} = -\delta(1, f') \Phi^\tau \begin{pmatrix} w_t \\ v_t |_{t,\theta} \end{pmatrix}.$$

$y_{t+\tau} |_t$ is then obtained from $y_{t+\tau} |_{t,\theta}$ in a manner analogous to the procedure outlined in Appendix 2, since η_{t+s}, ϵ_{t+s}, n_{t+s}, $s = 0, \ldots, \tau-1$ and independent of ϑ_t. From (8) we see that

$$\frac{\partial \Phi}{\partial h} = \begin{pmatrix} \beta_1 + \delta & \delta f' \\ 0 & 0 \end{pmatrix} .$$

This is used to obtain $\partial \Phi^T / \partial h$ in evaluating $\partial r_{t+\tau} / \partial h$. The resulting expression, however, does not seem to be too useful since $r_{t+\tau} |_t$ is complicated and probably has to be computed numerically.

4.4. Iterative Performance Improvement Scheme

Lacking sufficient information to carry out any sort of intertemporal optimization, firms may wish to adjust their h's nevertheless. Here, we can borrow the techniques of direct optimization of functions of several variables developed in the discipline of nonlinear programming and their extensions to stochastic function maximization by algorithms analogous to the one proposed by Kiefer and Wolfowitz to seek the maximum of a regression function. See, for example, Polyak [1972].

This is due to the fact that any firm's profit or loss over the past is a well-behaved function of the h's. We carry out our discussion for firm one. We take the t-th day as today. On the t-th market day, then, firm one knows how much profit and losses it has experienced on days 0, 1, ..., t. Denote the cumulative profit up to now by

$$L(h) = \sum_{\tau=0}^{t} [p_\tau^* - s_1(q_{1\tau})] q_{1\tau} .$$

Note that $L(\cdot)$ is quadratic in h, at least explicitly.

Suppose h^* is firm one's optimal adjustment step size. Expand $L(\cdot)$ into a Taylor series

$$L(h) = L(h^*) + \frac{1}{2} (h - h^*)' L_{hh} (h - h^*) + \dots .$$

Let ρ be a small positive number. Then

$$L(h+\rho) - L(h-\rho) = \frac{1}{2} [(h-h^*+\rho)' L_{hh} (h-h^*+\rho) - (h-h^*-\rho)' L_{hh} (h-h^*-\rho)] + \dots$$

$$= \rho' (L_{hh})(h-h^*) + \dots .$$

176

This relationship is the key relation[13] to allow us to show the convergence in probability and in mean square of h to h^*.

In our problem we need to show that $h \to h^*$ in some probabilistic sense when the individual h_j's are adjusted independently. This is analogous to the cyclic gradient method rather than the usual steepest ascent (descent) method which could also be carried out.

Firm one maximizes $L(h)$ by iterating on the adjustment step size using the data set covering the period $0, 1, \ldots, t$ by[14]

$$h_{1,m+1} = h_{1,m} + \frac{a_m}{c_m} [L(h_{1,m} + c_m) - L(h_{1,m} - c_m)]$$

where $h_{1,m}$ is the m-th iterate, a_m and c_m are such that

$$c_m \to 0, \quad \Sigma a_m = \infty, \quad \Sigma a_m c_m < \infty, \quad \Sigma a_m^2/c_m^2 < \infty$$

e.g., $a_m = 1/m^{1-\epsilon}$, $c_m = 1/2^{1/2-\eta}$ for some small $\epsilon, \eta > 0$.

We leave the technical verification of these convergence conditions to be completed elsewhere [Aoki, 1974].

The limit h_1^* of these iterations is the adjustment step size firm one should have employed in the light of the firm's past loss and profit record. Firm one could periodically repeat these iterations, say every week, utilizing all the data accumulated up to that time.

5. CONCLUSIONS

There are at least two alternatives to the dual optimization formulation described in this paper in deriving second best solutions. One is sketched in Sec. 4.4. The other is to separate the estimation of the unknown parameters from an approximate evaluation of the future profit expression, rather than to consider the combined estimation and profit maximization problem, or to postualte certain learning rates and obtain an approximate expression for $\mathcal{E}(J_t | \vartheta_t)$.

177

Although we have not discussed rational expectation, it will provide a result which can serve as a benchmark for this type of problem. The rational expectation assumption can easily be extended to cover this multi decision maker situation.

APPENDIX 1

EIGENVALUES OF Φ AND ASYMPTOTIC DISTRIBUTIONS

Let

$$\Phi_t = I + H_t B + \delta h_t e'$$

where

$$H_t = \text{diag}(h_{1t}, \ldots, h_{nt}), \quad h'_t = (h_{1t}, \ldots, h_{nt})$$

and where

$$e' = (1, \ldots, 1).$$

Suppose that firms do not change their adjustment step sizes once they are chosen. Then we can drop the time subscript from the matrices Φ_t, H_t and the vector h_t since they are all constant.

If the eigenvalues of Φ all have magnitude less than one, then the homogeneous solution of (7), i.e., the solution of

$$\Delta q_{t+1} = \Phi \Delta q_t$$

is asumptotically stable, $\Delta q_t \to 0$, as $t \to \infty$. Let $g(\lambda)$ be defined by

$$g(\lambda) = |\lambda I - \Phi|$$

$$= |(\lambda - 1)I - HB - \delta he'|$$

$$= \{1 - \delta \sum_{j=1}^{n} h_j / (\lambda - 1 - h_j \beta_j)\} \pi_{j=1}^{n} (\lambda - 1 - h_j \beta_j) .$$

Suppose we rename firms so that $0 > \theta_1 > \theta_2 \geq \ldots \geq \theta_n,$[15] where $\theta_j = h_j \beta_j$ we see that with $h_j < 0$ and $\max(\beta_j |h_j|, |h_n|\beta_n + \delta \sum_j |h_j|) < 2,$ the eigenvalues of Φ all lie within the unit disc in the complex plane. See [Wilkinson, 1965, Sec. 39].

We next give a sufficient condition for asymptotic stability with time varying h's. This condition is a slight generalization of Hukuhara's theorem (see [Miller, 1968, Sec. 1.3]).

We define the vector and matrix norm by

$$\|z\| = \sum_j |z_j| \qquad \text{where } z = (z_1, \ldots, z_n)'$$

and

$$\|A\| = \sum_j \sum_i |a_{ij}| \qquad \text{where } A = (a_{ij}) .$$

Suppose that h_{jt}, $j=1, \ldots, n$ are such that

$$h_{jt} = \bar{h}_j + k_{jt} .$$

In other words, k_{jt} is the deviation of the adjustment step size from the average step size of firm j. Defining

$$\bar{H} = \text{diag}(\bar{h}_1, \ldots, \bar{h}_n)$$

$$\bar{h} = (\bar{h}_1, \ldots, \bar{h}_n)' \qquad \text{etc. },$$

we write Φ_t as

$$\Phi_t = \Phi + \Psi_t$$

where

$$\Phi = I + \overline{H}B + \delta\overline{h}e'$$

and

$$\Psi_t = (H_t - \overline{H})B + \delta(h - \overline{h})e' \ .$$

Then

$$\|\Phi\| = \Sigma_{j=1}^{n}(1 + \overline{h}_j\beta_j) + \delta_n\Sigma|\overline{h}_j|$$

$$= n - \Sigma|\overline{h}_j|\beta_j + \delta n\Sigma|\overline{h}_j|$$

$$= n - \Sigma(\beta_j - \delta n)|\overline{h}_j|$$

and

$$\|\Psi_t\| = \Sigma_j |k_{jt}|(\beta_j + \delta n) \ .$$

Suppose $\overline{h}_j$'s are chosen in such a way that $\|\Phi\| < 1$. Such a choice is certainly possible. Since the eigenvalues of Φ are less than $\|\Phi\|$, Φ is asymptotically stable with such $\overline{h}$'s. We need the following theorem.

THEOREM. Let $\{z_t\}$ be generated by $z_{t+1} = (\Phi+\Psi_t)z_t$ where $\|\Phi\| < 1$ and $\Sigma_t \|\Psi_t\| < \infty$. Then $z_t \to 0$ as $t \to \infty$.

PROOF. There exists a number r such that $\|\Phi\| \leq r < 1$, by assumption. From the difference equation

$$z_t = \Phi^t z_o + \Sigma_{j=0}^{t-1} r^{t-1-j} \|\Psi_j\| \|z_j\| .$$

Denote

$$\|z_t\| \cdot r^{-t} \quad \text{by} \quad \|w_t\| .$$

Then

$$\|w_t\| \leq \|z_o\| + \frac{1}{r} \Sigma_{j=0}^{t-1} \|\Psi_j\| \cdot \|w_j\| .$$

From the difference equation version of the Bellman-Gronwall lemma (see Miller, Sec. 1.3), we see that

$$\|w_t\| \leq c \cdot \exp(\frac{1}{r} \Sigma_{j=0}^{t-1} \|\Psi_j\|).$$

From the assumption we thus establish the boundedness of $\|w_t\|$ for all t, hence $\|z_t\| \to 0$ as $t \to \infty$.

If k_{jt}'s are such that

$$\Sigma_{t=0}^{\infty} |k_{jt}| < \infty \quad \text{for all} \quad j = 1, \ldots, n ,$$

then, recalling that we name firms such that $\beta_n \leq \ldots \leq \beta_1$,

$$\Sigma_{jt=0}^{\infty} \|\Psi_t\| \leq (\beta_1 + \delta n) \Sigma_{t=0}^{\infty} |k_{1t}| < \infty,$$

and the asymptotic behavior of solutions of the difference equation $z_{t+1} = \Phi_t z_t$ is established. This result shows that if the firms' adjustment step sizes converge sufficiently fast[16] to their respective average values, then

$$\mathcal{E}(\Delta q_t) \to 0 \quad \text{as} \quad t \to \infty$$

181

if the average step sizes are such that $\|\Phi\| < 1$ holds.

From $\Delta p_\tau^* = 0$, $\tau = t, t+1, \ldots, t+n-1$, we obtain a set of n algebraic equations, assuming no exogenous disturbances,

$$0 = \begin{bmatrix} e' \\ e'\Phi \\ \vdots \\ e'\Phi^{n-1} \end{bmatrix} \Delta q_t .$$

If the rank of this matrix is n, then $\Delta q_t = 0$ follows from this set of equations, i.e., firm-by-firm output rates are at equilibrium.

From (7), it is easily seen that this rank condition is equivalent to that of none of β's being the same for the special case in which h_j is the same for all j. In other words, with at least two firms with the same supply price schedule slope, the industry wide equilibrium does not necessarily imply all firms output rates have reached the equilibrium rates.

Suppose now that all the eigenvalues of Φ lie within the unit disc. Let

$$z_t = \mathcal{E}(\Delta q_t)$$

and

$$\tilde{z}_t = \Delta q_t - z_t .$$

Then $\{\tilde{z}_t\}$ is generated by the stochastic difference equation

(1.1) $$\tilde{z}_{t+1} = \Phi \tilde{z}_t + \Delta \zeta_t .$$

Let $Z_t = \text{cov } \tilde{z}_t = \text{cov } \Delta q_t$. Then from (1.1),

(1.2) $$Z_{t+1} = \Phi Z_t \Phi' + \mathcal{E}(\Delta \zeta_t \tilde{z}_t') \Phi' + \Phi \mathcal{E}(\tilde{z}_t \Delta \zeta_t') + \text{cov}(\Delta \zeta_t) .$$

Suppose $\{\zeta_t\}$ are independently and identically distributed with mean zero and covariance Z. Assume further that $\tilde{z}_o$ is independent of ζ's. Recalling that $\Delta\zeta_t = \zeta_{t+1} - \zeta_t$ and from the independence assumption of $\tilde{z}_o$ we see that

$$\mathcal{E}(\tilde{z}_t \Delta\zeta_t') = -\mathcal{E}(\zeta_t \zeta_t')$$

$$= -\Sigma .$$

Equation (1.2) is rewritten then as

$$Z_{t+1} = \Phi Z_t \Phi' - \Sigma\Phi' - \Phi\Sigma + 2\Sigma,$$

$$Z_o = \Sigma_o .$$

The sequence $\{Z_{t+1}\}$ converges to a limit matrix Z^* for suitably small $|h|$'s, since $\|\Phi\|$ will be less than one. It is given as a positive (semidefinite) solution of

$$Z^* = \Phi Z^* \Phi' - \Sigma\Phi' - \Phi\Sigma + 2\Sigma .$$

Thus, if ζ's are normally distributed, then the distribution of $\{\Delta q_t\}$ converges to $N(0, Z^*)$. Under the same set of assumptions, q_t can be shown to be given by

$$q_t = q_0 + (I-\Phi)^{-1}(I-\Phi^{t+1})\Delta q_o + \rho_t$$

where

$$\rho_t \sim N(0, \Gamma_t)$$

and

$$\Gamma_t \to \Sigma + 2(I-\Phi)^{-1}\Sigma(I-\Phi)^{-1} .$$

APPENDIX 2
COMPUTATION OF $v_{t|t}$

We assume that δ is known and step sizes are held constant. Firm one's model of the market is

(2.1)
$$v_{t+1} = E(\theta)v_t + \delta\overline{h}(\theta)w_t + \epsilon_t + \delta\overline{h}(\theta)n_t$$

$$y_t = Cv_{t-1} + \begin{pmatrix} n_{t-1} \\ \eta_t + \delta h_1 n_t \end{pmatrix},$$

where $C = \delta\begin{bmatrix} -1 \\ h_1 \end{bmatrix}f'$ and where we use θ to denote the unknown parameters $(h_2, \ldots, h_n)$ that appear in E and $\overline{h}$. We use the notation y^t for $y_t, y_{t-1}, \ldots$. The information set $\mathcal{I}_t$ of firm one is $\mathcal{I}_t = \{y^t\}$. We assume conditional probability density functions exist for all the expressions we use. By the chain rule,

$$p(\theta, v_t, v_{t+1}, y_{t+1}|\mathcal{I}_t) = p(\theta, v_t|\mathcal{I}_t)p(v_{t+1}|\theta, v_t, \mathcal{I}_t) \cdot p(y_{t+1}|\theta, v_t, v_{t+1}, \mathcal{I}_t)$$

$$= p(\theta, v_t|\mathcal{I}_t)p(v_{t+1}|\theta, v_t)p(y_{t+1}|v_t) .$$

Also

$$p(\theta, v_{t+1}, y_{t+1}|\mathcal{I}_t) = p(y_{t+1}|\mathcal{I}_t)p(\theta, v_{t+1}|\mathcal{I}_{t+1}) .$$

Thus, we have a recursion formula for $p(\theta, v_t|\mathcal{I}_t)$,

(2.2)
$$p(\theta, v_{t+1}|\mathcal{I}_{t+1}) = \int p(\theta, v_t|\mathcal{I}_t)p(v_{t+1}|\theta, v_t)p(y_{t+1}|v_t)dv_t/p(y_{t+1}|\mathcal{I}_t) .$$

By definition

(2.3) $$v_{t+1|t+1} = \int v_{t+1} p(v_{t+1}|\vartheta_{t+1}) dv_{t+1}$$

where from (2.1),

(2.4) $$p(v_{t+1}|\vartheta_{t+1}) = \int p(\theta, v_{t+1}|\vartheta_{t+1}) d\theta .$$

Let

$$v_{t+1|t,\theta} = \mathcal{E}(v_{t+1}|\theta, \vartheta_t) .$$

From (2.2)

(2.5) $$v_{t+1|t,\theta} = E(\theta) v_{t|t,\theta} + \delta\bar{h}(\theta) w_t$$

where

$$v_{t|t,\theta} = \mathcal{E}(v_t|\theta, y^t)$$

is obtained by the usual recursive formula of the Kalman filter. From (2.3), (2.4) and (2.5)

$$v_{t+1|t+1} = \int v_{t+1|t,\theta} p(\theta, v_t|\vartheta_t) p(y_{t+1}|v_t) d\theta dv_t / p(y_{t+1}|\vartheta_t)$$

(2.6)
$$= \int \{E(\theta) v_{t|t,\theta} + \delta\bar{h}(\theta) w_t\} p(\theta, v_t|\vartheta_t) p(y_{t+1}|v_t) d\theta dv_t / p(y_{t+1}|\vartheta_t)$$

$$= \int \{E(\theta) v_{t|t,\theta} + \delta\bar{h}(\theta) w_t\} p(\theta|\vartheta_t) p(y_{t+1}|\theta, \vartheta_t) d\theta / p(y_{t+1}|\vartheta_t) .$$

In (2.6), $p(\theta|\vartheta_t)$ represents the "informational" state of firm one about the unknown parameter θ in its personal model of the market interaction.

Because of the nonlinearity present in $E(\theta)v_{t|t,\theta}$ it is not possible to obtain a closed form expression to this integral. In the above $p(y_{t+1}|\theta, \mathcal{I}_t)$ can be obtained in the usual way.

Note that even if v_{t+1} is exactly known, uncertainty is introduced into $v_{t+1|t}$ since from (2.5)

$$v_{t+1|t,\theta_1} - v_{t+1|t,\theta_2} = \{E(\theta_1) - E(\theta_2)\}v_t + \delta\{\overline{h}(\theta_1) - \overline{h}(\theta_2)\}w_t$$

$$= \delta\{\overline{h}(\theta_1) - \overline{h}(\theta_2)\}(f'v_t + w_t)$$

$$+ \text{diag}\{(h_2(\theta_1) - h_2(\theta_2))\beta_2, \ldots, (h_n(\theta_1) - h_n(\theta_2))\beta_n\}v_t.$$

This expression may be used in the min-max approach.

APPENDIX 3
INDUSTRY WIDE PROFIT MAXIMIZING OUTPUT

For use as a convenient benchmark against which the industry's performances can be judged, we obtain the expression for the profit maximizing outputs of n firms with no exogenous disturbances, when all the firms are under a single management with complete knowledge of their supply price schedules and $d(\cdot)$.

Suppose that $\Sigma_i q_{it}$ is given as a historical data. Assume that because of the adjustment cost (which is implicit in this model) only small adjustments are feasible.

The industry-wide profit maximization problem is restated then as

$$\max_{h_1, \ldots, h_n} \Sigma_{i=1}^{n}\{-s_i(q_{it} + \Delta q_{it}) + d(Q_t + \Sigma_i \Delta q_{it})\}(q_{it} + \Delta q_{it})$$

where q_{it}, $i=1, \ldots, n$ are given and where $\Delta q_{it} = h_i\{s_i(q_{it}) - d(Q_t)\}$. Then, we obtain as the first order condition

186

(3.1)

$$-s_i(q_{it}+\Delta q_{it}) + d(Q_t + \Sigma_j \Delta q_{jt})$$

$$+\{-s_i'(q_{it} + \Delta q_{it}) + d(Q_t + \Sigma_j \Delta q_{it})\}(q_{it} + \Delta q_{it}) = 0.$$

Under the assumption that h's are small in magnitude, we obtain up to $o(|h|)$,

$$\{-s_i'(q_{it}) + d'(Q_t)\}\Delta q_{it} + d'(Q_t)\Sigma_j \Delta q_{jt}$$

$$+\{-s_i''(q_{it})\Delta q_{it} + d''(Q_t)\Sigma_j \Delta q_{jt}\}q_{it}$$

(3.2)

$$+ \{-2s_i'(q_{it}) + d'(Q_t)\}\Delta q_{it} + d'(Q_t)\Sigma_j \Delta q_{jt}$$

$$+\{-s_i(q_{it}) + d(Q_t)\} = 0, \quad i=1,\ldots,n.$$

The second-order condition is given by

(3.3) $$\{-s_i''(q_{it}) + d''(Q_t)\}q_{it} + 2\{-s_i'(q_{it}) + d'(Q_t)\} < 0 .$$

It is convenient to write the optimal h's which solves (3.2) as

(3.4) $$h_{it}^* = \overline{h}_{it} + \tilde{h}_{it}$$

where

$$\overline{h}_{it} = N_i/D_i$$

$$N_i = -1+\{-s_i'(q_{it})+d'(Q_t)\}q_{it}/\{s_i(q_{it})-d(Q_t)\}$$

$$D_i = 2s_i'(q_{it})-d'(Q_t) + s_i''(q_{it})q_{it}$$

$$\tilde{h}_{it} = -\eta_t^* \{d'(Q_t) + d''(Q_t)\}/D_i$$

187

and where

$$\eta_t^* = \Sigma_{i=1}^n h_{it}^* = \{\Sigma_{i=1}^n N_i/D_i\}\Big/[1+\{d'(Q_t)+d''(Q_t)\}\Sigma_i 1/D_i].$$

When specialized to linear functions, it reduces to

$$\overline{h}_{it} = \{-s_i(q_{it})+p_t^*+(\beta_i+\delta)q_{it}\}/(2\beta_i+\delta)$$

and

(3.5)
$$\widetilde{h}_{it} = -\eta_t^* \delta/(2\beta_i+\delta) .$$

Equation (3.5) shows that firm i needs β_j, α_j, $j \neq i$, γ and δ to decide on the optimal output rate.

When $s_i(\cdot)$ and $d(\cdot)$ are affine, (3.4) gives rise to

$$\Delta q_{1t} = \Delta\overline{q}_{1t} + \Delta\widetilde{q}_{1t}$$

where

(3.6)
$$\Delta\overline{q}_{1t} = \{-(\beta_1+\delta)q_{1t} + p_t^* - s_1(q_{1t})\}/(2\beta_1+\delta)$$

and

$$\Delta\widetilde{q}_{1t} = \eta^* \delta(p_t^* - s_1(q_{1t}))/(2\beta_1+\delta)$$

where

$$\eta_t^* = [\Sigma\{-(\beta_i+\delta)q_{it} + p_t^* - s_i(q_{it})\}/(2\beta_i+\delta)]\Big/$$

$$[1 - \delta\Sigma 1/(2\beta_i+\delta)] .$$

NOTES

[1] By an economy with imperfect information we do not mean an economy of risk which does not involve any learning on the part of economic agents.

In economy of risk, all relevant information is assumed to be contained in some known joint probability distribution function which is a complete description of economy in a probabilistic sense. In this broader probabilistic sense, it still is an economy which perfect and complete information.

[2] This is called a decentralized information pattern in this paper.

[3] See Chapters III and IV of Aoki [1967] or Tse [1974] for further details.

[4] Another interesting question related to the topics of this paper is that of when and in what manner economic agents are forced to realize that their personal or subjective model of the economy are systematically denied or contradicted by observed data. See Hahn [1973] for a related view. The question is definitely a special case of the learning process in the sense that instead of modifying their subjective beliefs continually as new observation data becomes available, the original model is retained and the data is pooled until such time when the hypothesis of the original model is statistically accepted or rejected. This statistical hypothesis testing aspect will not be covered in this paper. See for example Aoki [1975].

[5] In a complete model the effort expended in reaching decisions must be incorporated in the utility function of economic agents at least implicitly. See for example Simon [1972].

[6] We consider the adjustment step size as the firm's decision-variable hence write it as h_t using the subscript t to indicate that h_t is the step size used on the t-th day. $h_t = h$ for all $t = 0, 1, \ldots, T$ for some finite $T > 0$ would be a special case to be considered later.

189

[7] The price adjusts "rapidly" during a market day according to an adjustment mechanism of the type

$$\Delta p_{i,t} = \lambda(D(p_{i,t}) - q_t), \quad i = 0, 1, \ldots$$

where i is the iteration index and where $D(\cdot)$ is a demand schedule, completing its adjustment within a single day. The price p_t^* thus obtained is the market clearing price at the end of the t-th market day.

[8] Let q_{jt}^* be such that $p_t^* = s_j(q_{jt}^*)$. Suppose that the supply price schedule is such that this output rate is uniquely determined. Then firm j's adjustment equation may equivalently be rewritten as

$$\Delta q_{jt} = h_{jt}[s_j(q_{jt}) - s_j(q_{jt}^*)] + \zeta_{j,t}$$

$$= h_{jt} \frac{\partial s_j}{\partial q}(q_{jt}^*)[q_{jt} - q_{jt}^*] + \zeta_{j,t}$$

provided either $s_j(\cdot)$ is affine or $q_{jt} - q_{jt}^*$ is sufficiently small if $s_j(\cdot)$ is not affine. We assume the former for simplicity, i.e., $s_j(q) = \alpha_j + \beta_j q$. Then the quantity adjustment equation (1) may be rewritten as

(1)'
$$\Delta q_{jt} = \gamma_j(q_{jt} - q_{jt}^*) + \zeta_{j,t}$$

where $\gamma_j = h_j \beta_j$ is the decision variable of firm j, and is the adjustment step size in closing the discrepancy between q_{jt} and q_{jt}^*. A nonstandard feature is that q_{jt}^* changes randomly with t and is affected by other firms. The adjustment equations (1) and (1)' are equivalent. We will use (1) in our discussion.

[9] With nonlinear supply price schedules, (5) is a linearized difference equation about some nominal time path.

190

[10]In other words, firm one assumes that other firms do not react to his occasional change in the step size very often. Although this assumption is analogous to that made in obtaining the Cournot solution of a duopoly problem, it is more general since this 'no reaction' assumption is not essential. To see this, rewrite Φ_t as $\Phi + \Psi_t$ as in Appendix 1. Firm one can then construct its personal model using $\Phi_t = \Phi + \Psi_t$ where firm one embodies as Ψ_t its belief on how likely other firms change their h's. In other words, firm one could have a class of possible adjustment step size changes as a class of possible Ψ_t with a subjective probability distribution over Ψ_t. Parameterizing this probability distribution by a vector ν in a compact set N, the problem may be formulated as a parameter adaptive decision problem. (In Appendix 2, θ would then include ν as its subvector.) An alternate procedure would be to assume $\|\Psi_t\| <$ const., and adopt a parameter adaptive min-max price prediction policy. This is quite reasonable since the h's of all firms come from a compact set in the n-dimensional Euclidean space by assumption. One needs to incorporate learning into the usual min-max scheme such as the one by Bertsekas and Rhodes [1973]. See also Appendix 2.

[11]When n_t is absent from (2) and consequently from (12), we cannot use the Kalman filter since one measurement is exact. In this case, we may use the method discussed by Rissanen [1967], for example.

[12]Alternately, we can assume $\Phi_t = \Phi + \varphi_t$ with $\|\varphi_t\| \le$ const. Then $p^*_{t+\tau \mid t}$ would be a closed interval on the real line instead of a point estimate.

[13]Other conditions on the boundedness of the second moments etc. are all satisfied for our problem (see Aoki [1974]).

[14]Assume other firms have not changed their adjustment step sizes. Thus, this procedure is useful in establishing the existence of Nash equilibrium.

[15]This ordering is used only in the proof. The main body of the paper is entirely independent of this ordering.

[16]For example $k_{jt} = 0(t^{-1-\delta})$, $\delta > 0$ suffices.

REFERENCES

Aoki, Masanao [1967], _Optimization of Stochastic Systems_, Academic Press, Inc., New York.

_____ [1975], "Inventory Level as a Signal to a Middleman with Imperfect Information," Working Paper No. 231, Department of Economics, Univ. Illinois, Feb. 10, 1975.

_____ [1974], "A stochastic Quantity Adjustment Model: An Example of Kiefer-Wolfowitz Like Stochastic Approximation Algorithm" presented at the North American Meeting of the Econometric Society, San Francisco, Dec. 28-30, 1974.

Bertsekas, D. P. and I. B. Rhodes [1971], "Recursive State Estimation for a Set Membership Description of Uncertainty," _IEEE Trans. Aut. Control_, _AC-16_, 117-128.

Britto, Ronald [1972], "Economic Systems Marked by Obsolescence of Information," Discussion Paper No. 29, Dept. of Economics, Univ. of Calif, Los Angeles.

Friedman, James W. [1971], "A Non-cooperative Equilibrium for Super-games," _Rev. Econ. Stud._ _38_, 1-12.

Hahn, F. [1973], _On the Notion of Equilibrium in Economics_, Cambridge Univ. Press.

Leijonhufvud, Axel [1974], "The Varieties of Price Theory: What Micro-foundations for Macrotheory," Discussion Paper No. 44, Dept. of Economics, Univ. of Calif., Los Angeles.

Lucas, Robert E., Jr. and E. C. Prescott [1971], "Investment Under Uncertainty," _Econometrica_, _39_, 659-683.

Miller, K. S. [1968], <u>Linear Difference Equations</u>, W. A. Benjamin, Inc.,
New York.

Polyak, B. T. and Ya. Z. Tsypkin [1972], "Pseudogradient Adaptation
and Training Algorithms," <u>Automation and Remote Control</u>, 45-68.

Rissanen, J. [1967], "An Algebraic Approach to the Problems of Linear
Prediction and Identification," Tech. Report, IBM Research Lab.,
San Jose, Calif.

Simon, H. A. [1972], "Theories of Bounded Rationality," in <u>Decisions
and Organization</u>, McGuire, C. B. and R. Rachner, eds., North
Holland, Amsterdam.

Tse, E. [1974], "Adaptive Dual Control Methods," 3 <u>Am. Econ. Soc.
Measurements</u>, 65-83.

Wilkinson, J. H. [1965], <u>Algebraic Eigenvalue Problem</u>, Clarendon Press,
Oxford, England.

Further Notes on the Allocation of Effort
Michael Rothschild

CONTENTS

1. INTRODUCTION

This paper continues the analysis of a non-optimizing model of administrative behavior which Roy Radner and I introduced elsewhere. The basic model is described briefly in section 2.1, the remainder of part 2 is given to a statement and explanation of the results of the present paper. These include: an exploration of the properties of an alternative concept of long run success; a generalization (to non-Markovian environments) of an earlier result which gives conditions under which "putting out fires" can succeed and a discussion of the costs and disadvantages of "putting out fires" in a particularly simple non-Markovian environment. The exotic terms of the preceeding sentence are defined as they are introduced. Proofs are given in part 3.

Lengthier discussion of motivation and interpretation will be found in Radner and Rothschild [1975], which I shall refer to below as RR, and in Radner [1975] which uses this model (and others of similar spirit) to analyze the problems of guiding technological change and choosing techniques of production.

2. STATEMENT OF RESULTS

2.1. A Model of the Allocation of Effort

In the paper mentioned, Roy Radner and I analyzed the following situation: An agent is in charge of I distinct activities. At time t the performance level of activity i is $U_i(t)$. Although the agent is responsible for all I activities, his ability to control them is severely limited. In the first place, regardless of his actions, the evolution of $U(t) = (U_1(t), \ldots, U_I(t))$ is stochastic. More importantly, he can only devote himself to one activity at a time and while his efforts are generally successful (attended activities tend to improve), their absence is likely to be harmful (neglected activities deteriorate). The agent's problem is to choose a rule for allocating his effort or attention among the various competing activities.

A formal version of this model is as follows: The allocation of the agent's effort at time t is determined by a vector $a(t) = (a_1(t), \ldots, a_I(t))$ satisfying $a_i(t) \geq 0$; $\Sigma\, a_i(t) = 1$. Here I shall consider only cases where the $a_i(t)$ are equal to 1 or 0; fractional allocations, which are discussed in RR, can arise from mixed strategies or because the agent is actually able to divide his attention among several activities. The allocation vector $a(t)$ affects the evolution of $U(\cdot)$ through its effects on the increments of $U(\cdot)$, $Z(t+1) \equiv U(t+1) - U(t)$. Thus, the distribution of $Z(t+1) = (Z_1(t+1), \ldots, Z_I(t+1))$ is determined by $a(t)$ and, possibly, by the past history of the process. We modeled the influence of the allocation of effort by assuming

196

(M.1) $$E\, Z_i(t+1) = a_i(t)\eta_i - (1-a_i(t))\xi_i$$

where η_i and ξ_i are given positive parameters. We further assumed that:

(M.2) the distribution of $Z(t+1)$ is determined solely by $a(t)$;

and that,

(M.2) given $a(t)$, the coordinates of $Z(t+1)$ are mutually independent.

In the sequel, I shall refer to assumptions (M.1), (M.2) and (M.3) as the Markov assumptions. In addition to these three assumptions we made some regularity assumptions very similar to the following conditions, which I shall adopt in this paper:

(R.1) $Z_i(t+1)$ is integer valued;

(R.2) $|Z_i(t+1)| < b$ for some $b > 0$;

and

if $H = \{h \in R^I \mid |h_i| = 1, \ i = 1, \ldots, I\}$,

(R.3) then there exists $\gamma > 0$ such that for all values of $a(t)$, all past histories of events up to and including time t, and $h \in H$,

$$\mathbb{P}\{Z(t+1) = h \mid a(t)\} > \gamma .$$

This last assumption has two purposes. It ensures that the stochastic process governing the evolution of $U(t)$ is not degenerate. Also, by stating that $U(t)$ can move in any direction, it eliminates the need for obvious qualifications and tiresome combinatoric arguments.

As usual, the underlying probability structure is represented by the triple $(\Omega, \mathfrak{F}, \mathbb{P})$. $\mathfrak{F}_o, \mathfrak{F}_1, \ldots, \mathfrak{F}_t, \ldots$ is a sequence of increasing sub-sigma fields of $\mathfrak{F}$; $\mathfrak{F}_t$ represents the events observed up to and including date t. Thus a variable dated t, such as $U(t)$, $a(t)$ or $Z(t)$, is $\mathfrak{F}_s$-measureable as long as $t \leq s$. I shall use a.s. as an abbreviation for events of $\mathbb{P}$ measure 1.

2.2. Alternative Concepts of Survival

This model can be used to analyze a number of different questions. One of the most natural is determining whether the manager can control all I activities simultaneously or whether his attempts to look after them all will lead naturally to disaster for one or more of the activities. Earlier we defined survival as keeping all indices above some arbitrary level for all time and asked whether or not it was possible to survive. Formally, if

$$(1) \qquad M(t) \equiv \min_i U_i(t),$$

survival is possible if

$$(2) \qquad \mathbb{P}\{M(t) > 0, \text{ all } t\} > 0 .$$

The notion of "being in control" is captured somewhat more sharply by a different notion. If

$$(3) \qquad \lim \inf M(t) = \infty, \quad \text{a.s.},$$

then I shall say the manager eventually succeeds. There are three reasons for believing that (3) is at least as interesting a property as (2). First it is more pleasing to know that events in which one is interested will occur almost surely than to know that there is some positive (but possibly very small) probability that they will occur. Secondly, one can show that if the manager eventually succeeds, things get better and better in the sense that for any arbitrary level of performance, L, and any $\varepsilon > 0$, there is a (non-random) time T such that with probability at least $1-\varepsilon$, $M(t) \geq L$ for all $t \geq T$. Finally eventual success implies there is, with arbitrarily high probability, a limit to how bad things get in the sense that for every $\varepsilon > 0$ there is a finite $B(\varepsilon)$ such that $M(t) \geq B(\varepsilon)$ for all t with probability at least $1-\varepsilon$. The following Proposition demonstrates that these are the implications of eventual success.

PROPOSITION 1. If $\lim\inf M(t) = \infty$, a.s. then

(i)   For every L, and every $\varepsilon > 0$, there exists $T(L, \varepsilon)$ such that

$$\mathbb{P}\{M(t) \geq L, \text{ all } t \geq T(L, \varepsilon)\} \geq 1-\varepsilon \ .$$

(ii) For every $\varepsilon > 0$, there exists $B(\varepsilon)$ such that

$$\mathbb{P}\{M(t) \geq B(\varepsilon) \text{ all } t\} \geq 1-\varepsilon \ .$$

All proofs are in Part 3.

The two concepts (2) and (3) are, despite their different meanings, quite closely related. Whether the manager can survive or will eventually succeed depends on two things: the distribution of the $Z(t)$'s and the rules used to determine the allocation of attention. In RR we showed for the Markov case, that there was a simple test for determining whether any policy could survive. Specifically, we showed that if

(4)
$$\bar{\zeta} \equiv (1 - \sum_{i} \frac{\xi_i}{\eta_i + \xi_i})/\sum_{i} (\eta_i + \xi_i)^{-1}$$

then $\bar{\zeta} > 0$ was a necessary and sufficient condition for the existence of any policy which has a positive probability of survival. It is trivial to adapt the argument of RR to prove that $\bar{\zeta} > 0$ is also a necessary and sufficient conditions for the existence of any policy which will eventually succeed. Thus $\bar{\zeta}$, a simple function of the conditional means of the distribution of the $Z_i(t)$, emerges as a natural measure of the difficulty of a task facing a manager. If $\bar{\zeta} \leq 0$ the task is impossible; nothing he does can lead survival. If $\bar{\zeta} > 0$, he can, if he chooses the right policy, eventually succeed.

If survival is possible, relatively simple policies can bring it about. In RR we described two. Both policies also will, if $\bar{\zeta} > 0$, eventually succeed. The first, balanced growth, is a behavior in which the allocation of effort is constant. Let

$$(5) \qquad \hat{a}_i = \frac{\bar{\zeta} + \xi_i}{\eta_i + \xi_i} ,$$

then $\Sigma \hat{a}_i = 1$ and if $\bar{\zeta} > 0$, $\hat{a}_i \geq 0$. Consider the behavior which simply sets $a_i(t) = \hat{a}_i$ for all i and t.

It is easy to see that, for the Markov case,

$$E[Z_i(t+1) | a_i(t) = \hat{a}_i] = \bar{\zeta}$$

so that the law of large numbers implies

$$\lim \frac{U_i(t)}{t} = \bar{\zeta} \quad \text{a.s.}$$

from which it follows that $\lim \frac{M(t)}{t} = \bar{\zeta}$ a.s.. Clearly this behavior will eventually succeed.

2.3. Putting Out Fires

Another simple rule which will eventually succeed when $\bar{\zeta} > 0$, is what we called "putting out fires." This is the policy in which all attention is allocated to the activity which is currently performing worst -- apparently a very common kind of administrative behavior. Formally we may define putting out fires by

(6)

(i)   if $U_i(t) \neq M(t)$, then $a_i(t) = 0$;

(ii) if $U_i(t) = M(t)$ and $a_i(t-1) = 1$, then $a_i(t) = 1$;

(iii) if neither (i) nor (ii) holds, then $a_i(t) = 1$ for $i =$ the smallest j such that $U_j(t) = M(t)$.

A notable feature of putting out fires behavior is that, in contrast to the constant proportions behavior described above, it can be pursued without knowledge of the parameters determining the distribution of $Z(t+1)$.

RR proved, again for the Markov case, that if $\overline{\zeta} > 0$ and putting out fires is followed, then the policy will eventually succeed (and survival is possible).

The purpose of this paper is to extend and qualify these results, which seem at once too weak and too strong. They appear too weak because they are restricted to the rather special Markov case; they are too strong because they seem to imply that putting out fires, which is often criticized as being a poor administrative strategy, is as good a rule as any in the sense that putting out fires will eventually succeed when any thing will; if putting out fires fails, nothing will work. These two defects are related. Putting out fires is, I believe, thought to be a bad strategy because it involves too much changing about and such changes are costly. These costs cannot be modeled easily within the Markov framework. Suppose the Markov assumptions are replaced by the much weaker assumptions below, which state in essence only that allocating effort to an activity leads to expected gains and withholding effort causes expected losses:

(G.1) $$E[Z_i(t+1) | a_i(t) = 1, \; \mathcal{F}_t] \geq \eta_i$$

(G. 2) $\qquad -\beta > E[Z_i(t+1)|a_i(t) = 0, \ \mathfrak{Z}_t] \geq -\xi_i$

where β, η_i and ξ_i are given positive numbers. Then, if $\bar{\zeta}$ is defined as in (1.4) above, its positivity is still a sufficient condition for putting out fires to succeed eventually.

THEOREM 1:   Define for each i

(7) $\qquad \zeta_i \equiv (1 - \sum_{j \neq i} \frac{\xi_i}{\eta_j + \xi_j})/\sum_{j \neq i} (\eta_j + \xi_j)^{-1}$.

If there is "putting out fires", assumptions (R.1-3) and (G.1-2) are satisfied, and if $\zeta_i > 0$ for $i = 1, \ldots, I$, then

$$\liminf \frac{U_i(t)}{t} \geq \bar{\zeta} \quad a.s. \quad i = 1, \ldots, I,$$

and if $\bar{\zeta} > 0$, then

$$\liminf M(t) = \infty \quad a.s.$$

Note that $\bar{\zeta} > 0$ implies $\zeta_i > 0$ for $i = 1, \ldots, I$ but that the converse does not hold; even for the Markov case this result is a slight strengthening of Theorem 3 of RR.

2.4. Costs of Putting out Fires

We now consider a model in which following putting out fires behavior may be ill-advised because of a cost involved in switching from one activity to another; in such a situation, wise policies would, as putting out fires does not, economize on the number of such switches. The simplest possible model is the following: Suppose that the allocation of effort is indivisible so that $a_i(t) = 0$ or $a_i(t) = 1$. Let $m(t)$ be the activity to which effort is allocated at time t. Let $s(t)$ be the number of consecutive periods immediately preceeding (but excluding) period t during which attention has been allocated to activity $m(t)$. Thus if

202

$m(t) = a_i(t)$ while $m(t-1) \neq a_i(t)$, then $s(t) = 0$; if $m(t) = m(t-1) = $,
..., $m(t-\tau) = a_i(t)$ while $m(t - (\tau+1)) \neq a_i$, then $s(t) = \tau$.

Now suppose that, given $\mathcal{F}_t$,

(8.a)   the distribution of $Z(t+1)$ is determined by $a(t)$ and $s(t)$,

and

(8.b) $E\, Z_i(t+1) = a_i(t)(\eta_i + \delta_{is(t)}) - (1-a_i(t))\xi_i$,

where for each i, $\{\delta_{is}\}$ is a bounded sequence of non-negative numbers
such that

(9.a) $\delta_{io} = 0$,

(9.b) $\delta_{is} \leq \delta_{i,s+1}$,

and

(9.c) $\delta_{is} > 0$ for some s .

The specification (8) and (9) captures the notion that there is
a cost to switching attention often and that there are increasing returns
to continuing to do the same thing. I shall show this formally below.
The criterion used to measure quality of performance is the long run rate
of growth of the $U_i(t)$'s   which is defined to be

$$R_i \equiv \lim\, U_i(t)/t, \quad a.s.$$

when that limit exists. Recalling the definition of ζ_i, (7), the following theorem is the first result about growth rates.

THEOREM 2:   Suppose assumptions (8) and (9) hold and putting
out fires is followed. If $\zeta_i > 0$, $i=1,\ldots,I$, then the growth rates R_i
exist and are equal to one another. This common growth rate, R^1, exceeds $\overline{\zeta}$.

It is appropriate to examine the costs of putting-out-fires be-havior as contrasted with behaviors which involve less frequent real-locations of attention. Consider in particular the following class of be-haviors which I shall call putting-out-fires-with-delay d or simply d -- delay behaviors:

(10.a)   i)   If $s(t-1) < d-1$, then $a_i(t) = a_i(t-1)$.

(10.b)   ii)   If $s(t-1) \geq d-1$, then putting-out-fires behavior is followed.

If $d = 1$ then (10) is simply putting out fires. If d exceeds unity then the agent is required to attend an activity d consecutive times before switching to a new activity. The consequence of following a d-delay behavior is very similar to that of putting out fires.

THEOREM 3:   If a d-delay behavior is followed and if $\zeta_i > 0$, i=1,...,I then all activities grow at a common rate $R^d > \overline{\zeta}$.

To show that putting out fires, or more generally unnecessary switching of attention is costly, it would be nice to show that R^d is monotone increasing in d. I have not been able to do this[1] however, a somewhat weaker result in the same spirit can be proved.

THEOREM 4:   Under the conditions of Theorem 3, the limit $R^\infty = \lim_{d \to \infty} R^d$ exists and $R^d < R^\infty$ for all finite d.

Theorem 4 shows that if (9) holds then putting out fires is a policy which leads to a lower growth rate than other policies which change al-locations less frequently. This paper closes with a demonstration that the costs of too frequent switching may be more dramatic; specifically, I give an example where putting out fires cannot survive but for large enough d, putting out fires with a delay of d will eventually succeed. Let $\xi > 0$ and $\eta > 0$ be such that

$$(I - 1) \frac{\xi}{(\eta+\xi)} < 1$$

while

$$I \frac{\xi}{(\eta+\xi)} > 1$$

or

(11)
$$I^{-1}\eta - (1 - I^{-1})\xi < 0$$

If for all i, $\eta_i = \eta$ and $\xi_i = \xi$, then $\bar{\zeta}_j > 0$, $j=1,\ldots,I$ and $\bar{\zeta} < 0$.
Choose δ so that

(12)
$$I^{-1}\eta - (1-I^{-1})\xi + \delta > 0 .$$

Fix $S > 0$ and suppose that for all i

$$\delta_{is} = \begin{cases} 0, & \text{for } s < S \\ \\ \delta, & \text{for } s \geq S . \end{cases}$$

Theorem 3 implies that if a d-delay policy is adopted, all activities grow at the rate R^d .

The symmetry of the example implies that

(13)
$$R^d = I^{-1}\eta - (1 - I^{-1})\xi_i + a_S^d \delta$$

where a_S^d is the relative frequency of the event $M(t) = i$ and $s(t) \geq S$. For fixed d, a_S^d is a function of S, in fact $\lim\limits_{S \to \infty} a_S^d = 0$; (11) implies it is possible to pick S so that $R^1 < 0$. If the common rate of growth of all activities when putting out fires is followed, R^1, is negative then $\lim\limits_{i} U_i(t) \to -\infty$ a.s. and survival is not possible.

However, for S fixed, $\lim\limits_{d \to \infty} a_S^d \to 1$ so that (12) implies $R^\infty > 0$; with S fixed there is a $\hat{d}$ such that $R^d > 0$ for all $d > \hat{d}$. $R^d > 0$ implies for all i $\lim\limits_i U_i(t) = +\infty$ which in turn implies the d-delay policy eventually succeeds.

3. PROOFS

3.1. Proposition 1

(i) Let $\omega \in \Omega$ be any realization of the stochastic process. Let $M(t, \omega)$ be the value of M at time t for ω. Consider $Y_t(\omega) = \text{Min}[M(t,\omega), L+\delta]$ for some $\delta > 0$. Then $Y_t \to L+\delta$ a.s. and Egorov's Theorem implies that for every $\varepsilon > 0$ there is a set F with $\mathbb{P}(F) \geq 1-\varepsilon$ such that $Y_t(\omega) \to L+\delta$ uniformly on F. The conclusion follows.

(ii) Assumption (R.2) implies $|M(t) - M(t-1)| < b$. Fix L and ε and let $B(\varepsilon) = L - T(L, \varepsilon)b$. The conclusion follows.

3.2. Theorem 1

The proof of Theorem 1 follows from the following proposition which is of some independent interest. Let $D(t) \equiv \max\limits_{i \in I} U_i(t) - \min\limits_{j \in I} U_j(t)$.

PROPOSITION 2. Under the conditions of Theorem 1 there exist positive numbers G, H, and K, such that, if s is a date for which $D(s) \geq G$ and $(s+T^*)$ is the first subsequent date for which $D(s+T^*) < G$ then

$$\mathbb{P}\{T^* > n \mid \mathfrak{F}_s\} \leq He^{-nK}, \quad n \geq 0.$$

REMARK. This implies that $E(T^*)$ is finite as

$$ET^* = \sum_n \Pr\{T^* \geq n\} \leq \sum_n He^{-nK} = \frac{H}{(1-e^{-K})} \cdot$$

PROOF OF THEOREM 1. We may without loss, set s = 0.

LEMMA 1.　　Proposition 2 implies

$$\frac{U_i(t)}{t} - \frac{U_j(t)}{t} \to 0, \quad \text{a.s.}$$

PROOF.　　Since $|U_i(t) - U_j(t)| < D(t)$, it will suffice to show $\frac{D(t)}{t} \to 0$ a.s.　No generality is lost if it is assumed that $D(0) \le G$. Let $A_0 = 0$ and for $n=1,2,\ldots$ define B_n as the first date $t > A_{n-1}$ such that $D(t) > G$ and A_n as the first date $t > B_n$ such that $D(t) \le G$. If $B_n \le t < A_n$, then

$$D(t) \le D(B_n - 1) + (t - B_n + 1)b$$

$$\le G + (A_n - 1 - B_n + 1)b$$

$$= G + (A_n - B_n)b,$$

and hence

$$\frac{D(t)}{t} \le \frac{G}{t} + \frac{A_n - B_n}{t}b \le \frac{G}{t} + \frac{A_n - B_n}{n}b \ .$$

Thus $\lim \sup \frac{D(t)}{t} \le \lim \sup \left[\frac{G}{t} + \frac{A_n - B_n}{n}b \right] = b \lim \sup \frac{A_n - B_n}{n}$.

To prove the Lemma, it will suffice to show that

$$\lim \sup \frac{A_n - B_n}{n} = 0 \quad \text{a.s.}$$

For any $\varepsilon > 0$, let E_n be the event that $\frac{A_n - B_n}{n} \ge \varepsilon$ and define $\mathscr{G}_{n-1} \equiv \mathcal{F}_{B_n}$.

Proposition 2 implies $\mathbb{P}\{(A_n - B_n) \ge n\varepsilon \,|\, \mathscr{G}_{n-1}\} \le H\,e^{-Kn\varepsilon}$.　　Let X_n be the indicator of E_n, and $\mu_n = E[X_n \,|\, \mathscr{G}_{n-1}] \le H\,e^{-Kn\varepsilon}$; then $\Sigma \mu_n < \infty$. We conclude from Freedman [1973, p. 919, Proposition (32)] that $\Sigma X_n < \infty$ a.s.　In other words, almost surely, only a finite number of the events E_n occur or $\lim \sup \dfrac{B_n - A_n}{n} < \varepsilon$, a.s. Since this holds

for all $\varepsilon > 0$, it follows that $\lim \sup \dfrac{B_n - A_n}{n} = 0$ a.s.

LEMMA 2. Let $\overline{U}(t) = \sum\limits_i w_i U_i(t)$ where $w_i = (\eta_i + \xi_i)^{-1} / \sum\limits_j (\eta_j + \xi_j)^{-1}$.

Then $\lim \inf \dfrac{\overline{U}(t)}{t} \geq \overline{\zeta}$ a.s.

PROOF. Let $\overline{Z}(t+1) = \overline{U}(t+1) - \overline{U}(t)$; then $\overline{Z}(t+1) = \sum w_i Z_i(t+1)$

and

$$E \overline{Z}(t+1) = \sum_i w_i E Z_i(t+1)$$

$$\geq \sum_i w_i [a_i(t)\eta_i - (1 - a_i(t)\xi_i]$$

$$= \sum_i w_i [a_i(t)(\eta_i + \xi_i) - \xi_i] = \overline{\zeta} .$$

Thus if $\overline{\mu}(t) = E[\overline{Z}(t) \mid \mathfrak{F}_{t-1}]$, $\overline{\mu}(t) \geq \overline{\zeta}$. Consider

$$\frac{\overline{U}(t)}{t} = \frac{\displaystyle\sum_1^t \overline{Z}(\tau)}{t} = \frac{\displaystyle\sum_1^t \overline{Z}(\tau)}{t \displaystyle\sum_1^t \overline{\mu}(\tau)} \cdot \frac{\displaystyle\sum_1^t \overline{\mu}(\tau)}{t}$$

$$\geq \overline{\zeta} \; \frac{\displaystyle\sum_1^t \overline{Z}(\tau)}{t \displaystyle\sum_1^t \overline{\mu}(\tau)}$$

Since

$$\lim \frac{\displaystyle\sum_1^t \overline{Z}(\tau)}{t \displaystyle\sum_1^t \mu(\tau)} = 1 \text{ a.s. } [\text{Freedman, 1973, Theorem (40)}]$$

it follows that

$$\lim \inf \frac{\overline{U}(t)}{t} \geq \overline{\zeta} \text{ a.s.},$$

which proves Lemma 2.

To prove Theorem 1 it remains only to observe that, for every k,

$$\overline{\zeta} \leq \lim \inf \frac{\overline{U}(t)}{t} = \lim \inf \sum_i w_i \frac{U_i(t)}{t}$$

$$= \lim \inf \sum_i w_i \frac{U_k(t)}{t} = \lim \inf \frac{U_k(t)}{t}, \text{ a.s.}$$

The next to the last step follows from Lemma 1.

PROOF OF PROPOSITION 2.   The proof is by induction on I. Clearly the proposition holds for $I = 1$. The induction step, that if it holds for $I = J-1$ then it is true for $I = J$, closely parallels the proof of Proposition 2 in RR. As in that paper, the proof is given in three Lemmas.

LEMMA 3.   Suppose $\mathcal{K}$ is any proper subset of $\mathcal{J} = \{1, \ldots, J\}$, that $\mathcal{K}'$ is the complement of $\mathcal{K}$ in $\mathcal{J}$ and that putting out fires is practiced on the activities in $\mathcal{K}$ while no effort is allocated to those in $\mathcal{K}'$. Then there is a (non-random) T such that

(14.a) $$E \min_{k \in \mathcal{K}} U_k(t) \geq \min_{k \in \mathcal{K}} U_k(0) + 1 \text{ for all } t \geq T$$

(14.b) $$E \max_{k \in \mathcal{K}'} U_k(t) \leq \max_{k \in \mathcal{K}'} U_k(0) - 1 \text{ for all } t \geq T.$$

T can be chosen so that (14) holds for any $\mathcal{K}$ properly contained in $\mathcal{J}$.

PROOF.   Consider the activities in $\mathcal{K}$ alone.   Let

(15) $$\overline{\zeta}_{\mathcal{K}} \equiv (1 - \sum_{k \in \mathcal{K}} \frac{\xi_k}{\eta_k + \xi_k}) / \sum_{k \in \mathcal{K}} (\eta_k + \xi_k)^{-1}$$

209

Comparing (15) and (7) we see that $\bar{\zeta}_{\mathcal{X}} > 0$ whenever $\zeta_j > 0$, $j=1,\ldots,I$ so that the induction hypothesis implies Proposition 2, and thus Theorem 1, holds when putting out fires is followed on the activities in $\mathcal{X}$ alone. Thus, for any $k \epsilon \mathcal{X}$

$$(16) \qquad \liminf \frac{U_k(t)}{t} \geq \bar{\zeta}_{\mathcal{X}} \; ; \; a.s.$$

and

$$(17) \qquad \liminf \frac{1}{t} \min_{k\epsilon\mathcal{X}} U_k(t) \geq \bar{\zeta}_{\mathcal{X}} \; a.s.$$

Since the increments of $U_k(t)$ are uniformly bounded by b,

$$\left| \min_{k\epsilon\mathcal{X}} \frac{U_k(t)}{t} \right| \leq b \; ;$$

we may apply the Lebesgue Monotone convergence theorem and the Fatou-Lebesgue theorem to conclude that

$$\liminf E \frac{1}{t} \min_{k\epsilon\mathcal{X}} U_k(t) \geq \bar{\zeta}_{\mathcal{X}}$$

and

$$E \liminf \frac{1}{t} \min_{k\epsilon\mathcal{X}} U_k(t) \geq \bar{\zeta}_{\mathcal{X}} .$$

It follows that

$$\liminf E \min_{k\epsilon\mathcal{X}} U_k(t) \to +\infty ,$$

and there exists $T_{\mathcal{X}}$ such that $t > T_{\mathcal{X}}$ implies

$$E \min_{k\epsilon\mathcal{X}} U_k(t) > \min_{k\epsilon\mathcal{X}} U_k(0) + 1.$$

If no attention is paid to an activity then (G. 2) states that $E Z_k(t) < -\beta$. It follows in a straightforward way from Theorem (40) of Freedman [1973] that,

210

$$\lim \sup \max_{k \in \mathcal{X}'} \frac{U_k(t)}{t} \leq -\beta.$$

Another application of Lebesgue and Lebesgue-Fatou produces

$$\lim \sup E \max_{k \in \mathcal{X}'} U_k(t) \rightarrow -\infty ,$$

so that there is a $T'_{\mathcal{X}}$ such that $t > T'_{\mathcal{X}}$ implies

$$E \max_{k \in \mathcal{X}'} U_k(t) < \max_{k \in \mathcal{X}'} U_k(0) - 1.$$

Letting $T = \max (\max(T_{\mathcal{X}}, T'_{\mathcal{X}}))$ where $\mathcal{X}$ ranges over all proper subsets of $\mathcal{J}$ completes the proof.

LEMMA 4.   Let $D(t) = \underset{i}{Max} \ U_i(t) - \underset{j}{min} \ U_j(t)$, and $G = 2JT(b+1)$; if $D(0) > G$, then $E \ D(t) < D(0) - 2$ where T is as in Lemma 1.

PROOF.   This lemma is identical to and has the same proof as Lemma 2 of RR.

LEMMA 5.   Suppose $G < D(0) < 2 Jb+G$. Let T^* be the first t such that $D(T^*) \leq G$. There exist H and K such that $\mathbb{P}(T^* > t) \leq H \ e^{-Kt}$.

PROOF.   Let $D = D(0)$ and consider the random variables $X_n \equiv D(nT) - D[(n-1)T)]$, where T is as in Lemma 1.

Let $\mathcal{L}_n = \mathcal{F}_{nT}$; $\mathcal{L}_n$ is an increasing sequence of sigma fields and X_n is $\mathcal{L}_n$-measurable. Furthermore, if $Y_n = \overset{n}{\underset{m=1}{\Sigma}} X_m$, then $D(nT) = D + Y_n$. Let $C = G - D$. Then $-C \leq 2bJ$. If $Y_n \leq C$ then $D(nT) \leq G$. Let N^* be the first N such that $Y_{N^*} \leq C$. It will suffice to show that there exist H' and K' such that for all $n > 2JB$

211

(18) $$\mathbb{P}\{N^* > n\} \leq H'e^{-K'n} \ .$$

The random variables X_n, Y_n have the following properties

(19) $$|X_n| \leq B$$

where $B = 2JTb$ and Lemma 2 implies $E[X_n | Y_{n-1} > C] < -2$.
Let

$$W_n \equiv \frac{X_n + B}{2B}$$

$$S_n \equiv \sum_1^n W_m = \frac{Y_n + nB}{2B}$$

$$R_n \equiv E[W_n | \mathcal{J}_{n-1}] \ .$$

Suppose

(20) $$n > 2Jb \geq -C \ ;$$

if $N^* > n$, then $Y_n > C$ and $R_m < \dfrac{-2+B}{2B}$ for $m = 1, \ldots, n$ so that

$$S_n > \frac{C+nB}{2B} \equiv a_n \quad \text{and} \quad \sum_1^n R_m < \frac{n(-2+B)}{2B} \equiv b_n \ .$$

Since (20) implies $a_n > b_n$ we may use (4.b) of Freedman [1973] to conclude that

(21) $$\mathbb{P}[N^* > n] \leq \exp\left[-\frac{(a_n - b_n)^2}{a_n}\right] \ .$$

Note that $(a_n - b_n)^2/2a_n = (C + 2n)^2/4B(C + nB) = ((C + 2n)/4B)f(n)$ where $f(n) = (C + 2n)/(C + B_n)$, an increasing function of n since $B > 2$. It follows from (20) that $(a_n - b_n)^2/2an \geq ((C + 2n)/4B)f(-c) = ((c + 2n)/4B)(B-1)^{-1}$. Thus (21) implies $\mathbb{P}\{N^* > n\} < \exp-[(C + 2n)/4B(B-1)]$, for $n > 2Jb$. This is (18) with $H' = \exp-[C/4B(B-1)]$ and $K' = (2B(B-1))^{-1}$. This proves Proposition 2.

3.3. Theorem 2

Again the proof follows from a proposition of some independent interest.

Let $V_i(t) \equiv U_i(t) - M(t)$, $V(t) = (v_1(t), \ldots, V_I(t))$ and consider the Markov chain

$$(22) \qquad C(t) = (m(t), s(t), V(t)) .$$

PROPOSITION 3. $C(t)$ is positive recurrent.

PROOF OF THEOREM 2. Since $C(t)$ is positive recurrent, the long run relative frequency of the events $m(t) = i$ and $s(t) = s$ converges almost surely to the invariant probability of that event, say a_{is}. Since $C(t)$ has a single class, the a_{is} are strictly positive numbers; furthermore $\sum_{i=1}^{I} \sum_{s=0}^{\infty} a_{is} = 1$. Let $\bar{a}_i = \sum_{s=0}^{\infty} a_{is}$. Then a straightforward generalization of Theorem 2.b of RR implies that, R_i exists for all i and that

$$(23) \qquad R_i = \bar{a}_i \eta_i - (1-\bar{a}_i)\xi_i + \sum_{s=1}^{\infty} a_{is}\delta_{is} .$$

Now suppose $R_i > R_j$ for some i and j. Recall that

$$V_i(t) = U_i(t) - M(t) \geq U_i(t) - U_j(t) .$$

But this last quantity diverges to $+\infty$ almost surely, which contradicts

213

Proposition 3. Therefore all activities must grow at the same rate.

It only remains to show that this common rate, R^1, exceeds $\bar{\zeta}$.
Recall from (5) that there exists a set of numbers $\hat{a}_i$ such that $\sum \hat{a}_i = 1$ and

$$(24) \qquad \hat{a}_1 \eta_i - (1-\hat{a}_i)\xi_i = \bar{\zeta}, \quad i=1,\ldots,I .$$

Since $\sum_i \bar{a}_i = 1$ it follows that there is an index j such that $\bar{a}_j \geq \hat{a}_j$.
Combining (23) and (24) we get

$$\bar{\zeta} = \hat{a}_j \eta_j - (1-\hat{a}_j)\xi_j \leq \bar{a}_j \eta_j - (1-\bar{a}_j)\xi_j$$

$$< \bar{a}_j \eta_j - (1-\bar{a}_j)\xi_j + \sum_{s=1}^{\infty} \delta_{js} a_{js} = R^1 .$$

The second inequality is strict since (9.c) and the fact that all a_{js}'s
are strictly positive imply $\sum_{s=1}^{\infty} \delta_{js} a_{js} > 0$.

PROOF OF PROPOSITION 3. Since $C(t)$ has a single class, it
will suffice to show that the expected time to return to a finite set of
states is finite. As before, let $D(t) \equiv \max_i U_i(t) - \min_j U_j(t) = \max_i V_i(t)$.
Let G be as in Proposition 2 above. Let B be the set of states,
(m, s, V), such that $\max_i V_i < G$. Let A be the set of states in B
such that $s = 0$. The number of states in A is finite; I will prove
Proposition 3 by showing that the expected time to return to A is finite.
Suppose $C(t_0) \in A$, and let t_1 be the first date $t > t_0$ such that
$C(t_1) \notin A$; if $t_1 + T$ is the first date $t > t_1$ such that $C(t_1 + T) \in A$, then
what must be proved is that $ET < \infty$. I assume, without loss of generality, that $t_1 = 0$. Let n_1 be the first date $t > 0$ such that $C(n_1) \notin B$.
Let N_1 be the first date $t > n_1$ such that $C(N_1) \in B$. Define n_2, N_2,
n_3, N_3, ... similarly. In an obvious terminology call the period N_k
to $n_{k+1} - 1$ the length of time of the kth visit to B. During the kth
visit to B the process either visits A or leaves B without visiting A.

(Recall that $A \subset B$.) Let k^* be the first k such that $C(t)$ visits A during its kth visit to B; k is, of course, random. From these definitions it follows that $T \leq N_{k^*+1}$ so that it will suffice to show that $E\, N_{k^*+1} < \infty$. This is accomplished in three Lemmas.

LEMMA 6. There is an L such that $E\, N_k \leq kL$ for all k.

PROOF. By assumption $D(0) < G$. If $D(t)$ increases by 1 for $t = 1, 2, \ldots, G$ then $D(G) \geq G$ and n_1, the first date t at which $D(t) \geq G$, is less than G. By (R.3) the probability of this happening is at least γ^G so that $\mathbb{P}(n_1 \geq G) \leq 1 - \gamma^G$. Similarly if $D(t)$ increases by 1 for $t = G+1, G+2, \ldots, 2G$, then $D(2G) \geq G$. Again the probability of this happening is at least γ^G. Thus $\mathbb{P}\{n_1 \geq 2G\} \leq (1 - \gamma^G)^2$. In general,

$$\mathbb{P}\{n_1 \geq \ell\, G\} \leq (1 - \gamma^G)^\ell$$

for $\ell = 1, 2, \ldots$, so that $E\, n_1 \leq G(1 - \gamma^G)/\gamma^G$. Note that this bound is independent of $C(0)$. The same argument shows that $E(n_k - N_{k-1}) \leq G(1 - \gamma^G)/\gamma^G$ for $k = 1, 2, \ldots$.

Now consider $E(N_1 - n_1)$. Since $\zeta_j > 0$, for $j = 1, \ldots, I$, Proposition 2 implies there is an H_1 such that $E(N_1 - n_1) < H_1$. Similarly for any k there is an H_k such that $E(N_k - n_k) < H_k$. Since for all k, $D(n_k) \leq G + b$ it is clear from the proof of Proposition 2 (see in particular Lemmas 4 and 5) that there is an H such that $H_k \leq H$ for all k. Therefore $EN_k \leq kL$ where

$$L = H + G(1 - \gamma^G)/\gamma^G .$$

LEMMA 7. $Ek^* < \infty$.

PROOF. Suppose $C(N_k) = (\hat{m}, \hat{s}, \hat{V})$. Since $C(N_k) \in B$, $\hat{V}_j - \hat{V}_{\hat{m}} < G$ for $j = 1, \ldots, I$. Suppose the level of performance of activity $\hat{m}$ increases by 1 during each of the periods $N_k+1, \ldots, N_k+G$ while the

215

level of performance on all other activities does not change. Then, it is easy to verify that $C(t)$ will visit A during its kth visit to B. The probability of this happening is (because of (R.3)) at least γ^G. This estimate is independent of k and $C(N_k)$; the conclusion follows.

LEMMA 8. $EN_{k^*+1} < \infty$.

PROOF. Let $k^{**} = k^* + 1$. Then $Ek^{**} < \infty$. I shall show that $EN_{k^{**}} \leq LEk^{**}$ where L is as in Lemma 6. Let $X_k = N_k - N_{k-1}$, $L_k = E(X_k \mid \mathfrak{I}_{N_{k-1}})$, and $Y_k = X_k - L_k$. Then $E(Y_k \mid \mathfrak{I}_{N_{k-1}}) = 0$ and the sequence $T_k = Y_1 + Y_2 + \ldots + Y_k$ is a martingale. Since

$$E\left[|T_{k+1} - T_k| \mid \mathfrak{I}_{N_k} \right] = E\left[|Y_k| \mid \mathfrak{I}_{N_k} \right] = E\left[|X_{k+1} - L_{k+1}| \mid \mathfrak{I}_{N_k} \right]$$

$$\leq E\left[|X_{k+1}| \mid \mathfrak{I}_{N_k} \right] + E\left[|L_{k+1}| \mid \mathfrak{I}_{N_k} \right]$$

$$= E\left[X_{k+1} \mid \mathfrak{I}_{N_k} \right] + L_{k+1} = 2L_{k+1} < \infty,$$

it follows from Proposition 5.33 of Breiman [1968, p. 99] that $ET_{k^{**}} = ET_1 = 0$. However, $T_{k^{**}} = \sum_1^{k^{**}} Y_k = \sum_1^{k^{**}} X_k - \sum_1^{k^{**}} L_k \geq N_{k^{**}} - k^{**}L$. Thus $0 = ET_{k^{**}} \geq EN_{k^{**}} - LEk^{**}$ or $EN_{k^{**}} \leq LEk^{**}$ as was to be proved.

3.4. Theorem 3

Theorem 3 follows immediately and familiarly from

PROPOSITION 4. If a d-delay behavior is followed and if $\zeta_j > 0$, $j=1,\ldots,I$ then the Markov chain $C(t)$ defined in (22) is positive recurrent.

PROOF OF PROPOSITION 4. If $\zeta_i > 0$ for all i, the proof of Proposition 2 can be trivially adapted so that its conclusion holds under the assumptions (8) and (9) when a policy of putting out fires with delay d is followed. Proposition 2 is essentially all that was needed to prove Proposition 3 above. The rest of the proof goes through unchanged for this case.

3.5. Theorem 4

PROOF. The proof is given first under the assumption that for all i

(25)
$$\delta_{io} = 0, \quad \delta_{is} = \delta_i > 0, \quad s > 0 .$$

Afterwards I discuss how to extend the argument to the more general specification (9).

Fix d. Proposition 4 implies the long run frequency of occurrence of the event $M(t) = i$ and $s(t) = s$ converges to the invariant probability a_{is}^d. Thus,

(26)
$$R^d = \bar{a}_i^d \eta_i - (1-\bar{a}_i^d)\xi_i + \delta_i \sum_{s=1}^{\infty} a_{is}^d$$

where

$$\bar{a}_i^d = \sum_{s=0}^{\infty} a_{is}^d .$$

Let $\bar{b}_i^d = \sum_{s=1}^{\infty} a_{is}^d$, the probability that $m(t) = i$ and $s(t) > 0$. Then (26) can be written as

(27)
$$R^d = \bar{a}_i^d(\eta_i + \delta_i) - (1-\bar{a}_i^d)\xi_i - (\bar{a}_i^d - \bar{b}_i^d)\delta_i$$

Note that $(\bar{a}_i^d - \bar{b}_i^d) = a_{io}^d > 0$, the probability of the joint event $m(t) = i$ and $s(t) = 0$. Let $\hat{b}$ be the set of weights such that $\Sigma \hat{b}_i = 1$ and, for all i,k,

$$\hat{b}_i(\eta_i + \delta_i) - (1 - \hat{b}_i)\xi_i = \hat{b}_k(\eta_k + \delta_k) - (1 - \hat{b}_k)\xi_k .$$

Let R^∞ denote the value of this common sum. I will show that

(28)
$$R^\infty > R^d .$$

217

Since both $\sum_i \bar{a}_i^d = \sum_i \hat{b}_i = 1$, there is a k such that $\bar{a}_k^d \leq \hat{b}_k$ so that

$$R^d = \bar{a}_k^d(\eta_k + \delta_k) - (1 - \bar{a}_k^d)\xi_k - a_{ok}^d \delta_k$$

$$< \bar{a}_k^d(\eta_k + \delta_k) - (1 - \bar{a}_k^d)\xi_k$$

$$\leq \hat{b}_k(\eta_k + \delta_k) - (1 - \hat{b}_k)\xi_k = R^\infty .$$

This proves (28).

To complete the proof we only need show

$$(29) \qquad\qquad \lim_{d \to \infty} a_{io}^d = 0$$

since (27), (28) and (29) imply that $\lim_{d \to \infty} \bar{b}_i^d = \hat{b}_i$ and $\lim_{d \to \infty} R^d = R^\infty$.

Recall that a_{io}^d is just the invariant probability of the event that $M(t) = i$ and attention has just begun to be allocated to i at time t. Now it is well known that the invariant or stationary probability of an event A is just equal to $[ET_A]^{-1}$ where T_A is the time to return to A. (See, for example, Breiman [1968, Proposition 6.38, p. 123].)

When A^d is the event that $M(t) = i$, $s(t) = 0$, and a d-behavior is followed, then T^d, the time to return to A^d, is always greater than d; thus $\lim_{d \to \infty} E(T^d) = \infty$ from which (29) follows.

This argument can be adapted to deal with the more general specification (9) in an obvious way. By assumption the sequences $\{\delta_{is}\}$ are monotone increasing and bounded. Let $\bar{\delta}_i = \lim_{s \to \infty} \delta_{is}$. Then $R^\infty = b_i^*(\eta_i + \bar{\delta}_i) - (1 - b_i^*)\xi_i$ where the b_i^* are chosen so that $\sum_i b_i^* = 1$ and

$$b_k^*(\eta_k + \bar{\delta}_k) - (1 - b_k^*)\xi_k = b_i^*(\eta_i + \bar{\delta}_i) - (1 - b_i^*)\xi_i .$$

Choose any set of $\tilde{\delta}_i$ such that $\tilde{\delta}_i < \bar{\delta}_i$. Let $\tilde{b}_i$ be a set of weights that $\Sigma \tilde{b}_i = 1$ and $\tilde{b}_k(_k + \tilde{\delta}_k) - (1 - \tilde{b}_k)\xi_k = \tilde{b}_i(\eta_i + \tilde{\delta}_i) - (1 - \tilde{b}_i)\xi_i$. Call this common sum $\tilde{R}$. Then it is straightforward although tedious to show that $\lim_{d \to \infty} \inf R^d > \tilde{R}$. This completes the proof.

NOTE

[1]There is a monotonicity property which is fairly easy to establish. Suppose that $\zeta_i \geq 0$, $i=1,\ldots,I$ and that the manager is allowed to redirect his effort only at time periods 0, d, $2d$, $3d$, $\ldots$ etc. Suppose further that when effort is redirected putting out fires is followed. Then if $a_i(nd)$ is the activity to which effort is allocated from period $(n-1)d$ to period $nd+1$ and

$$Z_i^n \equiv U_i(nd) - U_i((n-1)d+1)$$

it is easy to see that

$$EZ_i^n = a_i(nd)(d\eta_i + \sum_{i=0}^{d-1} \delta_{is}) - (1 - a_i(nd))d\xi_i \;.$$

Let $\eta_i^d = \eta_i + (\sum_{i=0}^{d-1} \delta_{is})/d$. Then it follows immediately from Theorem 3 of RR that $\lim \dfrac{U_i(t)}{t} = \bar{\zeta}^d$, where

$$\bar{\zeta}^d \equiv \left[1 - \sum_i \frac{\xi_i}{\eta_i^d + \xi_i} \right] \Big/ \sum_i (\eta_i^d + \xi_i)^{-1}$$

It is clear from the definition that $\bar{\zeta}^d$ is monotone increasing in d; since the δ_{is} are bounded, $\bar{\zeta}^d$ converges. I am indebted for this observation to Martin Hellwig.

REFERENCES

Breiman, Leo [1968], <u>Probability</u>, Addison Wesley (Reading, Mass.).

Freedman, David [1973], "Another Note of the Borel-Cantelli Lemma and the Strong Law." Annals of Probability, Vol. 1, No. 6, pp. 910-925.

Radner, Roy [1975], "A Behavioral Model of Cost Reduction." Bell Journal of Economics and Management Science, Vol. 6, No. 1.

Radner, Roy and Michael Rothschild [1975], "On the Allocation of Effort." Journal of Economic Theory, Vol. 10, No. 3.

I am indebted to Roy Radner for many discussions of the topics presented here. Some of the most important ideas are due to him. Martin Hellwig and Richard Quandt made helpful comments on earlier drafts. The National Science Foundation partially supported this research.

On Multi- and Ultrastable States in
Hierarchical Multilevel Multigoal Systems (abstract)
Christer Carlsson

ABSTRACT

The multiple goal behaviour of men and organizations is traditionally approximated by a single technically convenient criterion - as in linear programming, optimal control, in neoclassical microeconomic models. This paper outlines some principles, based on an utilization of multi- and ultrastable system states, that could possibly describe decision-making when it involves the fulfillment of a multiplicity of goals.

The system's concept is used as a conceptual frame for the discussion. A system is defined as an entity formed by a hierarchical set of activity units, which is made multilevel by sets of aggregating interrelations and co-ordinating intrarelations. The goals are defined as subsets of the value sets of the activity units; on the basis of this definition a multilevel system can be made multigoal. Within this conceptual framework some principles for multilevel, multigoal control are formulated and discussed; control is defined to be the activity of some control device that leads the system, in finite time, to attain the goals.

The principles found in the discussion were tested in an experimental system's model - of a multilevel, multigoal and hierarchical structure - which was programmed in Fortran and made operative on an IBM 1130 computer. The test results, although quite preliminary, suggest that the approach could be a way to find operative solutions to the multigoal problem.

REFERENCES

Ackoff, R. L. [1971], Towards a System of Systems Concepts. Management Science, Vol. 17, No. 11, pp. 661-671.

Ackoff, R. L. and E. F. Emery [1972], On Purposeful Systems, Chicago-New York.

Ashby, W. R. [1969], Principles of the Self-Organizing System. In Buckley, W. (ed.): Modern Systems Research for the Behavioral Scientist, Chicago, pp. 108-118.

_____ [1972], Design for a Brain, London.

Boltjanski, W. G. [1971], Matematische Methoden der Optimalen Steuerung, Leipzig.

Carlsson, C. C. [1974], A Study of the System's Concept in a Control Problem Context. Memo-Stencil, Nr 12, Åbo.

Clason, W. E. [1971], Elsevier's Dictionary of Computers, Automatic Control and Data Processing, New York.

Klir, G. J. [1969], An Approach to General Systems Theory, New York.

Mesarovic, M. D., D. Macko and Y. Takahara [1970], Theory of Hierarchical, Multilevel Systems, New York-London.

Raiffa, H. [1970], Decision Analysis, Reading, Massachusetts.

Rosenkranz, F. [1973], Deterministic Solution and Stochastic Simulation of a Simple Production-Inventory Model. Zeitschrift für Operations Research, Band 17, pp. B 141 - B 152.

Taschdjian, E. [1974], The Entropy of Complex Dynamic Systems, Behavioral Science, Vol. 19, Nr 2, pp. 93-99.

Adaptive Utility
Richard M. Cyert and Morris H. DeGroot

CONTENTS

1. INTRODUCTION

The two central components of a decision problem under uncertainty are the decision maker's subjective probabilities, which characterize his knowledge and beliefs, and his subjective utilities, which characterize his preferences and tastes. In the usual development of decision theory and descriptions of decision making, provision is made for the decision maker to change his probabilities in the light of new information, but no provision is made for him to change his utilities in the light of such information. As a result, examples such as the "Allais paradox" have been constructed which show that a decision maker may make a sequence of choices which are inconsistent with any fixed utility function.[1] Attempts to allow for such inconsistencies in the choices of a decision maker have led to the development of stochastic models of choice behavior and the notion of a stochastic utility function.[2]

It is our belief that the concept of learning can be applied to utilities as well as to probabilities. For example, when utility is a weighted average of several variables, we will argue that the particular weights used in the utility function are subject to change as a result of learning through experiencing particular values of the variables. The common use of utility functions assumes that an individual can calculate accurately the utility he will receive from any specified values of the variables. We are proposing instead the concept of an adaptive or dynamic utility function in which the utility that will be received by the individual from specified values of the variables is to some extent uncertain, and the expected utility from these values will change as a result of learning through experience.

We postulate a process in which the individual envisions the consequences of an event and derives in his mind the expected utility that he will realize from those consequences. A decision may be made on the basis of this expected utility but actually experiencing the consequences may result in the realization of a significantly different level of utility.[3] As a result of this experience, the expected utility of similar consequences will be changed and another decision under the same circumstances may be quite different. Once it is recognized that utilities can change by virtue of experience, it becomes important to incorporate these concepts in the theory of decision making.[4]

In this paper we shall attempt to present a full description of the impact of adaptive utility functions on the theory of decision making and to present some formal models for incorporating adaptive utility into the standard theory.

2. EXPECTED AND REALIZED UTILITY

In classical utility theory, a utility function is assumed to exist for any individual decision maker.[5] It is also assumed that this function is fully known to the individual so that it is even possible for him to make hypothetical choices. Thus, the demand curve for a product can be determined by having each consumer indicate the quantity he would purchase given different prices. After a decision is made, it is assumed that the utility realized by the decision maker is the amount indicated by the utility function. Thus, it is implicitly assumed that the utility that the individual expects from a particular decision is the utility realized when the decision is made. There are no surprises with respect to the amount of utility received. There is no gap between the expectation and the utility realized for each possible set of values of the variables in the utility function. There is only one utility function. It is known by the decision maker and it accurately reflects the utility that will be realized from the consequences of a particular event.

In the approach that we are taking it is assumed that there are two types of utility functions. The first one is represented by the concept of expected utility. Here the individual may have a complete utility function for consequences that have not been experienced previously, but for which the individual estimates his expected utility. This utility function is somewhat analogous to the a priori probability distribution that is used in Bayesian analysis. We assume that the individual is capable of deriving expected utility for any consequences that may be relevant to him. One way that this expected utility might be derived for any particular consequence or specified values of the variables in the utility function would be for the individual to utilize mathematical expectation. He would construct a probability distribution for the different amounts of utility he might realize from the specified values of the variables and then calculate the mathematical expectation of this distribution. This value would become a point on the expected utility function which is composed of all such points. We do not believe that each individual actually goes through such calculations in determining his expected utility function. Rather we believe that the expected utility function is a heuristic used by the decision maker and is not typically derived by him from the kind of detailed calculation just described. However it is derived, the expected utility function becomes the basis for the individual's decision-making behavior.

Once a decision is made, and the individual experiences the consequences, the actual utility experienced is compared with the expected utility. There can be a gap between these utilities. For example, in trying out a new food or in buying a new product, the prior expectation may not be realized. In a different type of problem, an individual may have an expected utility for the net revenue he will receive from selling a product, such as a house, at a particular price. However, the actual experience of having the price offered to him in the market may result in a new expected utility that is different from the previous one, and he may reject a price that he had expected to accept. As another example, assume that an individual buying a house prefers one with particular characteristics. However, he may find that the actual utility of a specific house that has different characteristics may exceed his expected utility of one with the original characteristics at the same price, and he may decide to purchase a house that does not conform to his initial specifications.

The result of the difference between the actual and expected utility is that the individual modifies the expected utility function when it is relevant for future decisions. In order to treat the problem formally, which we do in subsequent sections, we will assume that the expected utility function has been derived from the calculation of mathematical expectations as described earlier, and that this function is modified by the standard Bayesian analysis. This updating of the expected utility function could be based on a variety of assumptions, depending on the type of information extracted by the individual from the realized utility. For example, the individual might be able to perceive only that the actual utility was above or below the expected value and must apply Bayes theorem to these limited observations to determine a new expected utility function.

We do not explore the trivial case of modification in which the actual and expected functions can be brought into conformity on the basis of a few observations. This would be the case if the actual utility function depended on a small number of parameters which could be determined exactly from a small number of observations. Rather, we shall consider utility functions in which there is some element of randomness that

226

prevents the parameters from ever being determined exactly.

The approach that we are postulating concentrates on the inter-actions between these two functions--the expected utility function and the actual function. It should be emphasized that we assume that the individual is capable of comparing the actual realized utility with the expected utility of the consequences of an event.

3. MAXIMIZING EXPECTED UTILITY

If the individual does not know his utility function and gains infor-mation through experience, what kind of process does he follow to gain the maximum utility? Our assumption is that he has the objective of maximizing expected utility. Suppose, as in the classical theory of decision making under uncertainty, that an individual must choose a decision δ from some available class Δ of possible decisions, and that each decision $\delta \in \Delta$ induces a probability distribution $P(\delta)$ on a given space R of possible consequences r. (More precisely, δ in-duces a probability distribution $P(\delta)$ on a given σ-field of subsets of R.) In the classical theory, it is assumed that there exists a real-valued utility function V defined on the space R such that one decision δ_1 is preferred to another decision δ_2 if and only if $E[V|P(\delta_1)] > E[V|P(\delta_2)]$, where $E[V|P(\delta_i)]$ denotes the expectation of V with respect to the distribution $P(\delta_i)$. If a decision δ must be chosen from a specified subset Δ_0 of the set Δ, then one will be chosen for which $E[V|P(\delta)]$ is a maximum, assuming that such a decision exists.

In accordance with this theory, if an individual could simply choose a consequence r from a given available subset of R, he would choose one for which $V(r)$ was a maximum. The theory indicates that this choice would be straightforward and could be made without difficulty because there are no elements of uncertainty in the decision. Uncertainty enters the classical theory only if the individual is uncertain about the consequence that will result from at least one of the available decisions that he might consider. Thus, this theory assumes that an individual's

preferences among sure things are fixed, and then determines his preferences among probability distributions involving the same consequences.

In our approach, however, there are no sure things. A person who
can choose a consequence, or reward, from among an available set of
rewards may have difficulty making a choice because he is uncertain
about the utility of each of the rewards. Thus, regardless of whether the
reward is a meal at a new restaurant, a new household appliance, a stock
certificate, or twenty dollars, the utility of the reward will be uncertain.
Therefore, the utility that the person does assign to a reward should itself be regarded as an expected utility. Here, the expectation is taken,
formally or heuristically, over the possible values that the utility of the
reward might have, and is taken with respect to the person's subjective
distribution for these possible values. Thus, from our point of view, an
individual will typically be uncertain about the actual utility of any particular consequence, no matter how well specified that consequence
might be.

Nevertheless, in a single period decision problem in which the
individual must choose a decision δ from some specified subset Δ_0 of
Δ, it is irrelevant whether $V(r)$ is the actual utility that will be realized
from the consequence r or merely the expected utility that will be real-
ized from r. In either case, $E[V|P(\delta)]$ will be the overall expected
utility from choosing the decision δ, and the individual will try to
choose a decision that maximizes $E[V|P(\delta)]$.

However, in a multiperiod decision problem in which the individual
must choose decisions from Δ_0 repeatedly, the definition and underlying structure of the function V can be important. In a multiperiod
problem of this type, the individual will try to maximize the expectation
of some function, such as the sum, of the utilities that are realized in
each period. This maximization must, in general, now be a sequential
process. The individual will typically be able to increase the total utility realized over the entire process by explicitly taking into account the
fact that the utility $V(r)$ he assigns to a particular consequence r at

the beginning of the process is merely an expectation and may be higher or lower than the actual utility he would realize from r in any given period. By exploring the actual utilities of various consequences in the early stages of the process, the individual can learn about his utility function. This learning will result in the elimination of some or all of the uncertainty that is present in his utility function. He can thereby make decisions in later periods that will have a high probability of yielding conformance between actual utility and expected utility.

To formalize our description, consider a process with n periods and suppose that in each period, a decision maker must choose a decision $\delta \in \Delta$ after observing the consequences of the preceding periods. Let u_i denote the utility function for period i (i = 1, ..., n). The function u_i is defined on the space R of possible consequences. It is assumed that the decision maker is uncertain about the exact values of the function u_i and that this uncertainty is represented by the presence in the function u_i of a parameter θ whose value is unknown. Thus, if the consequence r occurs in period i, the realized utility will be $u_i(r|\theta)$. The parameter θ will in general be a vector taking values in some parameter space Θ.

For i = 1, ..., n, we shall let r_i denote the consequence that occurs in period i, and we shall assume that the total utility U over the entire process is simply the sum of the utilities realized in each of the n periods. Thus, we assume that $U = \sum_{i=1}^{n} u_i(r_i|\theta)$.

As is typical in statistical decision problems, we shall also assume that the probability distribution on the space R induced by each decision $\delta \in \Delta$ is not completely known and depends on a vector parameter φ. We shall let $P(r|\varphi, \delta)$ denote that distribution. The parameter φ will, in general, also be a vector taking values in a parameter space Φ. In some problems, some of the components of φ may be related to, or even identical with, some of the components of θ. In other problems, the parameters θ and φ may be completely unrelated.[6]

229

At the beginning of the process, the available information about the values of θ and φ can be represented by specifying a joint prior distribution $\xi(\theta, \varphi)$ for these parameters. If θ and φ were completely unrelated, this joint prior distribution would be a product distribution of the form $\xi_1(\theta)\xi_2(\varphi)$.

In the first period, there are two types of information that become available to the decision maker. First, after he has chosen a decision δ_1 in period 1, he observes which consequence r_1 actually occurs. Second, he gains some information about the utility $u_1(r_1 \mid \theta)$ that he actually receives from r_1 in period 1. In general, he will not be able to learn the exact numerical value of $u_1(r_1 \mid \theta)$, but will only be able to learn this value subject to error. For example, he might learn only whether this value is greater than or less than his prior expected value $\int_\Theta u_1(r_1 \mid \theta)d\xi_1(\theta)$, where $\xi_1(\theta)$ denotes the marginal prior distribution of θ.

Together, these two types of information lead to a posterior joint distribution of θ and φ that serves as the relevant prior distribution when a decision $\delta_2 \in \Delta$ is chosen in the second period. The decision maker must choose a sequence of decisions $\delta_1, \ldots, \delta_n$ that will maximize the expected total utility $E(U)$.

In general, the optimal decision δ_1 in the first period of this multiperiod problem will be different from the decision specified by the myopic rule which considers only the first period and ignores future periods. It will, in general, also be different from the decision specified by the rule which ignores possible changes in utility and assumes that the same expected utility function which pertains to the first period will also pertain to all future periods. Indeed, even in a two-period problem in which the parameters θ and φ are independent, and the information obtained about θ in the first period does not depend on which decision δ_1 is chosen or which consequence r_1 occurs, the decision maker must take possible changes in utility into account when choosing δ_1. This fact can be shown as follows:

230

Suppose that θ and φ are independent under their joint prior distribution, and that information about θ is obtained at the end of the first period by observing the value x of a random variable X whose distribution $F(x|\theta)$ depends on θ but does not depend on which decision δ_1 was chosen or on which consequence r_1 occurred.[7] Then the information obtained about θ is independent of the information obtained about φ, and it follows that θ and φ will again be independent under their joint posterior distribution. We shall let $\xi_1'(\theta)$ and $\xi_2'(\varphi)$ denote the posterior distributions of δ and φ, given δ_1, r_1, and x. If a particular decision δ_2 is then chosen on the second (and final) period, the expected utility resulting from this decision will be

(1)
$$\int_\Phi \int_\Theta \int_R u_2(r|\theta)dP(r|\varphi, \delta_2)d\xi_1'(\theta)d\xi_2'(\varphi)$$
$$= \int_\Phi \int_R v_2(r|x)dP(r|\varphi, \delta_2)d\xi_2'(\varphi) .$$

Here $v_2(r|x)$ is the expected utility function for the second period, as determined by the relation

$$v_2(r|x) = \int_\Theta u_2(r|\theta)d\xi_1'(\theta) .$$

Since the posterior distribution $\xi_1'(\theta)$ depends on x, so also will the expected utility function $v_2(r|x)$, and we have explicitly exhibited this dependence in the notation we are using. Next, for any possible decision δ_2, we can use the conditional distribution $P(r|\varphi, \delta_2)$ of r_2 given φ, together with the marginal distribution $\xi_2'(\varphi)$ of φ, to determine the marginal (or predictive) distribution $\overline{P}(r|\delta_2)$ of r_2. Since the posterior distribution $\xi_2'(\varphi)$ depends on the decision δ_1 that was chosen in the first period and on the observed consequence r_1, this marginal distribution should more properly be written as $\overline{P}(r|\delta_2, \delta_1, r_1)$. The expected utility (1) can now be expressed as follows:

(2)
$$\int_R v_2(r \mid x) d\overline{P}(r \mid \delta_2, \delta_1, r_1)$$

At the beginning of the second period, a decision δ_2 should be chosen for which the integral (2) is a maximum. We shall let

(3)
$$U_2(\delta_1, r_1, x) = \sup_{\delta_2 \in \Delta} \int_R v_2(r \mid x) d\overline{P}(r \mid \delta_2, \delta_1, r_1).$$

Then it follows from backward induction that at the beginning of the process, a decision δ_1 should be chosen for which the following expression is maximized:

(4)
$$\int_\Phi \int_\Theta \int_R u_1(r \mid \theta) dP(r \mid \varphi, \delta_1) d\xi_1(\theta) d\xi_2(\varphi)$$
$$+ \int_\Phi \int_R \int_\Theta \int_X U_2(\delta_1, r_1, x) dF(x \mid \theta) d\xi_1(\theta) dP(r_1 \mid \varphi, \delta_1) d\xi_2(\varphi).$$

The important feature of this result from our present point of view is that when the decision maker chooses δ_1, he must consider the full range of possible new expected utility functions $v_2(r \mid x)$ that might be obtained from the observation x. It should be noted that both δ_1 and δ_2 will be different from the decisions that would be optimal in traditional theory. The optimal decisions in traditional theory would be based solely on the available information about φ. It is clear that the optimal δ_2 in our approach will be different from the one in the traditional theory because of the new information about θ that becomes available from x. It should be emphasized, moreover, that even though the decision maker has no control over the information about θ that will be generated in the first period, the optimal δ_1 in our approach will also be different from the one in the traditional theory.

In a more general problem, the space R_i of possible consequences in period i, the space Δ_i of possible decisions in period i, and the distribution $P_i(r_i \mid \delta_i, \varphi)$ induced on R_i by each decision $\delta_i \in \Delta_i$ can

232

depend on the decisions that were chosen in preceding periods and on the consequences that were observed in those periods. Also, the total utility over the n periods can be an arbitrary function $U(r_1, \ldots, r_n \mid \theta)$ of the entire observed sequence of consequences. An optimal sequence of decisions that takes into account the adaptive nature of the utility functions can again be determined by backward induction.

4. UTILITY EFFECTS IN DEMAND THEORY

Demand theory is an area for which our approach has important implications. Although the standard analysis of consumption in terms of indifference curves is general enough to admit changes in the utility function, these changes have typically been ignored. Since change in the utility function is an integral part of our approach, we shall demonstrate how the standard analysis can include such changes.

Consider the choices of two commodities made by a particular household or individual. Let M denote the income of the household in a given period, let p and q denote the prices of the two commodities in that period, and let x and y denote the amounts of the commodities that are consumed in that same period. The values of x and y will be chosen to maximize the household's utility function $U(x, y)$ subject to the budget constraint $px + qy = M$.

The standard economic analysis[8] proceeds as follows: The utility function U determines a family of nonintersecting indifference curves in the xy-plane. In Figure 1, two of these indifference curves are denoted I_1 and I_2. In that figure, the line AB represents the budget constraint $px + qy = M$. The amounts x and y to be consumed are specified by the point $F = (x_1, y_1)$ at which the line AB is tangent to the indifference curve I_1.

Now suppose that the household's utility function changes from U to a different function U^*. The new utility function U^* will determine a new family of indifference curves. In Figure 1, the curve I_1^* represents one of the new indifference curves. In particular, I_1^* is the

233

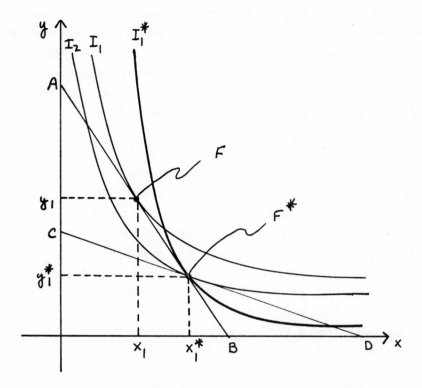

FIGURE 1: The change in utility is equivalent to a change in the price-income situation

new indifference curve that is tangent to the line AB. Thus, the consumption of the household will shift from the values x_1 and y_1 to the value x_1^* and y_1^* which are the coordinates of the point F^*.

It is also shown in Figure 1 that the <u>utility</u> <u>effect</u>, which results from changing the utility function from U to U^*, is equivalent to the effect of changing prices and income while retaining the original utility function. As indicated in the figure, among the original family of indifference curves, the curve I_2 passes through the point F^* and the line CD is tangent to the curve I_2 at the point F^*. Therefore, if the household retained its original indifference curves and its consumption had to

satisfy the budget constraint represented by the line CD, then the household would consume the amounts x_1^* and y_1^* specified by the point F^*.
It follows that changing the utility function from U to U^* is equivalent
to retaining the original utility function and changing the income and
prices to new values M^*, p^*, and q^* such that $M^*/p^* = C$ and
$M^*/q^* = D$. Clearly, there are an infinite number of different sets of
values of M^*, p^*, and q^* which satisfy these two equations.

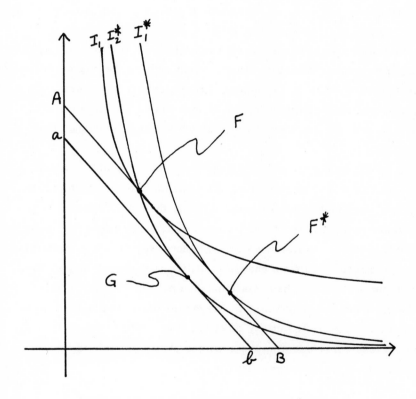

FIGURE 2: The income effect of a change in utility

Another way to think of the utility effect is illustrated in Figure 2.
The curves I_1 and I_1^*, and the points F and F^*, are as before. The

curve I_2^* is the indifference curve in the new family which contains the point F. Since both the points F and G lie on the curve I_2^*, the household is now indifferent between these points. The line ab is parallel to AB and tangent to the curve I_2^*. The point of tangency is denoted by G. Therefore, if the income of the household were reduced from M to the amount represented by the budget constraint ab, the household could still attain a consumption G equivalent to its original consumption F. Thus, from the point of view of the household, this income difference p(A - a), or equivalently q(B - b), can be regarded as the <u>income effect</u> of the change in utility.

By analogy with the traditional economic analysis, we can say that we have represented the utility effect, which induces the change in consumption from F to F^*, as the sum of the following two effects: (1) a substitution effect which incudes the change from F to G along the curve L_2^*, and (2) the income effect which induces the change from G to F^*.

It should be noted that since both the points F and F^* satisfy the budget constraint, and income and prices are held fixed, the point F^* must always yield a higher level of utility than F in the new family of indifference curves; and it must always yield a lower level of utility in the old family of indifference curves. Therefore, the income effect as defined here resulting from a change in utility must always be positive.

In our approach we have distinguished between the actual utility and the expected utility functions. The curves drawn in Figures 1 and 2 are based on the expected utility function. The change from F to F^* would result from adapting the expected utility function in light of the experienced utility at the point (x_1, y_1).

5. FORMAL EXTENSION TO k COMMODITIES

Consider now the choices of k commodities $(k \geq 2)$ made by a particular household or individual. Let M again denote the income of the household in a given period, let $p_1, \ldots, p_k$ denote the prices of the commodities in that period, and let $x_1, \ldots, x_k$ denote the amounts of the commodities that are consumed in that period. The values of $x_1, \ldots, x_k$ will be chosen to maximize the household's utility function $U(x_1, \ldots, x_k)$ subject to the budget constraint $\sum_1^n p_i x_i = M$.

Suppose now that the household changes its consumption from $x_1, \ldots, x_k$ to $x_1^*, \ldots, x_k^*$. This change could be the result of a change in income, a change in the price of at least one of the n commodities, or a change in the household's utility function. It is well-known[9] that under standard regularity conditions, the choices $x_1, \ldots, x_k$ of the household will satisfy the following relations, as well as the budget constraint:

$$(5) \qquad \frac{U_1}{p_1} = \frac{U_2}{p_2} = \ldots = \frac{U_k}{p_k} \, ,$$

where $U_i = \frac{\partial U}{\partial x_i}$. Thus, there is typically a wide class of combinations of income, prices, and utility that will result in a particular set of values of $x_1, \ldots, x_k$.

For example, suppose that the values of $x_1, \ldots, x_k$ must be positive and that

$$(6) \qquad U(x_1, \ldots, x_k) = \sum_{i=1}^k \alpha_i \log x_i,$$

where $\alpha_i > 0$ for $i = 1, \ldots, k$ and $\sum_{i=1}^k \alpha_i = 1$. It is easily found that the optimal choices of $x_1, \ldots, x_k$, subject to the constraint $\sum_{i=1}^k p_i x_i = M$ are

$$(7) \qquad x_i = M \, \frac{\alpha_i}{p_i} \quad \text{for } i = 1, \ldots, k.$$

A change in the value of x_i means that there must have been a change in the value of M, p_i, or α_i. From the point of view of the consumer, a change from $\alpha_1, \ldots, \alpha_k$ to $\alpha_1^*, \ldots, \alpha_k^*$ in the utility function is equivalent to a change in prices from $p_1, \ldots, p_k$ to $p_1^*, \ldots, p_k^*$, where $p_i^* = \dfrac{p_i \alpha_i}{\alpha_i^*}$ for $i = 1, \ldots, k,$ and income M is held fixed. More generally, the change from $\alpha_1, \ldots, \alpha_k$ to $\alpha_1^*, \ldots, \alpha_k^*$ is equivalent to any change in prices from $p_1, \ldots, p_k$ to $p_1^*, \ldots, p_k^*$ and in income from M to M^* that satisfies the following relations:

$$\frac{p_i^*}{M^*} = \frac{p_i}{M} \cdot \frac{\alpha_i}{\alpha_i^*} \quad \text{for } i = 1, \ldots, k .$$

On the other hand, a change in prices from $p_1, \ldots, p_k$ to a new set $p_1^*, \ldots, p_k^*$ is equivalent uniquely to a change in income from M to $M^* = M \sum_{i=1}^{k} \dfrac{\alpha_i p_i}{p_i^*}$ accompanied by a change in weights from $\alpha_1, \ldots, \alpha_k$ to

$$\alpha_i^* = \frac{M}{M^*} \frac{p_i}{p_i^*} \alpha_i \quad \text{for } i = 1, \ldots, k .$$

6. LEARNING ABOUT UTILITIES BY A BAYESIAN PROCESS

In this section we shall demonstrate in a demand theory context how utility functions are learned through Bayesian analysis. Assume two commodities with prices p and q and consumption x and y. Let the utility function be

(8) $$U(x, y \mid \alpha) = \alpha \log x + (1 - \alpha) \log y,$$

where $0 < \alpha < 1$. Suppose that the consumer is uncertain about the exact value of α and assigns a prior p.d.f. $\xi(\alpha)$ to this value. Thus, although it is unrealistic, we are assuming that the learning process we have described has resulted in the consumer's knowledge of the general form of his utility function but not the exact weights.

If the consumer is going to choose x and y in only a single period, then he should choose the values for which the expected utility $E[U(x, y \mid \alpha)]$ is a maximum. Since

(9) $E[U(x,y\,|\alpha)] = E(\alpha)\log x + [1 - E(\alpha)]\log y,$

the consumer can simply replace the uncertain value of α in his utility function by its expectation $E(\alpha)$. The optimal choices of x and y would, therefore, be

(10) $$x = \frac{E(\alpha)}{p}\,M \quad \text{and} \quad y = \frac{1 - E(\alpha)}{q}\,M\,.$$

We shall now consider a process with more than one period. After the consumer chooses the values of x and y in a given period and consumes those amounts of the two commodities, his experience will lead him to formulate a new posterior p.d.f. of α. The consumer should realize that the more quickly he can learn the precise value of α, the greater will be the utility that he can attain from his choices of x and y in each period. Because of this learning process, it will not be optimal in general to choose x and y in each period in accordance with (10), but rather to choose x and y to increase the rate of learning in order to maximize the total utility to be attained from the entire multi-period process. We shall now present two examples based on plausible models for the learning process. In the first example, the optimal choices of x and y in each period can be made in accordance with (10), and in the second example they cannot.

Example 1. At the beginning of each period, the consumer has an expectation $E(\alpha)$ for α. Therefore, after he has chosen the values of x and y to be used in a given period, his expectation $E[U(x,y\,|\alpha)]$ for the utility that he will realize in that period is given by Equation (9). We shall assume that after he has consumed the amounts x and y, he can determine whether the actual utility he has realized is larger than, smaller than, or equal to the expected utility given by (9).

The actual utility $U(x,y\,|\alpha)$ is given by Equation (8). Therefore, we are assuming that at the end of the given period, the consumer can determine which one of the following three relations is correct:

(i) $U(x, y \,|\, \alpha) > E[\, U(x, y \,|\, \alpha)]$,

(ii) $U(x, y \,|\, \alpha) < E[\, U(x, y \,|\, \alpha)]$,

(iii) $U(x, y \,|\, \alpha) = E[\, U(x, y \,|\, \alpha)]$.

It follows from Equations (8) and (9) that these three relations are equivalent, respectively, to the following three relations:

(i) $[\, \alpha - E(\alpha)]\,(\log x - \log y) > 0$,

(ii) $[\, \alpha - E(\alpha)]\,(\log x - \log y) < 0$,

(iii) $[\, \alpha - E(\alpha)]\,(\log x - \log y) = 0$.

If $x \neq y$, then determining which one of these three relations is correct is equivalent to determining whether $\alpha > E(\alpha)$, $\alpha < E(\alpha)$, or $\alpha = E(\alpha)$. Therefore, if the amounts x and y consumed in a given period are not equal, the consumer will be able to determine whether the actual value of α is greater than, less than, or equal to the expectation $E(\alpha)$ that he held at the beginning of the period.

Suppose now that $x = y$ in a given period. In this case, it follows from Equations (8) and (9) that

(11) $$U(x, y \,|\, \alpha) = E[\, U(x, y \,|\, \alpha)] = \log x.$$

Therefore, the consumer will not gain any information about the value of α from the realized utility. He knows in advance that the realized utility will be equal to the expected utility.

The essential feature of this example is that the information that the consumer learns about α in any period does not depend on the values of x and y that he chooses in that period, provided that $x \neq y$. Therefore, it will be optimal for him to proceed by choosing x and y in each period to maximize his expected utility in that period, in accordance with Equation (10), provided that Equation (10) does not yield $x = y$. If Equation (10) does specify that $x = y$ in a given period, then strictly speaking there will be no optimal values of x and y in that period.

The values $x = y$ will yield the maximum expected utility for that period but will yield no information whatsoever about the value of α. A procedure that will be almost optimal in this situation will be to choose x and y only very slightly different from each other. With such values for x and y, the expected utility in the given period will be very close to the maximum expected utility that could be obtained by choosing $x = y$ and, in addition, the consumer will learn whether the actual value of α is greater than, less than, or equal to $E(\alpha)$.

Example 2. We shall continue to assume that the utility function has the form given in Equation (8). However, suppose now that instead of the special form for the learning process that we have just considered, we assume that this process has the following alternative form: After he has consumed any particular amounts x and y in a given period, the consumer can determine whether he would have preferred a slightly larger value of x and a slightly smaller value of y, or a slightly smaller value of x and a slightly larger value of y. In more precise terms, we shall assume that the consumer can determine whether the derivative $\frac{\partial U(x,y)\,|\alpha)}{\partial x}$ of his utility function, evaluated at the particular values of x and y consumed in the given period, is positive, negative, or zero. We shall now derive some implications of this assumption.

The amounts x and y consumed in any period satisfy the relation

(12)
$$y = \frac{1}{q}(M - px) .$$

Therefore, it follows from Equation (8) that

$$\frac{\partial U(x,y\,|\alpha)}{\partial x} = \frac{\alpha}{x} + \frac{1-\alpha}{y} \cdot \frac{\partial y}{\partial x}$$

$$= \frac{\alpha}{x} - \frac{1-\alpha}{y} \cdot \frac{p}{q}$$

$$= p\left(\frac{\alpha}{px} - \frac{1-\alpha}{qy}\right) .$$

241

It can be seen from Equations (12) and (13) that the three relations

(i) $\quad \dfrac{\partial U(x, y \mid \alpha)}{\partial x} > 0,$

(ii) $\quad \dfrac{\partial U(x, y \mid \alpha)}{\partial x} < 0,$

(iii) $\quad \dfrac{\partial U(x, y \mid \alpha)}{\partial x} = 0,$

are equivalent, respectively, to the following three relations:

(i) $\quad \alpha > \dfrac{px}{M},$

(ii) $\quad \alpha < \dfrac{px}{M},$

(iii) $\quad \alpha = \dfrac{px}{M}.$

Hence, in this process, the consumer can determine which one of these relations is correct.

In a problem with n periods, a sequence of optimal decisions for the consumer can be found by backward induction. Since the information about α which the consumer gains in each period depends on his choice of x (and y) in that period, the optimal values of x and y in a given period will not typically be the values given by Equation (10).

7. CONCLUSIONS

It should be clear that this paper represents only the beginning exploration into an important topic. The concept of a well-defined utility function is central to most theories of decision making. At the same time the empirical work on decision making indicates that human decision makers do not have well-defined utility functions.[10] Our approach has been an attempt to use the utility concept in a manner that is closer to actual behavior. We have removed the constraints that require the decision maker to have immediate knowledge of his utility function.

In our approach the individual is assumed to be capable of determining an expected utility for the consequences of some event and to be capable of comparing the expected value with the actual value when the consequences are experienced. One criticism that can be made of the approach we have taken is that it represents the activity that preceded the standard theory. In other words, even if we are correct, our approach only justifies the traditional approach by showing how utility functions are learned.

We would not accept this criticism for several reasons. First, some of the population being analyzed at any time will be in the process of learning their utility functions, and this fact must be incorporated in any theory. Second, it is not clear that a utility function ever becomes completely known since there will be consequences never experienced by the individual. Finally, we do not believe that the utility function ever becomes completely stable. Individuals are always seeking new experiences as part of their nature. Knight[11] has referred to this aspect as "explorative activity." We try to deal with it in a formal way by utilizing a random variable in the utility function. One implication of this idea is that the standard concept of a stable equilibrium needs to be modified. The only equilibrium possible would be some kind of stochastic equilibrium.

The notion of explorative activity and utility being known only through experience is consistent with casual empiricism. We have reference to the fads in style, food, automobiles, soaps, and other products in the economy. Only a small number of the new products can lay claim to legitimate technical improvements over older products. In the marketing literature such shifts have been institutionalized in the concept of a product life cycle.[12] In other words, it is expected that products will have a limited life, partly because of preference changes.

One of the obvious concerns of an approach that challenges the existence of utility functions is whether it is possible to have an analytic science of decision making. In this paper we have made a start toward a positive answer.

243

NOTES

1. M. Allais [1953: pp. 503-546], L. J. Savage [1954: pp. 101-103], M. H. DeGroot [1970: pp. 93-94].

2. R. Quandt [1956: pp. 507-536], G. M. Becker, M. H. DeGroot, and J. Marschak [1963: pp. 41-55], R. D. Luce and P. Suppes [1965: pp. 249-410].

3. Cf. H. A. Simon [1955: pp. 99-118]. Simon has put this well: "The consequences that the organism experiences may change the pay-off function--it doesn't know how well it likes cheese until it has eaten cheese."

4. Cf. H. S. Witsenhausen [1974: pp. 91-94]. In this paper, Witsenhausen emphasizes the need to incorporate these concepts in problems of long range planning.

5. J. von Neumann and O. Morgenstern [1947: Theory of Games and Economic Behavior, Second Edition], M. H. DeGroot, op. cit.

6. For example, the parameter θ which determines how much utility or enjoyment an individual will derive from ordering a steak dinner at a particular restaurant will be closely related to the parameter φ which determines whether or not the restaurant prepares good steak dinners. As another example, the parameter θ which determines how much utility an individual will realize from owning a stock that yields a particular gain is only slightly related to the parameter φ representing external conditions which determine whether or not the stock will yield that gain.

7. The random variable X will in general be a function of the actual utility received from the realized consequence. For example, as mentioned earlier, X may be an indicator of whether the actual utility is greater or smaller than the expected utility for that consequence. The assumption made in the text that $F(x|\theta)$ does not depend on which consequence occurs is special and need not be retained in the general theory.

244

8.   Cf. K. J. Cohen and R. M. Cyert [1965].

9.   E. E. Slutsky [1915: pp. 1-26].

10.   H. A. Simon, op. cit.

11.   F. H. Knight [1935: pp. 22-23], quoted in G. J. Stigler [1946: p. 65].

12.   Cf. O. C. Nord [1963: Chapter 1], P. Kotler [1967: Chapter 13].

REFERENCES

Allais, M. [1953], "Le comportement de l'homme rationnel devant le risque: Critique des postulats et axioms de l'école Americaine," Econometrica, Vol. 21, pp. 503-546.

Becker, G. M., M. H. DeGroot and J. Marschak [1963], "Stochastic models of choice behavior," Behavioral Science, Vol. 8, pp. 41-55.

Cohen, K. J. and R. M. Cyert [1965], Theory of the Firm: Resource Allocation in a Market Economy, Prentice-Hall, Inc., Englewood Cliffs, New Jersey.

DeGroot, M. H. [1970], Optimal Statistical Decisions, McGraw-Hill Book Co., New York.

Knight, F. H. [1935], The Ethics of Competition, Harper, New York.

Kotler, P. [1967], Marketing Management, Prentice-Hall, Englewood Cliffs, New Jersey.

Luce, R. D. and P. Suppes [1965], "Preference, utility, and subjective probability, " Handbook of Mathematical Psychology (ed. by Luce, Bush, and Galanter), Vol. 3, pp. 249-410, John Wiley and Sons, Inc., New York.

Nord, O. C. [1963], Growth of a New Product: Effects of Capacity Acquisition Policies, The M.I.T. Press, Cambridge, Mass.

Quandt, R. [1956], "Probabilistic theory of consumer behavior," Quarterly Journal of Economics, Vol. 70, pp. 507-536.

Savage, L. J. [1954], The Foundations of Statistics, John Wiley and Sons, Inc., New York, pp. 101-103.

Simon, H. A. [1955], "A behavioral model of rational choice," Quarterly Journal of Economics, Vol. 69, pp. 99-118.

Slutsky, E. E. [1915], "On the theory of the budget of the consumer," Giornale degli Economisti, Vol. LI, pp. 1-26. Reprinted in Readings in Price Theory (ed. by Stigler and Boulding), Richard D. Irwin, Inc., Chicago, 1952, pp. 27-56.

Stigler, G. J. [1946], The Theory of Price, The Macmillan Co., New York.

von Neumann, J. and O. Morgenstern [1947], Theory of Games and Economic Behavior, Second Edition, Princeton University Press, Princeton, New Jersey.

Witsenhausen, H. S. [1974], "On the uncertainty of future preferences," Annals of Economics and Social Measurement, Vol. 3, pp. 91-94.

This research was supported in part by the National Science Foundation under Grant GS-42648X. The authors thank Timothy McGuire and Milton Harris for their critical reviews of the paper and suggestions for improvement.

Convergence of Adaptive Decisions
Frederic B. Shipley II

CONTENTS

1. INTRODUCTION

This paper considers an extension of the basic decision problem under uncertainty to the case of inadequate information. In such a situation the decision maker is unable to associate a single consequence with each act he can take and each state of nature that can occur. Intuitively, this lack of knowledge could arise from several sources--imperfect perception of the alternative actions available, imperfect information about the possible states of the environment, inability to specify the functional relationship between act-state pairs and outcomes, or a limited computational ability.

This extension assumes importance when we consider the complexity of commonplace decision problems under certainty. The game of chess, for example, has only three possible outcomes--win, lose or draw for WHITE--and it is conceptually possible to calculate all the possible sequences of moves since there are only a finite number. Once the strategies are known, assuming both players behave rationally, the game is trivial. In discussing this situation, von Neumann and Morgenstern [1953, p. 125] make the following observation: "But our proof, which

247

guarantees the existence of one (and only one) of these alternatives [win, lose or draw for WHITE] gives no practically useful method to determine the true one. This relative, human difficulty necessitates the use of those incomplete heuristic methods of playing that constitute 'good' chess. . ."

This "relative, human difficulty" becomes more acute when we introduce uncertainty. Simon (1972) has estimated that there are 10^{120} moves in chess that would have to be evaluated. Even the most sophisticated chess-playing computer programs evaluate no more than 1,000 moves at a time. It seems desirable then to formulate a model of decision making with inadequate information and relate it to the usual economic models of rational behavior. In doing so one of the first questions that must be answered is whether a model of "bounded rationality" approaches the economic model of complete rationality as we "loosen the bounds". An affirmative answer to that question is provided here. This offers some further justification for viewing the expected utility model, not only as a normative criterion, but also as an approximate description of choice behavior.

In the next section we introduce some notation, present the model formally and discuss the knowledge required to make rational decisions. Section 3 discusses some technical questions regarding measurability and integrability; the fourth section introduces set-valued random variables and the decision making mechanism. Section 5 establishes the important convergence result and in the last section the significance of the result is explored and some open problems discussed.

2. A FORMAL MODEL OF BOUNDED RATIONALITY

The basic elements of any decision problem are a set X of feasible actions x, a set S of <u>states of the environment</u> s together with a σ-field Σ of <u>events</u> (subsets of S), a set C of <u>consequences</u> c, and an <u>outcome function</u> $\rho : X \times S \rightarrow C$, which determines the outcome that arises when the action x is chosen and the state s occurs.

248

A state of nature specifies a complete history of the (economic) environment from the beginning to the end of the economic system in question.

The decision maker has preferences for different outcomes, represented by a complete transitive binary relation $\gtrsim_C$ over C; and certain beliefs about his environment, represented by a countably additive probability measure π on the measurable space (S, Σ).

Formally, then a <u>decision-maker</u> (or <u>agent</u>) is a quadruple $\{X, (S, \Sigma, P), C, \gtrsim_C\}$. If there is a (non-decreasing) numerical function $u: C \to \mathbb{R}$ (a utility function) such that $c_1 \gtrsim c_2$ iff $u(c_1) \geq u(c_2)$, the agent is said to be <u>representable</u>. The expected utility model (Savage [1954], DeGroot [1970] or Fishburn [1970])[1] deals with a representable agent whose preferences and beliefs satisfy axioms that guarantee that he prefers an action x to an action y--denoted $x \gtrsim y$--if and only if,

$$(1) \qquad \int_S u[\rho(x, s)]dP(s) \geq \int_S u[\rho(y, s)]dP(s) .$$

However, if the set X is sufficiently rich the agent might not be able to distinguish all the actions available to him. Following Marschak [1963] we may conceptualize this situation by looking at a partition Z of X into <u>perceptually equivalent actions</u> ζ. Each equivalence class ζ thus represents a set of actions between which the decision maker can perceive no distinction. The partition Z^*, under which every set $\zeta = \{x\}$, a singleton, represents <u>perfect perception</u>; the partition Z_0; under which the only set $\zeta = \{X\}$, the whole space, represents <u>null perception</u>. We let $\mathcal{Z} = \{Z_\alpha \mid \alpha \varepsilon \mathcal{A}\}$ denote a class of partitions of X and assume Z^* and Z_0 are both in $\mathcal{Z}$.

Analogously the agent may only be aware of a certain class N of events η-a measurable partition of S-that can occur. We define N^* representing <u>perfect information</u>[2] and N_0 representing <u>null information</u> or <u>ignorance</u> as above. We let $\mathcal{N} = \{N_\alpha \mid \alpha \varepsilon \mathcal{A}\}$ denote a class of (measurable) partitions of S and assume N^*, $N_0 \varepsilon \mathcal{N}$.

We will say that the <u>structure of choice information</u> available to the agent is the pair of partitions (Z_α, N_α), $\alpha \varepsilon \mathcal{A}$. In what follows we shall only provide definitions for $\mathcal{Z}$ since completely analogous definitions hold for $\mathcal{N}$. We also note that it is not possible to consider a partition W on the product space $X \times S$ since we need to insure that the projections on each of the factor spaces are partitions and this would not be generally true. We could consider the product space and impose some kind of independence conditions to ensure the projections are partitions, but this seems a rather roundabout way to accomplish what we do directly here.

DEFINITION 1. Let Z_α and Z_β be in $\mathcal{Z}$. We say that Z_α is <u>finer</u> than Z_β, which we denote by $Z_\alpha \underset{\sim}{\leq}_f Z_\beta$, iff for every $\zeta_\alpha \varepsilon Z_\alpha$ there exists $\zeta_\beta \varepsilon Z_\beta$ such that $\zeta_\alpha \subseteq \zeta_\beta$.

This definition involves a slight abuse of language. Strictly speaking we should say Z_α is <u>no coarser</u> than Z_β. We adopt the simpler convention of Definition 1 and will say Z_α is <u>strictly finer</u> than Z_β when $Z_\alpha \underset{\sim}{\leq}_f Z_\beta$ and for some $\zeta_\alpha \varepsilon Z_\alpha$ there is a $\zeta_\beta \varepsilon Z_\beta$ such that $\zeta_\alpha \subset \zeta_\beta$.[3] The class $\mathcal{Z}$ clearly has a unique greatest element Z^* and a unique least element Z_0 when ordered by $\underset{\sim}{\leq}_f$. The relation of fineness is, moreover, reflexive and transitive, but being a partial order is not complete.

The concept of increasing fineness clearly conveys some of the intuitive idea of being more informative. If the partition Z_α is finer than Z_β then every equivalence class of actions that can be distinguished under Z_β can also be distinguished under Z_α and if Z_α is strictly finer than Z_β, more can be.

As Radner [1968, p. 38] points out in a temporal context, if the agent did not forget any information he had previously, he would have an <u>increasingly finer</u> (or <u>expanding</u>) information structure. We shall be primarily interested in expanding structures of choice information in the remainder of this paper. This may be a rather strong requirement since we have introduced no way of evaluating the value of gathering more information.

It seems justified, however, as a first step since for a given decision problem with inadequate information it is necessary for the agent to acquire an expanded structure of information in order to behave according to economic models of rationality. The net effect then is simply to help ensure that we can eventually solve the problem in which we are interested. For discussions of fineness as a measure of informativeness, see McGuire [1972], Marschak and Radner [1972, especially Chapter 2], Mount and Reiter [1974] and Reiter [1974].

Marschak [1963] introduced the notion of relevance that we want to consider now. The following comments should motivate the idea. If the set of states is defined in such detail that a single action yields the same consequence for several different states then the agent gains nothing from knowing that those individual states can occur. Conversely, if the agent's knowledge of the set of states is so coarse that any equivalence class of states yield several consequences for a given action, then he needs more information to make "rational" decisions. The notion of relevance expresses the minimal knowledge necessary to make rational decisions.

Before proceeding we must consider how to relate the agent's choice information to the outcomes he can distinguish. For a given pair (Z_α, N_α) in $(\mathcal{Z}, \mathcal{N})$ we define an <u>outcome correspondence</u>[4]

$$(2) \qquad \xi_\alpha : Z_\alpha \times N_\alpha \to A(C)$$

where for every $\zeta \, \varepsilon \, Z_\alpha$ and $\eta \, \varepsilon \, N_\alpha$, $\xi_\alpha(\zeta, \eta) \subseteq C$, and where $A(C)$ denotes the set of nonempty subsets of C. Since ξ_α is defined for all $Z_\alpha \, \varepsilon \, \mathcal{Z}$, $N_\alpha \, \varepsilon \, \mathcal{N}$, we have a set of outcome correspondences Ξ which is called an <u>outcome condition</u> if it satisfies

$$(3) \qquad \xi_\alpha(\zeta, \eta) = \bigcup_{x \, \varepsilon \, \zeta} \ \bigcup_{s \, \varepsilon \, \eta} \rho(x, s), \quad \zeta \, \varepsilon \, Z_\alpha, \ \eta \, \varepsilon \, N_\alpha \, .$$

We will only consider a set Ξ that is an outcome condition, and will use ξ_α to indicate that ξ_{Z_α, N_α} is defined on $Z_\alpha \times N_\alpha$.

DEFINITION 2. The pair of partitions (Z_α, N_α) is <u>outcome-relevant-for</u> ρ iff it satisfies:

(i) (Z_α, N_α) is <u>sufficiently fine (s.f.) for</u> ξ_α -- that is for every x_1, $x_2 \, \varepsilon \, \zeta$, s_1, $s_2 \, \varepsilon \, \eta$,

$$(4) \qquad \xi_\alpha(x_1, s_1) = \xi_\alpha(x_2, s_2), \quad \zeta \, \varepsilon \, Z_\alpha, \quad \eta \, \varepsilon \, N_\alpha .$$

(ii) (Z_α, N_α) is <u>sufficiently coarse (s.c.) for</u> ξ_α that is, for every ζ, $\zeta' \, \varepsilon \, Z_\alpha$ and η, $\eta' \, \varepsilon \, N_\alpha$,

$$\xi_\alpha(\zeta, \eta) = \xi_\alpha(\zeta', \eta), \quad (\eta \, \varepsilon \, N_\alpha) \Longrightarrow \zeta = \zeta', \quad \text{and}$$

(5)

$$\xi_\alpha(\zeta, \eta) = \xi_\alpha(\zeta, \eta'), \quad (\zeta \, \varepsilon \, Z_\alpha) \Longrightarrow \eta = \eta' .$$

Marschak [1963, Theorem V] has shown that there is a unique outcome-relevant pair (Z^ρ, N^ρ) defined by

$$Z^\rho = \{\zeta^\rho \mid x, x' \, \varepsilon \, \zeta^\rho \text{ iff } \rho(x, s) = \rho(x', s), \, s \, \varepsilon \, S\}$$

(6)

$$N^\rho = \{\eta^\rho \mid s, s' \, \varepsilon \, \eta^\rho \text{ iff } \rho(x, s) = \rho(x, s'), \, x \, \varepsilon \, X\} .$$

We may coarsen these partitions by only considering those equivalence classes of actions (or states) between which the agent is not indifferent--or, if he is representable, those classes yielding different utility levels.

As before, let $u : C \to \mathbb{R}$ and define $v : X \times S \to \mathbb{R}$, a <u>payoff function</u>, by $v = u \circ \rho$, thus $v(x, s) = u[\rho(x, s)]$. For every ξ_α, define $\psi_\alpha : Z_\alpha \times N_\alpha \to A(\mathbb{R})$ by

(7)
$$\psi_\alpha(\zeta, \eta) = \bigcup_{x \varepsilon \zeta} \bigcup_{s \varepsilon \eta} v(x, s), \quad \zeta \varepsilon Z_\alpha, \quad \eta \varepsilon N_\alpha .$$

We then have definitions of sufficient fineness and coarseness for ψ_α and the existence of the unique payoff-relevant partition pair, which we will denote by (Z_∞, N_∞), given by

(8)
$$Z_\infty = \{\zeta_\infty \mid x, x' \varepsilon \zeta_\infty \text{ iff } v(x, s) = v(x', s), \quad s \varepsilon S\}$$

$$N_\infty = \{\eta_\infty \mid s, s' \varepsilon \eta_\infty \text{ iff } v(x, s) = v(x, s'), \quad x \varepsilon X\} .$$

We remark that completely analogous definitions hold for <u>prefer-ence-relevance</u>, and we will call the pair (Z_α, N_α) <u>outcome</u>--(or <u>payoff-</u>) <u>adequate</u> if it is at least s.f. for ξ_α (respectively ψ_α).

There are thus five basic elements in any decision problem under uncertainty:

(i) The basic spaces X and (S, Σ),

(ii) The outcome space C,

(iii) The payoff function $v : X \times S \to \mathbb{R}$,

(iv) The agent's beliefs P, and

(v) The structure of choice information (Z_α, N_α), $a \varepsilon \mathcal{A}$.

This allows us to state precisely that knowledge the agent needs in order to act according to the expected utility model: he must know the payoff-relevant partitions Z_∞ and N_∞, he must know the mapping $\psi_\infty : Z_\infty \times N_\infty \to A(\mathbb{R})$, and his beliefs must be summarized by the prob-ability measure[5] P. Finally, he must have sufficient computational power to use this knowledge and compute the expected utility of the dif-ferent actions available to him.

The decision problem under inadequate information is then a sit-uation in which the agent's knowledge is limited to: the inadequate parti-tions Z_α and N_α, the payoff correspondence $\psi_\alpha : Z_\alpha \times N_\alpha \to A(\mathbb{R})$, and his beliefs which may be represented by the (conditional) probability measure defined on $(N_\alpha, \Sigma(N_\alpha))$, where $\Sigma(\cdot)$ denotes the σ-algebra generated by $(\cdot)$.

This model thus encompasses all three possible causes of lack of knowledge mentioned earlier and so seems to be a useful formalization of what Simon [1972] has called "bounded rationality". It should be noted that the lack of computational capacity is really what gives rise to the case of inadequate information. Presumably the agent will compute as long as it is economically worthwhile. If we thus reinterpret the payoff function as net of computing costs, it is economically justified to compute the payoff-relevant information if the agent has the capacity. If he doesn't, then he must be unable to and would only know a payoff-inadequate partition pair.

The payoff-relevant structure of choice information thus assumes an important role in this model of bounded rationality. Given payoff-inadequate knowledge, the agent does not know the basic underlying relationship between the action taken, the state that occurs and the payoff received. Because this functional relationship, determined by the payoff function v, is unknown the agent cannot make a decision by assigning a probability distribution over the payoffs determined by the pair $(\zeta_\alpha, \eta_\alpha)$ and maximizing expected utility. By not knowing the payoff-relevant partitions (Z_∞, N_∞), the possibility of his behaving rationally is truly limited, for he has no way of going from a probability assessment over the payoffs determined by some $(\zeta_\alpha, \eta_\alpha)$ to actions $x \in \zeta_\alpha$. This breaking of the functional link between actions, states and payoffs is what makes this model of bounded rationality formally and conceptually different from the usual economic choice model.

We end this section by considering a two-period consumption-investment allocation problem.

EXAMPLE 1. Consider an agent who must allocate his resources (wealth) between a risky asset (common stock) and a safe, or riskless asset (cash). This situation is quite general for Cass and Stiglitz [1970] have given broad conditions under which the separation of the investment decision (which of many risky securities to purchase) and the consumption-investment allocation may be made optimally.

Arrow [1965] was one of the first to consider this problem in which the agent's objective is to maximize the expected utility of his terminal (next period) wealth and the only characteristics of interest are the assets' monetary returns and the probability distribution of those returns.

For simplicity we will consider here an example in which the only inadequacies arise in the agent's knowledge of the set S of states.[6] Suppose the agent has $100 to allocate between a stock and cash, but his economic forecast is such that he can only distinguish two events-- "recession" and "expansion" and his beliefs are that each has a probability of occurrence 1/2. Buying the stock will yield a return between -$50 and +$10 if the event recession occurs (depending of course on the magnitude of the recession which the agent simply cannot specify) and between +$11 and -$50 if expansion occurs. Cash has zero return in both events. We can summarize the decision problem in the following table.

TABLE 1.

EVENTS ACTS	η_1=RECESSION (p=1/2)	η_2=EXPANSION (p=1/2)
STOCK	-$50 to +$10	+$11 to +$50
CASH	-0-	-0-

If the agent's utility function is linear in wealth, then the expected utility of choosing the stock is the range $1/2(50) + 1/2(111)$ to $1/2(110) + 1/2(150) = 80.5$ to 130; the expected utility of holding cash is 100. We will adopt a simple (optimistic) decision rule and show that as the agent's information improves, his choices improve, and indeed converge to the maximum expected utility.

3. MEASURABILITY AND INTEGRABILITY OF SET-VALUED MAPPINGS

Since the utility function is by definition real-valued, our analysis is simplified considerably. The integrability of set-valued mappings has been studied by a number of authors beginning with Aumann [1965]. We shall draw on these result throughout this section.

The payoff function $v : X \times S \to \mathbb{R}$ may be viewed as a random variable, for every $x \varepsilon X$; that is the function $v(x, \cdot) : (S, \Sigma) \to (\mathbb{R}, \mathcal{B}(\mathbb{R}))$ given by $v(x, \cdot) = v(x, s)$, $x \varepsilon X$, where $\mathcal{B}(\mathbb{R})$ denotes the Borel σ-field of $\mathbb{R}$. It is now necessary to examine conditions under which the payoff correspondence ψ_α can be viewed as a <u>random correspondence</u>--that is, a measurable set-valued mapping.

Consider a partition N_α of S. We say that N_α is a <u>measurable partition</u> of S if for each event $\eta \varepsilon N_\alpha$, $\eta \varepsilon \Sigma$. We denote by Σ_α the σ-field generated by N_α, and by Σ^* and Σ_α^* the completion with respect to π of Σ and Σ_α, respectively. We remark that Σ_α (Σ_α^*) is a sub-σ-field of $\Sigma(\Sigma^*)$. We assume $\{N_\alpha \mid \alpha \varepsilon \mathcal{A}\}$, defined as in Section 2, is a set of measurable partitions of S. From now on we will consider a sequence--that is, the index set $\mathcal{A} = \mathbb{N}$, the set of positive integers-- of measurable partitions of S and we note that the set $\{\Sigma_n\}_{n \varepsilon \mathbb{N}}$ is an increasing sequence of sub-σ-fields of Σ--that is $\Sigma_n \subseteq \Sigma_{n-1}$.

DEFINITION 3. Dentoe by $\psi_n^x : N_n \to A(\mathbb{R})$, the correspondence given by $\psi_n^x(\eta) = \psi(x, \eta)$, $x \varepsilon X$. We say that the correspondence ψ_n^x is <u>measurable</u> if the graph of ψ_n^x,

$$(9) \qquad G(\psi_n^x) = \{(\eta, y) \varepsilon N_n \times \mathbb{R} \mid y \varepsilon \psi_n^x(\eta)\}$$

belongs to the product σ-field $\Sigma_n \otimes \mathcal{B}(\mathbb{R})$, for every $x \varepsilon X$.

Given the correspondence $\psi_n^x : N_n \to A(\mathbb{R})$, a <u>selector</u> of ψ_n^x is a function $f^x : N_n \to \mathbb{R}$ such that $f^x(\eta) \varepsilon \psi_n^x(\eta)$. A selector is <u>measurable</u> if $f^x(\eta) \varepsilon \psi_n^x(\eta)$ a.s. $[P_n]$ and f is measurable with respect to Σ_n. A measurable selector is integrable if $E|f^x(\eta)| < \infty$; the set of all integrable selectors of ψ_n^x is denoted by L_{ψ_n}. The integral of ψ_n^x is defined by

(10)
$$\int_{N_n} \psi_n^x(\eta)dP_n = \{\int_{N_n} f^x(\eta)P_n \mid f^x \varepsilon L_{\psi_n^x}\} .$$

Now in the definition of the decision problem with inadequate information, we may, following Marschak and Radner [1972], consider the agent's information about the events that might occur as arising from some signals about the economic environment--such as economic statistics, forecasts, etc. It is thus natural to assume that the evolution of the economy is governed by some basic probability law P defined on (S, Σ) and that the agent forms his beliefs based on some set of economic signals Y. Then one can assume that there is a function $\eta : S \rightarrow Y$ that associates each given state of the environment with some economic datum. The agent's beliefs will then be represented on the measurable space (N_n, Σ_n) by the measure π_n induced by the mapping η - that is, for every $\eta \varepsilon N_n$

$$\pi_n(\eta) = P(s \varepsilon \eta \mid y),$$

$$= P[\eta^{-1}(y)] .$$

If the agent knew the true payoff function v then the decision problem would be well-defined under the traditional economic model of rationality. Since the agent only knows the correspondence ψ_n^x we must develop a choice rule and examine its properties. First, however, we present some technical results concerning ψ_n^x.

For the remainder of the paper we assume that the decision problem under the traditional model of rationality has a solution. In particular, suppose the function $v^x : S \rightarrow \mathbb{R}$ is integrable for all $x \varepsilon X$ and suppose that the partitions N_n of S form a tree--that is, $N_0 = \{S\}$, $N_n \lesssim_f N_{n-1}$ --see Radner [1968, pp. 36-38].

LEMMA 1. Let the decision problem be given as above. Then for every n, ψ_n^x is a measurable correspondence.

PROOF. Let F be open in $\mathbb{R}$, we must show $(\psi_n^x)^w(F) = \{\eta \, \varepsilon \, N \mid \psi(\cdot, \eta) \cap F \neq \phi, \, x \, \varepsilon \, X\}$ is $\Sigma(N_n)$-measurable. Now for every $\eta \, \varepsilon \, N$, $n \, \varepsilon \, \Sigma$. so if we can write $(\psi_n^x)(F) = \bigcup_{i=1}^{\infty} \eta_n^i$, $\eta^i \, \varepsilon \, N$, the proof will be complete. $(\psi_n^x)^w(F) = \bigcup_{n} \bigcup_{s \varepsilon \eta} \{s \, \varepsilon \, S \mid v(\cdot, s) \cap F \neq \phi, \, x \, \varepsilon \, X\}$ and since v is measurable and $F \, \varepsilon \, \mathcal{B}$, the set $(v^x)^{-1}(F) = \{s \, \varepsilon \, S \mid v(\cdot, s) \, \varepsilon \, F, \, x \, \varepsilon \, X\} = \{s \, \varepsilon \, S \mid v(\cdot, s) \cap F \neq \phi, \, x \, \varepsilon \, X\}$ is in Σ, and since N_α is a measurable partition of S, the set $\bigcup_{s \varepsilon \eta} (v^x)^{-1}(F)$ is in $\Sigma(N_\eta)$. Thus so is $(\psi_\eta^x)^w(F)$ as an at most finite union of measurable sets. Q.E.D.

COROLLARY 1. Let $N = \lim_{n \to \infty} N_n$ be defined by

(11)
$$N = \{\eta(s) \mid \text{for every } s \, \varepsilon \, S, \, \eta(s) = \lim_{n \to \infty} \eta_n(s)\},$$

where the limit is taken setwise. Then $\psi^x : N \to A(\mathbb{R})$ is $\Sigma(N)$ measurable.

PROOF. Since $N = \{\eta(s) \mid (s \, \varepsilon \, S)\eta(s) = \lim_{n \to \infty} \eta_n(s)\} = \{\eta(s) \mid \text{for every } s \, \varepsilon \, S \, \, \eta(s) = \bigcap_{n=1}^{\infty} \eta_n(s)\}$, then for any open F in $\mathbb{R}$

$(\psi^x)^w(F) = \{\eta \, \varepsilon \, N \mid \psi(\cdot, \eta) \cap F \neq \phi, \, x \, \varepsilon \, X\} =$

$$\bigcap_{n=1}^{\infty} \{\eta \, \varepsilon \, N_n \mid \psi_n(\cdot, \eta) \cap F \neq \phi, \, x \, \varepsilon \, X\} \, \varepsilon \, \Sigma(N)$$

since each of these sets in in N_n. Q.E.D.

LEMMA 2. If for every n, N_n is a measurable partition of S, then N as defined by (11) is a measurable partition of S--that is, $\eta \, \varepsilon \, N$ implies $\eta \, \varepsilon \, \Sigma$.

PROOF.

$$N = \{\eta(s) \mid \text{for every } s \, \varepsilon \, S, \, \eta(s) = \lim_{n \to \infty} \eta_n(s)\}$$

$$= \{\eta(s) \mid \text{for every } s \, \varepsilon \, S, \, \eta(s) = \bigcap_{n=1}^{\infty} \eta_n(s)\}$$

since the N_n are expanding information structures. But $\eta_n(x) \varepsilon N_n \subseteq \Sigma$ by assumption and since Σ is a σ-field $\bigcap\limits_{n=1}^{\infty} \eta_n(s) \varepsilon \Sigma$. Q.E.D.

Thus the payoff correspondence is indeed well-defined as a random correspondence on (N_n, Σ_n) and since the sequence $\{N_n\} \to N$, a measurable partition of S we can legitimately speak of $(N, \Sigma(N))$ as a measurable space. In particular we will be interested in the case when $N = N_\infty$ the payoff-relevant partition of S.

4. RANDOM PAYOFF CORRESPONDENCES AND DECISION OPERATORS

Our major result concerns the definition of a decision operator, a mechanism for making decisions with inadequate information, and its characterization as a submartingale correspondence. To do so we must first extend some definitions for stochastic processes to set-valued stochastic processes. The definitions for stochastic processes may be found in Doob [1953] or Meyer [1966]; we provide the necessary modifications here.

We wish to characterize random correspondences as martingales or submartingales, but a major problem in doing so is how to characterize the constant expectation or increasing expectation property of these processes. We give a definition only for submartingales since that is the case we shall be interested in.

DEFINITION 4. Let (S, Σ, P) be a (subjective) probability space, (Σ_i) $i \varepsilon I$ an increasing family of sub-σ-fields of Σ, and (ψ_i) $i \varepsilon I$ a family of real random correspondences. Then the system $((S, \Sigma, P),(\psi_i)$ $i \varepsilon I)$ is called a <u>real set-valued stochastic process.</u>

DEFINITION 5. Let $((S, \Sigma, P), (\psi_i)$ $i \varepsilon I)$ be a real set-valued stochastic process adapted to an increasing family (Σ_i) $i \varepsilon I$ of sub-σ-fields of Σ. Then the process is called a <u>submartingale correspondence</u> with respect to the family Σ_i if

    (a) Each random correspondence ψ_i is integrable, and

    (b) For every pair i, j of elements of I such that $i \le j$, we
        have

$$\begin{aligned}
\inf_{x \varepsilon \zeta_i^*} \psi_i^x &\le \inf_{x \varepsilon \zeta_j} E(\psi_j^x \mid \Sigma_i) \\
&\le \sup_{x \varepsilon \zeta_i^*} \psi^x \le \sup_{x \varepsilon \zeta_j} E(\psi_j^x \mid \Sigma_i) .
\end{aligned}$$

(12)

REMARK 1. One of the questions that must be answered concerns the existence of the random correspondence $E(\psi_j^x \mid \Sigma_i)$. We will make assumptions that will allow us to apply the Debreu-Schmeidler Radon-Nikodym theorem for positive-closed-convex-valued correspondences, Debreu and Schmeidler [1972]. The notion of measurability we use is somewhat different than that used by Debreu and Schmeidler [1972], but Debreu [1967, (4.2) - (4.4)] gives conditions under which they are equivalent. These conditions are assumed in Theorem 1.

REMARK 2. Condition (b) seems to capture the increasing expectation property that is the characteristic of submartingales. Intuitively, it says that the worst payoff from a decision based on Σ_i is worse than the expectation of the actions later (i.e., at $j \ge i$). Also the best expectation of the actions later is better than the best payoff of a decision based on Σ_i.

REMARK 3. We must also give meaning to condition (a). Following Debreu [1967, especially section 6] we will say that a correspondence $\varphi : X \to Y$ is __integrable__ if the function $\mathfrak{F} : X \to \mathcal{K}$, the set of nonempty compact subsets of Y, given by $\mathfrak{F}(x) = \{\varphi(x)\}$, is integrable as a function (see, for example Ash [1972]). Debreu [1967] has shown that the integral defined in the above way is equivalent to that defined in (10).

It is well-known (see, for example, Doob [1953], Theorem 4.15) that a submartingale converges, and we would like to extend this result to submartingale correspondences. Moreover, we would like to verify that when the agent acquires payoff-relevant information then the limit of the sequence is the utility function and the agent's behavior may be rationalized by expected utility maximization.

We first complete the specification of the decision problem under inadequate information and define a decision operator. Then we verify

that the decision operator is a submartingale correspondence and state
and prove the convergence result.

Since we want to relate rationality with inadequate information to
expected utility maximization, we must obviously use some form of expected utility computation in our definition of rationality. We consider
the following simple case (which is an extension to uncertainty of Definition 5(a) in Shipley [1973b]).

DEFINITION 6. Let X be the set of feasible actions and let
$\mathcal{P} = \{Z_n\}_{n=1}^{\infty}$ be a class of partitions of X. A <u>decision operator</u> D_n
selects for every perceptually equivalent class of actions ζ a subclass
of chosen actions, called the <u>decision set</u>. That is,

$$D_n : Z_n \mapsto \mathcal{P}(Z_n) \, ,$$

when $\mathcal{P}(Z_n)$ denotes the power set of Z_n.

We will adopt the following simple and optimistic notion of rationality. As Theorem 2 will show any definition of rationality that can be
characterized as a submartingale correspondence has the property that it
converges to expected utility rationality. We conjecture that a maximin
kind of operator has this property, but the simple decision rule given
below will illustrate the method.

DEFINITION 7. A decision operator D_n is called <u>rational</u> (<u>ex-
pected utility sense</u>) or briefly <u>E. U. rational</u> iff, given partitions Z_n
and N_n,

$$D(Z_n) = \{\zeta_n \, \varepsilon \, Z_n \mid \text{for every } \zeta_n' \, \varepsilon \, Z_n, \, \exists x \, \varepsilon \, \zeta_n \text{ such that}$$

(13)

$$\int_{N_n} \psi_n^x(\eta) \, dP_n \geq \int_{N_n} \psi_n^y(\eta) \, dP_n, \quad y \, \varepsilon \, \zeta_n'\} \, .$$

The decision operator D_n is called <u>sequentially E. U. rational</u> if (13)
holds for all n.

Finally for our convergence results we will look at the <u>decision</u> <u>correspondences</u>, the random correspondences,

$$\Psi_n : Z_n \times N_n \rightarrow A(\mathbb{R}),$$

given by

(14) $$\Psi_n(\zeta, \eta) = \psi_n(\zeta, \eta); \ \zeta \in D(Z_n) .$$

First of all, we note that the decision correspondence is nonempty.

PROPOSITION 2. Let X be a set of feasible actions, Z_α a partition of X and D_α a decision operator on Z_α. Then if the expected utility problem has a solution--i.e., there is an $x^*\ \varepsilon X$ satisfying equation (1)-- $D_\alpha \neq \phi$.

PROOF. This follows immediately from Lemma 1 in Shipley [1973a]. Q.E.D.

We will show that if the agent chooses "rationally"--that is, according to Definition 6--then the decision correspondences form a submartingale correspondence. Before proceeding to the proof, we offer an intuitive explanation.

This definition of rationality may be regarded as optimistic since it requires that the agent choose the class of actions containing that action which yields the highest expected utility, conditional on his knowledge of S--that is, knowing Σ_i. It will be seen, however, that the significance of this restriction is considerably diminished when the requirement that the agent be able to acquire payoff-relevant information is added. For with this latter requirement other weaker definitions of rationality that could be characterized as submartingale correspondences could be adopted with the same convergence results holding. The promise of finding the same convergence results for less complex decision rules, however, makes this first step worthwhile because it illustrates the convergence mechanism and the importance of the motion of payoff-relevance.

THEOREM 1. Let $\{(Z_n, N_n)\}_{n=1}^{\infty}$ be a sequence of pairs of partitions of the sets X and S, respectively, such that for every $i \leq j$ we have $Z_j \leq_f Z_i$ and $N_j \leq_f N_i$. Suppose that the decision correspondences Ψ_n, $n \in \mathbb{N}$, defined by (14) are countably additive, π-continuous and positive-compact-convex-valued. Then the sequence $\{\Psi_n\}_{n=1}^{\infty}$ is a submartingale correspondence.

PROOF. By Debreu-Schmeidler [1972, Theorem 2] the existence of $E(\Psi_j^x \mid \Sigma_i)$ in Definition 5(b) is guaranteed. Condition (a) is satisfied since by assumption the function $v : X \times S \to \mathbb{R}$ is integrable. Thus only the chain of inequalities in (12) remains to be verified. We first note that for any $i < j$ $\Psi_j^x \subseteq \Psi_i^x$ because $\{N_n\}$ is increasingly finer. Now $\Psi_j(\zeta, \eta) = \psi_j(\zeta, \eta)$, $\zeta^* \in D(Z_j)$ and D is E. U. sequentially rational, so

$$\inf_{x \in \zeta^*} \Psi_i^x = \inf_{x \in \zeta^*} \psi_i(\zeta, \eta), \; \zeta \in D(Z_j) \leq \inf_{x \in \zeta^*} \psi(\zeta_j, \eta_i), \; \eta_i \in N_i, \; \text{since} \; \eta_i \subseteq \eta_j.$$

This implies $\inf_{x \in \zeta^*} \Psi_i^x \leq \inf_{x \in \zeta^*} E(\Psi_j^x \mid \Sigma_i)$, since the inequality above holds for every set $\eta \in N_i$, $\pi(\eta) > 0$. Analogously $\sup_{x \in \zeta^*} \Psi_i^x \leq \sup_{x \in \zeta^*} E(\Psi_j^x \mid \Sigma_i)$.

It thus remains only to verify that the intermediate inequality holds--that is, $\inf_{x \in \zeta_i} E(\Psi_j^x \mid \Sigma_i) \leq \sup_{x \in \zeta_i^*} \Psi_i^x$. Again since $i \leq j$ implies $\eta_j \subseteq \eta_i$, we have for every $x \in X$ $\inf_{x \in \zeta_i} E(\Psi_j^x \mid \Sigma_i) \leq \inf_{x \in \zeta_i} \Psi_j^x$, $\zeta_i \in D(Z_i) \leq \psi_i^x$, $x \in \zeta_i$, $\zeta_i \in D(Z_i) \leq \sup_{x \in \zeta_i} \Psi_i^x$. Q.E.D.

This completes the proof of Theorem 1, and prepares us for the proof of the main convergence result.

5. CONVERGENCE OF SUBMARTINGALE CORRESPONDENCES

A standard reference for the martingale convergence theorem is Doob [1953] and Meyer [1972]. We are interested in the following extension and particular application.

THEOREM 2. Let $\{\Psi_n, \Sigma_n, n = 1, 2, \ldots\}$ be a submartingale correspondence, defined on the probability space (S, Σ, P), satisfying all the hypotheses of Theorem 1. Set $\Sigma_\infty = \Sigma(\bigcup\limits_{n=1}^{\infty} \Sigma_n)$. Then

(i) $\Psi_\infty = \lim\limits_{n\to\infty} \Psi_n$ exists almost surely;

(ii) If (Z_∞, N_∞) is payoff-relevant, then $\Sigma_\infty = \Sigma$

$\Psi_\infty(\zeta, \eta) = v(x, s)$, $x \varepsilon \zeta$, $s \varepsilon \eta$, $\zeta \varepsilon Z_\infty$, $\eta \varepsilon N_\infty$; and

(iii) $\max\limits_{\zeta \varepsilon Z_\infty} \int_{N_\infty} \Psi_\infty(\zeta, \eta)dP(\eta) = \max\limits_{x \varepsilon X} \int_{S} v(x, s)dP(s)$.

Some further comments are in order before we proceed to the proof of Theorem 2. First of all, we assume that the subjective probability measure P is atomless. This is not a significant restriction since, for example, Savage's axioms [1972] imply this. Now it is well-known (see, for example, Aumann [1965] or Debreu [1967]) that is the measure P is atomless the range of values of the integral is a convex set. Since ψ_n maps into $\mathbb{R}$, this means that $\int\Psi_n$ is an interval. Moreover, if we assume that the payoff function v is bounded (see Fishburn [1971] for a discussion of this) then the range of $\int\Psi_n$ is also bounded since the measure P is finite. Thus in order to ensure that Ψ_n is compact-convex valued we only need assume that Ψ_n is closed. This assumption was made in Theorem 1. Finally we note that if Ψ_n is closed-valued for every n, then Ψ_∞ is also as the intersection of compact sets.

PROOF. (of Theorem 2.) The proof proceeds by a series of steps which may be of independent interest and so are identified individually as lemmas.

LEMMA 4. If (Z_∞, N_∞) is payoff-relevant, then $\Sigma_\infty = \Sigma$.

PROOF. Since $\Sigma_\infty \subseteq \Sigma$ we only need show the reverse inclusion. Let $E \varepsilon \Sigma$, we must show $E \varepsilon \Sigma_\infty$. Now since N_∞ is payoff-relevant, for every $\zeta \varepsilon Z_\infty \Psi_\infty(\cdot, \eta) = v(\cdot, \eta)$, a constant. Moreover, v is measurable with respect to Σ and hence

$$\Psi_\infty^w(B) = \{\eta \varepsilon N_\infty \mid \Psi(\cdot, \eta) \cap B \neq \phi\} =$$

$$v^{-1}(B) = \{s \varepsilon S \mid v(\cdot, s) \varepsilon B\} \varepsilon \Sigma . \qquad Q.E.D.$$

LEMMA 5. $\Psi_\infty = \lim_{n\to\infty} \Psi_n$ exists a.s.

PROOF. Let $\Psi^* = \limsup_{n\to\infty} \Psi_n$ and $\Psi_* = \liminf_{n\to\infty} \Psi_n$.

We proceed by contradiction--that is, assume $P\{\Psi^* > \Psi_*\} > 0$. Now $\{\Psi^* > \Psi_*\} = \bigcup_{\substack{r,s\,\varepsilon\,Q \\ r < s}} B(r, s) = \{\Psi^* > s > r > \Psi_*\}$. Since this is a countable union, one of the events $B(s, r)$ must have positive probability, for the union to have positive probability. We recall (Chow, Robbins and Siegmund [1971], p. 15) that if $a_1, a_2, \ldots, a_n$ are any real numbers and (r, s) a nonempty interval, then the number of <u>upcrossings</u> of (r, s) by $a_1, \ldots, a_n$ is the number of times that the values a_k, $1 \le k \le n$ pass from being $\le r$ to being $\ge s$. More formally, let $t_0 = 0$ and for all m, t_m is the least $k > t_{m-1}$ (if any) for which

$$a_k \le r \quad (m \text{ odd})$$

$$a_k \ge s \quad (m \text{ even}).$$

Then the number of upcrossings is β, where 2β is the largest even index m for which t_m is defined.

Now on the interval $B(r, s)$ the number of upcrossings β by $\Psi_1, \ldots, \Psi_n, \ldots$ tends monotonically to $+\infty$ with n, and so $\lim_{n\to\infty} E\beta_n = +\infty$. But the Upcrossing Inequality (Chow, Robbins and Siegmund [1971], Lemma 2.3) $E(\beta_n) < (s-r)^{-1}$

$$[\sup_{x\varepsilon\zeta_n^*} E\Psi_n^+ + |r|] < \infty, \quad \text{where } \Psi_n^+ = \max\{0, \inf_{x\varepsilon\zeta^*} \{\Psi_n\}\},$$

which is integrable since Ψ_n is. Thus $\sup_{x\varepsilon\zeta_n^*} E\Psi_n^+ < \infty$ since Ψ_n is, so the inequality follows. This contradiction shows that $P\{\Psi^* > \Psi_*\} = 0$. Q.E.D.

LEMMA 6. Let the sequence $\{(Z_n, N_n)\}$ of pairs of partitions converge to a limit (Z_∞, N_∞) which is payoff-relevant. Then the correspondence Ψ_∞ defined in (i) of Theorem 2 is such that

$$(15) \qquad \Psi_\infty(\zeta, \eta) = v(x, s), \quad x \varepsilon \zeta, \quad s \varepsilon \eta, \quad \zeta \varepsilon Z_\infty, \quad \eta \varepsilon N_\infty;$$

and so $\max_{\zeta \varepsilon Z_\infty} \int_{N_\infty} \Psi_\infty(\zeta, \eta) dP(\eta) = \max_{x \varepsilon X} \int_S v(x, s) dP(s)$, a.s. $[P]$.

PROOF. Now $\Psi_\infty(\zeta, \eta) = \lim_{n \to \infty} \Psi_n(\zeta, \eta)$ and for every n, $Z_n \leq_f Z_{n-1}$, and $N_n \leq_f N_{n-1}$, hence $\Psi_n(\zeta, \cdot) \subseteq \Psi_{n-1}(\zeta, \cdot)$ for every $\eta \varepsilon N_n$ and $\Psi_n(\cdot, \eta) \subseteq \Psi_{n-1}(\cdot, \eta)$ for each $\zeta \varepsilon Z_n$. Therefore, $\lim_{n \to \infty} \Psi_n(\zeta, \cdot)$ and $\lim_{n \to \infty} \Psi_n(\cdot, \eta)$ are well defined. Moreover, $\Psi_n(\cdot, \cdot)$ is closed-valued and hence a compact interval, for each n, so that $\Psi_\infty = \bigcap_{n=1}^{\infty} \Psi_n$ exists and is closed-valued--indeed compact.

Finally since (Z_∞, N_∞) is payoff-relevant, we have, for all $\zeta \varepsilon Z_\infty$, $\eta \varepsilon N_\infty$, $\Psi_\infty(\zeta, \eta) = v(x, s)$, $x \varepsilon \zeta$, $s \varepsilon \eta$. Now since $\Sigma_\infty = \Sigma$, $\eta \varepsilon N_\infty$, $P_\infty(\eta) = P\{s \mid s \varepsilon \eta\}$; also since $\Psi_\infty(\zeta, \eta)$ is compact-valued and $P_\infty = P$ is finite

$$\int_{N_\infty} \Psi_\infty(\zeta, \eta) dP_\infty(\eta) = \int_S v(x, s) dP(s)$$

and is compact. Therefore the maximum over $\zeta \varepsilon Z_\infty$ exists and because $\Psi_\infty(\zeta, \eta)$ is payoff-relevant, (15) holds and since the functions are equal, the integrals are almost usrely equal, hence

$$\max_{\zeta \varepsilon Z_\infty} \int_{N_\infty} \ldots = \max_{x \varepsilon X} \int_S \ldots \quad \text{a.s. } [P] . \qquad \text{Q.E.D.}$$

6. DECISION PROBLEMS WITH INADEQUATE INFORMATION AND EXPECTED UTILITY MAXIMIZATION

The formal structure we have used and have concentrated on in the last section may have obscured the economic significance of the problem we have tried to solve. For a decision maker faced with inadequate information to make a decision by maximizing the expected utility of his choice, the correct procedure to follow is not clear. Indeed there is a whole literature stemming from at least the time of Laplace. Laplace in fact suggested that when a person was faced with such a situation he proceed as if all outcomes were equally likely--the Principle of Insufficient Reason. We have not tried here to examine particular principles and techniques for making such choices, but only to see if the payoff correspondence converged as the choice information available to the agent improved.

The payoff-correspondence ψ_n is the set-valued version of the payoff function v. We have shown that as the partitions Z_n and N_n get finer--and thus convey more information--then the agent's payoff improves. But the agent might only be able to specify a range of utility values for each act-event pair he can distinguish. This might occur because the investor is unable to identify (and assign probabilities to) different events $E \subseteq S$ that yield different dollar outcomes (and hence different utility payoffs). By being able to characterize ψ_n as set-valued mapping into $\mathbb{R}$, we have been able to use special properties of $\mathbb{R}$--for example, that a convex set in $\mathbb{R}$ must be an interval (possibly degenerate). However, by this formal characterization we can say that we have provided the basis for a theory of "bounded rationality". We have shown that in a rigorous sense such a theory must converge to the expected utility approach as the amount of information and capacity for information processing increases. This seems to us to offer new support for the expected utility approach--no longer as a merely normative criterion, but now as a rigorously defined approximation to actual choice behavior.

NOTES

[1] The axiom systems given by these authors differs. Savage's is the classic exposition and Fishburn follows him, while pointing out that Savage's axioms imply the utility function is bounded. DeGroot presents an axiom system that does not imply boundedness along with an additional axiom that guarantees it. In what follows we will need the boundedness assumption, so we follow Savage.

[2] Since the term information has come to be associated with random events outside the agent's control, we use it only for the partition N although it could just as appropriately be applied to Z.

[3] We use "$\subseteq$" to denote containment and possible equality and "$\subset$" to denote strict containment.

[4] A set-valued mapping is a (possibly empty-valued) function from a set X to the power set of a set Y--symbolically $f : X \to \wp(Y)$. A correspondence ϕ is a nonempty set-valued mapping--thus $\phi : X \to A(Y)$. The definitions we give for ξ, ψ ensure that the use of the term correspondence is justified.

[5] We use the term probability measure to mean a countably additive measure. This is not universal. Savage's axioms [1972, cover] only imply that π is finitely additive. Dubins and Savage [1965] develop a complete theory of gambling based only on finite additivity. Moreover, even some texts on probability and measure theory [Ash, 1972] warn that a physical justification for countable additivity has not yet been found. Mathematical probability theory, has, from the formulation of Kolmogorov in 1933, been based on this assumption. This seems to be a classical example of when mathematical convenience wins out over philosophical purity. We should note, however, that Villegas [1964] has introduced axioms--chiefly monotone continuity--that are sufficient to guarantee countable additivity. Fine [1971] has recently introduced a condition that is necessary and sufficient in the presence of Savage's axioms.

^{6} Indeed we may remark here that the entire model could be specified in this way by suitably broadening the set of states to include perceptual difficulties. This would make the partial correspondence $\psi(\cdot, s)$
single-valued as a mapping from actions to payoffs - for a given state s.
Thus all lack of information would be reflected in the partitions N_α of
S. Such a reinterpretation would, however, not allow any consideration
of interrelations among perceptual and informational difficulties.

REFERENCES

Arrow, K. J. [1959], "Rational Choice Functions and Orderings".
Economica, N.S., 26.

_____ [1965], Aspects of the Theory of Risk-Bearing. Helsinki:
Yrjo Johnssonin saatio.

Artstein, Z. [1972], "Set-Valued Measures". Transactions of the American Mathematical Society, 165.

Ash, R. B. [1972], Real Analysis and Probability. New York: Academic
Press.

Aumann, R. J. [1965], "Integrals of Set-Valued Functions". Journal of
Mathematical Analysis and Applications, 12.

Cass, D. and J. E. Stiglitz [1970], "The Structure of Investor Prefer-
ences and Asset Returns and Separability in Portfolio Allocation:
A Contribution to the Pure Theory of Mutual Funds". Journal of
Economic Theory, 2.

Castaing, C. [1967], "Sur les multi-applications mesurables". Revue
Francaise Informatique et Recherche Operationelle, 1.

_____ [1969], Le theoreme de Dunford-Pettis generalise". Comptes
Rendus Academie Sciences de Paris, 268.

Chow, Y. S., H. Robbins and D. Siegmund [1971], Great Expectations:
The Theory of Optimal Stopping. New York: Houghton-Mifflin.

Datko, R. [1970], "Measurability Properties of Set-Valued Mappings in
a Banach Space". SIAM Journal of Control, 8.

269

Debreu, G. [1967], "Integration of Correspondences". Fifth Berkeley Symposium on Mathematical Statistics and Probability. Lucien LeCam and Jerzy Neyman, ed. Berkeley: University of California Press.

_____ and D. Schmeidler [1972], "The Radon-Nikodym Derivative of a Correspondence". Sixth Berkeley Symposium on Mathematical Statistics and Probability. Lucien LeCam, Jerzy Neyman and Elizabeth L. Scott, eds. Berkeley: University of California Press.

DeGroot, M. H. [1970], Optimal Statistical Decisions. New York: McGraw-Hill Book Co.

Doob, J. L. [1953], Stochastic Processes. New York: John Wiley and Sons.

Dubins, L. E. and L. J. Savage [1965], How to Gamble If You Must: Inequalities for Stochastic Processes. New York: McGraw-Hill Book Co.

Dunford, N. S. and J. T. Schwartz [1957], Linear Operators, Part I. New York: Wiley-Interscience.

Fine, T. [1971], "A Note on the Existence of Quantitative Probability". Annals of Mathematical Statistics, 42.

Fishburn, P. C. [1970], Utility Theory for Decision Making. New York: John Wiley and Sons.

Halmos, P. R. [1950], Measure Theory. New York: Van Nostrand-Reinhold.

Himmelberg, C. J. and F. S. VanVleck [1969], "Some Selection Theorems for Measurable Functions". Canadian Journal of Mathematics, 21.

Hurwicz, L. [1969], "Optimality and Informational Efficiency in Resource Allocation Processes". In Arrow, K. J., S. Karlin and P. Suppes (eds.), Mathematical Methods in the Social Sciences, Stanford: Stanford University Press.

Kuratowski, K. and C. Ryll-Nardzewski [1965], "A General Theorem on Selectors". Bulletin de L'Academie Polonaise de Sciences, 13.

Loève, M. [1963], Probability Theory, 3rd edition. New York: Van
Nostrand-Reinhold.

Luce, R. D. and D. H. Krantz [1971], "Conditional Expected Utility".
Econometrica, 39.

Marschak, J. [1963], "The Payoff-Relevant Description of States and
Acts". Econometrica, 31.

_____ [1971], "Economics of Information Systems". Journal of the
American Statistical Association, 66.

_____ and R. Radner [1972], Economic Theory of Teams. Cowles
Foundation Monograph No. 22. New Haven: Yale University
Press.

McGuire, C. B. [1972], "Comparison of Information Structures".
Chapter 5 in McGuire and Radner [1972].

_____ and R. Radner [1972], Decision and Organization: A Volume
in Honor of Jacob Marschak. Amsterdam: North-Holland Publishing Co.

Meyer, P. A. [1966], Probability and Potentials, Waltham, Mass.:
Blaisdell Publishing Co.

Mount, K. and S. Reiter [1974], "The Informational Size of Message
Spaces". Journal of Economic Theory, 8.

Neveu, J. [1965], Mathematical Foundations of the Calculus of
Probability. San Francisco: Holden-Day.

Parthasarathy, T. [1972], Selection Theorems and Their Applications.
Lecture Notes in Mathematics, Vol. 263, Berlin: Springer-Verlag.

Radner, R. [1968], "Competitive Equilibrium Under Uncertainty".
Econometrica, 36.

Reiter, S. [1974], "Informational Efficiency of Iterative Processes and
the Size of Message Spaces." Journal of Economic Theory, 8.

Robinson, S. M. and R. H. Day [1970], "Economic Decisions with
Lexicographic Utility". Social Systems Research Institute Working Paper 7047, University of Wisconsin.

Savage, L. J. [1954], The Foundations of Statistics. New York: John Wiley and Sons. Revised edition Dover [1972].

Sen, A. K. [1971], "Choice Functions and Revealed Preference". Review of Economic Studies, 38.

Shipley, F. B. [1973a], "A Theory of Choice Under Conditions of Inadequate Information". Unpublished Ph.D. Dissertation, Northwestern University.

Shipley, F. B. [1973b], "A Formal Model of Bounded Rationality". Center for Business and Economic Research, University of Tennessee, Working Paper No. 11.

Simon, H. A. [1972], "Theories of Bounded Rationality". Chapter 8 in McGuire and Radner [1972].

Smith, T. E. [1972], "On the Existence of Most-Preferred Alternatives." Regional Science Research Institute Discussion Paper No. 68. (mimeographed).

Villegas, C. [1964], "On Qualitative Probability σ-Algebras". Annals of Mathematical Statistics, 35.

von Neumann, J. and O. Morgenstern [1953], Theory of Games and Economic Behavior. 3rd edition Princeton: Princeton University Press. Paperback edition: New York: John Wiley and Sons [1966].

The revision of this paper was partially supported by a Faculty Research Fellowship while the author was at the College of Business Administration, University of Tennessee, Knoxville. The author would like to thank Professors Richard Day and Theodore Groves and the members of his dissertation committee - Professors Baron, Camacho and Prakash - for many helpful comments and suggestions that resulted in a much clearer presentation. They should not be held responsible for the outcome.

Approximate Minimization of Noncovex Integral Functionals (abstract)

J.P. Aubin and I. Ekeland

ABSTRACT

1. THE CONTINUOUS PROBLEM

Denote by Ω a bounded open subset of $\mathbb{R}^n$ and by X a convex subset of some Banach space U. Denote by φ and a_j $(1 \leq j \leq m)$ functions from $\Omega \times X$ into $\mathbb{R}$ which are continuous in ξ for almost every fixed $\omega \epsilon \Omega$, and measurable in Ω for every fixed $\xi \epsilon X$. Assume moreover that there exist $c \epsilon L^1(\Omega)$, $\alpha \epsilon [1, +\infty[$, and $M \epsilon \mathbb{R}$ such that

(1)
$$\begin{cases} |\varphi(\omega, \xi)| \leq c(\omega) + M \|\xi\|^\alpha \\ \\ |a_j(\omega, \xi)| \leq c(\omega) + M \|\xi\|^\alpha \end{cases}$$

It follows easily from the Lebesgue convergence theorem that the mappings:

$$f: L^\alpha(\Omega; X) \to \mathbb{R}$$

$$A: L^\alpha(\Omega; X) \to \mathbb{R}^m$$

defined by:

(2)
$$\begin{cases} f(x) = \int_\Omega f(\omega, x(\omega))d\omega \\ \\ A(x) = \{\int_\Omega a_j(\omega, x(\omega))d\omega\}_{1 \leq j \leq m} \end{cases}$$

are continuous in the norm topology.

We now introduce a convex and lower semi-continuous mapping $g : \mathbb{R}^m \to \mathbb{R}U\{+\infty\}$, and we consider the following minimization problem:

$$(3) \qquad v = \inf_{x \in L^\alpha(\Omega;X)} [\int_\Omega \varphi(\omega, x(\omega))d\omega + g(\int_\Omega A(\omega, x(\omega))d\omega)] \ .$$

Its Lagrangian is the functional on $L^\alpha(\Omega;X) \times \mathbb{R}^m_+$ defined by:

$$(4) \qquad L(x,p) = \int_\Omega \varphi(\omega, x(\omega))d\omega + \langle p, \int_\Omega A(\omega, x(\omega))d\omega \rangle - g^*(p)$$

where $g^*(p) = \sup_{\xi \in \mathbb{R}^m} \{\langle p, \xi \rangle - g(\xi)\}$.

We shall prove that there exists a Lagrange multiplier for problem (3), i.e. some $\bar{p} \in \mathbb{R}^m_+$ such that:

$$(5) \qquad v = \inf_{x \in L^\alpha(\Omega;X)} L(x, \bar{p})$$

Define the "lack of convexity" $\rho(f)$ of a function $f : X \to \mathbb{R}$ by:

$$(6) \qquad \rho(f) = \sup_{\substack{\text{convex} \\ \text{combinations}}} \{f(\Sigma \alpha_i x_i) - \Sigma \alpha_i f(x_i)\}$$

and assume that:

$$(7) \qquad \begin{cases} \text{ess sup}_{\omega \in \Omega} \ \rho[\varphi(\omega, \cdot)] < +\infty \\[2mm] \text{ess sup}_{\omega \in \Omega} \ \rho[a_j(\omega, \cdot)] < +\infty \ \text{ for } 1 \le j \le m \end{cases}$$

Lastly, in the case where the mapping A is not linear, to every pair (c^-, c^+) of vectors in $\mathbb{R}^m$ we associate the function on $\mathbb{R}^m$ defined by:

(8) $$g(\eta; c^-, c^+) = \inf\{g(\zeta)\,|-c^- \le \eta-\zeta \le c^+\}$$

and the perturbed minimization problem

(9) $$v(c^-,c^+) = \inf_{x \in L^\alpha(\Omega;x)} \{\int_\Omega \varphi(\omega,x(\omega))d\omega + g(\int A(\omega,x(\omega))d\omega; c^-,c^+)\} \ .$$

Note that $v = v(0,0)$. We shall assume that:

(10) $\begin{cases} \text{(i)} \quad \text{either } A \text{ is a linear operator} \\[2ex] \text{(ii)} \quad \text{or the mapping } (c^-,c^+) \mapsto v(c^-,c^+) \text{ is l.s.c. at } (0,0). \end{cases}$

THEOREM 1. Assume hypotheses (1), (7) and (10) as well as the constraint qualification:

(11) $$0 \in \text{Interior of } (\text{dom } g - A(X)).$$

Then there exists a Lagrange multiplier $\overline{p}$.

Note that the measurable selection theorem (e.g. Ekeland-Teman [1975] or Kuratowski and Ryll-Nardzewski [1965]) implies that:

$$\inf_{x \in L^\alpha(\Omega;X)} L(x,p) = \int_\Omega \inf_{\xi \in X} \{\varphi(\omega,x) + g \circ A(\omega,x)\}dx \ .$$

2. THE DISCRETE PROBLEMS

Let h be some small parameter, and $\mathcal{e}_h = \{T_h^j\}_j$ a partition of Ω in a finite number of subsets T_h^j, such that:

(12) $$|\mathcal{e}_h| = \max_j \text{ meas } (T_h^j) \to 0 \text{ as } h \to 0$$

Denote by $L_h(\Omega; x)$ the space of step functions $\Omega \to X$, constant over each member of $\mathcal{E}_h$. We approximate the minimization problem (3) by:

$$
\begin{aligned}
(13) \quad v_h &= \inf_{x_h \in L_h(\Omega;X)} \left\{ \int_\Omega \varphi(\omega, x_h(\omega)) d\omega + g(\int_\Omega A(\omega, x_h(\omega)) d\omega \right\} \\
&= \inf_{\{\xi_h^j\}_j} \left\{ \Sigma_j \int_{T_h^j} \varphi(\omega, \xi_h^j) d\omega + g(\Sigma_j \int_{T_h^j} A(\omega, \xi_h^j) d\omega) \right\}
\end{aligned}
$$

With every pair (c^-, c^+) of vectors in $\mathbb{R}^m$, we associate the perturbed minimization problem:

$$
(14) \quad v_h(c^-, c^+) = \inf_{x_h \in L_h(\Omega; x)} \left\{ \int_\Omega \varphi(\omega, x_h(\omega)) d\omega + g(\int_\Omega A(\omega, x_h(\omega)) d\omega; c^-, c^+ \right\}
$$

The following result can then be proved via the Shapley-Folkman theorem (e.g. Aubin and Ekeland [1974], Starr [1967]).

THEOREM 2. Consider the vectors c_h^- and c_h^+ in $\mathbb{R}^m$ with components =

$$
(15) \quad
\begin{cases}
c_{h,j}^- = (m+1) \underset{\omega \in \Omega}{\text{ess sup}} \ \rho[-a_j(\omega, \cdot)] \, |\mathcal{E}_h| \\
c_{h,j}^+ = (m+1) \underset{\omega \in \Omega}{\text{ess sup}} \ \rho[a_j(\omega, \cdot)] \, |\mathcal{E}_h| \ .
\end{cases}
$$

If the assumptions of theorem 1 are satisfied, there exists $p_h \in \mathbb{R}_+^m$ such that:

$$
(16) \quad v_h(c_h^-, c_h^+) \leq \inf_{x_h \in L_h(\Omega, X)} L(x_h, p_h) + (m+1) \underset{\omega \in \Omega}{\text{ess sup}} \ \rho[\varphi(\omega, \cdot)] \, |\mathcal{E}_h|.
$$

3. AN APPROXIMATION THEOREM

THEOREM 3. If the assumptions of theorem 1 are satisfied, there exists a subsequence p_h satisfying (16) and converging towards a

Lagrange multiplier $\bar{p}$ satisfying (5) as $h \to 0$.

PROOF. We always have $\displaystyle\inf_{x \in L^{\alpha}(\Omega;X)} L(x,p) \le v$. If A is linear, then $c_h^- = c_h^+ = 0$ and $v \le v_h \le v_h(c_h^-, c_h^+)$. If A is nonlinear, the lower semi-continuity (assumption (10)) implies that, for every fixed ϵ, there exists h_1 such that

(17) $\qquad v \le v(c_h^-, c_h^+) + \epsilon \le v_h(c_h^-, c_h^+) + \epsilon$ when $h \le h_1$.

Putting (16) and (17) together, we get:

(18) $\qquad v \le \displaystyle\inf_{x_h \in L_h(\Omega,X)} L(x_h, p_h) + \epsilon + N|\mathcal{E}_h|$

where $N = (m+1)$ ess $\displaystyle\sup_{\omega \in \Omega} [\varphi(\omega, \cdot)]$.

We then show by use of the constraint qualification (11) that the set of $p_h \in \mathbb{R}_+^m$ satisfying (16) is bounded. We can then extract a subsequence p_h converging towards $\bar{p} \in \mathbb{R}_+^m$.

Lastly, the continuity of the mappings f and A and the lower semi-continuity of g, imply that:

(19) $\qquad \displaystyle\inf_{x_h \in L_h(\Omega,X)} L(x_h, p_h) \le \inf_{x \in L^{\alpha}(\Omega,X)} L(x,\bar{p}) + \epsilon$ when $h \le h_2$.

By (18) and (19)

$$v \le \inf_{x \in L^{\alpha}(\Omega,X)} L(x,\bar{p}) + 2\epsilon + M|\mathcal{E}_h| \quad \text{where } h \le h_0 .$$

Hence, the result. ∎

The reader is referred to Aubin and Ekeland [1974] for detailed proofs.

REFERENCES

Arrow, K. and F. Hahn [1971], General competitive analysis, Holden
Day.

Aubin, Jean-Pierre and Ivar Ekeland [1974], "Estimates of the duality gap
of non-convex optimization problems," Mathematics Research
Center, Technical Summary Report #1491.

Ekeland-Temam [1975], Convex analysis and variational problems,
North Holland-Elsevier, to appear.

Ekeland, Ivar [1974], Une estimation a priori en programmation non
convexe. CR. Acad. Sci. Paris 279 (149-151).

Kuratowski and Ryll-Nardzewski [1965], "A general theorem on selectors",
Bulletin de l'academie polanaise des sciences, 13, pp. 397-403.

Perles, M. and R. Aumann [1965], A variational problem arising in
economics, J. Math. Anal. and Appl. 11 (488-503).

Starr, R. [1967], Quasi-equilibria in markets with non-convex preferences,
Econometrica 37 (25-38).

Equilibrium under Uncertainty and Bayesian Adaptive Control Theory
Sanford Grossman

CONTENTS

1. INTRODUCTION

In recent years, interest in optimal decisions under uncertainty has been growing at an ever accelerating rate. Simultaneously, econometricians have been concerned with constructing models of markets in which the participants are acting optimally over time subject to uncertainty. The recent surveys by Dreze [1972] and Nerlove [1972] aptly demonstrate both the current interest and the unsolved problems that researchers face. Many recent articles on the theory of the firm under uncertainty either assume the firm is a monopolist (e.g., Mills [1959], Dhrymes [1964], Leland [1972], Zabel [1970]) or assume that the firm under study is competitive, but has a subjective probability distribution about a future price (e.g., Leland [1972], Sandmo [1971], Stigum [1969]). In the latter case, little or nothing is said about how firms form subjective probability distributions. In this paper, Bayesian stochastic control theory and the theory of rational expectations will be synthesized to show how competitive firms can rationally form subjective probability distributions about a future price, and further, how actual market allocations and prices move over time when firms do so.[1]

The literature on dynamic stochastic control theory traditionally concerns itself with the determination of a sequence of policies (e.g., investment or other input plans) which are optimal with respect to a well specified, known objective function. However, the objective function of firms in a competitive industry (which is usually taken to be expected discounted profits) depends upon the time path of prices of outputs and inputs which is market determined. At time zero, those future prices are usually unknown. Hence, stochastic control theory alone will not provide a solution for the optimal policies. That is, the optimal policies will depend upon the price forecasting rule the firms use. Similarly, in modeling markets, it is often assumed that economic decision makers choose optimal decisions based on one or another ad hoc forecasting rule (e.g., Zabel [1969]). One forecasting rule popular in econometric models in adaptive expectations (see e.g., Cagan [1956], Friedman [1957], Nerlove [1958]). In the adaptive expectations model the decision-maker assumes that the price (e.g. price at which a producer can sell his output) in period t is a weighted average of past prices.

It is essential to note that associated with the choice of a particular forecasting rule by firms is a series of optimal input allocations that, along with random factors (e.g., the weather, illness), results in a sequence of final outputs being supplied to the market. Then, in each period, competition generates an actual output price that clears the market. Hence firms' forecasts of prices play a role in generating an actual series of equilibrium (i.e., market clearing) prices. Realization of this point led Muth [1961] to define a rational price forecasting rule as one in which anticipated prices have the same probability distribution as the actual prices generated by the anticipations. Lucas and Prescott [1971] applied the rational price forecasting rule in a path breaking study of investment under uncertainty. They assume "that expectations of firms are rational, [in] that the anticipated price at time t is the same function of $(u_1, u_2, \ldots, u_t)$ [the random disturbances] as is the actual price. That is, we assume that firms know the true distribution of prices for all future periods." (p. 9.)

In this paper the rational expectation hypothesis is synthesized with Bayesian control theory to yield econometrically relevant models of markets subject to uncertainty. Section II considers a competitive market where random production and demand functions contain parameters whose values are not known precisely by economic agents. In such a market there is learning and experimentation. Each period there is learning as new data are received and the estimates of the parameters of demand and production functions are updated. This process leads to new input allocations by firms. There is experimentation in that today's allocations are made with regard to their effect on the precision of tomorrow's parameter estimates. For such a market, Section 2 derives optimum input policies from a Bayesian adaptive control functional equation under the assumption that the equilibrium price random variable is known for all future periods. The equilibrium price random variables are used by competitive firms in making optimal discounted expected profit decisions.

Section 3 is the core of the paper. There it is shown how firms can rationally form anticipations about prices in future periods. It is shown that firms can derive a sequence of anticipated price random variables which will be the actual price random variables generated each period by the market through the interaction of supply and demand. Simultaneously, optimal input plans for each firm are derived. Section 3 uses a technique which I believe is of wide applicability in economic applications of dynamic stochastic control theory. I derive an <u>equilibrium</u> functional equation. That is, the rational expectations model is used to derive the functional equation for each firm which is consistent with market clearing each period. In most applications of stochastic control theory, a firm's (or consumer's) functional equation is derived with no reference to market clearing (see, e.g., Douglas [1973], Hakansson [1969], Holt <u>et al</u>. [1960], Malinvaud [1969], Theil [1964]). Section 4 analyzes a special case of the model which demonstrates that a Rational Expectations price predictor must be more than unbiased in order to be an equilibrium price random variable. All of its moments must be consistent with conditions implied by market clearing and expected profit maximization. Section 4 also contains conclusions.

2. STATEMENT OF THE PROBLEM

Let each of the identical firms in a competitive industry have a production function:

$$(1) \qquad Q_t = f(x_t, \theta_t) .$$

x_t is a vector of inputs, Q_t is output, and θ_t is a vector of random variables. Hence, for a given vector of inputs x_t, output Q_t is a random variable. x_t could represent seed planted at the beginning of period t, θ_t could be a vector of exogenous, random environmental variables (e.g., weather), and Q_t could be the amount of corn harvested at the end of period t. For all t, let θ_t take on values in a set[2] Θ . The joint density function of $(\theta_0, \theta_1, \ldots, \theta_T)$ will be described below. For all t, the input set is a convex set X with non-negative elements (i.e. $x_t \in X$ for all $(t = 0, 1, 2, \ldots, T)$. In discussions below, $\Theta^K \equiv \Theta^{K-1} \times \Theta$, $K = 1, 2, 3, \ldots, T$, where $\Theta^0 \equiv \Theta$. Let $\theta^t \equiv (\theta_0, \theta_1, \ldots, \theta_{t-1}, \theta_t)$ denote an element of Θ^t. (Since the primary purpose of this paper is to present a new technique for modeling markets subject to uncertainty, the text will not dwell on technical points such as uniqueness and existence of maxima and the differentiability and integrability of various functions. Further, if a derivative or integral is written down, then it is assumed to exist.)

Let $\overline{Q}_t$ equal total industry output in period t divided by the number of firms producing output during that period. $\overline{Q}_t$ shall be referred to as per-firm output. We shall assume throughout the paper that the number of firms, N, is constant from period $t = 0$ to $t = T$. Hence we can specify demand as a function of per-firm output instead of total output. Let the price at which $N\overline{Q}_t$ will be demanded in period t be given by

$$(2) \qquad \overline{P}_t = D(\overline{Q}_t, \theta_t) .$$

Equation (2) is designed to model the situation where the price that consumers are willing to pay for a _given_ quantity depends on the outcome of a random variable. The market for ice-cream is a good example. The price that people are willing to pay for $N\overline{Q}_t$ units of ice cream depends on the weather, which is a random variable. Note that the same θ_t appears in both (1) and (2). This is done only for notational convenience. θ_t could be partitioned into $(\theta_{1t}, \theta_{2t}) \equiv \theta_t$, where f does not depend on θ_{2t} and D does not depend on θ_{1t}.

At the beginning of time t firms choose an $x_t \in X$ using all the information they have learned up to, but not including, time t. Let $\overline{P}^t \equiv (\overline{P}_0, \overline{P}_1, \ldots, \overline{P}_t)$, $\overline{Q}^t \equiv (\overline{Q}_0, \overline{Q}_1, \ldots, \overline{Q}_t)$, $x^t \equiv (x_0, x_1, \ldots, x_t)$, and $I^t \equiv (\overline{P}^t, \overline{Q}^t, Q^t, x^t)$. At the beginning of time t, firms know I^{t-1}. Firms never observe θ^t. Since _all_ firms base their decisions at time t on their own I^{t-1}, it seems reasonable to assume that the actual $\overline{Q}_t$ is a function of the I^{t-1} (for each firm) and θ_t (since, by (1), the Q_t of each firm depends on θ_t). I^{t-1} is the same for each firm because all firms are assumed identical. However, in order to define a competitive equilibrium, we assume that each firm believes that it does not affect $\overline{Q}_t$ by its own choice of x_t. Thus since all firms make their decisions concerning an optimal x_t based on I^{t-1}, and since $Q_t = f(x_t, \theta_t)$, we assume that firms believe $\overline{Q}_t$ is generated by

(3a) $$\overline{Q}_t(\theta^t) \equiv M_t(\overline{P}^{t-1}, \overline{Q}^{t-1}, \theta_t), \quad \text{for } t = 1, 2, \ldots, T,$$

(3b) where $$\overline{Q}^0(\theta_0) \equiv \overline{Q}_0(\theta_0) ,$$

(3c) $$\overline{P}^0(\theta_0) \equiv D(\overline{Q}_0(\theta_0), \theta_0),$$

(3d) $$\overline{P}_t(\theta^t) \equiv D(\overline{Q}_t(\theta_t), \theta_t) ,$$

where the functions $M_t(\cdot)$, and $\overline{Q}_0(\cdot)$ are assumed given to each firm, and $D(\cdot)$ is the demand function given by (2). The functions $M_t(\cdot)$ and

$\overline{Q}_0(\cdot)$, specify how firms form anticipations about $\overline{Q}_t$. In Section 3 equilibrium functions $M_t(\cdot)$ and $\overline{Q}_0(\cdot)$ will be derived.[3] If firms know $M_1(\cdot)$ and $\overline{Q}_0$, then $\overline{Q}_0(\cdot)$ determines $\overline{P}^0(\cdot)$ by (3c). $\overline{Q}_1(\cdot)$ is then determined from (3a) using (3b) and (3c). This $\overline{Q}_1(\cdot)$ is then used in (3d) to determine $\overline{P}_1(\cdot)$. Then $\overline{Q}_2(\cdot)$ is determined from (3a) using $\overline{P}^1 \equiv (\overline{P}^0, \overline{P}_1)$, and $\overline{Q}^1 \equiv (\overline{Q}_0, \overline{Q}_1)$ (note that $\overline{P}^0 \equiv \overline{P}_0$). In this way two sequences of functions $\{\overline{P}_t(\theta^t)\}$ and $\{\overline{Q}^t(\theta^t)\}$ are generated from $M_t(\cdot)$ and $\overline{Q}_0(\cdot)$. Note that given I^{t-1} (and hence $(\overline{P}^{t-1}, \overline{Q}^{t-1})$), $\overline{P}_t(\theta^t)$ is random only through θ_t.

Our objective is to model a competitive industry with firms that are uncertain about the price at which consumers will demand the total industry output. Further, each firm is uncertain about how much output a given set of inputs will yield. As time goes on the firms accumulate knowledge about market demand and about their own production functions. This process can be modeled by having firms learn about the distribution of θ_t, using I^{t-1}.

Let A^t be a subset of Θ^t on which the probability that $\theta^t \epsilon A^t$ is well defined. Assume that there exists a statistic

$$(4a) \qquad \hat{\theta}_t \equiv K(\hat{\theta}_{t-1}, \overline{P}_{t-1}, \overline{Q}_{t-1}, Q_{t-1}, x_{t-1}) ,$$

with $K(\cdot)$ a given function and $\hat{\theta}_0$ a given element of a given set $\hat{\Theta}$. Assume that for all t, $j = 0, 1, 2, \ldots, T$:

$$(4b) \qquad \mathrm{Prob}(\theta^t \epsilon A^t \mid I^{j-1}) = \mathrm{Prob}[\theta^t \epsilon A^t \mid \hat{\theta}_j),$$

so that $\hat{\theta}_j$ and I^{j-1} give equivalent information about θ^t. In what follows we shall require that the density of θ_t given $\hat{\theta}_t$ exists. (4a) is a sequential updating formula. At the end of period $t-1$, all firms get new information: $\overline{P}_{t-1}, \overline{Q}_{t-1}, Q_{t-1}, \overline{P}_{t-1}$ and $N\overline{Q}_{t-1}$ are the market price and quantity that are observed by all firms at the end of $t-1$. Note that we do not assume that θ_{t-1} is ever observed. Each firm also

284

observes its own output at the end of period $t-1$. When the data $(\overline{P}_{t-1},$ $\overline{Q}_{t-1}, Q_{t-1}, x_{t-1})$ are combined with the prior (to period $t-1$ data) param-eter $\hat{\theta}_{t-1}$, the function K gives the updated parameter $\hat{\theta}_t$. (4a) can be understood better by examining a Cobb-Douglas example. Suppose (1) and (2) are given by

(5a)
$$Q_t = x_t^{\alpha_1} e^{\alpha_t}$$

(5b)
$$\overline{P}_t = \overline{Q}_t^{\beta_2} e^{\beta_t}$$

or in logs

$$\log Q_t = \alpha_1 \log x_t + \alpha_t$$

$$\log \overline{P}_t = \beta_2 \log \overline{Q}_t + \beta_t .$$

Assume that α_t and β_t are independent normal variables, serially un-correlated, with mean zero and variance one. Then θ_t is the vector

$$\theta_t \equiv (\alpha_1 \beta_2 \alpha_t \beta_t) .$$

If α_1 and β_2 are unknown, and the uncertainty is represented by inde-pendent normal prior distributions at time $t-1$, with parameters, say $\hat{\theta}_{t-1}$, then the a posteriori beliefs about α_1 and β_2 will be represented by independent normal distributions with parameter, say $\hat{\theta}_t \cdot \hat{\theta}_t$ depends on the prior parameter $\hat{\theta}_{t-1}$ and the data $(Q_{t-1}, x_{t-1}, \overline{P}_{t-1}, \overline{Q}_{t-1})$, via Bayes rule. This can be seen from the following result. Let $\hat{\theta}_t \equiv (a_t, A_t, b_t, B_t)$, where (a_t, A_t) is the mean and variance of the prior on α_1, and (b_t, B_t) is the mean and variance of the prior on β_2 at time t. Then, by Bayes rule:

$$a_t = \frac{a_{t-1} + A_{t-1}(\log Q_{t-1})(\log x_{t-1})^2}{1 + A_{t-1}(\log x_{t-1})^2}$$

$$A_t = \frac{A_{t-1}}{1 + A_{t-1}(\log x_{t-1})^2}$$

(5c)

$$b_t = \frac{b_{t-1} + B_{t-1}(\log \overline{P}_{t-1})(\log \overline{Q}_{t-1})}{1 + B_{t-1}(\log \overline{Q}_{t-1})^2}$$

$$B_t = \frac{B_{t-1}}{1 + B_{t-1}(\log \overline{Q}_{t-1})^2}$$

Notice from (5c) that large values of $(\log x_{t-1})^2$ lead to very precise information about α_1. This is the experimental design aspect of the firm's decision problem. From (5c) $\hat{\theta}_t$ is seen to depend on $\hat{\theta}_{t-1}$, $\overline{P}_{t-1}$, $\overline{Q}_{t-1}$, Q_{t-1}, and x_{t-1}. Thus (5c) defines a function $K(\cdot)$, of the type given in (4a).

Note that $\hat{\theta}_t$ depends explicitly on the firm's input choice in period t-1, and implicitly on the firm's input choice in all previous periods (since $\hat{\theta}_{t-1}$ is a function of x_{t-2}, x_{t-3}, ..., x_1). $\overline{P}_{t-1}$ and $\overline{Q}_{t-1}$ are incorporated in (4a) to allow for updating the posterior distribution of the parameters of the demand curve. Note that since $\overline{P}_{t-1}$ and $\overline{Q}_{t-1}$ represent equilibrium random variables and perfirm input allocations, they are not under the control of any single firm. Nevertheless, we assume that each firm is able to find out what industry output and price are at the end of the period, and incorporate that data in its estimate of the industry demand curve.

(4a) incorporates learning and experimentation. There is learning as $\hat{\theta}_t$ is updated every period when new data are received. There is experimentation because $\hat{\theta}_t$ depends on, among other things, the firm's controls x_0, x_1, x_2, ..., x_{t-1}. Hence it may pay for a firm to experiment in period t (perhaps reducing profits in that period) since the experimentation could lead to improved parameter estimates that lead to higher profits in future periods.

We now define an individual firm's optimization problem. Let

$$(6) \qquad \bar{\pi}_t(x_t, \theta^t) \equiv \bar{P}_t(\theta^t) f(x_t, \theta_t) - w_t x_t,$$

where w_t is a vector of input prices that are non-random, known and exogenous to the industry in question, and $\bar{\pi}_t(x_t, \theta^t)$ is the firm's t^{th} period profit function. $w_t x_t$ is the inner product of the two vectors w_t and x_t. At each time t the firm uses all the information available to choose some $x_t \in X$. The information available is $\hat{\theta}_t$. Assume that for all t $\hat{\theta}_t$ takes on values in a set $\hat{\Theta}$. An input plan for period t is a function $\tilde{x}_t$, where $\tilde{x}_t : \hat{\Theta} \to X$. Note that the problem is being structured in such a way that the firm chooses a point in X as its tth period allocation <u>before</u> θ_t is realized. (Farmers plant x_t at the beginning of period t, before they know what the weather is in period t.) We assume that at time $t = 0$, each firm chooses a sequence of plans[4] $(x_0(\hat{\theta}_0), x_1(\hat{\theta}_1), \ldots, x_T(\hat{\theta}_T)) \equiv \{x_t\}$ to maximize

$$(7) \qquad E\left[\sum_{t=0}^{T} \beta^t \bar{\pi}_t(x_t, \theta^t) \mid \hat{\theta}_0 \right],$$

where the expectation is taken with respect to the joint distribution of $(\theta_0, \theta_1, \theta_2, \ldots, \theta_T)$ conditional on $\hat{\theta}_0$, which is given to the firm and assumed to satisfy (4), and β is the discount factor. Expected discounted profits has been a criterion much used in the literature on dynamic models of firms, so I will not attempt to defend its use except to note that the dynamic programming procedure that will be illustrated below relies heavily on the additivity of returns over time.[5] However, the procedure to be described could equally be applied to

$$E\left[\sum_{t=0}^{T} U_t[\bar{\pi}_t(x_t, \theta_0^t)] \mid \hat{\theta}_0 \right],$$

where the U_t are any twice continuously differentiable functions.

The Principle of Optimality can be used to solve for the optimum input plans. Let

$$(8) \quad V_t(\hat{\theta}_t) \equiv \max_{x_t, x_{t+1}, \ldots, x_T} E[\sum_{i=t}^{T} \beta^i \bar{\pi}_i(x_i, \theta^i) | \hat{\theta}_t]$$

$$(8a) \quad V_t(\hat{\theta}_t) = \max_{x_t, x_{t+1}, \ldots, x_T} E[\beta^t \bar{\pi}_t(x_t, \theta_0^t) + E[\sum_{i=t+1}^{T} \beta^i \bar{\pi}_i(x_i, \theta^i) | \hat{\theta}_{t+1}] | \hat{\theta}_t]$$

$$V_t(\hat{\theta}_t) = \max_{x_t} \{ E[\beta^t \bar{\pi}_t(x_t, \theta^t) + \max_{x_{t+1}, \ldots, x_T} E[\sum_{i=t+1}^{T} \beta^i \bar{\pi}_i(x_i, \theta^i) | \hat{\theta}_{t+1}] | \hat{\theta}_t] \}$$

where [6] the last equality follows from the fact that the conditional distribution of θ_t given $\hat{\theta}_t$ does not depend on $x_{t+1}, \ldots, x_T$, since $\hat{\theta}_t$ is not a function of these variables. Using (8) the last equality becomes

$$(9) \quad V_t(\hat{\theta}_t) = \max_{x_t} E[\beta^t \bar{\pi}_t(x_t, \theta^t) + V_{t+1}(\hat{\theta}_{t+1}) | \hat{\theta}_t] \ .$$

Set

$$(10) \quad V_{T+1}(\hat{\theta}_{T+1}) \equiv 0,$$

since T is the last period. The expectation in (9) is taken with respect to the conditional distribution of θ^t and $\hat{\theta}_{t+1}$ given $\hat{\theta}_t$. Given $\hat{\theta}_0$, (9) and (10) can be used to solve for the optimum input plans $\hat{x}_0(\hat{\theta}_0)$, $\hat{x}_1(\hat{\theta}_1)$, $\ldots$, $\hat{x}_T(\hat{\theta}_T)$. Note that $x_t(\hat{\theta}_t)$ is defined as the maximizer of $E[\beta^t \bar{\pi}_t(x_t, \theta^t) + V_{t+1}(\hat{\theta}_{t+1}) | \hat{\theta}_t]$. If the maximum for a given $\hat{\theta}_t$ is not attained for some $x \in X$, then $x_t(\hat{\theta}_t)$ does not exist. Further, if the maximum is not unique for a given $\hat{\theta}_t$, then $x_t(\hat{\theta}_t)$ is not a function from $\hat{\Theta} \to X$. In line with the expositional nature of this paper we assume throughout that for each $\hat{\theta}_t$ a unique maximum is attained by some $\hat{x}_t(\hat{\theta}_t) \in X$. Note that $\hat{x}_t(\hat{\theta}_t)$ is implicitly a function from $\Theta^{t-1} \to X$ since $\hat{\theta}_t$ is a statistic which is a function of $(\theta_0, \theta_1, \theta_2, \ldots, \theta_{t-1})$, as given in (4). From (6), $\bar{\pi}_t(x_t, \theta^t)$ depends on $\bar{P}_t$. Since we have not specified

$\overline{P}_t$, the problem in (9) and (10) cannot be solved for the optimal policies. The next section is devoted to showing how optimal plans $\{x_t^o\}$ and equilibrium prices $\{P_t^o\}$ can be derived jointly, just as competitve equilibrium (supply and demand) problems are solved in non-random contexts.

3. SELF-FULFILLING EXPECTATIONS

From (6), t^{th} period profits are seen to depend on the ith period price random variable. Hence the profit maximizing plan $\{x_t\}$ depends on the sequence of price random variables anticipated $\{P_t\}$. Suppose the identical firms anticipate a particular sequence of prices $\{\overline{P}_t\}$. Then $\overline{\pi}_t = \overline{P}_t f(x_t, \theta_t) - w_t x_t$ could be substituted into (9) and a profit maximizing input plan could be found. Label this plan $\{\overline{x}_t\}$.

It need not be true that $\{\overline{x}_t\}$ and $\{\overline{P}_t\}$ are consistent. If the firms use $\{\overline{x}_t\}$, then the actual price in the market will be given by

$$(11) \qquad \hat{P}_t \equiv D[\, f(\overline{x}_t, \theta_t), \theta_t \,] \ .$$

Inconsistency arises since the actual price random variable, $\hat{P}_t$ need not equal the anticipated price random variable, $\overline{P}_t$. (That the price will be given by (11) follows from the assumption of no storage of output, and that in each period, for whatever realization of θ_t, a price will be determined such that the whole quantity produced is sold.) Another way of stating the inconsistency is that the anticipated per-firm output $\overline{Q}_t$, need not equal the actual per-firm output $f(\overline{x}_t, \theta_t)$. That is, the functions $M_t(\cdot)$ in (3) need not be equilibrium functions in that they generate $\overline{P}_t$ in such a way that the optimal input plans $\overline{x}_t$ need not generate the $\overline{Q}_t$ implied by M_t. The inconsistency, $\hat{P}_t \neq \overline{P}_t$, implies an irrationality on the part of firms anticipating a price sequence $\{\overline{P}_t\}$. All firms make their plans $\{\overline{x}_t\}$ under the assumption that $\{P_t\} = \{\overline{P}_t\}$, while the plans $\{\overline{x}_t\}$ generate a market price sequence different from $\{\overline{P}_t\}$. A rational plan $\{x_t^o\}$ would be made on the assumption that prices are given by $\{P_t^o\}$, $\{\overline{Q}_t^o\}$, where

289

(12) $$P_t^o(\theta^t) \equiv D[\overline{Q}_t^o(\theta^t), \theta_t],$$

and

(13) $$\overline{Q}_t^o(\theta^t) \equiv f[x_t^o(\hat{\theta}_t), \theta_t] .$$

In this case firms assume the price sequence is $\{P_t^o\}$ and choose plans $\{x_t^o\}$ that maximize expected profits when $P_t = P_t^o$, $t = 0, 1, \ldots, T$. Further, the plans are not self-contradictory since the sequence of inputs $\{x_t^o\}$ generates through (12) (market clearing), a sequence of price random variables $\{P_t^o\}$ which is the same as the one used to calculate the optimal plan. (13) requires that anticipations about per-firm output random variables be correct. Note that (13) gives the equilibrium functions M_t^o as follows (see (3)):

(14) $$M_t^o(P^{o\,t-1}, \overline{Q}^{o\,t-1}, \theta_t) \equiv f(x_t^o(\hat{\theta}_t^o), \theta_t),$$

where

(15) $$\hat{\theta}_t^o \equiv K(\hat{\theta}_{t-1}^o, P_{t-1}^o, \overline{Q}_{t-1}^o, \overline{Q}_{t-1}^o, x_{t-1}^o), \quad \hat{\theta}_o^o \equiv \hat{\theta}_o.$$

In (15), the arguments of $K(\cdot)$ are the equilibrium values of the arguments of $K(\cdot)$ in (4a). Note that $\overline{Q}_{t-1}^o$ appears twice in (15) because, in equilibrium all of the identical firms must choose the same x_t^o (which generates their outputs, each equal to the per-firm output $\overline{Q}_t^o$).

    With the above comments in mind, we formally define a self-fulfilling expectations (SFE) equilibrium as three sequences of functions $\{P_t^o\}$, $\{x_t^o\}$, and $\{\overline{Q}_t^o\}$, where $P_t^o : \Theta^t \to \mathbb{R}^+$, $x_t^o : \hat{\Theta} \to X$, and $\overline{Q}_t^o : \Theta^t \to \mathbb{R}^+$, such that for all $t = 0, 1, \ldots, T$:

(16a) $$\overline{Q}_t^o(\theta^t) = f(x_t^o(\hat{\theta}_t^o), \theta_t) \qquad \text{for all } \theta^t$$

(16b) $$P_t^o(\theta^t) = D[\overline{Q}_t^o(\theta^t), \theta_t] \qquad \text{for all } \theta^t,$$

and for any sequence $\{x_t\}$ such that $x_t : \hat{\Theta} \rightarrow X$:

(17) $$E[\sum_{t=0}^{T} \beta^t [P_t^o f(x_t^o, \theta_t) - w_t x_t^o] | \hat{\theta}_o^o] \geq E[\sum_{t=0}^{T} \beta^t [P_t^o f(x_t, \theta_t) - w_t x_t] | \hat{\theta}_o].$$

The expectation on the left hand side of (17) involves $x_t^o(\hat{\theta}_t^o)$, and assumes $\hat{\theta}_t^o$ is given by (15). The expectation on the right hand side of (17) involves $x_t(\hat{\theta}_t)$ and $\hat{\theta}_t$ is given by $\hat{\theta}_t = K(\hat{\theta}_{t-1}, P_{t-1}^o, \overline{Q}_{t-1}^o, Q_{t-1}, x_{t-1})$, where $\hat{\theta}_o$ is given and equal to $\hat{\theta}_o$ and $Q_{t-1} \equiv f(x_{t-1}, \theta_{t-1})$. Thus, the left hand side of (17) is the expected profit with anticipations $\overline{Q}_t^o$, P_t^o and inputs x_t^o. The right hand side of (17) is the expected profits to be derived from an alternative input plan $\{x_t\}$ under the same anticipations; $\overline{Q}_t^o$, P_t^o. Thus, (17) is the condition that if a firm has anticipations $\{\overline{Q}_t^o, P_t^o\}$, then $\{x_t^o\}$ is its optimal policy. (16) requires that the policy $\{x_t^o\}$ generate, through market clearing the sequences $\{P_t^o\}$ and $\{\overline{Q}_t^o\}$.

The above definition[7] has been called "Rational Expectations" when used by Lucas and Prescott [1971] in an analysis of investment which did not consider Bayesian learning and experimentation.[8] The term "Self-fulfilling Expectation" was used by Brock [1972] in the study of perfect foresight models (models of non-random markets in equilibrium over time). Radner [1970] and [1972] introduced randomness and considered general equilibrium over time with incomplete futures markets, and used the term "consistent expectations."

We now describe an algorithm which can be used to calculate the equilibrium and also illustrates in more detail what goes on in the model.

Returning to equation (9), we consider the problem at the last period when each firm knows $\hat{\theta}_T^o$. First, define, for $t = 0, 1, 2, \ldots, T$,

(18) $$\pi_t(x_t, \theta_t) \equiv P_t^o f(x_t, \theta_t) - w_t x_t .$$

Note that (16) implies that P_t^o depends only on $\hat{\theta}_t^o$ and θ_t. Then from (12) and (13):

(19)
$$V_T(\hat{\theta}^o_T) = \max_{x_T} E[\beta^T \pi_T(x_T, \theta_T) \mid \hat{\theta}^o_T] \,.$$

The expectation is taken with respect to the density of θ_T given $\hat{\theta}^o_T$, $\phi(\theta_T \mid \hat{\theta}^o_T)$. Hence, since $\phi(\theta_T \mid \hat{\theta}^o_T)$ does not depend on x_T (see (15)), an interior maximum occurs when

(20)
$$E[\beta^T \frac{\partial \pi_T}{\partial x_T} (x^o_T, \theta_T) \mid \hat{\theta}^o_T] = 0, \quad \text{which implies}$$

(21)
$$E[P^o_T \frac{\partial f}{\partial x_T} (x^o_T, \theta_T) \mid \hat{\theta}^o_T] = w_T \,.$$

But P^o_T must satisfy (16), so (21) becomes

(22)
$$E[D[f(x^o_T, \theta_T), \theta_T] \frac{\partial f}{\partial x_T} (x^o_T, \theta_T) \mid \hat{\theta}^o_T] = w_T \,.$$

If $\hat{\theta}^o_T$ were known, then (22) could be solved for x^o_T and (16) could be used to determine P^o_T. Then x^o_T and P^o_T so determined would have the property that x^o_T maximizes expected profits given that firms anticipate a price random variable P^o_T, and when firms use the input x^o_T, market clearing in period T implies the price random variable P^o_T. Firms fulfill their expectations about market price.

At time $t = 0, 1, \ldots, T-1$, $\hat{\theta}_T$ is not known. From (15) $\hat{\theta}^o_T$ depends on data that is not known until the end of period $T-1$. The solution to (22) is a plan that tells the firm what inputs to use in period T, given that at the beginning of the period, $\hat{\theta}^o_T$ has a particular value. That is, the firm acts sequentially, both learning and experimenting. It doesn't have to commit itself to an input choice for period T until the beginning of period T. Hence the firm's decision at that time will depend on what it has learned up until then (which is data fathered about the distribution of θ_T). For period $T-1$, the firm faces:

(23)
$$V_{T-1}(\hat{\theta}^o_{T-1}) = \max_{x_{T-1}} E[\beta^T \pi_{T-1}(x_{T-1}, \theta_{T-1}) + V_T(\hat{\theta}_T) \mid \hat{\theta}^o_{T-1}] \,,$$

where $\hat{\theta}_T \equiv K(\hat{\theta}^o_{T-1}, P^o_{T-1}, \overline{Q}^o_{T-1}, Q_{T-1}, x_{T-1})$, and $Q_{T-1} = f(x_{T-1}, \theta_{T-1})$. Thus the firm can affect $\hat{\theta}_T$ by its choice of x_{T-1}. This is the experimental design aspect of the firms decision problem. $P^o_{T-1} = D(\overline{Q}^o_{T-1}, \theta_{T-1})$, and $\overline{Q}^o_{T-1}$ will be determined below jointly with x^o_{T-1}. $\hat{\theta}^o_{T-1}$ is assumed given at this stage. Since $\hat{\theta}_{T-1}$ does not depend on x_{T-1}, the distribution of θ_{T-1} does not depend on x_{T-1}. Hence a necessary condition for an interior maximum is:

(24)
$$E[\beta^{T-1}P^o_{T-1} \frac{\partial f(x^o_{T-1}, \theta_{T-1})}{\partial x_{T-1}} \,|\hat{\theta}^o_{T-1}] =$$

$$= \beta^{T-1}w_{T-1} - E[\frac{\partial V_T(\hat{\theta}_T)}{\partial x_{T-1}} \,|\hat{\theta}^o_{T-1}].$$

Using (16), (24) can be written:

(25)
$$E[\beta^{T-1}D[f(x^o_{T-1}, \theta_{T-1}), \theta_{T-1}] \frac{\partial f}{\partial x}(x^o_{T-1}, \theta_{T-1}) \,|\hat{\theta}^o_{T-1}] =$$

$$= \beta^{T-1}w_{T-1} - E[\frac{\partial V_T(\hat{\theta}_T)}{\partial x_{T-1}} \,|\hat{\theta}^o_{T-1}] .$$

Suppose period $T-1$ is the beginning period (i.e., $T = 1$). Then firms know the statistic $\hat{\theta}^o_{T-1}$ at the beginning of period $T-1$. Note that

(26)
$$\frac{\partial V_T(\hat{\theta}_T)}{\partial x_{T-1}} = \frac{\partial V_T}{\partial \hat{\theta}_T} \frac{\partial \hat{\theta}_T}{\partial x_{T-1}} .$$

Since the market will clear in period T, the solution to (22), $x^o_T(\hat{\theta}_T)$, is the firm's optimal policy for period T. Hence V_T is given by

(27)
$$V_T(\hat{\theta}_T) = E[\beta^T[P^o_T f(x^o_T(\hat{\theta}_T), \theta_T) - w_T x^o_T(\hat{\theta}_T)] \,|\hat{\theta}_T]$$

$$= \beta^T[\int_\Theta P^o_T f(x^o_T(\hat{\theta}_T), \theta_T)\phi(\theta_T|\hat{\theta}_T)d\theta_T - w_T x^o_T(\hat{\theta}_T)].$$

293

(28)

$$\frac{\partial V_T}{\partial \hat{\theta}_T} = \beta^T \int_\Theta P_T^O \frac{\partial f(x_T^O(\hat{\theta}_T), \theta_T)}{\partial x_T} \frac{dx_T^O}{d\hat{\theta}_T} \phi(\theta_T | \hat{\theta}_T) d\theta_T -$$

$$-\beta^T w_T \frac{dx_T^O}{d\hat{\theta}_T} + \beta^T \int_\theta P_T^O f(x_T^O, \theta_T) \frac{\partial \phi(\theta_T | \hat{\theta}_T)}{\partial \hat{\theta}_T} d\theta_T \cdot$$

(29)

$$= \beta^T \frac{dx_T^O}{d\hat{\theta}_T} \cdot E[P_T^O \frac{\partial f(x_T^O, \theta_T)}{\partial x_T} - w_T]|\hat{\theta}_T] + \beta^T \int [P_T^O f(x_T^O, \theta_T)$$

$$- w_T x_T^O] \frac{\partial \phi(\theta_T | \hat{\theta}_T)}{\partial \hat{\theta}_T} d\theta_T \cdot$$

From (21) the first term on the right of (29) is zero. Note that in deriving (28) and (29), we have used the fact that $x_T^O(\hat{\theta}_T)$ is _not_ a function of θ_T, since $\hat{\theta}_T$ is not a function of θ_T. In deriving the second term on the right, in (29), we have used the fact that $\phi(\theta_T | \hat{\theta}_T)$ is a probability density function for each $\hat{\theta}_T$. Hence $\int_\Theta \phi(\theta_T | \hat{\theta}_T) d\theta_T \equiv 1$, which implies $\int_\Theta \frac{\partial \phi}{\partial \hat{\theta}_T} (\theta_T | \hat{\theta}_T) d\theta_T \equiv 0$. Note that P_T^O depends on the $\hat{\theta}_T$ of the average firm, not on the $\hat{\theta}_T$ of the firm solving the maximum problem here. That is, in finding $\frac{\partial V_T}{\partial x_{T-1}} = \frac{\partial V_T}{\partial \hat{\theta}_T} \frac{\partial \hat{\theta}_T}{\partial x_{T-1}}$, we have assumed that each firm knows that its own period $T-1$ control (x_{T-1}) will not affect P_T^O, but all of the firms $T-1$ controls together determine P_T^O. (Note that $\frac{\partial \hat{\theta}_T}{\partial x_{T-1}}$ is a matrix and $\frac{\partial V_T}{\partial \hat{\theta}_T}$ is a row vector, hence $\frac{\partial V_T}{\partial x_{T-1}}$ is a row vector with the same number of components as the number of rows in $\frac{\partial \hat{\theta}_T}{\partial x_{T-1}}$.) With the above comments in mind, (21) can be used to rewrite (29) as:

(30) $\quad \dfrac{\partial V_T}{\partial \hat{\theta}_T}(\hat{\theta}_T) = \beta^T \int\limits_\Theta [\, P_T^o f(x_T^o(\hat{\theta}_T),\, \theta_T) - w_T x_T^o(\hat{\theta}_T)\,]\, \dfrac{\partial \phi}{\partial \theta_T}(\theta_T|\hat{\theta}_T)d\theta_T$

(31) $\quad = \beta^T \int\limits_\Theta D[\, f(x_T^o(\hat{\theta}_T),\, \theta_T),\, \theta_T]\, f(x_T^o(\hat{\theta}_T),\theta_T)\, \dfrac{\partial \phi}{\partial \theta_T}(\theta_T|\hat{\theta}_T)d\theta_T\,.$

Rewrite (4a) as

(32) $\quad \hat{\theta}_t = K(\hat{\theta}_{t-1}, P_{t-1}^o, \overline{Q}_{t-1}^o, Q_{t-1}, x_{t-1}) \equiv g(\hat{\theta}_{t-1}, \theta_{t-1}, x_{t-1}, x_{t-1}^o),$

where $g(\cdot)$ is derived by noting that $P_{t-1}^o = D[\,f(x_{t-1}^o, \theta_{t-1}), \theta_{t-1}]$, $\overline{Q}_{t-1}^o = f(x_{t-1}^o, \theta_{t-1})$ and x_{t-1}^o is the equilibrium input plan for period $t-1$. Then it is consistent with (15) to define $\hat{\theta}_t^o$ by:

(33) $\quad\quad\quad \hat{\theta}_t^o \equiv g(\hat{\theta}_{t-1}^o, \theta_{t-1}, x_{t-1}^o, x_{t-1}^o),$

which is the value of the function $g(\hat{\theta}_{t-1}, \theta_{t-1}, x_{t-1}, x_{t-1}^o)$ when $x_{t-1} = x_{t-1}^o$. $\hat{\theta}_t^o$ is the statistic a single firm would have if it acted just as all the other identical firms acted and there was equilibrium in period $t-1$. Using (26), we can define[9]

(34)
$$v_T(\hat{\theta}_{T-1}^o, \theta_{T-1}, x_{T-1}^o) \equiv \dfrac{dV_T(\hat{\theta}_T^o)}{dx_{T-1}}$$
$$\dfrac{\partial V_T(\hat{\theta}_T^o)}{\partial \theta_T} \cdot \dfrac{\partial g(\hat{\theta}_{T-1}^o, \theta_{T-1}, x_{T-1}^o, x_{T-1}^o)}{\partial x_{T-1}}$$

Hence (25) can be written:

(35)
$$E[\, \beta^{T-1} D[\,f(x_{T-1}^o, \theta_{T-1}), \theta_{T-1}]\, \dfrac{\partial f(x_{T-1}^o, \theta_{T-1})}{\partial x_{T-1}}\, |\hat{\theta}_{T-1}^o\,] =$$
$$\beta^{T-1} w_{T-1} - E[\, v_T(\hat{\theta}_{T-1}^o, \theta_{T-1}, x_{T-1}^o)\, |\hat{\theta}_{T-1}^o\,]\,.$$

For any given $\hat{\theta}_{T-1}^o$, (35) is an equation in x_{T-1}^o. Suppose that the equation has a unique solution for each $\hat{\theta}^O_{T-1}$; then it can be solved for an x^O_{T-1} which is a function of $\hat{\theta}^O_{T-1}$. Since we assumed that T-1 was the first period, $x^O_{T-1}(\hat{\theta}^O_{T-1})$ is some element of the input set. Hence, given the prior vector $\hat{\theta}^O_{T-1}$ we have solved for a deterministic input control for the first period. The second period's problem (Tth period here) has already been solved, conditional on $\hat{\theta}^O_T$. The optimal plan is $x^O_T(\hat{\theta}^O_T)$, (see (22) and (33)). Defining $P^O_T = D[f(x^O_T, \theta_T), \theta_T]$, $P^O_{T-1} = D[f(x^O_{T-1}, \theta_{T-1}), \theta_{T-1}]$ leads us to note that x^O_{T-1}, x^O_T maximize expected two period profits when the equilibrium price random variables are P^O_T, P^O_{T-1} (see (22) and (33)). Further, if all firms carry out their plans, then market prices will be given by P^O_T, P^O_{T-1}. Hence firms' anticipated prices are generated in the market by allocations which the firms make based on their anticipations.

Suppose T is arbitrary positive integer, then by induction on j,

$$(36) \quad \begin{aligned} E[\beta^{T-j}D[f(x^O_{T-j}, \theta_{T-j}), \theta_{T-j}] &\frac{\partial f(x^O_{T-j}, \theta_{T-j})}{\partial x_{T-j}} \,|\hat{\theta}^O_{T-j}] = \beta^{T-j}w_{T-j} \\ &- E[v_{T-j+1}(\hat{\theta}^O_{T-j}, \theta_{T-j}, x^O_{T-j}) \,|\hat{\theta}^O_{T-j}] \end{aligned}$$

gives the equilibrium plans $x^O_t(\hat{\theta}^O_t)$, where j = 0, 1, 2, ..., T and $\hat{\theta}^O_o$ is a given vector. As in (34), for t = 0, 1, ..., T

$$(37) \quad v_t(\hat{\theta}^O_{t-1}, \theta_{t-1}, x^O_{t-1}) \equiv \frac{dV_T}{dx_{T-1}}(\hat{\theta}^O_t) = \frac{\partial V_t}{\partial \hat{\theta}_t}(\hat{\theta}^O_t) \cdot \frac{\partial g}{\partial x_{t-1}}(\hat{\theta}^O_{t-1}, \theta_{t-1}, x^O_{t-1}, x^O_{t-1})$$

Using an argument similar to (27) - (31),

$$(38) \quad \frac{\partial V_t}{\partial \hat{\theta}_t}(\hat{\theta}^O_t) = \int [\beta^t D[f(x^O_t, \theta_t), \theta_t]f(x^O_t, \theta_t) + V_{t+1}(\hat{\theta}^O_{t+1})]\frac{\partial \phi(\theta_t | \hat{\theta}^O_t)}{\partial \hat{\theta}_t} \, d\theta_t ,$$

where

$$(39) \quad V_{T+1}(\hat{\theta}^O_{T+1}) \equiv 0 .$$

The actual calculation of $x_t^o(\hat\theta_t^o)$, moves backwards in time. Take $j=0$ in (36); then since $V_{T+1} \equiv 0$, $v_{T+1} \equiv \underline{0}$. Hence (36) determines $x_T^o(\hat\theta_T^o)$, from which (9) determines[10] $V_T(\hat\theta_T^o)$. Then (37), (38) and (39) are used to determine the function $v_T(\hat\theta_{T-1}^o, \theta_{T-1}, x_{T-1}^o)$. Let $j=1$ in (36) and use the function v_T to solve for $x_{T-1}^o(\hat\theta_{T-1}^o)$. This is used in (9) to determine[11] $V_{T-1}(\hat\theta_{T-1}^o)$ and the procedure continues until $x_o^o(\hat\theta_o^o)$ is determined. If P_t^o is defined as

$$(40) \qquad\qquad P_t^o \equiv D[\, f(x_t^o(\hat\theta_t^o),\ \theta_t),\ \theta_t\,]\ ,$$

then $\{x_t^o,\ P_t^o\}$ is the required equilibrium. That is, with P_t^o defined as in (40), and $\pi_t(x_t,\ \theta_t)$ defined as in (18), $\{x_t^o\}$ solves

$$(41) \qquad V_t(\hat\theta_t^o) = \max_{x_t} E[\,\beta^t \pi_t(x_t, \theta_t) + V_{t+1}(\hat\theta_{t+1}) \,|\hat\theta_t^o\,],\quad t = 0,\ 1,\ 2,\ \ldots,\ T,$$

where (39) holds, $\hat\theta_o^o$ is a given vector, and $\hat\theta_t$ is given in (32). Thus we have proved:

THEOREM. If there is a solution to (16) and (17), with x_t^o positive for all t, then x_t^o solves (36). If $P_t^o \equiv D[\, f(x_t^o,\ \theta_t),\ \theta_t\,]$, and $\overline{Q}_t^o \equiv f(x_t^o,\ \theta_t)$, then $\{\overline{Q}_t^o,\ x_t^o,\ P_t^o\}$ is an equilibrium.

The sequence $\{x_t^o,\ P_t^o\}$ has the property that if firms anticipate the price sequence $\{P_t^o\}$ and use that sequence to find optimal input plans, the the optimal input plans will be x_t^o, $t = 0,\ 1,\ 2,\ \ldots,\ T$. Further, $P_t^o = D[\, f(x_t^o,\ \theta_t),\ \theta_t\,]$, so the input plans x_t^o generate, through market-clearing, the same price random variables that firms anticipate.

The algorithm detailed above makes feasible the solution of Bayesian control problems in economics without the use of ad hoc assumptions about future prices, such as adaptive expectations. It can be applied to many of the control problems that study only the individual firm, and say nothing about how the market affects the subjective probability distributions that firms have about future prices (many of the articles referenced in Leland [1972] provide candidates for the application of the Rational Expectations model).

If there are inventories or inputs like capital, the model is not greatly changed. In the case of a capital input the only change is that the input space, X, depends on time through a capital accumulation equation. Since depreciation is usually not considered random, the input space, X, at time t will have a deterministic relation to the input space in period t-1. In the case of inventories, a cost of storage function must be added to $V_T(\hat{\theta})$. The problem is complicated by the possibility of speculation on the part of consumers, once we allow output to be non-perishable. That makes demand equations of the form given in (2) unacceptable. If consumer speculation is ignored (as it usually is in inventory models) the model given here is directly applicable (see Scarf [1963] for some relevant models).

4. A SPECIAL CASE AND CONCLUSIONS

The equilibrium $\{x_t^o, P_t^o\}$ is easy to calculate when the demand function is random but the production function is not, i.e.,

$$(42) \qquad\qquad P_t = D(\overline{Q}_t, \theta_t), \qquad \text{and}$$

$$(43) \qquad\qquad Q_t = f(x_t).$$

In this case all learning is about the demand curve--the production function is deterministic. Learning occurs through updating $\hat{\theta}_t$ via (32). However, since we are considering the case of competitive firms, none of which can affect the market price, $\hat{\theta}_t$ is not a function of x_{t-1}. That is, since only D depends on θ_t, the only source of information about θ_t is contained in P_t and $\overline{Q}_t$ (the output of the average firm). Since individual firms cannot affect P_t or $\overline{Q}_t$, they cannot affect the only source of information about θ_t, $\hat{\theta}_t$. Since $\hat{\theta}_t$ does not depend on x_{t-1},

$$v_t \equiv \frac{\partial V_t}{\partial \hat{\theta}_t} \frac{\partial \hat{\theta}_t}{\partial x_{t-1}} \equiv 0. \quad \text{Hence, (36) becomes:}$$

(44) $$E[\, D[\, f(x_t^o),\ \theta_t)]\ |\hat{\theta}_t^o\,]\ \cdot\ \frac{\partial f}{\partial x}(x_t^o)\ =\ w_t, \quad \text{for } t=0,1,2,\ldots,T.$$

Since $P_t^o = D[\, f(x_t^o(\hat{\theta}_t^o)),\ \theta_t\,]$, (44) is in the usual form: expected price multiplied by marginal product equals the relevant factor price. Note that $E[\, P_t^o\,|\hat{\theta}_t^o\,]$ is a rational expected price unlike the "expected" price that is usually referred to in the adaptive expectations literature. However, Muth [1961] showed that under some circumstances the "expected" price generated by an adaptive expectations model is the same as $E[\, P_t^o\,|\hat{\theta}_t^o\,]$.

(44) can be written as

(45) $$E[\, P_t^o\,|\hat{\theta}_t^o\,]\ \frac{\partial f}{\partial x}\,(x_t^o)\ =\ w_t\ .$$

(45) has the property that if a firm knows the expected price in period t, $E[\, P_t^o\,|\hat{\theta}_t^o\,]$, then it can solve for its tth period optimal input vector x_t^o. That is, the only property of the equilibrium price distribution that a firm need know is the mean (first moment). In this very special case it is possible to write supply functions for firms. Let

(46) $$\overline{P}_t^o \equiv E[\, P_t^o\,|\hat{\theta}_t^o\,]\ .$$

From (42)

(47) $$\overline{P}_t^o = E[\, D(\overline{Q}_t,\theta_t)\,|\hat{\theta}_t^o\,]$$

From (45) and (46)

(48) $$\overline{P}_t^o\ \frac{\partial f}{\partial x}\,(x_t^o)\ =\ w_t\ .$$

(48) implicitly defines a supply function. Assume that, for each $\overline{P}_t^o$, (48) has a unique solution for x_t^o, then there is a function $x_t^o(\overline{P}_t^o)$ which gives the optimal input allocation for $\overline{P}_t^o$. Let

(49)
$$Q_t^s(\overline{P}_t^o) \equiv f(x_t^o(\overline{P}_t^o)),$$

then $Q_t^s(\overline{P}_t^o)$ is the firm's supply function. Supply is a function only of the expected price. (49) and (47) together determine the tth period equilibrium price under the market clearing assumption that

(50)
$$Q_t^d(\overline{P}_t^o, \hat{\theta}_t^o) = \overline{Q}_t^s(\overline{P}_t^o).$$

$Q_t^d(\overline{P}_t^o, \hat{\theta}_t^o)$ is the function that is derived when (47) is solved for $\overline{Q}_t$ as a function of $\overline{P}_t^o$. The relevant implicit function exists if $D(\overline{Q}_t, \theta_t)$ is assumed a strictly decreasing function of $\overline{Q}_t$ for each θ_t; here $\overline{Q}_t$ is not random by (43). The solution to (50) $\overline{P}_t^o(\hat{\theta}_t^o)$ is the expected equilibrium price in period t. It is the mean of the equilibrium price distribution from (45). $\overline{P}_t^o(\hat{\theta}_t^o)$ gives the effect of learning on the time path of expected prices. Thus it shows how competitive dynamics can be generated through learning without the use of ad hoc expectations assumptions.

The above simplification is made possible by the assumption that the production function is not random (see (43)). Under that assumption it was possible to show that supply is a function only of the mean of the market price distribution. Baron [1970] was unable to prove that supply can be written as a function of only the mean price and was forced to assume this result. (In fact, Baron's equation (13), p. 468, implies that in general, a firm's supply will depend on all of the moments of the price distribution. Hence his assumption on the top of p. 472, that supply is a function of the expected price, is puzzling.)

Unfortunately once production is random the above simplification is lost. Consider the beginning of the Tth period. Let $\hat{\theta}_T^o$ be given. (22) gives the equation for the equilibrium input,

(51)
$$E[D[f(x_T^o, \theta_T), \theta_T] \frac{\partial f(x_T^o, \theta_T)}{\partial x_T} | \hat{\theta}_T^o] = w_T$$

or equivalently,

$$(52) \qquad E[\, P^o_T \; \frac{\partial f(x^o_T, \; \theta_T)}{\partial x_T} \; |\hat{\theta}^o_T\,] = w_T$$

Suppose a firm is given $E[\, P^o_T | \hat{\theta}^o_T\,]$. The firm will not be able to solve (52) for its optimal input x^o_T unless P^o_T is independent of θ_T, or $\frac{\partial f(x_T, \; \theta_T)}{\partial x_T}$ is not a function of θ_T. The first possibility is precluded by the fact that all firms are identical and subject to the same random variable, θ_T. If the second possibility does not hold, then $E[\, P^o_T | \hat{\theta}^o_T\,]$ does not contain enough information to solve (52).

This has implications for the growing econometric literature on rational expectations. Suppose firms make allocations, acting as if they know next period's price with certainty. Let the price used be the mean of the equilibrium price distribution. Further, let the firms be maximizing expected profits. Then the firms can still be acting irrationally. Rationality does not mean the use of unbiased predictors. A related point has been made in an econometric context by Grossman [1972]. We have shown here that rationality means the use of the price predictor

$$(53) \qquad P^o_T = D[\, f(x^o_T(\hat{\theta}^o_T), \; \theta_T), \; \theta_T\,]$$

in solving (52), where $x^o_T(\hat{\theta}^o_T)$ is the solution to (51). (This is obviously redundant, but that is because the expectations used here are internal to the model.) Further, P^o_T is the kind of anticipated price random variable that the recent literature on the theory of the firm under uncertainty should be referring to. Sandmo [1971] assumes that: "The firm's beliefs about the sales price can be summarized in a subjective probability distribution." p. 65. He says nothing about where the probability distribution comes from. Baron [1970] writes"

> Two other factors related to price uncertainty have con-
> siderable import on output. First is the nature of the prob-
> ability distribution [on market price] assessed by the firms...

Second is the information available to the firm regarding the
distribution of price... Assume that the firm believes that
the process generating price is normal with known variance
σ_p but unknown mean $\bar{P}$ ... As information is obtained,
..., it is likely that the best estimate of $\bar{P}$ will change,
so output can either increase or decrease.

A further treatment of the effects of probability distributions and information are [sic] beyond the scope of this
brief discussion... p. 471.

The preceding sections have sketched a method for modeling competitive markets subject to uncertainty. Firms in such a market will be
learning, experimenting and forecasting, while making input allocation
decisions. I have shown how equilibrium price random variables $\{P_t^o\}$
and equilibrium input plans $\{x_t^o\}$ can be defined and calculated. The
equilibrium $\{x_t^o, P_t^o\}$ has the self-fulfilling property that if a firm chooses
the equilibrium input plans $\{x_t^o\}$, then that plan will yield the highest
expected profit possible, given that future prices are generated by $\{P_t^o\}$.
Learning and experimentation are taken into account in the expected profit maximization problem that $\{x_t^o\}$ solves when prices are generated by
$\{P_t^o\}$. Further, if the competitive firms choose the input plans $\{x_t^o\}$,
then market prices will be generated by $\{P_t^o\}$ via market clearing each
period.

The above characteristics of the model lead to a theory of competitive dynamics and a general approach to the econometric modeling of
markets subject to uncertainty. If the sequence of random variables
$\{\theta_t\}$ representing uncertainty is such that the conditional distribution
of θ_t given $\theta_{t-1}, \theta_{t-2}, \ldots, \theta_0$ has a sufficient statistic $\hat{\theta}_t$, then
individual firms learn and experiment by updating $\hat{\theta}_t$ from period to
period (using Bayes theorem). Competitive dynamics are generated by
that updating since x_t^o and P_t^o are functions of the equilibrium sufficient
statistic, $\hat{\theta}_t^o$. Hence the functions $x_t^o(\hat{\theta}_t^o)$ and $P_t^o(\hat{\theta}_t^o, \theta_t)$ can be used
to derive the path of input plans and price random variables as a function
of the path of $\hat{\theta}_t^o$. The price random variable P_t^o is the "momentary
equilibrium" discussed by Radner [1970]. If $\hat{\theta}_t^o$ converges in probability

302

to a constant, $\hat{\theta}^o$, as $t \to \infty$, then $P_t^o(\hat{\theta}_t^o, \theta_t) \equiv D[\,f(x_t^o(\hat{\theta}_t^o,\theta_t),\theta_t)]$ can be used to derive the long run equilibrium in the market after all learning and experimentation cease. The long run price will be a random variable $P_t^o(\hat{\theta}^o, \theta_t)$, where the density of θ_t is given by $\emptyset(\theta_t | \hat{\theta}^o)$.

NOTES

[1]Like Stigum [1969] and Diamond [1967], I assume that there are no contingent commodity markets of the type discussed by Arrow [1964]. While Diamond assumes that equilibrium is attained by trading in the stock market, my model makes no explicit mention of a stock market. Lucas and Prescott [1971] has pointed out that the rational expectations equilibrium is not inconsistent with stock market equilibrium of the type considered by Diamond.

[2]Θ is a subset of $\mathbb{R}^n$, the n dimensional Euclidean vector space.

[3]$\overline{Q}_t(\theta^t) = f(\overline{x}_t, \theta_t)$, where $\overline{x}_t$ is the input vector that each of the identical firms choose. This choice is based on the observed data $\overline{P}^{t-1}$ and $\overline{Q}^{t-1}$. Thus if this choice function, $\overline{x}_t(\overline{P}^{t-1}, \overline{Q}^{t-1})$, were well defined, then $M_t(\overline{P}^{t-1}, \overline{Q}^{t-1}, \theta_t)$ could be defined as $f[\overline{x}_t(\overline{P}^{t-1}, \overline{Q}^{t-1}), \theta_t]$. Since we cannot define an equilibrium $\overline{x}_t(\cdot)$ before defining an individual firms optimization problem, we assume M_t is given to firms in this section and represents their anticipations about $\overline{Q}_t$.

[4]The function, x_t, is called a plan. The sequence $\{x_t\}$ is called a sequence of plans. Sometimes, to shorten sentences, I refer to $\{x_t\}$ as a plan. The context will make clear what is intended.

[5]The reader can find a defense of the criterion in Hirshleifer [1965] and Lucas [1971].

[6](11a) follows from $E[\,E[\,\sum_{i=t+1}^{T} \beta^i \pi_i(x_i, \theta_i) | \hat{\theta}_{t+1}]\, | \hat{\theta}_t] = E[\,\sum_{i=t+1}^{T} \beta^i \pi_i(x_i, \theta_i) | \hat{\theta}_t]$, which follows from (6) and (7), and the well known fact that if X and Y

are any two random variables and g is any function of X and Y, then $E[E[g(X,Y)|X]] = E[g(X,Y)]$ (provided all the expectations exist). We are able to move the max operator across the expectation operator because $x_{t+1}, \ldots, x_T$ are functions of θ_t, not elements of X.

[7] The above definition assumes that all firms are identical. This is done in order to make possible the actual calculation of such equilibria later on in the paper. The generalization to N possibly different firms is straightforward, but will not be considered here.

[8] Cyert and DeGroot [1974] have analyzed dynamic Bayesian Rational Expectations using a simple interesting model of the firms. Crawford [1973] has also considered a "Rational Expectations" definition with Bayesian learning, but without experimentation, in a different context from the one given here.

[9] $\dfrac{dV_T}{dx_{T-1}}(\hat{\theta}_T^o)$ is the derivative of V_T with respect to x_{T-1} evaluated at $\hat{\theta}_t = \hat{\theta}_t^o$.

[10] The maximization in (9) obviously does not need to be repeated
$$V_T(\hat{\theta}_T^o) = E[\beta^T \pi_T(x_T^o(\hat{\theta}_T^o), \theta_T)|\hat{\theta}_T^o] .$$

[11] That is, $V_{T-1}(\hat{\theta}_{T-1}^o) = E[\beta^{T-1}\pi_{T-1}(x_{T-1}^o(\hat{\theta}_{T-1}^o), \theta_{T-1}) + V_T(\hat{\theta}_T^o)|\hat{\theta}_{T-1}^o]$.

REFERENCES

Arrow, K. J. [1964], "The Role of Securities in the Optimal Allocation of Risk-Bearing," Rev. Econ. Stud., 86, 91-96.

Baron D. [1970], Price Uncertainty, Utility and Industry Equilibrium in Pure Competition," Int. Econ. Rev. 11, pp. 463-80.

Brock, W. [1972], "On Models of Expectations that Arise from Maximizing Behavior of Economic Agents Over Time," J. Econ. Theory, 5, 348-76.

Cagan, P. [1956], "The Monetary Dynamics of Hyperinflation," pp. 23-
117 in M. Friedman, ed., Studies in the Quantity Theory of Money.
Chicago: University of Chicago Press.

Crawford, [1973], "Implications of Learning for Economic Models of
Uncertainty," International Economic Review, Vol. 14, No. 3.

Cyert, R. and M. DeGroot [1974], "Rational Expectations and Bayesian
Analysis," Journal of Political Economy, 82, 521-536.

Dhrymes, P., [1964], "On the Theory of the Monopolistic Multiproduct
Firm Under Uncertainty," Int. Econ. Rev., 5, 239-57.

Diamond, P. A. [1967], "The Role of a Stock Market in a General Equilibrium Model with Technological Uncertainty," Amer. Econ. Rev.,
57, 759-76.

Douglas, A. J. [1973], "Stochastic Returns and the Theory of the Firm,"
Amer. Econ. Rev., 63, 129-133.

Dreze, J. [1972], "Econometrics and Decision Theory," Econometrica,
40, 1-18.

Dreze, J. and J. Gabszewicz [1967], "Demand Fluctuations, Capcaity
Utilization and Prices," Operations Research Verfahren III, 119-
141.

Friedman, M. [1957], A Theory of the Consumption Function. Princeton:
Princeton University Press.

Grossman, S. J. [forthcoming], "Rational Expectations and the Econo-
metric Modeling of Markets Subject to Uncertainty: A Bayesian
Approach," Manuscript, 1972. Forthcoming in the Journal of
Econometrics, 1975.

Hakansson, N. [1969], "Optimal Investment and Consumption Strategies
Under Risk, An Uncertain Lifetime and Insurance," Int. Econ. Rev.,
10, 443-66.

Hirshleifer, J. [1965], "Investment Decision Under Uncertainty: Choice
Theoretic Approaches," Quart. J. of Econ., 79, 509-536.

Holt, C., Modigliani, Muth, and Simon [1960], Planning Production,
Inventories, and Work Force. Prentice Hall, Inc.: Englewood
Cliffs, N. J.

Leland, H. [1972], "The Firm and Uncertain Demand," Amer. Econ. Rev. ,
  62, 278-91.

Lucas, R. and E. Prescott [1971], "Investment Under Uncertainty,"
  Econometrica, 39, 659-83.

Malinvaud, E. [1969], "First Order Certainty Equivalence," Econometrica, 37, 706-18.

Mills, E. [1959], "Uncertainty and Price Theory," Quart. J. of Econ. ,
  73, 116-29.

_____ [1962], Price, Output and Inventory Policy: A Study in the
  Economics of the Firm and Industry. New York: Wiley.

Muth, J. F. [1961], "Rational Expectations and the Theory of Price
  Movements," Econometrica, 29, 315-335.

Nelson, R. [1961], "Uncertainty, Prediction and Competitive Equilibrium,"
  Quart. J. of Econ. , 75, 41-62.

Nerlove, M. [1958], The Dynamics of Supply: Estimation of Farmers'
  Response to Price. Baltimore: The Johns Hopkins Press.

_____ [1972], "Lags in Economic Behavior," Econometrica, 40, 221-
  52.

Radner, R. [1970], "Problems in the Theory of Markets Under Uncertainty,"
  Amer. Econ. Rev., 60, 454-60.

_____ [1972], "Existence of Equilibrium of Plans, Prices, and Price
  Expectations in a Sequence of Markets," Econometrica 40, 289-304.

Sandmo, A. [1971], "On the Theory of the Competitive Firm under Price
  Uncertainty," Amer. Econ. Rev. , 61, 65-73.

Scarf, H. [1963], "A Survey of Analytic Techniques in Inventory Theory,"
  pp. 185-225, in H. Scarf, et al. , Multistage Inventory Models
  and Techniques. Stanford: Stanford University Press.

Stigum, B. [1969], "Competitive Equilibria Under Uncertainty," Quart.
  J. of Econ. , 83, 533-561.

_____ [1969], "Entrepreneurial Choice Over Time Under Conditions of
  Uncertainty," Int. Econ. Rev. , 10, 427-442.

Theil, H. [1964], Optimal Decision Rules for Industry and Government.
Amsterdam: North-Holland Publishing Co.

Zabel, E. [1969], "The Competitive Firm and Price Expectations," Int.
Econ. Rev. , 10, 467-478.

_____ [1970], "Monopoly and Uncertainty," Rev. Econ. Stud., 37
205-20.

Department of Economics, University of Chicago and
H. G. B. Alexander Research Foundation, Graduate School of
Business, University of Chicago. Research financed in part
by the National Science Foundation, Grant GS-2347, and by
the H. G. B. Alexander Endowment Fund. The author is grateful
to Arnold Zellner for advice and encouragement throughout the
writing of this paper, and to Theodore Groves for helpful comments on a previous draft. The author assumes full responsibility for any errors.

Market Adjustment with Adaptive Supply and Pricing Decisions
William R. Porter

CONTENTS

1. INTRODUCTION

An unsolved problem in microeconomic thoery is the explanation of how market prices are adjusted by participating economic agents so as to move the market toward an equilibrium. Dissatisfaction with tâtonnement processes that use an outside auctioneer has led to several attempts to incorporate the participating agents explicitly into the price setting process, Rothschild [1973]. These attempts have succeeded in finding non-tâtonnement adjustment mechanisms that converge to a market equilibrium, and they clearly illustrate many of the difficulties involved in decentralizing the price setting task. However, they do not allow the agents to learn from or adapt to the situations they are encountering.

Intuition strongly suggests that the agents' beliefs will change during a market adjustment process. Economic theory, however, has assumed perfect knowledge so long that methods for handling partial knowledge and changing beliefs have not been developed to the point where we can model the adaptive learning and decision-making that is certainly going on in an adjusting market.

The purpose of this paper is to describe and analyze a market adjustment mechanism, based on the work of Mirman and Porter [1974], that evolves out of the interaction of the adaptive behavior of agents on both sides of the market. The market analyzed here is a labor market where:

(1) there is imperfect knowledge about wages and wage-supply relationships;

(2) decisions by agents are made independently and are based on accurate but partial information which has been acquired;

(3) employment contracts are for only one period in length and are made at the beginning of each period,

(4) firms are price-setters only and workers are price-takers only. The analysis is a continuation of previous studies of optimal behavior under uncertainty, optimal sample size determination, and job search under imperfect knowledge.

2. PREVIOUS MARKET ADJUSTMENT STUDIES

Precedents for the present undertaking developed along several different lines after the appearance of George Stigler's "Economics of Information" [1961]. Stigler dealt with the problem of an agent who is faced with a known price distribution from which he can sample at a known sampling cost to obtain a favorable trade offer. He put forth a method which allowed the agent to calculate a priori the otpimal number of observations he should collect before trading. McCall [1965] and Nelson [1970] improved on Stigler's method by using sequential sampling. Recent works in statistical decision theory have suggested adaptive sequential sampling methods that allow an agent to sample optimally from an unknown distribution. The agent uses his latest observations to alter sequentially his beliefs about the distribution from which he is sampling.

310

Several authors, Mortensen [1970], Lucas and Rapping [1970], Phelps [1970], Lucas and Prescott [1973], have attempted to incorporate some of the results of optimal price search or optimal sampling into models of the labor market, making some attempt to explain the behavior on both sides of the market. None of these, however, are couched in terms of the behavior of the agents themselves.[1] Fisher [1972] and Diamond [1971] on the other hand have attempted to explain the market adjustment process in terms of agent behavior, and have succeeded in obtaining processes which converge to a market equilibrium. Neither used optimal search techniques for their searching agents. Moreover, their models were designed with the object of obtaining convergence to a single, point equilibrium, and that has led to some rather awkward and poorly motivated assumptions about the behavior of the agents.

3. AN OVERVIEW OF THE ANALYSIS

The work presented here is not an attempt to find a process which converges to any particular type of equilibrium. The point of view is rather to determine the type of process that emerges from the interaction of many independent agents each of whom has very simple but naturally motivated rules of behavior. We assume that firms set their wage offers but must bear the cost of hiring all workers who accept their offer, which may be more or fewer workers than their desired level. Workers search for the highest wage they can find but must bear the cost of searching. Firms cannot search and workers cannot set wage offers. The problem for the firm is that of trying to determine the wage offer that will attract the optimal number of workers. The problem for the worker is to balance his perceived gains with the cost of search. Both the workers and the firms develop strategies designed to deal optimally with the type of institutional constraints placed upon them and the type of periodic information they can obtain.

The market is analyzed in a periodic framework where each type of agent is able to replay his strategy in the light of his most recent

311

information. At the beginning of the period there exists a population of wage offers outstanding in the market. These are the wage offers that have been set, one by each firm, at the end of the preceding period. The workers, who are all employed in some pattern among the firms in the market at wages they accepted at the end of last period, begin sampling from the current population of wage offers. The cost of sampling is perfectly known to each worker, and he uses that knowledge plus a sequential sampling method to decide when to stop sampling and accept his best offer. The job acceptance is for his employment next period. By the end of the current period each worker has accepted one of the wage offers and has contracted to work at the corresponding firm next period. The firms then observe the number of worker acceptances they have obtained at their current wage offer and use this to determine whether they should offer a higher or lower wage next period. The new wage offers form the next period market wage population from which the workers will again sample.

The aggregate behavior of the agents produces a time sequence of wage and employment patterns. Its properties depend on the random sampling variation of the worker search activity and upon the nature of the population being sampled. Workers are sampling from a population of wage offers. This population determines the random properties of the workers' acceptance pattern. As the firms base their new wage offers on the number of acceptances they get at their old wage offers, the old wage population determines the random sampling properties of the new wage population. For this reason the market adjustment of vectors of wage offers is a Markov process. We find that this Markov process has a stable, stationary probability distribution to which the process will converge regardless of the initial state of the market.

This market equilibrium is different from the equilibrium of a static, pure competition market. It is neither a single state nor a single wage equilibrium. Instead it is one characterized by periodically changing wage vectors whose components are normally not equal and by constantly shifting patterns of employment. It is the long run structure of this fluctuation that exhibits regularity in equilibrium, and it is this type of regularity that is analyzed. Indeed, we can determine what proportion of time the market will spend in each possible wage and employment pattern in the long run.

The reason that the market adjustment activity does not come to a stop is because the agents never attain perfect knowledge. The workers continue to canvass firms for the best offer they can find. If all the wage offers happen to be the same so that each worker obtains a sample containing equal wages, then workers will be indifferent among the firms they have sampled and will accept jobs randomly. However this will in all likelihood leave some firms short of workers and others with excess workers, and a wage adjustment will occur which will move the market away from the single wage offer. If the firms all knew that the wage was unique and that they would in the long run do just as well if they all kept the same wage offer then there would be no further wage change; however, we do not endow the firm with this type of knowledge, nor do we allow the possibility of collusion. Wages, therefore, continue to move. One can speculate that if the firms were to hold the wage population constant at a single wage offer then the workers might learn through time that they were sampling from this type of fixed population and adjust their strategy accordingly. However the workers are sampling from a periodically changing population, therefore their assumed strategy is appropriate even if they have memories.

The equilibrium is one that is established by the agents' continuing efforts to adjust to something that is changing in ways they do not understand. The pattern of the change is of course determined by their joint behavior, however the agents neither control nor understand this pattern because they are each operating individually and independently. This type of model captures much of the realism which is lost in the perfect knowledge model. Price here is not something that is set by an invisible force and then passively reacted to by agents who see it as fixed. In this market price setting is used by one group of agents to advertise

313

to and to communicate with another group of agents. The group that does not set prices actively seeks out price differentials and responds to them. The active role of prices in a continuous allocative and informational process is clearly brought out.

4. A FORMAL MODEL OF A LABOR MARKET HAVING A FINITE NUMBER OF AGENTS

4.1. Behavior of the Workers

ASSUMPTION W1: <u>Lifespan and numbers</u>. There are n workers with infinite lifespans.

ASSUMPTION W2: <u>Goal and information</u>. During the current period the worker tries to maximize his expected income for next period net of his search costs for the current period. He obtains all of his information about the "true" current wage population, $w(t) = (w_1(t), \ldots, w_m(t))$ consisting of one wage for each of the m firms, by canvassing firms to get wage offers. We assume that canvassing is equivalent to drawing random observations from the "true" population, $w(t)$. The worker uses his random sample of wage offers to form his subjective distribution of the wage population and to decide when to stop searching. Once he decides to stop searching he accepts the maximum wage offer in his sample. If he has obtained more than one offer equal to the maximum he accepts the earliest one obtained.

ASSUMPTION W3: <u>Sampling and subjective probability</u>. Let α_k^{it} be the kth wage offer sampled by worker i in period t. Consider a K element sample $(\alpha_1^{it}, \alpha_2^{it}, \ldots, \alpha_k^{it}) = (_1\alpha_K^{it})$, in which $\alpha_k^{it} = w^j(t)$ for some j, where j is the kth firm sampled by worker i in period t. We assume that the subjective probability distribution for worker i is a two parameter distribution: $f_{itK}(w) = f(w \mid \bar{\alpha}_K^{it}, S_K^{it})$, where $\bar{\alpha}_k^{it}$ and S_K^{it} are the sample mean and the sample variance of the K-element sample, $(_1\alpha_K^{it})$. $f(w \mid \bar{\alpha}_K^{it}, S_K^{it})$ is a continuous density function on $0 \leq w < \infty$ having mean and variance equal to $\bar{\alpha}_K^{it}$ and S_K^{it}.

ASSUMPTION W4: <u>Sampling and search cost</u>. The search cost is a function only of the sample size K. The search cost function $C(K)$ is assumed to have the following properties:

(1) $C(1) = C(2) = 0.$

(2) $C(K+1) - C(K) > C(K) - C(K-1), \quad K \geq 2.$

(3) $\lim_{K \to \infty} [C(K+1) - C(K)] = \infty.$

The function $C(K)$ is perfectly known by each worker. The worker begins each period by obtaining the first two free sample wage offers. This allows him to form his initial subjective probability distribution which he then uses to begin his sequential sampling procedure.

From these assumptions we can formulate an adaptive sequential decision procedure for the worker. Since all workers are identical and any period is representative the superscripts i and t will be supressed. Let $\hat{\alpha}_K$, $\overline{\alpha}_K$ and S_K be the maximum wage, the mean wage, and the wage variance for the sample $(_1\alpha_K)$. Once the worker has a wage sample large enough to allow him to form a subjective probability distribution on wages (i.e. for $K \geq 2$) he will determine before obtaining the next wage offer whether he should stop sampling and accept the highest wage he now has or continue to sample more wage offers. If he stops sampling his net income will be $\hat{\alpha}_K - C(K)$. If he continues to sample his expected net income will be at least $E(\hat{\alpha}_{K+1} \mid \hat{\alpha}_K) - C(K+1)$, where

$$E(\hat{\alpha}_{K+1} \mid \hat{\alpha}_K) = \hat{\alpha}_K \int_0^{\hat{\alpha}_K} f(w \mid \overline{\alpha}_K, S_K)dw + \int_{\hat{\alpha}_K}^{\infty} wf(w \mid \overline{\alpha}_K, S_K)dw$$

is the workers' expected maximum wage offer if one more offer is obtained given that $\hat{\alpha}_K$ is his present maximum wage offer. Therefore the worker will sequentially apply the following decision rule:

Stop searching, if $\hat{\alpha}_K - C(K) \geq E(\hat{\alpha}_{K+1} \mid \hat{\alpha}_K) - C(K+1)$.

Continue searching, otherwise.

If the decision is to stop searching at K then the worker will accept some offer $w_j(t)$ in his sample such that $w_j(t) = \hat{\alpha}_K$. If the decision is

315

to continue searching then the worker will obtain α_{K+1} and replace

$$\hat{\alpha}_K \quad \text{with} \quad \hat{\alpha}_{K+1} = \max(\hat{\alpha}_K, \ \alpha_{K+1})$$

$$\overline{\alpha}_K \quad \text{with} \quad \overline{\alpha}_{K+1} = (K\overline{\alpha}_K + \alpha_{K+1})/(K+1)$$

and S_K with $S_{K+1} = 1/K \ \sum_{i=1}^{K+1} (\alpha_i - \overline{\alpha}_{K+1})^2$. He will use these new values to again decide whether to stop or continue searching. The sequence of sample wage offers which is obtained in this way will be called the worker's <u>sample sequence</u>. The sample size K at which the worker decides to stop searching will be called the <u>stopping size</u> of the sample sequence, and a sample sequence which terminates in a stop-searching decision will be called a <u>terminating sequence</u>. This decision rule makes the stop-searching decision whenever the current net income is greater than the expected net income after only one more offer is obtained. It seems that this could lead to a premature stop-searching decision in some cases since the expected net value of additional offers is not considered.

However, due to the assumption about the increasing marginal cost of sampling and the fact that the expected sample maximum increases at a decreasing rate as the sample size increases, this rule will not lead to a premature stop-searching decision, Porter [1974, pp. 16-18].

Denote the probability that the worker, searching in population w(t), will accept the wage offer $w_j(t)$ from firm j by $p_j(w(t))$. $p_j(w(t))$ is then equal to the probability that the worker will draw from w(t) one of the stopping sequences where $w_j(t)$ appears as the first offer equal to the sample maximum. It can then be shown that $p_j(w(t))$ is a probability density function on j = 1, ..., m for any $w(t) \in R^m$, Porter [1974, p. 20].

4.2. <u>Behavior of the Firms</u>

ASSUMPTION F1: <u>Lifespan and numbers.</u> There are. m identical firms with an infinite lifespan.

316

ASSUMPTION F2: _Productivity of labor._ All firms have identical perfectly known marginal revenue product of labor functions V(L) defined by:

$$V(L) = a-L, \quad \text{where } L = \text{the number of workers employed}$$
at the firm during the period, [2]
$$a > n .$$

ASSUMPTION F.3: _Constraints and information._ Firms set their own wage offer each period but must hire exactly the number of workers who accept their offer for the duration of the next period. The offer is set at the beginning of each period and must stand until the end of the period. Firms do not have knowledge of the offers of other firms, how- ever they do know that workers accept the highest wage offer they obtain each period, therefore the firm believes it can affect its number of accept- ances by changing its wage offer. Each firm can set only one wage offer each period, and that wage can be any real number.

REMARK. At first glance the assumption that each firm must hire all the workers who accept its offer seems very unrealistic. However, within the model there is very little difference between the firm that is so constrained and the one that isn't. In each case the firm must attempt to set the wage level that will attract the optimal number of workers. If more workers accept than are desired the firm will have incentive to lower its wage next period whether or not it is required to hire all who accept this period. Also if the firm is receiving fewer acceptances than desired it will have an incentive to raise its offer in both cases. Therefore the essential nature of the firm's adjustment process is the same under either assumption, but the one we use simplifies some of the analysis.

ASSUMPTION F.4: _Periodic wage adjustment._ Firms use their wage offer as a means of worker recruitment. They periodically set their next period wage offer based on their current level of acceptances com- pared with their desired employment level at the current wage offer. The periodic wage adjustment for firm j is defined by:

317

$$w_j(t + 1) = w_j(t) + \beta(D(w_j(t)) - A_j(t))$$

(1)

$$= (1 - \beta)w_j(t) + \beta(a - A_j(t))$$

where $D(w_j) = a - w_j$ is the firm's desired employment level at wage w_j, $0 < \beta < \dfrac{n}{n+m}$, and $A_j(t) =$ the number of workers who accept wage $w_j(t)$ in period t.

REMARK. This assumption that the firm adjusts its wage offer according to a linear function of its current excess demand may seem unsatisfactory since it is not shown here that this type of linear adjustment is the result of a profit maximization strategy used by the firm. It is, of course, possible to describe a reasonable framework of beliefs which if held by a profit maximizing firm would lead to this linear adjustment rule. A specific example of such a framework is set forth in Porter [1974, pp. 42-44]. It is important to keep in mind that in general profit maximization would not lead to this linear adjustment rule. It is assumed here in order to simplify the exposition. However in general it is possible to carry out the analysis of the market adjustment whenever the wage adjustment is a well-defined function of the firm's excess demand.

4.3. The Market Process

ASSUMPTION M1: Uniform contract period. The contract periods are institutionally set to be the same for all agents (i.e., having the same beginnings and duration).

ASSUMPTION M2: Independence of workers. Workers sample and accept offers independent of each other; the sampling process can always be accomplished during one period.

ASSUMPTION M3: Impossibility of bankruptcy. No firm or worker can ever become bankrupt.

The market acceptance vector is a member of the set

$$\mathcal{A} = \{A := (A_1, \ldots, A_m) \mid \sum_{j=1}^{m} A_j = n;\ A_j \geq 0,\ j = 1, \ldots, m\} .$$

The Market wage vector $w(t)$ is a member of R^m (Euclidean m-space) each period.

Applying the wage adjustment formula (1) to all firms in the market we obtain the market wage vector adjustment formula:

$$w(t + 1) = (1 - \beta)w(t) + \beta(a\ell - A(t)),$$

(2)

where $\ell = (1, 1, \ldots, 1)$ having m components.

From (2) we can write the expression for the probability that the market wage vector will change from any point $u \in R^m$ to any point $v \in R^m$ in exactly one period. Denote this probability as $p_{v/u}$.

$$p_{v|u} = P(a\ell - \frac{1}{\beta} v + \frac{1-\beta}{\beta} u \mid u) =$$

(3)
$$= \begin{cases} \dfrac{n! \; \Pi_{j=1}^{m}[\, p_j(u)]^{A_j}}{\Pi_{j=1}^{m} A_j!} & , \text{ for } A \in \mathcal{Q} \\ \\ 0 & , \text{ for } A \notin \mathcal{Q} \end{cases}$$

where $A = a\ell - \frac{1}{\beta} v + \frac{(1-\beta)}{\beta} u$.

From this we can define the stochastic transition function

(4) $\qquad p(u, V) = \sum_{v \in V} p_{v|u}$ for any $u \in R^m$ and $V \subset R^m$.

5. ANALYTICAL RESULTS

We may now state the main results concerning existence and stability. First we observe the following.

$P(u, V)$ is defined for any $u \in R^m$ and $V \subset R^m$. Given u, $P(u, V)$ is a probability measure on R^m for all $u \in R^m$. $P(u, V)$ is independent of t. Therefore $(R^m, p(u, V))$ is a stationary Markov process.

Define the following. Let

$$E = \{w \in R^m \mid \sum_{j=1}^{m} w_j = ma - n; \ a - n \leq w_j \leq a, \ \text{all } j\}.$$

For any two points $x, v \in R^m$ define

$$d(x, v) = \max_{j \in \{1, 2, \ldots, m\}} |x_j - v_j|.$$

For any $z \in R^m$, define $N_\delta(z) = \{w \in R^m \mid d(w, z) < \delta\}$ and $X = \{w \in R^m \mid \sum w_j = n, \ w_j \geq 0, \ \text{all } j\}$. Let $\vec{a} = (a, a, \ldots, a)$. Then $E = \vec{a} - X$.

PROPOSITION 1: If $w(t) \in R^m$ then for all $\{A(\tau)\} \in \Pi_{\tau=t}^{\infty} \mathcal{A}$ there exists an S such that $w(t + s) \in E$, for all $s > S$. (For convenience we shall say that as $s \to \infty$, $w(t + s) \in E$).

PROOF.

$$w(t + s) = (1 - \beta)^s w(t) + \beta \sum_{\tau=1}^{s} (1-\beta)^\tau (\vec{a} - A(t + s - \tau)).$$

Now
$$\lim_{s \to \infty} (1 - \beta)^s w(t) = 0. \quad \lim_{s \to \infty} (\beta \sum_{\tau=1}^{s} (1 - \beta)^\tau) \vec{a} = \vec{a}.$$

$$\sum_{j=1}^{m} (\beta \sum_{\tau=1}^{s} (1 - \beta)^\tau A_j(t + s - \tau)) = (\beta \sum_{\tau=1}^{s} (1 - \beta)^\tau) n = [1 - (1 - \beta)^{s+1}] n.$$

Hence, as $s \to \infty$, $\beta \sum_{\tau=1}^{s} (1 - \beta)^\tau A(t + s - \tau) \in X$. Therefore as $s \to \infty$ $w(t + s) \in \vec{a} - X = E$. Q.E.D.

PROPOSITION 2. Given $w(t) \in R^m$, $z \in E$, and $\delta > 0$ then $\exists$ a finite sequence $\{A(\tau)\}_t^{t+s}$, $A(\tau) \in \mathcal{A} \ni w(t+s+1) \in N_\delta(z)$ where $w(t+s+1) = (1 - \beta)^{s+1} w(t) + \alpha \sum_{\tau=0}^{s} (1 - \beta)^\tau (\vec{a} - A(t + s - \tau))$.

PROOF. Let $x = \vec{a} - z$. Then $x \in X$ by definition of E. From the expression for $w(t + s + 1)$ it can be seen that

$$d(w(t + s + 1), Z) \leq d((1 - \beta)^{s+1} w(t), 0)$$
$$+ d((\beta \sum_{\tau=0}^{s} (1 - \beta)^\tau) \vec{a}, \vec{a})$$
$$+ d(\beta \sum_{\tau=0}^{s} (1 - \beta)^\tau A(t + s - \tau), x).$$

320

It is easily seen that $\exists$ a positive integer $K_1 \ni d((1 - \beta)^{s+1}w(t),\ 0) <$ $\delta/3$, for all $s \geq K_1$ and $\exists$ a positive integer $K_2 \ni d((\beta \sum_{\tau=0}^{s}(1-\beta)^{\tau})\vec{a},\ \vec{a})$ $< \delta/3$, for all $s \geq K_2$ since $(\beta \sum_{\tau=0}^{s}(1-\beta)^{\tau})\vec{a} = [1 - (1 - \beta)^{s+1}]\vec{a}$. For any sequence $\{A(\tau)\}_t^{t+s}$ define $q_k(t + s) = \beta \sum_{\tau=0}^{s}(1 - \beta)^{\tau}A_k(t + s - \tau)$, $k = 1, 2, \ldots, m$. We now construct a sequence $\{A(\tau)\}_t^{t+s}$ that will casue $q(t + s)$ to be close to x. The sequence will be constructed backwards. Let

$$A_k(t + s) = \max_{J \in \{0, 1, \ldots, n\}}\{J \leq n - \sum_{i=1}^{k-1}A_i(t+s) \mid \beta J \leq x_k\},$$

$$k = 1, \ldots, m .$$

Then define:

$$A_k(t + s - \tau) = \max_{J \in \{0, 1, \ldots, n\}}\{J \leq$$

$$\leq \sum_{i=1}^{k-1}A_i(t + s - \tau) \mid \beta(1 - \beta)^{\tau}J \leq x_k - q_k(t + s - (\tau - 1))\} ,$$

$$k = 1, \ldots, m; \ \tau = 1, \ldots, s .$$

Using this constructions for $\{A(\tau)\}_t^{t+s}$ we see that it is not possible for

$$\sum_{k=1}^{m}A_k(t + s - \tau) > n, \quad \tau = 0, 1, \ldots, s .$$

Moreover

$$\sum_{k=1}^{m}A_k(t + s - \tau) < n$$

implies that

$$\beta(1 - \beta)^{\tau} > x_k - q_k(t + s - \tau),$$

all k. (If this were not so, then $A_k(t+s - \tau)$ would be at least one unit

321

larger.) This implies that

$$m\beta(1 - \beta)^T > \sum_k x_k - \sum_k q_k(t + s - \tau)$$

which implies that

$$m\beta(1 - \beta)^T > n - n[1 - (1 - \beta)^{T+1}] .$$

As

$$\sum_k q_k(t + s - \tau) \leq \sum_k \beta \sum_{\tau=0}^t (1 - \beta)^T A_k(\tau)$$

$$\sum_k q_k(t + s - \tau) \leq \beta n \sum_{\tau=0}^t (1 - \beta)^T$$

$$= n[1 - (1 - \beta)^{T+1}] .$$

Hence, $m\beta > n(1 - \beta)$ which implies that $\beta > \dfrac{n}{n+m}$ which contradicts Assumption F.4 that $\beta < \dfrac{n}{n+m}$. Hence $\sum_{k=1}^m A_k(t + s - \tau) = n$, all τ. Also by construction $0 \leq q_k(t + s - \tau) \leq x_k$, $k = 1, \ldots, m$, $\tau = 0, \ldots, s$. Hence

$$\sum_{k=1}^m q_k(t + s - \tau) = \sum_{k=1}^m \beta \sum_{\tau=0}^s (1 - \beta)^T A_k(t + s - \tau)$$

$$= n\beta \sum_{\tau=0}^s (1 - \beta)^T = n[1 - (1 - \beta)^{T+1}],$$

and, since $\sum_{k=1}^m x_k = n$,

$$d(q(t + s), x) \leq n(1 - \beta)^{s+1} .$$

Therefore, $\exists$ a positive integer K_3 such that, using the method of constructing $\{A(\tau)\}$ outlined in above,

$$d(\beta \sum_{\tau=0}^s (1 - \beta)^T A(t + s - \tau), x) < \delta/3 \text{ for all } s \geq K_3 .$$

322

Hence we know that $\exists$ a sequence $\{A(\tau)\}_t^{t+s}$, $s \geq \max\{K_1, K_2, K_3\}$ such that $w(t + s + 1) \in N_s(z)$. Q.E.D.

PROPOSITION 3. $E = \vec{a} - X$ is the unique ergodic set for the Markov process of Proposition 2.

PROOF. No point outside of E can be an ergodic state, by Proposition 1. Every open subset of E has positive probability of containing the state vector after a sufficient number of period has elapsed, by Proposition 2. Q.E.D.

PROPOSITION 4. The Markov process is non-cyclic.

PROOF. Suppose $w(t) = v = (v_1, v_2, \ldots, v_m) \in E$, where $a - v_i =$ a non-negative integer, $i = 1, \ldots, m$, and $\sum_{i=1}^m (a - v_i) = n$. If $A(t) = \vec{a} - v \in \mathcal{A}$, which has positive probability of occurring, then $w(t + 1) = (1 - \beta)v + \beta(\vec{a} - (\vec{a} - v)) = (1 - \beta)v + \alpha v = v = w(t)$. Q.E.D.

PROPOSITION 5. There is a unique stationary probability distribution $\pi(V)$ which is positive on all open subsets V of E and zero on all sets $V \subset R^m \ni V \cap E = \emptyset$.

PROOF. Existence is established by Theorem 5.7, Doob [1953, p. 214] where conditions D of p. 192 holds if we define $\varphi(V) = \int_V dw / \int_E dw$. Uniqueness follows since by Proposition 3 the ergodic set is unique and by Proposition 4 it is non-cyclic. By Proposition 2 $\pi(V)$ is positive on all open $V \subset E$ and by Proposition 1 $\pi(V)$ is zero on all $V \subset R^m \ni V \cap E = \emptyset$. Q.E.D.

PROPOSITION 6. The expected vector of the limiting distribution is $E_\pi W = \int_Q w\pi(w)dw = (a - \frac{n}{m}, a - \frac{n}{m}, \ldots, a - \frac{n}{m})$.

PROOF. By symmetry, since all firms are identical $E_\pi w_i = E_\pi w_j$, and $\sum_{i=1}^m E_\pi w_i = ma - n$.

6. COMMENT ON STOCHASTIC EQUILIBRIA AND PERFECT MARKETS

It is interesting to note that the stochastic equilibrium has an average market wage that is strictly determined by the market supply and demand. Therefore we see that even though there is a great deal of wage

323

and employment movement the average market wage is constant and equal to what the single wage would be if it were a classical perfect knowledge market. Wage variation among firms in particular periods and wage pattern fluctuation through time are due to the imperfect knowledge and search process but the average wage is constant and determined by classical market forces even in the face of imperfect knowledge.

NOTES

[1]Mortensen, Lucas and Rapping, and Phelps do not explain the distribution of real wages which is the cause of their worker search each period. Lucas and Prescott use a tatonnement type auctioneer to set price within markets.

[2]This form of the marginal revenue product curve corresponds to the class of concave quadratic total revenue product functions. Any linear downward sloping marginal revenue product curve can be represented in this form by adjusting the units in which either value or labor are measured. The condition $a > n$ is imposed so that under no circumstances will the marginal revenue product of labor be negative.

REFERENCES

Diamond, P. A. [1971], "A Model of Price Adjustment," Journal of Economic Theory, 3.

Doob, J. L. [1953], Stochastic Processes, Wiley, New York.

Fisher, F. M. [1970], "Quasi-Competitive Price Adjustment by Individual Firms: A Preliminary Paper," Journal of Economic Theory, 2.

_____ [1972], "On Price Adjustment Without an Acutioneer," Review of Economic Studies.

Lucas, R. E. and E. C. Prescott [1973], "Equilibrium Search and Unemployment," Carnegie-Mellon working paper.

Lucas, R. E. and L. A. Rapping [1970], "Real Wages, Employment, and Inflation," in E. S. Phelps et al., Micro-economic Foundations of Employment and Inflation Theory, Norton, New York.

McCall, J. J. [1965], "The Economics of Information and Optimal Stopping Rules," Journal of Business, 38, 300-317.

_____ [1970], "Economics of Information and Job Search," Quarterly Journal of Economics, 84, 113-126.

Mirman, L. J. and Porter, W. R. [1974], "A Microeconomic Model of the Labor Market under Uncertainty," Economic Inquiry, 12, 135-145.

Mortensen, D. T. [1970], "A Theory of Wage and Employment Dynamics," in E. S. Phelps et al., Microeconomic Foundations of Employment and Inflation Theory, Norton, New York.

Nelson, P. [1970], "Information and Consumer Behavior," Journal of Political Economy, 78.

Phelps, E. S. [1970], "Money Wage Dynamics and Labor Market Equilibrium," in E. S. Phelps et al., Microeconomic Foundations of Employment and Inflation Theory, Norton, New York.

Porter, W. R. [1974], "Labor Market Adjustment Under Imperfect Knowledge," unpublished doctoral dissertation, Cornell University, Ithaca, New York.

Rothschild, M. [1973], "Models of Market Organization with Imperfect Information: A Survey," Journal of Political Economy, 81, 213-225.

Stigler, G. J. [1961], "The Economics of Information," Journal of Political Economy, 69, 312-325.

Demand for Labor in a Dynamic Theory of the Firm
William J. Scanlon and Charles C. Holt

CONTENTS

1. INTRODUCTION

This paper develops a theory describing the decisions made by business firms impinging directly on the labor market. Many economic and business problems have been studied intensively and are found characteristically to involve dynamics, uncertainty, actions in anticipation, and actions in response to past errors. Unfortunately, rigorous dynamic programming solutions of these problems are often of uncomputable size and the optimal strategies are difficult to abstract. Hence, the economist's tactic of assuming optimal behavior as the source of theory about actual behavior may not be workable. However, when the payoff function of a decision problem can be approximated by a quadratic function and its constraints can be approximated by linear equations, the direct solution for optimal strategies in the form of decision rules is possible as the result of certainty equivalence. Tremendous simplification is obtained in this special case by the proof that the decision solution under certainty applies to the uncertainty case as well, provided that expected value

forecasts are used. Thus, it is unnecessary to deal with stochastic processes in making the dynamic decision analysis. Forecasts of exogenous
variables can be made quite separately.

The development of the decision rules affecting the labor market
can be perceived as a mutli-stage procedure, as described in the work
on investment decisions by Chang and Holt. The first stage consists of
solving a static optimization problem in which the firm assumes all external conditions are fixed and adjustment costs are neglected in determining the optimal levels for various decision variables. In the second
stage, the firm chooses a dynamic strategy for the adjustment process
toward its optimal position taking into account the trade-off between
costs associated with adjustment and those arising from operating at non-
optimal levels. We have characterized the dynamic optimization as being
the result of independent recursive decisions by separate departments
within the firm. A production-sales department sets prices, production,
and shipment rates, while the personnel department uses the production
targets as inputs into its decisions on the desired level of the workforce
and wage level. Because of our concern for the labor market, we focus
exclusively on the decisions of the personnel department. The dynamic
decision process of the personnel department is portrayed as a two-phase
procedure. First, it sets the desired level of its workforce along with
wages, and then uses the desired workforce level in decision rules for
vacancies and layoffs in the second. Its objective in the latter stage is
to use these variables which it actually controls to equate the expected
workforce size with the desired size; the actual workforce is stochastic.

2. STATIC MODEL OF THE FIRM

We postulate a modified neoclassical model of the firm with no
restrictions on whether it is a competitor or possesses monopoly power
in either product or factor markets. The firm's profit-maximizing decisions are constrained by various functions governing demand, supply of
factors, and production relations. The basic equations are:

328

$$(1) \quad P = \alpha_o O^{\alpha_1} D^{\alpha_2} Z^{\alpha_3} \qquad \text{Product Demand}$$

$$(2) \quad D = \left(\frac{I}{B}\right) \qquad \text{Service Quality}$$

$$(3) \quad G = \beta_o L^{\beta_1} K^{\beta_2} e^{\beta_3 t} (qL)^{\beta_4} \qquad \text{Production Function}$$

$$(4) \quad W = \gamma_o \left(\frac{V}{U}\right)^{\gamma_1} L^{\gamma_2} \overline{W} \qquad \text{Labor Supply}$$

$$(5) \quad r = \rho_o (i)^{\rho_1} I^{\rho_2} \qquad \text{Inventory Costs}$$

$$(6) \quad b = \tau_o B^{\tau_1} \quad 0 > \tau_1 \geq -1 \qquad \text{Backlog Costs}$$

$$(7) \quad q = \xi_o \left(\frac{V}{U}\right)^{\xi_1} \left(\frac{W}{\overline{W}}\right)^{\xi_2} \qquad \text{Turnover Rate}$$

where:

P is the price of the firm's product;

O is the orders received by the firm;

D is an index of service quality;

Z is a proxy for all other factors influencing demand;

I is inventory on hand;

B is backlog of unfilled orders;

G is production per period;

L is labor used per period;

K is the level of capital services available;

t is time;

W is the wage rate of the firm;

V/U is the aggregate vacancy-unemployment ratio in the labor market;

$\overline{W}$ is the average wage rate in the labor market for labor used by the firm;

r   is cost of maintaining inventory per period;

i   is a short term interest rate;

q   is the turnover rate consisting of the quit rate plus the rate of terminations for cause.

Product demand represents one modification from standard theory in that the firm influences the quantity demanded through dimensions other than price.[1] Thus, the orders, O, a business receives in any period are related to the price of its product, P, the quality of the product it provides, D, and a set of other factors influencing demand, summarized in the index Z. Ideally, "quality" would include delivery time, workmanship, reliability, etc., which lead consumers to distinguish between firms producing otherwise homogenous products and maintain brand loyalty. However, only the role of delivery time will be made explicit in this model. Quality is inversely related to the delivery lag, which in turn varies directly with the backlog of orders a firm has on hand when a new order is received and inversely with its current inventory.

Z is a proxy for a variety of demand influences. These include income, competitors' prices, prices of other goods, tastes, etc. For oligopolistic firms, it may not be appropriate to regard Z as completely exogenous since other firms and individuals may react to the firms' decisions.

The firm's profit function involves the usual concept of net revenues with the exception that there are two components to the cost of labor. The first is the wage which must be paid directly to the workers and the second is an indirect cost arising from the loss of output associated with recruiting and training newly hired workers on the job. This cost can be regarded as an investment in specific human capital for each worker, necessary before he can be fully productive. This investment will be assumed to be a joint product with the firm's usual product output in a manner similar to that employed by Toikka and Tachibanaki. Hence, the production function has been written to reflect the loss of product output associated with training. β_4 is assumed to be less

330

than 0, indicating the reduction in output available from a labor force of any given size as the resources diverted to training new hires increases. In setting the wage rate, the firm will consider the trade-off between raising wages to minimize turnover and keeping wages low to reduce the total wage bill. Firms requiring larger specific human capital investments than the average level needed by other employers will find a relatively high wage policy advantageous in reducing their turnover costs.

By adopting a wage policy which takes into account turnover costs, the firm may find that it has more willing applicants than it needs to replace the flow of separated workers. Because of the training costs involved with each new hire and the sensitivity of quits to the wage rate, the firm would make no attempt to reduce wages to the point where the number of willing applicants equalled the needed replacements.[2]

The firm distinguishes among workers according to occupation and other characteristics which may influence productivity, training, and turnover. As the supplies of different types of labor shift and the relative costs change, the firm adjusts the composition of its workforce. These adjustments lead to the observation of simultaneous layoffs and vacancies by a profit-maximizing firm when market conditions change. Even in the steady state, turnover and recruiting occur continuously. All this suggests that some of our relationships should be elaborated to show different classes of labor according to productivity and turnover propensities. In particular, we will rewrite:

$$(3A) \qquad G = \tilde{\beta}_o \prod_{i=1}^{N} (q_i L_i)^{\beta_{4_i}} L_i^{\beta_{1_i}} K^{\beta_2} e^{\beta_3 t}$$

$$(4A) \qquad W_i = \gamma_{oi} \left(\frac{V}{U}\right)^{\gamma_{1_i}} L_i^{\gamma_{2_i}} \overline{W}$$

$$(7A) \qquad q_i = \xi_{oi} \left(\frac{V}{U}\right)^{\xi_{1_i}} \left(\frac{W_i}{\overline{W}}\right)^{\xi_{2_i}}$$

Distinguishing workers by discrete classes, of course, only approximates the actual differences among workers which occur along continuous dimensions. If the firm is able to perceive these actual differences more precisely than indicated by the discrete approximation, it may not alter the distribution of workers by type or the wages it pays them for small changes in market conditions. Rather, it will vary its hiring standards by setting different minimum productivity requirements for each type, and thereby it can adjust the real wage to reflect market conditions.[3]

The firm's equilibrium position is one in which the rate of production, inventory, backlog, and the workforce are at the optimal levels, and, therefore, the following relationships hold.

$$(8) \qquad 0 - S = B_t - B_{t-1} = \emptyset$$

$$(9) \qquad G - S = I_t - I_{t-1} = \emptyset$$

$$(10) \qquad \dot{L} = h - q = \emptyset ,$$

where S is the rate of shipments and h is the new hire rate.

The firm's profits are then:

$$(11) \qquad \pi = PG - \sum_{i=1}^{N} W_i L_i - rI - bB,$$

which, by substitution of equations (1), (2), (3A), (4A), (5), (6), and (7A), yields:

$$(12) \qquad \pi = a_1 \left(\frac{V}{U}\right)^{a_2} \left(\frac{I}{B}\right)^{a_3} Z^{a_4} \prod_{i=1}^{N} L_i^{a_{5i}} K^{a_6} e^{a_7 t} - \sum_{i=1}^{N} \gamma_{oi} \left(\frac{V}{U}\right)^{\gamma_{1i}} L_i^{\gamma_{2i}+1} \overline{W}$$

$$- p_o i^{p_{1i}} I^{p_2+1} - \tau_o B^{\tau_1+1} .\,[4]$$

For determining the optimum, the capital stock will be treated as fixed.[5] The presumption is that the lead time involved in adjusting the level of capital is so long relative to the lead needed for other decisions of the firm that in making the latter, the stock may be regarded as predetermined. As the derived profit function has incorporated all the constraints, the firm optimizes by finding the unconstrained maximum of (12). The first order conditions for an optimum are linear in the logarithms and may be solved to yield the reduced form:

$$(13) \qquad \begin{bmatrix} \ell n \underline{L}^* \\ \ell n I^* \\ \ell n B^* \\ \ell n S^* \end{bmatrix} = [A] \begin{bmatrix} 1 \\ \ell n \left(\dfrac{V}{U} \right) \\ \ell n(K) \\ \ell n(\overline{W}) \\ \ell n(i) \\ \ell n(Z) \\ t \end{bmatrix}$$

where $\underline{L}^*$ is a $1 \times N$ vector of optimum levels for the different types of labor and A is a $(3+N) \times 7$ matrix of coefficients. Substitution in our original relations will yield the optimum levels for prices, wages, production, and the turnover rate.

3. DYNAMIC MODEL OF THE FIRM

Next, we consider the dynamic situation in which the firm's market environment is changing continuously, and hence, the optimal position also is changing. If adjustments were costless, the firm would want to move to its desired levels immediately, whenever its current position were different. However, adjustment costs are often substantial and increase with the speed of adjustment, (see Holt, et al.). Hence, the firm wishes to smooth its adjustments toward this moving target. Determining these

333

dynamic optimal decisions involves combining the analysis of the static optimum with the dynamic adjustment costs. This two-stage suboptimization approximates the fully dynamic optimal strategy.[6]

It would be conceivable for the firm to make all dynamic decisions simultaneously. However, the decision rules which would result from attempting to minimize total adjustment and disequilibrium costs for a model with as many decisions as this would be extremely complex, combining information on a large number of forecasted and lagged values of the different variables.[7] Because the actual decision processes are not that sophisticated, it can be assumed that the dynamic decisions of the firm can be partitioned into two sets. The first set regarding prices, production, and shipment rates is the responsibility of the production-sales department. The second, which includes vacancy levels, layoffs, wages, is controlled by the personnel department.[8]

The analysis of the personnel department is handled in two stages. First, the optimal work force decisions are obtained as if these variables were directly controlled.[9] Second, the implementation of these decisions through vacancies and layoffs is determined. The personnel department is assumed to minimize several types of costs. First are the disequilibrium costs associated with having the actual level of the workers of each type and their wage rate deviating from the long run optimal levels. Secondly, there are overtime and slacktime costs arising from having the actual workforce deviating from the efficient level for current production. Third, there are adjustment costs associated with altering the number of workers or the wage rate. Finally, there are a set of costs connected with non-firm initiated turnover and recruitment errors.

The dynamic costs the personnel department is assumed to minimize can be written as follows:

$$C = \sum_{t=0}^{T} \rho^t \sum_{i=1}^{N} [C_{1i}(\tilde{L}_{it} - L_{it}^*)^2 + C_{2i}(W_{it} - W_{it}^*)^2 + C_{3i}(\tilde{L}_{it} - L_{it}^d)^2$$

(14)
$$+ C_{4i}(\tilde{L}_{it} - L_{it-1})^2 + C_{5i}(W_{it} - W_{it-1})^2 + C_{6i}(\tilde{q}_{it})^2$$

$$+ C_{7i}(d_{it})^2 + C_{8i}(W_{it} - \overline{W}_t - C)^2]$$

where $\tilde{L}_{it}$ is the dynamically desired number of workers of type i in time period t;

L_{it}^* is the static optimal number of workers of type i in time period t;

L_{it}^d is the efficient number of workers of type i needed to produce the actual output planned in period t;

L^{it} is the actual number of workers of type i in time period t;

$\tilde{q}_{it}$ is the number of workers of type i who quit in time period t;

d_{it} is the number of workers of type i who are discharged in time period t.[10]

Costs associated with the firm's production rate and workforce, as noted, are tied together inextricably. Changing the production rate involves altering the size or intensity of use of the workforce with the accompanying recruitment and training expenditures and overtime or slacktime costs. For the long run, the firm will adjust its workforce toward the level $\underline{L}^*$. However, for the current period, the firm is concerned about its workforce in relation to the production rate. The production function provides the technologically optimal workforce for any production rate and can be inverted to determine the current workforce needs, $\underline{L}^d$. For the dynamic analysis, we linearize the production function so that when inverted we find:

(15)
$$L_{it}^d = \hat{\beta}_o + \hat{\beta}_1 K_t + \hat{\beta}_2 G_t + \hat{\beta}_3 t + \sum_{j \neq i} \hat{\beta}_{4j} L_{jt}$$

The costs of deviating from $\underline{L}^d$, C_{3i}, are likely to be quite large as they involve expenditures for overtime or slacktime.

When a segment of the workforce is expanding, the costs represented by C_{4i} involve the recruitment and training of the additional personnel and their integration into the production processes. If a segment is being contracted through layoffs or discharges, the cost involves the benefits and other compensation which must be paid to furloughed workers and the potential loss of firm specific human capital in the case that those laid off find other work before being recalled.

Paralleling the costs of altering any part of the workforce's size are the costs of maintaining it at a given level. Workers who quit or are discharged must be replaced and the associated recruitment and training expenses incurred. The costs are expected to be different for the two types of turnover. The costs of a quit, C_{6i} presumably involve the lost service of a fully-trained, qualified worker and the need for a new worker to be trained completely to replace the quitter's productive capcaity. The discharged worker was presumably less than fully productive, so that his replacement may require less training to restore the productive capacity of the workforce. However, in addition to the services lost, the costs of a discharge, C_{7i}, will include various forms of severance expense, principally unemployment insurance contributions, while none will be incurred for quits, which are voluntary actions of the worker.

Discharges arise from the inability of the firm to have perfect foresight concerning a worker's productive potential when he is hired. The firm will know soon after they come to work whether most workers are adequate and the largest proportion of discharges should follow closely the time a group of workers is hired. If firms discharge workers as soon as it is evident that they are unsatisfactory, it would be expected that, for workers hired at one point in time, the proportions discharged in subsequent periods would be declining. So it will be reasonable to regard current discharges as a distributed lag of former hires:

$$(16) \qquad d_{it} = \sum_{T=0}^{T} \delta_{oi} \lambda_i^T H_{it-T} .$$

Hence,

$$(17) \qquad d_{it} = \lambda_i (\delta_{oi} H_{it} + d_{it-1}) .$$

Quits, as described in Section I, are related to the relative wage of the firm and labor market conditions. Linearizing the quit function, we have:

$$(18) \qquad \tilde{q}_{it} = \hat{\xi}_{oi} + \hat{\xi}_{1i} \left(\frac{V}{U_t} \right) + \hat{\xi}_{2i} (W_{it} - \overline{W}_{it}) + \hat{\xi}_{3i} L_{it-1} .$$

Reducing the total costs of turnover is possible by adjusting the wage rate to limit quits and increase the quality of recruits so discharges are less likely. However, the firm must be concerned about the long-term effects and the immediate payroll costs of its wage policy. Wage increases by an individual firm may be followed with a lag by wage increases of other firms leaving the firm in the same relative position with respect to wages as before its first increase. If there had not been a shift in product demand allowing a compensating price increase, long-run profits will be diminished. Even if the market wage does not respond, the firm would incur additional future costs as it tried to reduce wages to the equilibrium level since these actions would trigger quits and cause a loss of morale and productivity. Thus, the costs represented by C_{2i} and C_{5i} will have a dampening effect on the use of wages to control turnover.

The firm is also concerned in setting the wage rate with respect to its influence on the duration of vacancies. As the firm determines its hiring needs for more distant future points, its uncertainty regarding when the new hires report to work and the forecasts of its needs for those workers increases.[11] Thus, firms desire to reduce the expected duration of vacancies. A vacancy has a probability of being filled at any moment which is a function of the relative wage of the firm and labor market conditions. The duration of vacancies will tend to be an exponential distribution so that both its expected value and variance can be decreased by increasing the per-period probability of filling a vacancy. The firm can probably do so by increasing its wage relative to the market wage.

The expression involving C_{8i} includes a negative constant, because the recruitment and forecasting costs are not necessarily symmetric. As the firm's wage declines relative to the market wage, the costs of recruitment increase. When the firm's wage is high, relative to the market wage, the problem of finding workers diminishes, but costs increase more rapidly, because of the higher wage bill.

The cost structure presented in (14) can be minimized by solving the system of 2NT equations which form the first order conditions. This system could be solved analytically using the Z-transform method described in Hay and Holt. However, its size probably makes a numerical solution more efficient. In either case, the solution would be of the form:

$$(19) \qquad \begin{bmatrix} \underset{\sim}{\underline{L}}_t \\ \underline{W}_t \end{bmatrix} = [\,B\,] \begin{bmatrix} \underline{L}^* \\ \underline{W}^* \\ \underline{L}^d \\ \dfrac{\underline{V}}{\underline{U}} \\ \underline{W} \\ \underline{L}_{t-1} \\ \underline{W}_{t-1} \\ \dfrac{d_{t-1}}{1} \end{bmatrix}$$

where $\underset{\sim}{\underline{L}}_t$ and $\underline{W}_t$ are $N \times 1$ vectors of the decisions for the current period;

$\underline{L}^*$, $\underline{W}^*$, and $\underline{L}^d$ are $NT \times 1$ vectors of forecasted optimal levels
of L_{it}^*, W_{it}^*, and L_{it}^d for $i = 1, \ldots, N$ and $t = 1, \ldots, T$;
$\underline{\dfrac{V}{U}}$ and $\underline{W}$ are $T \times 1$ vectors of forecasted values of labor
market conditions in period t, $t = 1, \ldots, T$;
$\underline{L}_{t-1}$, $\underline{W}_{t-1}$, and $\underline{d}_{t-1}$ are lagged values of workforce, wage
rates and discharges.

B is a $[2N] \times [3NT + 2T + 3N+1]$ matrix of coefficients.

The wage decisions can be implemented directly, but control of the labor force is inherently indirect through control of vacancies and layoffs.

4. VACANCY AND LAYOFF DECISIONS

In the last section, a decision rule was derived for the number of workers of each type under a hypothesis of dynamic cost minimization. However, the firm does not completely control the number of workers, because workers' decisions with respect to job acceptances, quits, and retirements are only partially affected by a firm's actions. What the firm presumably attempts is to equate the expected number of the workers it employs with the desired size workforce in each time period through the decisions under its direct control, namely the vacancy stock and lay-offs.[12] For simplicity, we will drop, in this section, the i subscript and consider the vacancy and layoff rules for one type of worker. The same analysis applies directly to each type.

A first approximation to a vacancy decision rules might specify the vacancy stock as the difference between the existing workforce and the desired. Designating the existing workforce as L_t, vacancies would be:

$$(20) \qquad V_t = \tilde{L}_t - L_t .$$

However, this rule would result in an expected workforce less than the desired size unless the firm constantly had a queue of qualified applicants ready to start work immediately, so that the duration of a vacancy would be zero. It is more plausible to expect that a nonzero lead time will exist between the moment the need for additional workers is perceived and the process of recruitment, job acceptance, and reporting to work can be completed. If this lead time involves a period τ, then the vacancy stock at any given moment, t, should reflect the expected labor shortage at time $t + \tau$, which would occur in the absence of recruiting:

$$(21) \qquad V_t = \tilde{L}_{t+\tau} - L_{t+\tau} .$$

Greater insight into the composition of the vacancy stock can be obtained by deriving alternative expressions for the two terms above. First, the desired workforce at time $t+\tau$ will differ from the desired workforce at time t by the growth desired over the period of length τ. So the first term in (21) can be expressed as:

$$(22) \qquad \tilde{L}_{t+\tau} = \tilde{L}_t + \dot{L}\tau ,$$

where $\dot{L}$ is the desired growth rate of the workforce per unit of time.

The actual workforce which will be available at time $t + \tau$ will equal the present workforce less turnover in the form of quits, retirements, and discharges occuring during the period τ. Then:

$$(23) \qquad L_{t+\tau} = L_t - q\tau - d\tau .$$

Combining (21) and (22), we find that the stock of vacancies which will produce an expected workforce at time $t + \tau$ equal to the desired level is:

$$(24) \qquad V_t = (\tilde{L}_t - L_t) + (q + d)\tau + \dot{L}\tau .$$

These components may be described as the current shortage of workers for present production needs, the replacements needed for turnover during

340

the lead time, and the new workers needed for growth during the lead time.

The vacancy stock will contain vacancies created at many different points in the past. If previous forecasts of workforce needs were accurate and the variance of vacancy duration is small, the current shortage component should be relatively small as well. However, as noted in the previous section, the vacancy durations are distributed exponentially so that a small variance would imply a short mean duration also. Thus, all three components of vacancies would be small under these circumstances and the total stock of vacancies will not be large when recruitment time is short.

When the mean and the variance of the vacancy duration is large, the vacancy rule implies that firms engage in labor hoarding at some times and experience shortages at others. The larger variance of duration means firms will be less sure of the arrival time of new workers. When some vacancies are unexpectedly filled very quickly, workers hired in anticipation of turnover or growth may report for work before the need for their services actually occurs. Thus, the firm appears to be hoarding labor since it is employing both some workers expected to quit and their replacements, and workers who are slated for planned future production. The firm accepts these additional costs because it believes the early filling of vacancies is simply a stochastic phenomenon. In these circumstances, the costs of temporarily paying the additional workers must be weighed against the possibility of incurring costs from future labor shortages.

The vacancy decision rule we have specified will be operable as long as the calculated vacancy stock remains positive (for the particular type of labor). When the vacancy stock is negative, the present workforce is too large taking into account both current production needs and anticipated turnover and growth, so the firm will lay off some excess workers.

The number of workers laid off depends upon the relationship of the firm's decision period to the average recruitment time, τ. When recruitment time is shorter than the decision period, the firm will lay off the workers required to bring the workforce to the desired level at the end of the decision period.

If expected recruitment time is longer than the decision period, the firm may defer some layoffs and incur the costs of additional slack time, if these costs are less than those of laying off these workers and recruiting replacements.[14] Recruitment time will lengthen only as the labor market tightens so only firms moving counter to the general cyclical condition and contemplating layoffs in a tight market will be concerned about the layoff decisions when recruiting time exceeds the decision period.

The layoff decision rule can then be written as:

$$(25) \qquad \ell_t = \begin{cases} (L_t - \tilde{L}_t) - (q + d)\tau - \dot{L}\tau & \text{if } \tau > t_\delta \\[2em] (L_t - \tilde{L}_t) - (q + d)t_\delta - \dot{L}t_\delta & \text{otherwise} \end{cases}$$

where t_δ is the length of the decision period.

A separate vacancy and layoff decision rule will exist for each type of worker. It is conceivable that within a single firm there will exist, simultaneously, vacancies for one type of worker, while layoffs of another type are proceeding. Shifts in the supplies of different worker types may make it profitable to change the relative proportions of worker types. It can be expected that generally when simultaneous layoffs and vacancies do occur, they are for categories of workers which are not close substitutes. This will be true because the advantages to be gained in the short run by changing the proportions of close substitutes through increased productivity will be outweighed by the larger costs associated with layoffs, recruitments, and training.

5. AGGREGATION

Before proceeding to the estimation of our model, two notes should be made about the question of aggregating the derived relationships to correspond to existing data. First, the model was specified and developed theoretically in terms of the individual firm. Since micro time series on the relevant variables are not readily available at the firm level, it will be necessary to aggregate across firms to the industry level. Since the decision rules are linear, such aggregation results in the familiar biasing of coefficients.[15] We will not be able to interpret the estimated parameters as unbiased estimates of the expected value of the corresponding firm parameters because it would be unreasonable to assume either the equality of parameters across firms or a constant distribution of the industry aggregate variables accross firms through time.

A second problem arises involving aggregation in connection with the different types of labor. Since we have postulated a Cobb-Douglas production function, it would be possible, given the proper data, to construct a consistent aggregate index of labor inputs.[16] Data on the workers actually employed by type would be available on an industry basis. However, as our theory suggests, the number of workers employed is not necessarily equal to either the equilibrium level or the desired number in a dynamic sense. Adjustments to the total employed must be made for the number of unfilled vacancies and the rate of non-firm initiated separations. No measures of these latter variables is available disaggregated by worker type. Therefore, we have chosen to use a simple unweighted index of workers recognizing that it is a biased estimate of the labor input.

The major result of this aggregation of the labor input will be to obscure the dynamic wage strategy of the firm. There are a variety of constraints, involving unions, legislation, morale, etc., on the freedom of firms to alter the nominal wage rate as a response to changes in labor market tightness. As noted, when market conditions shift moderately,

343

the firm can adjust the real wage by altering the hiring standards it uses in selecting workers. For larger changes in market conditions, it will need to alter the composition of the workforce by type and perhaps the nominal wage rate as well. The fluctuations that we observe in the average nominal wage will reflect a mixture of both these latter effects. Unfortunately, their relative importance will be indeterminate and no information on the variation in hiring standards is available.

6. EMPIRICAL ESTIMATES

To test our theory of dynamic decisions for vacancies and layoffs, we have estimated these decision rules for the total manufacturing sector and for the aggregations of durable and nondurable goods producing industries.[17] The purpose of our test is to ascertain if the variables suggested by this theory are significant determinants of these decisions and if the decision rules would provide good predictions for the actual decision variables. The vacancy and layoff decisions as described in (24) and (25) depend on the dynamically desired workforce level, which in turn, is related to the static optimal workforce and wage rate. In order to eliminate these unobservables from our decision rules a multistage procedure was employed. In the first, the reduced form relations for the static optimal workforce and wage rate as described in (13) are estimated using a measure of the optimal workforce based on the actual level of vacancies and turnover. The predicted values from these equations are then used as estimates of the unobserved optimal values. Secondly, the expression for the dynamically desired workforce (19), containing the estimated optimal values, is substituted into the decision rules for vacancies and layoffs, equations (24) and (25), which are then estimated.

6.1. Equilibrium Workforce and Wage Rate Estimates

Among the determinants of the dynamic decision variables, the static equilibrium levels of the workforce and the wage rate are not observed directly. However, it can be assumed that the firm's decisions

344

result in the actual levels of these variables approximating the equilibrium level on average.[18] The reduced form equilibrium relationships described in (13) can then be fit for the wage rate and the workforce.[19] For the wage relation, the dependent variable is the observed hourly wage rate adjusted to exclude overtime. This measure does not allow distinguishing shifts in the real wage due to changes in hiring standards as distinct from changes in the money wage. For the workforce equation, it was assumed that the dynamic desired workforce level would approximate the equilibrium workforce. While neither of these variables is observed directly, the vacancy relationship (24) suggests $\tilde{L}$, the dynamic desired workforce, can be derived from observable quantities. Solving for $\tilde{L}$, we have:

$$(26) \qquad \tilde{L}_t = L_t + \hat{V}_t - (q + d)\tau - \dot{L}\tau \ .$$

Because this is an aggregate relationship for all types of workers, $\hat{V}_t$ is net vacancies, namely reported vacancies less layoffs. We can observe all the components of (26) with the exception of the desired growth rate of the workforce, $\dot{L}$. However, since our data is for discrete intervals, the growth component would involve expansions in periods beyond the current period so that if the mean vacancy duration were shorter than our observed interval, the growth component can be ignored. Two sets of empirical estimates indicate the mean duration is quite short, so we have excluded this component from our estimate of (26).[20]

The desired labor force will then be approximated by:

$$(27) \qquad \tilde{L}_t = L_t + \hat{V}_t - (q + d)\tau \ .$$

As our measure of τ, the average duration of vacancy, we have used the ratio of the vacancy stock to the number of hires.[21] This now serves as the dependent variable in our estimate of equation (13).

345

Among the predetermined variables, all except the demand proxy Z and the capital stock are readily available. Z was postulated as representing all influences on demand other than price and a single dimension of product quality, delivery time. We take advantage of the fact that the observed flow of orders, price and inventory-backlog levels define the demand curve to write Z as:

$$(28) \qquad Z = \left\{ \alpha_o^{\alpha_0} \alpha_1 \left(\frac{I}{B} \right)^{\alpha_2} p^{-1} \right\}^{\frac{1}{\alpha_3}} . \qquad 22$$

Taking logs of (28), we then eliminate $\ell n(Z)$ from the reduced form equations (13).

Because data on the capital stock disaggregated by industry and observed at frequent intervals is rather limited, we have chosen to exclude this variable from our equations. The influence of the growth of the capital stock should be captured adequately by the time trend we have included. Indeed, for one of the capital measures available, the Federal Reserve's Index of Manufacturing Capacity, the logarithm of this variable is almost perfectly collinear with a time trend.

The results from estimating the modified reduced form equation are presented in Table 1.[23] The model performs very well for desired labor for the durable goods industries and total manufacturing, and reasonably well for the nondurable industries. As these equations are reduced form relationships, the parameters do not have any structural interpretations. When significant, the parameters all have intuitively reasonable signs.[24] The desired workforce varies directly with cyclical indicators such as the $\ell n \left(\frac{V}{U} \right)$ or $\ell n(i)$. Increased product demand raises the desired workforce level as seen by the positive coefficients on $\ell n(0)$ and $\ell n(P)$. While theory suggested that $\ell n \left(\frac{I}{B} \right)$ would have a positive influence on product demand and, hence, labor demand, the coefficients when significant are negative. However, it must be remembered that when actual inventory and backlog are not at equilibrium levels, firms may begin adjusting them before changing the workforce size in response to a change in product demand.

TABLE 1

Variable	EQUILIBRIUM WORKFORCE			EQUILIBRIUM WAGE RATE		
	Total Manufacturing	Durable Goods	Nondurable Goods	Total Manufacturing	Durable Goods	Nondurable Goods
Constant	7.910 (4.195)	11.692 (5.010)	6.561 (3.005)	-1.500 (-1.599)	-1.386 (-1.328)	-1.209 (-1.902)
$\ell n\left(\dfrac{V}{U}\right)$	0.021* (3.100)	0.030* (3.491)	0.0143 (1.550)	-0.005 (-1.69)	-0.009* (-2.592)	-0.001 (-0.609)
$\ell n(\bar{W})$	-0.151 (-0.465)	-0.698 (-1.700)	0.104 (0.251)	0.445* (2.800)	0.383** (2.123)	0.479* (4.260)
$\ell n(i)$	0.032* (3.993)	0.025 (1.913)	0.034* (3.623)	-0.001 (-0.181)	-0.002 (-0.405)	-0.0001 (-0.021)
$\ell n(0)$	0.151* (4.941)	0.172* (6.262)	0.191* (4.276)	-0.007 (-0.668)	0.016 (1.473)	-0.059* (-5.507)
$\ell n(P)$	0.393* (3.847)	0.090 (0.792)	0.164** (2.190)	0.020 (0.311)	0.052 (0.912)	-0.042 (-1.494)
$\ell n\left(\dfrac{I}{B}\right)$	-0.066* (-3.080)	-0.191* (-5.264)	0.026 (0.731)	-0.004 (-0.420)	-0.002 (-0.142)	-0.0002 (-0.021)
t	-0.0004 (-0.215)	0.003 (1.218)	-0.001 (-0.698)	0.003* (3.249)	0.003* (2.954)	0.003* (4.649)
R^2	0.939	0.948	0.758	0.989	0.995	0.997
$F^{\dagger}$	121.42	145.63	26.01	999.75	2125.55	3206.09
D.W.	1.331	1.216	0.889	1.561	1.403	1.828
Period	196904-197312	196904-197312	196904-197312	196707-197312	196707-197312	196707-197312

t-statistics are in parenthesis.
* indicates the coefficient is significant at the 0.01 level.
** indicates the coefficient is significant at the 0.05 level.
† Degrees of freedom for the workforce regressions are (8, 49) and for the wage rate regressions (8, 70).

The desired wage rate regressions reported in Table 1 have been corrected for a first order autoregressive structure in the error term. That wages are serially correlated on a monthly basis is not surprising, given the institutional strictures on their movements. Collective bargaining agreements fix wages for long periods, while worker resistance prevents considerably downward movement. As noted in Section 2, the firm has two means with which to control the real wage, namely the nominal wage rate and hiring standards. We anticipate that the latter are used more extensively to cope with cyclical fluctuations.

Aggregation across worker types and using an average wage rate as the regressand has a demonstrable effect on the coefficients obtained. For the vacancy-unemployment ratio, a positive relationship with the wage rate would be anticipated. However, the estimated coefficients all have negative signs though only one is significant. The observed effect probably stems from a counter cyclical movement in the average quality of workers as inexperienced, low productivity and low wage workers are hired when the market is tight and the senior, more productive and higher paid workers are retained when the market slackens and layoffs occur.

A similar aggregation effect can be seen in the coefficients on orders. This coefficient is positive for the durable goods industries and negative for the nondurables. The former sign probably stems from durable manufacturers maintaining a more homogeneous workforce because of higher skill requirements, while the sign of the latter reflects the dominance of the compositional changes in the workforce over any change in offered wage rates in the response of nondurable manufacturers to changes in orders.

The regression results indicate the stability of relative wages. The wage rate in the total private sector alone explains virtually all the variation. This variable itself is almost a simple time trend so that the nominal wage rate exhibits little movement, except steady growth through time. These findings suggest there is no need for a dynamic decision rule for wages. Firms apparently determine their nominal wage policy for the long run and use hiring standards to vary the real wage in response to short run fluctuations. If either hiring standards or the real wage were observable, it would be useful to investigate the dynamic strategies used in setting them.

6.2. Estimates of Vacancy and Layoff Decision Rules

We will ignore, as in the last section, the growth component, $\dot{L}\tau$. We can obtain $\tilde{L}_t$ from the derivation of the dynamically desired workforce in (19). Separations other than layoffs $(q_t + d_t)$, can be approximated by a function of the tightness of the labor market represented by the vacancy-unemployment ratio, $\frac{V}{U}$, the relative wage $\frac{W_t}{\overline{W}_t}$, and the size of last period's workforce, L_{t-1}:

$$(29) \qquad (q_t + d_t) = f\left[\left(\frac{V}{U}\right), \left(\frac{W_t}{\overline{W}_t}\right), L_{t-1}\right]$$

The mean duration of a vacancy, τ, can be approximated as a function of the first two variables:

$$(30) \qquad \tau = g\left[\left(\frac{V}{U_t}\right), \left(\frac{W_t}{\overline{W}_t}\right)\right]$$

The decision period is assumed equal to our observation period. Substitution of (19), with the predicted values of $\underline{L}^*$ and $\underline{W}^*$ from our estimate of (14), along with (29) and (31) into (24) and (25) and taking a linear approximation results in decision rules for vacancies and layoffs of the form:

$$(31) \qquad \begin{bmatrix} V_t \\ \ell_t \end{bmatrix} = [\, B' \,] \begin{bmatrix} \underline{L}^* \\ \underline{W}^*_d \\ \underline{L} \\ \left(\dfrac{V}{U}\right) \\ \overline{W} \\ L_{t-1} \\ W_{t-1} \\ d_{t-1} \\ 1 \end{bmatrix}$$

Where B' is a $2 \times (5T + 4)$ matrix of coefficients;

$\underline{L}^*$ and $\underline{W}^*$ are a $T \times 1$ vector of the forecasts of the equilibrium values of the total workforce and average wage rate in the current and $T-1$ future periods from our regressions of (14);

$\underline{L}^d$ is a $T \times 1$ vector of forecasts of the workforce for projected production requirements in the same periods;

$\left|\dfrac{V}{U}\right|$ and $(\overline{W})$ and $T \times 1$ vectors of forecasts of the labor market condition and average wage rate in the same period; and

L_{t-1}, W_{t-1}, d_{t-1} are the lagged values of the industry's work-force, wage rate, and number of discharges.

The structure of linear decision rules is such that the coefficients on forecasted values of future conditions are declining in absolute value, so that forecasts of more distant future events can be excluded from the decision rule without appreciably altering actual decisions. Hence, we have trunacted the vectors of future forecasts at $(t + 5)$.

Since business firms do not have perfect foresight in making decisions, but often must rely on imprecise guesses of future conditions, we decided to use quarterly moving averages of actual values as proxies of the firm's forecasts. The coefficients on these variables are then

350

estimates of the sum of the coefficients on the corresponding monthly forecasts within each future quarter.

The forecasted (quarterly average) production rate and a time trend were substituted for L^d, the optimal workforce for production, on the assumption that it could be approximated by inverting a production function involving these variables.

Estimation of the decision rules with the entire set of variables in the theoretical specification may involve problems of spurious correlation and multicollinearity. The former could arise from including the current period's vacancy-unemployment ratio in the forecast of labor market conditions because manufacturing vacancies may have a greater impact on our measure of aggregate vacancies than they do on the true level.[25] To avoid possible spurious correlation in our vacancy decision rule, we excluded the vacancy-unemployment ratio for the current period from our regression.

To the extent that there are seasonal patterns in sales and in the availability of factor supplies, a portion of the seasonal effects will be reflected in the production and desired workforce levels entering our decision rules. There may be additional seasonal effects due to variations in the supplies of labor. Hence, we have added a set of seasonal variables to the decision rules.[26]

The regression results for each industry group for the vacancy and layoff decisions are presented in Table 2. The very significant F statistics for the relationship as a whole with the small number of significant individual coefficients indicates, even with our prior exclusions, the amount of remaining multicollinearity is high.[27]

Vacancies appear to respond to the variables in the decision rule in ways consistent with our theory.[28] Larger optimal workforce and production levels generally lead to increased vacancies.[29] A larger current labor force has a net positive effect indicating that the increased turnover associated with a larger workforce outweights the depressant effect workforce size would have on additional recruitment. The influence of both

351

TABLE 2

	VACANCY DECISION RULE			LAYOFF DECISION RULE		
Variable	Total Manufacturing	Durable Goods	Nondurable Goods	Total Manufacturing	Durable Goods	Nondurable Goods
Constant	-1491.270 (-1.326)	-1117.395 (-1.885)	-1383.227 (-3.272)	4255.600 (1.255)	2948.427 (1.251)	1416.145 (0.932)
L_1^*	0.031 (1.498)	0.028 (1.431)	0.035 (1.878)	-0.039 (-0.628)	0.024 (0.308)	-0.066 (-0.982)
L_2^*	-0.012 (-0.471)	-0.016 (-0.821)	0.011 (0.458)	-0.129 (-1.694)	-0.042 (-0.541)	-0.189** (-2.151)
G_1	0.200 (0.881)	0.113 (0.424)	0.212 (1.220)	-0.273 (-0.397)	-1.809 (-1.712)	-2.003 (-3.205)
T	-7.075 (-1.072)	-6.081 (-1.740)	-5.472** (-2.152)	22.665 (1.138)	20.078 (1.445)	2.141 (0.234)
$\left(\frac{V}{U}\right)_1$	3484.7* (3.091)	3043.9* (4.318)	434.351 (1.075)	-4979.2 (-1.464)	-4578.7 (-1.634)	-327.365 (-0.225)
$\left(\frac{V}{U}\right)_2$	1115.4 (1.0371)	827.566 (1.252)	418.192 (1.485)	6096.8 (1.878)	836.709 (0.318)	739.602 (0.730)
$\overline{W}$	3.971 (1.137)	3.320 (1.794)	2.257 (1.814)	-8.494 (-0.806)	-8.830 (-1.140)	1.127 (0.252)
L_{t-1}	0.005 (0.428)	0.004 (0.345)	0.019 (1.491)	0.160* (3.941)	0.104* (2.360)	0.171* (3.776)
W_{t-1}	-65.824 (-0.617)	-13.091 (-0.243)	69.119 (1.280)	-397.119 (-1.234)	-173.674 (-0.809)	-194.858 (-1.004)
d_{t-1}	0.001 (0.017)	-0.219** (-2.017)	-0.032 (-0.824)	-0.167 (-0.719)	-0.162 (-0.376)	0.021 (0.148)
F(Seasonals)	3.13*	5.00*	3.44**	4.75*	2.65**	3.18**
R^2	0.968	0.975	0.953	0.823	0.788	0.740
F(15, 36)	108.04	138.84	73.86	17.63	14.25	11.14
D.W.	1.747	1.651	1.778	1.760	2.159	1.933
Period	196904-197306	196904-197306	196904-197306	196904-197306	196904-197306	196904-197306

L_1^* is a moving average of L_t^*, L_{t+1}^*, and L_{t+2}^*.
L_2^* is a moving average of L_{t+3}^*, L_{t+4}^* and L_{t+5}^*.
G is a moving average of G_t, G_{t+1}, G_{t+2}.
$\left(\frac{V}{U}\right)_1$ is a moving average of $\left(\frac{V}{U}\right)_{t+1}$, $\left(\frac{V}{U}\right)_{t+2}$, and $\left(\frac{V}{U}\right)_{t+3}$.
$\left(\frac{V}{U}\right)_2$ is a moving average of $\left(\frac{V}{U}\right)_{t+4}$, $\left(\frac{V}{U}\right)_{t+5}$, and $\left(\frac{V}{U}\right)_{t+6}$.
$\overline{W}$ is a moving average of $\overline{W}_t$, $\overline{W}_{t+1}$, and $\overline{W}_{t+2}$.
*Indicates the coefficient is significant at the 0.01 level.
**Indicates the coefficient is significant at the 0.05 level.

the firm's own wage and the general market wage level is also consistent with our theory. The higher the firm's relative wage, the fewer vacancies, as the firm finds it easy to recruit new workers. But, as the market wage rises with the firm's wage fixed, the level of vacancies rises because of the longer duration.

Layoffs respond negatively to the forecasted optimal workforce size and production rates are, as expected, the opposite of the effect of vacancies.[30] The firm's own wage rate has a positive influence reflecting the increased cost of slack time. The market wage and the first quarter aggregate vacancy-unemployment ratio reduce layoffs among the durable industries. In part, this may be because these variables indicate the reduced probability that a firm will be able to recall its workers before they find other jobs or will be able to fill new vacancies. Surprisingly though, forecasts of a tight labor market two quarters hence increases current layoffs. $(V/U)_1$ and $(V/U)_2$ have similar effects among nondurable producers, but the forecasted market wage affects layoffs positively. While no ready explanation is available for the result, the very small t-ratio indicates it is not a cause of great concern.

The nondurable industries also have a positive sign on lagged discharges as opposed to the negative one for the durable industries. The positive sign may indicate the use of discharges as a form of covert layoff in order to avoid some of the unemployment compensation costs associated with layoffs. As noted in the analysis of wage rates, there is considerable variation in the size of the workforce in the nondurable industries. This would mean a larger fraction of workers was on some form of probationary status or has limited job tenure. Under these circumstances, employers would have an easier time reducing their workforce through discharges instead of layoffs.

7. CONCLUSIONS

We have found the complex dynamics of the firm's demand for labor could be modeled facilely only by simplification of the decision processes through conditional suboptimization, quadratic costs, linear constraints, and certainty equivalence. The adaptive responses of firms in the labor market in correcting for past deviations from optimal levels and in the behavior of workers were developed in the form of dynamic decision rules for wage rates, vacancies, and layoffs, the variables under the firm's direct control.

Empirically, we tested the decision rules and concluded that if firms follow the strategy developed here in adjusting the real wage rate, they must be using hiring standards rather than the nominal wage rate as the adjusting mechanism. For vacancies and layoffs, the decision rules were found to fit actual decisions quite well. Expectation variables for changes in optimum workforce levels generally produced the anticipated changes in the vacancy stock or layoff rate. Limitations of data in terms of both appropriate variables for all the theoretical concepts of the model and excessive aggregation prevented a full-scale, rigorous test of the structural elements of the theory. However, the results suggest the approach developed here provides a means for greater understanding and measurement of the processes occuring in the labor market.

NOTES

[1] A similar demand relationship was presented by Zarnowitz in examining price and backlog responses to excess demand.

[2] This behavior, strictly speaking, implies the firm's profit-maximization problem should regard the labor supply function as an inequality rather than equality constraint and should be solved using nonlinear programming. However, as a practical matter, the deviations of a solution using that method and classical optimization techniques are likely quite small, because the cost savings of reduced turnover are small in comparison to increases associated with higher levels.

[3]A discussion of the role of both hiring standards and nominal wage rates in determining the real wage is contained in Hall.

4

$$a_1 = \alpha_o \tilde{\beta}_o^{1+\alpha_1} \left\{ \prod_{i=1}^{N} \frac{\beta_{4i} \xi_{2i}^{\beta_{4i}}}{\xi_{oi} \gamma_{oi}} \right\}^{1+\alpha_1}$$

$$a_2 = (1+\alpha_1) \sum_{i=1}^{N} \beta_{4i}(\xi_{1i} + \xi_{2i} \gamma_{1i})$$

$$a_3 = \alpha_2$$

$$a_4 = \alpha_3$$

$$a_{5i} = (1+\alpha_1)(\beta_{4i}(\gamma_{2i}\xi_{2i}) + \beta_{1i})$$

$$a_6 = \beta_2(1 + \alpha_1)$$

$$a_7 = \beta_2(1 + \alpha_1)$$

[5]The optimal capital capacity can, of course, be included in this analysis (see Chang and Holt).

[6]Models developing dynamic decision rules recognizing disequilibrium and adjustment costs have appeared in Eisner and Strotz, Holt, et al., Hay, Treadway, Chang and Holt, and Lee. The model presented here, as point out earlier, follows most closely the method of Chang and Holt, but emulates Lee in putting particular stress on the determination of vacancies and in using linear approximations for the constraint relationships to insure that the decision rules form a linear system.

[7]Lee, it should be noted, did model the firm as minimizing total costs, but in developing his decision rules he put restrictions on the variables entering each decision. The restrictions were derived from an analysis of approximate costs and a numerical solution of the decision rule system.

355

[8] The segmentation of the firm's decisions along these lines is suggested by the results obtained by Lee. He found decisions regarding the workforce and wages were most sensitive to labor market conditions and production rates, while decisions regarding prices and shipments were related almost completely to demand conditions and independent of the labor market. Partitioning of short-term decision making does not imply the absence of significant interactions among departments. The dynamic decisions of separate departments are linked since disequilibrium costs associated with one department's decision variables reflect costs incurred throughout the firm because of the department's disequilibrium. In addition, decisions from one department may recusively affect those of other departments.

[9] The use of the workforce as a decision variable assumes that the firm has this variable completely within its control. In fact, the workforce is determined by the flows of quits, hires, layoffs, and discharges. Only the latter two are completely determined by the firm. Hires involve a joint decision between workers and the firm and quits are unilateral decisions by workers. However, as the firm can strongly influence quits and hires by the wages it offers, we will regard them as a predictable constraint in this phase of the analysis.

[10] Note we distinguish between $\tilde{L}_{it}$ and L_{it} because, as noted earlier, the actual size of the workforce is not under the firm's direct control.

[11] See Lee for an extensive discussion of the point.

[12] The role of vacancies in equating desired and expected workforce levels was first explored in Holt and David.

[13] The longer the average recruiting lead time τ, and associated variance, the greater is the total cost of sporadic excesses and shortages of labor. Both will cause declines in labor productivity through imbalances of the workforce relative to production requirements.

[14]In practice, firms do engage in temporary layoffs and use recalls to bring the workforce back to the desired level in later periods. However, decisions of this type would involve a more thorough analysis of the probabilities of filling a vacancy through recall versus recruitment and their impact on the decision process. We have not extended the analysis to consider this aspect here.

[15]See Theil.

[16]See Berndt and Christensen.

[17]The discussion of empirical work on this model contained here is an abbreviated version of that reported in Scanlon and Holt.

[18]This assumption is reasonable, given the linear decision rule framework which results in decisions which smooth fluctuations from long run equilibrium levels and result in smaller per period deviations.

[19]As noted in the previous section, we have aggregated over the different types of workers because of the absence of disaggregate vacancy or turnover information.

[20]These estimates are presented in Scanlon and Holt.

[21]The results obtained are not sensitive to the choice of the duration measure, since the turnover from quits and discharges each month is not a large fraction of the total workforce.

[22]A large number of variables, such as personal income, other industry prices, proxies for taste, etc., could be included in Z. However, since we are concerned only with estimating the reduced form for the wage rate and the workforce, we employ this method which was also used by Chang and Holt when using a similar product demand function.

[23]Sources of data for all variables are presented in Scanlon and Holt.

[24]We do not have estimates of the structural parameters so that it was not possible to anticipate a priori the signs of all the reduced form coefficients.

[25]The only available measure of the total level of vacancies in the economy for the sample period is the Help-Wanted Index collected by The Conference Board. This index which is the number of newspaper help-wanted advertisements is collected only in selected major cities where manufacturers employ a larger share of the labor force than the national average. Secondly, manufacturers may rely more heavily upon newspaper advertising as a recruiting device than industries using more skilled workers.

[26]The set consists of four sinusoidal variables, two with periodicity of twelve months and two of six months.

[27]In part to reduce multicollinearity and to eliminate the risk of spurious correlation between the aggregate vacancy-unemployment ratio and vacancies, we tested the exclusion of $(V/U)_1$ and $(V/U)_2$. The hypothesis of whether $(V/U)_1$ and $(V/U)_2$ should, in fact, be excluded was rejected in all cases at the 0.01 level for the vacancy relationships but could not be rejected for layoffs. The effect of exclusion on the remaining coefficients is discussed in Scanlon and Holt.

[28]We did not analytically solve the dynamic optimization problem, nor did we have structural parameter or cost estimates, so again we could not postualte, a priori, the expected signs.

[29]For the durable goods industry, L_2^* has a depressing insignificant effect, but when $(V/U)_1$ and $(V/U)_2$ were excluded, it became both positive and significant.

[30]Again, for the durable goods industries, the signs on the optimal work-force forecasts are mixed when the labor market variables are included, but both are negative when the latter are omitted.

REFERENCES

Berndt, E. R. and L. R. Christensen [1973], "The Internal Structure of Functional Relationships: Separability, Substitution, and Aggregation," Review of Economic Studies, Vol. XL, No. 123, pp. 403-410.

Chang, J. C. and C. C. Holt [1973], "Optimal Investment Orders Under Uncertainty and Dynamic Costs: Theory and Estimates," The Southern Economic Journal, Vol. XXXIX, No. 4.

Eisner, R. and R. H. Strotz [1963], "Determinants of Business Investments," in Impacts of Monetary Policy, by the Commission on Money and Credit, (Englewood Cliffs: Prentice Hall).

Hall, R. E. [1974], "The Process of Inflation in the Labor Market," Brookings Papers on Economic Activity, 2, pp. 343-393.

Hay, G. A. [1970], "Production Price, and Inventory Theory," American Economic Review, Vol. LX, No. 4, pp. 531-545.

Hay, G. A. and C. C. Holt [1975], "A General Solution for Linear Decision Rules: An Optimal Dynamic Strategy Applicable Under Uncertainty," Econometrica, Vol. 43, No. 2, pp. 231-259.

Holt, C. C. and M. H. David [1966], "The Concept of Job Vacancies in a Dynamic Theory of the Labor Market," in The Measurement and Interpretation of Job Vacancies; A Conference Report of the National Bureau of Economic Research (New York: Columbia University Press).

Holt, C. C., F. Modigliani, J. F. Muth and H. A. Simon [1960], Planning Production, Inventories, and Work Force, (Englewood Cliffs: Prentice Hall).

Lee, K. S. [1969], "Employment Decision of Manufacturing Firms in Response to Demand Fluctuations: An Econometric Study," unpublished Ph. D. dissertation, University of Wisconsin.

Scanlon, W. J. and C. C. Holt [1974], "Demand for Labor in a Dynamic Theory of the Firm," The Urban Institute, Working Paper 350-68.

Theil, H. [1965], Linear Aggregation of Economic Relations, North Holland.

Toikka, R. and T. Tachibanaki [1974], "The Economics of Human Capital and Labor Turnover," The Urban Institute, Working Paper 350-67.

Treadway, A. B. [1970], "Adjustment Costs and Variable Inputs in the Theory of the Competitive Firm," Journal of Economic Theory, Vol. 2, No. 4, pp. 329-347.

Zarnowitz, V. [1962], "Unfilled Orders, Price Changes, and Business Fluctuations," Review of Economics and Statistics, Vol. XLIV, No. 4, pp. 367-394.

This research was supported by funds from the Office of Manpower Research, U. S. Department of Labor, under Grant No. 92-11-72-36, to The Urban Institute, and by the National Science Foundation and the Ford Foundation. Opinions expressed are those of the authors and do not necessarily represent the views of The Urban Institute or its sponsors. The authors wish to acknowledge the able research assistance of Jacqueline Taylor and the helpful comments of their colleagues, Ralph Smith, Richard Toikka, and Jean Vanski. Any errors remain their responsibility.

Productivity Increase as a Learning Process (abstract)
Karl O. Faxén

ABSTRACT

A substantial part of productivity increase is due to "technical progress". This factor may best be seen as including an element of "social learning". The rate at which new methods of production actually are applied and the organization of work is adjusted to the use of new machinery etc. is dependent upon changes in social variables.

As part of a research project in industrial democracy detailed observations on changes in the organization of work during time periods of 3 years or more were made on a number of member firms of the Swedish Employers' Confederation. Productivity was measured at department level primarily in terms of quantity of product per manhour. This measure was sometimes supplemented by such variables as reject rates, tool costs per manhour or personal allowance time. An economic volume index was occasionally used instead of a physical measure of production. In all case studies, changes in the allocation of tasks and in methods of work were related to developments in frames of reference and patterns of information among blue collar workers as well as among supervisors and salaried staff, for instance planners. A change in organization, such as for instance transfer of responsibility for planning inside each week from the planning department to supervisors and to groups of workers, is coupled with widening the workers' frames of reference to include the interrelationships between operations in a group of machines during a week. The planners, on the other hand, learn more about deviations between plans and actual performance when they have to discuss weekly planning with workers and cannot prescribe norms for each job separately. Such deviations might result from variations in the quality of materials, known to workers but not previously to planners.

If the workers' detailed knowledge about work conditions is to be used in an efficient decision-making process, the motivation of each worker has to be related to performance at group or department level over some period of time rather than at individual level for each job separately. Major obstacles to a positive development in this direction were found to be:

1) efforts to preserve an unchanged identity in the work rôle. Such observations were made both among workers, supervisors and salaried staff.

2) traditional negative expectations about possible reactions as result of changes in the work rôles of other groups in the organization.

3) inadequate or insufficient feed-back information on limited changes in attitudes and performance of other groups at a social distance from one's own group.

A change in the pay system for blue-collar workers was seen as initiating a process of re-thinking and re-orientation over a wide range of variables, including social relationships between groups of employees. In many cases, productivity increased considerably when pay was related to group or department performance even when individual monetary incentives were weakened. Such a change in the pay system was so important that it could sometimes overcome the obstacles mentioned above and start an adaptive process, including a sequence of changes in the work organization, leading to an enlargement of the workers' frames of reference and a stepwise increase in information and co-operation. Both positive and negative examples of adaptive processes in work organizations were given in the paper, as well as an outline for a model for sequence analysis in terms of information, motivation and identity.

The full text is obtainable upon request from Dr. Karl O. Faxén, Swediwh Employers' Confederation, Box 16120, Stockholm 16, Sweden.

Diffusion of Innovations under Imperfect Competition
Alessandro Cigno

CONTENTS

1. INTRODUCTION

Detailed empirical studies of North American and Western European economies[1] have produced considerable evidence that the speed of diffusion of innovations and factor reallocation affects both the level and the growth rate of output per capita.   They have also shown that economic fluctuations have an adverse effect on the rate of growth of output per unit of input, with the obvious implication that aggregate demand management may influence "technical progress." Yet, generation after generation of neo-classical growth theories have invariably come to the conclusion that, given the rate of unemployment, the level of output per capita is determined solely by the share of investment in the national product, and its growth rate solely by exogenous changes in technology. Nor could it be otherwise, given the underlying assumptions of an aggregate production function (or one for each generation of capital-goods), which by definition rules out any misallocation of resources, and of perfect competition, which does not justify any deliberate delay in the widest application of the latest technical discoveries.

It is only in Kaldor's theory of economic growth[2] that we find imperfect competition explicitly assumed, and the aggregate production function replaced by a dynamic equation, the technical progress function, reflecting in its parameters the system's ability to adapt to changes in technical knowledge. Kaldor's approach has been often criticised, with some reason, for lacking any empirical basis or clear micro-economic explanation, but it still seems to me to be a step in the right direction towards interpreting an imperfect economic reality. In the present paper, I hope to show that a modified version of the technical progress function fits aggregate data better than a production function, and to offer a micro-economic justification for the existence of such a function.[3]

2. A MACRO-ECONOMIC RELATIONSHIP

A technical progress function is described by Kaldor as a relation between the growth rates of some aggregate measure of output per capita, y, and some aggregate measure of capital per capita, k,

$$(1) \qquad \frac{1}{y} \frac{dy}{dt} = f\left(\frac{1}{k} \frac{dk}{dt}\right), \quad f' > 0, \quad f'' < 0,$$

reflecting in its parameters the economic system's "... ability to invent and introduce new techniques of production [Kaldor, 1960, p. 265]" and shifting upwards every time that there is "... a burst of new inventions [Kaldor, 1960, p. 268]".[4] Several forms of this function were tested by Yucer [1971], using U.K. data, but they all performed very poorly. One may therefore suspect that (1) is incorrectly stated. Indeed, Kaldor's own discussion of the assumptions lying behind the function points to a possible way of restating it.

According to its propounder, the technical progress function should reflect "... not only 'inventiveness' in the strict sense, but the degree of dynamism of the economy in the broader sense - which includes not only the capacity to think of new ideas, but the readiness of those in charge of production to adopt new methods of production [Kaldor, 1960, p. 266]." To my mind, this can only mean there is a lag between the first application of a new idea and its widespread adoption - hardly surprising in a world where new products are usually protected by patents and brand names. Without such a lag the technical progress function would only reflect 'inventiveness in the strict sense' - i.e., the rate of progress in the state of the arts at a point in time - and it would then be none other than a differential form of aggregate production function.[5]

Kaldor also contends that any distinction between increases in labour productivity due to an improvement in the state of knowledge, and increases in labour productivity due to an increase in the amount of capital per worker within a given state of knowledge is arbitrary and artificial. The latter, in fact, "... inevitably entails the introduction of superior techniques which require 'inventiveness' of some kind, though these need not necessarily represent the application of basically new principles or ideas [Kaldor, 1960, p. 266]." According to this view, not only a change in the relationship between y and k, but also a change in k would reflect innovative effort. Hence, one may deduce, the same lag should apply to the effects of both types of change.

In order to test these hypotheses, I began by estimating three discrete-time forms of technical progress function. The first, in ascending order of generality,

$$(2) \qquad \frac{y_{t+1}}{y_t} = A \left(\frac{k_{t+1}}{k_t} \right)^{\alpha} , \quad 0 < \alpha < 1,$$

is obtained by logarithmic differencing of a Cobb-Douglas production function in per-capita form shifting over time. Here A and α are constants, and the subscripts denote time periods. Given the usual interpretation of an aggregate production function, (2) implies that productivity responds without delay to every change in the state of knowledge or in the way in which the existing knowledge is applied. The second,

$$(3) \qquad \frac{y_{t+1}}{y_t} = A^{\eta} \left(\frac{k_{t+1}}{k_t} \right)^{\alpha\eta} \left(\frac{y_t}{y_{t-1}} \right)^{1-\eta} , \quad 0 < \eta \leq 1,$$

is obtained from the first one by applying a distributed lag, with constant elasticity of response η, to equation (2). If η were equal to unity, (3) would obviously be the same as (2), but any lower (positive) value would imply slow diffusion of innovations. The third, finally,

$$(4) \qquad \frac{y_{t+1}}{y_t} = A^{\eta \Delta T_t^{(1)}} \left(\frac{k_{t+1}}{k_t}\right)^{\alpha \eta} \left(\frac{y_t}{y_{t-1}}\right)^{1-\eta} ,$$

is a generalisation of (3), based on the assumption that changes in the state of knowledge are related to changes in the general economic climate as reflected in the level of economic acticity. The variable $T^{(1)}$ is accordingly defined in such a way that it increases by one unit every time that aggregate demand increases, and remains constant otherwise. This equation reduces to the previous one if aggregate demand is always increasing.

In its most general form, the econometric model consisted of a logarithmic transformation of (4),

$$(5) \qquad \Delta \ln y_t = \eta (\ln A) \Delta T_t^{(1)} + \alpha \eta \Delta \ln k_t + (1-\eta) \Delta \ln y_{t-1} + \Delta \ln u_t$$

with error term $\Delta \ln u$, and of an autoregressive equation,

$$(6) \qquad \Delta \ln u_t = \sum_{i=1}^{n} \mu_i \, \Delta \ln u_{t-i} + \Delta \ln \epsilon_t$$

where the μ-s are constants, and the error $\Delta \ln \epsilon$ is assumed to be normally and independently distributed.[6] The possibility of serial correlation was therefore accounted for, and its effect hopefully eliminated from the estimates. Equations (2) and (3) were estimated likewise, by setting η and $\Delta T^{(1)}$ in (5) equal to unity as appropriate.

The data used were G.D.P. and fixed capital at constant prices, and total employment in the U.K. from 1900 to 1969 (war years excluded). Similar data for the manufacturing sector, covering only the period from 1948 to 1969, were also used.[7] Annual observations were taken in both cases to avoid picking up some short-term demand phenomenon. Where the U.K. economy as a whole was concerned, regressions were initially run for the sub-periods 1900-13, 1921-38 and 1948-69 separately, but the estimates for the first two sub-periods turned out to be very similar, so the 1900-38 data were pooled together. The $\bar{R}^2$ and the t-tests show that the lagged equations perform better than the unlagged one, and that (4) has the edge over (3), but none of them can be said to fit the data well, and none of the estimates passes the significance test at the 5% level. It may, therefore, be inferred that the use of differenced forms is not justified by the data.

The obvious next step was to investigate the relationship between the absolute values of y and k. Testable hypotheses were obtained by indefinite summation (the finite calculus analogue of integration) of (2), (3) and (4):

$$(2') \qquad\qquad y_t = CA^t k_t^\alpha \, ,$$

$$(3') \qquad\qquad y_t = C^\eta A^{\eta t} k_t^{\alpha\eta} y_{t-1}^{1-\eta}$$

and

$$(4') \qquad\qquad y_t = C^\eta A^{\eta T_t} k^{\alpha\eta} y_{t-1}^{1-\eta} \, ,$$

where C is a constant determined by initial conditions. As for the shift variable T, two alternative hypotheses were tested in addition to the one already discussed under the label of $T^{(1)}$:[8]

T = constant, implying that fundamental innovations take place only at the very outset of each of the sub-periods considered, 1900-13 and 1948-69;

$T = T^{(1)}$, defined as before, which implies that the development of new methods and ideas is strictly synchronized with their application;

367

$T = T^{(2)}$, so defined that each increase in aggregate demand shifts the technical progress function by an amount proportional to the time elapsed since the last increase in aggregate demand, thus implying that basic research proceeds at its own pace irrespective of whether it is immediately applied or not.

The econometric model is now

(5') $$\ln y_t = \eta \ln C + \eta (\ln A) T_t + \alpha \eta \ln k_t + (1-\eta) \ln y_{t-1} + \ln u_t ,$$

(6') $$\ln u_t = \sum_{i=1}^{n} \mu_i \ln u_{t-i} + \ln \epsilon_t .$$

With η constrained to unity and $T = t$ the model becomes that of an ordinary Cobb-Douglas production function shifting with time. Hence, I shall refer to the constrained estimates as the aggregate production function hypothesis, against which the technical progress function hypothesis, represented by the unconstrained estimates, is to be tested. With η not constrained to unity the constant term C turned out to be statistically insignificant for the manufacturing sector, and was therefore dropped from the appropriate equation.

Figures I, II and III show the observed time-path of y against those predicted by the aggregate production function and by the best fitting of the technical progress functions, namely, equation (4') with T equal to $T^{(2)}$. Although the $\overline{R}^2$ are very high for both the technical progress function and the aggregate production function, it is clear from the diagrams that the former captures the movement of labour productivity more faithfully than the latter. The t-tests, for their part, show that the estimates of the technical progress functions are in each case at least as reliable as those obtained under the competing hypothesis. As for the fact that the best estimates of the technical progress functions are obtained using $T^{(2)}$, this supports the hypothesis of unabated research

FIGURE I: <u>Productivity in the U.K. economy</u>.   1900-38

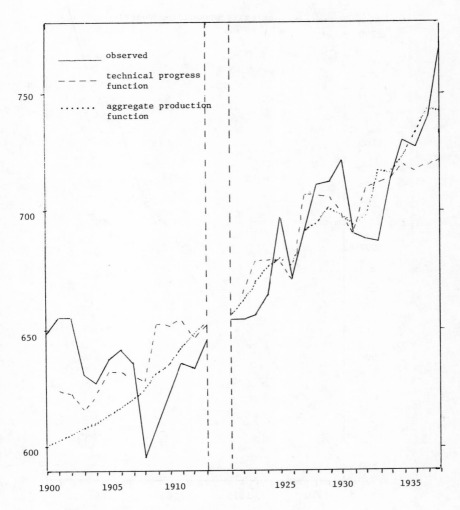

FIGURE II: <u>Productivity in the U.K. economy</u>. 1948-69

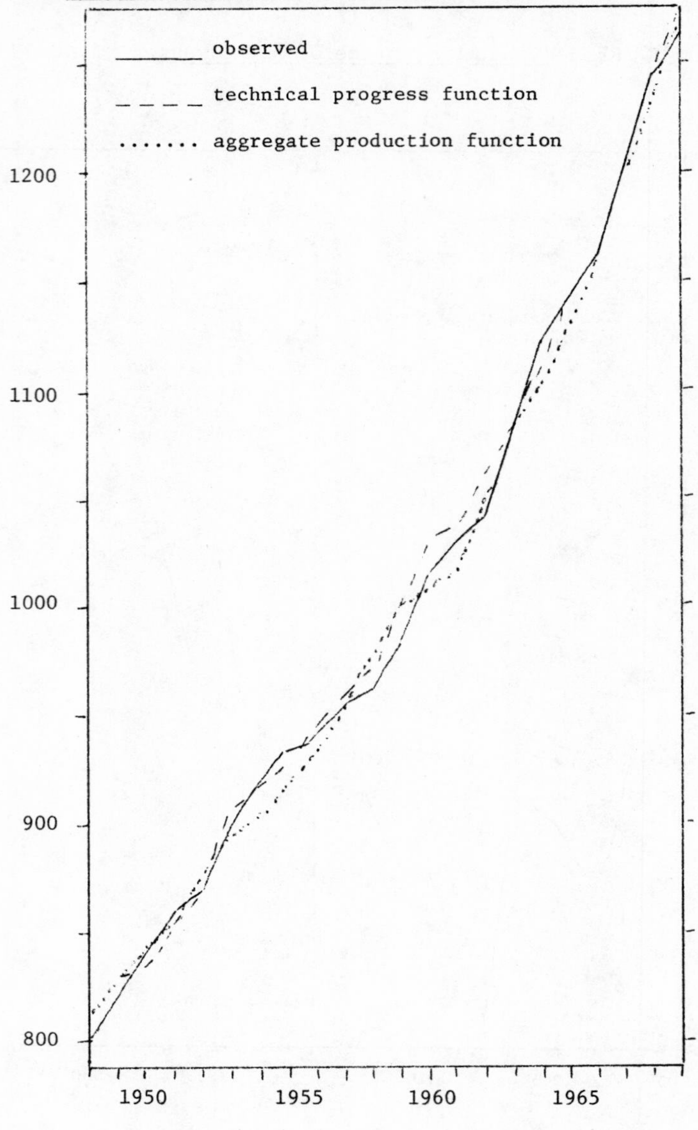

<u>SOURCE</u>: Cigno [1974, Appendix A, Table Al].

FIGURE III: <u>Productivity in the U.K. manufacturing sector.</u> 1948-69

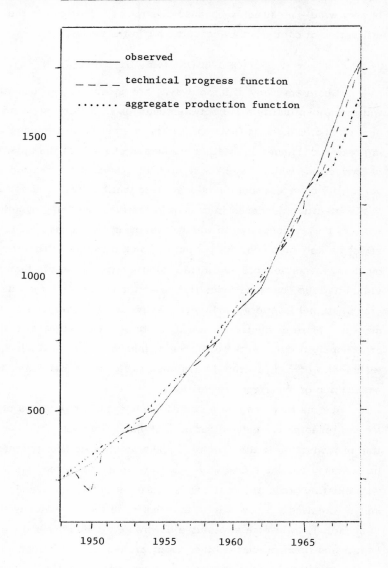

<u>SOURCE</u>: Cigno [1974, Appendix A, Table A2].

during recessions. We must be careful, however, not to take the estimates for the first sub-period too seriously, because their range of error is very wide - presumably because of strong fluctuations in the rate of utilisation of capital, not accounted for in the model.

3. A MICRO-ECONOMIC INTERPRETATION

There are many different ways, not necessarily incompatible, in which one can justify a lag between changes in the organization of production and changes in factor productivity - not to be confused with a lag between changes in relative prices and changes in the organization of production, which may have to do with imperfect information and irreversibility of investment decisions. One that has received some attention in the literature descends from Arrow's learning-by-doing hypothesis [Arrow, 1967], according to which investment would have a cumulative effect on its own productivity. But one would expect to find the learn-by-doing principle more applicable to humanity as a whole than to individual nations, because industrial patents and personal know-how often cross national frontiers, and older discoveries are everyone's patrimony anyway. More productive seems to me to be an enquiry into the effects of monopoly pricing on the diffusion of innovations - particularly as the technical progress function is designed to fit into models based on the assumption of imperfect competition.

Let us then imagine a situation where the final stages of technological research are carried out by individual firms, so that every new line of production is the exclusive preserve of some firm or other. A new product may provide a new way of satisfying a need already catered for with existing products, or it may be aimed at satisfying - and, in a sense, creating - a new want. In either case the innovator is a monopolist facing, for a time at least, a downward sloping demand curve. Labour and finance, on the other hand, are perfectly homogeneous, and any product that is used as a factor of production is also employed - perhaps in different combinations with other factors - by many different firms, so that nobody enjoys any monopsony power.

At any time there may be one or many firms producing a particular good, but each firm can only produce one good at a time. The output of each firm is a continuous function of the labour employed and of the stock of a durable intermediate product called 'capital'. This function is linear-homogeneous and may differ from one firm to the other only by a multiplicative constant. If two products satisfy the same want - say, private transportation - their production functions will be identical, but each product requires a specific type of capital, and each type of capital consists of, or is made with, a specific combination of the products of other firms. In the long run a firm can therefore alter the proportion in which capital and labour are combined, but it can never change the composition of its capital stock without also changing the nature of its final product.

Now let Y_{ij} denote total expenditure on the j-th of the products which contribute to satisfy the i-th want, K_{ij} the value (cost) of the total capital stock held by the firm or firms producing it, and L_{ij} the number of workers employed by them. In long-run equilibrium, if firms are profit maximizers,

$$(7) \qquad \frac{K_{ij}}{L_{ij}} = \frac{\alpha_{ij}}{1-\alpha_{ij}} \ \frac{w}{r} \ , \quad 0 < \alpha_{ij} < 1,$$

and

$$(8) \qquad \frac{Y_{ij}}{L_{ij}} = \frac{1 + \pi_{ij}}{1 - \alpha_{ij}} \ w, \quad 0 \leq \pi_{ij} < \infty,$$

where α_{ij} and $1-\alpha_{ij}$ are the production elasticities of capital and labour, respectively, w is the wage rate, r is the rate of interest, and π_{ij} is the net profit margin (or "mark-up") over the total cost of the product in question. As α_{ij} will be the same in every firm for the assumptions made earlier, this means that the capital/labour ratio is, in value terms, the same for every product and for every firm. The net-profit, on the other hand, will vary with the elasticity of the demand function facing the producer, β_{ij},

$$(9) \qquad \pi_{ij} = \frac{1}{1 + \beta_{ij}} \quad , \quad -\infty \leq \beta_{ij} < -1.$$

Hence, unless all the markets are perfectly competitive, the productivity of labour in value terms cannot, in general, be expected to be the same for each firm.

It follows from (7) and (8) that the average capital/labour ratio of the system,

$$(10) \qquad k \equiv \frac{\sum_i \sum_j K_{ij}}{\sum_i \sum_j L_{ij}} = \frac{K_{ij}}{L_{ij}} \quad \text{for all } i \text{ and } j,$$

does not depend on its degree of monopoly, as reflected in the average net profit margin,

$$(11) \qquad \pi \equiv \frac{\sum_i \sum_j Y_{ij}}{\sum_i \sum_j (rK_{ij} + wL_{ij})} - 1,$$

while the average productivity of labour,

$$(12) \qquad y \equiv \frac{\sum_i \sum_j Y_{ij}}{\sum_i \sum_j L_{ij}},$$

obviously does. On the other hand, no patent or brand-name can preserve a monopoly for ever: any product is liable to imitation, and even the best guarded production secret is eventually cracked. If the flow of innovations were to dry up, and no fresh monopolies were therefore established, a situation would then eventually arise where every firm would face a perfectly elastic demand function. In such a competitive situation net profits would be zero and the productivity of labour in value terms would be the same in every firm.[9] Using an asterisk to denote the competitive value of a variable, we can then write

374

(13)
$$y^* = \frac{Y^*_{ij}}{L^*_{ij}} \quad \text{for all i and j.}$$

Given the competitive allocation of aggregate demand among the various wants to be satisfied, it is now obvious that y^* depends only on k, because the competitive value of labour productivity is the same for every firm, and every firm has the same capital/labour ratio anyway. In particular, if we choose the unit of measurement of each product so that its competitive price is unity, and assume the production functions to be such that

(14)
$$Y^*_{ij} = (a_i K^*_{ij})^{\alpha} L^{*1-\alpha}_{ij} \quad \text{for all i and j,}$$

where a_i and α are constants, then, given (10), (12) and (13), we can write[10]

(15)
$$y^* = (ak)^{\alpha}, \quad \text{where} \quad a \equiv \left\{ \sum_i a_i^{\alpha} \, \frac{\sum_j Y^*_{ij}}{\sum_i \sum_j Y^*_{ij}} \right\}^{1/\alpha} .$$

In interpreting (15) we must be careful not to think of this as an aggregate production function, determining the actual productivity of the system. All we have here is a tendential relationship, determining the value that y would take if all monopolistic restrictions on the supply of new products were lifted - or, to put it differently, if the latest inventions and discoveries had the widest application allowed by consumer preferences. We should therefore regard (15) as a kind of technological frontier - keeping in mind, however, that y^* is not necessarily the highest value of y for each particular value of k, since it may well be possible to find a noncompetitive set of relative prices such that y is higher and k is the same. What is at a maximum along the frontier is the elasticity of y with respect to k, equal to the physical elasticity of the output of each firm with respect to its capital stock,

$$(16) \qquad \frac{k}{y^*} \frac{\partial y^*}{\partial k} = \alpha .$$

Conditions (7) and (8), in fact, imply

$$(17) \qquad \frac{K_{ij}}{Y_{ij}} \frac{\partial Y_{ij}}{\partial K_{ij}} = \frac{\alpha}{1 + \pi_{ij}} \quad \text{for all } i \text{ and } j,$$

whence, given (12),

$$(18) \qquad \frac{k}{y} \frac{\partial y}{\partial k} < \alpha \quad \text{for } y \neq y^* .$$

Any movement along the frontier signals innovation, but a change in k alone means that the new product is just an improved version of an existing one, while a change in "a" implies satisfaction of a new want.

To determine the actual value of y, we must now specify the relation between this variable and y^*. If y^* were constant - i.e., if there were no further innovations - the imitation process would tend to bring the system to its technological frontier. This movement would be gradual, because of the different time involved in imitating different kinds of products - ranging from very short, in the case of innovations based on fairly simple new ideas, to very long, in the case of innovations based on the results of complex scientific research. The time-path of y is therefore likely to be asymptotic to that of y^*, which means that the rate of change in y decreases as the system gets nearer to the frontier. But not every adjustment hypothesis is consistent with the rest of the assumptions. A linear form such as

$$(19) \qquad \Delta y = \varepsilon (y^* - y), \quad 0 < \varepsilon < 1,$$

for example, would not do because, given (15), it implies

$$(20) \qquad \frac{k}{y} \frac{\partial y}{\partial k} = \alpha,$$

376

whether y is equal to y^* or not - thus contradicting (18). On the other hand, a log-linear form such as

(21) $$\Delta \log y = \eta(\log y^* - \log y), \quad 0 < \eta < 1,$$

would be quite acceptable because, taken together with (15), it implies

(22) $$\frac{k}{y} \frac{\partial y}{\partial k} = \alpha\eta \quad \text{for } y \neq y^* .$$

From (15) and (22) we get

(23) $$y_{t+1} = a_t^{\alpha\eta} k_t^{\alpha\eta} y_t^{1-\eta}$$

which is the equation of our technical progress function (4') for

(24) $$CA^T \equiv a^\alpha .$$

We can now give the parameters of the technical progress function, and their numerical estimates (see table below), a precise interpretation. There are two elasticities, α and η. The first determines the potential change in y following a change in a or k - i.e., the effect that an innovation would eventually have if the imitation process were allowed to run its full course. The second determines the pace at which y adjusts to its new potential level following an innovation, and is, therefore, a measure of the speed of diffusion of innovations. Not surprisingly, given that all the production functions have the same elasticities, the estimate of α is roughly the same for the manufacturing sector as for the economy as a whole. But the estimate of η is lower in manufacturing, where innovations are more often a result of sophisticated research and new products are consequently harder to imitate. The immediate effect of a change in y or k depends on the product of the two elasticities, $\alpha\eta$, because the change in y depends not only

<u>Estimates[a] of A-1, α and η (1948-69)</u>

	A-1	α	η
Manufacturing sector[b]	0.10	0.68	0.49
All sectors[c]	0.01	0.65	0.56

(a) derived from the regression coefficients of the technical
progress equations used to construct Figures II and III.

(b) source: Cigno [1974, Appendix C, Table IV(iv), n = 0]

(c) source: Cigno [1974, Appendix C, Table III(iv), n = 1]

on the innovators' productivity, governed by α, but also on their share
of aggregate demand, governed by η.

We can also explain the statistical association between changes
in aggregate demand and changes in the term CA^T which we now know
to reflect introduction of completely new goods. The demand functions
for these goods being unknown, it is, in fact, quite natural that entrepreneurs should want to wait for signs of a general increase in demand
before embarking on such a risky venture.[11] But it is only the timing of
innovations that responds to fluctuations in aggregate demand, not the
research effort that feeds the innovations. The potential rate of growth
in a^{α} (i.e., the rate at which this term would increase if aggregate demand never faltered) is in fact a constant, equal to A-1. Understandably,
the estimate for A is much higher in the manufacturing sector (towards
which most of the research effort is directed) than in the U.K. economy
as a whole.

4. SOME DYNAMIC IMPLICATIONS

By expanding equation (23) in infinite series,

(25) $$y_t = (a_t k_t)^{\alpha\eta} (a_{t-1} k_{t-1})^{\alpha\eta(1-\eta)} (a_{t-2} k_{t-2})^{\alpha\eta(1-\eta)^2} \cdots,$$

it becomes clear that the productivity of labour at any point in time is determined by the system's entire history of investment and innovation, not just by the quantity of equipment and technical knowledge accumulated by that date. The reason, of course, is that the full effect of a change in a or k is not felt until the rate of production of the new goods has reached its full competitive level - and that may never happen, not even approximately, if another change in aggregate demand or in w/r triggers off a new wave of innovations before the effect of the previous one has had time to work itself out. Hence, there may be a different level of labour productivity for each conceivable way of timing the introduction of a given list of new goods and the accumulation of a given stock of capital. As the time-paths of aggregate demand and of the interest rate are influenced by government actions, it may be interesting to investigate the effects of some alternative patterns of economic policy on the productivity of the system.

The solution sequence of the difference equation (23) can be written as

$$(26) \qquad y(t) = \overline{y}(t)\left\{\frac{y(0)}{\overline{y}(0)}\right\}^{(1-\eta)^t},$$

where $\overline{y}(t)$ is a limit sequence, towards which y converges as t tends to infinity. In general, the value of $\overline{y}$ at each point in time depends on both the levels and the rates of change of a and k at that time. In particular, if

$$(27) \qquad a_t = a_o \quad \text{and} \quad k_t = k_o \quad \text{for all} \ t,$$

thus implying that aggregate demand and w/r are held constant, the function is

$$(28) \qquad \overline{y} = (ak)^\alpha$$

Hence, in this case, y has a long-term tendency to become the same as y^*. On the other hand, if

(29) $$a_t = a_o \lambda^t \text{ and } k_t = k_o \mu^t \text{ for all } t,$$

thus implying that it is only the percentage rates of change in aggregate demand and w/r that are kept constant, then

(30) $$\bar{y} = (\lambda\mu)^{\alpha(1 - \frac{1}{\eta})} (a \ k)^\alpha$$

which means that y only tends to become proportional to y^*.[12] But in either case the elasticities of y with respect to a and k tend to become equal to α.

These results need careful interpretation. According to our assumptions, the degree of monopoly of the system is subject to two opposite forces: innovation, that creates monopolies, and imitation, that destroys them. If (27) applies, which means that there are no innovations after period 0, any monopolies that may have existed in that period are gradually washed away by the rising tide of imitations. As this process goes on, the production elasticity tends to become the same for each firm in value as in physical terms, and the system tends to approach its technological frontier, where the elasticities of y with respect to a and k are at a maximum. But this result has no practical interest, because it only holds for as long as a and k are constant: if either of these were to change, new monopolies would be created and the system would slip away from the frontier.

The situation is quite different if (29) applies. Here innovations do occur and the production elasticities do not tend to become the same for every firm. The system cannot, therefore, reach its technological frontier, but the flow of new products is such that innovation and imitation are, in a sense, in balance. What happens is then that the degree of monopoly, as measured by the average mark-up, tends to become a constant.[13] Hence, y tends to grow in proportion to y^*, giving the impression that innovations have the same immediate effect on both variables, while in reality each change of y is the cumulated effect of all past changes in a and k. Consequently, only the absolute level of y tends to be affected by the value of η, while its growth rate tends to be the highest possible, as if innovations had instant diffusion.[14]

Our search for a relationship that would replace the aggregate production function thus ends with an ironical twist: if we define the aggregate production function as a steady-state relationship between output and capital per capita, then (30) is such a function. But an aggregate production function so defined can only be used to make comparisons between different points of the same growth path, or between different paths with the same growth rate. Any argument about the stability of the growth path, or the transition from one growth path to another, should properly be based on the technical progress function, of which the aggregate production function is a particular solution. For the same reason, a production function can be directly fitted to time-series of aggregate output, capital and employment only if the system is, and always has been, in steady state[15] - in every other case the values of its parameters will have to be inferred from those of the technical progress function.

NOTES

[1]See, for example, Denison [1962, 1967] or Caves [1968].

[2]See Kaldor [1960], and Kaldor and Mirrlees [1961].

[3]The data and econometric results referred to in the text are reported in detail in the statistical appendices of Cigno [1974].

[4]In the Kaldor-Mirrlees version, where substitutability of capital for labour is ruled out, the function is assumed to apply to current investment only; see Kaldor and Mirrlees [1961].

[5]Black [1962], who was the first to study the technical progress function, came to the conclusion that this does not imply the existence of an aggregate production function only if (1) is non-linear. If (1) is linear,

$$\frac{1}{y}\frac{dy}{dt} = a + b(\frac{1}{k}\frac{dk}{dt}) ,$$

its integral with respect to t is in fact the Cobb-Douglas production function

$$y(t) = Ce^{at}k(t)^b ,$$

where a, b and C are constants. On the other hand, if (1) is not linear, y depends on the rate of change, as well as the level, of k, and such a relationship cannot be described as a production function in the usual sense; the same conclusion is reached by Solow [1967]. But the same is true if the technical progress function is a higher-order differential equation (linear or not) or in the case of a distributed lag. Besides, Black's argument applies only to continuous changes. In discrete time the relation between the growth rates of y and k,

$$\frac{\Delta y}{y} = (1+a)\left\{\frac{\Delta k}{k} + 1\right\}^b - 1 ,$$

obtained by logarithmic differencing of

$$y = C(1+a)^t k^b$$

is non-linear.

[6]The model was estimated by an iterative method that approximates a maximum likelihood solution if the number of observations is 'large' relative to n; see Hendry [1970]. No trace of higher than second order (n = 2) autocorrelation was found in any of the equations, see Cigno [1974, Appendix B].

[7]For the manufacturing sector the employment figure reflects the number of hours actually worked, while for the economy as a whole it is only the number of heads; see Cigno [1974, Appendix A].

[8]The new set of estimates is in Cigno [1974, Appendix C]. For the manufacturing sector $T^{(1)}$ and $T^{(2)}$ are the same as t because the demand for manufactures never stopped growing between 1948 and 1969.

[9]This view of the process of economic development is strongly reminiscent of Schumpeter's [1934], and rests crucially on the assumption that the production functions are linear-homogeneous. Under increasing returns to scale the monopolist could in fact discourage competition by setting the price for its product at such a level, that the entry of another efficiently sized producer would wipe out the net profit.

[10]From (10), (12) and (13) we get

$$K_{ij}^* = Y_{ij}^* \frac{\sum\limits_i \sum\limits_i K_{ij}^*}{\sum\limits_i \sum\limits_j Y_{ij}^*} \quad \text{and} \quad L_{ij}^* = Y_{ij}^* \frac{\sum\limits_i \sum\limits_i L_{ij}^*}{\sum\limits_i \sum\limits_j Y_{ij}^*} .$$

Hence, given (14),

$$\frac{\sum\limits_i \sum\limits_j Y_{ij}^*}{\sum\limits_i \sum\limits_j L_{ij}^*} = \left\{ \frac{\sum\limits_i \sum\limits_j K_{ij}^*}{\sum\limits_i \sum\limits_j L_{ij}^*} \right\}^{\alpha} \frac{\sum\limits_i \sum\limits_j a_i Y_{ij}^*}{\sum\limits_i \sum\limits_j Y_{ij}^*}$$

or

$$y^* = k^{*\alpha} \frac{\sum\limits_i \sum\limits_j a_i Y_{ij}^*}{\sum\limits_i \sum\limits_j Y_{ij}^*} = k^{\alpha} \frac{\sum\limits_i \sum\limits_j a_i Y_{ij}^*}{\sum\limits_i \sum\limits_j Y_{ij}^*} .$$

[11]Schumpter too found a theoretical and empirical connection between the upturn of the business cycle and innovative activity [Schumpeter, 1934]. But, according to Schumpeter, it is the crowding of major innovations around particular dates (due to their mutual interdependence) that causes

383

the surge of economic activity, not the other way round. In reality, what has probably happened, at least since Keynesian times, is that firms have responded to each government announcement of expansionary monetary and fiscal measures by both increasing capital expenditure and starting new lines of production. Some indirect support for this interpretation comes from the fact that my model performs better in the post-war period, where aggregate demand acts as a proxy for government-induced business confidence, than in the previous one.

[12]Two special cases of steady growth may be worth mentioning. One is

$$\mu = \lambda^{\frac{\alpha}{1-\alpha}} \;,$$

in which case the value of the capital/output ratio tends to become a constant, and (30) simplifies to

$$\bar{y} = \lambda^{1-\frac{1}{n}} (ak)^{\alpha} \;.$$

The other is

$$\mu = \lambda^{-1} \;,$$

in which case the value of labour productivity tends to become a constant, and (30) reduces to (28).

[13]In Kaldor's models the degree of monopoly, assumed constant, only appears as a boundary condition, thus implying that the average mark-up may in effect be higher than required by profit maximization. This assumption cannot be challenged within the context of the earlier model [Kaldor, 1960], where marginal conditions are studiously avoided. But in the Kaldor-Mirrlees model [1961] this boundary condition comes into conflict with a scrapping rule for capital-goods, which implies equality

between the marginal productivity of labour and the wage rate. Nuti [1969] pointed out the inconsistency and suggested replacing both conditions with a marginal revenue condition appropriate to a monopolistic situation. Nuti's condition differs from my (8) only in that he assumes gross, instead of net, profit maximization. In any case, the degree of monopoly cannot be determined within either the Kaldor or the Kaldor-Mirrlees model, where it is simply assumed to be a constant determined by custom, while I have shown it to depend on the rate and speed of diffusion of innovations. But we should not make the mistake of taking y/y^* for a measure of the degree of monopoly, because the physical composition of y is different from that of y^*, and their ratio is not the same as the average profit margin.

[14] In the U.K., where labour productivity has grown more or less steadily since World War II, Caves found that "... although the growth of productivity...has recently been in line with its growth in other industrial nations, the U.K. level seems to be lower. This fact confirms the direct evidence of considerable inefficiency in the organisation of business enterprises and in the use of the labour force... [Caves, 1968, p. 491]".

[15] The estimates of α that I obtained under the aggregate production function hypothesis were in fact biased downwards, and close to the estimates of $\alpha\eta$ obtained under the technical progress function hypothesis; see Cigno [1974, Appendix C].

REFERENCES

Arrow, K. J. [1967], "The Economic Implications of Learning by Doing", Review of Economic Studies.

Black, J. [1962], "The Technical Progress function and the Production Function," Economica.

Caves, R. E. and Associates [1968], Britain's Economic Prospects, The Brookings Institution.

Cigno, A [1974], Diffusion of Innovations under Imperfect Competition: An Adaptive View of Technical Progress, Workshop Paper No. 7508, Social Systems Research Institute, Madison.

Denison, E. F. [1962], The Sources of Economic Growth in the U.S. and the Alternatives Before Us. Supplementary Paper No. 13, Committee for Economic Development.

_____ [1967], Why Growth Rates Differ, The Brookings Institution.

Hendry, D. F. [1970], The Estimation of Economic Models with Autoregressive Errors, Ph.D. Dissertation, University of London.

Kaldor, N. [1960], "A Model of Economic Growth", Economic Journal, 1957; reprinted in Essays in Economic Stability and Growth.

Kaldor, N. and J. A. Mirrlees [1961], "A New Model of Economic Growth", Review of Economic Studies.

Nuti, D. M. [1969], "The Degree of Monopoly in the Kaldor-Mirrlees Growth Model", Review of Economic Studies.

Schumpeter, J. A. [1934], The Theory of Economic Development (transl. by R. Opie), Harvard University Press.

_____ [1939], Business Cycles, McGraw-Hill.

Solow, R. M. [1967], "Some Recent Developments in the Theory of Production", in M. Brown (ed.), The Theory and Empirical Analysis of Production, N.B.E.R.

Yucer, O. [1971], On the Theory and Measurement of Technical Progress in Growth Models, M. Soc. Sc. Dissertation, University of Birmingham.

Autonomous Control of the Economic System: A Survey (abstract)
András Simonovits

ABSTRACT

Traditional economic theory concentrates on the price mechanism, while, in reality other mechanisms also play important roles in the control sphere of complex economies. These include directive planning and order-stock mechanisms. The latter are examples of the general class of autonomous control mechanism specified by Kornai and Martos [1973]. This paper summarizes contributions to the analysis of order-stock mechanisms in which a dynamic Leontief model is used to represent the underlying technology of the economy.

Autonomous controls are those with two fundamental properties: (1) each component of the control vector of the system belongs to a unique decision maker and (2) only directly observable information is used. The main problems of research involved in their study are the existence of autonomous control rules that (1)" will ensure the survival and permanent functioning of the system; (2) that are stable with respect to normal paths; and (3) that are economically efficient.

Kornai and Martos [1973] demonstrated (1) and (2) in their model. (See also Dancs, Hunyadi and Sivák [1973].) Virág [1971] established positive probabilities for survival over finite intervals for a stochastic generalization of the Kornai-Martos model. Bródy [1973] developed stability for similar models with alternative assumption about the technology and initial stocks. Kornai and Simonovits [1974] establish the existence of a von Neumann ray, local stability, and viability for a new model. Related theoretical work is Sargan [1958] and Leontief [1961], Metzler [1941] and Lovell [1962], McFadden [1969] and Aoki [1972].

REFERENCES

Aoki, M. [1972], "On Feedback Stabilizability of Decentralized Dynamic Systems," Automatica, Vol. 8, pp. 163-173.

Arrow, K. and Hurwicz, L. [1960], "Decentralization and Computation in Resource Allocation," in Essays in Economics and Econometrics. Chapel Hills: University of North Carolina Press.

Augustinovics, M. [1972], "A Twin-Pair of Models for Long-Term Planning," in Input-Output Techniques, ed. by A. Brody and A. P. Carter. Amsterdam: North-Holland.

Brody, A. [1973], "On Control Models," (In Hungarian), Szigma, VI, pp. 93-103.

Dancs, I., Hunyadi, L. and Sivák, J. [1973], "Control Based on Stock Signals in a Leontief-Type Economy," (In Hungarian), Szigma, VI, pp. 185-208.

Gelfond, A. O. [1952], Calculus of Differences, (In Russian), Moscow-Leningrad.

Kornai, J. [1971, Anti-Equilibrium, Amsterdam: North-Holland.

_____ and Martos, B. [1971], "Vegetativ Müködesü Gazdasag Rendszer," (In Hungarian), Manuscript and Szigma, IV., pp. 35-41.

_____ [1973], "Autonomous Control of the Economic System," Econometrica, Vol. 41, No. 3, pp. 509-528.

Kornai, J. and Simonovits, A. [1975], "Control Problems in Neumann-economies," (In Hungarian), To appear in Szigma, VIII.

Leontief, W. W. [1961], "Lags and Stability of Dynamical Systems" and "A Rejoinder," Econometrica, Vol. 29, No. 4, pp. 659-669 and 674-675.

Lovell, M. C. [1962], "Buffer-Stock, Sales Expectations and Stability: A Multi-Sector Analysis of the Inventory Cycle," <u>Econometrica</u>, Vol. 30, pp. 267-296.

McFadden, D. [1969], "On the Controllability of Decentralized Macro-economic Systems: The Assignment Problems," in <u>Mathematical Systems, Theory and Economics I.</u>, pp. 221-239. Springer-Verlag.

Martos, B. [1973], "Comments on the Paper by Dancs-Hunyadi-Sivak," (In Hungarian), <u>Szigma</u>, VI., pp. 209-210.

Sargan, J. D. [1958], "The Stability of the Leontief Dynamic Model," <u>Econometrica</u>, Vol. 26, pp. 581-592.

_____ [1961], "Lags and Stability of Dynamical Systems -- A Reply," <u>Econometrica</u>, Vol. 29, No. 4, pp. 671-674.

Virág, I. [1971], "The Autonomous Functioning of an Economic System with Stochastic External Consumption," (In Hungarian), <u>Szigma</u>, IV., pp. 261-268.

Modelling Discrete Adaptive Behavior in the Chemical Process Industries
Gary J. Powers

CONTENTS

ABSTRACT

In predicting the adaptive behavior of an economic system it is necessary to model how the monetary and material flows change within a given system as well as how the system structure itself changes. Changes in the system structure occur due to substitution of known alternatives, the invention of new processes or products, or changes in market or legislative constraints. These types of structural changes have been difficult to handle in economic modelling. The changes involve discrete variables and are strongly tied to the technological basis of the system. In addition, the number of designs which are potential solutions is very large. These designs require a large amount of time to generate and evaluate and skilled practitioners are usually used to generate the alternate designs.

Recent work on the computer-aided synthesis and analysis of processes for the chemical process industries portends a new method for investigating the possible adaptive changes which occur in the structure of economic systems. A paradigm is presented for the systematic invention of networks of processes which represent the chemical process industry. An economic model is derived which describes both the changes in continuous flows within a given chemical processing network as well as changes in the network topology. Extensions of this approach to other industries are discussed.

1. INTRODUCTION

In most attempts at modelling the adaptive behavior of economic systems the basic structure of the system is assumed invariant. That is, the topology of the material and monetary flows within the system network is not allowed to change. With this assumption adaptation occurs through changes in the flows in the various branches within the system.[1] Given the structure of the system the optimization of system performance can be thought of as occurring at two levels. Figure 1 illustrates this situation. At the first level of optimization discrete and continuous variables (degrees of freedom) associated with the synthesis and analysis of the system are varied to give a more desirable performance. The optimization over continuous variables (the flows in the network) has been carried out for a large number of systems and a number of fairly powerful techniques exist for this type of analysis. The continuous models of the system are based on the conservation of material, energy, momentum and money. The balances are commonly written for steady-state conditions although a number of dynamic models have been developed. These models are usually constrained to operate within certain physical and legislative boundaries. When properly formulated there are more variables than equations in these models. Hence optimization is used to select values for the degress of freedom for the system. The evaluation used for guiding the optimization depends on the objective function selected for the problem. This objective function depends in part on the utility function of the person or persons performing the analysis.

In many analyses the constraints and utility function are assumed to be fixed for the time scale under study. This assumption can be

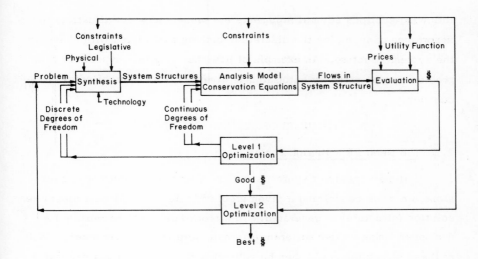

Figure 1.   THE SYNTHESIS AND ANALYSIS OF PROCESSING SYSTEMS.

    The problem is transformed into plausible structural solutions by discrete decisions made during the synthesis activity.   The performance of the structures is predicted and evaluated during analysis and evaluation.   The degrees of freedom in both the synthesis and analysis steps are adjusted in a first level of optimization.   A second level of optimization is used to adjust the problem description, the utility function, and physical and legislative constraints.

removed if another level of optimization is considered.   This second level of optimization is concerned with learning (adjusting) the forms and values of the problem statement, physical and legislative constraints, and the utility function.   Cyert and DeGroot [1975] investigate how the utility function could change in a duopoly situation and Rudd [1975] illus- trates several mechanisms for changing physical and legislative con- straints in the chemical process industries.   While these two levels of optimization can be employed in the study of economic systems it is al- most always assumed that the topology of the system does not change. That is, the synthesis part of Figure 1 is almost never included.   In the

393

following sections several arguments are presented which illustrate the importance of including the discrete decisions associated with changing the system structure. An example of how the synthesis aspects of this problem can be partially automated is given for the chemical process industries.

2. SYNTHESIS OF SYSTEM STRUCTURE

2.1. The Need for a Design Theory

The synthesis of system structure means that a number of decisions are made concerning a given problem statement so that a plausible solution (structure) is generated. This procedure could be repeated a number of times so that different alternate solutions are produced. Each of these structures could then be subjected to the continuous parameter optimization discussed above. If the synthesis part of the solution procedure is <u>not</u> included predictions of economic behavior will most probably be in error. The reasons for error are the following

a) The optimization over continuous variables is obviously limited by the particular structure used for the system. (Another system structure may have better properties even without the continuous parameter optimization)

b) Changes in the basic definition of the problem and in the physical and legislative constraints which apply during synthesis can have major effects on the system's economic performance.

c) Technology can change very rapidly and give rise to new and potentially more attractive system structures.

Prior attempts to include the synthesis of the system structure have been generally unsuccessful due to the lack of a sufficiently general and quantitative design theory. Without this theory it is necessary to employ rather large teams of professional designers who carry out the synthesis activities for a small number of cases. The cost of this analysis is often very high and without a design theory the results are generally of a very speculative nature. Over the last ten years a more quantitative theory for design has been developed. This new design theory has at its roots non-numerical problem-solving, operations research, computer science, and the more special purpose modelling and problem-solving techniques developed in disciplines like chemical, electrical, and civil engineering and architecture. In the following sections I briefly outline the design theory that is developing for the chemical process industries. A brief example is then presented which illustrates how this theory, when embodied in computer programs, can be used in the adaptive economic modelling of the chemical process industries.

2.2. General Design Theory

Consider the problem

$$P(\overline{v}_c, \overline{v}_s) = 0$$

where $\overline{v}_c$ is a vector of continuous variables and $\overline{v}_s$ is a vector of structural (discrete) variables. One possible representation for this problem is the State-Space Representation. The state-space representation operator R_s can be applied to $P(\overline{v}_c, \overline{v}_s) = 0$ to produce a new representation for the problem.

$$R_s(P(\overline{v}_c, \overline{v}_s) = 0) \rightarrow P(\overline{v}_c, \overline{S}_i, \overline{S}_g) = 0$$

The structural variables have been represented as vectors of initial and goal states. An element of the state vector is a vector of state characteristics

$$S_i = \overline{C}_n$$

An element of the characteristic vector is an atom selected from the problem space

$$C_i \equiv A$$

Operators are defined for the problem domain which change one state into another.

$$O_j(\overline{S}_\ell) = \overline{S}_k$$

subject to

$$\overline{X}_{O_j} = 1$$

where $\overline{X}_{O_j}$ is a constraint on the application of operator O_j.

$$\overline{X}_{O_j} \equiv \overline{C}_{n, O_j}$$

and

$$\overline{X}_{O_j} = 1 \text{ if } \overline{C}_{n, O_j} = \overline{C}_{S_\ell}$$

$$= 0 \text{ otherwise}$$

The characteristics of the states $\overline{S}_\ell$ must match those required by the operator O_j before the operation can be applied.

A solution to the discrete part of the problem $P(\overline{v}_c, \overline{S}_i, \overline{S}_g) = 0$ is obtained when the difference D between the states is zero.

$$\overline{D}_{\overline{S}_i, \overline{S}_g} = \overline{C}_{n, S_i} - \overline{C}_{n, S_g} = 0$$

The solutions to the problem are given by

$$\psi = \sum_{\text{Path}} O_j(\overline{S}_k)$$

such that

$$\overline{D}_{S_i, S_g} = 0$$

$$\overline{X}_{O_j} = 1$$

The optimal solution to the problem $P(\overline{v}_s, \overline{S}_i, \overline{S}_g) = 0$ is

$$\psi^* = \underset{\psi}{\text{Max}}\{\overline{I}\}$$

where $\overline{I}$ is the objective function for the system. In representing a problem in this manner it is necessary to define $\overline{S}_i$, $\overline{S}_g$, $\overline{C}_n$, $\overline{O}_j$, and $\overline{X}_{O_j}$. The definitions will depend on the particular technological and economic system being analyzed. The state-space is defined below for the synthesis of chemical processes.

2.3. Chemical Process Synthesis

One definition of the chemical process synthesis problem is:

$\overline{S}_g \equiv$ desired products

$\overline{S}_i \equiv$ available raw materials

$$\overline{C}_n \equiv \begin{cases} C_1(MT) & = \text{molecular type(s) in a stream} \\ C_2(AMT) & = \text{amount of a stream} \\ C_3(CONC) & = \text{concentration of each molecular type (species) in a} \\ & \quad \text{stream} \\ C_4(T) & = \text{temperature of a stream} \\ C_5(P) & = \text{pressure of a stream} \\ C_6(PH) & = \text{phase(s) of a stream} \\ C_7(F) & = \text{form(s) of a stream (the size(s) and shape(s) of the} \\ & \quad \text{various phases are defined).} \end{cases}$$

397

$$
\overline{O}_j \equiv \begin{cases}
O_1 & = & \text{React} \\
O_2 & = & \text{Split (tee)} \\
O_3 & = & \text{Mix} \\
O_4 & = & \text{Separate} \\
O_5 & = & \text{Change temperature} \\
O_6 & = & \text{Change pressure} \\
O_7 & = & \text{Change phase} \\
O_8 & = & \text{Change form}
\end{cases}
$$

The characteristics of a state are given by C_1 through C_7. Each of these characteristics corresponds to a major physical or chemical attri- of the state. Specification of all of these characteristics supplies the information required to uniquely determine the gross physical and chemical status. Operators O_1 through O_8 define the major functions performed in chemical processing systems. Operator O_1 (React) is responsible for changing the molecular type (C_1) of a state. There is a physical and chemical correspondence between molecular type and all the other characteristics of a state. Hence React could be used to change any one or more of the state characteristics. The generality of the React operator is what makes the design of chemical processing systems a very challenging activity. The search for the appropriate React operator is often the key research and development activity.

The operators O_2 and O_3, Split and Mix, are primarily used for changing the amount and concentration (Mix only) of a state. Operator O_4 (Separate) is used to produce two or more states whose concentrations have been changed. Operators O_5 through O_8 simply change the physical characteristics of temperature, pressure, phase, and form of a state.

Each of these operators is subject to a number of constraints. The constraints are shown below. The most constrained operator is React. The highly constrained nature of this operator is due to the fact that the mechanistic steps in the chemical transformations are constrained by energy, concentration, and conformation in the reaction media. Hence it is necessary to have the appropriate molecular types, any amount greater than zero, appropriate concentration, temperature, and pressure ranges, and the necessary phases and forms. The major task in the synthesis of a chemical process it to satisfy these constraints in an economical manner.

$$
\bar{X}_{O_j} \equiv
\begin{cases}
X_{O_1 \text{ REACT}} = 1 \text{ for}
\begin{bmatrix}
C_1(\text{MT}) = \begin{cases} \text{Required Species (including} \\ \text{catalysts) Present and} \\ \text{Absence of Prohibited Species} \end{cases} \\[6pt]
C_2(\text{AMT}) > 0 \\
C_3(\text{CONC}) = \{C_{3,\text{lower}} \leq C_3 \leq C_{3,\text{upper}}\} \\
C_4(\text{T}) = \{C_{4,\text{lower}} \leq C_4 \leq C_{4,\text{upper}}\} \\
C_5(\text{P}) = \{C_{5,\text{lower}} \leq C_5 \leq C_{5,\text{upper}}\} \\
C_6(\text{PH}) = \text{liquid, gas, solid, or a combina-} \\ \qquad\qquad\text{tion of these phases.} \\
C_7(\text{F}) = \text{specified shapes or sizes of the} \\ \qquad\qquad\text{phases.}
\end{bmatrix} \\[10pt]

X_{O_2 \text{ SPLIT}} = 1 \text{ for AMT} > 0 \\[6pt]

X_{O_3 \text{ MIX}} = 1 \text{ for}
\begin{bmatrix} \text{AMT}, S_1 > 0 \\ \text{AMT}, S_2 > 0 \end{bmatrix}
\begin{array}{l} \text{Operator } O_3(\text{MIX}) \text{ operates} \\ \text{on two states to produce one} \\ \text{state} \end{array} \\[10pt]

X_{O_4 \text{ SEPARATE}} = 1 \text{ for}
\begin{bmatrix} \text{AMT} > 0 \\ \text{CONC}_n > 0 \quad \text{i.e. must have a mixture} \\ \text{PH} = \text{proper phases} \end{bmatrix} \\[10pt]

X_{O_5 \, \Delta T} = 1 \text{ for AMT} > 0 \\[4pt]
X_{O_6 \, \Delta P} = 1 \text{ for AMT} > 0 \\[4pt]
X_{O_7 \, \Delta PH} = 1 \text{ for AMT} > 0 \\[4pt]
X_{O_8 \, \Delta F} = 1 \text{ for}
\begin{bmatrix} \text{AMT} > 0 \\ \text{PH} = \text{two phases or solid} \end{bmatrix}
\end{cases}
$$

$\bar{I} \equiv$ PROFIT = f(Raw materials, Utilities, Equipment, Labor, Safey, Flexibility, Controllability)

This particular definition of the chemical process synthesis problem uses a functional definition of an operator. These operators are very general and could be performed by a number of different specific means. The procedures for generating and selecting a given specific means for carrying out the function defined by an operator are described in Powers and Rathore [1974]. The exact nature of the constraints which are applicable to a given operator depends on the specific means used to carry out the operation. For example, the operator REACT has the function of changing one molecular type into another. The exact constraints $\overline{X}_{REACT} = 1$ which apply to O_{REACT} depend upon the specific reaction used.

2.4. Constraint Satisfaction

If the application of a given operator (call it the primary operator either functional or equipment) to a state is in violation of a constraint, the operator could be rejected or a new subproblem defined. The subproblem is the removal of the constraint violation. Operators could be applied to the state until it satisfied the constraints required for the application of the primary operator. Let $O_k(S_\ell)$ be the primary operator. For this operator

$$\overline{X}_{O_k(S_\ell)} = 1$$

and the state characteristics $C_1, \ldots, C_q$ are in violation. The new subproblem SP could be

$$SP(S_i, S_g) = SP((C_1, \ldots, C_q = 0, C_q, \ldots, C_n = 1)_i, (C_1, \ldots, C_n = 1)_g)$$

where the characteristics of the initial state are $C_1, \ldots, C_n$ and the constraints $C_1, \ldots, C_q$ are in violation for the application of the primary operator O_k to state S_ℓ. The goal state characteristics have all the constraints satisfied for the operator O_k. This subproblem can be solved in the same manner as the original problem. That is,

$$\bar{\psi}(SP(S_i, S_g)) = \bar{O}_j(S_i, S_g)$$

such that

$$\bar{D}_{g,i} = 0$$

and

$$X_{\bar{O}_j} = 1$$

where S_i and S_g are defined for the subproblem. This procedure is recursive in that it may be necessary to generate other subproblems within the subproblem in order to apply an operator to satisfy a constraint at a higher level. The operators and their constraints form the technological basis for synthesis. The definition of the initial and goal states define the problem. Each of the previous operators can be elaborated to define the more specific nature of the system structure. Fortunately a hierarchy of problems exists in the design of chemical processing systems. The hierarchy means that partial solutions to complex chemical processing problems can be used to bound the objective function values of the complete solutions. The details of the operators and constraints are given in a number of books and only one operator will be discussed here.

3. REACTION PATH SYNTHESIS

In the chemical industry the basic economic structure is dominated by a network of chemical and physical transformations which convert raw materials into a number of intermediates and final products including energy. The common methods for predicting the economic behavior of this type of chemical process industry is to formulate a continuous variable model of the flow of materials in this reaction network. The behavior of

this network for changing prices and demands can then be investigated.
Most models of this type do not allow for substitution of raw materials,
new products, and changes in the reaction network. [2]

An approach which will allow the generation of new networks of
reactions has been developed recently. What is required is a way to
mathematically represent molecules, their functions, and their potential
reactions. The representation of the molecules defines the initial states
(raw materials) and goal states (desired products). The potential reactions
are operators which can be applied to the states to create possible reaction path networks which solve the given problem. Several chemists have
worked on this problem over the past ten years. Professor E. J. Corey at
Harvard University has developed a series of computer programs which
carry out reaction path synthesis for complex molecules commonly synthesized in laboratories. Professor J. B. Hendrickson at Brandeis University
has developed a somewhat more general theory which is applicable to all
classes of organic reactions. Professor Hendrickson's models have served
as the basis for a program written by R. Jones for the laboratory synthesis
of DNA. This program is currently being extended to handle industrial
networks of reactions. Examples of the output of these programs are given
in Figures 2, 3, and 4. This theory of reaction path synthesis allows the
inclusion of changing network structure in an economic model.

Consider the following small example. The monomer vinyl chloride has been used for over seventy-five years in the manufacture of poly-
vinylchlordie polymers. The polymer is used in the "vinyl" covering used
on chairs and car seats, in plastic pipe, for phonographic records, for
coating wire, in floor coverings, rain wear, and so on. Some of the reaction paths to vinyl chloride generated using our synthesis program are
shown in Figure 4. These paths were generated completely automatically
without guidance or specific intervention by the program operator. [3]

One pathway in the network was used extensively in the early production of vinyl chloride.

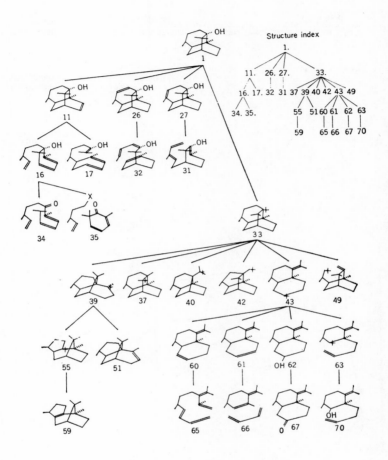

Figure 2. REACTION PATHS TO PATCHOLI ALCOHOL.

This set of paths was produced by the LAHSA
program at Harvard University [Corey, 1969].

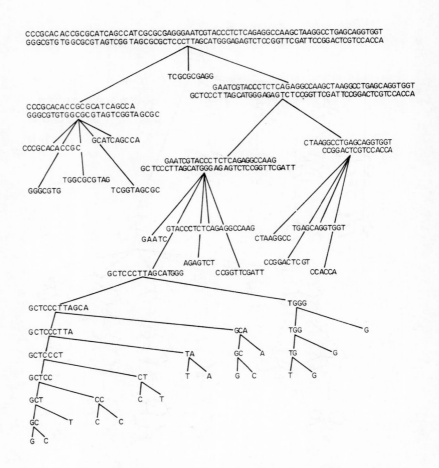

Figure 3. PART OF ONE REACTION PATH TO THE DNA FOR THE ALAINE t-RNA FROM YEAST.

This pathway was generated by the SINASYN program at Carnegie-Mellon University [Powers and Jones, 1973].

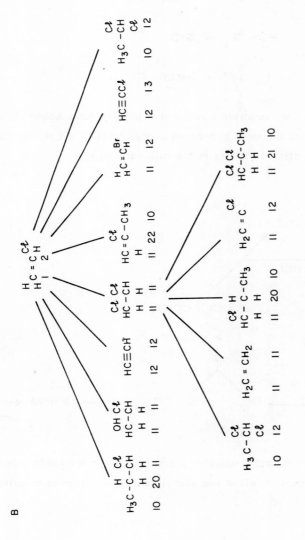

Figure 4. A SET OF REACTION PATHS FOR THE PRODUCTION OF VINYL CHLORIDE MONOMER.

405

$$HC \equiv CH + HC\ell \rightarrow HC\ell\,C = CH_2$$

$$CaC_2 + H_2O \rightarrow HC \equiv CH$$

$$H_2 + C\ell_2 \rightarrow 2HC\ell$$

$$NaC\ell + H_2O \rightarrow NaOH + C\ell_2 + H_2$$

As the demand for vinyl chloride increased it became more economic to reduce the amount of the more expensive acetylene $(HC \equiv CH)$ by substituting ethylene $(HC = CH)$ as in the following paths.

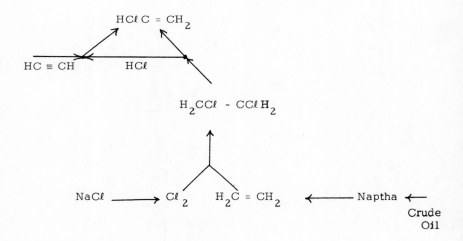

Still higher demand for vinyl chloride produced further economic incentive to substitute ethylene for all of the acetylene. The following reaction path resulted.

$$HC\ell\,C = CH_2$$

$$H_2C\ell\,C - CC\ell\,H_2$$

$$HC\ell$$

$$NaC\ell \longrightarrow C\ell_2 \qquad H_2C = CH_2 \longleftarrow Naptha \longleftarrow Crude\ Oil$$

As the pollution control constraints (legislative) tightened on the discharge of byproduct $HC\ell$ and as the price of $C\ell_2$ increased the following pathway became more economical:

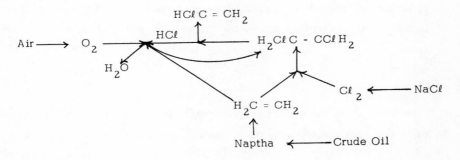

The byproduct $HC\ell$ is converted into 1, 2-dichloroethane which is re-
cycled back through the process thus recovering raw materials and avoiding pollution problems.

This historical sequence of changes in one small part of the
chemical process industry is representative of the types of changes in
system structure that can occur. Simple models, based solely on the
flows and prices for a single given reaction network, would not be able
to predict the shifts in system structure described above.[4] The chemical
process industry is currently in a very dynamic state. The rapidly increasing price of crude oil is greatly intensifying the search for alternate
raw materials and reaction paths. Any models which might be used to
predict the future economic state of affairs in the chemical industries

407

will have to be aware of potential changes in the system structure. A quantitative design theory such as the one presented here for the chemical process industries, has the potential for predicting the shifts which could occur in this system structure.

A basic research effort directed toward the development and use of these design theories is now underway at the Design Research Center at Carnegie-Mellon University. The research group includes engineers, computer scientists, psychologists, operations researchers, and economists. They are looking at basic problems in <u>representation</u> and <u>search</u> techniques as well as at problems in the synthesis of <u>energy efficient,</u> <u>fault tolerant,</u> and <u>pollution free systems</u>. One of the goals of this group is to put the technology required for the synthesis of the structure of an industry into a form that can be readily used in economic system modelling.

NOTES

[1] The topology of the system may change in a trivial way in that the flows of one or more streams may go to zero.

[2] While what I propose here goes beyond current modelling techniques, I do not mean to imply that the flows in the chemical reaction network have been defined. In fact there is a surprising lack of knowledge of the current network structure itself. The problem of obtaining a meaningful material balance for the chemical industry will continue to limit the effectiveness of economic models of this industry.

[3] Of course, the paths represent our general thinking on reaction paths as embodied in the program.

[4] The recent discovery of the carcinogenic nature of vinyl chloride monomer may add further constraints (safety legislation) during its manufacture. For example, it may become necessary to operate parts of the process

under low pressures to avoid small leaks of vinyl chloride. A major change such as this in operating conditions could shift attention to low pressure reactions which are different from those discussed above.

REFERENCES

Corey, E. J. and W. Todd Wipke [1969], _Science,_ 166, 178.

Corey, E. J., R. D. Cramer III and W. J. Howe [1972], "Computer-Assisted Synthetic Analysis for Complex Molecules. Methods and Procedures for Machine Generation of Synthetic Intermediates," _J. Am. Chem. Soc.,_ 94, 421.

Cyert, Richard M. and M. DeGroot [1975], "Adaptive Utility," in this volume.

Hendrickson, James B. [1971], "A Systematic Characterization of Structures and Reactions for Use in Organic Synthesis," _J. Am. Chem. Soc.,_ 93: 22, p. 6847.

Powers, G. J. and R. L. Jones [1973], "Reaction Path Synthesis Strategies," _AIChE Journal,_ Vol. 19, No. 6, p. 1204.

Powers, G. J. and D. F. Rudd [1974], "A Theory for Design in Chemical Engineering," Proceedings of the Conference on Design Theory, Columbia University, ed. W. Spillers.

Rudd, D. F., G. J. Powers and J. J. Siirola [1973], _Process Synthesis,_ Prentice-Hall, Englewood, N. J.

Rudd, D. F. [1975], "Long Range Adaptive Mechanisms in the Process Industries," in this volume.

Modelling the Development of the Intermediate Chemicals Industry
Dale F. Rudd

CONTENTS

1. INTRODUCTION

The central problem in industrial development is the projection of past experiences into a coherent plan for future development. The accuracy with which we perceive the forces at work in an economy determines the success in developing new industry and maintaining the vigor of developed industry.

We distinguish between a <u>description</u> of industrial development and a <u>theory</u> of development. Description is a first step towards understanding, but a mere compilation of statistics and historical data can give little insight into the future response of the industry. A theory of industrial development serves to integrate the economic, technical and behavioral forces at work into a simulation of the industrial dynamics which captures the dominant features of the developing industry.

Here we examine the difficulties in formulating a theory of development for the intermediate chemicals industry. The characteristics of the industry that attract attention are its large size, the extensive technical redundancy, the great flexibility and the frequent development of new technology. In the course of a few years whole sections of the industry can change and adapt to new conditions. We examine this adaptive mechanism.

2. SCOPE AND NATURE OF THE INDUSTRY

Figure 1 illustrates the transformation of natural gas and crude oil into consumer products. Although this is an overly simplified picture of the operations of a small segment of the E. I. duPont de Nemours and Company, certain features of the industry are apparent. Processing begins with relatively few basic raw materials, expands into a complex network of anonymous chemicals, and converges to materials that serve specific functions in the economy. Basic raw materials are not converted directly to consumer products, but pass through a complex series of transformations that compose the intermediate chemicals industry.

Hundreds of separate organizations engage in some segment of the processing. In the United States close to 400 major companies are involved in the transformation of basic chemicals into chemicals ready for the consumer market. The two leading producers of each of the top 100 intermediate organic chemicals include 50 separate companies, and the annual output of the materials ranges from 3 billion pounds to less than 10 million pounds. From crude oil alone over three thousand separate chemical compounds are made.

However, if we stand back far enough the organizational details blur and a broad pattern comes into focus. Raw materials enter a complex sequence of transformation to be converted into finished molecules to be consumed by the economy. The study of this industry as a whole can be likened to the study of global weather patterns, a study that sacrifices the day-to-day accuracy of local weather forecasting with the hope of understanding the larger patterns upon which the local weather is super-imposed. We seek to understand the global and long range

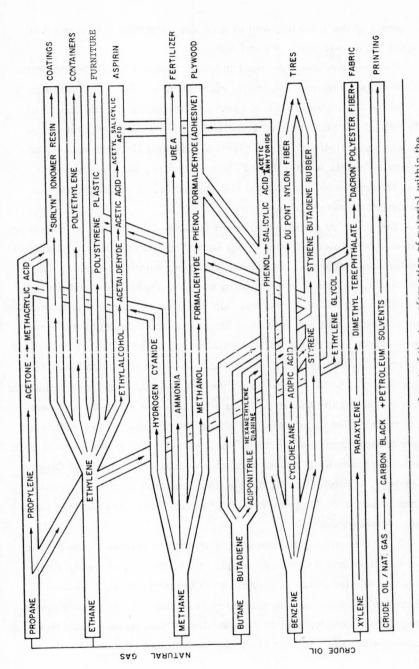

Figure 1. A schematic representation of part of the transformation of material within the duPont Company. From duPont Context, No. 2, 1974, E. I. duPont de Nemours and Company, Wilmington, Delaware.

413

development of the industry, and in this way determine the forces that influence the development of local industry.

The intermediates chemical industry provides the molecular building blocks that enter into the manufacture of thousands of consumer products. In the U.S. petrochemical raw materials alone are the source of nearly half of the plant nutrients, half of the fibers, 80 per cent of the rubber and essentially all of the plastics. Table 1 lists the primary organic raw materials for the United States industry, some of the major organic intermediates and organic end chemicals. A similar listing of inorganic chemicals could be made.

The scope of our direct concern is limited on the left by molecules that appear in natural deposits or are formed by the primary processing of raw materials. Ethylene, propylene, methane, butane, benzene, coal, air, minerals, and water are the kinds of basic chemicals that form the left-hand boundary of the industry. On the right our concern is limited by the molecules that are consumed directly in the manufacture of consumer products. Acrylonitrile, the building-block for Orlon fiber, certain synthetic rubber and plastics, is an example of the right-hand boundary of the industry. Basic molecules on the left and building-block molecules on the right bound the industry. Figure 2 traces the ethylene molecule as it is transformed to intermediate molecules and to finished molecules that are consumed by the economy, showing only part of the complex path the molecule takes as it passes through the industry. Chemical Origins and Markets, a publication of the Stanford Research Institute, contains over eighty pages of diagrams similar to Figure 2 that map out this extremely complex industry.

Figure 3 outlines the network of industries related to the production of only five end molecules: acrylonitrile, phenol, styrene, vinyl-acetate and ethylene glycol. Within each industry block, a number of alternate technologies can be used to convert the materials. Any realistic study of the development of the industry to manufacture these five molecules, must include over sixty chemical transformations involving

PRIMARY ORGANICS

Table 1. Major Organic Chemicals

	PRODUCTION VALUE (MILLIONS OF DOLLARS)
1. ETHYLENE	526.4
2. BENZENE	256.1
3. PROPYLENE	243.0
4. TOLUENE	125.0
5. ACETYLENE	109.1
6. N-BUTENES	68.1
7. XYLENES,	81.6
8. ISOBUTYLENE	48.8
9. NAPHTHALENE	37.6
10. FURFURAL	18.8
11. CRESOLS	18.6

from Chemical Origins and Markets
Stanford Research Institute
Menlo Park, California, 1967,
(estimated data for 1970)

ORGANIC INTERMEDIATES

1. STYRENE	304.7
2. BUTADIENE	256.5
3. ETHYLENE OXIDE	275.3
4. DIMETHYL TEREPHTHALATE	228.0
5. ETHYLENE DICHLORIDE	233.7
6. ETHYLBENZENE	212.0
7. ADIPIC ACID	171.0
8. N-BUTYRALDEHYDE	191.7
9. VINYL CHLORIDE MONOMER	177.8
10. ACETIC ANHYDRIDE	163.0
11. ETHYL ALCOHOL	114.0
12. ACRYLONITRILE	121.3
13. PHENOL	122.9
14. ISOPROPYL ALCOHOL	120.6
15. METHYL ALCOHOL	133.5
16. ACETIC ACID, SYNTHETIC	106.2
17. P-XYLENE	101.6
18. FORMALDEHYDE (37% BY WEIGHT)	99.2
19. PROPYLENE OXIDE	95.3
20. POLYETHER POLYOLS (PROPYLENE OXIDE BASE	104.0
21. ACETALDEHYDE	86.4
22. METHYL METHACRYLATE MONOMER	88.8
23. ACETONE CYANOHYDRIN	96.0
24. CAPROLACTAM	88.2
25. PHTHALIC ANHYDRIDE	78.5
°	
°	
°	10.7
86. DIETHANOLAMINE	11.2
87. NONENE (TRIPROPYLENE)	10.5
88. TRIETHANOLAMINE	10.4
89. POLYETHYLENE GLYCOL	

ORGANIC END CHEMICALS

1. NYLON 66 FIBERS	845.4
2. POLYESTER FIBERS	883.0
3. POLYETHYLENE RESINS	763.4
4. POLYBUTADIENE-STYRENE (SBR) ELASTOMERS	553.4
5. RAYON	367.5
6. POLYETHYLENE TEREPHTHALATE (FOR FIBERS AND FILMS)	488.9
7. POLYURETHANES, CELLULAR	467.5
8. CELLULOSE ACETATE AND TRIACETATE FIBERS	423.5
9. POLYVINYL CHLORIDE AND COPOLYMER RESINS	429.4
10. NYLON POLYMERS (FOR FIBERS)	406.0
11. TETRAETHYL AND TETRAMETHYL LEAD	350.9
12. NYLON 6 FIBERS	315.0
13. CELLULOSE ACETATE (FOR FIBERS AND PLASTICS)	276.8
14. ACRYLIC AND MODACRYLIC FIBERS	226.8
15. PHENOLIC AND OTHER TAR ACID RESINS	239.6
16. CELLOPHANE	227.8
17. POLYPROPYLENE PLASTICS	182.7
18. ALKYD RESINS	165.7
19. POLYSTYRENE RESINS (RUBBER MODIFIED)	198.2
20. POLYESTER FILM	216.0
21. POLYESTER RESINS (UNSATURATED)	175.8
22. ACRYLIC RESINS[a]	218.4
23. UREA-FORMALDEHYDE RESINS	200.0
24. ETHYLENE GLYCOL	203.0
25. POLYSTYRENE RESINS (UNMODIFIED)	155.7
°	
°	
°	
106. ASCORBIC ACID (VITAMIN C)	16.3
107. STYRENE-ACRYLONITRILE COPOLYMER (SAN) RESINS	11.2
108. DICHLOROTETRAFLUOROETHANE (FLUOROCARBON 114)	11.2
109. MONOETHANOLAMINE	11.0

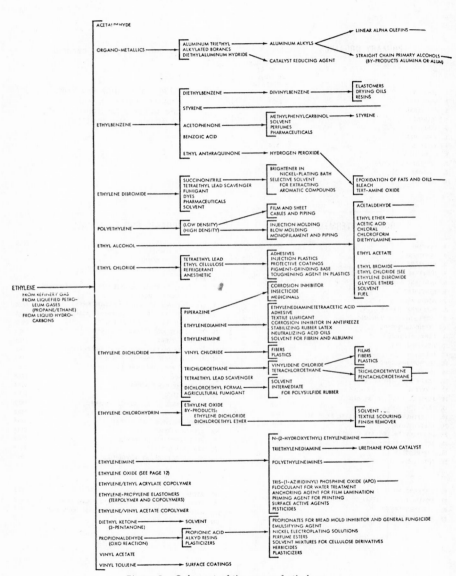

Figure 2. Only part of the uses of ethylene

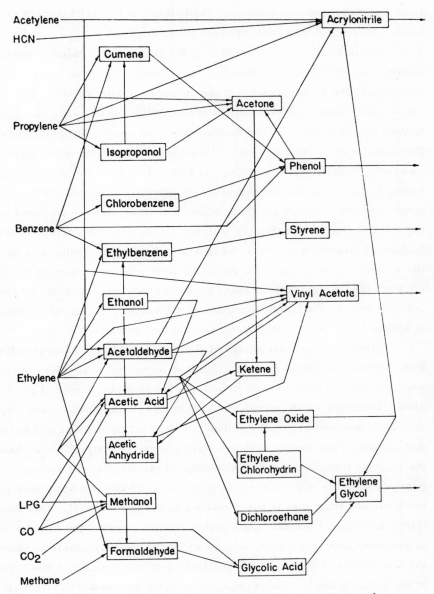

Figure 3. The network of industries related to the production of five finished molecules. Each industry block contains several alternate processes.

more than forty chemical species. The industry is orders of magnitude more complex than that small segment shown in Figure 3.

There are two characteristics of the industry that deserve early mention, anonymity and adaptibility. Great segments of the industry are anonymous, the products reaching the consumer in altered form. The annual production of acrylonitrile is over 2 billion pounds, and all of this is used within industry as the building block for man-made fibers, synthetic rubber and plastics. Acetic anhydride and salicyclic acid appear as asprin, hexamethylene diamine and adipic acid enter the economy as nylon, and so it is with the thousands of materials produced and consumed within the industry. These anonymous molecules are produced for the function they can perform by building fibers, bleaching and cleaning, by forming protective coatings, as fuel additives and so forth. Few of these functions are unique to a particular molecule, and a current list of products from the industry includes molecules that are available, low in cost and best fit the functional needs of the economy at this time. There is a wide flexibility for substitution among the chemicals.

However, a greater source of flexibility within the industry arises from the fact that two or more combinations of raw materials often can be used to make the same product molecule. For example, identical acrylonitrile molecules can be manufactured from propylene, ammonia and air, from acetylene and hydrogen cyanide, and from ethylene oxide and hydrogen cyanide. The surplus of cheap propylene in the early 1960's shifted the industry towards the first combination of raw materials; however, possible shortage of petrochemical feedstocks can cause a shift back to the acetylene route that is based on coal as the raw material. This flexibility in chemical reaction route occurs commonly within the industry and is a primary long range mechanism by which the industry adapts to changing conditions. A change in the availability of raw material in one sector of the industry can be compensated for by using completely different sets of raw materials to accomplish the same processing task. This technical redundancy illustrated in Figure 4 is essential to the long-range adjustment

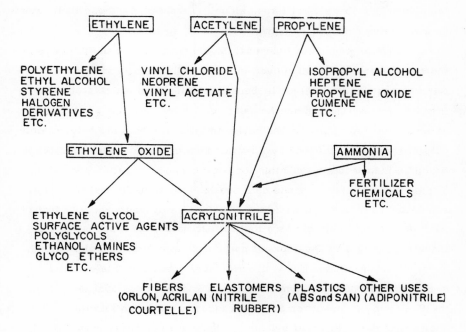

Figure 4. Partial structure of the economy involving acrylonitrile.

of the industry to the changing economy it serves.

History reveals little trend towards stability. External forces, such as the current energy crisis, and internal forces, such as the development of a new chemical reaction path to acrylonitrile, buffet the industry and cause continuing changes. A central problem in industrial development and long range planning is the prediction of the course the industry ought to take to be in the best position to serve the economy. This requires more than a superficial knowledge of the industry.

3. DYNAMIC MODELS OF INDUSTRIAL DEVELOPMENT

The course of industrial development is controlled by the interaction of technical, economic and behavioral forces. An understanding of the chemistry and engineering alone is as ineffective as understanding the economic or behavioral forces alone. We show how these fit together as a recursive model of industrialization.

A basic premise in industrial development is that the problems are too complicated for solution over an extended horizon, and that decision-makers constrain themselves by benavioral rules that afford protection from errors in estimation and forecasting. Decision making consists of various short run optimizations based on the belief that the only credible data is short-run, followed by a limited number of major strategic moves based on judgements of possible long-run consequences. A simulation of the technical and economic data available to decision-makers and a simulation of their response to the data forms a dynamic model of industrial development suitable as a tool for estimating the response of the industry to proposed development policies or to anticipated disruptions.

Day and Nelson [1973] describe applications of this economic model of industrial development to the U.S. bituminous coal industry, the U.S. and Japanese iron and steel industry and to an interregional analysis of the U.S. Steel industry. These are industries with limited technical alternatives, but the successes in economic modelling (illustrated in Figure 5) are sufficient to suggest this pattern of analysis as appropriate to the study of the highly complex intermediate chemicals industry. The premise is that similar behavioral patterns govern the decision-making of those who guide the development of the intermediate chemical industry, even though they interact with a much more technically complex system.

Figure 6 outlines the flow of information in the recursive model of the intermediate chemicals industry. The demands of the economy for food, fibers, fuel and other materials and the availability of raw materials drive the industrial dynamics, and determine the cast of molecules that are to enter and leave the industry. For example, the demand for fiber in the economy reflects into the industry as a demand for the finished molecules from which fibers can be made. The first step in modelling is the conversion of the demands of the economy for the materials to perform

420

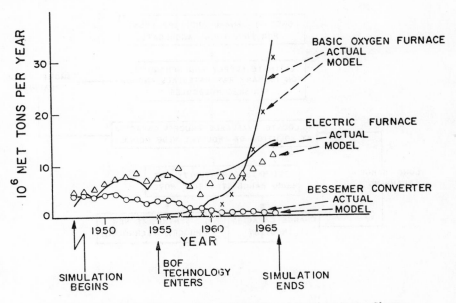

Figure 5. Actual and simulated U.S. Steel Production - Shows
ability to track an industry. R. H. Day and J. P. Nelson,
Journal of Econometrics 1[1973], 155-190.

the variety of aggregate functions into the specific data on the supply and
demand of particular molecules.

In the short-run, say in the matter of a year or less, the industry
can respond by allocating the existing process capacity optimally. A
reasonable criterion is the allocation of process capacity to meet the
supply and demand constraints at the minimum total production cost.
This short-range planning can be modelled by a massive linear program.

The short-range planning model can point to the need for long-
range strategic moves. These long-range moves involve the change in
the process capacity of the industry, the development of new processes
and the change in the spectrum of molecules capable of meeting the functional needs of the economy. These long-range adjustments occur in a
time scale of 5 to 15 years. We outline the methods for detecting these

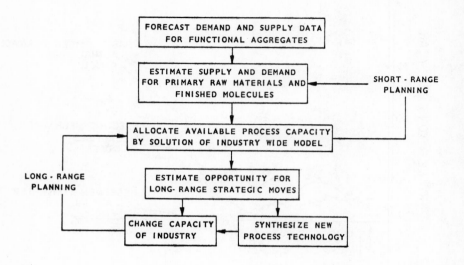

Figure 6. Flow of Information in the Model
of Industrial Development

strategic moves, discuss the modelling of the adoption, adjustment, obsolescence and obsoleteness phases of the changes in industrial capacity and examine the theories of process design that lead to new process technology.

We continue on the conjecture that it is possible to model the forces that cause these short-run and long-run adjustments in the industry, and with the hope that the modelling will give insight into the development policies to insure the future health of the industry.

4. INTERFACE BETWEEN ECONOMY AND INDUSTRY

Figure 7 shows the total demand for antifreeze in the United States from the 1930's to the 1960's; this curve parallels the growth of

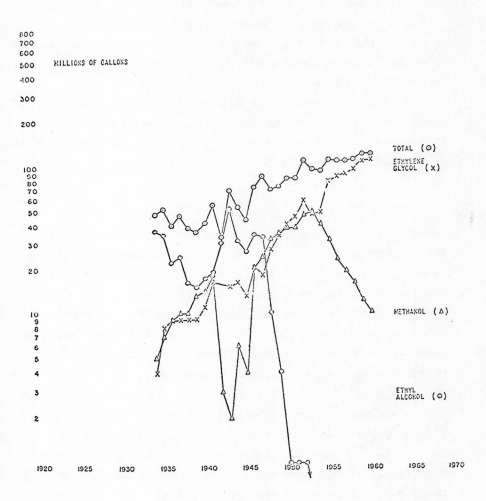

Figure 7. The substitution of ethylene glycol for ethyl alcohol and methanol within the automotive antifreeze functional aggregation.

the use of the internal combustion engine in automotive and industrial use. Also shown is the cast of molecules used to perform the antifreeze function. Ethylene glycol, methanol and ethyl alcohol have shared this responsibility. The first move we must take in modelling the industry is to convert the demand for a general aggregate function, such as the need for antifreeze, into the demand for specific molecules.

Let b_i be the demand for a specific finished molecule i, F_j be the demand by the economy for materials to perform the function j, and f_{ij} be the amount of finished molecule i required to form one unit of the material needed for function j. Then

$$b_i = \sum_j f_{ij} F_j$$

where j ranges over all functions in the economy. For example, the need for antifreeze is an F_j, the fraction of the antifreeze function performed by ethylene glycol is an f_{ij}, and to determine the b_i all the needs for ethylene glycol in the economy must be summed.

The first step in the modelling of the industry is to determine reasonably accurate estimates of the supply and demand for primary raw materials and finished molecules. This is accomplished by accepting the results of economy wide models that forecast the F_j and by estimating the f_{ij} from a technical study of the materials involved.

While economic studies can forecast changes in the demands for fiber, food, fuel, plastics and other materials, the forecast is more difficult for the particular cast of chemical building-blocks needed to serve these functions in the economy. Rarely does the economy demand a particular molecule, rather the economy demands the function the molecule can perform. Typically, similar products can be made from a wide choice of chemical building-block molecules and the current demand for a particular molecule is the result of a combination of price, availability and function in the economy. For example, cotton is the number one single fiber in the U.S. but the non-cellulosic man-made fibers will probably

pass cotton in popularity in the next few years. Of the 17 man-made
fibers shown in Table 2 available to the textile industry, there are several
thousand variations, each tailored to specific end use. The fiber industry
adapts by substitution within these functional aggregates, and the industries that supply the building-blocks for man-made fibers must respond.

An interesting problem in substitution is arising with the recent
discovery of the cancer producing property of vinyl chloride, the monomer
of polyvinyl chloride used in film, fiber and structural plastics. Should
the use of vinyl chloride be banned, the industry must respond by the
increased production of intermediates capable of filling the role that
vinyl chloride now plays in the economy. The reduction of vinyl chloride
production will be accompanied by a corresponding increase in the production of other molecules. What molecules these will be can be estimated by examining the possibility for substitution within functional
aggregates.

Using as a base the forecast long range trends in the nation's
need for materials in the various functional aggregates, we must determine
the probable mix of materials within each aggregate. This estimates the
production required of each of the wide variety of chemical intermediates.
We illustrate how this is accomplished for several important outlets for
the products of the chemicals industry.

Fiber. The world production of synthetic fibers exceeds three
million tons with the U.S.A. responsible for 38 per cent, Western Europe
31 per cent, Japan 18 per cent and other countries 13 per cent. Nylon holds
the major share of the market with about 40 per cent of the production,
polyesters about 30 per cent and acrylic 20 per cent. Polyolefins, polyvinyl alconol, polyvinyl chloride, elastomeric materials and flourine-
based products account for the remainder. The synthetic fibers account
for about 15 per cent of the total fiber market that includes cotton, wool,
the man-made cellulose fibers and synthetics.

By the mid 1970's the world's consumption of apparel fibers should
increase to 22 million tons and the share taken by synthetics should be

Table 2. The 17 Major classes of man-made fibers

Generic Name	Monomer or Polymer	First Commerical U. S. Producer	Year
Rayon	Regenerated cellulose	The American Viscose Corp. (now FMC Corp.)	1910
Acetate	Cellulose acetate (80% acetylated)	Celanese Corp. of America (now Celanese Corp.)	1924
Rubber	Natural or synthetic	U.S. Rubber Co. (now Uniroyal, Inc.)	1930
Glass	Glass	Owens-Corning Fiberglas Corp.	1936
Nylon	Polyamide	E. I. dePont de Nemours and Co.	1939
Vinyon	> 85% Vinyl chloride	The American Viscose Corp. (now FMC Corp.) and Union Carbide Corp.	1939
Saran	Vinylidene chloride	Firestone Plastics Co. (now Firestone Synthetic Fibers and Textiles Co.)	1941
Metallic	Metal, coated metal, and metallic coated	Dobeckmun Co. (production since absorbed by Dow Badische Co.)	1946
Modacrylic	35-85% Acrylonitrile	Union Carbide Corp.	1949
Acrylic	> 85% Acrylonitrile	E. I. duPont de Nemours and Co.	1950
Polyester	Ester of dihydric alcohol and terephthalic acid	E. I. duPont de Nemours and Co.	1953
Triacetate	Cellulose acetate (97% acetylated)	Celanese Corp. of America (now Celanese Corp.)	1954
Spandex	Urethane	E. I. duPont de Nemours and Co.	1959
Olefin	Ethylene, propylene, or other olefin	Hercules Powder Co. (now Hercules, Inc.)	1961
Anidex	Monohydric alcohol / acrylic acid ester	Rohm and Haas Co.	1969

at least 25 per cent. Synthetic fibers should begin to replace hard fibers
such as flax, jute and hemp. The world market for synthetic fibers may
be on the order of 6 million tons.

The raw materials for synthetic fiber production include:

Fiber	Required Molecules
nylon	adipic acid, hexamethylene diamine, caprolactam
polyesters	ethylene glycol, terephthalic acid
acrylic	acrylonitrile
polypropylene	propylene

Today the chances are not too great for the development of synthetic fibers with properties that differ readically from the existing fibers.
While advances will occur in weaving and knitting, dying, permanent
press properties, and nonwoven fabrics, the chemicals industry will not
be greatly influenced by these consumer product developments. The
growth of the market for adipic acid, hexamethylene diamine, caprolactam,
ethylene glycol, terephthalic acid, acrylonitrile, propylene and others in
the fibers industry will probably follow the growth of the fiber demands.

Plastics and Resins. Starting with the billard ball and celluloid
collar of the last century, plastic and resin manufacture has grown to a
world-wide, billion dollar industry. Celluloid was patented in 1870 and
Bakelite was introduced by Union Carbide in 1909. But it was the research
and development which occurred during and after World War II that formed
the technical base of this rapidly emerging industry. In 1969 in the U.S.
along, 19 billion pounds of plastics were produced, valued at 3.8 billion.

Chemists have learned to manipulate the molecular structure of
plastics so that they can be tailored to the requirements of the end use.
Further, they can be manufactured from petroleum products very cheaply.
Finally, plastics resist corrosion to an unusual degree. These properties
have led to revolutionary changes in the paint and coating industry, the
packaging industry, the house-wave industry and others.

The plastics fall into two broad classes, thermoplastics and thermosets. The thermoplastics which are soluble and capable of repeated softening and hardening include polystyrene, polyvinyl chloride, polyethylene, polypropylene, and polyvinylidene. The thermosets which are insoluble and infusible include the phenolics, melamines, epoxies and styrene based polyesters.

Polytheylene is the largest volume plastic in the world and the United States. The United States produced nearly half of the world wide production of 12 billion pounds in 1970. Styrene plastics rank second with a U.S production of 3.8 billion pounds. Third is polyvinyl chloride with polypropylene and the phenolics following. The intermediate chemicals needed in plastics and resin production are:

Plastic and resin	Required Molecules
polyolefins	ethylene, propylene
polystyrene	styrene
polyvinyl	vinyl chloride
polyester resins	ethylene glycol, propylene glycol, maleic anhydride
epoxy resins	epichlorohydrin, diphenylolpropane
nylon	adipic acid, hexamethylene diamine, caprolactam
polyurethane resins	toluene diisocyanate, polyethers
polycarbonates	diphenylolpropane, phosgene diphenol carbonate
polyformaldehyde	formaldehyde
phenol formaldehyde resin	phenol, formaldehyde

Natural and Synthetic Rubber. Three decades ago natural rubber claimed the United States' elastomer market supplying all but the minute 0.4% claimed by synthetic rubber. Now natural rubber has only 20% of

428

the market and synthetics dominate with 80% of the market. Over 2.7 million tons of rubber are consumed annually in the United States.

Synthetic rubber is manufactured from ethylene, propylene, butadiene, styrene and other products of the chemical and petroleum industries. In 1931 duPont introduced the first synthetic elastomer, Neoprene, a polychloroprene, and soon afterwards Thiokol Corporation introduced a polysulfide rubber called Thiokol. However, the first general purpose synthetic rubber was styrene-butadiene rubber (SBR) developed by Standard Oil of New Jersey, the four major tire companies, and the U.S. Government in a crash program during World War II. Since World War II great strides have been made in the elastomer industry and synthetics with a wide range of properties have been developed.

Synthetic rubber finds its way into the manufacture of power transmission belts, hoses, wire and cable sheathing, building sheeting, and other rubber products. However, about 65% of all elastomers went into the manufacture of tires in the United States, and that dominance of the tire industry as a consumer is even more pronounced for certain elastomer types.

The major intermediates consumed in elastomer production are:

elastomer	required molecule
SBR	butadiene, styrene
Neoprene	acetylene, chlorine, butadiene
nitrile rubber	butadiene, acrylonitrile
butyl rubber	isobutylene
stereo specific rubbers	butadiene, isopentene, propylene, ethylene

Forecasts in the demand for the variety of finished molecules are based on forecasts of the demand for the various functional aggregates of the economy. Changes in the need for fibers, plastics and resins, elastomers and other classes of materials influence the demand for the finished molecule to a varying degree. To a sufficient approximation the forecasts might be made by determining the current production that goes into each functional aggregate and then assuming that the demand for each production category follows the forecast changes in the functional aggregate.

These forecasts must be tempered by an assessment of the expected technical developments that will open the possibility for future substitutions within the aggregates. Forecasts of functional aggregate distribution that extend much beyond a decade are apt to be unreliable, as Figure 7 shows in the case antifreeze materials used over the past four decades. While the total antifreeze consumption follows the general increase in automotive use, the relative use of ethylene glycol, methanol, and ethyl alcohol follows a more complex pattern of change that we would hesitate to predict.

It is by perturbation of the coefficients f_{ij} and F_j that the following kinds of questions are asked of the model of industrial development.

"A reduction in the use of the tetraethyl lead in gasoline as an antiknock agent will free ethylene for other uses. However, the antiknock function in motor fuels will then be performed by aromatic compounds thereby increasing the demands on limited benzene supply, perhaps, causing shortages in synthetic rubber. What disruptions in the industry might obtain?"

5. SHORT RANGE ALLOCATION MODEL

In the short run the industry seeks to use its existing process capacity most effectively to convert available resources into the products in current demand. Short-range adjustments are made rapidly, perhaps on a year to year schedule, and can be modelled as a linear programming allocation [Stadtherr, 1974].

Three constraints exist, the available supply of raw materials $\underline{A}$, the existing demand for finished molecules $\underline{B}$ and the available processing capacity $\underline{C}$.

The chemical transformations possible within the industry can be thought of as R chemical reactions $r_1, r_2, r_3, \ldots, r_R$. These involve S chemical species $s_1, s_2, s_3, \ldots, s_S$. The species combine in definite proportions in each reaction to produce other species in definite proportions. Thus, the inputs and outputs from each reaction are constrained. This can be expressed by the stoichiometric or yield coefficients α_i^j for each species s_i in a reaction r_j. The α_i^j are positive for products and negative for reactants. Each reaction is described by the chemical reaction equation

$$\sum_i \alpha_i^j s_i = 0.$$

For the industry this information forms a matrix with thousands of elements. In general the matrix will be sparse with most of the entries being zero.

The model includes parameters x_j which denote the amount of each unit reaction r_j in use during a given planning period. The x_j are constrained by the available process capacity c_j

$$0 \le x_j \le c_j, \quad j = 1, 2, \ldots, R .$$

In addition to the constraints on x_j imposed by process capacity limits, the available feed stocks constrain x_j. That is x_j is constrained by the amount of available limiting feed stocks of the several species s_i^j needed in the reaction r_j. The amount of s_i^j required by x_j units of reaction r_j is

$$\begin{cases} -\alpha_i^j x_j & \text{if } \alpha_i^j < 0 \\ 0 & \text{otherwise} . \end{cases}$$

The amount of s_i^j produced by x_j units of reaction r_i is

$$\begin{cases} \alpha_i^j x_j & \text{if } \alpha_i^j > 0 \\ \\ 0 & \text{otherwise .} \end{cases}$$

For basic raw materials species s_i,

$$-\sum_j \alpha_i^j x_j \le a_i$$

and for product aggregates species s_i,

$$\sum_j \alpha_i^j x_j \ge b_i \, ,$$

where a and b are raw material and product amounts. The total production of species s_i must not be less than the total consumption of that species. That is,

$$\sum_{\alpha_i^j < 0} - \alpha_i^j x_j \le \sum_{\alpha_i^j > 0} \alpha_i^j x_j \quad \text{for } i = 1, 2, \ldots, s.$$

These then are the physical constraints within which the industry must function.

During each short-range planning period the amounts x_j of each reaction are to be adjusted to meet the short-range suboptimization goal. One criterion is the minimization of the total cost of production

$$\underset{i=1,2}{\text{Min}} \sum_R \gamma_i x_i$$

where γ_i is the cost of running a unit of reaction r_i. The solution of this linear program gives the optimal use of existing industrial capacity. In our preliminary study of the Mexican industry the objective was changed to that of minimizing imported materials [Rivas, 1974].

432

Figure 8 illustrates the structure of the simple five product part of the industry shown in Figure 3. The solution to the linear programming allocation model trims the network of feasible processes down to those active in the minimum cost allocation, Figure 9. This short run allocation model is fine-tuned by adjusting the economic parameters to match the observed performance of the industry.

It is an approximation to consider the capacity C for the manufacture of a given material to be fixed even in the short run, since there is the possibility of changing the operation of a process so that it serves a purpose other than that currently performed. For example, acetylene can be produced by the pyrolysis of naphtha in the Wulff process and the Farbwerke Hoechst high-temperature process (HTP). In the HTP process vaporized naphtha is reacted for 0.002 to 0.003 seconds at high temperatures and is then quenched by a spray of cold oil. Ethylene and acetylene are coproducts in the weight ratio of from 1 to 1 to 1.5 to 1 depending on the final reaction temperature.

A shift in the price and demand for acetylene and ethylene would result in a short-run shift in ratio of ethylene to acetylene produced thus giving more production of one of these coproducts than is possible by current capacity data. Many processes have this flexibility, and this leads to an economic dependence of the stoichiometric coefficients and a non-linear programming model. However, there is a question as to the detail that need be included to capture the gross adjustments of the industry.

This short-range planning model is consistent with the basic hypothesis of business behavior expressed by Bower [1970].

"Wnile everyone realizes that the long-run return is the objective, the only quantitative data is short-run, so that observed behavior usually consists of various sorts of short-run optimization and/or a limited number of major moves justified by judgements of long-run strategic consequences."

433

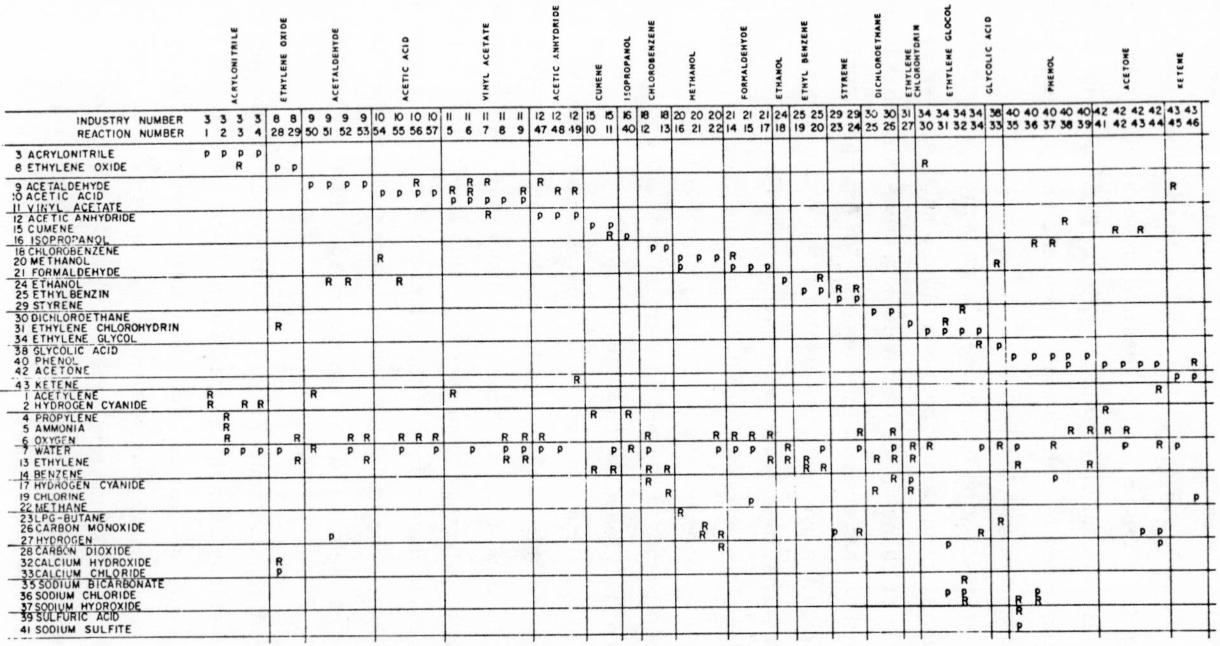

Figure 8. Input/output structure of five finished molecule portion of industry. Actual industry is two orders of magnitude more complex. (Courtesy of M. Staidkerr).

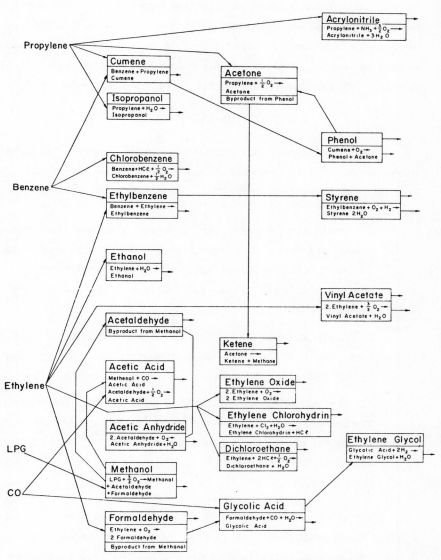

Figure 9. Solution to short range planning model for industry of Figure 2.

The linear programming model described above models the short-run optimizations; but to examine the possible long-run strategic moves requires a much deeper understanding of the forces at work in the economy. In the long-run the constraints (A, B and C) on resource supply, product demand and process capacity change, and new process technology emerges. We examine the forces that cause these changes.

6. DETECTION OF STRATEGIC MOVES

The short-range adjustments of the industry are modelled by the linear programming allocation of the available process capacity. The long-range adjustments alter the short-range allocation problem in three ways.

1. Substitutions occur within the aggregate supply and demand constraints A and B. For example, a shift might occur in the fraction of the fiber needs met by Nylon and Acrylic fibers, changing the demand for the finished molecules used in these synthetic fibers.

2. The capacity of the industry is altered to eliminate bottle-necks that limit the short-range allocation. By the investment in new technology the capacity constraints C can be altered.

3. New technology is developed to utilize surplus raw materials, to ease shortages of intermediates and so forth. The new technology can change the entire structure of the industry by adding new elements to the matrix of chemical reactions that describes the industry.

The short-range allocation of available process capacity forms a _primal_ linear program the _dual_ of which establishes shadow prices that define local economic criteria to be used to identify sites for process modification, in the same way that purchase and sales price are used, along with investment costs, to establish the economic attractiveness

436

of proposed engineering activities

primal	dual
Min $\underline{\Gamma} \cdot \underline{x}$	Max $\underline{w} \cdot \underline{d}$
$\underline{\underline{E}} \cdot \underline{x} \geq \underline{d}$	$\underline{w} \cdot \underline{\underline{E}} \leq \underline{\Gamma}$
$\underline{x} \geq 0$	$w \geq 0$

where the elements in the primal problem correspond to the stoichio-metric, raw material and finished molecule constraints, the processing costs and the allocation of capacity in the original problem. The new vector $\underline{w}$ in the dual problem forms the shadow prices, generated auto-matically during the solution of the primal problem, one price for each constraint in the primal problem. The shadow prices have the following useful properties.

1. If a constraint does not influence the optimal short-range performance of the industry, its shadow price is zero.

2. A non-zero shadow price is equal to the change in the optimal cost of the industry-wide production caused by a unit change in the corresponding constraint.

Other post-optimal studies can be performed to identify certain limited classes of long-range strategic moves.

In addition to the shadow prices and similar post-optimal in-dicators of the sensitivity of the short-range model to changes in defini-tion, surplus of intermediate materials attract attention. When material is available in surplus, attempts will be made to create the technology to upgrade the surplus into materials in short supply. Unfortunately, this adaptive mechanism tampers with the left-hand side of the con-straint matrix, and little guidance is available from linear programming theory on the effects of such structural changes in the problem. The recent work of Saidikowski [1974] holds the promist of an interactive programming capability to resolve these difficulties, but the study of this adaptive mechanism remains heuristic.

The substitution within functional aggregates is not modelled in this study, and is assumed to be an external force to which the industry responds. The diffusion of capacity change in the industry is presumed to follow the classic models of industrial dynamics. The synthesis of new technology can be performed on a case study basis to see how the industry might respond to a completely new technology, the new technology becoming one of the technical alternatives entering into the industrial development model above.

The size of the industry limits the modelling of long-range changes to only certain selected industries. Those industries whose capacity constraints are active during the short-range allocation are obvious candidates for capacity change studies, and unconsumed materials within the industry attracts attention as a site of the synthesis of new technology. This becomes a second level optimization problem on the parameters A, B, C and α in the linear allocation problem, the properties of which are not completely understood.

7. CHANGES IN INDUSTRY CAPACITY

There are fundamental differences between the changing capacity of an existing industry and the introduction of new process technology. The former involves familiar technology with less resistance to adoption should the economics be attractive. The latter involves unfamiliar technology which often is not adopted initially at the same rate as familiar technology regardless of its economic promise.

A further difference is that a new technology can change the entire structure of the industry by opening up new pathways. The consequences of new technology often cannot be seen locally and an economy wide model is needed to determine the results of the new structure of the industry. However, let us examine the competition among existing technical alternative, and the mechanism by which industry-wide capacity changes.

438

To diffuse into the economy an innovation must in theory be more economical than current practice and the investment capital must be available to bring the technology into being; but other factors constrain the behavior of decision makers, according to Day [1969].

"The first is a resistance to adopting a new technique because of the time required to learn its use and perfect its application in existing firms. The second in unwillingness to make decisions to expand capacity in any one year purely on considerations of capitalized values and cost differentials, because of doubts about future capacity requirements and the possibility of future, superior innovations. We represent the first by a set of behavioral adoption constraints and the second by a set of behavioral adjustment constraints on investment activity levels. Together they place an upper bound on the growth in capacity of any given technique that resembles the diffusion curves often observed in studies of technological change. The adoption constraints are given a simple form in which the upper bound on investment in a given technique is proportional to the past period's capacity of that technique. The idea is that learning is proportional to exposure, and exposure is measured by existing capacity. These constraints are almost always equated in the early stages of adoption".

"The investment adjustment constraints also place an upper bound on the investment in a given period. They are based on the hypothesis, often used in other econometric models, that capacity is adjusted toward the current conception of the desirable capacity in the technique in question. In this model, desired capacity is taken to be proportional to the sales forecast of final commodities already described above. Investment is constrained to be not more than some given proportion of the difference between this amount and current capacity".

These concepts lead to the phase diagram for an individual capital good shown in Figure 10 taken from Day and Nelson [1973]. Given the initial capacity at time i, the capacity at time $t + 1$ is constrained to fall within the shaded area. The adoption constraint states that learning is proportional to exposure and that exposure is proportional to existing capacity, and the adjustment constraint places an upper bound on the capacity, that bound being proportional to the sales forecast. The lower bound is the capacity decumulation rate determined by the physical depreciation of obsolete technology.

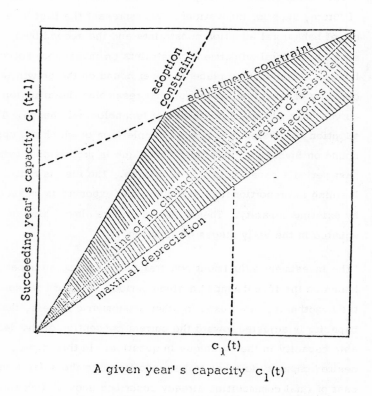

Figure 10. Phase diagram for the expansion of a technology

A <u>modern</u> industry has a trajectory along the upper boundary of
this region. If the trajectory is the interior of the shaded region and is
at the maximum rate for a competing technology, the former technology
is <u>obsolescent</u>. If no new investment is made in a technology the trajectory follows the lower curve, and the technology is <u>obsolete.</u>

This leads to four distinct phases of industrial development:
(1) <u>adoption</u> where the rate of expansion is proportional to the number
of plants that have successfully used the new technology, (2) <u>adjustment</u>
where the growth is restricted by expected demand and the fear of over-
specialization, (3) <u>obsolescence</u> where investment fills our capacity
needed to meet short-run objectives while the firm is learning about
another superior technique and (4) <u>obsoleteness</u> where the capacity is
allowed to run down at its maximum rate.

The time scales at which these forces operate is determined by
the time lags in the construction of new capacity, once the technology
has been demonstrated on the commerical scale. A longer time scale
occurs during the transition from laboratory to pilot plant to demonstration of full-scale feasibility.

In summary, three general forces are in operation in the diffusion
of new technology into the economy: (1) <u>Economic forces</u> that attract
capital towards the current concept of optimal technology, (2) <u>behavioral
forces</u> that restrict the movement of capital towards the short-run optimal
technology, and (3) <u>dynamic forces</u> that limit the speed at which new
capacity can be brought into being.

We examine the extent to which this model of industrial development explains the diffusion of chemical innovations through the process
industries. Towards that end we study the historical evidence on the
acceptance of innovations in the manufacture of acrylonitrile. The analysis of this evidence leads to a general model for the probable impact on
the economy of proposed chemical innovations.

Acrylonitrile was a laboratory curiosity from its discovery in 1893
until World War II when it was used in a copolymer with butadiene in the

manufacture of oil resistant synthetic rubber. Orlon, one of the first acrylic fibers was introduced in 1950, and the demand for acrylonitrile grew. More recently acrylonitrile-butadiene-styrene (ABS) plastics found use in automotive parts, pipe and fittings and major appliances. Currently fiber production consumes 61% of the U.S. production, co-polymer resins 18%, nitrile rubber 9% and other use, including the production of adioponitrile (an intermediate in nylon 66 manufacture) 11%.

Figure 11 illustrates the history of the production technology. Acrylonitrile was first made in the U.S. by American cyanamid from ethylene oxide and hydrogen cyanide,

$$C_2H_4O \quad + \quad HCN \quad = C_3H_3N + H_2O$$
ethylene oxide hydrogen cyanide acrylonitrile

and later from acetylene and hydrogen cyanide.

$$C_2H_2 \quad + \quad HCN \quad + \quad C_3H_3N$$
acetylene hydrogen cyanide acrylonitrile

In the 1950's Union Carbide entered with the ethylene oxide process, and Monsanto, duPont and Goodrich came in with the acetylene process.

In the late 1950's James Idol discovered the propylene route that uses the then cheap and plentiful co-product from ethylene manufacture.

$$C_3H_7 \quad + \quad NH_3 \quad + 3/2 O_2 = \quad C_3H_2N \quad + 3 H_2O$$
propylene ammonia oxygen acrylonitrile water

In 1960 Standard Oil of Ohio (SOHIO) began producing acrylonitrile by this intrinsically economic process. The rapid growth of ethylene manufacture to meet the demand for polyethylene plastics assured a continuing supply of cheap propylene, and now this propylene-ammonia process and other propylene based technology are the only ones used in the U.S. The price of acrylonitrile dropped from a historic high of 38 cents per pound to the current 12 cents per pound.

In Figure 11 we observe the obsolescence of the acetylene route between 1960 and 1964 when the capacity of this familiar technology was increasing in spite of the existence of the more economical but less familiar propylene route. Obsoleteness of the acetylene route began in 1964 and the last processes were closed down in 1972. The propylene route shows the classic adoption dynamics between 1960 and about 1966 in which the rate of increase of capacity is proportional to existing capacity. In 1966 the total capacity exceeded the demand, and the adjustment phase began in which growth is restricted by demand considerations.

In this example we see the adoption, adjustment, obsolescence and obsoleteness phases of development in the chemical intermediates industry. The recent studies of Saxena [1974] on other intermediates show similar patterns of growth and decay controlled by economic and behavioral forces. These studies given credence to the attempts to model the response of the industry to changes in the economic, demand and supply picture. The long range changes in industry capacity of the past may be projected into the future with this model of the forces at work.

The growth in the acceptance of products made from acrylonitrile is reflected in the rapid increase in the demand for acrylonitrile shown in Figure 12. The economy has its influence on the industry by providing the production goals for the intermediates, and the industry influences the economy by discovering the technology that dropped the price of acrylonitrile to 12 cents per pound. However this drop in price was possible because propylene is a coproduct in the production of ethylene, an intermediate then experiencing a rapid increase in demand.

However, while the changes in process capacity are an important adaptive mechanism, the invention of new technology is an even more important mechanism. In the early 1950's Standard Oil of Ohio began a research program to find use for their surplus propylene, and this led to the propylene route to acrylonitrile. A 1955 projection of the industry-wide capacity of the ethylene oxide and actylene routes to acrylonitrile,

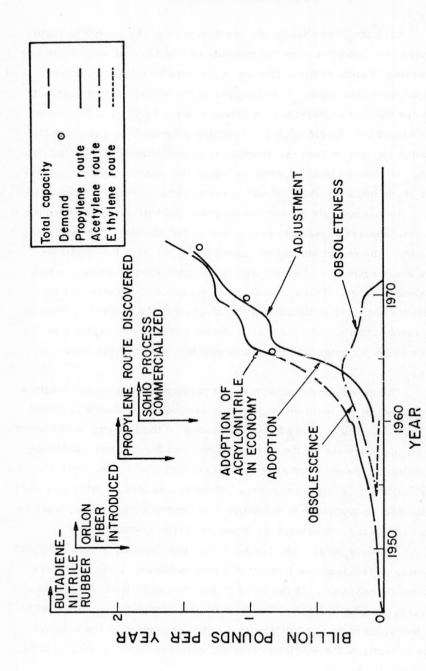

Figure 11. History of Acrylonitrile Technology. R. Saxena, Private Communication.

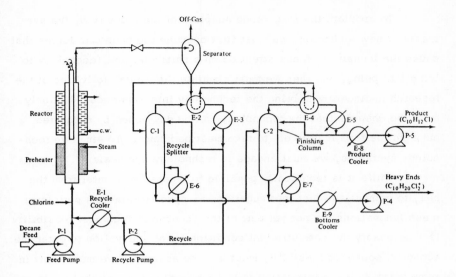

Figure 12. Process flow sheet direct chlorination of n-Decane (R. R. Hughes)

without the knowledge of the soon to be discovered propylene route, would have been meaningless. Somehow the synthesis of new technology must enter into a model of development of the chemicals industry.

8. SYNTHESIS OF NEW TECHNOLOGY

The mere expansion and reduction of the process capacity of the industry is an evolutionary adaptive mechanism that causes no great surprises in the performance of the industry. However, the creation of a new technology can have the revolutionary effect of changing the basic structure of the industry. The opportunities and problems perceived during short-range planning are the motivating forces that drive the changes in industry wide process capacity and the search for new technology. The evolutionary changes are conservative, relatively risk free and fairly easily modelled, and the revolutionary changes are far more difficult to implement, capable of far greater effect, and exceptionally difficult to model.

To simulate the long-range adaption of the industry by the synthesis of new technology we must first examine the economic forces that
cause the industry to focus attention on a particular new technology to
bring into being, and then we must simulate the mental activities of the
research engineers who bring the technology into existence. Not only
must the chances that the technology can be developed by estimated,
but also the form it is likely to take must be known. To simulate technology synthesis, we must engage in technology synthesis.

While it is technically possible to create fresh water from the
sea, to convert sawdust into sugar and to make protein from petroleum
these innovations are not yet part of the economy. Technical feasibility
is a necessary but not sufficient condition for an innovation to enter the
economy; economic feasibility must also be assured. We must know in
some detail how the innovation is to be accomplished, so that costs can
be estimated. Essentially, the innovation must be carried through to
the preliminary engineering design, before it can take its place as one
of the technical alternatives available for diffusion into the economy.

Considerable progress has been made in the last decade in the
theory of process synthesis and design, and, while the creative skills
of the experienced engineer are still very much a part of this activity,
sufficient theoretical guidance is available to consider process development to be a mechanism of economic adaptation capable of being modelled.
The experienced engineer is part of the model [Powers 1972, Hendry et
al. 1973, Rudd, Powers and Siirola, 1974].

Given the need for a special transformation of materials, candidate process concepts are synthesized. The concepts are then analysed to determine their probably operating characteristics. Then the
processes are optimized by iteration through the synthesis and analysis
cycle until the final process design is obtained. By the application of
these concepts of process development, a proposed new technology is
transformed into an estimate of its technical and economic characteristics

with sufficient accuracy to determine the impact the technology might have on the economy should it be brought into being.

By simulating the development of new technology and examining its acceptance by the economy, we model one of the major strategic moves the industry can make to adapt its structure.

However, it is useful to begin with an example of the kind of information that must be generated to determine the economic impact of a proposed technology. We wish to contemplate the introduction of a chemical transformation of decane into monochlorodecane, a technology that already exists in one form

$$C_{10}H_2 + Cl_2 = C_{10}H_{21}Cl + HCl .$$

To assess the impact of this technology on the economy we need to know the cost of performing the reaction. To determine the cost the process must be created to the level of sophistication shown in Figure 12, from which the following estimate can be made.

		$/LB	% OF TOTAL
I.	Capital costs	$4,000,000	
II.	Annual operating costs	$4,400,000/yr	
	Amortization of capital	$600,000/yr	
III.	Product cost	$0.05/lb of MCD	
	Capital costs	0.006	12
	Raw materials	0.035	71
	Utility	0.003	5
	Labor	0.005	10
	Other	0.001	2
	Total	0.050	

Table 3. Estimated economics of producing 100 million pounds per year of monochlorodecane by process of Figure 12 (R. R. Hughes).

To create the process flow sheet the original design synthesis task is transformed into a hierarchy of subgoals that penetrate the synthesis problem to overcome the severe and overwhelming combinatorial problems the engineer faces, the modern theory of which is patterned after current work in artificial intelligence and pattern recognition [Powers, 1975].

In brief outline, flow sheet synthesis occurs by the solution to these basic problems. First the chemical reaction path is established. This is the sequence of reactions which best transforms the raw materials into the products on the industrial scale. The second problem is one of species allocation in which a mapping of material flow is proposed from raw material and reaction site sources to product, waste and reaction site destinations. During species allocation the easiest set of separation problems are sought. The third problem is the selection of the physical and chemical phenomena which best accomplish the separation problems which arose from the species allocations. The final problem is task integration in which the several separate reaction and separation phenomena are integrated by the reuse of energy and material.

The synthesis of the technology to support the chemistry for the production of monochlorodecane from decane and chlorine results in the eight plausible processes shown in Figure 13. To estimate the economics of these process candidates each must be analysed in some detail.

The process concepts are then converted into the cost surfaces shown in Figure 14. We see that as the economic and operating environment change Flowsheet 1, 3 and 6 alternate as the superior technology, and that from the surface of superior designs it is possible to estimate the cost of converting decane and chlorine into monochlorodecane. Such a study provides the economic and technical detail required to assess the penetration of this reaction path into the economy.

448

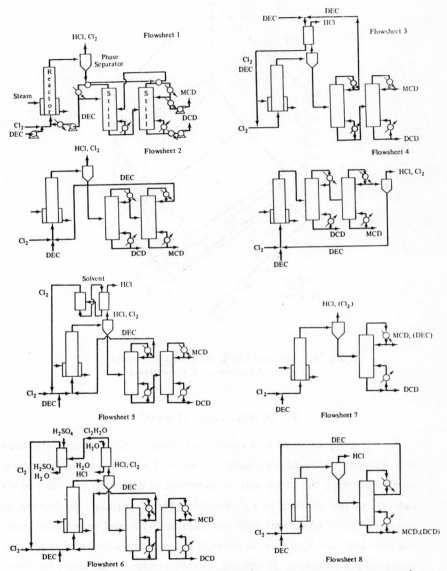

Figure 13. Preliminary flowsheets for the technology to convert decane and chlorine into monochlorodecane.

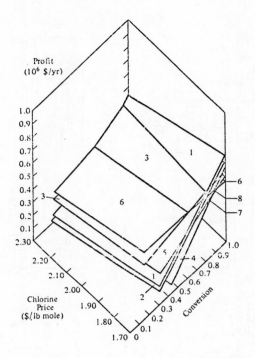

Figure 14. Venture profit surfaces for eight monochlorodecane processes

9. CONCLUDING REMARKS

The objective of this continuing study of the intermediate chemical industry is the development of a general model of the industry capable of tracking the historical development of a particular sector of the industry or the industry in a particular national setting. By fine-tuning the model to fit historical data and running the model beyond the present time into the future, a forecast is made of the effects of industrial development policies. Hopefully, policy errors can be made and corrected on paper rather than concrete and steel.

The striking features of the intermediate chemicals industry include the large size of any problem of interest, the enormous redundancy of technical alternatives available to accomplish the same subgoal within the industry and the ability to innovate and create new technology with success in a relatively short span of time. The hope of modelling the development of the industry rests in the transformation of the enormous complex interdependencies into short range linear programming allocation model applied recursively as the economic and behavioral forces change the coefficients and constraints to simulate long range changes. Superimposed on these mathematical simulations is a man-machine simulation of the creation of new technology.

To be reported in the near future are the results of studies on the development of the Mexican chemicals industry, the role new chemical technology plays in development, the adaptive capacity of the industry, the behavioral constraints in the acceptance of new technology, and the resolution of infeasible development problems. These delve deeper into the several special problems identified here.

ACKNOWLEDGEMENTS

The support of the Mathematics Research Center of the University of Wisconsin and the Midwest Consortium for International Activities is acknowledged. Discussions with R. H. Day, J. Rivas, R. Saidikowski, M. Stadtherr, R. Saxena, C. C. Watson and D. May contributed to this manuscript.

REFERENCES

Bower, J. L. [1970], "Planning within the Firm," American Economic Review, 60, 186-194.

Day, R. H. and T. Groves (Editors) [1975], Adaptive Economic Models, Academic Press.

Day, R. H. and P. E. Kennedy [1970], "Recursive Decision Systems, An Existence Analysis," Econometrica, 38, 666-681.

Day, R. H. et al. [1969], "Recursive Programming Models of Industrial Development and Technical Change," in Input-Output Techniques, Canter and Brody (eds.), North Holland Press, 1970.

Day, R. H. and J. E. Nelson [1973], "A Class of Dynamic Models for Describing Industrial Development", Journal of Economics, 1, 155-190.

Hendry, J. E., D. F. Rudd and J. D. Seader [1973], "Synthesis in the Design of Chemical Processes," AIChE Journal, 19, 1.

Powers, G. J. [1973], "Heuristics in Process Development", Chem. Engr. Progress.

——————— [1975], "Modelling Discrete Adaptive Behavior in Chemical Process Industries", in this volume.

Rivas, J. R. and D. F. Rudd [1974], IMIQ Meeting, Guadalajahar.

Rudd, D. F., G. J. Powers and J. J. Siirola [1973], Process Synthesis, Prentice-Hall.

Saidikowski, R. [1974], private communication.

Saxena, R. [1974], private communication.

Stadtherr, M. [1974], private communication.

Siirola, J. J. and D. F. Rudd [1971], "Computer-Aided Synthesis of Chemical Process Designs", Ind. Engr. Chem. Fund., 10, 353.

Economic Adjustments under Noncompetitive Pricing
Hukukane Nikaido

CONTENTS

1. INTRODUCTION

1.1. Summary of the Results

The market price mechanism is expected to implement an efficient resource allocation through the parametric function of prices. This idealized mechanism worked well in the good old day's competitive economy where every agent was a price-taker. It achieved resource allocation by reconciling individual ex ante price-taking behaviors of all agents, producers as well as consumers, and integrating them to mutually consistent feasible actions in the economy.

In the contemporary economy involving more or less monopolistic characteristics, however, the function is no longer perfect owing to the

453

presence of price-making agents, especially, among producers. Nonetheless, in order for the price mechanism to work, even though imperfectly, there must be price-taking agents. For otherwise all agents would
intend to make prices, while nobody would take them as given parameters,
and no transaction could result. Thus the economy whose working depends
on a price mechanism includes price-takers. Their behaviors are functions
of prices and therefore can more or less be controlled by agents making
the prices. A demand or supply function with prices as arguments, available to a price-making agent, is an integration of behaviors of some price-
taking agents behind it. He is thereby capable of controlling their behaviors by price adjustment.

Today, the price mechanism still works but imperfectly. Disequilibrium in the sense of imbalance of demand and supply does not necessarily result in a price adjustment that would reduce the excess demand
or supply toward an equilibrium. Demand is brought in balance to supply
through output adjustments rather than price adjustments. Prices function
as price-makers' instruments to regulate the size and distribution of national income, that is, distribution between workers and capitalists on
one hand and that among capitalists in various sectors on the other.

This view was developed somewhat extensively by the author in
two forthcoming works (Nikaido [forthcoming, a, b]). In particular, it
is shown in the first of these that sectoral levels of output can be uniquely and stably determined at any possible price situation to meet the corresponding effective demand for goods. Thereby the capitalists can potentially regulate income distribution by way of controlling prices.

Some dynamics in output adjustments of this kind was also included. However, the exploration was not thoroughly done. The purpose
of this paper is to supplement the dynamics in two typical adjustment
processes, namely, adjustment under full cost pricing and that under perceived profit maximization. The case where the system Jacobian matrix possesses a uniformly column dominant negative diagonal, is then considered
and stability is established using a result due to Karlin ([1959], Chap. 9,

Th. 9.5.1.). The existence and uniqueness of a solution are also discussed for this case.

1.2. Basic Working of the Economy

The economy is depicted as a Leontief system of the standard type having an input coefficients matrix

(1) $$A = (a_{ij}),$$

where a_{ij} denotes the amount of the i th good to produce one unit of the j th good in the j th sector with no joint production under constant returns to scale, $i, j = 1, 2, \ldots, n$. A is a nonnegative matrix and will be assumed to be indecomposable whenever required.

If labor is taken as a numeraire on the assumption of no money illusion, the price vector p is essentially determined by setting up a vector of sectoral profit per unit ouput π in the equation[1]

(2) $$p' = p'A + \ell' + \pi',$$

where ℓ is a given labor inputs vector, which is positive given the indispensability of labor. The solution $p = \sigma$ of equation (2) for $\pi = 0$ is the economy's labor value vector.

Let $F(p)$ be the demand vector of workers and $G(p, s_1, s_2, \ldots, s_j, \ldots, s_n)$ be the demand vector of capitalists' households, where s_j is the profit of the j th sector. Let further $L(p)$ be the supply of labor at p.

For a predetermined nonnegative profit per unit output vector π, which determines p in (2), the gross output vector $x = (x_i)$ is determined by:

J. B. Say's Case

(3) $$x = Ax + F(p) + G(p, \pi_1 x_1, \pi_2 x_2, \ldots, \pi_n x_n).$$

Keynesian Case

(4) $$x = Ax + F(p) + G(p, \pi_1 x_1, \pi_2 x_2, \ldots, \pi_n x_n) + \omega d$$

both subject to full employment requirement

(5) $$L(p) = \ell'x \, ,$$

where $d \geq 0^2$ is a given constant investment composition vector and ω is a nonnegative scalar indicating the level of investment.

In the work previously cited it was shown that the output levels, including ω, are uniquely determinate under appropriate conditions on F, G and L. The profit per unit output vector π therefore determines the output vector x and the scale of investment ω. They are thereby functions of π, $x = x(\pi)$ and $\omega = \omega(\pi)$, which are termed objective demand functions. Thus capitalists as producers are potentially capable of regulating the state of the economy by controlling π. Determination of π is ultimately dependent on monopolistic competition among sectors in one of its alternative forms, including, e.g., joint maximization of surplus value or aggregate profit, Cournot-Negishi noncooperative perceived profit maximization and so forth.

1.3. Dynamic Adjustments

In the economy whose basic working is characterized above, disequilibrium in the sense of excess demand for or supply of goods induces adjustments in output toward equilibrium, rather than changes in the prices of goods. Prices need not be sensitive to the imbalance of demand and supply. They are more apt to change through visible hands of producers. How the visible hands perform depends on the entrepreneurial behaviors of producers. A typical case of such a pricing is full cost pricing at fixed mark-up rates. It will be shown in Subsections 2.2 and 2.3 that the profit per unit output vector converges to an equilibrium state and that the sectoral output levels also converge to their equilibrium levels determined by equation (3) or (4) subject to (5), if output is adjusted in the direction of the excess of demand over supply while prices change on the full cost principle.

Another kind of the adjustment of the profit per unit output vector takes place in a dynamized process of the Cournot-Negishi noncooperative ex ante perceived profit maximization. Subsection 2.4 discusses convergence to a Cournot-Negishi solution along the objective demand schedules on the assumption that output adjustments to balance demand and supply are instantaneous.

1.4. Uniform Diagonal Dominance

In Nikaido [forthcoming, a] fundamental workability of the economy, namely, existence and uniqueness of solution, is established by virtue of the Brouwer fixed point theorem and certain univalence theorems due to Gale and myself [1965]. However, the Jacobian matrices of the relevant mappings have dominant diagonals for a set of weights constant throughout their domains. This fact simplifies the discussion for workability. It is remarkable that the existence and uniqueness of a solution can be proved simultaneously under this kind of uniform diagonal dominance. In Section 3 are presented a number of results in this line, including the one just mentioned.

2. DYNAMIC PROCESSES

2.1. The Assumptions

The following conditions are assumed:

(P) A is productive enough to meet positive amounts of final demand for goods. That is to say, the Hawkins-Simon conditions hold so that $I - A$ is invertible and $(I - A)^{-1}$ is nonnegative, where I is the identity matrix.

(W.1) $F(p) = (F_i(p))$ is a nonnegative, continuously differentiable vector-valued function of the positive price vector p.

(W.2) The identity holds:

(6) $$p'F(p) = L(p),$$

which implies, among other things, the nonnegativity and continuous differentiability of $L(p)$.

(W.3) $L(p)$ tends to zero when p_j ($j = 1, 2, \ldots, n$) tend to $+\infty$ simultaneously.

(W.4) $L(\sigma) > 0$.

(C.1) $G(p, s_1, s_2, \ldots, s_n) = (G_i(p, s_1, s_2, \ldots, s_n))$ is a nonnegative, continuous, vector-valued function of the positive p and nonnegative s_j's.

(C.2) Each component function G_i has continuous partial derivatives, and those with respect to s_j satisfy

(7) $$G_{ij} = \frac{\partial G_i}{\partial s_j} \geq 0 \quad (i, j = 1, 2, \ldots, n),$$

that is, there are no inferior goods for capitalists' households.

(C.3) For J. B. Say's case there holds the identity

(8) $$p'G(p, s_1, s_2, \ldots, s_n) = \sum_{j=1}^{n} s_j .$$

(C.4) For the Keynesian case the average propensity of capitalists' households to spend is uniformly less than unity, that is, there is a constant θ such that $1 > \theta > 0$ and

(9) $$p'G(p, s_1, s_2, \ldots, s_n) \leq \theta \sum_{j=1}^{n} s_j .$$

(C.5) For the Keynsian case the marginal propensities of capitalists' households to spend are not larger than unity, that is

(10) $\quad \dfrac{\partial}{\partial s_j} \; p'G = \displaystyle\sum_{i=1}^{n} p_i \dfrac{\partial G_i}{\partial s_j} \; \leqq 1 \quad (j = 1, \, 2, \, \ldots, \, n) \; .$

There are immediate consequences from these assumptions. First of all, it is noted that in J. B. Say's case the full employment requirement (5) automatically follows from equation (3). For premultiplication of (3) by p' gives rise to (5) because of (2), (6) and (8).

Second, in view of the fact that ω is determined in equations (4) and (5) so that potential underemployment or labor-shortage equilibrium is avoided, the Keynesian case can be reduced to J. B. Say's case as long as the static workability of the economy is concerned. In fact this can be done by introducing an adjusted G function

$$G^{*}(p, \, s_1, \, s_2, \, \ldots, \, s_n) = G(p, \, s_1, \, s_2, \, \ldots, \, s_n)$$

(11)

$$+ \; \omega(p, \, s_1, \, s_2, \, \ldots, \, s_n)d$$

and formulating (3) for it, where

(12) $\quad \omega(p, \, s_1, \, s_2, \, \ldots, \, s_n) = \{\displaystyle\sum_{j=1}^{n} s_j - p'G(p, \, s_1, \, s_2, \, \ldots, \, s_n)\}/p'd \; .$

It is readily verified that G^{*} satisfies (C. 3) by construction, and (C. 2)

$$\dfrac{\partial G_i^{*}}{\partial s_j} = \dfrac{\partial G_i}{\partial s_j} + (1 - \dfrac{\partial}{\partial s_j} \; p'G)/p'd \geqq 0$$

by (7) and (10).

2.2. Output Adjustments Under Full Cost Pricing: J. B. Say's Case

Under full cost pricing the j th sector prices the j th good by adding a profit margin to the current direct material and labor cost by $100 \, \delta_j$ per cent. Then, the prices change over time conforming to

$$\dot{p}_j = \mu_j \text{ times the } j \text{ th component of}$$

(13) $$R(p) = p'A(I + D) + \ell'(I + D) - p'$$

$$(j = 1, 2, \ldots, n),$$

where a dot means differentiation with respect to time, and μ_j are speeds of adjustment and

(14) $$D = \begin{pmatrix} \delta_1 & & & O \\ & \delta_2 & & \\ & & \ddots & \\ O & & & \delta_n \end{pmatrix}.$$

Output is adjusted in the direction of excess of demand over supply, and the adjustment is represented by

$$\dot{x}_i = \lambda_i \text{ times the } i \text{ th component of}$$

(15) $$Q(x, p) = Ax + F(p) + G(p, \pi_1 x_1, \pi_2 x_2, \ldots, \pi_n x_n) - x$$

$$(i = 1, 2, \ldots, n)$$

where λ_i are speeds of adjustment and

(16) $$\pi' = (p'A + \ell')D.$$

THEOREM 1. If the mark-up rates δ_i are small enough to permit $I - A(I + D)$ to have a nonnegative inverse, the movements of p and x determined by (13) and (15) are stable, and p and x converge to unique $\hat{p}$ and $\hat{x}$, respectively.

PROOF. (In this proof as well as in those following the basic assumptions will be used whenever required without explicit reference to them each time.) First of all, it is noted that the price movement is independent of and separated from the output movement, whereas the

460

latter depends on the former. The convergence of the price vector to a unique equilibrium price vector $\hat{p}$ determined by

(17) $$\hat{p}' = \hat{p}'A(I + D) + \ell'(I + D)$$

is well known. In fact, the invertibility of $I - A(I + D)$ with a nonnegative inverse implies the unique determination of $\hat{p}' = \ell'(I+D)\{I-A(I+D)\}^{-1}$ on the static side and the negative real parts of all eigenvalues of $A(I + D) - I$ on the dynamic side, and thereby ensures the convergence.

The moving price vector, which has started at a positive initial price vector, remains positive forever in the course of its convergence to $\hat{p}$. For $\dot{p}_j$ will be positive whenever p_j becomes too small by (13). This ensures, in particular, the positivity of the changing profit per unit output vector π' by (16). If the initial position of the output vector $x(0)$ is nonnegative, (15) generates an adjustment process forever. For $\dot{x}_i$ will be nonnegative by (15) and the positivity of π' whenever x_i reaches zero while x having remained nonnegative. Therefore it makes sense to see where the adjustment process will lead.

Equation (3) has a unique solution $x = \hat{x}$ for $p = \hat{p}$ and the corresponding $\pi = \hat{\pi}$, as established in my previously cited book or as will be shown alternatively in Section 3 below. It will be proved that the changing output vector converges to this $\hat{x}$.

To this end, first of all, let us examine the boundedness of x. The prices, which converge to the components of $\hat{p}$ while remaining positive, are bounded uniformly away from zero by common positive constants. Hence $L(p)$ is also bounded by continuity.

Let

$$\Lambda = \begin{pmatrix} \lambda_1 & & & O \\ & \lambda_2 & & \\ & & \ddots & \\ O & & & \lambda_n \end{pmatrix}$$

$$M = \begin{pmatrix} \mu_1 & & & O \\ & \mu_2 & & \\ & & \ddots & \\ O & & & \mu_n \end{pmatrix} .$$

Then, premultiplication of $\Lambda^{-1}\dot{x}$ by p' gives

$$\frac{d}{dt}(p'\Lambda^{-1}x) = \dot{p}'\Lambda^{-1}x + p'(A - I)x + p'F + p'G$$

(18)
$$= \dot{p}'\Lambda^{-1}x + (\dot{p}'M^{-1} - \ell' - \pi')x + L(p) + \pi'x$$

$$= L(p) - \{\ell' - \dot{p}'(\Lambda^{-1} + M^{-1})\}x$$

by (13), (15) and (16) together with (6) and (8). Since p and $\dot{p}$ tend to $\hat{p}$ and zero, respectively,

$$\ell' - \dot{p}'(\Lambda^{-1} + M^{-1}) \geqq \varepsilon p'\Lambda^{-1} \quad (\varepsilon = \text{a positive constant})$$

for large t. Hence (18) implies

(19)
$$\frac{d}{dt}(p'\Lambda^{-1}x) \leqq L(p) - \varepsilon p'\Lambda^{-1}x$$

when t becomes large, which ensures the boundedness of $p'\Lambda^{-1}x$ by that of $L(p)$. From this follows the boundedness of $\hat{p}'\Lambda^{-1}x$, whence that of x by its nonnegativity.

Next let us evaluate the Jacobian matrix of the compound system of (13) and (15), whose elements are bounded along the bounded trajectories of x and p. The Jacobian matrix is evaluated as

(20)
$$\begin{pmatrix} \Lambda & O \\ O & M \end{pmatrix} \begin{pmatrix} A + \left(\dfrac{\partial G_i}{\partial s_j}\right)\Pi - I & N \\ O & (I + D)A' - I \end{pmatrix}$$

where

$$\Pi = \begin{pmatrix} \pi_1 & & & O \\ & \pi_2 & & \\ & & \ddots & \\ O & & & \pi_n \end{pmatrix}$$

and $N = (n_{ij})$ is a square matrix of order n and n_{ij} is the partial derivative of the right-hand side of the i th equation in (15) with respect to p_j.

Now, partially differentiating (3) with respect to s_j, we have

(21)
$$p'\left(\frac{\partial G_i}{\partial s_j}\right) = (1, 1, \ldots, 1) .$$

Then, (13) and (21) imply

$$p'\left\{A + \left(\frac{\partial G_i}{\partial s_j}\right)\Pi - I\right\} = \mathring{p}'M^{-1} - \ell' ,$$

so that

(22)
$$\hat{p}'\left\{A + \left(\frac{\partial G_i}{\partial s_j}\right)\Pi - I\right\} \leqq -\frac{\ell'}{2} < 0'$$

along the trajectory for large t.

Additionally, $\hat{p}'(|n_{ij}|)$ is bounded along the trajectory, and hence

(23)
$$m'\{(I + D)A' - I\} + \hat{p}'(|n_{ij}|) \leqq -c' < 0'$$

for constant positive vectors m and c by the invertibility of $I - A(I+D)$ with a nonnegative inverse.

Note that

$$A + \left(\frac{\partial G_i}{\partial s_j}\right)\Pi \quad \text{and} \quad (I + D)A'$$

463

are nonnegative matrices under (7). Then (22) and (23) imply that the Jacobian matrix has a negative dominant diagonal with respect to column sum with the weight vector

$$(\hat{p}'\Lambda^{-1}, \quad m'M^{-1})$$

along the trajectory for large t. Therefore, following the idea of Karlin [1959, Chap. 9, Th. 9.5.1.] and defining the Liapounov function

$$V(x, \; p) = \sum_{i=1}^{n} (\hat{p}_i/\lambda_i) \, |\lambda_i Q_i(x, \; p)| + \sum_{j=1}^{n} (m_j/\mu_j) \, |\mu_j R_j(p)|$$

we can show that

$$\frac{d^+ V}{dt} \leqq - \sum_{j=1}^{n} (\ell_j/2) \, |\lambda_j Q_j(x, \; p)| - \sum_{i=1}^{n} c_i \, |\mu_i R_i(p)|$$

along the trajectory for large t, where d^+/dt denotes one-sided differentiation. Hence the convergence of x to $\hat{x}$ follows. This completes the proof of Theorem 1.

2.3. Output Adjustments Under Full Cost Pricing: The Keynesian Case

The adjustment process applies to J. B. Say's case transformed from the Keynesian case through (11) as well. In such a situation, however, ω is adjusted instantaneously following the adjustments of x and p. This is somewhat unsymmetrical.

In order to adjust ω in a manner similar to x let us assume that ω changes in the direction of excess of total profit over the sum of spending from profit and investment demand. Then

$$\dot{\omega} = \lambda_0 [\pi'x - p'\{G(p, \; \pi_1 x_1, \; \pi_2 x_2, \; \ldots, \; \pi_n x_n) + \omega d\}]$$

(24)
$$\dot{x}_i = \lambda_i \text{ times the } i \text{ th component of}$$

$$Q(\omega, \; x, \; p) = Ax + F(p) + G(p, \; \pi_1 x_1, \; \pi_2 x_2, \; \ldots, \; \pi_n x_n) + \omega d - x$$

$$(i = 1, \; 2, \; \ldots, \; n)$$

while the behavior of p is regulated by (13) as before.

THEOREM 2. Under the same conditions on δ_j as in Theorem 1, the movements of ω, x and p determined by (13) and (24) are stable, and there will be convergence of ω, x and p to unique $\hat{\omega}$, $\hat{x}$ and $\hat{p}$ determined by equations (4), (5) and (17).

PROOF. A sketch of an analogous proof will be given. p tends to $\hat{p}$ while remaining positive, as in Theorem 1. x_i and ω will never become negative, and can be generated without limit. The nonnegativity of ω follows from $\dot{\omega} \geq 0$ whenever ω reaches zero while x, ω having remained nonnegative, since $\pi'x - p'G \geq (1 - \theta)\pi'x \geq 0$ by (9). The nonnegativity of x is ensured for similar reasons.

It can readily be verified in the light of (6) that equation (5) is equivalent to

$$\pi'x = p'(G + \omega d)$$

under equation (4). Hence the critical point of the compound system of (13) and (24) is uniquely determined as $\hat{\omega}$, $\hat{x}$ and $\hat{p}$ by (4), (5) and (17), to which the convergence of the solution is asserted.

The boundedness of the solution can be seen as follows. The boundedness of ω will immediately follow by the first equation in (24) regulating $\dot{\omega}$ once x proves bounded. Next the boundedness of x can be seen by considering the following inequality, similar to (19),

$$\frac{d}{dt}p'\Lambda^{-1}x + \lambda_0^{-1}\dot{\omega} \leq L(p) - \varepsilon p'\Lambda^{-1}x,$$

which holds for large t and a positive constant ε, and the fact that the first equation in (24) implies $(1 - \theta)\pi'x < \omega p'd$ in case $\dot{\omega} < 0$.

The Jacobian matrix of the compound system of (13) and (24) is evaluated as

$$(25) \begin{pmatrix} \lambda_0 & 0 & 0 \\ 0 & \Lambda & 0 \\ 0 & 0 & M \end{pmatrix} \begin{pmatrix} -p'd & \pi' - p'\left(\dfrac{\partial G_i}{\partial s_j}\right)\textstyle\prod & \\ d & A + \left(\dfrac{\partial G_i}{\partial s_j}\right)\textstyle\prod - I & N \\ 0 & 0 & (I + D)A' - I \end{pmatrix}$$

where $N = (n_{ij})$ is an $(n + 1) \times n$ matrix. It is noted that

$$\pi' - p'\left(\frac{\partial G_i}{\partial s_j}\right)\textstyle\prod \geq 0'$$

by (10). Clearly

$$p'd > 0, \quad d \geq 0$$

$$A + \left(\frac{\partial G_i}{\partial s_j}\right)\textstyle\prod \geq 0, \quad (I + D)A' \geq 0 .$$

Finally, the Jacobian matrix has a negative dominant diagonal with respect to column sum with the positive weight vector

$$(\rho, \hat{p}', m') \begin{pmatrix} \lambda_0^{-1} & 0 & 0 \\ 0 & \Lambda^{-1} & 0 \\ 0 & 0 & M^{-1} \end{pmatrix}$$

along the trajectory for large t, provided a scalar $\rho > 1$ and a positive vector m are suitably chosen, similarly as in Theorem 1. Thereby Karlin's method can be applied. This completes the proof.

2.4. Adjustments Toward the Cournot-Negishi Solution

It is now assumed that output is adjusted instantaneously in response to the predetermined profit per unit output vector toward the level determined by the objective demand function $x(\pi)$. Nonetheless producers

466

need not know the true shapes of the objective demand schedules. They perceive subjective demand schedules and try to price their product so as to maximize the expected profit along the schedules. But the economy must find itself on the objective demand function, so long as all the markets are actually cleared. Thus, the Cournot-Negishi solution is defined to be such a point on the objective demand function that all producers are simultaneously maximizing their expected profits there. For a detailed discussion see Nikaido [forthcoming, a]

Let

$$(26) \qquad q_j = p_j - \eta_j(p, x)(y_j - x_j) \quad (j = 1, 2, \ldots, n)$$

be an inverse demand function perceived by the j th sector when supply x is currently cleared at the prices p. q_j is the expected price when the planned output y_j is supplied. The perceived demand functions are downward-sloping, so that $\eta_j(p, x) > 0$.

The j th sector maximizes the expected profit

$$\{(1 - a_{jj})q_j - \sum_{i \neq j} a_{ij}p_i - \ell_j\}y_j .$$

The maximization is worked out subject to the nonnegativity constraint $y_j \geq 0$. Nonetheless it always results in marginal conditions with vanishing derivatives, yielding

$$(27) \qquad (1 - a_{jj})q_j - \sum_{i \neq j} a_{ij}p_i - \ell_j = (1 - a_{jj})\eta_j y_j$$

$$(j = 1, 2, \ldots, n).$$

The right-hand side in the j th equation of (27) is the profit per unit output expected by the j th sector which is evaluated as

$$(28) \qquad \pi_j(p, x) = \frac{1}{2}\{(1 - a_{jj})\eta_j(p, x)x_j + \pi_j\}$$

$$(j = 1, 2, \ldots, n)$$

467

The Cournot-Negishi solution is a situation such that

(29) $$\pi_j = \pi_j(p, x(\pi)) \quad (j = 1, 2, \ldots, n)$$

and is obtained as a fixed point under the mapping $\pi \to (\pi_j(p, x(\pi)))$.

Now, assume producers price goods in the direction of their expectation (28) while the economy is moving on the objective demand function. Then, the actual profit per unit output changes conforming to

(30)
$$\dot{\pi}_j = \alpha_j(\pi_j(p, x(\pi)) - \pi_j)$$

$$(j = 1, 2, \ldots, n) .$$

If $\eta_j(p, x)$ are continuous for positive p and nonnegative x, system (30) is well-behaved, since $\dot{\pi}_j \geq 0$ when π_j reaches zero while π having started at a nonnegative initial position and remained nonnegative.

Now, suppose for simplicity that η_j are positive constants. Then, (30) is explicitly given as

(31)
$$\dot{\pi}_j = \alpha_j((1 - a_{jj})\eta_j x_j(\pi) - \pi_j)$$

$$(j = 1, 2, \ldots, n),$$

where the speeds of adjustment α_j are rearranged so as to include $1/2$.

THEOREM 3. The solution π of equation (31) converges to a Cournot-Negishi solution, provided the η_j are sufficiently small.

PROOF. It has already been noted that π remains nonnegative. $p \geq \sigma > 0$ for the labor value vector σ when $\pi \geq 0$. Therefore $x(\pi)$ is bounded for $\pi \geq 0$ by continuity, (5) and (W.3). Therefore the solution π of equation (30) is bounded. $x(\pi)$ has continuous partial derivatives, which are therefore bounded along the trajectory. Hence the Jacobian matrix of (31) has a negative dominant diagonal with respect to column sum with constant positive weights along the trajectory provided the η_j are sufficiently small. The convergence to a critical point can thereby be proved by Karlin's method. Q.E.D.

3. SYSTEMS HAVING UNIFORMLY DOMINANT DIAGONALS

3.1. Uniformly Dominant Diagonals

As is well known, a square matrix $T = (t_{ij})$ has a dominant diagonal, if there are positive weights α_i such that

$$(32) \qquad \alpha_j |t_{jj}| > \sum_{i \neq j} \alpha_i |t_{ij}| \qquad (j = 1, 2, \ldots, n).$$

Alternatively, T has a dominant diagonal, if there are positive weights α_j such that

$$(33) \qquad \alpha_i |t_{ii}| > \sum_{j \neq i} \alpha_j |t_{ij}| \qquad (i = 1, 2, \ldots, n).$$

The two definitions are equivalent, since both are equivalent to the fulfillment of the Hawkins-Simon conditions by the matrix (t_{ij}^*) whose elements are given by

$$t_{ij}^* = \begin{cases} |t_{ii}| & \text{if } i = j \\ \\ -|t_{ij}| & \text{otherwise.} \end{cases}$$

For general information about dominant diagonals we may consult McKenzie [1960].

If T, whose elements are functions defined on a set, has a dominant diagonal throughout the set, the weights α_i in (32) are generally different from palace to place in the set. Thus in the case of a matrix whose elements are functions we may strengthen diagonal dominance to

DEFINITION 1. T has a uniformly dominant diagonal with respect to column sum (abbr. c-u.d.d.), if there are constant positive weights α_i such that (32) holds uniformly.

DEFINITION 2. T has a uniformly dominant diagonal with respect to row sum (abbr. r-u.d.d.), if there are constant positive weights α_j such that (33) holds uniformly.

It goes without saying that both versions of uniform diagonal dominance need not be equivalent. Uniform diagonal dominance remarkably simplifies discussion not only of stability but also of static workability (uniqueness and/or existence of a solution).

3.2. Uniqueness by Uniform Diagonal Dominance

Consider a system of equations

$$(34) \qquad f_i(x) = 0 \qquad (i = 1, 2, \ldots, n)$$

where the functions on the left-hand side are continuously differentiable in a convex domain X of the n-dimensional Euclidean space.

THEOREM 3. If the Jacobian matrix of (34) has a c-u.d.d. in X, then its solution is unique.

PROOF. Let

$$f_{ij}(x) = \frac{\partial f_i}{\partial x_j} \qquad (i, j = 1, 2, \ldots, n).$$

The diagonal elements f_{jj} never vanish but are of a definite sign. Therefore, it may be assumed by replacing f_j by $-f_j$ if necessary that the Jacobian matrix has a positive c-u.d.d.

Suppose that there are two solutions $a = (a_j)$ and $b = (b_j)$ of (34). If $a_j < b_j$ for some components j, we can perform linear transformations $x_j \rightarrow -x_j$, $f_j \rightarrow -f_j$ simultaneously for all such j. The Jacobian matrix of the transformed system still has a positive c-u.d.d. on the new transformed convex domain. Therefore we may assume,

470

without loss of generality, that $a \geq b$.

Define

$$\phi(t) = ta + (1 - t)b \qquad (1 \geq t \geq 0) .$$

Then, in view of the positive c-u.d.d.,

$$\frac{d}{dt} \sum_{i=1}^{n} \alpha_i f_i(\phi(t))$$

$$= \sum_{j=1}^{n} \sum_{i=1}^{n} \alpha_i f_{ij}(\phi(t))(a_j - b_j)$$

$$\geqq \sum_{j=1}^{n} (\alpha_j f_{jj} - \sum_{i \neq j} \alpha_i |f_{ij}|)(a_j - b_j) > 0 ,$$

which contradicts

$$\sum_{i=1}^{n} \alpha_i f_i(a) = \sum_{i=1}^{n} \alpha_i f_i(b) = 0 .$$

Q.E.D.

THEOREM 4. If the Jacobian matrix of (34) has a r-u.d.d. in X, then its solution is unique.

PROOF. It suffices to consider such two solutions a and b of (34) having a positive r-u.d.d. that $a \geq b$, as in Theorem 3. Let

$$\theta = \max_{j} \frac{a_j - b_j}{\alpha_j} = \frac{a_k - b_k}{\alpha_k} > 0 .$$

Then, in view of the positive r-u.d.d.,

$$\frac{d}{dt} f_k(\phi(t)) = \sum_{j=1}^{n} f_{kj}(\phi(t))(a_j - b_j)$$

$$\geqq f_{kk}(a_k - b_k) - \sum_{j \neq k} |f_{kj}|(a_j - b_j)$$

$$\geqq \theta(f_{kk}\alpha_k - \sum_{j \neq k} |f_{kj}|\alpha_j) > 0 ,$$

which contradicts

$$f_k(a) = f_k(b) = 0.$$

Q.E.D.

3.3. Existence and Uniqueness by Uniform Diagonal Dominance

Further strengthening of uniform diagonal dominance enables us to establish existence and uniqueness simultaneously in a simple way along with the idea in Nikaido [1972].

In this subsection the functions in equation (34) are assumed to satisfy the following conditions. (A) Their common domain is the non-negative orthant, namely, the set of all nonnegative x. (B) The off-diagonal elements of the Jacobian matrix are nonpositive

$$(35) \qquad f_{ij}(x) \leq 0 \quad (i \neq j)$$

and (C)

$$(36) \qquad f_i(x) \leq 0$$

whenever the i th component of x is zero.

Now we have

THEOREM 5. If the Jacobian matrix has a positive c-u.d.d. in the further stringent sense that

$$(37) \qquad (\alpha_1, \alpha_2, \ldots, \alpha_n)(f_{ij}(x)) \geq (\beta_1, \beta_2, \ldots, \beta_n)$$

uniformly for positive constants α_i, β_i, then equation (34) has a unique solution.

PROOF. The proof will be worked out by induction on n simultaneously for existence and uniqueness. If n = 1, system (34) consists of a single equation of a scalar variable

472

(38)
$$f_1(x) = 0$$

(37) in this case is specified to $\alpha_1 f_{11}(x) \geq \beta_1$, whence $f_{11}(x) \geq \beta_1/\alpha_1 > 0$ uniformly. Hence $f_1(x)$ monotonically increases without limit, as x increases from zero toward infinity. Thus a solution exists by continuity, since $f_1(0) \leq 0$ by (C), and the solution must be unique by monotonicity.

Suppose now the truth of the assertion for n - 1. For convenience of discussion let us rewrite (34) as

(39)
$$f_i(x_1, x_2, \ldots, x_{n-1}, x_n) = 0 \quad (i = 1, 2, \ldots, n-1)$$

(40)
$$f_n(x_1, x_2, \ldots, x_{n-1}, x_n) = 0$$

and consider the system of equations in the n-1 variables $x_1, x_2, \ldots, x_{n-1}$, (39), for each fixed nonnegative value of x_n.

This system satisfies all the assumptions of the theorem. In fact, (A), (B) and (C) are automatically met. Its Jacobian matrix is the principal submatrix J_n of order n-1 in the upper left corner of that of the original system. Since (37) holds and $f_{nj}(x) \leq 0$ (j < n) by (35), we have

(41)
$$(\alpha_1, \alpha_2, \ldots, \alpha_{n-1}) J_n \geq (\beta_1, \beta_2, \ldots, \beta_{n-1}) \cdot$$

Therefore, (39) has a unique solution $(x_1, x_2, \ldots, x_{n-1})$ for each fixed nonnegative value of x_n by the induction hypothesis for n-1, whence these x_j (j = 1, 2, $\ldots$, n-1) are functions of x_n

(42)
$$x_j = g_j(x_n) \quad (j = 1, 2, \ldots, n-1)$$

which satisfy by construction

(43)
$$f_i(g_1(x_n), g_2(x_n), \ldots, g_{n-1}(x_n), x_n) = 0 \quad (i = 1, 2, \ldots, n-1)$$

identically for $x_n \geq 0$.

Let

(44) $\qquad g(x_n) = f_n(g_1(x_n), g_2(x_n), \ldots, g_{n-1}(x_n), x_n)$.

Then equation (34) has a unique solution if and only if

(45) $\qquad\qquad\qquad\qquad g(x_n) = 0$

is uniquely solvable in the nonnegative unknown x_n.

$\qquad$ The rest of the proof is to see that equation (45) satisfies all the assumptions of the theorem for $n = 1$. In fact, (A) is clearly met, while (B) is meaningless. (C) is also met, since

$$g(0) = f_n(g_1(0), \ g_2(0), \ \ldots, \ g_{n-1}(0), \ 0) \leq 0$$

by (C) for the original system. Equations (35) and (37) imply that $(f_{ij}(x))$ is invertible with a nonnegative inverse, whence

(46) $\qquad (\alpha_1, \ \alpha_2, \ \ldots, \ \alpha_n) \geq (\beta_1, \ \beta_2, \ \ldots, \ \beta_n)(f_{ij}(x))^{-1}$.

$\qquad$ Let the elements of the n th column of $(f_{ij}(x))^{-1}$ be $h_{in}(x)$ $(i = 1, \ 2, \ \ldots, \ n)$, which are nonnegative. Then, from (46) follows in particular

$$\alpha_n \geq \sum_{i=1}^{n} \beta_i h_{in}(x) \geq \beta_n h_{nn}(x),$$

which reduces to

(47) $\qquad\qquad\qquad\qquad \alpha_n \geq \beta_n \dfrac{\det J_n}{\det(f_{ij}(x))}$.

Clearly $\det(f_{ij}(x)) > 0$ and $\det J_n > 0$ by the Hawkins-Simon conditions.

Hence (47) can be written as

(48)
$$\alpha_n \frac{\det(f_{ij}(x))}{\det J_n} \geqq \beta_n .$$

Now, the n-1 functions (42) are continuously differentiable by the implicit function theorem, and, upon differentiation, we have

$$\frac{dg}{dx_n} = \frac{\det(f_{ij}(x))}{\det J_n}$$

evaluated for the functions (42). Hence

$$\alpha_n \frac{dg}{dx_n} \geqq \beta_n$$

by (48). Thus all the assumptions are satisfied and equation (45) is uniquely solvable by virtue of the assertion for $n = 1$ already proved. Q.E.D.

THEOREM 6. If the Jacobian matrix has a positive r-u.d.d. in the further stringent sense that

(49)
$$(f_{ij}(x)) \begin{pmatrix} \alpha_1 \\ \alpha_2 \\ \vdots \\ \alpha_n \end{pmatrix} \geqq \begin{pmatrix} \beta_1 \\ \beta_2 \\ \vdots \\ \beta_n \end{pmatrix}$$

uniformly for positive constants α_j, β_j then equation (34) has a unique solution.

PROOF. The proof can be worked out in essentially the same way as in Theorem 5 and is left to the reader.

It is finally remarked that the static workability of the basic economy is within the reach of Theorem 5. In fact, if the i th component of the excess of the left-hand side over the right-hand side in (3) is denoted by $f_i(x)$, equation (3) is rewritten as equation (34), with the corresponding Jacobian matrix

$$(f_{ij}(x)) = I - \left(A + \left(\frac{\partial G_i}{\partial s_j}\right) \Pi \right).$$

Assumptions (A), (B) and (C) are clearly met. Moreover

$$p'(f_{ij}(x)) = \ell'$$

holds as a special case of (37). Therefore Theorem 5 can be applied. The Keynesian case (4), (5) can be transformed to J. B. Say's case, as was already noted.

NOTES

1. Here, as well as in the sequel, a prime denotes transposition.
2. Here, as well as in what follows, the following semi-order for vectors $x = (x_i)$, $y = (y_i)$ will be used:

$$x \geqq y \text{ if } x_i \geqq y_i \quad (i = 1, 2, \ldots, n)$$

$$x \geq y \text{ if } x \geqq y, \quad \text{and } x \neq y$$

$$x > y \text{ if } x_i > y_i \quad (i = 1, 2, \ldots, n).$$

REFERENCES

Gale, D. and H. Nikaido [1965], The Jacobian Matrix and Global Univalence of Mappings, Mathematische Annalen, 159, No. 2.

Karlin, S. [1959], Mathematical Methods and Theory in Games, Programming and Economics, Vol. I, Addison-Wesley.

McKenzie, L. W. [1960], Matrices with Dominant Diagonals and Economic Theory, Mathematical Methods in Social Sciences 1959, Stanford University Press.

Nikaido, H. [1972], Relative Shares and Factor Price Equalization, Journal of International Economics, Vol. 2, No. 3.

_____ [forthcoming, a], <u>Monopolistic Competition and Effective</u> <u>Demand</u>, Princeton University Press.

_____ [forthcoming, b], What is an Objective Demand Function ?, Zeitschrift für Nationalökonomie.

This work was supported by the Japan
Economic Research Foundation

Equilibrium in Stochastic Economic Models
Mukul Majumdar

CONTENTS

1. INTRODUCTION

The purpose of this paper is, first, to discuss briefly some conceptual problems in defining an equilibrium or a steady state in stochastic models in economics. Secondly, I analyze a dynamic model of resource allocation under uncertainty that has direct relevance to some practical planning problems. From this point of view, the present piece is a continuation of research reported in Majumdar [1972]. In the present model, the planner follows the classical rule of price-adjustment by raising the price when there is excess demand and lowering the price when there is excess supply. However, stocks of commodities can be carried over from one period to the next. Inventories are explicitly recognized in price setting since total supply at date t is not just current inflow of goods, but the sum of such inflow and the stocks carried over from the past period. My main concern is the existence of an equilibrium in the sense of a time-invariant joint distribution of stocks and prices.

There are interesting open questions related to the stability of this system. Moreover, very little is known about the optimality of a stochastic equilibrium. The nature of a stochastic equilibrium may be quite different qualitatively from that of its deterministic counterpart. This is illustrated in the last section by means of the familiar neoclassical aggregative optimal growth model. It would of course be interesting and desirable to throw light on some properties of a stochastic equilibrium that are of economic interest. Results of any significant generality have not been obtained so far, at least in the present context.

2. EQUILIBRIUM CONCEPTS IN STOCHASTIC ECONOMIC MODELS

2.1. Equilibrium and Uncertainty, A Brief Overview

Much of the analytical work in economic theory is devoted to characterization of some sort of an 'equilibrium' or 'a steady state'. An equilibrium is typically a state of the system satisfying some basic consistency conditions that make it self-perpetuating once it is attained. Perhaps the simplest example is that of an equilibrium in a single market in which demand and supply of the commodity are functions of the price of that commodity alone. An equilibrium price vector has the property that planned demand equals planned supply. In particular, if the prevailing market price is an equilibrium price, there will be no pressures for bringing about a change in the price. The rigorous formulation of the theory of the more general Walrasian equilibrium in which all markets are cleared simultaneously in a competitive economy has posed quite challenging mathematical questions and has been one of the most active areas of research in the past two decades. Part of the interest in the static theory has surely been due to the fact that a Walrasian competitive equilibrium enjoys some fundamental efficiency properties. An equilibrium is in the core, in particular it is Pareto optimal; moreover, when we ask ourselves how to characterize an efficient decentralized economy, it turns out to be a competitive equilibrium relative to a suitable price system.

In dynamic models of intertemporal resource allocation, it is often shown that optimal paths of capital accumulation happen to converge to paths that are stationary or time invariant in some sense. Examples of such limiting steady states are the (modified) golden rule program and the von Neumann path (along which the highest rate of growth is attained consistent with the condition that the proportion among different sectors remains the same over time). It is fair to say that such stability properties along with the normative implications have contributed as much to the importance of equilibrium analysis as the desire to study the logical coherence and consistency of a model itself.

Motivation behind the various attempts to go beyond the framework of equilibrium analysis under perfect certainty has come from different sources. In one direction, the point of departure has been the model of Arrow and Debreu (see Chapter 7 of Debreu's Theory of Value [1959]) that suggested a possible generalization of the standard Walrasian model to allow for uncertainty (by a suitable redefinition of the commodity space). The inadequacies of this approach have been spelled out in the literature[1] and naturally subsequent research was directed to developing more satisfactory models. In talking about the market price of a good at different dates and different states of the environment, the Arrow-Debreu model required in principle "a complete system of insurance and future markets which appears to be too complex, detailed and refined to have any practical significance." Similarly, the theory did not take account of at least three important institutional features of a modern economy-- money, the stock market and active markets at every date. Consequently, some of the major macroeconomic questions related to these institutions cannot be easily dealt with in the Arrow-Debreu framework. An interesting literature treating equilibrium with a sequence of spot markets has been developed, and efficiency properties of such temporary equilibria under uncertainty have also been studied.

Another important direction has been the literature related to informational aspects of uncertainty. The Arrow-Debreu approach required all agents to have the same information structures. Along with general equilibrium models with agents having distince information structures, there has been exhaustive analysis of simpler--often partial equilibrium models of agents making decisions on the basis of imperfect information. Stimulated by Stigler's well-known paper "The Economics of Information" [1961], answers to quite specific questions have been sought, by assuming away many of the complexities usually faced in a general equilibrium system. While there is some overlapping of ideas and techniques, I shall not attempt to relate what follows to this important literature. The interested reader is referred to the survey by Rothschild [1973]. I shall start with the example of a static exchange economy in which the preferences and endowments of the agents are random. The structural simplicity of the model enables one to derive strong results and provides an extremely convenient framework for bringing out some of the fundamental conceptual difficulties one has to face in developing a theory of equilibrium under uncertainty.

2.2. Random Exchange Economies

It is not clear that a single equilibrium concept is useful or interesting in all stochastic cases, even if it happens to exist (i.e., is consistent with the assumptions of the model). The usual properties of a deterministic equilibrium may not simply be consistent when randomness is present. This is most easily seen in the framework of a random exchange economy, studied by Hildenbrand [1971], Bhattacharya and Majumdar [1973] and others. Recall that in the standard deterministic model of an exchange economy, an agent α is completely described by his demand function d reflecting his tastes and preference and his endowment e. The following notation will be used in the discussion. R_+ (resp. R_{++}) is the set of non-negative (resp. positive) reals. An ℓ-vector $x = (x_i)$ is strictly positive, written $x >> 0$, if x_i is in R_{++} for all $i = 1, 2, \ldots, \ell$. It is non-negative, written $x \geq 0$, if x_i is in R_+ for all i. R_+^ℓ (resp. R_{++}^ℓ) is the set of all non-negative (resp.

strictly positive) ℓ-vectors. $P = \{x \varepsilon R^{\ell}, \; x >> 0, \; \sum_{i=1}^{\ell} x_i = 1\}$. $\overline{P}$ is the closure of P. For two ℓ-vectors $x = (x_i)$ and $y = (y_i)$, $\langle x, y \rangle = \sum_{i=1}^{\ell} x_i y_i$. For an ℓ-vector x, $\|x\|$ is the standard Euclidean norm.

A <u>demand</u> <u>function</u> $d : P \times R_{++} \to R_+^{\ell}$ satisfies

    a) d is continuous

    b) $\langle p \cdot d(p, w) \rangle = w$ for each p in P and w in R_{++}

    c) if a sequence (p_n, w_n) in $P \times R_{++}$ converges to some (p, w) in $(\overline{P} \backslash P) \times R_{++}$, then $\|d(p_n, w_n)\|$ tends to ∞.

The last condition (c) describes the desirability of all goods while (b) requires that the budget constraint be satisfied (i.e., the value of the commodity vector d demanded at the price vector p and wealth w must be equal to the wealth). Let M be the set of all demand functions and G be a compact subset of R_{++}^{ℓ}. G is taken to be the set of all admissible endowments. An agent α is formally described as a point $d = (d, e)$ in $M \times G$, the space of all characteristics. If the agents behave competitively, the wealth w and excess demand $\xi(\alpha, p)$ of an agent $\alpha \equiv (d, e)$ corresponding to a price vector $p >> 0$ are given by $w \equiv \langle p, e \rangle$ and $\xi(\alpha, p) \equiv d(p, w) - e$ respectively. The total excess demand for the whole economy $\mathcal{E}$ corresponding some $p >> 0$ is given by $\xi_{\mathcal{E}}(p) = \sum_{\alpha} \xi(\alpha, p)$. Thus $\xi_{\mathcal{E}}(p)$ is the sum of the individual excess demand vectors. An equilibrium $p^* >> 0$ satisfies $\xi_{\mathcal{E}}(p^*) = 0$. One can show (see e.g., Debreu [1970]) that the set of all equilibrium price vectors is non-empty.

To introduce stochastic elements, a <u>random</u> <u>agent</u> α is a ($\mathcal{F}$-measurable) map from $(\Omega, \mathcal{F}, \mu)$ with values in the space of characteristics $M \times G$. The set $M \times G$ can be taken to be a metric space. Let $\hat{\mathcal{F}}$ be the Borel σ-field of $M \times G$. We assume that for any F in $\hat{\mathcal{F}}$, $\alpha^{-1}(F)$ belongs to $\mathcal{F}$. Ω is to be interpreted as the set of all states of the environment. Each ω of Ω completely specifies the characteristics $\alpha(\omega)$ of the agent α. The simplest interpretation is to say that the preferences depend on ω, which presumably describes all factors like climatic conditions affecting the agent. For a random exchange economy $\mathcal{E}$ consisting of a finite number of agents, the total excess demand corresponding to any $p \gg 0$ is random and is given as $\xi(\omega, p) = \sum_{\alpha(\omega)} \xi(\alpha(\omega), p)$.

It is easy to construct examples with just two states ω_1 and ω_2, such that there is no $p^* \gg 0$ satisfying $\xi(\omega_i, p^*) = 0$ for both $i = 1, 2$. Of course, by appealing to the measurable choice theorem it is straightforward to assert the existence of a <u>random price equilibrium</u> i.e., of a ($\mathcal{F}$-measurable) function $p(\cdot)$ from Ω into P such that $\xi(\omega, p(\omega)) = 0$ for a.e.ω. The problem of characterizing the distribution of (a suitably normalized) random price equilibrium was discussed in Bhattacharya and Majumdar [1973]. Of course, even in a dynamic context, one can try to characterize alternative paths of market clearing prices (with proper attention paid to questions like nonuniqueness of equilibrium prices).

An alternative concept of equilibrium suggests itself--instead of requiring market clearance at each state, one may insist only on excess demand being zero (or small) "on the average". It has been shown that if (a) the agents are stochastically independent and (b) if $\mathcal{E}_n$ is an increasing sequence of economies such that the probability distributions of all the agents[2] belong to a compact set,[3] then there is a sequence (p_n) of price vectors such that a) $E\xi_{\mathcal{E}_n}(\cdot, p_n) = 0$ for all n, i.e., expected excess demand corresponding to p_n is zero and b) for any $\delta > 0$, $\mu\{\omega \in \Omega : |\xi_{\mathcal{E}_n}(\ , p_n)|/N_n \leq \delta\}$ goes to one as n tends to infinity, N_n being the total number of agents in $\mathcal{E}_n$, i.e., per capita excess demand in $\mathcal{E}_n$ converges in probability to zero. If one is interested in such an equilibrium concept, one must recognize <u>that in such an equilibrium the plans of some agents may well be inconsistent with probability one</u>. If one is serious about a possible application of such a concept to dynamic situations, one has to provide some explanation of how the market is going to react is excess supply (or demand) shows up persistently and if (in absolute terms) it is of significant magnitude. I shall

484

come back to this point later on. A deeper difficulty with such a concept is brought out by Föllmer's analysis [1974]. If the preferences of the agents depend on a common factor (like climatic conditions), they are likely to be highly correlated. Thus, the assumption of stochastic independence is far from innocuous. Föllmer has presented a systematic analysis of stochastic dependence in a model with a countably infinite set of agents represented by Z^v (where Z is the set of integers and v is any positive integer greater than or equal to one). An agent $\alpha(\cdot)$ can be influenced only by his "neighbors" $N(\alpha) = \{b : \|b - a\| = 1\}$. It is quite difficult to formalize adequately the various facets of the complex process of interaction among agents, and Föllmer has attempted to capture "multidirectional interaction" among agents. He has shown that if interaction is sufficiently weak or the structure of interaction is sufficiently simple ($v=1$), one can prove the existence of a price vector p such that (roughly speaking) per capita excess demand converges to zero in probability. More interestingly, he has given an example of a class of economies with just two states of the environment, and $v=2$ in which such an equilibrium almost never exists. Things are worse for a larger value of v, as the structure of interaction gets more complex. Nonexistence is the typical rule when the agents have the propensity to go with the trend as reflected in the states of their neighbors. Thus, the existence of this type of equilibrium seems to depend criticallly on absence of Bandwagon effects or the well-known psychology associated with bank-runs and galloping inflations.

Both the concepts discussed above have immediate relevance to the problem of price-setting under uncertainty. Of course, if the prices have to be set without the knowledge of which state of the environment will obtain, the concept of a random price equilibrium is likely to be of little use. If the planner can approximate the true distribution of the random excess demand corresponding to any given p, then rules like "set a $p \gg 0$ such that expected excess demand is zero, and per capita excess demand is very likely to be small" may provide helpful guidelines.

On the other hand, it would certainly be useful to know how much prices are going to vary from one state of the environment to another if markets are to be cleared. If such variations seem excessively large, appropriate regulations of the endowments (or supply) might be undertaken to stabilize the situation. For another ingenious application of the concept of an equilibrium in the average sense see Malinvaud [1972]. However, it is perhaps quite unnecessary to emphasize the formal distinction between the two types of equilibrium--in one case, the price vector is itself a random variable, in the other it is not. Whether one prefers one to the other depends on the nature of application one has in mind.

3. EQUILIBRIUM AS AN INVARIANT DISTRIBUTION

3.1. Background

In this section I shall concentrate on the concept of an equilibrium as an invariant distribution of the relevant variables in the stochastic models. Such an equilibrium concept has some appeal from a purely descriptive point of view. For the usual model of price determination under certainty, observed price changes are simply inconsistent with the markets being in equilibrium. As Rothschild has observed, "variety and volatility of prices, the commonplaces of our experience that led Stigler to formulate his original model, disappear from the scene once equilibrium is established. This is unfortunate, since these phenomena do not seem to be disappearing from the world. If our theories are to apply to situations in which distributions of prices persist, we are going to have to develop broader equilibrium concepts." Results on the existence, uniqueness and stability of such a stochastic equilibrium have been obtained for many different models (see, e.g., Majumdar and Green [1972], Lucas and Prescott [1974], Brock and Mirman [1972]).[4] I shall first formulate a simple model of resource allocation under uncertainty and prove the existence of a stochastic equilibrium. Interestingly enough, the nature of such a stochastic equilibrium may well be qualitatively different from its deterministic counterpart. This point is most easily brought out by using the aggregative model of capital accumulation which I take up in Section 4. There I shall sketch a method of proving the existence of a stochastic steady state that is applicable to more general models with multiple capital goods. It is convenient to recall at this point a few definitions and results from the theory of Markov processes before the formal models are set up.

3.2. Some Results from the Theory of Markov Processes

Let $\mathfrak{X} = \{x_n\}_{n>0}$ be a Markov Process with a state space S, a compact subset of R^{ℓ}, and a stationary transitional kernel $\lambda(x, F)$ defined on $S \times \mathcal{B}$, where $\mathcal{B}$ is the Borel σ-field of S. By definition, $\lambda(x, F)$ satisfies (i) for each $x \varepsilon S$, $\lambda(x, \cdot)$ is a probability distribution on $\mathcal{B}$ and (ii) for each $F \varepsilon \mathcal{B}$, $\lambda(\cdot, F)$ is $\mathcal{B}$-measurable. The interpretation of $\lambda(x, \cdot)$ is simply that it gives the conditional distribution of x_{n+1} given $x_n = x$, i.e., $\lambda(x, F)$ is the probability that x_{n+1} belongs to F given $x_n = x$. The kernel and the initial distribution π_0 of x_0 determine the distribution of $\mathfrak{X}$. If π_n is the distribution of x_n, the distribution π_{n+1} of x_{n+1} is determined simply by taking for any F in $\mathcal{B}$,

$$(3.1) \qquad \pi_{n+1}(F) = \int_S \lambda(\cdot, F) d\pi_n .$$

An invariant distribution π^* of $\mathfrak{X}$ satisfies for each F in $\mathcal{B}$

$$(3.2) \qquad \pi^*(F) = \int_S \lambda(, F) d\pi^* .$$

Thus, if the distribution of x_n happens to be π^*, then the distribution of all x_m, $m \geq n+1$ will be π^*. In fact, if the initial distribution of x_0 happens to be π^*, the process is stationary. We shall use the following

PROPOSITION 3.1. Let $\mathfrak{X}$ be a Markov process with a compact state space S, a subset of R^ℓ. Suppose that for any sequence x_n in S converging to x in S, one has the sequence $\lambda(x_n,)$ of probability distributions converging weakly to $\lambda(x,)$. Then an invariant distribution of the Markov process necessarily exists.

For the sake of completeness, let us see how Proposition 3.1 follows from a more general result in the theory of Markov Process. Let $C(S)$ be the space of all real valued continuous functions on S. For any f in $C(S)$ define the iterates f_t on S for $t \geq 1$, with $f_0 \equiv f$ as

$$(3.3) \qquad f_t(x) = \int_S f_{t-1} d\lambda(x,) \ .$$

First, check that under our assumption for any f in $C(S)$, f_t belongs to $C(S)$ for all $t \geq 1$. For $t = 1$, let x_n be any sequence in S converging to x_0 in S. Since $\lambda(x_n,)$ converges weakly to $\lambda(x_0,)$ it follows that $\int_S f d\lambda(x_n,)$ converges to $\int_S f d\lambda(x_0,)$ implying (from (3.3)) that $f_1(x_n)$ converges to $f_1(x_0)$. By the same argument, f_t belongs to $C(S)$ for all $t \geq 2$. The fundamental theorem of Yosida [1966, p. 395] states that under this condition, a necessary and sufficient condition for the nonexistence of an invariant measure is that

$$\lim_{T \to \infty} \frac{1}{T} \sum_{t=0}^{T} f_t(x) = 0 \quad \text{for all } x \text{ in } S \ .$$

But taking g to be the indicator function of S, one has trivially,

$$\lim_{T \to \infty} \sum_{t=0}^{T} g_t(x) = 1 \quad \text{for } \underline{\text{all}} \ x \text{ in } S.$$

This establishes proposition 3.1.

Some additional properties of a Markov process satisfying the conditions of Proposition 3.1 are known. The set of all invariant distributions is compact and convex. There is a subset S_0 of S having the property that $\pi^*(S_0) = 1$ for $\underline{\text{any}}$ invariant measure π^* such that

$$\lim_{T \to \infty} \frac{1}{T} \sum_{t=0}^{T} f_t(x)$$

exists for all x in S_0 and all f in $C(S)$. Indeed, for any x in S_0, there is a set $\hat{S}_x$ containing x such that $\lambda(y, \hat{S}_x) = 1$ for all y in $\hat{S}_x$ having the property that there is essentially one invariant measure on $\hat{S}_x$, i.e., $\hat{S}_x$ cannot be decomposed into parts A and B with $\pi^*(A) > 0$, $\pi^*(B) > 0$ for some invariant measure π^* and $\lambda(x, B) = 0$ for all x in A and $\lambda(y, A) = 0$ for all y in B.

3.3. A Dynamic Allocation Process

In the static model described above the excess demand in the competitive economy corresponding to a price vector $p \gg 0$ is itself a random vector. Suppose that the initial price vector is chosen according to a distribution π_0. At any date t given any price $p \gg 0$, the excess demand is $\xi(\omega_t, p)$ where ω_t is independently and identically distributed according to some probability measure μ (which does not depend on t or p). Furthermore there is an adjustment function g such that

$$(3.4) \qquad\qquad p_{t+1} = g(p_t, \xi(\omega_t, p_t))$$

where g was assumed to be a continuous sign preserving function (i.e., $p_{t+1} - p_t$ has the same sign as $\xi(\omega_t, p_t)$) satisfying some other requirement. The price adjustment process (3.4) was studied in Green and Majumdar [1972]. A stochastic equilibrium of the process was simply defined as a time invariant distribution of the prices p_t. A major inadequacy of the model was a complete lack of specification of the behavior of the stocks of commodities in or out of the equilibrium. Since excess demand was not required to be zero or small even in some average sense, and perishability of all commodities within each period is manifestly awkward to assume, it is natural to enquire whether an adjustment process can be developed that allows for durable goods that are transferable from

489

period to period, and price adjustment takes appropriate note of the inventories. My purpose is to sketch the simplest possible extension. The equilibrium concept is still meaningful, and to isolate conceptual from purely technical difficulties, I shall consider a model with a single commodity. However, by using the strong assumptions on the demand functions made in Green and Majumdar [1972], it is almost routine to work out a version with many commodities.

It should perhaps be emphasized that there is no optimization involved in the adjustment contrary to many other models in economics. The problem is one of pure allocation of an essential commodity among its users by suitably adjusting its price. Uncertainty is introduced in the picture by making the new supply at any period a random variable, the distribution of which depends on the stock in the previous period.

In order to get a possible interpretation of the model, consider a planned economy which has a serious balance of pyaments problem. The foreign exchange available for use (depends on factors like foreign aid, international prices and demand conditions for exports, etc.) is chanelled into different departments. While there is a fixed official exchange rate, each department is allowed to set its own shadow price to facilitate allocation among its customers. The amount that the manager of a particular department is allotted is random, depending upon the priorities decided on by the Central Planning Board, but does depend on the stock in the previous period. If the stock was sufficiently high, no new supply is made available to this department. On the other hand, each department is required to maintain a critical minimal level, so as to avoid a complete loss of confidence in the official exchange rate and to meet any emergency created, e.g., by needs of defence or food imports. The specific assumptions made below can be easily understood if this interpretation of the model is kept in mind. Naturally, other interpretations can also be suggested.

I shall make two simplifying assumptions. First, the storage of the resource under consideration is costless and there is no depreciation.

In terms of the interpretation suggested above, I can say that the interest earnings of the foreign exchange held just pay for the costs of keeping accounts. Secondly, the resource manager must maintain a minimal level $\underline{s}$ of the stock in any period. If at the given price p_t in period $D(p_t)$ - s_t is below $\underline{s}$, (i.e., total demand cannot be satisfied without the stock going below the critical level), the quantity $s_t - \underline{s}$ is simply rationed among the potential customers by following some simple rule (it can be divided equally, or can be distributed on a "first come first served" basis). I do not allow for excess demand to be carried forward. It will undoubtedly be of interest to generalize the model in this direction. The stock in period t is given by

$$s_t = \max[\, s_{t-1} - D(p_{t-1});\ \underline{s}\,] + x_t$$

(3.5)

$$s_1 = s_0 + x_1 \text{ for some fixed } s_0 > \underline{s}$$

where $D(p_{t-1})$ is the total demand corresponding to price p_{t-1} set in the previous period. Thus, $s_{t-1} - D(p_{t-1})$ is simply excess supply (if any) from the previous period. x_t is the fresh supply in period t. It is a random variable whose distribution depends on s_{t-1}, the stock in period $t-1$. Some restrictions will be made on the conditional distributions. First, I make the following assumption on the demand function:

ASSUMPTION 3.1. D is a continuous function from R_+ to R_{++} which is monotonically decreasing in p. There is some $\tilde{p} > 0$ such that $D(\tilde{p}) > \underline{s}$ and as p tends to infinity $D(p)$ goes to zero.

The nature of the random variable x_t is made precise by the following assumption:

ASSUMPTION 3.2. There is a time invariant stochastic kernel φ on $R_+ \times \tilde{\mathcal{B}}$ where $\tilde{\mathcal{B}}$ is the Borel σ-field of R_+ such that

(a) for each s in R_+, $\varphi(s,\ )$ is a probability distribution on $\tilde{\mathcal{B}}$. For each F in $\tilde{B}$, $\varphi(\ , F)$ is $\tilde{\mathcal{B}}$-measurable.

491

(b) there is a number $\tilde{s} > 0$, $\tilde{s} > \underline{s}$ such that for all $s \geq \tilde{s}$, $\varphi(s, \ )$ assigns mass 1 to 0.

(c) If s_n in R_+ converges to s in R_+, $\varphi(s_n, \ )$ converges weakly to $\varphi(s, \ )$.

(d) For some $A > 0$, $x_t \leq A$ irrespective of s.

The distribution of x_t given $s_{t-1} = s$ is given by $\varphi(s, \ )$. Note that this does not depend on t. If the stock in period t-1 exceeds $\tilde{s}$, there will be no fresh supply in period t. Moreover, the fresh supply is uniformly bounded and the distributions satisfy a continuity requirement.

At date t, the resource manager has to set the price of the re-source without knowing the precise value of x_t. Thus, his available in-formation consists of the values of s_{t-1} and p_{t-1} and the total demand in period t-1. Since he does not know the exact quantity of new supply, he cannot in general set a price so as to equate supply and demand. I shall analyze the implications of the classical "sign preserving rule" according to which the manager should raise (or lower) price according as excess demand in the previous period is positive (or negative). An alternative possibility is to set prices so as to equate demand (according to the function D(p)) with expected supply. It will be of interest to compare alternative rules, but that is beyond the scope of the present paper. We thus have

$$p_t = g(p_{t-1}, Q_{t-1})$$

where $Q_{t-1} \equiv D(p_{t-1}) - s_{t-1}$ and the following assumptions on the adjust-ment rule are made:

ASSUMPTION 3.3. g is a continuous function from $R_+ \times R$ with values in R_+ that is sign-preserving in Q, i.e., g(p, Q) - p has the same sign as Q.

ASSUMPTION 3.4. There is some constant $M > 0$ such that $|g(p, Q) - p| \leq M$ for any p and any Q.

492

Assumption 3.4 imposes a restriction on the speed of adjustment and avoide awkward problems with discrete time formulations.

It is known that the process $z_t = (p_t, s_t)$, the evolution of which follows the pattern described above, is Markovian (see, e.g., Norman [1972, p. 24]). Let π_0 be the distribution of s_0, the initial stocks, and $\lambda(z, F)$ be the kernel of the process. Given our assumptions, it is not difficult to see that there is a compact set C in R^2 such that $\lambda(z, C) = 1$ for all z in C. A stochastic equilibrium of the process is, as usual, an invariant distribution π^* (in the sense of satisfying (3.2)) such that if z_t has the distribution π^*, so will be the distribution of z_{t+i}, for all $i \geq 1$. Existence of a stochastic equilibrium will follow from Proposition 3.1 since the required continuity properties are immediate. In fact, the compact set C can simply be taken as $[\underline{s}, \tilde{s}+A] \times [0, \underline{p} + M]$ where $\underline{p}$ is the price vector such that $D(p) \leq \underline{s}$ for all $p \geq \underline{p}$. The existence of such a $\underline{p}$ follows from Assumption 3.1. Note that if $s_t \leq \tilde{s}$, then $s_{t+1} \leq \tilde{s} + A$. On the other hand, $\tilde{s} + A \geq s_t \geq \tilde{s}$ implies that $s_{t+1} = \max[s_t - D(p_t), \underline{s}]$ since $x_{t+1} = 0$. But this means that $s_{t+1} \leq s_t$ (since $D(p_t) > 0$ and $\tilde{s} > \underline{s}$) leading to the bound $s_{t+1} \leq \tilde{s} + A$. Of course, $s_t \geq \underline{s}$ implies $s_{t+1} \geq \underline{s}$. If $p_t \leq \underline{p}$, then $p_{t+1} \leq \underline{p} + M$. On the other hand, $\underline{p} + M \geq p_t > \underline{p}$ would imply $D(p_t) < \underline{s} \leq s_t$. This, in turn, by the sign preserving property would give us $p_{t+1} - p_t \leq 0$ ($p_{t+1} - p_t$ having the same sign as $D(p_t) - s_t$) implying $p_{t+1} \leq \underline{p} + M$. Thus the following proposition is verified:

PROPOSITION 3.2. Under Assumptions 3.1 through 3.4, there exists a stochastic equilibrium.

Since the state space C is compact, the results on the ergodic decomposition mentioned earlier are applicable and statements about the asymptotic properties of the time-averages can be made. It would however be more interesting to see whether by using the special structure of the model, some other properties of invariant measures can be derived that can throw some light on the behavior of stocks, excess demands, etc. when the process is in fact in equilibrium. Even in the simpler price adjustment model, global stability (in the sense of the distribution π_t of prices at date t converging to an invariant distribution independently of the initial distribution) was obtained under highly restrictive conditions on the adjustment rule and the demand functions.[5] It may be possible, however, to make some progress by making stronger assumptions on the family $\phi(s, \cdot)$ of conditional distributions. But a reasonably satisfactory stability result has not yet been obtained.

It is possible, however, to consider variations of the usual sign preserving rule. If the resource manager has a desired level or a "target" stock to which he attempts to stay as close as possible, he may ignore $D(p_{t-1}) - s_{t-1}$ and simply raise (or lower) the price according as s_{t-1} is lower than (resp. higher than) the target. However, if the initial stock is low enough, and fresh supply is absent or inadequate, such a rule may lead to continuous increase in price over time and an equilibrium may not exist. On the other hand, if the resource manager starts lowering the price as soon as "current" excess supply reflected in $s - D(p_{t-1})$ is greater than or equal to some preassigned magnitude and the adjustment function is continuous, a stochastic equilibrium can still be shown to exist. To avoid unnecessary duplication, such modifications are not presented.

4. STOCHASTIC EQUILIBRIUM IN THE NEOCLASSICAL GROWTH MODEL

With a Markovian structure, the existence of a stochastic equilibrium in the sense of a time invariant distribution of the relevant variables seems to follow from reasonable boundedness and continuity properties. As I have indicated earlier, for the stochastic adjustment processes that have been experimented with, our knowledge of the properties of the model in such an equilibrium is far from satisfactory. Indeed, the existence question itself is likely to be much more challenging mathematically in the absence of Markovian structures. I am not aware of any result or model in any general setting related to the present framework of analysis.

While the stability results related to the adjustment processes described above have so far not been very exciting, it should be mentioned that there are other models in which significant progress has been made in showing that a stochastic equilibrium is globally stable adding to its significance. My framework so far has been microeconomic, in the conventional sense. Fortunately, the concepts and techniques have wider application. As a final illustration, I shall briefly discuss how the well-known "turnpike theory" of capital accumulation can be extended to take account of uncertainty: Consider first the simplest model of Brock and Mirman [1972]. The problem is:

$$\text{"to maximize } \underset{\sim}{\mathrm{E}} \left(\sum_{t=0}^{\infty} \delta^t u(c_t) \right)$$

(4.1) $$\text{subject to } c_t + x_t = f(x_{t-1}, r_{t-1}(\cdot))$$

$$c_0 + x_0 = s > 0, \quad c_t \geq 0, \quad x_t \geq 0, \quad 0 < \delta < 1 \,,$$

where c_t, x_t are per capita consumption and capital respectively and s is the initial per capita stock of the producible good. The utility and production functions are supposed to have the standard strong assumptions about differentiability and strict concavity guaranteeing the existence of an interior solution; $r_t(\cdot)$ is a sequence of independent and identically distributed random variables assuming values in a compact interval $[a, b]$ in R_{++}.

It is not difficult to show that the stochastic process of optimal capital accumulation satisfies

(4.2) $$x_t(\cdot) = H(x_{t-1}(\cdot), r_{t-1}(\cdot))$$

where H is continuous for each value of r_{t-1}. Using the boundedness assumption of r_t, and a well-known boundedness property of the neoclassical model, it is straightforward to verify that the process $x_t(\cdot)$ is

Markovian with a compact state space in R_+, and indeed the kernel satisfies the continuity property of Proposition 3.1. It follows that s stochastic steady state exists. Note that this argument is applicable to a much wider class of models, e.g., the stochastic version of the class of multisector models considered by McKenzie and others where such boundedness properties hold. Moreover, a detailed examination of the structure of optimal policy enabled Brock and Mirman to show that the stochastic steady state is globally stable, i.e., the sequence of distributions of $x_t(\cdot)$ converges weakly to a unique invariant distribution, independently of the initial stock, as t goes to infinity. The technique of Brock and Mirman does not seem to apply easily to models with more than one capital good. However, with a strong convexo-concavity restriction on the Hamiltonian, analogous to the conditions of Cass and Shell [1974] for deterministic models, a global stability result can still be obtained (see Brock and Majumdar [1974]).

However, even in the simplest one good model,[6] the stochastic steady state is not independent of the utility function. This is in sharp contrast to the standard deterministic case in which the steady state $\bar{x}$ to which the optimal per capita capital sequence converges is determined solely by the condition $f'(\bar{x}) = \frac{1}{\delta}$, and thus, is completely independent of the utility function. Thus, the reformulation of optimal growth models to take account of uncertainty not only enhances the degree of realism, but also leads to an essential and interesting difference in the nature of the steady state.

ACKNOWLEDGEMENT

I wish to thank Professor W. A. Brock, R. N. Bhattacharya, J. Green, R. Radner, and H. Wan for helpful discussions. This research was supported by N.S.F. Grant GS-44279 to Cornell University.

FOOTNOTES

[1]See, e.g., Radner [1970] and Stigum [1969].

[2]The distribution of $\underset{\sim}{\alpha}$ is the probability measure μ defined as $\mu(F) =$ $\mu\{\omega \ \varepsilon \Omega : \alpha(\omega) \ \varepsilon F\}$ for any F in $\tilde{\mathfrak{F}}$.

[3]We endow the set of all probability measures with the weak topology. Compactness refers to compactness in the weak topology. See, e.g., Billingsley [1968].

[4]It should be mentioned that there are continuous time adjustment processes with additive and multiplicative random shocks disappearing on the average. Conditions under which the process converges to a price vector that is an equilibrium without these shocks have been given. See, e.g., Weintraub [1970].

[5]The strong "contraction" assumptions ensured that the distribution of p_t is asymptotically the same, irrespective of the initial distribution. See, e.g., Majumdar [1972].

[6]This observation is due to Brock.

REFERENCES

Bhattacharya, R. N. and M. Majumdar [1973]: "Random Exchange Economies", Journal of Economic Theory, Vol. 6, 37-67.

Billingsley, P. [1968]: Convergence of Probability Measures, John Wiley; New York.

Brock, W. A. and M. Majumdar [1974]: "Asymptotic Stability Results for Multisector Models of Optimal Growth when Future Utilities are Discounted", Cornell Discussion paper (forthcoming).

Brock, W. A. and L. J. Mirman [1972]: "Optimal Economic Growth and Uncertainty: The Discounted Case", Journal of Economic Theory, Vol. 4, 479-513.

Cass, D. and K. Shell, "The Structure and Stability of Competitive Dynamical Systems", (unpublished).

Debreu, G. [1959]: Theory of Value, John Wiley; New York.

_____ [1970]: "Economies with a Finite Set of Equilibria", Econometrica, Vol. 38, 387-392.

Föllmer, H. [1974]: "Random Economies with Many Interacting Agents", Journal of Mathematical Economics, Vol. 1, 51-63.

Green, J. and M. Majumdar [1972]: "The Nature of Stochastic Equilibria", to appear in Econometrica.

Hildenbrand, W. [1971]: "Random Preferences and Equilibrium Analysis", Journal of Economic Theory, Vol. 3, 414-429.

Lucas, R. E. and E. C. Prescott [1974]: "Equilibrium Search and Unemployment", Journal of Economic Theory, Vol. 7, 188-209.

Majumdar, M. [1972]: "Equilibrium and Adjustment in Random Economies", Technical Report No. 58, Institute for Mathematical Studies in Social Sciences, Stanford University, Stanford, California.

Malinvaud, E. [1972]: "The Allocation of Individual Risks in Large Markets", Journal of Economic Theory, Vol. 4, 312-328.

Norman, M. [1972]: Markov Processes and Learning Models, Academic Press, New York.

Radner, R. [1970]: "Problems in the Theory of Markets under Uncertainty", American Economic Review, Vol. 2, 454-460.

Rothschild, M. [1973]: "Models of Market Organization with Imperfect Information: A Survey", Journal of Political Economy, Vol. 69, 213-225.

Stigum, B. [1969]: "Competitive Equilibrium under Uncertainty", Quarterly Journal of Economics, Vol. 83, 533-561.

Stigler, G. [1961]: "The Economics of Information", Journal of Political Economy, Vol. 69, 213-225.

Weintraub, E. [1970]: "Stochastic Stability of a General Equilibrium Model", American Economic Review, Vol. LX, 380-385.

Yosida, K. [1966]: "Functional Analysis", Springer Verlag, New York.

Temporary Walrasian Equilibrium in a Monetary Economy
Bryce Hool

CONTENTS

1. INTRODUCTION

Recently, an increasing amount of attention has been focused on the problem of integrating money into general equilibrium theory. This problem is best viewed in the context of the development of dynamic models of monetary economies and an attempt to close the gap between micro- and macro-economic monetary theory. The purpose of this paper is to outline the progress that has been made in this direction by applying the Hicksian temporary equilibrium method in a Walrasian framework.[1]

A dynamic model of a monetary economy must have certain minimal features. First, there must be a genuine time element, a non-trivial evolution of the economy with genuine uncertainty about the future. Second, the model must indeed be a model of a monetary economy as opposed to some other form of economic organization. Third, there must be a decision mechanism which incorporates an individual's response to market signals and his expectations about the uncertain future. This is so regardless of the degree of decision-making sophistication attributed to the individual; even the most simplistic, myopic rules must be formally included. Fourth, there must be a concept to describe the state of the economy at a given point in time (some form of equilibrium, for example).

Usually this choice will be reciprocal to the selection of market signals appropriate to the decision process.

The requirement of evolution under uncertainty leads naturally to consideration of a sequential economy, one which operates over an arbitrary sequence of elementary time periods, without a complete system of Arrow-Debreu markets in each period. In general, monetization of the economy must be achieved through the introduction of institutional (i.e., non-behavioral) constraints on exchange. These should reflect the aspects of trading, such as the requirement that money be on one side of any transaction, which are intrinsic to monetary economies. An individual's expectations about the uncertain future can be represented by a mapping which associates, with each set of relevant past and present observations, a probability distribution over future unknowns. The individual then chooses a plan over some horizon with the objective of maximizing expected utility. The selection of market variables or their relative speeds of adjustment, and the corresponding definition of an equilibrium state for the economy, tends to be the main feature distinguishing between the possible approaches. Here we shall retain the Walrasian framework and the corresponding Hicksian concept of temporary equilibrium, with prices adjusted by a tâtonnement process to equilibrate all markets in each period.

In Section 2 we develop a basic model of a perfectly competitive pure exchange monetary economy along the above lines, and indicate in Section 3 various ways in which it can be modified to take account of other economic phenomena. In Section 4 we present some summary remarks.

2. THE BASIC MODEL

In the context of a sequence economy, the individual's decision problem will involve the maximization of some objective function (such as the expected utility of his consumption stream over some horizon), subject to a sequence of trading constraints. Consider the simplest case of a perfectly competitive pure exchange economy where the objects of choice in each period are a vector of non-durable consumption goods, x, and a final money balance, m. Suppose money is the only store of value. Then, if p is the vector of money prices and ω an initial endowment, both of N consumption goods, there is a budget equation in each period:

$$(1) \qquad p_t \cdot x_t + m_t = p_t \cdot \omega_t + m_{t-1} \qquad (t = 1, 2, \ldots) .$$

It has been clearly pointed out by Clower [1967] that the classical budget constraint is not sufficient by itself to represent the trading opportunities available to an individual in a monetary economy. In particular, money enters the constraint symmetrically with other commodities and is therefore analytically indistinguishable from them. Consequently, money does not play a special role as the medium of exchange; the constraints (1) are those of a barter economy. To model the special exchange property of money we can follow Clower and dichotomize the budget constraint into one on money expenditure and one on money income. The main impact derives from the expenditure constraint which requires that the total cost of an individual's purchases in a given period be no greater than his initial stock of money:

$$(2) \qquad p_t \cdot [x_t - \omega_t]^+ \leqq m_{t-1} \qquad (t = 1, 2, \ldots)^2$$

Money income from the sale of consumption goods $(p_t \cdot [x_t - \omega_t]^-)$ forms all or part of the cash balance available for expenditure in the succeeding period. This is jointly implied by (1) and (2).

Uncertainty about the future will be confined to prices. Thus, in the constraint sequences (1) and (2), only the first-period prices (p_1) are known; each individual will have expectations about the prices which will prevail in the future. To simplify matters we shall take the individual's horizon to be two periods. This does not mean that the economy 'ends' after period 2 but rather that the individual is boundedly rational, making plans only one period into the future. There is no methodological problem concerning what happens to money in period 2 since, at the beginning of that period, individuals will adjust their horizons and revise their plans in the light of the additional information they will have received.

The individual's expectations about the prices which will prevail in the second period are represented by a mapping ψ which associates, with each admissible current price system, a probability measure on the set of admissible price systems in period 2. Formally, $\psi : P_1 \to \mathcal{M}(P_2)$, where P_t is the space of admissible prices in period t and $\mathcal{M}(P_2)$ the space of all probability measures on $(P_2, \mathcal{B}(P_2))$, $\mathcal{B}(P_2)$ denoting the Borel σ-field of P_2. For B in $\mathcal{B}(P_2)$, $\psi(B; p_1)$ denotes the probability of B given that p_1 is the price system in period 1. [3]

If we assume that the individual's consumption set in each period is R_+^N, the positive cone of the commodity space, the constraints on his choice of (x_1, m_1) are therefore

$$p_1 \cdot x_1 + m_1 = p_1 \cdot \omega_1 + m_0$$

(3)
$$p_1 \cdot [x_1 - \omega_1]^+ \leq m_0$$

$$(x_1, m_1) \geq 0 .$$

Given p_1 and the choice of m_1, the constraints on his planned consumption x_2 in the second period are, for each p_2 in supp $\psi(p_1)$ (i.e., for each price system to which he assigns a positive probability),

$$p_2 \cdot x_2 = p_2 \cdot \omega_2 + m_1$$

(4)
$$p_2 \cdot [x_2 - \omega_2]^+ = m_1$$

$$x_2 \geq 0 . [4]$$

Define $A(p_2, m_1) \equiv \{x_2 \in R_+^N \mid p_2 \cdot x_2 = p_2 \cdot \omega_2 + m_1$ and $p_2 \cdot [x_2 - \omega_2]^+ = m_1\}$. Suppose the individual has a von Neumann-Morgenstern utility function for consumption streams, $u(x_1, x_2)$. Then, given p_1 and a choice (x_1, m_1) in the first period, there is, for each p_2 in supp $\psi(p_1)$, at least one x_2 which maximizes $u(x_1, x_2)$ subject to $x_2 \in A(p_2, m_1)$. Define $\varphi(x_1, m_1, p_2) \equiv \{(x_1, x_2) \mid u(x_1, x_2) \geq u(x_1, x_2') \forall x_2' \in A(p_2, m_1)\}$ and $u(\varphi(x_1, m_1, p_2)) \equiv u(x_1, x_2)$ for some $(x_1, x_2) \in \varphi(x_1, m_1, p_2)$. The individual should therefore choose in period 1 the pair (x_1, m_1) which maximizes the expected utility function

$$(5) \qquad v(x_1, m_1, p_1) \equiv \int_{P_2} u(\varphi(x_1, m_1, p_2)) d\psi(p_2; p_1),$$

subject to (3). The solution to this problem is the individual's demand.

We observe from (5) that money and prices enter the individual's objective function, which thus reflects a generalized real balance effect. The demand for money is a "transactions - precautionary" demand arising from the desire to hold effective purchasing power in a future with unknown prices.

A temporary monetary equilibrium is a monetary price system and a list of final demands for consumption goods and money which are individually optimal, given expectations, and clear all markets (including the residual market for money).

The mathematical formalization of the basic decision framework and Hicksian temporary equilibrium structure is due to Grandmont [1971]. The first attempt to introduce a money expenditure constraint into this structure was that of Grandmont and Younès [1972], who used a modification of (2), namely

$$p_t \cdot [x_t - \omega_t]^+ \leq m_{t-1} + \beta p_t \cdot [x_t - \omega_t]^-, \quad \beta \text{ given}, \quad 0 \leq \beta \leq 1.$$

This reduces to (2) or (1) when β is 0 or 1, respectively. When

$\beta > 0$, the individual has access to a positive fraction of the proceeds from his current-period sales.

Attention has been given mainly to the problem of existence of a temporary monetary equilibrium. Since this is essentially reduced to a single-period problem (the maximization of expected utility, as described above) it is semi-static. The adaptive behavior of the economic system is largely suppressed; the present is linked with the past (implicitly) and the future (explicitly) through expectations together with money, the intertemporal store of value. In a monetary economy the existence problem centers on the need to establish a positive exchange value for money in equilibrium, as was made clear by Hahn [1965], and is found to depend crucially on price expectations.

Grandmont and Younès proved the existence of a temporary equilibrium in their model for the range $0 < \beta \leq 1$, using an assumption which restricts the sensitivity of expectations to current prices, namely that[5]

(a)   the family $\{\psi(p_1): p_1 \epsilon P_1\}$ is uniformly tight; i.e.,

$\forall \epsilon > 0$, $\exists$ a compact $C_\epsilon \subset P_2$ such that $\psi(C_\epsilon; p_1) > 1-\epsilon$,

$\forall p_1 \epsilon P_1$.

The assumption (a) requires essentially that expectations be inelastic. In the case of subjectively certain expectations (where, for each p_1 in P_1, all the probability is concentrated on a single p_2 in P_2), the condition (a) implies the existence of a compact subset C of P_2 such that $\psi(C; p_1) = 1$, $\forall p_1 \epsilon P_1$.

In Hool [1974a], existence of temporary equilibrium is established for the model described above (i.e., with the expenditure constraint (2)) using an assumption which allows expectations with, at most, unitary elasticity, namely

(b) $\exists(k_1, k_2)$ such that for any sequence $\langle p_1^n \rangle$ in P_1 with $\| p_1^n \| \to +\infty$,

$$\lim_{n \to \infty} \int_{P_2} \frac{p_{1k_1}^n}{p_{2k_2}} \, d\psi(p_2; p_1^n) > \frac{u'_{k_1}(\omega)}{u'_{N+k_2}(\omega)} \, ,$$

where k is the commodity index, $\omega = (\omega_1, \omega_2)$, and $u_k'(x)$ denotes the marginal utility of k at x. The condition (b) requires that, in the limit, the average relative price of some commodity in the first period compared with some commodity in the second be greater than the ratio of their marginal utilities in the initial endowment sequence. It is precisely a limiting form of the classical condition for desirability of substitution in the case of two commodities and two dates. The class of unit-elastic expectations, admitted by (b), includes several examples common in the literature on monetary theory, such as (i) Patinkin's assumption (in Patinkin [1965]) that current prices are expected to hold in the future (i.e., $\psi(p_1; p_1) = 1$, $\forall p_1 \epsilon P_1$), (ii) linear adaptive expectations, and (iii) linear homogeneous expectations. The latter form can be essential if there is to be no "money illusion" (see Grandmont [1971]). But, while the absence of money illusion is not ruled out, it is apparent from (5) that it will not be a general property of demand behavior.

The analysis in Hool [1974a] provides an answer to Hahn's question regarding the existence, under reasonable conditions, of equilibrium in a neo-Walrasian monetary model such as Patinkin's. In that case, the condition (b) becomes (if we take $k_1 = k_2 = k$ for simplicity):

(b') for some commodity k, $u_{N+k}'(\omega) > u_k'(\omega)$,

which requires that, taking into account his time preference, the individual is relatively poorly endowed with some commodity k in the second period compared with the first. This must hold for at least one consumer if temporary equilibrium is to exist. More generally, the analysis indicates that unitary elasticity marks the boundary between those expectations (more precisely, those elasticities of expectations) which are consistent with the existence of a temporary monetary equilibrium and those which are not. This conforms to intuition since we would expect inflationary or deflationary trends to be aggravated by elastic expectations, moderated by inelastic expectations.

3. EXTENSIONS

The basic model presented in Section 2 can easily be extended to incorporate other aspects of economic activity.

We can consider an economy in which production takes place. The sequential framework then facilitates the explicit consideration of production technologies with intertemporal characteristics and production plans which must be based on unknown future prices for inputs and out-puts. In the simple case of a two-period horizon, a production process might combine commodity inputs (including labor) in the first period to produce outputs in the second; input prices will be known, output prices unknown. (See, for example, Sondermann [1971] and de Montbrial [1971]).

The process of exchange among producers and consumers can be formalized by introducing market intermediaries and marketing technol-ogies. The technologies will typically have both atemporal and inter-temporal characteristics (intertemporal because of storage, at least) and should distinguish the nature (in particular, the origin or destination) of the various commodities. The modelling of such marketing technologies will reflect real transactions costs.

More generally, we can include the various classes of economic participants (consumers, producers, market intermediaries) under the collective title of economic agents. These agents will have decision frameworks of the type described in Section 2 for consumers. They will be subject to trading constraints of the form of (1) and (2) and will be further constrained by their respective 'technologies' (consumption sets, production sets, marketing sets).

A particular form of market intermediation is the financial inter-mediation of a central banking authority. Apart from the facilitation of borrowing and lending (in the absence of a general banking system), the primary objective of a central bank will be to control, or to influence, monetary parameters such as the money supply or the interest rate. A model which features alternative policies for a central bank has been studied by Grandmont and Laroque [1972].

506

The introduction of financial assets (in addition to money) leads
to considerations of liquidity and speculation. Younès [1973a] has demonstrated the existence of a temporary monetary equilibrium when there
is another financial asset, bearing interest, provided it is less liquid
than money. For his set of assumptions (including, in particular, inelasticity of interest rate expectations), the existence of a liquidity trap is
a necessary condition for the existence of equilibrium. In Hool [1974b],
emphasis is on the speculative demand for money when there is an alternative asset which is as liquid as money but has uncertain future value
and hence the possibility of capital gains or losses. Interest rates are
implicitly determined by the asset prices, which are uncertain in the future. The method of proof of existence of a temporary monetary equilibrium uses the same approach as Hool [1974a] and obviates the need to
assume inelasticity of price and interest rate expectations. While the
existence of a "speculative trap" is consistent with the set of assumptions sufficient for the existence of equilibrium, it is not a necessary
consequence.

Rather than restrict trading to current commodities and financial
assets, one can allow the possibility of trading in claims on future commodities, as in Green [1973]. Difficulties in establishing the existence
of equilibrium arise from the fact that, without institutional limits (such
as collateral requirements), trades are not bounded below. This problem
is confronted also in Hool [1974b]. Essentially, there must be future
asset prices, assigned positive probability by the individual, which would
give negative profit to asset-holding.

Dusansky, Kalman and Wickström [1974] have investigated a model of an economy with both monetary and barter exchange in which transactions costs are explicit. They consider costs which are linear in quantities traded and are expressed in money units, independently of prices.
They establish the existence of a temporary equilibrium and derive generalized comparative statics properties of the model.

507

Finally, there is nothing to preclude the introduction into the basic model of price rigidities (such as minimum wages). However, if prices in general are fixed in the short run we are no longer in the Walrasian framework; in the temporary equilibrium context, the Hicksian fixprice method becomes appropriate. In any given period it will no longer be the case in general that markets equilibrate, that actual demands and supplies are the desired demands and supplies.

4. REMARKS

It is clear from the studies reported on above that the consideration of a sequential trading economy and temporary equilibria, rather than a static economy and once-and-for-all equilibrium, opens the way, within a Walrasian framework, for several new features. In particular, it becomes possible to model monetary economies. The role of money as a medium of exchange can be made explicit, thereby providing an endogenous reason for the holding of money: the desire to hold effective purchasing power. This contrasts with other explanations to account for the holding of money, such as Patinkin's random payment mechanism, which are necessarily exogenous to models in which there is no analytical distinction between money and other commodities. Since it is possible to establish the existence of a temporary monetary equilibrium under conditions on price expectations which do not preclude Patinkin's simplifying assumption (that future prices are expected with certainty to be identical with current prices), there is not necessarily any internal inconsistency in the foundations of Patinkin's comparative statics analysis. However, while price expectations might be such that a temporary monetary equilibrium exists, there might also be money illusion, since the expected utility function ((5) of Section 2) is not in general homogeneous of degree zero with respect to nominal money balances and current prices.

In view of the developments described in Sections 2 and 3, the main residual inadequacy of neo-Walrasian monetary theory would seem to be the intrinsic notion of a Walrasian market, with a behind-the-scenes auctioneer finding equilibrium prices via a tâtonnement process. Keeping price and quantity adjustments in the background suppresses important features of the dynamic behavior of the system. There is clearly a need to make these more explicit. On the other hand, the general structure of temporary equilibrium analysis is premised upon a sequential market structure and can easily be carried over to frameworks other than the Walrasian. The general formulation (due to Grandmont) of the short-run decision mechanism, incorporating uncertain expectations, provides a method for linking the uncertain future with current actions which can be adapted to alternative specifications of the economic environment.

NOTES

[1] By restricting thus the scope of the paper, we shall be neglecting some important contributions to the theory of money and general equilibrium. Particular mention should be made of the transaction cost approach (see, for example, the papers of Hahn [1971], Kurz [1974 a, b, c], Heller [1974], Heller and Starr [1973] and Starr [1970, 1974]), and Keynesian disequilibrium theory approach (see, for example, Clower [1965, 1967], Leijonhufvud [1968, 1973], Benassy [1973] and Younès [1970, 1973b]).

[2] $[x]^+$ is defined to be the vector whose k^{th} element is max $(0, x_k)$; $[x]^- \equiv [-x]^+$.

[3] The mapping ψ, defined in this general way, is taken as datum for the individual. While we shall require restrictions on ψ which will ensure the existence of a temporary equilibrium, we shall not be concerned with the question of whether or not the expectations are rational in some sense. On this question see, for example, the paper by Grossman in this volume, and the references cited there.

[4] We have explicitly omitted m_2 since it will always be planned to be zero.

[5]In fact, since they deal with the case of subjective certainty, Grandmont and Younès use the point-expectation equivalent referred to below. Assumption (a) was introduced by Grandmont [1971].

REFERENCES

Benassy, J.-P. [1973], "Disequilibrium Theory," C.R.M.S. Working Paper No. 185, University of California, Berkeley.

Clower, R. W. [1965], "The Keynesian counter-revolution: a theoretical appraisal," in Hahn and Brechling [1965].

_____ [1967], "A reconsideration of the micro-foundations of monetary theory," Western Economic Journal, 6.

Debreu, G. [1959], Theory of Value, Wiley, New York.

Dusansky, R., P. J. Kalman and B. A. Wickström [1974], "General equilibrium and comparative statics in an exchange economy with money, price uncertainty and transactions costs." Working Paper No. 116, SUNY (Stony Brook).

Grandmont, J.-M. [1971], "Short-run equilibrium analysis in a monetary economy," C.E.P.R.E.M.A.P. Discussion Paper, Paris.

Grandmont, J.-M., and G. Laroque [1972], "On money and banking," CORE Discussion Paper, Université Catholique de Louvain, to appear in Review of Economic Studies.

Grandmont, J.-M. and Y. Younès [1972], "On the role of money and the existence of a monetary equilibrium," Review of Economic Studies, 39.

Green, J. R. [1973], "Temporary general equilibrium in a sequential trading model with spot and futures transactions," Econometrica, 41.

Hahn, F. H. [1965], "On some problems of proving the existence of an equilibrium in a monetary economy," in Hahn and Brechling [1965].

Hahn, F. H. and F. Brechling [1965], editors, The Theory of Interest Rates, Macmillan.

Hahn, F. H. [1971], "Equilibrium with transaction costs," Econometrica, 39.

Heller, W. P. [1974], "The holding of money balances in general equilibrium," Journal of Economic Theory, 7.

Heller, W. P. and R. M. Starr [1973], "Equilibrium in a monetary economy with non-convex transactions costs," Technical Report No. 110, Institute for Mathematical Studies in the Social Sciences, Stanford University, Stanford, California.

Hicks, J. R. [1939], Value and Capital, Clarendon Press, Oxford.

_____ [1965], Capital and Growth, Clarendon Press, Oxford.

Hool, R. B. [1974a], "Money, expectations and the existence of a temporary equilibrium," SSRI Working Paper No. 7425, University of Wisconsin, Madison.

_____ [1974b], "Money, financial assets and general equilibrium in a sequential market economy," unpublished Ph D. dissertation, University of California, Berkeley.

Kurz, M. [1974a], "Equilibrium in a finite sequence of markets with transaction cost," Econometrica, 42.

_____ [1974b], "Equilibrium with transaction cost in a single market exchange economy," Journal of Economic Theory, 7.

_____ [1974c], "Arrow-Debreu equilibrium of an exchange economy with transaction cost," International Economic Review, 15.

Leijonhufvud, A. [1968], "On Keynesian economics and the economics of Keynes," Oxford University Press, London.

_____ [1973], "Effective demand failures," Swedish Journal of Economics.

de Montbrial, T. [1971], "Intertemporal general equilibrium and interest rates theory," Working Paper No. CP-322, Center for Research in Management Science, University of California, Berkeley.

Patinkin, D. [1965], Money, Interest and Prices, Harper and Row.

Sondermann, D. [1971], "Temporary competitive equilibrium under uncertainty," C.O.R.E., Louvain.

Starr, R. M. [1970], "Equilibrium and demand for media of exchange in a pure exchange economy with transaction cost," Cowles Foundation Discussion Paper No. 300, Yale University.

_____ [1974], "The price of money in a pure exchange monetary economy with taxation," Econometrica, 42.

Younès, Y. [1970], "Sur une notion d'équilibre utilisable dans le cas où les agents économiques ne sont pas assurés de la compatibilité de leurs plans," C.E.P.R.E.M.A.P., Paris.

_____ [1973a], "Money and interest in a short-run Walrasian equilibrium," paper presented to the M.S.S.B. Workshop, University of California, Berkeley.

_____ [1973b], "on the role of money in the process of exchange and the existence of a non-Walrasian equilibrium," C.E.P.R.E. M.A.P., Paris.

Mathematical Models for a Theory of Money and Financial Institutions
Martin Shubik

CONTENTS

1. INTRODUCTION

This paper serves to lay out an approach and set of models and problems for the development of a theory of money and financial institutions. A previous paper "An Informal Guide to Some Papers on a Theory of Money and Financial Institutions," Shubik [1974a] serves as a guide to the various papers and publications relevant to the type of modeling presented here. These references supply much of the discussion needed to link this approach to the economic problems which are modeled here. Several of the papers contain analyses of models and proofs that are needed. They are referred to directly. Here we concentrate on setting up the formal models together with the appropriate notation for mathematical analysis of economies controlled in disequilibrium by money and financial institutions.

2. PLAYERS (TRADERS, CONSUMERS, PRODUCERS, BANKERS, ETC.)

In the various models players may be modeled as

(a) Strategic "live" participants with both strategic choices and utility functions.

(b) Mechanisms with no freedom of strategic choice and no utility functions -- i.e. -- as merely part of the rules.

(c) <u>Dummies</u> who may have utility functions but have no strategic freedom.

(d) <u>Nature</u> with no utility function but strategic freedom (if probabilities are assigned to Nature's choices this amounts to making Nature into a mechanism).

3. BASIC ELEMENTARY ECONOMIC ELEMENTS

In the models which follow up to as high as eight "elementary particles" may play a role. Four of them do not involve contracts and contingencies or time interlinkages, but four of them do. Four of them do not involve more than one party, four of them involve two or more parties. Two of them are "real" and six are paper. In a separate publication the details of these eight items are discussed [Shubik, 1974b].

The four elements which do not involve contracts are:

$$\text{"real"} \begin{cases} \text{goods} \\ \\ \text{services} \end{cases}$$

$$\text{paper} \begin{cases} \text{fiat money} \\ \\ \text{ownership paper (shares, stocks, deeds, etc.)} \end{cases}$$

Each of these items has associated with it a different form of paper which is a contract among two or more individuals and which link one period of time with another:

Associated with "goods" are "futures contracts"

Associated with "services" are "service contracts"

Associated with "fiat money" are "debt contracts"

Associated with "ownership papers" are "warrants, options, puts and calls"

Models can be built involving far fewer than the eight instruments. Difficulties can be separated out and the policy adapted here is to do so.

The creation of contracts as economic instruments introduces legal and societal problems in defining what to do if an economy reaches a state at which the conditions specified in a contract cannot be met. Thus methods which specify how insolvency, or failure to meet any contract, can be cured must form an integral part of the rules (thus a "mathematical institutional economics" emerges in the sense that the mathematical requirements for the complete definition of the model requires the specification of laws and institutions to fully define the process).

Given all laws then an 8×8 transition matrix linking t and t+1 can be described. Figure 1 shows these transitions when no failures

t+1 \ t	Goods	Services	Fiat Money	Ownership Paper	Future Contracts	Service Contracts	Debt Contracts	Puts, Calls, Warrants
Goods	X							
Services								
Fiat Money			X					
Ownership Paper				X				
Futures Contracts	X							
Service Contracts		X						
Debt Contracts			X					
Puts, Calls, Warrants				X				

Figure 1

of contract are encountered. It may be noted that the distinguishing feature between "goods" and "services" is the possibility for inventorying.
A service at time t will not exist at time t+1; a good at time t is
transformed, in general, to a somewhat different type of good at t+1.

It is possible that a fully dynamic economic system with desirable dynamic properties will only need the first four elements and one
contract. The others do exist and an eight dimensional space that can
be defined appears to include as mixtures all financial instruments that
exist or have existed.

4. COMMODITIES, FINANCIAL INSTRUMENTS AND PREFERENCES

In the various models, in general it will be assumed that m
goods and services exist and up to six financial instruments exist. It
may be necessary in some models to explicitly distinguish goods and
services and different types of goods such as those which are public,
those which are indivisible, those which do not enter directly into consumer preferences (pure production goods) and so forth. These distinctions will be made whenever they are directly relevant.

Suppose we consider an economic model with T discrete time
periods. (We may later wish to consider $T \to \infty$.)

It is assumed that there are n individuals in the economy and
that each individual has a completely ordered set of preferences defined
on an outcome space specified below. It is further assumed that each
individual's preferences can be represented by a utility function which
is concave (implying risk neutraility or risk aversion unless otherwise
specified). Furthermore as a modeling simplification it is assumed that
the individual's utility functions are separable between time periods.

The preference structure is defined on R^{m+5} where preferences
must be specified for all outcomes in the positive orthant and also for
outcomes involving contracts in the negative (-) as well as the positive
(+) axis.

517

A contract is basically a <u>two party</u> instrument, thus merely in order to obey simple laws of conservation we must have an accounting scheme where any contract which appears as an asset (+) on one set of accounts must appear as a liability (-) on another set of accounts. Furthermore to avoid double-counting we must take care in correctly accounting for the presence of both goods and ownership paper (such as shares) associated with these goods. In most societies the set of actions with respect to goods and ownership paper are not the same.

It is my belief that an adequate model of an economy with financial instruments and institutions must be such that accounting plays a natural and integrated role in the development of a theory of economic behavior. The models presented here have this property.

Let there be n individuals in an economy; m "real" goods and services, two nontime dated financial instruments (fiat money and ownership paper)[1] and three financial instruments which are contracts. For simplicity, we regard these contracts as only two party paper although three or more party paper is not uncommon. The addition of more than two parties to a contract is a complication which does not appear to be called for at this stage in model building.

We define the utility function of individual i to be of the form

$$(1) \quad u_i = \sum_{t=1}^{T} \beta_i^{t-1} \varphi_i (q_{1,t}^i, \; q_{2,t}^i, \; \cdots, \; q_{m,t}^i; f_{1,t}^i, \; f_{2,t}^i, \; c_{\Delta t}^{ij}, \; d_{\Delta t}^{ij}, \; e_{\Delta t}^{ij}).$$

The notation is as follows:

$q_{j,t}^i$ = the amount of good j held by player i at time t.

$f_{1,t}^i$ = the amount of fiat money held by player i at time t.

$f_{2,t}^i$ = the amount of ownership paper held by player i at time t.

$d_{\Delta t}^{ij}$ = the amount of goods[2] or services contracts between i and j at the start of period t and due at the end of period t.

$c_{\Delta t}^{ij}$ = the amount of money or debt contracts between i and at the start of period t and due at the end of period t.

$e_{\Delta t}^{ij}$ = the amount of warrants or puts or calls between i and j at the start of period t and due at the end of period t.

Two comments are called for. The word "amount" has been used concerning the financial instruments. The measures must be specified.

$f_{1,t}^i$ - the amount of fiat money is expressed in units of fiat money.

$f_{2,t}^i$ - the amount of ownership paper is expressed as a percentage claim on the physical assets regarded as an indivisible unit.[3]

$d_{\Delta t}^{ij}$ - the amount of a goods (or services) contract is expressed in terms of the quantity of goods to be delivered. In a more complex model a "future" might involve a payment of money at time t in return for a right to pay a price p_t^* at period $t+k$ for the delivery at time $t+k$ of the quantity $q_{j,t+k}$.

$c_{\Delta t}^{ij}$ - the amount of a debt contract is expressed in the quantity of fiat money due at any period. This will involve accrual rules for multi-period debt contracts. For simplicity we begin by considering instruments which have a life only from t to $t+1$. By renegotiation new contracts can be made to connect $t+1$ to $t+2$ and so forth.

$e_{\Delta t}^{ij}$ - the amount of a warrant can be measured most simply in terms of the amount of the ownership paper to be delivered at time $t+k$. A slightly more complicated and realistic measure is the amount of money p_t^* to be paid at period $t+k$ for the delivery at time $t+k$ of an amount $f_{2,t+k}$ of the ownership paper.

The three contracts each bear two names. As noted above the names may indicate two active players. If however a banking system is constructed which has the bank or other lending or depository institution

519

as a mechanism or part of the rules of the game one part of the balance of the contract will be out of the player set.

The notation $c_{\Delta t}^{ij}$ has been adopted so that Δt signifies that i contracts to borrow from j at the start of period t with the promise to settle at the end of t. This simplification will not cause any particular limitations when we wish to consider longer term loans, or if we wish to change the length of time periods. The tree diagram shown as Figure 2 gives one form in which we may imagine that trade takes place. In different specific models the details of the order of trade, production, and consumption must be spelled out.

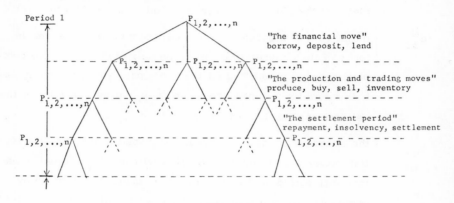

Figure 2

In Figure 2 the symbol $P_{1,2,\ldots,n}$ means that all players move simultaneously (or at least without information of each others acts). The idea of contract reflected in this model is that of a short term financing of trade for consumption. Finance for investment might require long term finance. The only condition on the order of the moves noted above is that the financial move must be before the trading moves of the player. Settlement could be before or after consumption. The major difference in these choices are that if settlement is before consumption, unconsumed goods can be claimed if contracts are violated. If settlement is after consumption there are less goods available for use in insolvency settlements.

4.1. Fiat Money and Commodity Money

In Section 4 the strategic characterization of a money is given. Here a distinction is made between a fiat money and a commodity money in terms of its consumption worth and durability properties.

A commodity money has the strategic properties of a money, but the consumption properties of a real good. An example might be a bar of salt or brick of tea. A fiat money has the strategic properties of a money but no intrinsic consumption worth.

As a fiat money will not be defined for negative amounts (a debt instrument is not the same as fiat money -- the statement "I owe $10" means that a contract, implicitly or explicitly exists for the delivery of $10), there is no need to consider preferences for negative amounts of money. Because debt instruments may be measured in terms of money one could try to measure both money and debt on the same axes. This creates more complications than it avoids. This should certainly be clear for commodity money. A debt instrument for 10 pounds of gold to be delivered which cannot be honored does not mean that the individual has -10 pounds of gold. It means that a contract cannot be honored and it is that which must be evaluated.

4.2. A Simplification

We leave out of the utility functions both fiat money and ownership paper. For the first set of models we consider only one contract that is the debt contract. Thus we can simplify equation (1) replacing it by:

$$
(2) \qquad u_i = \sum_{t=1}^{T} \beta_i^{t-1} \varphi_i(q_{1,t}^i, \; q_{2,t}^i, \; \ldots, \; q_{m,t}^i; \; c_{\Delta t}^{i,j}) \, .
$$

By leaving out contracts other than those which involve money for money we remove from consideration other "futures" markets which may exist in various economies. This simplification needs to be removed later.

It must be stressed that although the utility function shown in (2) involves only m+1 items (m goods and one financial instrument) there are m+3 items in the model (m goods fiat money, ownership paper and debt).

If the economic system functions without the failure of any contract, i.e. if all contracts are all balanced at each period then at the end of each period they will net to zero and we can in general consider that except for positions of insolvency which may lead to bankruptcy or other cures for the failure to honor contract, the utility functions depends only on the "real" commodities, i.e. it is essentially of the form:

$$(3) \qquad u_i = \sum_{t=1}^{T} \beta_i^{t-1} \varphi_i(q_{1,t}^i, \ q_{2,t}^i, \ \ldots, \ q_{m,t}^i, \ 0) \ .$$

4.3. Insolvency, Bankruptcy and Feasibility

When a system evolves, it is logically possible if contracts exist, that a state may be reached at which an individual is unable to honor a contract that falls due. If the contract is between two players then the double entry system will show that the time of settlement entries of $c_{\Delta t}^{ij}$ and $-c_{\Delta t}^{ij}$ which cannot be immediately cancelled. Special rules must be invoked to effect an alternative settlement.

The simplest and most nonspecific way of taking insolvency and bankruptcy into account is to define the utility functions to include contracts which are not wiped out by the full settlement of their conditions. This somewhat avoids the task of describing precisely what happens. If we do this it is important to note that we evaluate the utilitarian worth of contracts which are not completely honored at or immediately after the violation of contract is cured, i.e. after the contract is removed from the books, destroyed and replaced by a settlement.

In actuality conditions of insolvency may lead to the replacement of one contract by another, or a series of contracts and partial payments in different forms. Eventually if an individual is not merely insolvent but cannot meet his debts even with more time to do so, bankruptcy or other procedures wipe out the contract. In the process of doing so the contract is annihilated and replaced eventually by nothing or some combination of goods, services, money and ownership paper. Going to jail or being put to death are possibilities which have arisen and they could be modeled if need be. But the attitude adopted here is that the first approximation is to include the contracts in the utility function and the second approximation is to produce a transition matrix of the variety shown in Figure 1 where however transitional probabilities must be specified for the transformation of a contract into another contract and/or partial payments in money, goods or ownership paper. The transitional probabilities are not given a priori but should emerge as a part of the solution of the game. Further discussion is needed and must be given when specific models are described.

5. ON MONEY: COMMODITY OR FIAT

The distinction between a "money" and other goods or services is essentially strategic and not in its characteristic as a consumption item.

The distinction between a commodity money and a fiat money is essentially in terms of its consumption worth and not its strategic properties.

In an economy with m+1 commodities we may select one commodity to serve as a "money" which means that we will select a model of trade in which the set of strategies of each individual with respect to the monetary commodity will be different from their strategies with respect to the other commodities.

A well known key example of a strategic requirement for a money is to consider trade in which for m+1 commodities there are only m markets in which each market involves an exchange of that commodity for the monetary commodity. By requiring trade in the "money," m markets can be used for trade instead of $m(m+1)/2$. The specific structure of the markets and methods of trade will influence the needs for and strategic properties of a money. This is discussed further in Section 5 on markets.

The distinction between a commodity money and a fiat money is that the former will appear as a component in the utility function and the latter will not.

A small problem is faced in the modeling of a commodity money in a multistage model. If, for example, a bar of salt is used as a commodity money, it will yield utility in consumption but not in storage. Thus although it may appear within the utility function, the amount that should appear there is that which is consumed,[4] not that which is inventoried. Following this distinction through, in general, it may be shown that the use of a commodity money instead of a paper money is less efficient inasmuch as it ties up inventories of a consumable (or productive input) for strategic or trade purposes whereas paper backed by law could serve the same purpose.

6. ON MARKETS AND MONEY

The concept of money is intimately related with the concept of a market. It plays a key role in the simplification of market structures and in the operations of markets. It serves as a powerful information aggregation device and decentralization mechanism.

6.1. Futures Markets

It is possible to consider an economy or a game which lasts for a finite number of time periods as though it all were to take place in a single time period. In using this type of transformation (replacing a game in extensive form by a game in strategic form) it is mathematically feasible (but not necessary) to imagine that all future contingent markets exist. Arrow and Debreu use this device. Suppose that an economy has m commodities, T time periods and k different states each period (such as rain or sunshine then we could imagine the existence of mTk markets, one for each commodity at each time period under all contingencies. This formulation gives us the chance to describe an essentially dynamic (T period) evolutionary process as a static model of enormous

size. Having done this it is possible to use well developed methods
from static theory to derive certain properties of the equilibrium states
of the system.

There is an alternative approach to modeling multiperiod markets
this involves making the assumption that virtually no futures markets exist. It may be that in order to take care of differing subjective probabilities concerning future chance events that different futures contracts
must be distinguished. This possibility however should not be considered as an a priori assumption but should emerge from the development
of the theory. To start with we consider only a debt futures contract.
Thus for an economy with T time periods, k different states of nature
each period and m goods, we consider an enlarged market with m goods,
fiat money, ownership paper and debt contracts. This gives us a dynamic system with m+2 markets only one of which is directly time
linked.

Consideration of risk and the meaning of optimality may call for
the distinction of two types of debt contract, a loan and an insurance
policy. This will be considered in reference to specific models.

6.2. Money, Prices and the Form of Trade

Money is intimately related to the concept of a market but prices
are not. The general equilibrium model has as a central feature the existence of prices in a closed, non-strategic, non-institutional static context. In contradistinction virtually all attempts to model oligopolistic
behavior have resulted in the formulation of strategic models of trade and
production. In particular virtually all of the oligopoly models have been
open models with money and goods flowing in or out with no modeling
needed to preserve laws of conservation. They have been strategic (and
implicitly dynamic) and in order merely to well define these models it has
been necessary to specify completely the manner of trade or the markets.
Thus, for example, the Cournot model utilizes quantity as a strategic
variable; the models of Bertrand, Edgeworth, and Chamberlin utilize

individual price naming. Other models consider both price and quantity as simultaneous variables [Levitan and Shubik, 1970]. Different oligopoly models have been constructed where production variation, innovation and other economic variables have been considered [Chamberlin, 1950].

In the building of all of these models because they are strategic they call for a specification of all positions of disequilibrium as well as equilibrium. This makes it mandatory to describe the details of trade and markets.

A trained theorist might balk at the idea of having to specify a specific market mechanism. After all there are thousands of specific institutions and we might easily become lost in institutional detail. Unfortunately we do not have the alternative of leaving out this step. Leaving out the market mechanism is not a successful way to avoid institutional detail. It leaves us with an incomplete model.

The solution to the dilemma noted above which is suggested here (and previously by Shubik [1972a] and Shapley and Shubik [1974a] is that we start with two or three specific models of markets, see what they imply, see what their limitations are, then branch out later to study the sensitivity of the results to market variations). An adequate mathematical instutional economics should help us to explore the properties of the optimal design of institutions (where "optimal" is adequately defined).

The simplest model of a market for the generation of price (not necessarily efficient price) can be based on the Cournot market model. This will be clearly "unrealistic" but it provides a well defined method for both introducing a monetary mechanism and embedding a strategic model of oligopoly into a closed economy. In specifying the models we return to the special role of money.

6.3. Markets and the Role of Money

Consider an economy with k+1 commodities with n individuals; each individual i with an endowment $(A_1^i, A_2^i, \ldots, A_{k+1}^i)$. Suppose that all individuals are required by a rule of the game to offer for sale at k

warehouses all of their endowments of the first k commodities. This
is illustrated in Figure 3. There will be A_j units of the jth commodity
for sale where $A_j = \sum_{i=1}^{n} A_j^i$ for $j = 1, \ldots, k$.

The rules of the game require that each individual buy the quantities of the k goods he intends to consume by bidding for them in terms
of the $k+1^{st}$ commodity. Strategically the distinction between the $k+1^{st}$
commodity and the others is that all trade involves a set of k two sided
markets where the $k+1^{st}$ commodity exchanges for all of the other commodities. The essence of the "money role" in the markets is that it is
the commodity that appears in all trades.

Several features are unreasonable about this model. All of them
can be relaxed or otherwise accounted for. They are

(1) this model does not allow for some barter,

(2) individuals must sell all their goods through the markets,

(3) individuals must buy in money without credit available to
them even if they own many assets,

(4) individuals must bid quantities of money without being
exactly sure of what they can buy.

A model with mixed markets to permit some trade through barter
and partial exchange using money and anonymous markets can be defined
but to begin with the ruling out of barter appears to be a reasonable simplification.

The requirement that individuals must sell all of their goods each
period, even if they buy them back will be relaxed in the second model.
Although the requirement that all goods are required to go through the
market every time period may appear to be strange and "unreal" it has
the economic and accounting benefit that income can now be measured
accurately every period because all goods in the economy are monetized
in the markets (capital gains and losses cannot be hidden). The mathematical benefit from this model is that the strategies of the players are
relatively simple.

In some sense the contrast between the model of trade using a money and the general equilibrium model without an explicit form of money or credit is that in the first, no credit is granted to the individual even if he has many assets he wishes to sell. Whatever he buys must be paid for in cash. In contrast in the general equilibrium model the constraint is an overall budget constraint. It is as though the individual is instantaneously credited for all of the assets he wishes to sell. The budget constraint is less restrictive than a constraint to trade using money or no more restrictive. Hence if we wish to make the model with money have less restrictive trading constaints than that imposed by the money holdings of the individuals we must introduce credit. This is done, and the nature of a credit instrument has already been noted in Section 2.

There is a curious and counterintuitive feature to the bidding mechansim which apparently has individuals assign quantities of money to markets without knowing the price of the items they are buying. I claim

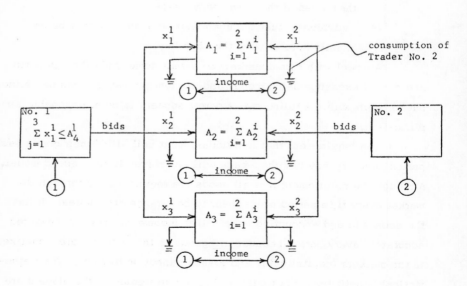

Figure 3

that upon reflection this is not as strange as it might seem. In particular if there are many individuals in the market and the market has a history, last period's price may serve as a guide to determining this period's allocation. There probably is no such thing as <u>the</u> <u>correct</u> <u>model</u> for price formation; there are many and they differ for many institutional and special information processing or other detailed reasons. No matter how the system is modeled, if we assume that prices and quantities sold evolve out of market forces then someone has to act without the economic environment being perfectly given to him.

An alternative but more complicated model of bidding can be formalized as follows: All individuals can send to or hold back from the markets any amount they wish. Thus each, without knowledge of the actions of the others sends in his goods to the markets. Then they all bid to buy the amount for sale.

Information conditions, time lags and communication conditions are all important, but for a start we begin with the simplest situation; the decisions are as shown in Figure 4. This signifies that effectively each chooses the amounts he wishes to sell and his bidding strategies simultaneously.

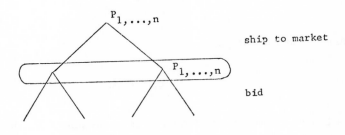

Figure 4

A third model in which each also names a price for his goods and the market determines a final price has been studied and used experimentally by Shubik [1974c].

6.4. Income and Sales

The market mechanism sketched in Figure 3 has not yet been fully described. We have not stated how the money flows back.

Suppose we were to regard the trading economy[5] we are describing as a parlor game or a game which can actually be played experimentally. In order to simplify accounting and record keeping we might give each player a receipt for the commodity he delivers. Thus against the delivery of 10 tons of wheat he is given a nonnegotiable warehouse receipt. After the market has sold all the goods and price has been determined he gives his receipt to the market manager and obtains his income from the sale of his goods.

For ease in illustration we consider the first model where individuals are required to sell all of their goods. Suppose that player i allocates his spending so that he spends x^i_j on good j. Then the total expenditure on good j will be:

$$(4) \qquad x_j = \sum_{i=1}^{n} x^i_j .$$

The total amount of good j for sale is

$$(5) \qquad A_j = \sum_{i=1}^{n} A^i_j .$$

Thus the market price is:

$$(6) \qquad p_j = x_j / A_j .$$

The income derived by individual i from the sale of his goods will be:

$$(7) \qquad \sum_{j=1}^{k} p_j A^i_j .$$

The amount of the monetary commodity in the ownership of the ith individual is defined as a residual after expenditures have been made and income received.

(8)
$$q^i_{k+1} = A^i_{k+1} - \sum x^i_j + \sum_{j=1}^{k} p_j A^i_j \,.$$

7. RULES OF THE GAME AND INFORMATION CONDITIONS

The monetary system and the financial institutions are the neural network of an economy. They are the carriers of much of its information content. Can this somewhat rhetorical statement be operationalized and given a mathematical structure? To a great extent the answer is yes and it lies in modeling the extensive form.

The introduction of exogenous uncertainty takes place by having "Nature" move with given probabilities. Uncertainty about the rules of the game can be introduced in a manner first used by Vickery [1961] and generalized independently by Harsanyi [1968]. Each player is considered to be one of a class of players who is chosen with given probabilities to play at the start of the game. Thus after the selection each player knows who he is, but the others are not quite sure of his identity in the sense that they have only a probability distribution on his utility function or strategic limitations or other characteristics.

In general these models may be extremely sensitive to some information conditions and not to others. There is no easy a priori test. However, many of the cases which can be generated appear to have their counterparts in economic life. For example suppose that an individual is uncertain about his income next period can he arrange his purchases so that he goes into the market before or after this uncertainty is removed? The extensive form for the first is shown in Figure 5a, and the second 5b. Nature moves second in 5a and first in 5b. The merchant capitalist who must spend even though he does not know if his ship will return safely provides an example of 5b. The full specification and import of this distinction will be made in formal models in Section 11.

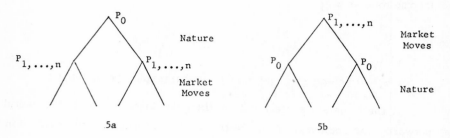

Figure 5

7.1. Aggregation Coding and Macroeconomics

Economic models involving groups of individuals specifying strategies frequently have moves or strategies which (unlike most abstract
games) provide a natural way to aggregate information. For many economic purposes (though clearly not all) the aggregate number indicating
all consumer spending may be as valuable as a detailed breakdown of the
spending of each consumer. For a bank making loans to an individual,
his debt outstanding and various aggregate indicators of loanable funds
may well provide an optimal information structure.

If we are studying individual behavior in mass markets where the
size of the individual with respect to the whole market is small then
there are some indications [Shubik, 1973a] that aggregate information
loses little or nothing for the individual actor.

It is my belief that macroeconomic models and theory may be derived naturally from aggregating information conditions in the microeconomic models discussed here. In general it is meaningless to talk about
aggregating information because usually no natural metric is suggested
with makes the addition of moves feasible. For economic games it frequently can be done.

8. SOLUTION CONCEPTS

So far the discussion has been limited to describing economic
models and modeling markets and trading procedures without discussing

how the traders behave, or should behave. We now must consider what solution criteria we wish to apply. Before turning directly to this question it should be noted that for many purposes the specification of the model alone may be regarded as the solution to the economic problem at hand, or may be a major part of the solution.

People including economists tend to attach undue importance to that which they do well. Thus there is a danger that among highly mathematically trained theorists the emphasis is placed upon the mathematical proof of theorems while the value of building the appropriate model, correctly mathematizing it and conjecturing what the theorems might be and what aspects of the models appear to be interesting or worth exploring; are regarded as secondary. My skills are in the latter and as such I am probably biased towards unduly stressing the latter at the expense of the former. Yet neither position is sound scientifically. The skills are different and the requirements of economic analysis call for both. A failure to understand this leads to sterile economic theory full of uninteresting theorems on the one hand or taxonomies and potentially interesting descriptions without the needed depth of analysis on the other hand.

8.1. Cooperative, Noncooperative and Mechanistic Solutions

The approach adopted here will be to adapt the noncooperative equilibrium solution concept or to consider behavioral mechanisms which provide the dynamics for the multistage models. Two other alternatives could be followed. We could consider an expressly cooperative approach as has been exemplified in the solution of the core [Gillies, 1959] or the value [Shapley, 1953]. In order to do this we would need to cast the models in coalitional form. This may be worth doing, although it must be noted that because of the presence of market mechanisms[6] which introduce an interconnection among the traders, the c-game property of the characteristic function [Shapley and Shubik, 1973a] is destroyed, i.e. it makes the characteristic function or coalitional representation of the game less trustworthy as an adequate reflection of the underlying economic structure.

The reasons for not following the cooperative solutions at this point are several.

(1) With markets the characteristic function or other coalitional forms of representation are hard to justify.

(2) The very essence of the role of money and financial institutions appears to lie in the dynamics and the cooperative representations of the economy viewed as a game do not reflect this well.

(3) The implicit or explicit assumption in cooperative models that the solution is constrained to be Pareto optimal is too strong. We should hope to deduce rather than assume optimality.

In particular it is my belief that one of the prime roles of the rules or laws for the operation of an economy with contracts is to achieve quasi-cooperation in a system which can be described as behavioristically noncooperative. But the system design provides for self policing which enables optimal outcomes to be achieved without the necessity for particularly high levels of cooperation or communication.

Another alternative to considering cooperative solutions is to try to utilize the price system of Walras as developed by Arrow, Debreu and others in a direct extension. It is my belief that although this approach may yield some results, it is an inadequate approach for several reasons.

(1) It is nonstrategic. Individuals are assumed to have no strategic freedom (even to commit errors).

(2) It provides an inadequate model with which to introduce nonsymmetric information conditions.

(3) It does not provide a natural model for intermixing oligopolistic and purely competitive sectors.

(4) It fails to meet a key test of modeling. If we try to describe a competitive market as a game to be played there is no unique way to do so. The model is insufficiently defined (as Arrow and Debreu [1954 and 1974a] discovered in their

534

attempt). The lack of definition hinges upon whether prices are meant to be assumed or deduced from the model.

It is conjectured here that all of the results which can be obtained by using variants of the Walrasian models can be obtained by using a noncooperative solution concept and studying an appropriately defined limiting behavior. This solution concept however and the models to which it applies do not suffer from the weaknesses of the competitive price system models. They yield results for nonsymmetric information and for mixed competitive or oligopolistic markets.

It is my belief that the attempts to modify the competitive equilibrium Walrasian model to account for monetary, financial and informational phenomena are not unlike the attempts to modify the Ptolemaic model in astronomy. It may conceivably be done, but a parsimonious explanation lies in going to a different model.

In the remaining discussion we confine our attention to the noncooperative or to behavioral solutions.

8.2. Noncooperative Equilibria and State Strategies

The concept of a noncooperative equilibrium solution to an economic problem was first introduced by Cournot [1897]. The general definition is due to Nash [1952]. Suppose that we have a game in extensive form where there are points in the game tree at which all players have perfect information, i.e. at which they can identify exactly where they are. At each of these points the game can be partitioned into a set of subgames. A perfect equilibrium point is in equilibrium in all subgames [Selten, 1960]. Much of the work in control theory and dynamic games utilizes a solution concept close to that of a perfect noncooperative equilibrium.

Paradoxically although the concept of a perfect equilibrium appears to be associated with relatively high levels of information, the control theory approach apparently depends upon a somewhat parsimonious state description and essentially aggregated information. This appears to be closely linked to the remarks made in 7.1 on aggregation and macroeconomic models.

In general, to start with, when we discuss solutions our attention is first focussed upon perfect equilibria. It should however be noted that a perfect equilibrium is not necessarily the same as a stationary state equilibrium. Individuals frequently talk about a stationary state when they have in mind a special model (such as a simple matrix game or a trading economy) which is repeatedly played over many periods. A great amount of confusion can arise from a failure to recognize differences in the definitions of commonly used phrases. In order to avoid the confusion here I merely note that the concept of a stationary state equilibrium is not rigorously defined until it is needed.

Suppose we were to consider the possibility of an economy that is constantly under the influence of exogenous random events (as economists do not -- and probably should not -- try to include in their models all aspects of human affairs such as the social, political and psychological factors these could be considered as supplying a random exogenous influence). Then our interest in economic dynamics might be in the study of systems which tend towards an equilibrium even though they may never reach an equilibrium. Our prime concern may be with paths of adjustment and movement in disequilibrium states. These distinctions, however, must be made clear in the investigation of specific models.

8.3. Historical Strategies and Information

A game which is solved for its perfect equilibrium points may also possess other equilibrium points. These other equilibria will arise from strategies which utilize more information or "history" about the previous progress of the game than do the strategies which give the perfect equilibria. The strategies needed for a perfect equilibrium are state strategies, in the sense that they depend only upon knowing where you are, not how you arrived at that position. A historical strategy makes use of information concerning the path to a position in the game. The distinction

536

has been made in detail elsewhere and simple examples have been given [Shubik, 1974d].

A simple verbal example may at least help to describe the difference and to suggest that for different economic problems either state or historical strategies may be relevant. One policy on which loans can be made is to lend to only those who currently have assets worth considerably more than the loans. This requires little information about the individuals in order to give the lender a certain level of security. A different lending policy might be to lend based upon information concerning the past history of the individual in repaying debts. This may require considerably more information.

8.4. Behavioral Solutions and Disequilibrium

Both the noncooperative and competitive price system solutions can be regarded as special cases of a broader class of updating mechanisms which are based upon behavioral considerations which may involve more than mere maximization. For example we might wish to consider myopic behavior in which the individual forecasts future change from the immediate past and tries to maximize immediate revenues based on this information.

It is easy to specify myriads of ad hoc system updating rules which invoke no maximization operators whatsoever. It is however not so easy to offer either empirical or normative justification for most of them.

The importance of considering behavioral mechanisms is nevertheless two fold. First they provide a class of solution concepts which may be considerably easier to solve for than say a competitive equilibrium (if it exists) or a noncooperative equilibrium. Second they tend, by their very formulation, to lay their stress on process rather than equilibrium. They provide laws of motion for the system rather than seek ways to down-play dynamics and disequilibrium.

A symptom of the difference between a behavioral approach and one say, involving an equilibrium model is given by the use of forward updating methods for generating the solution or time path of behavior and the use of backward induction. For example a common technique used for solving finite stage dynamic programs is to start at the last period and work backwards.

Attempts by economists to describe a price system dynamics by introducing excess supply or demand functions and then defining the movement of prices as depending upon the size of the gap in supply or demand can be regarded as attempts to replace the originally formulated optimization problem by a dynamically formulated behavioral system. It is my opinion that such an approach might be successful if the economic models included trade in financial instruments and had the financial system modeled together with the physical economic system in such a way that many of the feedbacks, controls and adjustments took place through the financial (or a central planning) mechanism. Without such a modification it appears to me that economic models whose dynamics derive from perceived lack of balance in the goods and services sectors alone are not adequate models of any economy.

8.5. On Optimality and Feasibility

There is considerable confusion in the discussion of optimality and feasibility by economists and others. This confusion arises for several considerably different reasons.

(1) Can long term preferences be defined ?

(2) Can the Pareto set be defined in the presence of uncertainty ?

(3) How does market structure influence feasibility ?

(4) How do differing levels of information influence the perception of optimality ?

The first and possibly most profound level at which disagreement might appear between the economists and others is that the assumption frequently made by the economist that it is meaningful to consider that an individual might look at his welfare in terms of a preference ordering over both current and future events is unreasonable. It may be argued that it is far more reasonable to assume that individuals update their preferences.

Although I am much more sympathetic to the behavioral point of view as providing a better overall model of man, I nevertheless am willing to support the economists' view that as a first approximation in application to some economic problems the assumption of the existence of preferences is a useful place to start.

Once we have accepted the existence of a preference ordering, the existence of a utility function defined up to a linear transformation appears to me to be clearly a natural next step. Arrow and Debreu offer the alternative which involves an enormous expansion of the set of outcomes. This particular expansion, while logically sound appears to me to be unsatisfactory as a method of modeling. Financial instruments exist specifically for the purpose to enable individuals to avoid having to deal with myriads of futures markets. Virtually all of the evidence from both behavior in general and economic markets in particular goes against a vast proliferation of futures trading.

The skilled economic theorist when confronted with evidence to the contrary may say that the real world contains "frictions" which do away with many of the future markets. This observation may well be valid, but the essence of a good approximation is that even though it is a simplification of reality it is still close to it. For this reason it is my belief that an adequate theory should have very few futures contracts rather than enormous numbers. As noted in Section 3 I believe that no more than four basic types of contracts are needed and (as noted in 4.2) a great deal can be developed allowing only one type of futures contract.

As has been observed in Section 4 we will assume the existence of utility functions. If we do so then optimality of a state can be defined in the utility or payoff space R^n as being on the Pareto optimal surface or "northeast" boundary of the feasible set of outcomes.

A set of outcomes which are feasible and optimal in one economic model may no longer be feasible in another closely related model. Thus for example, if we consider a model of exchange with no transactions costs and no constraints on trade we may be able to define a Pareto optimal set of outcomes all of which are feasible; if we compare this model with the one which has transactions costs the Pareto optimal set of the latter will be contained within the former because certain outcomes are no longer feasible. An easy and dangerous error which can be commited is to talk about the Pareto optimal set achievable in an economy with transactions costs as not being really optimal just because it does not coincide with the set that can be achieved if transactions costs were not a fact of life. This is about as meaningful as saying that the Pareto set in an economy in which there are costs to the production of steel is not "really Pareto optimal" because they are contained in the set for an economy where steel production is costless.

The presence of specific market structures or the absence of various futures markets may all impose limits on the feasibility of certain exchanges, hence may change the Pareto optimal set. It may well be useful to compare the Pareto optimal sets achievable in the various market models with the utopian model with all futures markets and no transactions costs. This may help us to derive a measure of the costs and worth of market organization and information.

It is technically feasible to define a game with incomplete information to solve it for its equilibrium points and to examine them in relation to the noncooperative equilibria of a game with complete information. In this manner a value for information can be established. However so far no general methods or results concerning the economic worth of information exist. We do not pursue this problem further at this time.

9. OTHER IMPORTANT FACTORS[7]

The development of an adequate economic dynamics which reflects both the physical and the information flow process of a society is an exercise in <u>mathematical</u> <u>institutional</u> economics. The institutions are the carriers of the information, control and financial processes. It is easy to make this observation, but it is difficult to go from such an observation to a parsimonious description which does not become bogged down in institutional detail.

9.1. The Approach Adopted

In order to avoid the considerable confusion which might arise in trying to handle too many features of the financial and information system simultaneously the approach adopted here is to construct a series of relatively specialized, oversimplified and "unrealistic" models in order to cope with the difficulties, one at a time, or at least not more than a few at a time.

The remaining parts of this section are devoted to sketching several of the more important factors which need to be investigated separately when possible.

9.2. The Actors

It is argued here (and elsewhere) [Shapley and Shubik, 1973b] that the description of an economy may, for many economic purposes, require the explicit introduction of several different types of economic agents or actors. In particular for many economic questions it is my belief that the following types need to be characterized separately. They are the:

(a) consumers,

(b) entrepreneurs,

(c) bureaucrats and administrators,

(d) financial agents and evaluators,

and (e) politicians.

Depending upon the question at hand there are several different ways in which each of these agents might be modeled using the categories suggested in Section 2, or even constructing elaborate behavioral models.

541

9.3. Banking

In several of the models being developed, the need for banking arises extremely naturally from considerations of Pareto optimality in a noncooperative game. However different functions for banking may emerge which call for the construction of several differentiated institutions. In particular we may wish to distinguish

(a) Internal Commerical Banking where any player can be a banker and (i) the lender cannot "create money," i.e. lend more than the amount of fiat he has on hand; (ii) the lender can create money.

(b) Internal But Differentiated Commercial Banking where only a distinguished class of players can be bankers who have strategic options not available to others.

(c) External Commerical Banking where the bank is either a mechanism or a special player with constraints or special rules concerning its use of banking profits and the role of the conservation of money and debt instruments.

(d) Central Banking where there is a banker's bank which is a mechanism or special player with a special goal and distinguished rules of operation which enable it to take actions that other bankers cannot take. In particular considerable care must be taken in describing the role of the central bank in the issue of fiat money.

(e) Investment Banking which can be (i) internal or (ii) external to the system (such as part of the government) where the stress is on risk evaluation and perception of the worth of new projects.

(f) International Banking poses a completely new set of problems involving the interrelationship between different fiat monies and individual nations as players. These problems are not discussed further in this paper.

In all of the above instances bank failure and various contract violation rules must be specified.

9.4. Insurance

Insurance also cannot be treated completely monolithically. The distinctions which are needed must cover the insurance company as

    (i)   a nondistinguished private player

    (ii)   a distinguished private player

    (iii) an external player (or mechanism).

A further distinction must be made concerning

    (i)   noncorrelated events (auto accidents)

and   (ii)   highly correlated events (plague, natural disaster).

Furthermore the role of insurers as risk evaluators must be reflected in the models. As with a full description of the banking function, so for the insurance function the rules concerning insurance company failure, other failures to meet contractual obligations, rules concerning reinsurance and rules describing the role of government must be specified in order to provide a sufficient operational definition of the system.

9.5. Production

Production must be modeled as a time consuming sequential process. There are obviously myriads of different partially parallel, partially sequential processes which are employed. Any cross section view of the economy gives an apparently simultaneous view of the activities involved in production. Thus at any point in time, some firms are hiring labor, others are buying raw materials, others are running the production lines and still others are shipping finished goods, or warehousing or stocking retailers.

The firm as an institution is an embodiment of the organization and information required to be the carrier of a production process. It is desirable to be able to distinguish the speed with which a firm can be created or destroyed as contrasted with the speed with which production

can take place given the existence of the firm. An economy with institutions is a nonconservative system. Reversing the conditions which
caused bankruptcy does not cause "unbankruptcy."

There are many ad hoc factors which must be accounted for in the
modeling of production in time. Not the least of which is that capital
goods of long duration provide "hostages" or security in the market for
loans. This preliminary and abbreviated discussion is given only to call
attention to the need for treating production as a seperate and important
factor in the development of adequate microeconomic models. In particular it is stressed that the roles of assets, production and financing are
closely interlinked.

9.6. Labor

Labor must be treated as a distinguished service, if for no other
reason than for the empirical and conceptual difficulties encountered in
trying to provide a satisfactory characterization of it as both a production and consumption input.

Frequently a good indication of the closeness of fit between economic theory and reality lies in the correspondence between the accounting schemes in theory and fact. The myriads of ways in which labor productivity can be concealed, unemployment disguised and quality of labor
varied indicate that there are deep difficulties in describing and accounting for this factor which differ from all other factors.

9.7. Government and Public Goods; Treasury and Taxation

Modern governments work through direct planning and physical
controls or through financial instruments. The interlinkage between micro
and macro-economics must come not merely in information aggregation as
noted in 7.1, but also in the introduction of governmental institutions and
public goods as part of the overall structure.

There are many types of public goods (as has been noted elsewhere). However as a first cut the simplest model might consist of

government as a mechanism with an exogenously given strategy or utility function which involves the raising of funds to provide for a supply of public goods. For even a simple model to have the property of computability or to be playable as a game it is necessary to specify the treasury, public financing and taxation mechanism no matter how elementary it may be. This type of model is not investigated further here.

9.8. Futures Markets, Contracts, Law and Accounting

In Section 3 it was suggested that at most four contracts are needed to provide time links for a dynamic economy which trades primarily in spot markets. At this point a stress on a feature in modeling is made. A criterion for the measure of success in modeling an economy with financial instruments and institutions should be how naturally do the models complement and fit in with those provided by law and accounting. Economics is not an all-encompassing discipline. The depth of description and analysis obtained in one area is invariably bought at the expense of gross simplification and the ignoring of detail elsewhere. Unless one has a mystic faith in an all-encompassing grand socio-political-economic model which is going to answer simultaneoulsy all questions concerning society, the polity and the economy, it is probably more reasonable to settle for models with exogenous features where inputs which need more detailed description and explanation based on other disciplines are not claimed to be explained.

The legal knowledge displayed here is slight and the handling of key concepts such as property rights and contracts is rudimentary. However more concern for these factors is given than is usual in most of economic theorizing. The full detail of legal questions concerning property rights and contracts is not immediately germaine to the models at hand and the projected analysis; nevertheless the connection between the law and the economic institutions and instruments needed to run an economy, is important and should be clearly identifiable in the economic models.

Economic control and equity in a free enterprise or in a centrally controlled economy depend delicately upon the accuracy and quality of economic accounting. The imperfections in all systems are clear today in the uses of myriads of tax shelters in free enterprise economies and in concealment of stocks, pricing distortions and accounting failures in all bureaucratic systems, whether they are privately run or part of the governmental structure.

The explicit introduction of financial instruments into the models of microeconomic theory provides an opportunity for achieving a closer integration of accounting and economics and a closer investigation of the underlying basic principles of both.

10. THE STATIC MODEL

In this and the remaining sections of this paper, discussion and commentary on the motivation for the type of models advocated in this paper is kept to a minimum. The emphasis is placed upon the construction and definition of a set of mathematical models whose analysis may help to justify the approach described above.

10.1. A Closed, One Period Trading Economy with Money and Credit

Let there be n individual traders (denoted by $i = 1, 2, \ldots, n$).

There are $m+1$ commodities. The $m+1^{st}$ commodity is distinguished as a money (see Section 5).

The distinction between a commodity money and a fiat or paper money may be made later by including or excluding the $m+1^{st}$ commodity as an argument in the utility functions of the traders.

There is one debt contract which is for money obtained at the start of trade to be repaid before consumption but after trade has taken place.

There is one distinguished "player" or $n+1^{st}$ player which is a mechanism known as a "bank", which may extend credit or accept deposits at a zero rate of interest.

Each trader i has a utility function or payoff function evaluated at the point of consumption, i.e. after trade and the settlement of contracts has taken place. This function has $m+2$ arguments, one for each commodity and one for the debt contract ($m+1$ arguments if the money is fiat). The indifference maps for each trader are defined on the non-negative orthant of the Euclidean space R^{m+2} for all components except the $m+2^{nd}$ dimension (the debt contracts). For this dimension both the positive and negative domain must be included to account for a final position which has some contracts which have not been settled (and hence may appear as negative on some accounts and positive on other accounts).

Let the initial amount of commodity j held by individual i be A_j^i and the final amount q_j^i.

The initial amount of credit held by all individuals is assumed to be zero. After the financial settlement after the market the amount of credit held will once more be zero unless it is not feasible to settle all accounts. In which case the worth of the resolution or "cure" for this state must be reflected in the utility functions.

Let the amount that i borrows from or deposits in the bank be $c_{\Delta t}^{i,n+1}$. It is important to note that because the bank has a nonsymmetric role in the game its "name" $(n+1)$ is always one of the two names that appear on the credit instrument. Borrowing or depositing takes place between an individual and the bank and not among individuals. It is easy to argue that sometimes individuals lend each other money; but here the argument is that as an approximation for what may go on in a modern economy it is not bad to consider the credit system as going through the bank.

Let the amount of credit held by individual i after settlement be $c^{i,n+1}$. The method for calculating this amount will be specified later.

Each trader attempts to maximize his payoff:

$$(9) \qquad \varphi_i(q_1^i, \ldots, q_m^i, q_{m+1}^i, c^{i,n+1}); \text{ where } q_j^i \geq 0 .$$

The strategic choices have not yet been specified.

Information Conditions and Extensive Form

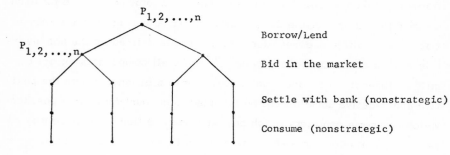

Borrow/Lend

Bid in the market

Settle with bank (nonstrategic)

Consume (nonstrategic)

Figure 6

Figure 6 (see also Figure 2) is a modified game tree where it is assumed that each individual takes his financial move (borrowing and lending) and his market move (bidding, spending, selling) without being informed of the actions of the others. After these strategic moves, two "automatic" moves take place. Debt contracts are settled and then consumption takes place.

As we are attempting to provide a completely well defined mathematical structure the assumptions concerning knowledge of the rules of the game must be made explicit. It is assumed that all individuals know their own preferences and know the preferences of all others. For the type of solution (a noncooperative equilibrium) first examined here it appears that the solution will be relatively insensitive to modifications of this assumption. This may not be so in a dynamic context.

The linkage of behavioral approaches and more traditional economic approaches come quite clearly in the information and knowledge assumptions made. Much of the description of mass economic behavior appears to imply low information conditions but this may not be made explicit in the economic theory formulations (such as the Arrow-Debreu treatment of general equilibrium) which essentially finesse having to make their assumptions explicit concerning knowledge of the rules of the game.

The Market Structure and Ownership

In Section 6 we have already discussed the need to completely specify the market mechanism. Shubik [1972a], Shapley [1974b], and Shapley and Shubik [1974a] have considered the simplest model with all nonmonetary goods offered for sale. This model is specified below and has been studied and solved in the papers referred to above. There are also several variants of a slightly more complicated nature in which each individual simultaneously is required to decide how much to offer to the market, what to borrow and what to bid.

Model 1a. Quantity Strategy--No Credit

There are n traders and each trader tries to maximize his payoff (given in equation (9)) where a strategy for a trader i is an allocation of money or a vector of m dimensions $(x_1^i, x_2^i, \ldots, x_m^i)$ such that:

$$(10) \qquad \sum_{j=1}^{m} x_j^i \leq A_{m+1}^i \quad \text{and} \quad x_j^i \geq 0 .$$

The amount of good j trader i will obtain is given by

$$(11) \qquad q_j^i = \frac{x_j^i}{x_j} A_j \quad \text{or} \quad q_j^i = 0 \quad \text{if} \quad x_j = 0 .$$

where $x_j = \sum_{k=1}^{n} x_j^k$ and $A_j = \sum_{k=1}^{n} A_j^k$.

The amount of money trader i will have at the end of the period is:

$$(12) \qquad q_{m+1}^i = A_{m+1}^i - \sum_{j=1}^{m} x_j^i + \sum_{j=1}^{m} p_j A_j^i$$

where $p_j = x_j/A_j$. Thus we can formulate the first noncooperative game as:

$$(13) \quad \underset{x^i}{\text{maximize}} \; \varphi_i \left(\frac{x_1^i A_1}{x_1}, \frac{x_2^i A_2}{x_2}, \ldots, \frac{x_m^i A_m}{x_m} ; A_{m+1}^i - \sum_{j=1}^{m} x_j^i + \sum_{j=1}^{m} p_j A_j^i \right)$$

$$i = 1, 2, \ldots, n$$

where $x^i = \sum_{j=1}^{m} x_j^i$.

It has been shown that a noncooperative equilibrium exists for this model if there are at least two players who have positive utility for any good.

Replication

Replace each trader of type i by k traders of the same type (i.e. identical traders). Now consider a new noncooperative game with kn traders analogous to the game shown in (13) with n traders. It has been shown that if there is "enough" money held by all individuals then there will be a noncooperative equilibrium point which "approaches" the competitive equilibrium in the sense that in the appropriate metric it is closer for successively larger replications.

If there is not "enough" money the above is not true. The shortage of money stops trade that would have been advantageous otherwise.

Fiat Money

When the money is assumed to be fiat the $m+1^{st}$ component in the utility functions drops out. The money is used for trade, but becomes worthless after trade. The meaning of "enough" money changes in this case. There is always enough as the system is homogeneous of order 0. The coincidence of the noncooperative equilibrium and the competitive equilibrium will depend upon the ratios of monetary holdings.[8]

If the ratios are appropriate the coincidence of the competitive equilibrium and the noncooperative equilibrium is immediate and does not require more than two traders of each type (this is not true for a market with more complex strategies where individuals do not have to offer all for sale).

Model 1b. Quantity Strategy and Credit

The simplest modification of Model 1a which reflects the role of credit is to relax condition (10). An individual is permitted to "spend more money" than he has. A way in which this can be stated more precisely is that in this model, with the permission of the bank he can jointly create a credit instrument which will be accepted at par with money when used in trade. The amount of bank money or debt created between an individual and the bank is:

(14)
$$c^{i,n+1}_{\Delta t} = A^i_{m+1} - x^i .$$

If the amount defined by (14) is negative the trader is a depositor in (or lender to) the bank. j As no interest payment is assumed in this model depositing and hoarding is not distinguished.

After trade has taken place it is assumed that debt contracts must be settled. The method is as follows: each individual calculates the sum $q^i_{m+1} - c^{i,n+1}_{\Delta t}$. If this is positive he is solvent and his payoff is:

(15)
$$\varphi_i(q^i_1, q^i_2, \ldots, q^i_m; q^i_{m+1} - c^{i,n+1}_{\Delta t}, 0) .^9$$

If the sum is negative define $c^{i,n+1} = q^i_{m+1} - c^{i,n+1}_{\Delta t}$ and the payoff is

(16)
$$\varphi_i(q^i_1, q^i_2, \ldots, q^i_m; 0, c^{i,n+1}) .$$

Shapley and Shubik has shown that for this game noncooperative equilibria exist and that under replication the approach of the noncooperative equilibrium to the competitive equilibrium can be established. In the papers referred to however the distinction between money and credit was not made as clearly as it needs to be to appreciate problems involving conservation or lack of conservation of money.

10.2. The Money Rate of Interest

Model 2. Quantity Bids, Credit and an Interest Rate

Suppose that individuals may borrow or deposit as they choose, but that there are charges associated with doing so. This game may be formulated in virtually the same way as Model 1b, except that two new parameters must be introduced:

ρ_1 - interest rate charged by bank on loans $(c_{\Delta t}^{i,n+1} > 0)$

ρ_2 - interest rate paid by bank on deposits $(c_{\Delta t}^{i,n+1} < 0)$.

At settlement each individual calculates the sum

$$(17) \qquad q_{m+1}^i - c_{\Delta t}^{i,n+1}(1 + \rho_1) \quad \text{if} \quad c_{\Delta t}^{i,n+1} > 0$$

$$(18) \qquad q_{m+1}^i - c_{\Delta t}^{i,n+1}(1 + \rho_2) \quad \text{if} \quad c_{\Delta t}^{i,n+1} < 0 .$$

(18) will always be positive, but (17) may be negative. When (17) is positive the payoff to trader i is:

$$(19) \qquad \varphi(q_1^i, q_2^i, \ldots, q_m^i; \; q_{m+1}^i - c_{\Delta t}^{i,n+1}(1 + \rho_1), \; 0)$$

a similar expression with ρ_2 replacing ρ_1 exists for (18). If (17) is negative then define $c^{i,n+1} = q_{n+1}^i - c_{\Delta t}^{i,n+1}(1 + \rho_1)$; the payoff is

$$(20) \qquad \varphi_i(q_1^i, q_2^i, \ldots, q_m^i; \; 0, \; c^{i,n+1}) .$$

Some Comments and Conjectures

This model has not yet been analyzed, however several observations may be made.

(a) For a commodity money and $\rho_1 > 0$ if any borrowing takes place which is not compensated for precisely by the appropriate amount of deposits then the system of the n traders is not conservative in commodity money. Hence we have either to postulate insolvency or bank failure to preserve conservation or to abandon conservation.

If loans exceed deposits by a ratio of ρ_2/ρ_1 the traders as a whole must lose part of the supply of commodity money to the bank. Thus the equilibrium in the system cannot be on the Pareto optimal set of the unconstrained trade model.

If deposits exceed loans by a ratio of ρ_2/ρ_1 then the bank is required to generate inputs of new commodity money at settlement.

(b) <u>Fiat Money</u>: Because fiat money is "just paper" or part of the rules of the game; the breaking of conservation laws on paper by the bank does not cause the creation of real goods (even though it may change price levels in a multistage game).

11. MONEY, CREDIT AND BANKING: DYNAMICS

In this and the next section a series of models are presented, only one of which has been fully investigated. Nevertheless it provides a prototype for the others and links immediately with the static models in Section 10.

11.1. One Commodity and Fiat Money

<u>Model 3.</u> The Simplest Dynamic Model -- Fiat Money, without Credit

An analogue to the pure trade model for many periods is one in which a perishable "manna" falls from heaven each period.

We may limit our analysis to one commodity by the simplifying (and somewhat unrealistic) device of requiring that although each individual may have an ownership claim to a fraction of the manna he does not have the opportunity to eat it directly but he must buy the good from a central warehouse. After all has been sold, the individuals obtain an income which equals their ownership claims on the money gathered by the warehouse. Thus we may define a circulation of income.

Suppose that there are n traders where each trader i has an ownership claim of α_i of the amount of consumer good available at any period. $(\sum_{i=1}^{n} \alpha_i = 1)$.

Suppose trade takes place for T time periods and that the amount of the consumer good or manna each period is given by $A_1, A_2, \ldots, A_T$ $(A_t \geq 0)$.

Let each trader i have an amount of a substance called "fiat money" γ_i to start with $(\gamma_i \geq 0)$. We could normalize the total amount so that $\sum\limits_{i=1}^{n} \gamma_i = 1,$ although it is not necessary to do so.

Each individual i has a utility function of the form:

$$(21) \qquad U_i(\tilde{q}^i) = \sum_{t=1}^{T} \beta_i^{t-1} \varphi_i(q_t^i) \quad i = 1, 2, \ldots, n$$

where q_t^i is the amount of the consumer commodity consumed by i during period t. The φ_i are assumed to be concave, and when we wish to consider $T \to \infty$ we must assume that the U_i remain bounded.

A strategy by individual i in the subgame to be played at time t is to name an amount of money he offers to the market to buy the manna.

Let his strategy be denoted by x_t^i $(x_t = \sum\limits_{i=1}^{n} x_t^i)$.

Market price will be

$$(22) \qquad P_t = x_t/A_t \, .$$

The number of units of manna he will obtain during period t is given by

$$(23) \qquad q_t^i = \frac{x_t^i}{P_t} = \frac{x_t^i}{x_t} A_t \quad (q_t^i = 0 \text{ if } x_t = 0) \, .$$

Let C_t^i be the cash holdings of individual i at the start of time t. Then $C_1^i = \gamma_i$ and in general:

$$(24) \qquad C_t^i = C_{t-1}^i - x_{t-1}^i + \alpha_i x_{t-1} \, .$$

We have the constraint that $0 \le x_t^i \le C_t^i$.

Figure 7 sketches the dynamic structure of the system with two traders.

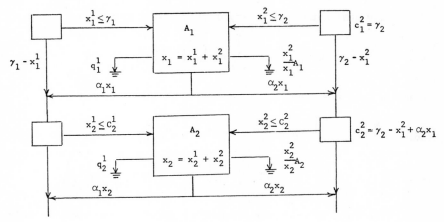

Figure 7

The solution concept we use is that of a perfect equilibrium or a Markovian equilibrium which has the property that the strategies are in equilibrium for every subgame.

For games with a finite horizon T, as fiat money is worthless at the end of time T we immediately know that it will all be spent at time T hence we can start a backwards induction.

An investigation of this model has been carried out by Shubik and Whitt [1973b]. In particular for $\beta_i = \beta$, $\varphi_i(q_t^i) = q_t^i$ and $A_t = A$ a closed form solution is obtained.

(a) For β_i not all the same the noncooperative equilibrium is not a Pareto optimal point in the unconstrained model.

(b) If $\beta_i = \beta$ and $\alpha_i = \gamma_i$ then there is a Pareto optimal stationary state where all spend everything.

11.2. One Commodity Money without Credit

Model 4. Commodity Money without Credit

Let there be an exogenous supply of perishable manna A_1, A_2, ..., A_T.

There is also a supply B^1, B^2, ..., B^n of commodity money which can be stored indefinitely at no cost or can be consumed at any time.

The utility function for any trader is given by:

(25)
$$U_i(\tilde{q}_1^i, \tilde{q}_2^i) = \sum_{t=1}^{T} \beta_i^{t-1} \varphi_i(q_{1,t}^i, q_{2,t}^i)$$

where $q_{1,t}^i = \dfrac{x_t^i}{x_t} A_t$ and

(26)
$$0 \le q_{2,t}^i \le C_t^i - x_t^i + \alpha^i x_t .$$

(27)
$$C_1^i = B^i \quad \text{and} \quad C_t^i = C_{t-1}^i - x_{t-1}^i + \alpha x_{t-1} - q_{2,t-1}^i .$$

There are several case distinctions which depend upon the information conditions. Possibly the simplest is that everyone bids for the consumer good simultaneously, the results of the market are announced then everyone simultaneously decides upon how much money he will "eat." This extensive form is shown in Figure 8.

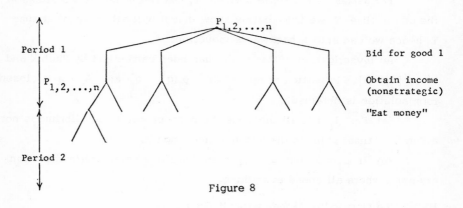

Figure 8

11.3. Money and Banking

Only the simplest bank is noted here which is an extension of the model in 10.1 for a multiperiod model.

Model 5. Fiat Money with Credit

The model is almost the same as Model 3 but with credit modifications. The extensive form is as in Figure 6, but for T periods.

Suppose the rate of interest charged or given by the bank for both loans and deposits is ρ. Furthermore individuals borrow or deposit, then spend without added information.

There are many strategic possibilities which cannot be ruled out a priori such as one individual borrowing to deny another funds; or hoarding even though there is a positive rate paid on deposits. We should expect that an adequate theory will rule out such cases as a result derived from not as an assumption of the thoery.

For simplicity however in the model constructed here several assumptions are made which must be rigorously established. They are (a) an individual borrows only to spend and (b) an individual will not hoard if the rate on deposits is positive.

There are n traders, each with an ownership claim of α_i on the consumer good available each period. These amounts are $A_1, A_2, \ldots, A_T$.

Each trader starts with γ_i of fiat money.

The bank will make any loan or accept any deposit. All contracts are short term they are settled at the end of the period in which they are made.

The bank is always in a position to pay its depositors by issuing bank money which may be regarded as a variant of fiat money. The distinction is worth making with care. When individual i borrows the amount $c_{\Delta t}^{i, n+1}$ from a bank one or two pieces of paper may be created. If the bank holds fiat money it may give him the amount $c_{\Delta t}^{i, n+1}$ in fiat money and keep the loan document (which for simplicity at this point we assume to be non-negotiable). The document calls for a repayment of the amount $c_{\Delta t}^{i,n+1}(1+\rho)$. In this instance only one piece of paper has been created.

Suppose instead that the bank as part of the rules of the game has the power to create paper. It issues to a borrower a piece of paper which is a negotiable debt instrument of its own which might be described as $c_{\Delta t}^{n+1,i}$ where by double entry bookkeeping

$$c_{\Delta t}^{n+1,i} \equiv c_{\Delta t}^{i,n+1} .$$

The bank's instrument however is accepted at par with fiat money. In this instance two pieces of two-party paper have been created, one of which adds to the money supply.

If at the end of a period an individual cannot meet his contract with the bank, unlike the bank he does not have the opportunity to roll over his loan. We could enlarge the utility function as has been suggested in 3.3. There is however an alternative which is to specify how the failure to meet contract is to be cured. In this simple example the following (somewhat harsh)rule is employed. He is no longer able to borrow until his loan is paid back.

Let u_t^i be the amount that individual borrows from or deposits in the bank $u_t^i > 0$ means a loan, $u_t^i < 0$ means a deposit.

If C_t^i is the initial financial position of trader i at the start of time t then the amount spent on the consumer good will be:

(28)
$$x_t^i = C_t^i + u_t^i$$

where

(29)
$$C_t^i = \max[(\alpha^i x_t + (1+\rho)u_t^i), \ 0] .$$

Suppose $c_t^{i,n+1} = \alpha^i x_t + (1+\rho)u_t^i < 0$, i.e. at the end of time t individual i fails to meet his obligation by $c_t^{i,n+1}$ then

$$c_{t+1}^{i,n+1} = c_t^{i,n+1}(1+\rho) - \alpha^i x_t \, .$$

As long as $c_t^{i,n+1} < 0$ then $u_t^i = 0$.

For a game of finite length we must still specify a penalty for ending the game with an unfulfilled contract thus we modify (21) to the form

(30)
$$U_i(\tilde{q}^i, \, c_T^{i,n+1}) = \sum_{t=1}^{T-1} \beta_i^{t-1} \varphi_i(q_t^i) + \beta_i^{T-1} \psi_i(q_T^i, \, c_T^{i,n+1}).$$

It is conjectured that there are noncooperative equilibria to this game which are the competitive equilibria in the unconstrained market.

A Simple Example

A simple two trader two-time period model helps to illustrate the market model with fiat money without and with banking.

Consider individual 1 who attempts to maximize

(31)
$$\Pi_1 = \frac{x}{x+y} + \beta A \left\{ \frac{1}{2} - x + \frac{x+y}{2} \right\}$$

and individual 2

$$\Pi_2 = \frac{y}{x+y} + \beta A \left\{ \frac{1}{2} - y + \frac{x+y}{2} \right\} \, .$$

This is a two period economy where each individual starts with an amount of $1/2$ of money. Each has the same ownership claim to the manna. This amount is $A_1 = 1$ in period 1 and $A_2 = A$ in period 2. The trade runs only for two periods. There is a discount factor β. A strategy for Trader 1 is to bid $x \leq 1/2$ in the first period and $\frac{1}{2} - x + \frac{x+y}{2}$ in the second period.

Solving (31) for maximal strategies we obtain

(32)
$$\frac{y}{(x+y)^2} = \frac{\beta A}{2}$$

or for a symmetric solution $x = y = 1/2\beta A$. This solution will hold for $\beta A \geq 1$, otherwise we would have $x = y = 1/2$. In particular we may note that for $\beta A < 1$, $x = y < 1/2$ which means that they both hoard during the first period. For example with $\beta = 1$, $A = 2$, $x = y = 1/4$, which means half of all money is hoarded during the first period.

Now we add a bank which is an outside mechanism which functions to accept deposits or make loans up until period $T-1$. In the simple example this means for the first period only.

If we assume that there is a noncooperative solution for which there is no hoarding of money we may then assume that an individual borrows to spend, or deposits excess funds in the bank. Let the bank have one interest rate ρ which it charges for loans or pays on deposits.

Let u, (v) = the amount borrowed or deposited by trader 1, (2). If this is positive it is a loan, negative a deposit. We may immediately write:

(33)
$$\Pi_1 = \frac{\frac{1}{2} + u}{1+u+v} + \frac{\beta A \left[\frac{1+u+v}{2} - (1+\rho)u \right]}{1 - \rho(u+v)}$$

and we have a similar expression for Π_2.

Solving for an optimal policy we obtain:

(34)
$$u = v = \frac{1 - \beta A(1+\rho)}{2\{\rho + \beta A(1+\rho)\}} \quad .$$

Using the same example as before suppose $\beta = 1$, $A = 2$ then for $\rho = 0$ $u = v = -1/4$ which means half of all money is deposited during the first period at an interest rate of zero.

Comments

It is relatively easy to set up and obtain a steady state equilibrium solution for T time periods by defining equations analogous to (33) and solving. However, this does not cover the rules needed to prevent unbounded borrowing. A fully specified general model must be more explicit on borrowing rules, and also needs insolvency and bankruptcy conditions to be specified. It is intended to discuss these details in a subsequent paper.

It should be noted that if $\rho \neq 0$ then whenever there is net borrowing or lending in the system the amount of money cannot be conserved without insolvency.

It should be further stressed that the money interest rate ρ is introduced as an exogenous control variable. It must be deduced from the theory that any particular values of ρ have any significant properties such as guaranteeing Pareto optimality of trade.

Because the bank in this model is a mechanism outside of the traders without a direct utility for consumption then the payment of interest to the bank does not imply any distribution of real resources to the bank.

If the system were in a Pareto optimal noncooperative equilibrium[10] without banking then it remains there regardless of ρ the money rate of interest, otherwise the value of ρ influences the speed of adjustment.

It appears that in a system where all individuals have the same "natural discount" β that somehow the money rate of interest will be linked in an important way to this number. But this is only one of several relevant variables which include depreciation rates, inventory costs, and growth in productivity.

When the dynamic system is weakly interlinked (as is the case in all of the examples given here) then there may easily be more than one money rate of interest which permits the noncooperative game to achieve outcomes which are Pareto optimal in the nonmonetary model. It is conjectured however that in general there will only be one efficient money rate ot interest associated with each competitive equilibrium in the non-monetary system. The qualification "in general" refers to economies where there are many time links such as durable goods. A further quali-fication is "neutral banking" which means that loans and deposits are instigated by the traders, not the banks. This somewhat loose wording can be made precise by defining the bank as a strategic dummy (like the "house" in Blackjack) who up to the rules of the game must accommo-date borrowers and lenders.

11.4. Productive Assets, Ownership Paper, a Stock Market and Fiat Money

Consider the simple example with two traders and T time periods where $\Pi_1 = \sum_{t=1}^{T} \beta_1^{t-1} x_t$ and $\Pi_2 = \sum_{t=1}^{T} \beta_2^{t-1} y_t$ where $1 > \beta_1 > \beta_2$. Suppose that there is a machine which does not depreciate and which produces one unit of output each period. We may consider an issue of ownership paper such that two traders each hold $1/2$ of the stock. The stock enti-tles each to a claim of $1/2$ of the income derived from selling the output.

It is easy to see that the competitive equilibrium in this economy is given by a policy where the trader with the highest discount consumes first until a switchover point is reached at which the other trader then consumes all for the rest of the market. It has been shown by Shubik [1973c] that without a stockmarket there is no noncooperative equilibrium giving the same distribution of consumption as the competitive equilib-rium. If the trader with the highest discount has any income or money after the switchover point there would be no enforcing mechanism within the market to prevent him from spending and thus destroying the equilib-rium.

Model 6

In the paper noted above a stockmarket is introduced in which the ownership paper can be sold and with it entitlements to further income.

It is shown that in this enlarged market the opportunity for the sale of ownership provides the means for obtaining a noncooperative equilibrium which is Pareto optimal and gives the same distribution as the competitive equilibrium. At the time of switchover of consumption the second trader has completely sold his shares and has neither money nor claims to income left.

As the formal model is presented elsewhere it is not reproduced here, however Figure 9 shows the moves in the game. In this first simple case with a stock market the rule that all shares must be offered for sale every period simplifies both the accounting of periodic income and the mathematical model.

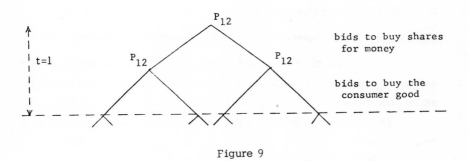

Figure 9

12. UNCERTAINTY AND INSURANCE

The need for an insurance institution appears with the introduction of exogenous or endogenous uncertainty. We will limit our remarks to exogenous uncertainty (rather than discuss risk favoring and mixed strategies).

The simplest two models which reflect the role of uncertainty can be obtained by assuming that each individual will obtain an amount of "manna" at period t with a given probability. In particular individual i will be the owner of $A^i_{j,t}$ amounts of manna at period t with a probability p^i_j where $\sum_{j=1}^{m} p^i_j = 1$.

Two important case distinctions must be made. They are illustrated by Figures 5a and 5b. In Figure 5b the individual traders have to make their market moves before they know what their ownership claims will be. After they have moved "Nature" moves and the market clears. This may appear to be somewhat unrealistic in the sense that individuals will be bidding before they know either their short term incomes or the amount of goods that will be available in the markets. It represents an extreme case of short term uncertainty.

The model in Figure 5a has the random move take place before the traders bid in the market. Thus they know their ownership claims and the total amount of goods that exist before they go into the market to bid.

12.1. Uncertainty without Insurance

Model 7a: No insurance, action with short term uncertainty

A set of simple two period models illustrate the qualititative properties of the closed dynamic models with uncertainty, but no insurance and no banking.

There are three states of the system and ownership claims on the "manna":

With probability $1/3$ supply is 1 and ownership $(1, 0)$
With probability $1/3$ supply is 1 and ownership $(0, 1)$
With probability $1/3$ supply is 2 and ownership $(1, 1)$.

Each trader wishes to maximize his expected income, and begins with $1/2$ unit of money,

$$
\begin{aligned}
\Pi_1 = &\frac{2}{3} \log\left(\frac{x}{x+y}\right) + \frac{1}{3} \log\left(\frac{2x}{x+y}\right) + \beta\left\{\frac{2}{9} \log\left(\frac{1}{2} - x\right) + \frac{1}{9}\log(1 - 2x)\right. \\
&+ \frac{2}{9} \log\left(\frac{1}{2} + y\right) + \frac{1}{9} \log(1 + 2y) + \frac{2}{9} \log\left(\frac{1}{2} + \frac{y-x}{2}\right) + \left.\frac{1}{9} \log(1+y-x)\right\} .
\end{aligned}
$$
(35)

Solving (35) for a symmetric noncooperative equilibrium we obtain

$$
\frac{y}{x(x+y)} = \frac{\beta}{3} \left(\frac{1}{\frac{1}{2} - x} + \frac{1}{\frac{1}{2} + \frac{y-x}{2}} \right)
$$
(36)

or

(37) $$\frac{1}{2x} = \frac{\beta}{3}\left\{\frac{1}{\frac{1}{2} - x} + \frac{1}{\frac{1}{2} + \frac{y-x}{2}}\right\} \text{ or } x = \frac{3 + 4\beta - \sqrt{16\beta^2 + 9}}{8\beta} \; .$$

For $\beta = 1$, $x = .25$ and $\Pi_1 = -.4447$.

Model 7b: No insurance, action with short term certainty

In this model nature moves first thus the players will each have to make a decision for each of the three states that the system may be in. Player 1 wishes to select numbers x_1, x_2, x_3 (the subscripts index the system state) to maximize

(38) $$\begin{aligned}
\Pi_1 = \frac{1}{3}&\left[\log\left(\frac{x_1}{x_1 + x_2}\right) + \beta\left(\frac{2}{3}\log\left(\frac{1}{2} - x_1\right) + \frac{1}{3}\log(1 - 2x_1)\right)\right] \\
+ \frac{1}{3}&\left[\log\left(\frac{x_2}{x_2 + y_2}\right) + \beta\left(\frac{2}{3}\log\left(\frac{1}{2} - y_2\right) + \frac{1}{3}\log(1 + 2y_2)\right)\right] \\
+ \frac{1}{3}&\left[\log\left(\frac{x_3}{x_3 + y_3}\right) + \beta\left(\frac{2}{3}\log\left(\frac{1 + y_3 - x_3}{2}\right) + \frac{1}{3}\log(1 + y_3 - x_3)\right)\right]
\end{aligned}$$

solving we obtain

(39) $$x_1 = \frac{-(1+\beta) + \sqrt{(1+\beta)^2 + 4\beta}}{4\beta} \; , \quad x_2 = \frac{1}{2} \text{ and } x_3 = \frac{1}{2\beta} \; .$$

For $\beta = 1$, $x_1 = \frac{-1 + \sqrt{2}}{2} = .207$, $x_2 = .5$ and $x_3 = .5$ similarly $y_1 = .5$, $y_2 = .207$ and $y_3 = .5$. Hence

$$\Pi_1 = \frac{1}{3}[\log(.2930) + \frac{2}{3}\log(.293) + \frac{1}{3}\log(.586)]$$

$$+ \frac{1}{3}[\log(.707) + \frac{2}{3}\log(.707) + \frac{1}{2}\log(1.414)]$$

$$+ \frac{1}{3}[\log(.5) + \log(.5)]$$

$$= -.6287.$$

565

We note here that the extra information lowers the expected equilibrium payoff. This appears to happen because the extra knowledge when the ownership claims are not equal enables the traders to damage each other apparently for immediate advantage.

Model 7c: Competitive Equilibrium with Full Uncertainty

This is the competitive equilibrium solution to Model 7a. Here we assume that 12 "contingent commodities" exist. They could be described as "apples in period 1 if states 1, 4 or 7 and apples in period 2 if states 1, 2, ..., 8 or 9. The endowments of Traders 1 and 2 are respectively,

$$(0, 1, 1; 0, 1, 1, 0, 1, 1, 0, 1, 1)$$

$$(1, 0, 1; 1, 0, 1, 1, 0, 1, 1, 0, 1) \, .$$

Let the commodities be $j = 1, \ldots, 12$ then Traders i's holdings of commodity j is x^i_j. Thus

(40) $$\Pi_i = \frac{1}{3} \sum_{j=1}^{3} \log x^i_j + \frac{1}{9} \sum_{j=4}^{12} \log x^i_j \, .$$

By symmetry $\Pi_1 = \Pi_2 = -.40137$, and the prices are:

$$(2, 2, 1; 2, 2, 1, 2, 2, 1, 2, 2, 1) \, .$$

12.2. Uncertainty with Insurance

We introduce an insurance agency which is an exogenous mechanism. In order to completely define its role we must specify whether it has a fund of fiat money at its disposal or if it is in a position to create money, or exactly how it underwrites its policies. The nature of the contract must be specified in complete detail concerning whether it is money for future money or whether it relates to other types of payments.

The simplest model is that of an exogenous insurance company which we may regard as being backed by the state who has unlimited possibilities for creating the fiat money needed to pay any claims on the company.

We assume that at any period t the company has the following information:

(i) it knows the amount of fiat money in the hands of each trader;

(ii) it knows the expected amount of the consumer good available next trading period and the expected ownership claims of each trader.

Let E_i be the expected ownership claim of trader i at any time t; and E be the expected overall amount of good for sale.

Let c_t^i be the amount of fiat money held by trader i at the start of time t. We consider a game where, before the random move the traders may buy insurance (in this simple model, the insurance agency is not a player and we limit our consideration to having players buy or not buy insurance, we need also to consider a more general model in which they can also sell insurance).

The insurance company sells a contract at a risk premium η ($\eta = 0$ is a fair bet) such that it will pay individual i the amount:

$$\frac{E_i}{E} (x_t + y_t) \left(\frac{1}{1+\eta}\right)$$

at the end of time t in return for his actual income from the market during time t. In this simple example the insurance company may be regarded as a factoring agency which offers a certain income against uncertain receivables.

The extensive form (for case a) is as shown in Figure 10.

We assume that the insurance policies can be purchased in any denomination thus in the two trader market the traders have a strategic variable w_t and z_t where $0 \leq w_t \leq 1$, $0 \leq z_t \leq 1$. The 0 values imply no insurance and the values of 1 imply an insurance of all income.

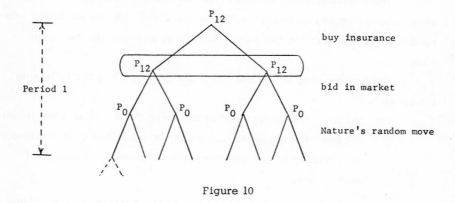

Period 1

buy insurance

bid in market

Nature's random move

Figure 10

<u>Model 8a.</u> Insurance and short term uncertainty

The payoff for Trader 1 is as follows

(41)
$$\Pi_1 = \frac{2}{3} \log\left(\frac{x}{x+y}\right) + \frac{1}{3} \log\left(\frac{2x}{x+y}\right) + \beta\left\{\frac{2}{9} \log(x_1) + \frac{1}{9} \log(2x_1)\right.$$
$$\left. + \frac{2}{9} \log(x_2) + \frac{1}{9} \log(2x_2) + \frac{2}{9} \log(x_3) + \frac{1}{9} \log(2x_3)\right\}$$

where
$$x_1 = w\left(\frac{x+y}{2}\right)\left(\frac{1}{1+\eta}\right) + (1-w)(\frac{1}{2} - x)$$

$$x_2 = w\left(\frac{x+y}{2}\right)\left(\frac{1}{1+\eta}\right) + (1-w)(\frac{1}{2} + y)$$

$$x_3 = w\left(\frac{x+y}{2}\right)\left(\frac{1}{1+\eta}\right) + (1-w)(\frac{1}{2} + \frac{y-x}{2})$$

and a similar expression exists for Trader 2.

The solution for a perfect equilibrium calls for Trader 1 to maximize over x and w and Trader 2 to maximize over y and z.

Let us make a guess that there are values of η such that in equilibrium both traders completely insure. If this were so we could rewrite (41) as:

568

$$(42) \quad \Pi_1 = \log\left(\frac{x}{x+y}\right) + \frac{1}{3} \log 2 + \beta \log\left(\frac{\frac{1}{2} - x + \frac{x+y}{2}\left(\frac{1}{1+\eta}\right)}{1 - (x+y)\left(\frac{\eta}{1+\eta}\right)}\right) + \frac{\beta}{3} \log 2 .$$

Solving for the symmetric solution we obtain

$$(43) \quad x = \frac{1+\eta}{2\{\beta(1+\eta) + \eta\}} .$$

For $\eta = 0$, $x = 1/2\beta$, and $\beta = 1/1+\eta$, $x = 1/2$. However substituting (43) into (42) we obtain immediately

$$(44) \quad \Pi_1 = \log \frac{1}{2} + \beta \log \frac{1}{2} + \frac{1}{3} (1+\beta) \log 2$$

for $\beta = 1$, $\Pi_1 = -.40137$. But this is precisely the same as the competitive equilibrium solution.

13. CONCLUSIONS: MATHEMATICAL INSTITUTIONAL ECONOMICS

13.1. Some Modeling Details

The approach adopted here stresses explicit detailed modeling to the point that if you cannot play the game described in a classroom or laboratory then it is not well defined. By adopting this approach several key obstacles to understanding monetary phenomena are overcome. In particular:

(1) Pecuniary externalities are real

(2) Tatonnoment processes are avoided

(3) The velocity of money is not a particularly important variable.

(1) Markets strategically connect trading groups. The specific nature of how this leads to pecuniary externalities has been discussed elsewhere [Shubik, 1971].

(2) There may well be myriads of different trading and production arrangements which lead to price formation. The tatonnoment process was

an unsatisfactory way of avoiding any of them. The approach here is only a start. It specifies one way of price formation. The next step calls for a sensitivity analysis over alternative procedures and some empirical guidance to choose among them.

(3) The model presented here has as a first approximation, a fixed time period. The velocity of money can only vary if individuals hoard it or save it. It is relatively easy to model time lags in payments which are either strategic or nonstrategic which would immediately create a "float" and introduce the timing of payments as a factor influencing velocity. But this appears to have little more significance than does the hoarding of inventories or lags in physical good distribution. In a hyper-inflation the speed at which an individual can run to the bank may be of some interest, but almost always other financial factors appear to be of more importance than velocity regarded as a strategic variable.

13.2. Rules, Institutions and Laws

The financial system including money, other financial instruments and institutions must be viewed holistically. Money is not defined without giving all of the rules for its operation in a financial process.

In our attempt to define process we are forced to define rules which amount to inventing institutions and laws. As most of these rules are for the guidance of the system in a disequilibrium state it is not surprising that most of them apparently disappear at a stationary equilibrium.

13.3. The Key Solution Concept Restated

Any solution concept to be adequate for the development of a theory of money and financial institutions must be defined for

(1) Nonsymmetric information conditions

and (2) few as well as many traders.

Furthermore the models to which the solution concept is applied must be defined for all states of the system -- not merely for the equilibrium states and local neighborhoods around them.

The noncooperative equilibrium has these properties and gives the competitive equilibrium results as a special case.

The noncooperative equilibrium however can be regarded as a special case of the broader scheme of behavioral mechanisms.

13.4. The Central Role of Information and Communication

Information clearly plays a central role. The institutions forming the financial infrastructure of a society may be viewed as information processing and communicating control devices. The approach adopted here is not yet sufficiently advanced to be able to handle many of the subtle features of communication but at least for a noncooperative game with an economic structure a way to evaluate the worth of information with respect to a solution concept is by having a solution concept defined for all information states and performing a sensitivity analysis with respect to changes in information. An example of this approach where more information had negative worth was given in the insurance models in Section 12.1.

13.5. On Mathematical Institutional Economics

The right mathematical model of economic process will call for the invention of the rudimentary institutions (such as banks, insurance companies and markets) to carry and control the processes. The differences among institutions the world over may depend upon detailed variables and special conditions not touched upon in the mathematical simplification. Nevertheless a mathematical institutional economics must be able to portray the essential features of institutions which exist or need to exist without an immediate need to proceed to great detail.

A mathematical institutional economics must be in harmony with an institutional economics in the sense that it should be relatively easy to reconcile the role of any actual institution with the theory. The added detail and special variables should be easy to spot and if need be incorporate in the theoretical framework.

A mathematical institutional economics should be in harmony with mathematical economics. A key test here is whether or not it gives the same results to well understood problems and gives more results elsewhere.

NOTES

[1] Although these forms of paper do not involve contracts between two individuals they may be regarded as forms of social contract where their laws of operation are defined in the rules of the game.

[2] At this level by aggregating goods and services we also aggregate goods and service contracts.

[3] A separate detailed discussion is needed to distinguish appropriately, aggregations of divisible goods, economic institutions and indivisible goods.

[4] A further difficulty remains with the meaning of consumption value derived from the holding of an asset. Does the possesion of a gold bar in one's bank vault yield a stream of value until it is used in trade? This is a well known problem in the modeling of stocks and flows and can be dealt with ad hoc.

[5] Production will be introduced later.

[6] Which are not present in the models of trade as barter or direct exchange.

[7] For those directly interested in the models, this section could be skimmed or skipped on first reading.

[8] There may be more than one competitive equilibrium in the unconstrained system; however it should be noted that the introduction of fiat money appears to offer a way for selecting among these equilibria.

[9]There is a problem with this formulation inasmuch as we have implicitly assumed that the bank always redeems its debt instruments for commodity money.

[10]and Pareto optimal in the nonmonetary model.

REFERENCES

Arrow, K. J. and G. Debreu [1954], "Existence of an Equilibrium for a Competitive Economy," Econometrica, Vol. 22, 265-290.

Chamberlin, E. H. [1950], The Theory of Monopolistic Competition. Cambridge: Harvard University Press, 6th ed., 1950 (originally published 1933).

Cournot, A. A. [1897], Researches into the Mathematical Principles of Wealth, New York: Macmillian (original in French, 1838).

Gillies, D. [1959], "Solutions to General Nonzero Sum Games," Ann. Math. Study, Vol. 40, 47-85.

Harsanyi, J. [1868], "Games with Incomplete Information Played by Bayesian Players, Part II," Management Science, Vol. 14, No. 5, 320-334.

Levitan, R. E. and M. Shubik [1970], "Duopoly with Price and Quantity as Strategic Variables." RC2920, Yorktown Heights, N.Y.

Nash, J. E., Jr. [1952], "Equilibrium Points in N-Person Games," Proc. Nat. Acad. Sci. U.S.A., Vol. 38, 886-893.

Selten, R. [1960], "Bewertung strategisher Spiele," Zeitschrift fur die gesemte Staatswissenschaft, 116, 221-282.

Shapley, L. S. [1953], "A Value for n Person Games," in Contributions to the Theory of Games II, Ann. Math. Studies 28, Princeton, University Press, 307-317.

Shapley, L. S. and M. Shubik [1973a], "Competition Welfare and the Theory of Games" (in process), Chapter 6, RAND R-904-NSF/6.
_____ [1973b], op. cit., Ch. 2, R-904-NSF/2.

——————————————————— [1974a], "Trade Using One Commodity as a Money," Cowles Foundation CF-40318.

Shapley, L. S. [1974b], "Noncooperative General Exchange," mimeographed.

Shubik, M. [1971], "Pecuniary Externalities: A Game Theoretic Analysis," American Economic Review, Vol. 59, No. 4, 713-718.

—————————— [1972a], "Commodity Money, Oligopoly Credit and Bankruptcy in a General Equilibrium Model," Western Economic Journal, Vol. X, No. 4, 24-38.

—————————— [1972b], "Competitive and Controlled Price Economies: The Arrow-Debreu Model Revisited," CFDP 337.

—————————— [1973a], "Information, Duopoly and Competitive Markets: A Sensitivity Analysis," Kyklos, Vol. 26, No. 4, 736-761.

—————————— and W. Whitt [1973b], "Fiat Money with One Nondurable Good and No Credit" in Topics in Differential Games, A. Blaquiere (ed.). Amsterdam: North Holland.

—————————— [1973c], "A Dynamic Economy with Fiat Money without Banking and with and without Production Goods," CFDP 364.

—————————— [1974a], "An Informal Guide to Some Papers on a Theory of Money and Financial Instiutions,"   Foundation CF-40531.

—————————— [1974b], "On the Eight Basic Units of a Dynamic Economy with Spot and Futures Markets," CFDP 367. (To appear in The Review of Income and Wealth.)

—————————— [1974c], "A Trading Model to Avoid Tatonnement Metaphysics," CFDP 368.

—————————— [1974d], "Money, Trust and Equilibrium Points for Games in Extensive Form," to appear in Zeitschrift fur Nationaloekonomie.

Vickrey, W. [1961], "Counterspeculation, Auctions and Competitive Sealed Tenders," Journal of Finance, Vol. 16, 8-37.

———————

The research described in this paper was undertaken by grants from the Office of Naval Research and from the Ford Foundation.

Index

A 5
B 6
C 7
D 8
E 9
F 0
G 1
H 2
I 3
J 4